About Pearson

Pearson is the world's learning company, with presence across 70 countries worldwide. Our unique insights and world-class expertise comes from a long history of working closely with renowned teachers, authors and thought leaders, as a result of which, we have emerged as the preferred choice for millions of teachers and learners across the world.

We believe learning opens up opportunities, creates fulfilling careers and hence better lives. We hence collaborate with the best of minds to deliver you class-leading products, spread across the Higher Education and Test Preparation spectrum.

Superior learning experience and improved outcomes are at the heart of everything we do. This product is the result of one such effort.

Your feedback plays a critical role in the evolution of our products and you can contact us at reachus@pearson.com. *We look forward to it.*

VRIO

"VALUE. RARITY. IMITABILITY. ORGANIZATION."

What Is It?

This book is not just a list of concepts, models, and theories. It is the first undergraduate textbook to introduce a **theory-based, multi-chapter organizing framework** to add additional structure to the field of strategic management.

"VRIO" is a mechanism that integrates two existing theoretical frameworks: the positioning perspective and the resource-based view. It is the primary tool for accomplishing internal analysis. It stands for four questions one must ask about a resource or capability to determine its competitive potential:

1. **The Question of Value:** Does a resource enable a firm to exploit an environmental opportunity, and/or neutralize an environmental threat?
2. **The Question of Rarity:** Is a resource currently controlled by only a small number of competing firms?
3. **The Question of Imitability:** Do firms without a resource face a cost disadvantage in obtaining or developing it?
4. **The Question of Organization:** Are a firm's other policies and procedures organized to support the exploitation of its valuable, rare, and costly-to-imitate resources?

What's the Benefit of the VRIO Framework?

The VRIO framework is the organizational foundation of the text. **It creates a decision-making framework for students** to use in analyzing case and business situations.

Students tend to view concepts, models, and theories (in all of their coursework) as fragmented and disconnected. Strategy is no exception. This view encourages rote memorization, not real understanding. VRIO, by serving as a consistent framework, connects ideas together. This encourages real understanding, not memorization.

This understanding enables students to better analyze business cases and situations—the goal of the course.

Within each chapter, the VRIO framework makes it possible to discuss the formulation and implementation of a strategy simultaneously.

Because the VRIO framework provides a simple integrative structure, we are actually able to address issues in this book that are largely ignored elsewhere—including discussions of vertical integration, outsourcing, real options logic, and mergers and acquisitions, to name just a few.

6 EDITION

STRATEGIC MANAGEMENT AND COMPETITIVE ADVANTAGE

Concepts and Cases

Jay B. Barney
The University of Utah

William S. Hesterly
The University of Utah

Arunaditya Sahay
Birla Institute of Management Technology, Greater Noida, UP

Srinivasan R. Iyengar
Jamnalal Bajaj Institute of Management, University of Mumbai

Pearson

Authorized adaptation from the United States edition, entitled *Strategic Management and Competitive Advantage*, 6th Edition, ISBN 978-0-13-474114-7, by Jay B. Barney; William S. Hesterly, published by Pearson Education, Inc © 2019.

Indian Subcontinent Adaptation

ISBN 978-93-615-9728-2

First Impression, 2024
Second Impression, 2025

This edition is manufactured in India and is authorized for sale only in India, Bangladesh, Bhutan, Pakistan, Nepal, Sri Lanka and the Maldives. Circulation of this edition outside of these territories is UNAUTHORIZED.

Published by Pearson India Education Services Pvt. Ltd, CIN: U72200TN2005PTC057128.

Head Office: 1st Floor, Berger Tower, Plot No. C-001A/2, Sector 16B, Noida - 201 301, Uttar Pradesh, India.
Registered Office: Featherlite, 'The Address' 5th Floor, Survey No 203/10B, 200 Ft MMRD Road, Zamin Pallavaram, Chennai – 600 044.
Website: in.pearson.com, Email: companysecretary.india@pearson.com

Printer: Gopsons Papers Pvt. Ltd., Noida.

Dedication

This book is dedicated to my wife, Kim, and our 11 grandchildren: Isaac, Dylanie, Audrey, Chloe, Lucas, Royal, Lincoln, Nolan, Theo, Cade, and Townes. They help me remember that no success can compensate for failure in the home.

—Jay B. Barney

This book is dedicated to my wife Denise and my soon to be 14 grandchildren: Ellie, Owen, Emerson, Cade, Elizabeth, Amelia, Eden, Asher, Lydia, Scarlett, Charlotte, Amos, and Claire.

—William S. Hesterly

This book is dedicated to my wife Geeta, my sons Arvind & Alind and all four grandchildren: Akanksha, Kaavya, Arushi and Shabnam.

—Arunaditya Sahay

This book is dedicated to Srividhya, Anusha and Adithya.

—Srinivasan. R. Iyengar

Brief Contents

Part 1: THE TOOLS OF STRATEGIC ANALYSIS

Part 2: BUSINESS-LEVEL STRATEGIES

Part 3: CORPORATE STRATEGIES

Contents

Part 1: THE TOOLS OF STRATEGIC ANALYSIS

CHAPTER 1 What Is Strategy and the Strategic Management Process? 2

CHAPTER 2 Evaluating a Firm's External Environment 30

CHAPTER 3 Evaluating a Firm's Internal Capabilities 68

End-of-Part 1 Cases

Part 2: BUSINESS-LEVEL STRATEGIES

CHAPTER 4 Cost Leadership 104

CHAPTER 7 Collusion 194

End-of-Part 2 Cases

Part 3: CORPORATE STRATEGIES

CHAPTER 8 Vertical Integration 218

Foreword to Indian Edition

In an increasingly competitive world buffeted by rapid technological change, firms need to make the right strategic choices in order to achieve profitable growth on a sustainable basis. While there is a plethora of strategy frameworks and tools, understanding which framework to use and when, and how to use the chosen framework appropriately is a challenge for most students. The classic text on Strategic Management and Competitive Advantage by Barney and Hesterly is one of the few texts that enables students to address this challenge effectively.

Context matters. Students in India using international texts often struggle with unfamiliar examples and case studies that come in the way of their comprehension and absorption. The Indian co-authors of this edition of Barney and Hesterly – Professors Arunaditya Sahay and Srinivasan R. Iyengar - have ensured that this problem is solved by providing a wide array of Indian examples and case studies. I am particularly impressed by the inclusion of material on leading Indian companies and conglomerates ranging from everyday names such as Mahindra and Godrej to new age companies such as Zomato, Zerodha and Oyo.

The coming together of leading scholars from the East and West in this book to produce a conceptually sound yet contextually relevant primer on strategy should enable an excellent and effective learning experience for Indian students.

Rishikesha T. Krishnan
Director & Professor of Strategy
Indian Institute of Management Bangalore

Preface

NEW TO THIS EDITION

What Should Be Included in a Strategic Management Text?

A very interesting question. Some books seem to think that the answer to this question is: Everything. And so, they get longer and longer each edition. Nothing dropped, plenty added.

We have taken a very different approach:

- Topics that are now covered more completely in non-strategic management texts are dropped.
- Models or frameworks that have proved to be theoretically unsound or empirically not substantiated are dropped.
- Strategic management models that provide important insights that have emerged over the last few years are added.

The result of all these changes is that the sixth edition of our text is just about the same length as the first edition, although the content of the sixth edition is dramatically different than all prior editions.

What Have We Dropped

Two elements have most obviously been dropped from this edition. In both cases, this decision was made, not because these are unimportant topics, but rather, because they are so important that non-strategic management text books have been written to address them.

- The "Strategy in the Emerging Enterprise" feature in each chapter has been dropped. As entrepreneurship teaching has become more important, these topics have been receiving enhanced coverage in entrepreneurship texts.
- The "International Strategies" chapter has been dropped. Again, this is not because international strategy is unimportant. Rather, it is so important that entire texts are dedicated to this topic.

What Has Been Added

By dropping these two topics, we were able to add two new chapters to this edition, while keeping the length of the book more or less the same.

- **Chapter Six: Flexibility and Real Options.** This chapter summarizes the latest theoretical and empirical work on the value of strategic flexibility. It describes the settings under which flexibility will create value, and how that value can be estimated.

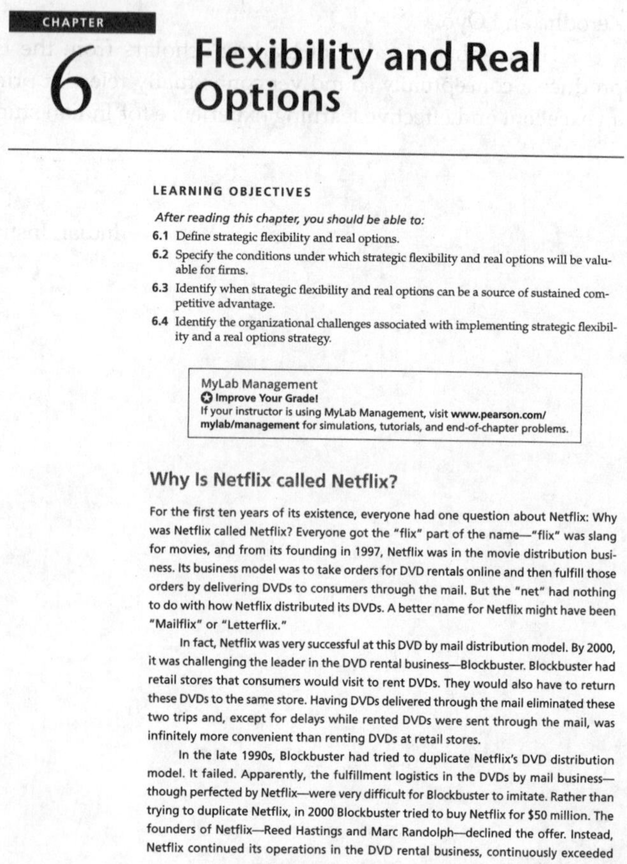

CHAPTER 6

Flexibility and Real Options

LEARNING OBJECTIVES

After reading this chapter, you should be able to:

6.1 Define strategic flexibility and real options.

6.2 Specify the conditions under which strategic flexibility and real options will be valuable for firms.

6.3 Identify when strategic flexibility and real options can be a source of sustained competitive advantage.

6.4 Identify the organizational challenges associated with implementing strategic flexibility and a real options strategy.

MyLab Management
Improve Your Grade!
If your instructor is using MyLab Management, visit **www.pearson.com/mylab/management** for simulations, tutorials, and end-of-chapter problems.

Why Is Netflix called Netflix?

For the first ten years of its existence, everyone had one question about Netflix: Why was Netflix called Netflix? Everyone got the "flix" part of the name—"flix" was slang for movies, and from its founding in 1997, Netflix was in the movie distribution business. Its business model was to take orders for DVD rentals online and then fulfill those orders by delivering DVDs to consumers through the mail. But the "net" had nothing to do with how Netflix distributed its DVDs. A better name for Netflix might have been "Mailflix" or "Letterflix."

In fact, Netflix was very successful at this DVD by mail distribution model. By 2000, it was challenging the leader in the DVD rental business—Blockbuster. Blockbuster had retail stores that consumers would visit to rent DVDs. They would also have to return these DVDs to the same store. Having DVDs delivered through the mail eliminated these two trips and, except for delays while rented DVDs were sent through the mail, was infinitely more convenient than renting DVDs at retail stores.

In the late 1990s, Blockbuster had tried to duplicate Netflix's DVD distribution model. It failed. Apparently, the fulfillment logistics in the DVDs by mail business—though perfected by Netflix—were very difficult for Blockbuster to imitate. Rather than trying to duplicate Netflix, in 2000 Blockbuster tried to buy Netflix for $50 million. The founders of Netflix—Reed Hastings and Marc Randolph—declined the offer. Instead, Netflix continued its operations in the DVD rental business, continuously exceeded

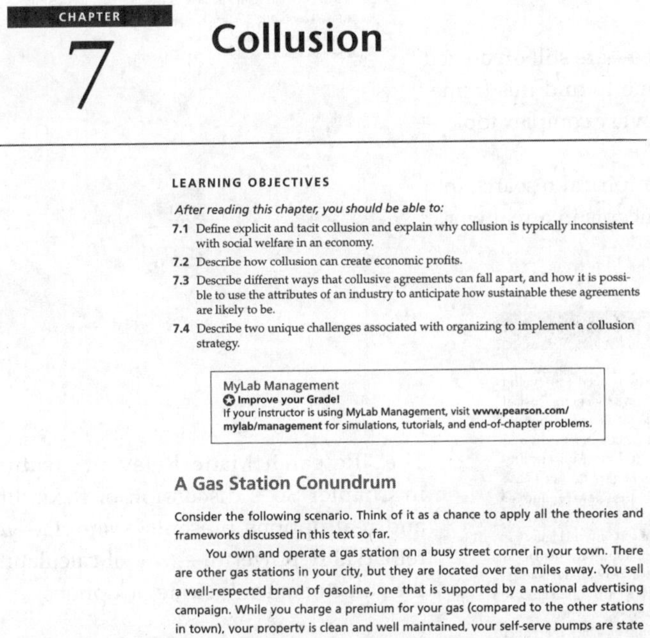
CHAPTER 7

Collusion

LEARNING OBJECTIVES

After reading this chapter, you should be able to:

7.1 Define explicit and tacit collusion and explain why collusion is typically inconsistent with social welfare in an economy.

7.2 Describe how collusion can create economic profits.

7.3 Describe different ways that collusive agreements can fall apart, and how it is possible to use the attributes of an industry to anticipate how sustainable these agreements are likely to be.

7.4 Describe two unique challenges associated with organizing to implement a collusion strategy.

MyLab Management
Improve your Grade!
If your instructor is using MyLab Management, visit **www.pearson.com/mylab/management** for simulations, tutorials, and end-of-chapter problems.

A Gas Station Conundrum

Consider the following scenario. Think of it as a chance to apply all the theories and frameworks discussed in this text so far.

You own and operate a gas station on a busy street corner in your town. There are other gas stations in your city, but they are located over ten miles away. You sell a well-respected brand of gasoline, one that is supported by a national advertising campaign. While you charge a premium for your gas (compared to the other stations in town), your property is clean and well maintained, your self-serve pumps are state

- **Chapter Seven: Collusion.** This chapter explores the economic—and ethical—implications of explicit and tacit collusion. Even if a particular firm chooses to not engage in collusion, it must still understand this strategy and its economic consequences, because some of its competitors may choose this strategy.

These two chapters have all the teaching elements (Learning Objectives, Opening case, Research made Relevant feature, Strategy in Depth feature, Ethics and Strategy feature, Challenge Questions, and a Problem Set) and are supported by cases, just like the other chapters in the book. However, they explore important strategic options that receive less attention in other texts.

Of course, the Indian edition has opening vignettes and closing case studies chapter-wise throughout the book have been updated or changed, as have the as per Indian context. The supporting cases and instructor's manual have also been updated. Given below is the list of Indian cases included:

Quick Glance at the list of Cases in Indian context

Chapter	Opening Vignette	Closing Case Study
1	From Delivery to Profit: Zomato's Strategic Wins	Bandhan… Rethinking, Reimagining Banking
2	AGEL's Strategic Growth and Industry Dominance	Jet Airways' Quest for Revival: A Strategic Analysis of the Aviation Industry
3	Biocon's Biopharmaceutical Breakthroughs	Strategic Shifts at L&T: Bridging Engineering with IT Innovation
4	DMart's Winning Formula: Everyday Low Pricing	Zerodha Way: Trading reimagined
5	Strategic Diversification: Royal Enfield's Route to Global Leadership	Will Paper Boat Sail through the Storm
8	JSW Steel's Strategic Mastery	PVR-INOX Integration: Navigating Challenges, Sustaining Growth
9	Mahindra Group: Diversified Growth and Global Reach	Godrej Group's Journey: From Locks to a Diverse Conglomerate
10	Infosys: Balancing Growth and Governance	OYO – Rise of Sharing Economy
11	From Alliance to Impact: Pfizer and BioNTech's Joint Venture in COVID-19 Vaccine Production	Accelerating India's Digital Transformation: Google and Bharti Airtel
12	Strategic Merger in Indian Finance: HDFC Ltd and HDFC Bank Unite	Asian Paints: All Great Things Start Small

What Remains the Same

"VRIO" – an integrative framework (see next page for details).

- Broad enough to apply in analyzing a variety of cases and real business settings.
- Simple enough to understand and teach.

VRIO

VRIO

VRIO

VRIO

All the chapters in the book—beginning with Chapter Three—are still organized around the VRIO framework. Students at all levels continue to find this framework helpful in thinking about and applying what can be a very complex topic—strategic management.

We also continue to integrate the latest theory and empirical research into the text—but in a way that helps students apply these concepts in a real world setting. Consider just two examples:

Research Made Relevant

Rita McGrath and Ian MacMillan argue that under conditions of uncertainty, managers should invest in a diversified range of projects that parallel many of the real options discussed in this chapter. These projects can be arrayed as in Figure 6.1.

In this figure, **technical uncertainty** refers to the extent to which managers understand the process by which a new product or service will be developed before that process is undertaken. Low technical uncertainty exists when managers know what kinds of skills and other

The Value of Real Options Thinking

resources they will need to develop a new product or service, the cost of acquiring these skills and resources, how to manage them effectively, and so forth. High technical uncertainty exists when managers do not know these things about a new product or service.

Market uncertainty, in Figure 6.1, refers to the extent to which managers understand how a new product or service will be received in the market. Low market uncertainty exists when managers know the price at which a product or service is likely to sell, the likely size

- The "Research Made Relevant" feature in Chapter Six's discussion of flexibility and real options presents a simple—yet remarkably powerful—way of calculating the value of a firm's strategic options

- The "Research Made Relevant" feature in Chapter Nine's discussion of the value of economies of scope cites the most recent research—some published in 2017—about this important issue.

Research Made Relevant

In 1994, Lang and Stulz published a sensational article that suggested that, on average, when a firm began implementing a corporate diversification strategy, it destroyed about 25 percent of its market value. Lang and Stulz came to this conclusion by comparing the market performance of firms pursuing a corporate diversification strategy with portfolios of firms pursuing a limited diversification strategy. Taken together, the market performance of a portfolio of firms that were pursuing a limited diversification strategy was about 25 percent

How Valuable Are Economies of Scope?

higher than the market performance of a single diversified firm operating in all the businesses included in this portfolio. These results suggested that not only were economies of scope not valuable, but, on average, efforts to realize these economies destroyed economic value. Similar results were published by Comment and Jarrell using different measures of firm performance.

Not surprisingly, these results generated quite a stir. If Lang and Stulz were correct, then diversified firms—no matter what kind of

We have also kept our most popular supporting cases, including True Religion, Harlequin, Walmart, and Starbucks among others. With only a couple of exceptions, the revised cases are shorter. In shortening the cases, we have mostly cut out historical and other peripheral background material. Two of the new cases, Collusion in Major League Baseball and Torrey Nano, require students to apply concepts from the new chapters in the book on collusion and flexibility. As has been true of all of the editions, the vast majority of the cases deal with companies and industries that students will find familiar and, we hope, stimulating to analyze and discuss.

With the introduction on the chapters on strategic flexibility and real options (Chapter Six) and collusion (Chapter Seven), the book continues to include the most up to date conceptual and analytical material in the field of strategic management, while presenting that material in an accessible and applicable way.

Solving Teaching and Learning Challenges

Some MBA and undergraduate business programs teach strategic management early in the curriculum, to give students a broad strategic perspective before they begin specializing in particular functional areas. Others teach strategic management later in the curriculum, after students have taken a deep dive into one or more functional areas.

Students in these different programs bring very different skill sets to the strategic management course. This book accommodates faculty and students in both kinds of programs.

Teaching in a "Strategy First" Curriculum

Faculty who teach in "strategy first" programs can emphasize the core text material in each chapter—and the associated cases—and de-emphasize the "Strategy in Depth" and "Research Made Relevant" features. This core material does not require much background in other business functions, and when it does, the required background is explained in detail. However, there is enough substance in this material to enable students to read and analyze the cases, and to apply strategic management ideas throughout their curriculum, and into their career choices.

Teaching in a "Strategy Last" Curriculum

Faculty who teach in "strategy last" programs can broaden their emphasis to include the "Strategy in Depth" and "Research Made Relevant" features. These features include most of the technical, economic, and mathematical discussions in the book—discussions that build directly on knowledge students should have received in their functional classes. These materials make it possible for students and faculty to go into much more analytical detail in discussing the cases, and help demonstrate how the ideas developed in other functional areas are relevant in strategic management.

Developing Employability Skills

Students who take the strategic management course often ask—how can this course enhance my employability? This question is answered in Chapter One of this book.

The VRIO framework is not just a tool for analyzing sources of competitive advantage for firms, it can also be used by students to assess whether or not they have a competitive advantage in the labor market. Consider the following:

- Is a student's knowledge of how to discount a firm's cash flow likely to be a source of competitive advantage in the labor market? This skill is valuable, but—because every business student in the world learn this skill—it is not rare, and thus will only be a source of competitive parity for a student.
- Is a student's ability to derive projected cash flows and an appropriate discount rate from a deep understanding of a firm's strategy likely to be a source of competitive advantage in the labor market? This skill is also valuable, but—in my experience—it is more rare, and thus potentially a source of competitive advantage.
- Which is more likely to be a source of competitive advantage for a student in the labor market: The ability to recite the "Five P's" in marketing or the ability to leverage their unique work experiences—either in a full time job or an

internship—with their education to analyze a firm's marketing strategy? The VRIO framework suggests the latter, not the former, approach will more likely be a source of competitive advantage.

Competing for a great job in the labor market is just another form of competition. Students who want to gain a competitive advantage in that market must build valuable, rare, and costly to imitate capabilities. As described in Chapter Three, these capabilities will typically need to be socially complex, path dependent, or causally ambiguous.

Put differently, this book is not just about corporate competitive advantage in the product market, it is also about a student's competitive advantage in the labor market.

Instructor Teaching Resources

At the Instructor Resource Center, *www.pearsoned.co.in/JayBBarney*, instructors can easily register to gain access to a variety of instructor resources available with this text in downloadable format. If assistance is needed, our dedicated technical support team is ready to help with the media supplements that accompany this text.

This program comes with the following teaching resources.

Supplements available to instructors at ***www.pearsoned.co.in/JayBBarney***	**Features of the Supplement**
Case Teaching Notes authored by William Hesterly from the University of Utah	• Case-by-case summaries • Examples and activities not in the main book • Study questions • Teaching plans • Case analysis and discussion
Instructor's Resource Manual authored by Ram Subramanian from the University of Florida	• Chapter-by-chapter summaries • Teaching points • Lecture guides for accompanying PowerPoint slides • Answers to challenge questions and problem sets in the book
PowerPoint Presentations authored by Ram Subramanian from the University of Florida	• Slides include graphs, tables, and equations from the textbook. • PowerPoints meet accessibility standards for students with disabilities. Features include, but not limited to: ▪ Keyboard and Screen Reader access ▪ Alternative text for images ▪ High color contrast between background and foreground colors

Acknowledgments

The following people were helpful in the development of this edition of the text: Stephanie Wall, Director of Portfolio Management; Neeraj Bhalla, Senior Sponsoring Editor; Sugandh Juneja, Content Producer; Melissa Feimer, Managing Producer; Becky Brown, Senior Product Marketer; and Liza Maria Borja, Shylaja.G, and Sreemeenakshi R, Project Managers at SPi Global.

Finally, this book would have never been finished without Tresa Fish. Thanks for everything, Tresa.

Preface to the Indian Edition

Conceptualized and developed by Jay B. Barney & William S. Hesterly from University of Utah, this title on "Strategic Management & Competitive Advantage" is a practical and skill-oriented book on Strategic Management. We are delighted to co-author this Indian Edition because we strongly believe in the educative value of interpretive discussions for the students.

This Indian edition offers variety of exciting collection of 24 case studies in the Indian context—every chapter containing one chapter-opening vignette and one end-of-chapter case study, respectively—allowing students to apply Strategic Management concepts and techniques for the intellectual and practical work of interpretive discussions. Participating in interpretive discussions can help teachers and students alike learn to use their minds with power and pleasure. Chapters 6 and 7 have been retained with US-original case studies for learners to understand the relevance of upcoming and latest concepts in Strategic Management.

The framework, annotated examples and appendixes can structure and guide students group work as they prepare questions, discussions, observe and analyse classroom experiments. Students gain confidence and skill through collaborative experimentation and development through case study discussions.

This book can prove useful for academicians and working professionals too for developing a shared vision and understanding of interpretive discussion and its flexible uses across various disciplines of Management like Marketing Strategy, Entrepreneurship, and so on.

We wish this book will become a primer for students, teachers, industry professionals, entrepreneurs and management consultants across the country to learn and practice the concept of Business Planning & Strategic Management.

—Arun Sahay & Srinivasan.R. Iyengar

Acknowledgments for the Indian Edition

We'd like to take this opportunity to thank the team at Pearson—Varun Goenka, Anindita Malhotra and Purushothaman C.—for their timely handling of the content and for helping us negotiate difficulties at every step of the way. Above all, we extend heartfelt gratitude towards Dr. Kasturi Naik for her contribution in this book.

About The Authors

JAY B. BARNEY

Jay Barney is currently a Presidential Professor of Strategic Management and holds the Lassonde Chair in Social Entrepreneurship at the Eccles School of Business at the University of Utah. He received his undergraduate degree from Brigham Young University, and his master's and Ph.D. degrees from Yale University. Previously, he served on the faculties at the Anderson Graduate School of Management at UCLA, the Mays School of Business at Texas A&M University, and as the Chase Chair for Excellence in Strategic Management at the Fisher College of Business at the Ohio State University. He has also served as a visiting scholar at INSEAD in Fontainebleau, France and as a visiting professor at the Said Business School at Oxford University, United Kingdom.

Most of Professor Barney's research focuses on how firms can gain and sustain competitive advantages. He has published over 100 articles in a variety of outlets, including the Harvard Business Review, the Sloan Management Review, the Strategic Management Journal, the Academy of Management Review, the Academy of Management Journal, and has published six books, including a novel titled *What I Didn't Learn at Business School: How Strategy Works in the Real World* (with Trish Gorman). He has published some of the most widely cited papers in the field of strategic management.

Professor Barney has won several awards for his research and writing, including the Irwin Outstanding Educator Award for the Business Policy and Strategy Division of the Academy of Management, the Scholarly Contributions Award for the Academy of Management, and three honorary doctoral degrees—from Lund University (Sweden), the Copenhagen Business School (Denmark), and Universidad Pontifica Comillas (Spain). He has also been elected to the Academy of Management Fellows and the Strategic Management Society Fellows and has won teaching awards at UCLA, Texas A&M, and Ohio State.

Professor Barney has also served as an officer of the Business Policy and Strategy Division of the Academy of Management, as a member of the board and later an officer of the Strategic Management Society, as an Associate Editor at the *Journal of Management*, as a Senior Editor at *Organization Science*, as a Co-editor at the *Strategic Entrepreneurship Journal*, and currently serves as Editor at the *Academy of Management Review*.

Professor Barney consults with companies and other organizations to help identify and leverage their sources of sustained competitive advantage. His over 50 clients have included Honeywell, Hewlett Packard, Texas Instruments, Koch Industries, Nationwide Insurance, Cardinal Health, and Columbus Public Schools.

WILLIAM S. HESTERLY

William Hesterly is the Associate Dean for Faculty and Research and the Dumke Family Presidential Chair of Strategic Management in the David Eccles School of Business, University of Utah. After studying at Louisiana State University, he received bachelors and master's degrees from Brigham Young University and a Ph.D. from the University of California, Los Angeles.

Professor Hesterly's research on organizational economics, vertical integration, organizational forms, and entrepreneurial networks has appeared in top journals including the *Academy of Management Review, Organization Science, Strategic Management Journal, Journal of Management*, and the *Journal of Economic Behavior and Organization*. His research has been mentioned on the front page of the *Wall Street Journal* and was featured prominently in Malcolm Gladwell's 2010 *New Yorker* article, "Talent Grab."

Professor Hesterly's research was recognized with the Western Academy of Management's Ascendant Scholar Award in 1999. Dr. Hesterly has also received best paper awards from the Western Academy of Management and the Academy of Management. Professor Hesterly has served on the editorial boards of *Strategic Organization, Organization Science* and the *Journal of Management*. He also served as the Senior Editor of *Long Range Planning*, the leading European journal in strategy.

Professor Hesterly has previously served as Associate Dean for Academic Affairs, Department Chair, and also as

Vice-President and President of the faculty at the David Eccles School of Business at the University of Utah. He was a founding member of the Strategic Human Capital Interest Group in the Strategic Management Society as well as a co-founder of the Utah-BYU Winter Strategy Conference.

Professor Hesterly has been recognized multiple times as the outstanding teacher in the MBA Program at the David Eccles School of Business and he has also been the recipient of the Student's Choice Award. He has also received the outstanding teacher awards in both the EMBA and PhD programs at the David Eccles School of Business.

Professor Hesterly has served as a consultant to *Fortune* 500 firms in the electronic, office equipment, paper, telecommunications, energy, aerospace, and medical equipment industries. He has also consulted with smaller firms in several other industries. He has taught in a variety of executive programs, both in universities and corporations.

ARUNADITYA SAHAY

Arunaditya Sahay, Professor of Strategic Management and Dean (Research), is a hard core business executive-turned-academician, who is an innovator, a corporate entrepreneur, a researcher, a teacher and an institution builder. Starting his career as an academician, he turned to the corporate world early in life wading his way to become the CEO of a large Public Sector Enterprise. In industry, he worked with many reputed companies during which he innovated many products, processes and business models getting patents and design registrations. In industry, he is known as a strategist, especially a Turnaround Manager. Returning to academics, he not only bagged the best researcher award but became champion in delivering MDPs in General Management that included Corporate Strategy, Turnaround Strategy, Innovation, Entrepreneurship, Sustainability and CSR. His consulting experience includes projects sponsored by the European Union, the Government of India, and some leading companies. He serves on the Boards of various universities and companies. He has to his credit 6 books and over 220 research/case publications.

Prof. Sahay is reachable at arun.sahay@bimtech.ac.in

SRINIVASAN R. IYENGAR

Srinivasan R. Iyengar is a multifaceted professional with roles spanning teaching, research, writing, training, speaking, and consulting. Currently, he serves as the Director and Professor at JBIMS, University of Mumbai. With a strong emphasis on continuous learning and knowledge sharing, Prof. Iyengar has authored ten textbooks covering various areas such as Strategic Management, Business Planning, Market Opportunities, Mall Management, and Strategic Retail Management, among others. He has contributed extensively to the field through articles, research papers, and case studies published in reputable national and international journals, magazines, and newspapers. Specializing in Strategic Management and Marketing, he holds a PhD in Management from Mumbai University. Dr. Iyengar's areas of expertise include Strategic Management, International Business, and Retail Shopper Behavior, and he brings over 24 years of combined corporate and academic experience to his work.

He may be contacted on rsrini@jbims.edu

PART

1 THE TOOLS OF STRATEGIC ANALYSIS

CHAPTER

1 What Is Strategy and the Strategic Management Process?

LEARNING OBJECTIVES

After reading this chapter, you should be able to:

1.1 Define strategy and describe the strategic management process.

1.2 Define competitive advantage and explain its relationship to economic value creation.

1.3 Describe two different approaches to measuring competitive advantage.

1.4 Explain the difference between emergent and intended strategies.

1.5 Discuss why it is important for you to study strategy and the strategic management process.

From Delivery to Profit: Zomato's Strategic Wins

In 2008, Deepinder Goyal and Pankaj Chaddah, founded Foodie Bay, a restaurant-listing-and-recommendation portal, that was rebranded as Zomato in 2010, expanding globally to become a multi-sided platform in the food tech industry. The company went public in July 2021, showcasing its significant growth and strategic acquisitions, including NexTable, a US online table reservation platform, and MapleGraph Solutions cloud-based PoS company. Zomato's vision encompasses enhancing the dining experience through technology, evident in its ventures like Zomato Book, Zomato Base, and acquisition of the quick commerce platform Blinkit (previously Grofers).

Zomato's strategic journey through FY2023 encapsulates a vivid narrative of strategic management, operational agility, and financial prudence, serving as an exemplary company for understanding the dynamics of the food tech industry. With its genesis as a restaurant discovery platform, Zomato transitioned into a multi-faceted entity, embodying the essence of a digital marketplace for food delivery, dining out, and culinary experiences. This evolution is underpinned by a meticulous adherence to the strategic management process and an innovative business model canvas that collectively propelled Zomato towards operational excellence and market leadership.

The fiscal year commenced with Zomato navigating through the challenges and opportunities inherent in the food tech sector. The first quarter of FY2023 was marked by a significant reduction in net loss to ₹185.7 crores, juxtaposed with a 67.44 percent year-on-year revenue surge, highlighting Zomato's strategic focus on growth and efficiency. The Gross Order Value (GOV) exemplified robust growth, attributed to an increase in order volumes and average order values, showcasing Zomato's ability to enhance its core operations while expanding its market footprint. As the year progressed, Zomato's strategic acquisition of Blinkit heralded its foray into quick commerce, integrating Blinkit's financials from the third quarter onwards. This strategic move not only diversified Zomato's revenue streams but also underscored its ambition to redefine the contours of instant delivery services. The adjusted revenue witnessed a remarkable 66 percent year-on-year growth, with a significant reduction in EBITDA loss, reflecting Zomato's operational resilience and strategic foresight.

Analysts projected a positive trajectory towards faster-than-expected profitability for Zomato, driven by strong revenue growth and strategic cost-cutting measures. Despite the seasonal variations and consumption trends impacting the sequential performance, Zomato's strategic initiatives were poised to foster a conducive environment for sustained profitability. The emphasis on revenue diversification, coupled with operational optimization, positioned Zomato to leverage its strategic advantages effectively. Central to this food tech giant's strategic approach, is a structured plan that details how it constructs, delivers, and captures value. The company's strategic plan comprehensively outlines the its unique selling points, targeted customer demographics, distribution methods, customer engagement strategies, sources of income, essential resources, main operational activities, strategic alliances, and overall financials. With this structured approach, the company skilfully addresses the complexities of the food tech sector, enhancing its service offerings, boosting customer interaction, and establishing critical partnerships to reinforce its market leadership.

Zomato's journey through FY2023 epitomizes a strategic alignment of vision, innovation, and execution, illustrating the efficacy of the strategic management process and the Business Model Canvas in navigating the volatile food tech landscape. As Zomato continues to evolve, its strategic endeavours offer valuable insights into balancing growth with financial sustainability, customer centricity with operational efficiency, and market expansion with consolidation.

REFERENCES

Goyal, D. (2023). *Q3FY23 shareholders' letter and results. Zomato.* Zomato Blog (February 9, 2023). Accessed from https://blog.zomato.com on March 12, 2024.

Nahar, P. K. (2023). *Zomato Q4 results preview: Strong revenue growth to lead faster-than-expected profitability. Business Today.* Business Today (May 19, 2023). Accessed from https://www.businesstoday.in on March 12, 2024.

Paluri, R. A., Jain, R. U., & Sankara Narayanan, R. (2022). *Zomato's race to capture the foodtech market. Emerald Emerging Markets Case Studies*, 12(2), 1-28. 10.1108/EEMCS-04-2020-0103.

Reuters (2023). *India's Zomato posts first-ever profit earlier than expected.* Reuters report (August 3, 2023). Accessed from https://www.reuters.com on March 12, 2024.

Singh, J. (2023). *Zomato: quick commerce on the menu. Emerging Markets Case Studies*, 13(2), 1-28. Emerald Publishing, the UK.

Wenger, M. (2022). *Strategic business models in the online food delivery industry-detailed analysis of the-order and delivery-business model* (Doctoral dissertation). Available at http://hdl.handle.net/10362/140006

Many of the elements of strategy discussed in this book are manifest in the Zomato story. Whether Zomato's advantage is likely to be sustainable is a question that can be answered with the models on internal strategic analysis presented in following chapters.

This and the other strategic management theories and models discussed throughout this book are, in the end, immensely practical. They can be used to understand why some firms are not able to survive, while others can survive and even pror. Understanding how to apply these theories and models will help in choosing where to work and how to be successful while at work.

Objective 1.1 Define strategy and describe the strategic management process.

Strategy and the Strategic Management Process

Although most can agree that a firm's ability to survive and prosper depends on choosing and implementing a good strategy, there is less agreement about what a strategy is and even less agreement about what constitutes a good strategy. Indeed, there are almost as many different definitions of these concepts as there are books written about them.

Defining Strategy

In this book, a firm's **strategy** is defined as its theory about how to gain competitive advantages.[1] A good strategy is a strategy that generates such advantages. Pokémon Go's theory of how to gain a competitive advantage focused on leveraging the traditional brand power of Pokémon with the new technological capabilities of augmented reality—largely an example of a product differentiation strategy discussed in Chapter 5 of this book.

Each of these theories—like all theories—is based on a set of assumptions and hypotheses about the way competition in an industry is likely to evolve and how that evolution can be exploited to earn a profit. The greater the extent to which these assumptions and hypotheses accurately reflect how competition in this industry evolves, the more likely it is that a firm will gain a competitive advantage from implementing its strategies. If these assumptions and hypotheses turn out not to be accurate, then a firm's strategies are not likely to be a source of competitive advantage.

But here is the challenge. It is usually very difficult to predict how competition in an industry will evolve, and so it is rarely possible to know for sure that a firm is choosing the right strategy. Therefore, a firm's strategy is almost always a theory: It's a firm's best bet about how competition is going to evolve and how that evolution can be exploited for competitive advantage.

The Strategic Management Process

Although it is usually difficult to know for sure that a firm is pursuing the best strategy, it is possible to reduce the likelihood that mistakes are being made. Research suggests that the best way to do this is for a firm to choose its strategy carefully and systematically and to follow the strategic management process. The **strategic management process** is a sequential set of analyses and choices that can increase the likelihood that a firm will choose a good strategy; that is, a strategy that generates competitive advantages. An example of the strategic management process is presented in Figure 1.1. Not surprisingly, much of this book is organized around this strategic management process.

A Firm's Mission

The strategic management process begins when a firm defines its mission. A firm's **mission** is its long-term purpose. Missions define both what a firm aspires to be in the long run and what it wants to avoid in the meantime. Missions are often written down in the form of **mission statements**.

Some Missions May Not Affect Firm Performance Most mission statements incorporate common elements. For example, many define the businesses within which a firm will operate—medical products for Johnson and Johnson; adhesives and substrates for 3M—or they can very simply state how a firm will compete in those businesses. Many even define the core values that a firm espouses.

Indeed, mission statements often contain so many common elements that some have questioned whether having a mission statement even creates value for a firm.[2] Moreover, even if a mission statement does say something unique about a company, if that mission statement does not influence behavior throughout an organization, it is unlikely to have much impact on a firm's actions. For example, while Enron was engaging in wide ranging acts of fraud[3], it had a mission statement that emphasized the importance of honesty and integrity.[4] Research suggests that, on average, mission statements do not affect a firm's performance.

Some Missions Can Improve Firm Performance Despite these caveats, research has identified some firms whose sense of purpose and mission permeates all that they do. These firms have included, for example, 3M, IBM, Hewlett-Packard, and Disney. Some of these **visionary firms,** or firms whose mission is central to all they do, have enjoyed long periods of high performance.[5] From 1926 through 1995, an investment of $1 in one of these firms would have increased in value to $6,536. That same dollar invested in an average firm over this same period would have been worth $415 in 1995.

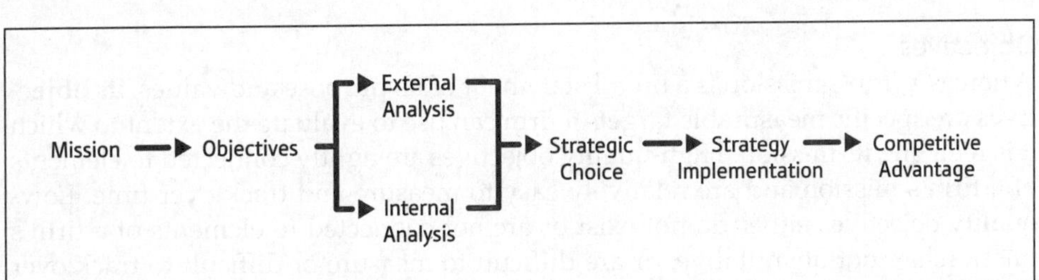

Figure 1.1 The Strategic Management Process

These visionary firms earned substantially higher returns than average firms even though many of their mission statements suggest that profit maximizing, although an important corporate objective, is not their primary reason for existence. Rather, their primary reasons for existence are typically reflected in a widely held set of values and beliefs that inform day-to-day decision making. While, in other firms, managers may be tempted to sacrifice such values and beliefs to gain short-term advantages, in these special firms, the pressure for short term performance is balanced by widespread commitment to values and beliefs that focus more on a firm's long-term performance.[6]

Of course, that these firms had performed well for many decades does not mean they will do so forever. Some previously identified visionary firms have stumbled more recently, including American Express, Ford, Hewlett-Packard, Motorola, and Sony. Some of these financial problems may be attributable to the fact that these formally mission-driven companies have lost focus on their mission.

Some Missions Can Hurt Firm Performance Although some firms have used their missions to develop strategies that create significant competitive advantages, missions can hurt a firm's performance as well. For example, sometimes a firm's mission will be very inwardly focused and defined only with reference to the personal values and priorities of its founders or top managers, independent of whether those values and priorities are consistent with the economic realities facing a firm. Strategies derived from such missions are not likely to be a source of competitive advantage.

Consider, for example, Yahoo. In 2008, Microsoft tried to buy Yahoo for $31 per share, a deal worth, in total, $44.6 billion. This represented a premium over Yahoo's market price at the time. Yahoo declined the offer, citing the strength of their global brand, recent investments in its advertising platform, and their ongoing strategy in concluding that Microsoft's offer undervalued Yahoo. In short, Yahoo remained committed to its mission and strategy, and remained independent.

Over the next several years, Yahoo's market value tumbled, reaching a low of less than $10 per share—well below the $31 per share Microsoft had offered. Finally, in 2013, Yahoo's valuations rose to equal what Microsoft had offered to buy it for in 2008.

But this valuation turned out to be difficult to maintain. While Yahoo continued as an independent company, its value continued to fall. Finally, in July of 2016, Verizon purchased Yahoo for $4.8 billion. In other words, by keeping focused on its mission and strategy, Yahoo destroyed almost $40 billion in value for its shareholders over an eight-year period of time.[7]

Obviously, because a firm's mission can help, hurt, or have no impact on its performance, missions by themselves do not necessarily lead a firm to choose and implement strategies that generate competitive advantages. Indeed, as suggested in Figure 1.1, while defining a firm's mission is an important step in the strategic management process, it is only the first step in that process.

Objectives

Whereas a firm's mission is a broad statement of its purpose and values, its **objectives** are specific measurable targets a firm can use to evaluate the extent to which it is realizing its mission. High-quality objectives are tightly connected to elements of a firm's mission and are relatively easy to measure and track over time. Low-quality objectives either do not exist or are not connected to elements of a firm's mission, are not quantitative, or are difficult to measure or difficult to track over time. Obviously, low-quality objectives cannot be used by management to evaluate how well a mission is being realized. Indeed, one indication that a firm is not that serious about realizing part of its mission statement is when there are no objectives, or only low-quality objectives, associated with that part of the mission.

External and Internal Analysis

The next two phases of the strategic management process—external analysis and internal analysis—occur more or less simultaneously. By conducting an **external analysis**, a firm identifies the critical threats and opportunities in its competitive environment. It also examines how competition in this environment is likely to evolve and what implications that evolution has for the threats and opportunities a firm is facing. A considerable literature on techniques for and approaches to conducting external analysis has evolved over the past several years. This literature is the primary subject matter of Chapter 2 of this book.

Whereas external analysis focuses on the environmental threats and opportunities facing a firm, **internal analysis** helps a firm identify its organizational strengths and weaknesses. It also helps a firm understand which of its resources and capabilities are likely to be sources of competitive advantage and which are less likely to be sources of such advantages. Finally, internal analysis can be used by firms to identify those areas of its organization that require improvement and change. As with external analysis, a considerable literature on techniques for and approaches to conducting internal analysis has evolved over the past several years. This literature is the primary subject matter of Chapter 3 of this book.

Strategic Choice

Armed with a mission, objectives, and completed external and internal analyses, a firm is ready to make its strategic choices. That is, a firm is ready to choose its theory of how to gain competitive advantage.

The strategic choices available to firms fall into two large categories: business-level strategies and corporate-level strategies. **Business-level strategies** are actions firms take to gain competitive advantages in a single market or industry. These strategies are the topic of Part 2 of this book and include cost leadership (Chapter 4), product differentiation (Chapter 5), and flexibility (Chapter 6). In addition, tacit collusion as a business level strategy will be discussed in each chapter of this book in Chapter 7. **Corporate-level strategies** are actions firms take to gain competitive advantages by operating in multiple markets or industries simultaneously. These strategies are the topic of Part 3 of this book. Common corporate-level strategies include vertical integration strategies (Chapter 8), diversification strategies (Chapters 9 and 10), strategic alliance strategies (Chapter 11), and merger and acquisition strategies (Chapter 12).

Obviously, the details of choosing specific strategies can be quite complex, and a discussion of these details will be delayed until later in the book. However, the underlying logic of strategic choice is not complex. Based on the strategic management process, the objective when making a strategic choice is to choose a strategy that: (1) supports the firm's mission; (2) is consistent with a firm's objectives; (3) exploits opportunities in a firm's environment with a firm's strengths; and (4) neutralizes threats in a firm's environment while avoiding a firm's weaknesses. If this strategy is implemented—the last step of the strategic management process—a strategy that meets these criteria is very likely to be a source of competitive advantage for a firm.

Strategy Implementation

Of course, simply choosing a strategy means nothing if that strategy is not implemented. **Strategy implementation** occurs when a firm adopts organizational policies and practices that are consistent with its strategy. Three specific organizational policies and practices are particularly important in implementing a strategy: (1) a firm's formal organizational structure; (2) its formal and informal management control systems; and (3) its employee compensation policies. A firm that adopts an organizational structure, management controls, and compensation policy that are consistent with and reinforce its strategies is more likely to be able to implement those strategies than a firm that adopts an organizational structure, management controls, and compensation policy that are inconsistent with its strategies. Specific organizational structures, management controls, and compensation policies used to implement the business-level strategies are discussed in Part Two of this book; ways that firms can implement corporate strategies are discussed in Part Three. Normally, the process of choosing and implementing a strategy are discussed in the same chapter. However, because so much has been written about implementing a diversification strategy, choosing this strategy is discussed in Chapter 9 while implementing it is discussed in Chapter 10.

Objective 1.2 Define competitive advantage and explain its relationship to economic value creation.

What is Competitive Advantage?

Of course, the ultimate objective of the strategic management process is to enable a firm to choose and implement a strategy that generates a competitive advantage. But what is a competitive advantage? In general, a firm has a **competitive advantage** when it can create more economic value than rival firms. **Economic value** is simply the difference between what customers are willing to pay for a firm's products or services and the total cost of producing these products or services. Thus, the size of a firm's competitive advantage is the difference between the economic value a firm can create and the economic value its rivals can create.[8]

Consider the two firms presented in Figure 1.2. Both these firms compete in the same market for the same customers. However, Firm I generates \$180 of economic value each time it sells a product or service, whereas Firm II generates \$150 of economic value each time it sells a product or service. Because Firm I generates more economic value each time it sells a product or service, it has a competitive advantage over Firm II. The size of this competitive advantage is equal to the difference in the economic value these two firms create, in this case, \$30(\$180 – \$150 = \$30).

However, as shown in the figure, Firm I's advantage may come from different sources. For example, it might be the case that Firm I's customers are willing to pay more for its products or services than are Firm II's customers. In panel A of the figure, Firm I's customers are willing to pay \$230 for the benefits they associate with Firm I's products or services, whereas Firm II's customers are only willing to pay \$200 for its products or services. Thus, even though both firms' costs are the same (equal to \$50 per unit sold), Firm I creates more economic value (\$230 – \$50 = \$180) than Firm II (\$200 – \$50 = \$150). Indeed, it is possible for Firm I, in this situation, to have higher costs than Firm II and still create more economic value than Firm II if these higher costs are offset by the willingness of Firm I's customers to pay more for its products or services.

Alternatively, as shown in panel B of the figure, the customers of these two firms may be willing to pay the same for Firm I and II's products or services (equal to \$210 in the figure) but these firms may have different costs. If Firm I's costs per unit are only \$30, it will generate \$180 worth of economic value (\$210 – \$30 = \$180). If Firm II's costs are \$60, it will generate only \$150 of economic value (\$210 – \$60 = \$150). Indeed, it might be possible for Firm I's customers to have a lower willingness to pay than Firm II's customers, and Firm I can still create more economic value than Firm II. This is possible as long as Firm

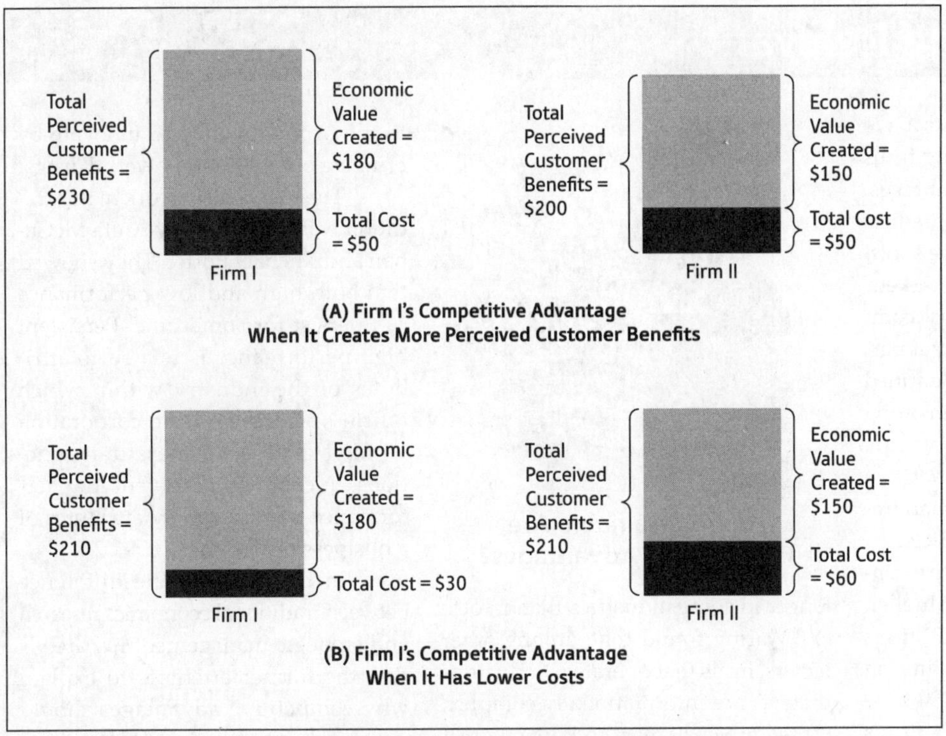

Figure 1.2 The Sources of a Firm's Competitive Advantage

I's disadvantage in customer willingness to pay is more than offset by its cost advantage.

A firm's competitive advantage can be temporary or sustained. As summarized in Figure 1.3, a **temporary competitive advantage** is a competitive advantage that lasts for a very short time. A **sustained competitive advantage**, in contrast, can last much longer. How long sustained competitive advantages can last is discussed in the Research Made Relevant feature. Firms that create the same economic value as their rivals experience **competitive parity**. Finally, firms that generate less economic value than their rivals have a **competitive disadvantage**. Not surprisingly, competitive disadvantages can be either temporary or sustained, depending on the duration of the disadvantage.

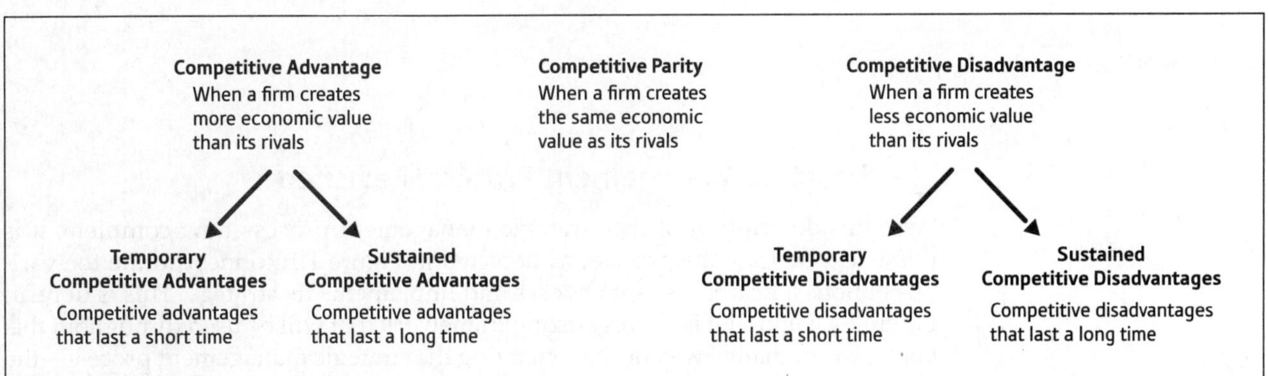

Figure 1.3 Types of Competitive Advantage

Research Made Relevant

For some time, economists have been interested in how long firms can sustain competitive advantages. Traditional economic theory predicts that such advantages should be short-lived in highly competitive markets. This theory suggests that any competitive advantages gained by a particular firm will quickly be identified and imitated by other firms, ensuring competitive parity in the long run. However, in real life, competitive advantages often last longer than traditional economic theory predicts.

One of the first scholars to examine this issue was Dennis Mueller. Mueller divided a sample of 472 firms into eight categories, depending on their level of performance in 1949. He then examined the impact of a firm's initial performance on its subsequent performance. The traditional economic hypothesis was that all firms in the sample would converge on an average level of performance. This did not occur. Indeed, firms that were performing well in an earlier period tended to perform well in later time periods, and firms that performed poorly in an earlier period tended to perform poorly in later time periods as well.

Geoffrey Waring followed up on Mueller's work by explaining why competitive advantages seem to persist

How Sustainable Are Competitive Advantages?

longer in some industries than in others. Waring found that, among other factors, firms that operate in industries that: (1) are informationally complex; (2) require customers to know a great deal to use an industry's products; (3) require a great deal of research and development; and (4) have significant economies of scale are more likely to have sustained competitive advantages compared to firms that operate in industries without these attributes.

Peter Roberts studied the persistence of profitability in one particular industry: the U.S. pharmaceutical industry. Roberts found that not only can firms sustain competitive advantages in this industry, but that the ability to do so is almost entirely attributable to the firms' capacity to innovate by bringing out new and powerful drugs.

The most recent work in this tradition was published by Anita McGahan and Michael Porter. They showed that both high and low performance can persist for some time. Persistent high performance is related to attributes of the industry within which a firm operates and the corporation within which a business unit functions. In contrast, persistent low performance was caused by attributes of a business unit itself.

In many ways, the difference between traditional economics research and strategic management research is that the former attempts to explain why competitive advantages should not persist, whereas the latter attempts to explain when they can. Thus far, most empirical research suggests that firms, in at least some settings, can sustain competitive advantages[9]

Sources: D. C. Mueller (1977). "The persistence of profits above the norm." *Economica*, 44, pp. 369–380; P. W. Roberts (1999). "Product innovation, product-market competition, and persistent profitability in the U.S. pharmaceutical industry." *Strategic Management Journal*, 20, pp. 655–670; G. F. Waring (1996). "Industry differences in the persistence of firm-specific returns." *The American Economic Review*, 86, pp. 1253–1265; A. McGahan and M. Porter (2003). "The emergence and sustainability of abnormal profits." *Strategic Organization*, 1(1), pp. 79–108.

The Strategic Management Process, Revisited

With this description of the strategic management process now complete, it is possible to redraw the process, as depicted in Figure 1.1, to incorporate the various options a firm faces as it chooses and implements its strategy. This is done in Figure 1.4. Figure 1.4 is the organizing framework that will be used throughout this book. An alternative way of characterizing the strategic management process—the business model canvas—is described in the Strategy in Depth feature.

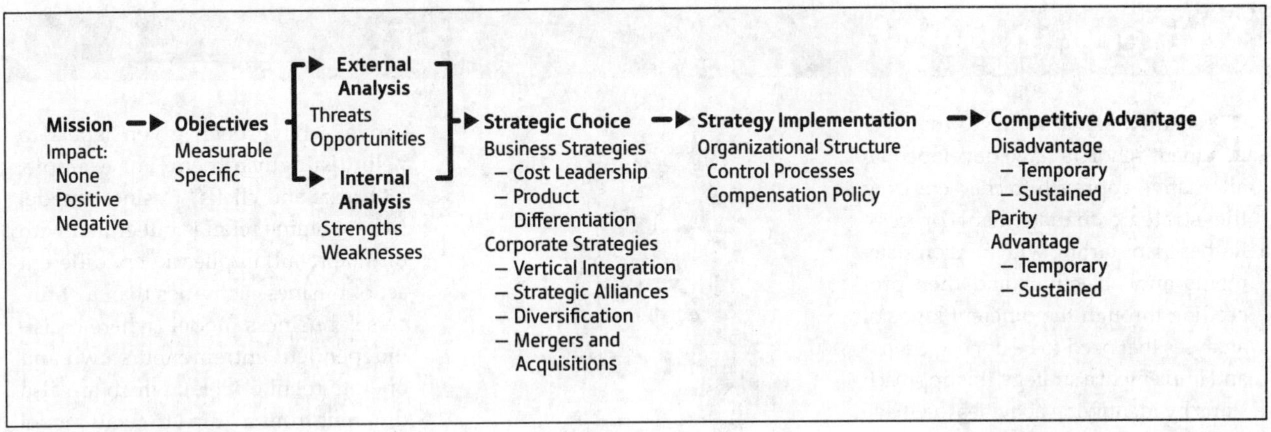

Figure 1.4 Organizing Framework

Measuring Competitive Advantage

Objective 1.3 Describe two different approaches to measuring competitive advantage.

A firm has a *competitive advantage* when it creates more economic value than its rivals. *Economic value* is the difference between what customers are willing to pay for a firm's products or services and the full cost of producing and selling these products or services. These are deceptively simple definitions. However, these concepts are not always easy to measure directly. For example, the benefits of a firm's products or services are always a matter of customer perception, and perceptions are not easy to measure. Also, the total costs associated with producing a particular product or service may not always be easy to identify or associate with a particular product or service. Despite the very real challenges associated with measuring a firm's competitive advantage, two approaches have emerged. The first estimates a firm's competitive advantage by examining its accounting performance; the second examines a firm's economic performance. These approaches are discussed in the following sections.

Accounting Measures of Competitive Advantage

A firm's **accounting performance** is a measure of its competitive advantage calculated by using information from a firm's published profit and loss and balance sheet statements. A firm's profit and loss and balance sheet statements, in turn, are typically created using widely accepted accounting standards and principles. The application of these standards and principles makes it possible to compare the accounting performance of one firm to the accounting performance of other firms, even if those firms are not in the same industry. However, to the extent that these standards and principles are not applied in generating a firm's accounting statements or to the extent that different firms use different accounting standards and principles in generating their statements, it can be difficult to compare the accounting performance of firms. These issues can be particularly challenging when comparing the performance of firms in different countries around the world.

One way to use a firm's accounting statements to measure its competitive advantage is with accounting ratios. **Accounting ratios** are simply numbers taken from a firm's financial statements that are manipulated in ways that describe various aspects of a firm's performance. Some of the most common accounting ratios that can be used to characterize a firm's performance are presented in Table 1.1.

Strategy in Depth

Recently, some strategic management scholars have developed an alternative approach to characterizing the strategic management process. Rather than starting with mission statements and objectives and then proceeding through the different kinds of analyses that need to be done to choose and implement a strategy, this approach starts by identifying activities that have an impact on the ability of a firm to create and appropriate economic value and then specifying exactly how a particular firm accomplishes these activities. The set of activities that a firm engages in to create and appropriate economic value, in this approach, is called a firm's **business model**. (see Required Reading: Business Model Development at the end of this chapter).

Probably the most influential approach to identifying a firm's business model was developed by Alex Osterwalder and Yves Pigneur in their book *Business Model Generator*. In the book, a generic business model—not unrelated to the generic value chains that will be introduced in Chapter 3 of this book—is presented. Because this approach enables managers to see the entire landscape of their business in a single page, this model is called the *business model canvas*. This canvas is reproduced in this feature.

The center of the canvas is dominated by a box labeled *Value Propositions*. A firm's value propositions are statements about how it will attempt to create value for its customers, customer problems it is trying to solve through its business operations, which customers it will focus on, and so forth. Identifying a firm's value propositions is very close to identifying its strategy, as presented in Figure 1.4.

Once a firm's value propositions are identified, they have important

The Business Model Canvas

implications for the *Key Activities* a firm needs to engage in, the *Key Resources* it needs to control to engage in those activities, and the *Key Partners* it needs to have to gain access to those resources. The value propositions also help determine critical *Customer Relationships*, the *Channels* a firm needs to use to reach those critical customers, and which *Customer Segments* a firm will address with its products or services.

If a firm's key activities, resources, and partners, on the one hand, and its customer relationships, channels, and segments, on the other hand, all support the execution of its value propositions, then these activities—collectively—will improve a firm's cost structure and revenue streams. Consistent with the definitions presented in this chapter, the difference between a firm's revenues and costs is a measure of the economic value created by a firm.

Different business models—as summarized by the business model canvas—have been given labels to help distinguish them. For example, a "bricks and clicks" business model (where online retail is integrated with off-line retail) implies a very different set of business activities than a "franchise" business model (where quasi-independent entrepreneurs own and operate retail outlets), which are also different from a "direct" retail model (where firms eliminate in-process inventory by having customers order each product sold), and so forth.

Some scholars have objected to the introduction of the canvas, arguing that it does not add anything fundamental to our understanding of the strategic management process. Others have suggested that some important components of that process—including, for example, organizing to implement a firm's strategy—are left out of the canvas. Others argue that competition is not well represented in the canvas—if large numbers of competing firms all adopt the same business model canvas, how is that canvas supposed to enhance the competitive position of any one of those firms? On the other hand, the canvas is a convenient way to summarize a wide variety of firm activities, how those activities are related to one another, and how they ultimately affect a firm's costs and revenues. And while the framework presented in Figure 1.4 will not be used to organize the material in the rest of this book, insights from the canvas approach will be incorporated throughout the book as appropriate[10].

Sources: A. Osterwalder and Y. Pigneur (2010). Business Model Generator. NY: Wiley. G. George and A. J. Bock (2011). The business model in practice and its implications for entrepreneurial research. *Entrepreneurship: Theory and Practice*, 35(1), 83–111. C. Zott, R. Amit, and L. Massa. (2010). The Business Model: Theoretical Roots, Recent Development, and Future Research. Working Paper 862, IESE, Barcelona, Spain.

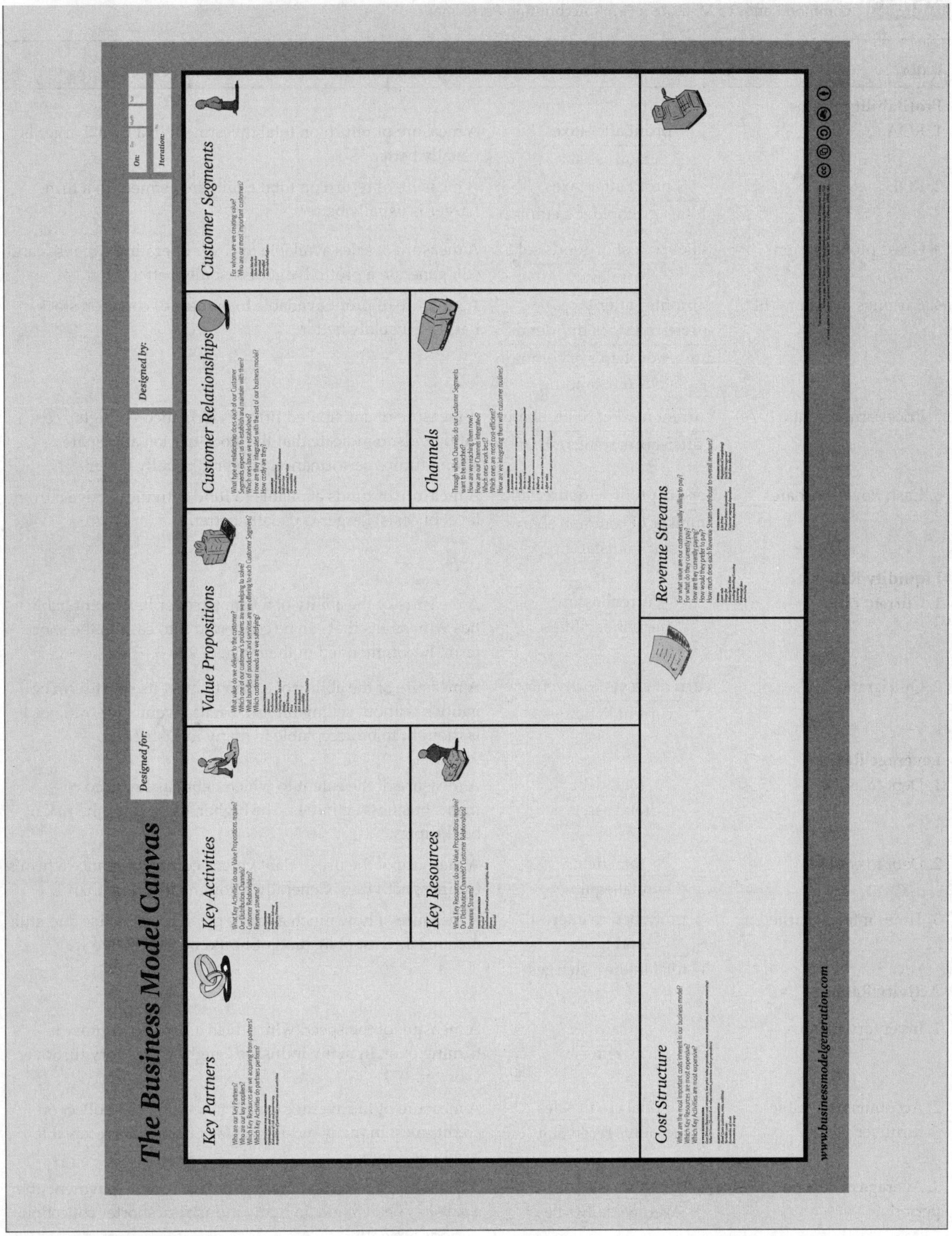
The Business Model Canvas
Designed for:
Designed by:
On:
Iteration:
Key Partners
Key Activities
Key Resources
Value Propositions
Customer Relationships
Channels
Customer Segments
Cost Structure
Revenue Streams
www.businessmodelgeneration.com

TABLE 1.1 Common Ratios to Measure a Firm's Accounting Performance

Ratio	Calculation	Interpretation
Profitability Ratios		
1. ROA	$\frac{\text{profit after taxes}}{\text{total assets}}$	A measure of return on total investment in a firm. Larger is usually better.
2. ROE	$\frac{\text{profit after taxes}}{\text{total stockholder's equity}}$	A measure of return on total equity investment in a firm. Larger is usually better.
3. Gross profit margin	$\frac{\text{sales} - \text{cost of goods sold}}{\text{sales}}$	A measure of sales available to cover operating expenses and still generate a profit. Larger is usually better.
4. Earnings per share (EPS)	$\frac{\text{profits (after taxes)} - \text{preferred stock dividends}}{\text{number of shares of common stock outstanding}}$	A measure of profit available to owners of common stock. Larger is usually better.
5. Price earnings ratio (p/e)	$\frac{\text{current market price/share}}{\text{after-tax earnings/share}}$	A measure of anticipated firm performance—a high p/e ratio tends to indicate that the stock market anticipates strong future performance. Larger is usually better.
6. Cash flow per share	$\frac{\text{after-tax profit} + \text{depreciation}}{\text{number of common shares stock outstanding}}$	A measure of funds available to fund activities above current level of costs. Larger is usually better.
Liquidity Ratios		
1. Current ratio	$\frac{\text{current assets}}{\text{current liabilities}}$	A measure of the ability of a firm to cover its current liabilities with assets that can be converted into cash in the short term. Recommended in the range of 2 to 3.
2. Quick ratio	$\frac{\text{current assets} - \text{inventory}}{\text{current liabilities}}$	A measure of the ability of a firm to meet its short-term obligations without selling off its current inventory. A ratio of 1 is thought to be acceptable in many industries.
Leverage Ratios		
1. Debt to assets	$\frac{\text{total debt}}{\text{total assets}}$	A measure of the extent to which debt has financed a firm's business activities. The higher, the greater the risk of bankruptcy.
2. Debt to equity	$\frac{\text{total debt}}{\text{total equity}}$	A measure of the use of debt versus equity to finance a firm's business activities. Generally recommended less than 1.
3. Times interest earned	$\frac{\text{profit before interest and taxes}}{\text{total interest charges}}$	A measure of how much a firm's profits can decline and still meet its interest obligations. Should be well above 1.
Activity Ratios		
1. Inventory turnover	$\frac{\text{sales}}{\text{inventory}}$	A measure of the speed with which a firm's inventory is turning over. In many industries, higher inventory turnover is better.
2. Accounts receivable turnover	$\frac{\text{annual credit sales}}{\text{accounts receivable}}$	A measure of the average time it takes a firm to collect on credit sales. In many industries, faster accounts receivable turnover is better.
3. Average collection period	$\frac{\text{accounts receivable}}{\text{average daily sales}}$	A measure of the time it takes a firm to receive payment after a sale has been made. In many industries, shorter collection periods are better.

These measures of firm accounting performance can be grouped into four categories: (1) **profitability ratios,** or ratios with some measure of profit in the numerator and some measure of firm size or assets in the denominator; (2) **liquidity ratios,** or ratios that focus on the ability of a firm to meet its short-term financial obligations; (3) **leverage ratios,** or ratios that focus on the level of a firm's financial flexibility, including its ability to obtain more debt; and (4) **activity ratios,** or ratios that focus on the level of activity in a firm's business.

Of course, these ratios, by themselves, say very little about a firm. To determine how a firm is performing, its accounting ratios must be compared with some standard. In general, that standard is the average of accounting ratios of other firms in the same industry. Using ratio analysis, a firm earns **above-average accounting performance** when its performance is greater than the industry average. Such firms typically have competitive advantages, sustained or otherwise. A firm earns **average accounting performance** when its performance is equal to the industry average. These firms generally enjoy only competitive parity. A firm earns **below-average accounting performance** when its performance is less than the industry average. These firms generally experience competitive disadvantages.

Consider, for example, the performance of Apple Inc. Apple's financial statements for 2015 and 2016 are summarized in Table 1.2. Losses in this table would be presented in parentheses. Several ratio measures of accounting performance are calculated for Apple in these two years in Table 1.3.

Apple's sales decreased from 2015 to 2016, from just under $234 billion to $215.6 billion. Apples profitability also fell over this period, with ROA dropping from .18 to .14. However, its gross margins remained almost constant, at .4 and .39 respectively. This suggests that while Apple's sales decreased, it did not engage in significant price cutting or shift its product mix to lower priced items. Lower sales revenues then generated lower levels of profit. Also, both Apple's Current and Quick ratios increased, suggesting that it increased its ability to meet any short-term obligations it might face. Finally, a nearly constant debt to total assets ratio

TABLE 1.2 Apple Inc.'s Financial Statements for 2016 and 2015 (numbers in millions of dollars)

	2016	2015
Net sales	215,639	233,715
Cost of goods sold	131,376	140,089
Gross margin	84,263	93,626
Selling, general, and administrative expenses	14,194	14,329
R & D expense	10,045	8,067
Total operating expenses	24,239	22,396
Operating income (loss)	60,024	71,230
Total income (loss), before taxes	61,372	72,515
Provision for taxes	15,685	19,121
Net income, after taxes	45,687	53,394
Inventories	2,132	2,349
Total current assets	106,869	89,378
Total assets	321,686	290,345
Total current liabilities	79,006	80,610
Total debt	193,437	170,990
Total shareholders' equity	31,251	27,416
Retained earnings	96,364	92,284

TABLE 1.3 Some Accounting Ratios for Apple Inc. in 2016 and 2015

	2016	2015
ROA	45,687/321,686 = .14	41,711/176,064 = 0.237
Gross profit margin		
Current ratio	106,869/79,006 = 1.35	89,378/80,610 = 1.11
Quick ratio		
Debt to assets	193,437/321,686 = .60	170,990/290,345 = 0.59

suggests that Apple did not take on any additional long term liabilities from 2015 to 2016.

Overall, the information in Tables 1.2 and 1.3 suggests that Apple Inc., in 2015 and 2016, was, financially speaking, very healthy, although 2015 was a better year than 2016.

Economic Measures of Competitive Advantage

The great advantage of accounting measures of competitive advantage is that they are relatively easy to compute. All publicly traded firms must make their accounting statements available to the public. Even privately owned firms will typically release some information about their accounting performance. From these statements, it is quite easy to calculate various accounting ratios. One can learn a great deal about a firm's competitive position by comparing these ratios to industry averages.

However, accounting measures of competitive advantage have at least one significant limitation. Earlier, economic profit was defined as the difference between what customers are willing to pay for a firm's products or services and the cost of producing and selling those products or services. However, one important component of cost is typically not included in most accounting measures of competitive advantage: the cost of the capital a firm employs to produce and sell its products or services. The **cost of capital** is the rate of return that a firm promises to pay its suppliers of capital to induce them to invest in the firm. Once these investments are made, a firm can use this capital to produce and sell products and services. However, a firm must provide the promised return to its sources of capital if it expects to obtain more investment capital in the future. **Economic measures of competitive advantage** compare a firm's level of return to its cost of capital instead of to the average level of return in the industry.

Generally, there are two broad categories of sources of capital: **debt** (capital from banks and bondholders) and **equity** (capital from individuals and institutions that purchase a firm's stock). The **cost of debt** is equal to the interest that a firm must pay its debt holders (adjusted for taxes) to induce those debt holders to lend money to a firm. The **cost of equity** is equal to the rate of return a firm must promise its equity holders to induce these individuals and institutions to invest in a firm. A firm's **weighted average cost of capital (WACC)** is simply the percentage of a firm's total capital which is debt, times the cost of debt, plus the percentage of a firm's total capital that is equity, times the cost of equity. Mathematically, a firm's WACC is:

$$\text{WACC} = (\text{market value of a debt/firm's market value}) \times \text{after tax cost of debt} + (\text{market value of equity/firm's market value}) \times \text{cost of equity} \quad (1.1)$$

The process for estimating these elements of a firm's WACC is discussed in any corporate finance text. The **cost of debt** is simply the interest a firm must pay on its debt. The **after-tax cost of debt** is equal to the cost of debt multiplied times one minus a firm's marginal tax rate (assuming that the interest on debt is tax deductible). The **cost of equity**, on the other hand, is equal to the return a firm promises to pay its equity holders for investing in a firm's equity. Usually, the cost of equity is estimated using the **Capital Asset Pricing Model (CAPM)** which can be written as:

$$\text{Cost of Equity} = \text{Risk Free Rate of Return} + \beta\,(\text{Expected Market Return} - \text{Risk Free Rate of Return}) \quad (1.2)$$

In this equation, the **risk-free rate of return** equals the interest earned on a risk-free asset (typically an investment in a government bond), the **expected market return** is the return an investor expects to receive from investing in a fully diversified portfolio of stocks, and $\boldsymbol{\beta}$ is how much riskier a particular firm's stock is, compared to a fully diversified portfolio. For many publicly traded firms, β is available online.

Conceptually, a firm's cost of capital is the level of performance a firm must attain if it is to satisfy the economic objectives of two of its critical stakeholders: debt holders and equity holders. A firm that earns above its cost of capital is likely to be able to attract additional capital because debt holders and equity holders will scramble to make additional funds available for this firm. Such a firm is said to be earning **above-normal economic performance** and will be able to use its access to cheap capital to grow and expand its business. In general, firms with competitive advantages earn above normal economic performance.

A firm that earns its cost of capital is said to have **normal economic performance**. This level of performance is said to be "normal" because this is the level of performance that most of a firm's equity and debt holders expect. Firms that have normal economic performance can gain access to the capital they need to survive, although they are not prospering. Growth opportunities may be somewhat limited for these firms. In general, firms with competitive parity usually have normal economic performance.

A firm that earns less than its cost of capital is in the process of liquidating. **Below-normal economic performance** implies that a firm's debt and equity holders will be looking for alternative ways to invest their money, someplace where they can earn at least what they expect to earn; that is, normal economic performance. Unless a firm with below normal performance changes, its long-term viability will come into question. Obviously, firms that have a competitive disadvantage generally have below normal economic performance.

Measuring a firm's performance relative to its cost of capital has several advantages for strategic analysis. Foremost among these is the notion that a firm that earns at least its cost of capital is satisfying two of its most important stakeholders: debt holders and equity holders. Despite the advantages of comparing a firm's performance to its cost of capital, this approach has some important limitations as well. For example, it can sometimes be difficult to calculate a firm's cost of capital. This is especially true if a firm is **privately held**—that is, if it has stock that is not traded on public stock markets or if it is a division of a larger company. In these situations, it may be necessary to use accounting ratios to measure a firm's performance. Moreover, some have suggested that although accounting measures of competitive advantage understate the importance of a firm's equity and debt holders in evaluating a firm's performance, economic measures of competitive advantage exaggerate the importance of these two particular stakeholders, often to the disadvantage of other stakeholders in a firm. These issues are discussed in more detail in the Ethics and Strategy feature.

Ethics and Strategy

Stockholders Versus Stakeholders

Considerable debate exists about the role of a firm's equity and debt holders versus its other stakeholders in defining and measuring a firm's performance. These other **stakeholders** include a firm's suppliers, its customers, its employees, and the communities within which it does business. Like equity and debt holders, these other stakeholders make investments in a firm. They, too, expect some compensation for making these investments.

On the one hand, some argue that if a firm maximizes the wealth of its equity holders, it will automatically satisfy all of its other stakeholders. This view of the firm depends on what is called the **residual claimants view** of equity holders. This view is that equity holders only receive payment on their investment in a firm after all legitimate claims by a firm's other stakeholders are satisfied. Thus, a firm's equity holders, in this view, only receive payment on their investments after the firm's employees are compensated, its suppliers are paid, its customers are satisfied, and its obligations to the communities within which it does business have been met. By maximizing returns to its equity holders, a firm is ensuring that its other stakeholders are fully compensated for investing in a firm.

On the other hand, some argue that the interests of equity holders and a firm's other stakeholders often collide and that a firm that maximizes the wealth of its equity holders does not necessarily satisfy its other stakeholders. For example, whereas a firm's customers may want it to sell higher-quality products at lower prices, a firm's equity holders may want it to sell low-quality products at higher prices; this obviously would increase the amount of money left over to pay off a firm's equity holders. Also, whereas a firm's employees may want it to adopt policies that lead to steady performance over long periods of time—because this will lead to stable employment—a firm's equity holders may be more interested in its maximizing its short-term profitability, even if this hurts employment stability. The interests of equity holders and the broader community may also clash, especially when it is very costly for a firm to engage in environmentally friendly behaviors that could reduce its short-term performance.

This debate manifests itself in a variety of ways. For example, many groups that oppose the globalization of the U.S. economy do so on the basis that firms make production, marketing, and other strategic choices in ways that maximize profits for equity holders, often to the detriment of a firm's other stakeholders. These people are concerned about the effects of globalization on workers, on the environment, and on the cultures in the developing economies where global firms sometimes locate their manufacturing and other operations. Managers in global firms respond by saying that they have a responsibility to maximize the wealth of their equity holders. Given the passions that surround this debate, it is unlikely that these issues will be resolved soon[11]

Sources: T. Copeland, T. Koller, and J. Murrin (1995). *Valuation: Measuring and managing the value of companies*. New York: Wiley; L. Donaldson (1990). "The ethereal hand: Organizational economics and management theory." *Academy of Review*, 15, pp. 369–381; and E. Freeman, J. Harrison, A. Wicks, B. Parmar, and S. de Colle (2010 Stakeholder Theory: The State of the Art. Cambridge: Cambridge.

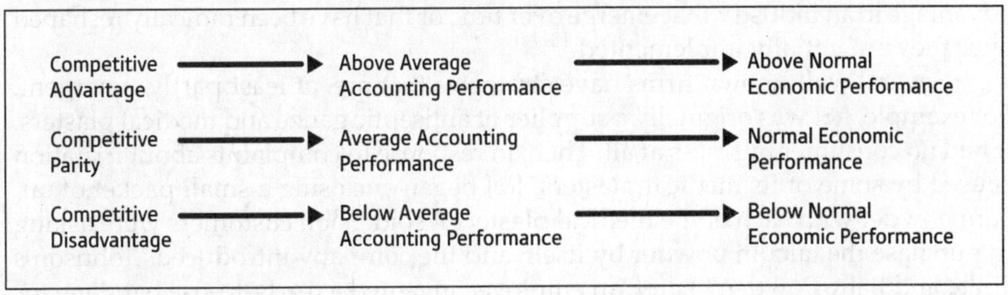

Figure 1.5 Competitive Advantage and Firm Performance

The Relationship Between Economic and Accounting Performance Measures

The correlation between economic and accounting measures of competitive advantage is high. That is, firms that perform well using one of these measures usually perform well using the other. Conversely, firms that do poorly using one of these measures normally do poorly using the other. Thus, the relationships among competitive advantage, accounting performance, and economic performance depicted in Figure 1.5 generally hold.

However, it is possible for a firm to have above-average accounting performance and simultaneously have below normal economic performance. This could happen, for example, when a firm is not earning its cost of capital but has above industry average accounting performance. Also, it is possible for a firm to have below-average accounting performance and above normal economic performance. This could happen when a firm has a very low cost of capital and is earning at a rate more than this cost, but still below the industry average.

Emergent Versus Intended Strategies

Objective 1.4 Explain the difference between emergent and intended strategies.

The simplest way of thinking about a firm's strategy is to assume that firms choose and implement their strategies exactly as described by the strategic management process in Figure 1.1. That is, they begin with a well-defined mission and objectives, they engage in external and internal analyses, they make their strategic choices, and then they implement their strategies. And there is no doubt that this describes the process for choosing and implementing a strategy in many firms.

For example, FedEx, a world leader in the overnight delivery business, entered this industry with a very well-developed theory about how to gain competitive advantages in this business. Indeed, Fred Smith, the founder of FedEx (originally known as Federal Express), first articulated this theory as a student in a term paper for an undergraduate business class at Yale University. Legend has it that he received only a "C" on the paper, but the company that was founded on the theory of competitive advantage in the overnight delivery business developed in that paper has done extremely well. Founded in 1971, FedEx had 2016 sales just over $50 billion and over 400,000 employees.[12]

Other firms have also begun operations with a well-defined, well-formed strategy but have found it necessary to modify this strategy so much once it is implemented in the marketplace that it bears little resemblance to the theory with which the firm started. **Emergent strategies** are theories of how to gain competitive advantage in an industry that emerge over time or that have been radically reshaped once they are initially implemented.[13]

Several well-known firms have strategies that are, at least partly, emergent. For example, J&J was originally a supplier of antiseptic gauze and medical plasters. It had no consumer business at all. Then, in response to complaints about irritation caused by some of its medical plasters, J&J began enclosing a small packet of talcum powder with each of the medical plasters it sold. Soon customers were asking to purchase the talcum powder by itself, and the company introduced "Johnson's Toilet and Baby Powder." Later, an employee invented a ready-to-use bandage for his wife. It seems she often cut herself while using knives in the kitchen. When J&J marketing managers learned of this invention, they decided to introduce it into the marketplace. J&J's Band-Aid products have since become the largest-selling brand category at J&J. Overall, J&J's intended strategy was to compete in the medical products market, but its emergent consumer products strategies now generate more than 40 percent of total corporate sales.

Another firm with what turns out to be an emergent strategy is the Marriott Corporation. Marriott was originally in the restaurant business. In the late 1930s, Marriott owned and operated eight restaurants. However, one of these restaurants was close to a Washington, D.C., airport. Managers at this restaurant noticed that airline passengers would come into the restaurant to purchase food to eat on their trip. J. Willard Marriott, the founder of the Marriott Corporation, noticed this trend and negotiated a deal with Eastern Airlines whereby Marriott's restaurant would deliver prepackaged lunches directly to Eastern's planes. This arrangement was later extended to include American Airlines. Over time, providing food service to airlines became a major business segment for Marriott. Although Marriott's initial intended strategy was to operate in the restaurant business, it became engaged in the emergent food service business at more than 100 airports throughout the world.[14]

Of course, one might argue that emergent strategies are only important when a firm fails to implement the strategic management process effectively. After all, if this process is implemented effectively, then would it ever be necessary to fundamentally alter the strategies that a firm has chosen?

In reality, it will often be the case that at the time a firm chooses its strategies, some of the information needed to complete the strategic management process may simply not be available. As suggested earlier, in this setting a firm simply must make its "best bet" about how competition in an industry is likely to emerge. In such a situation, a firm's ability to change its strategies quickly to respond to emergent trends in an industry may be as important a source of competitive advantage as the ability to complete the strategic management process. For all these reasons, emergent strategies may be particularly important for entrepreneurial firms.

Objective 1.5 Discuss why it is important for you to study strategy and the strategic management process.

Why you Need to Know About Strategy

At first glance, it may not be obvious why students would need to know about strategy and the strategic management process. After all, the process of choosing and implementing a strategy is normally the responsibility of senior managers in a firm, and most students are unlikely to be senior managers in large corporations until many years after graduation. Why study strategy and the strategic management process now?

In fact, there are at least three very compelling reasons why it is important to study strategy and the strategic management process now. First, it can give you the tools you need to evaluate the strategies of firms that may employ you. We have already seen how a firm's strategy can have a huge impact on its competitive advantage. Your career opportunities in a firm are largely determined by that firm's competitive advantage. Thus, in choosing a place to begin or continue your career, understanding a firm's theory of how it is going to gain a competitive advantage can be essential in evaluating the career opportunities in a firm. Firms with strategies that are unlikely to be a source of competitive advantage will rarely provide the same career opportunities as firms with strategies that do generate such advantages. Being able to distinguish between these types of strategies can be very important in your career choices.

Second, once you are working for a firm, understanding that firm's strategies, and your role in implementing those strategies, can be very important for your personal success. It will often be the case that expectations of how you perform your function in a firm will change, depending on the strategies a firm is pursuing. For example, as we will see in Part 2 of this book, the accounting function plays a very different role in a firm pursuing a cost leadership strategy versus a product differentiation strategy. Marketing and manufacturing also play very different roles in these two types of strategies. Your effectiveness in a firm can be reduced by doing accounting, marketing, and manufacturing as if your firm were pursuing a cost leadership strategy when it is actually pursuing a product differentiation strategy.

Finally, although it is true that strategic choices are generally limited to very experienced senior managers in large organizations, in smaller and entrepreneurial firms many employees end up being involved in the strategic management process. If you choose to work for one of these smaller or entrepreneurial firms—even if it is not right after graduation—you could very easily find yourself to be part of the strategic management team, implementing the strategic management process and choosing which strategies this firm should implement. In this setting, a familiarity with the essential concepts that underlie the choice and implementation of a strategy may turn out to be very helpful.

More broadly, the study of strategy and the strategic management process will help you develop a set of skills that will be helpful, no matter what your employment situation may be. For example, as you read the theories and models in the text and apply them to the analysis of cases, you will develop business communication skills with your classmates and your instructor as you try to convince them that your point of view is correct. You will have the opportunity to develop your critical thinking skills as you take the theories and models presented in this book and apply them to develop points of view about the cases you analyze. The cases are full of both qualitative and quantitative data. Analyzing them will enhance your data literacy. And finally, you will be able to confront some of the ethical issues in business, since each chapter includes a feature on ethics and strategy. Thus, in addition to learning about strategy and the strategic management process, the topics covered in this book will also increase your overall business knowledge, and help enhance your success in whatever career you choose.

Summary

A firm's strategy is its theory of how to gain competitive advantages. These theories, like all theories, are based on assumptions and hypotheses about how competition in an industry is likely to evolve. When those assumptions and hypotheses are consistent with the actual evolution of competition in an industry, a firm's strategy is more likely to be able to generate a competitive advantage.

One way that a firm can choose its strategies is through the strategic management process. This process is a set of analyses and decisions that increase the likelihood that a firm will be able to choose a "good" strategy, that is, a strategy that will lead to a competitive advantage.

The strategic management process begins when a firm identifies its mission, or its long-term purpose. This mission is often written down in the form of a mission statement. Mission statements, by themselves, can have no impact on performance, can enhance a firm's performance, or can hurt a firm's performance. Objectives are measurable milestones firms use to evaluate whether they are accomplishing their missions. External and internal analyses are the processes through which a firm identifies its environmental threats and opportunities and organizational strengths and weaknesses. Armed with these analyses, it is possible for a firm to engage in strategic choice. Strategies can be classified into two categories: business-level strategies (including cost leadership, product differentiation, flexibility, and tacit collusion) and corporate-level strategies (including vertical integration, strategic alliances, diversification, and mergers and acquisitions). Strategy implementation follows strategic choice and involves choosing organizational structures, management control policies, and compensation schemes that support a firm's strategies.

The ultimate objective of the strategic management process is the realization of competitive advantage. A firm has a competitive advantage if it is creating more economic value than its rivals. Economic value is defined as the difference between a customer's willingness to pay for a firm's products or services and the total economic cost of developing and selling that product or service. Competitive advantages can be temporary or sustained. Competitive parity exists when a firm creates the same economic value as its rivals. A competitive disadvantage exists when a firm creates less economic value than its rivals, and it can be either temporary or sustained.

Two popular measures of a firm's competitive advantage are accounting performance and economic performance. Accounting performance measures competitive advantage using various ratios calculated from a firm's profit and loss and balance sheet statements. A firm's accounting performance is compared with the average level of accounting performance in a firm's industry. Economic performance compares a firm's level of return with its cost of capital. A firm's cost of capital is the rate of return it had to promise to pay to its debt and equity investors to induce them to invest in the firm.

Although many firms use the strategic management process to choose and implement strategies, not all strategies are chosen this way. Some strategies emerge over time, as firms respond to unanticipated changes in the structure of competition in an industry.

Students need to understand strategy and the strategic management process for at least three reasons. First, it can help in deciding where to work. Second, once you have a job it can help you to be successful in that job. Finally, if you have a job in a small or entrepreneurial firm you may become involved in strategy and the strategic management process from the very beginning.

Challenge Questions

1.1. Some firms publicize their corporate mission statements by including them in annual reports, on company letterheads, and in corporate advertising. What, if anything, does this practice say about the ability of these mission statements to be sources of sustained competitive advantage for a firm?

1.2. Why would including a corporate mission statement on company letterhead or in corporate advertising be seen as a source of sustained competitive advantage?

1.3. Little empirical evidence indicates that having a formal, written mission statement improves a firm's performance. Yet many firms spend a great deal of time and money developing mission statements. Why?

1.4. Explain if it is possible to distinguish between an emergent strategy and an ad hoc rationalization of a firm's past decisions.

1.5. Both external and internal analyses are important in the strategic management process. Is the order in which these analyses are conducted important?

1.6. If the order of analyses is important, which should come first: external analysis or internal analysis?

1.7. Concerning external analysis and internal analysis, if the order of analyses is not important, why not?

1.8. Will a firm that has a sustained competitive disadvantage necessarily go out of business?

1.9. Will a firm with below average accounting performance over a long period necessarily go out of business?

1.10. Will a firm with below normal economic performance over a long period necessarily go out of business?

1.11. Can more than one firm have a competitive advantage in an industry at the same time?

1.12. Is it possible for a firm to simultaneously have a competitive advantage and a competitive disadvantage?

Problem Set

1.13. Write objectives for each of the following mission statements.

(a) We will be a leader in pharmaceutical innovation.
(b) Customer satisfaction is our primary goal.
(c) We promise on-time delivery.
(d) Product quality is our first priority.

1.14. Rewrite each of the following objectives to make them more helpful in guiding a firm's strategic management process.

(a) We will introduce five new drugs.
(b) We will understand our customers' needs.
(c) Almost all of our products will be delivered on time.
(d) The number of defects in our products will fall.

1.15. Do firms with the following financial results have below-normal, normal, or above-normal economic performance?

(a) ROA = 14.3%, WACC = 12.8%
(b) ROA = 4.3%, WACC = 6.7%
(c) ROA = 6.5%, WACC = 9.2%
(d) ROA = 8.3%, WACC = 8.3%

1.16. Do these same firms have below-average, average, or above-average accounting performance?

(a) ROA = 14.3%, Industry Avg. ROA = 15.2%
(b) ROA = 4.3%, Industry Avg. ROA = 4.1%
(c) ROA = 6.5%, Industry Avg. ROA = 6.1%
(d) ROA = 8.3%, Industry Avg. ROA = 9.4%

1.17. Is it possible for a firm to simultaneously earn above-normal economic returns and below average accounting returns? What about below-normal economic returns and above-average accounting returns? Why or why not? If this can occur, which measure of performance is more reliable: economic performance or accounting performance? Explain.

1.18. Examine the following corporate Web sites and determine if the strategies pursued by these firms were emergent, deliberate, or both emergent and deliberate. Justify your answer with facts from the Web sites.

(a) www.walmart.com
(b) www.homedepot.com
(c) www.cardinal.com

1.19. Using the information provided, calculate this firm's ROA, ROE, gross profit margin, and quick ratio. If this firm's WACC is 6.6 percent and the average firm in its industry has an ROA of 8 percent, is this firm earning above or below normal economic performance and above- or below-average accounting performance?

Net sales	6,134	Operating cash	3,226	Net other operating assets	916
Cost of goods sold	(4,438)	Accounts receivable	681	Total assets	5,161
Selling, general administrative expenses	(996)	Inventories	20	Net current liabilities	1,549
Other current assets	0	Long-term debt	300	Other expenses	(341)
Total current assets	3,927	Deferred income taxes	208	Interest income	72
Gross properties, plant, equipment	729	Preferred stock	0	Interest expense	(47)
Retained earnings	0	Provision for taxes	(75)	Accumulated depreciation	(411)
Common stock	3,104	Other income	245	Book value of fixed assets	318
Other liabilities	0	Net income	554	Goodwill	0
Total liabilities and equity	5,161				

Writing Assignments

1.20. Describe what visionary firms may do to earn substantially higher returns than average firms.

1.21. What is the relationship between a firm's business model and its value proposition?

CASE STUDY | Bandhan Bank: Rethinking, Reimagining Banking

Bandhan Bank's unique business model has fostered the development of differentiated and efficient operations processes. These processes facilitate seamless business operations while keeping necessary checks and controls in place. Recognizing the uniqueness of both micro banking and traditional banking, Bandhan has established its back-end operations and continues to refine these processes. A combination of a strong vision, effective management strategies, extensive banking experience, expertise in dealing with government regulations, and support from international organizations has propelled Bandhan Bank to become a leading success among new entrants in the banking sector.

How the Journey Began...

Chandra Shekhar Ghosh amazing journey started from working at his father's sweet shop to owning the largest micro-finance network in India in less than 15 years, and thereafter, venturing into the banking sector. After working with Village Welfare Society, a non-profit, in West Bengal for several years, Ghosh transformed his vision to empower poor women—microfinance. In 2001, he started his own company—Bandhan-Konnagar—to extend small loans to poor women, with a mere amount of ₹2 lakh, which were otherwise primarily sourced/borrowed from relatives. Ghosh remained committed to the core objective of providing financial products & services in unbanked rural areas, and to achieve the financial inclusion through women empowerment poverty alleviation through employment generation. Within 13 years, Bandhan has managed to establish its presence in 34 states and union territories with special focus on the eastern and underdeveloped states of Northeast India.

Current Landscape of the Indian Banking Sector

The Indian banking sector has showcased a remarkable recovery post-pandemic, with credit off-take surging to an 11-year high during FY2022–23. This growth was broad-based across various segments, including agriculture, industry, and personal loans. The sector's resilience is evident from the microfinance institutions' Gross Loan Portfolio (GLP) reaching ₹3.20 lakh crore, underscoring their role in financial inclusion. Notably, NBFC-MFIs accounted for a 39 percent share of this portfolio, indicating their critical support to low-income households. The banking industry now serves 6.4 crore unique borrowers, signifying the expansive reach of financial services across India.

Bandhan Bank's Strategic Growth and Digital Transformation

Bandhan Bank has significantly enhanced its service offerings through strategic partnerships with various mutual fund companies, bringing a wide range of investment products to its customers. The bank's aggressive push towards technology and digital innovation has led to 94 percent of transactions being conducted digitally. The introduction of digital banking platforms, such as corporate banking platform and online mutual fund services, has positioned Bandhan Bank as a leader in digital banking solutions. The bank's digital transactions, including 53 crore UPI transactions and a 31 percent digital origination of retail deposits, highlight its successful digital transformation journey.

Retail Banking: Embracing Digital Innovation

Bandhan Bank's initiatives, such as the launch of the mBandhan mobile app and a comprehensive internet banking platform, illustrate the bank's dedication to providing a seamless digital banking experience. These efforts are part of a broader industry trend towards digitalization, aiming to meet the evolving needs of customers and enhance the convenience and efficiency of banking services. The bank's digital transformation initiatives, including the Neo+ Digital Savings Account and the enhanced corporate banking platform, have been instrumental in attracting and retaining customers in the digital age.

Bandhan Bank's Milestones and Future Outlook

Bandhan Bank achieved remarkable milestones in FY2022–23, including reaching ₹1 lakh crore each in total deposits and advances, surpassing ₹2 lakh crore in total business, and expanding its customer base to 3 crores. The bank's strategic focus on portfolio diversification resulted in the housing finance portfolio growing to 25 percent of the total asset book. Moreover, commercial banking expanded to represent 35 percent of the total asset book, reflecting the bank's commitment to serving a broader range of customers. Geographical diversification efforts led to the addition of 360 new banking outlets, with a significant push towards expanding beyond the traditional markets of East and Northeast India.

Questions:

1. How has Bandhan Bank's comprehensive digital transformation, highlighted by the deployment of advanced digital banking platforms and services, contributed to its remarkable growth in customer base and financial metrics?
2. How have Bandhan Bank's targeted financial products and services, particularly in microfinance and commercial banking, advanced the agenda of financial inclusion across diverse demographic segments in India?
3. With the banking sector's rapid evolution towards digitalization, what strategic challenges does Bandhan Bank face in maintaining its competitive edge, and how can it leverage its digital initiatives to foster future growth and customer engagement?

References

Palo, S., & Chaudhari, S. R. (2023). *Bandhan Bank's Strategic CSR: Building Knowledge and Experience of Rural Microfinance.* NHRD Network Journal, 16(2), 138-152.

Suresh, K., & Pradhan, S. K. (2023). *Evaluation of Financial Performance of Banking Sector in India–A Camel Approach.* International Journal of Professional Business Review: Int. J. Prof. Bus. Rev., 8(5), 50.

Kumar, P., & Sharma, D. (2023). *Benchmarking the financial performance of Indian commercial banks by a hybrid MCDM approach.* International Journal of Process Management and Benchmarking, 15(3), 285-309.

Mathur, M., Bhamboo, U., & Sharma, P. (2023). *Financial Analysis of Private Sector Banks: Bankometer Model.* European Economic Letters (EEL), 13(3), 262-269.

Bandhan Bank. (2023). *Annual Report 2022–23.* Accessed from https://bandhanbank.com on March 11, 2024

Required Reading: Business Model Development

A company's blueprint for achieving its set objectives is encapsulated within its business model, which outlines the methodology for offering products or services, pinpointing the intended customer base, and projecting anticipated operational expenditures. In the rapidly evolving landscape marked by technological advancements and regulatory shifts, the necessity for companies to periodically reevaluate and refresh their business models is paramount to sustain competitiveness and relevance. Originating in the 1990s amid the digital revolution, particularly with the advent of the internet, the term "business model" has come to signify the strategic architecture of a business, detailing its approach to creating value, securing market share, managing costs, generating revenue, and establishing a competitive stance.

The importance of a well-defined business model is universally recognized, serving as the foundation for both emerging startups and long-established corporations alike. Scholars Chesbrough and Rosenbloom have provided a seminal definition of a business model as a systematic approach that transforms technological innovations into economic value for the market, delineating six essential components that encompass the offering's value proposition, the targeted customer segments, the operational cost framework, the potential for profit, the network of partners and stakeholders involved, and the strategies for outperforming competitors.

Components of Business Models

Further exploration into the domain of digital business models by Afuah and Tucci resulted in a comprehensive framework that includes mechanisms for profit generation, strategies for creating customer value, defining the scope of the market, establishing pricing models, identifying sources of revenue, outlining operational execution plans, leveraging organizational capabilities, and ensuring the sustainability of the business model over time. This multifaceted approach serves to elaborate on how a business intends to deliver unique value to its customers, carve out a niche in the market, streamline its cost structures, optimize profit margins, and cultivate a network of partnerships that enhance its value proposition and market presence.

Fundamentally, a business model articulates how a company intends to generate revenue by efficiently meeting customer needs. The discussion on the significance of business models, as highlighted by Joan Magretta, points to their widespread application with the introduction of personal computing and the development of sophisticated analytical tools like spreadsheets. An effective business model addresses several pivotal questions:

- Who is the target customer?
- What need is met for the customer?
- What offering will we provide to address that need?
- How does the customer gain access to that offering?
- What role will our business play in providing the offering?
- How will our business earn a profit?

Competitive Advantage: Gaining a competitive edge involves outperforming rivals by delivering more value to customers. This edge is marked by distinctiveness and differentiation from competitors. There are primarily two methods to secure such an advantage: One approach is to adopt a pricing strategy that enables a company to offer its products at lower costs compared to its rivals. Alternatively, an advantage can be secured through product differentiation, where the unique attributes of a product are highlighted, justifying a higher price due to perceived added value. Both approaches aim to enhance the value perceived by customers. By innovating in ways that are difficult or impossible for competitors to replicate, a company can establish a superior market position, leveraging this uniqueness to create significant value.

Innovation Strategies: Innovation intertwines knowledge and creativity to forge new value in processes, products, or services, offering novel solutions and methods. It manifests across various domains including product development, service enhancement, marketing approaches, organizational structures, and operational techniques. Central to innovation is the concept of novelty, which encompasses two critical elements: the generation of new value and the introduction of fresh knowledge. An innovative organization thrives on thinking beyond conventional boundaries, merging great ideas, a dedicated team, and a deep understanding of customer needs to stand out. It's not merely about having inventive ideas but about strategically combining those ideas with an engaged workforce to meet customer expectations. Innovation plays a pivotal role in securing a competitive edge in the business arena, serving as a core strategy for achieving market dominance globally. Instead of solely focusing on static strategic elements like competitive positioning or organizational size, the emphasis shifts towards understanding how companies dynamically establish and maintain advantageous positions over time.

Business Modelling A business model outlines a company's strategic approach, reflecting its adaptation to global shifts. Each company crafts its unique strategy to navigate and succeed in the international marketplace. However, a business model tends to be more broadly defined than a specific business strategy. Essentially, an effective business model delivers significant value to its customers and manages to capture a sustainable share of that value as revenue. Yet, simply having a robust business model does not guarantee a competitive edge. Business model innovation involves the creation of novel strategies for how businesses operate. This innovation may involve either emulating or modifying emerging strategies considering past approaches. The process of strategy comparison is crucial for developing innovative business models, but it also requires thorough analysis to ensure the maintenance of a competitive advantage.

End Notes

1 This approach to defining strategy was first suggested in Drucker, P. (1994). "The theory of business." *Harvard Business Review*, 75, September–October, pp. 95–105.

2 See Bart, C.K., and Beatz. (1998) "The relationship between mission statements and firm performance: An exploratory study," Journal of Management Studies, 35(6): 823–853; Bartkus, B., Glassman, M.; and McAfee, B. (2000) "Mission statements: Are they smoke and mirrors?" Business Horizons, November/December: 23–28; and Smith, M., Heady, R., Cason, P, and Cason K. (2003) "Do Missions Accomplish Their Missions?: An Exploratory Analysis of Mission Statement Content and Organizational Longevity," Journal of Applied Management and Entrepreneurship, 6(1): 75–96.

3 See www.enron.com.

4 See Emshwiller, J., D. Solomon, and R. Smith. (2004). "Lay is indicted for his role in Enron collapse." *The Wall Street Journal*, July 8, pp. A1+; Gilmartin, R. (2005). "They fought the law." *BusinessWeek*, January 10, pp. 82–83.

5 These performance results were presented originally in Collins, J. C., and J. I. Porras. (1997). *Built to last: Successful habits of visionary companies*. New York: HarperCollins.

6 Collins, J. C., and J. I. Porras. (1997). *Built to last: successful habits of visionary companies*.

7 Yahoo's story is summarized in "Yahoo Rejects Microsoft's Bid," CNET.com, retrieved on November 1, 2016; Nicholas Carlson, "Jerry Yang's Last Laugh," businessinsider.com, retrieved November 1, 2016; and "Verizon Buys Yahoo for $4.8 Billion," CNBC.com, retrieved November 1, 2016.

8 This definition of competitive advantage has a long history in the field of strategic management. For example, it is closely related to the definitions provided in Barney (1986, 1991) and Porter (1985). It is also consistent with the value-based approach described in Peteraf (2001), Brandenburger and Stuart (1999), and Besanko, Dranove, and Shanley (2000). For more discussion on this definition, see Peteraf and Barney (2004).

9 D. C. Mueller (1977). "The persistence of profits above the norm." *Economica*, 44, pp. 369–380; P. W. Roberts (1999). "Product innovation, product-market competition, and persistent profitability in the U.S. pharmaceutical industry." *Strategic Management Journal*, 20, pp. 655–670; G. F. Waring (1996). "Industry differences in the persistence of firm-specific returns." *The American Economic Review*, 86, pp. 1253–1265; A. McGahan and M. Porter (2003). "The emergence and sustainability of abnormal profits." *Strategic Organization*, 1(1), pp. 79–108.

10 A. Osterwalder and Y. Pigneur (2010). Business Model Generator. NY: Wiley. G. George and A. J. Bock (2011). The business model in practice and its implications for entrepreneurial research. *Entrepreneurship: Theory and Practice*, 35(1), 83–111. C. Zott, R. Amit, and L. Massa. (2010). The Business Model: Theoretical Roots, Recent Development, and Future Research. Working Paper 862, IESE, Barcelona, Spain.

11 T. Copeland, T. Koller, and J. Murrin (1995). *Valuation: Measuring and managing the value of companies*. New York: Wiley; L. Donaldson (1990). "The ethereal hand: Organizational economics and management theory." *Academy of Review*, 15, pp. 369–381; and E. Freeman, J. Harrison, A. Wicks, B. Parmar, and S. de Colle (2010 Stakeholder Theory: The State of the Art. Cambridge: Cambridge.

12 FedEx's history is described in Trimble, V. (1993). *Overnight success: Federal Express and Frederick Smith, its renegade creator*. New York: Crown.

13 Mintzberg, H. (1978). "Patterns in strategy formulation." *Management Science*, 24(9), pp. 934–948; and Mintzberg, H. (1985). "Of strategies, deliberate and emergent." *Strategic Management Journal*, 6(3), pp. 257–272. Mintzberg has been most influential in expanding the study of strategy to include emergent strategies.

14 The J&J and Marriott emergent strategy stories can be found in Collins, J. C., and J. I. Porras. (1997). *Built to last: Successful habits of visionary companies*. New York: HarperCollins.

CHAPTER

2 Evaluating a Firm's External Environment

LEARNING OBJECTIVES

After reading this chapter, you should be able to:

2.1 Describe the dimensions of the general environment facing a firm and how this environment can affect a firm's opportunities and threats.

2.2 Describe how the structure-conduct-performance (S-C-P) model suggests that industry structure can influence a firm's competitive choices.

2.3 Describe the five environmental threats and indicators of when each of these threats will enhance or reduce the attractiveness of an industry.

2.4 Discuss the role of complements in analyzing competition within an industry.

2.5 Describe four generic industry structures and specific strategic opportunities in those industries.

AGEL's Strategic Growth and Industry Dominance

Launched in 2015, Adani Green Energy Limited (AGEL) is a subsidiary of the Indian conglomerate Adani Group. Gautam Adani, the founder of AGEL, has been instrumental in the company's development focusing on renewable energy solutions within India and worldwide. The company was officially incorporated on January 23, 2016, under the Companies Act 2013, marking its formal entry into the renewable energy sector. It has demonstrated remarkable financial and operational performance in the fiscal year ending March 2023, signalling a strategic pivot in India's renewable energy landscape. The company's financial indicators, notably a 57 percent increase in EBITDA to ₹5,538 crore, with a 72 percent rise in cash profit to ₹3,192 crore, highlight its operational efficiency and capacity expansion. Such financial health is critical in AGEL's strategy to invest $20 billion in renewable energy, aiming for a 45 GW capacity by 2030—a move that not only emphasizes the group's commitment to sustainable energy solutions but also aligns with global efforts to combat climate change.

AGEL's strategic edge in the renewable sector is further highlighted by its operational capacity increase, with a significant addition of 2,676 MW in FY23. This capacity expansion, including the notable 2,140 MW of solar-wind hybrid plants in Rajasthan, plays a pivotal role in advancing India's decarbonization efforts. The introduction of advanced technologies like bifacial PV modules and horizontal single-axis tracking (HSAT) exemplifies AGEL's innovative approaches to optimizing energy capture and enhancing project performance. On a global scale, AGEL's achievement as the

second-largest solar PV developer, with a total solar capacity of 18.1 GW, reflects its competitive advantage in the renewable energy sector. This position is not just a testament to AGEL's operational success but also a strategic leverage in the global renewable energy market, highlighting its significant role in promoting large-scale renewable energy development.

The external environment for AGEL includes navigating the complex renewable energy development landscape in India, characterized by infrastructure, regulatory, and market dynamics. Despite the challenges of increasing competition and the need for sustainable financial strategies to support large-scale projects, AGEL's strategic investments and operational excellence have positioned it for continued growth. This strategic positioning is crucial as the company aims to contribute significantly to India's renewable energy ambitions, leveraging its scale, innovation, and sustainability practices. AGEL's strategic competitive advantage lies in its ability to scale operations, innovate, and efficiently manage its financial and operational resources. This advantage is crucial in an external environment that requires navigating infrastructural and regulatory challenges, as well as leveraging opportunities such as the Indian government's plans to significantly increase renewable energy capacity. AGEL's achievements and strategic focus not only support its growth but also enhance its role in driving India's energy transition, contributing to global efforts against climate change while pursuing economic growth and energy security.

REFERENCES

Acharya, N., & NR, S. (2024). *India's Adani Green Energy said on Monday its third-quarter profit more than doubled from a year earlier, helped by robust power sales to customers and higher capacity utilisation*. Reuters (January 29, 2024). Accessed from https://www.reuters.com on March 11, 2024.

Adani Green Energy Ltd. (2023). *Adani Green Energy Ltd announces FY23 Results reporting an EBITDA of Rs. 5,538 Cr, up by 57 percent YoY*. Adani Green Energy Ltd (May 1, 2024). Accessed from https://www.adanigreenenergy.com on March 11, 2024.

Adani Group. (2023). *Adani Green Energy Ranks Among Top 3 Global Solar PV Developer.* Adani Group Newsroom (December 6, 2023). Accessed from https://www.adanigreenenergy.com on March 11, 2024.

Aguilera, R. V., De Massis, A., Fini, R., & Vismara, S. (2024). *Organizational Goals, Outcomes, and the Assessment of Performance: Reconceptualizing Success in Management Studies.* Journal of Management Studies, 61(1), 1-36.

So, how efficient is the green energy industry? The level of competition among firms in this industry seems high—there are large numbers of competitors including AGEL, Tata Solar Power, Suzlon, and JSW will continue to grow, given that these companies understand that the demand for sustainable energy resources will increase in the future and their their offerings being relatively similar. New competitors continue to enter the industry, and some of these new entrants are assumably competitive "heavyweights" like Reliance New Energy. But it is yet to be seen if customers will have loyalties to particular energy provider. And, the value of the offering by the competing firms will depend on the growth of this category.

In short, this may be a tough place to decide profit.

This chapter presents a series of models and tools that can be used to evaluate the attractiveness of the industry within which a firm operates. It begins with a discussion of evaluating trends in a firm's broader environment and then shifts to understanding threats and opportunities within a firm's industry.

Objective 2.1 Describe the dimensions of the general environment facing a firm and how this environment can affect a firm's opportunities and threats.

Understanding a Firm's General Environment

Any analysis of the threats and opportunities facing a firm must begin with an understanding of the general environment within which a firm operates. This **general environment** consists of broad trends in the context within which a firm operates that can have an impact on a firm's strategic choices. As depicted in Figure 2.1, the general environment consists of six interrelated elements: technological change, demographic trends, cultural trends, the economic climate, legal and political conditions, and specific international events. Each of these elements of the general environment is discussed in this section.

In 1899, Charles H. Duell, commissioner of the U.S. patent office, said, "Everything that can be invented has been invented."[1] He was wrong. Technological changes over the past few years have had significant impacts on the ways firms do business and on the products and services they sell. These impacts have been most obvious for technologies that build on digital information—computers, the Internet, mobile phones, and so forth. Many of us routinely use digital products or services that did not exist just a few years ago. However, rapid technological innovation has not been restricted to digital technologies. Biotechnology has also made rapid progress over the past 10 years. New kinds of medicines are now being created. As important, biotechnology holds the promise of developing entirely new ways of both preventing and treating disease.[2]

Technological change creates both opportunity, as firms begin to explore how to use technology to create new products and services, and threats, as technological change forces firms to rethink their technological strategies.

A second element of the general environment facing firms is demographic trends. **Demographics** is the distribution of individuals in a society in terms of age, sex, marital status, income, ethnicity, and other personal attributes that may

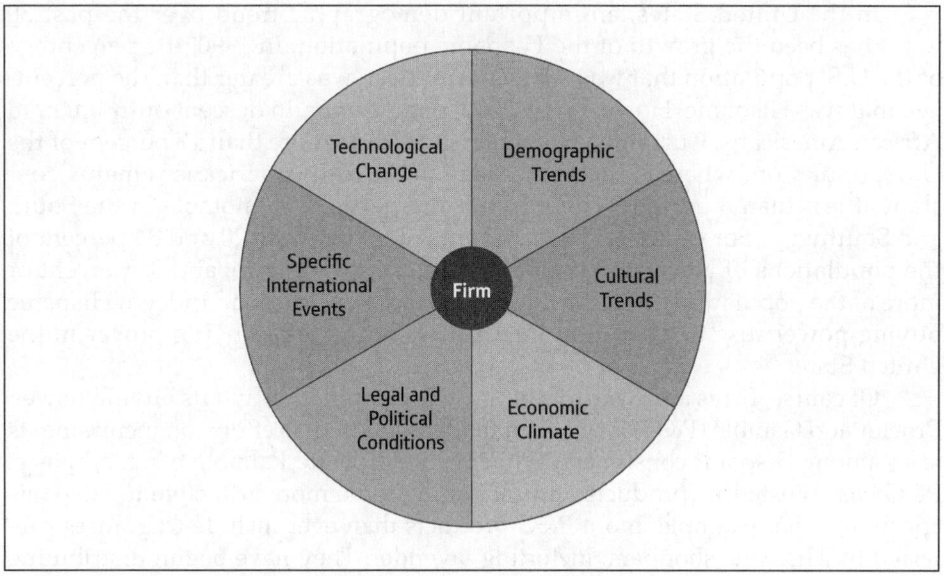

Figure 2.1 The General Environment Facing Firms

determine buying patterns. Understanding this basic information about a population can help a firm determine whether its products or services will appeal to customers and how many potential customers for these products or services it might have.

Some demographic trends are very well known. For example, most people have heard of the "baby boom generation" (born between 1946 and 1964), "generation X" (born between 1965 and 1976), the "millennial generation" (born between 1977 and 1995), and the "iGeneration" (born after 1996). While individuals within these generation categories can vary, research suggests some trends among these groups that can have important implications for business.[3]

For example, "baby boomers" have typically adopted a "buy now, pay later" attitude towards money and have often not saved enough for retirement. "Generation X," on the other hand tends to be very conservative with its money, and aggressively saves for the future. "Millennials," on average, earn to spend, and also do not save a great deal. The financial preferences of "iGen" aren't yet known, because they are only now entering their earning years.

Financial services companies must adjust their product offerings to be consistent with the interests of these different kinds of customers. For example, "baby boomers" have a hard time saving. Financial services that make the cost of saving lower—like automatic payroll deduction programs—will be popular among this generation of customers. "Generation X" customers, on the other hand, already save. What they are looking for are investment opportunities. "Millennials" don't currently save, but they also avoid debt. Helping this generation understand that saving is also a form of consumption is a big marketing challenge for financial services companies. Finally, while both Gen X and Millennials respond more to social media forms of marketing than Baby Boomers, Gen X customers are still very influenced by their customer experience when they visit a bank.[4]

In the United States, an important demographic trend over the past 30 years has been the growth of the Hispanic population. In 1990, the percentage of the U.S. population that was African American was greater than the percentage that was Hispanic. However, by 2000, people of Latin descent outnumbered African Americans. Currently, Hispanics constitute more than 17 percent of the U.S. population, whereas the percentage of African Americans remains constant at less than 8 percent. These trends are particularly notable in the South and Southwest. For example, Hispanics make up between 20 and 34 percent of the populations of Nevada, Arizona, Florida, and Colorado, and 35 percent or more of the population of California, Texas, and New Mexico.[5] Indeed, Hispanic buying power rose to $1 trillion in 2010, 9% of the total buying power in the United States.

Of course, firms are aware of this growing population and its buying power. Proctor and Gamble (P&G) is one firm that has focused its efforts on increasing its sales among Hispanic consumers. While behind Colgate-Palmolive in toothpaste, P&G has adjusted its products and marketing to be more attractive to Hispanic consumers. For example, more P&G products than ever include fragrances preferred by Hispanic shoppers, including lavender. They have begun distributing coupons in Spanish. And, they have begun hiring Latin spokespeople for some of their products—Eva Mendes for Pantene Shampoo and Jennifer Lopez for Venus Razors.[6]

A third element of a firm's general environment is cultural trends. **Culture** is the values, beliefs, and norms that guide behavior in a society. These values, beliefs, and norms define what is "right and wrong" in a society, what is acceptable and unacceptable, what is fashionable and unfashionable. Failure to understand changes in culture, or differences between cultures, can have a very large impact on the ability of a firm to gain a competitive advantage.

This becomes most obvious when firms operate in multiple countries simultaneously. Even seemingly small differences in culture can have an impact. For example, advertisements in the United States that end with a person putting their index finger and thumb together mean that a product is "okay"; in Brazil, the same symbol is vulgar and offensive. Ads in the United States that have a bride dressed in white may be very confusing to the Chinese because, in China, white is the traditional color worn at funerals. In Germany, women typically purchase their own engagement rings, whereas in the United States, men purchase engagement rings for their fiancées. And what might be appropriate ways to treat women colleagues in Japan or France would land most men in U.S. firms in serious trouble. Understanding the cultural context within which a firm operates is important in evaluating the ability of a firm to generate competitive advantages.[7]

A fourth element of a firm's general environment is the current economic climate. The **economic climate** is the overall health of the economic systems within which a firm operates. The health of the economy varies over time in a distinct pattern: Periods of relative prosperity, when demand for goods and services is high and unemployment is low, are followed by periods of relatively low prosperity, when demand for goods and services is low and unemployment is high. When activity in an economy is relatively low, the economy is said to be in **recession**. A severe recession that lasts for several years is known as a **depression**. This alternating pattern of prosperity followed by recession, followed by prosperity, is called the **business cycle**.

Throughout the 1990s, the world, and especially the United States, enjoyed a period of sustained economic growth. Some observers even speculated that the government had become so skilled at managing demand in the economy through adjusting interest rates that a period of recession did not necessarily have to follow a period of sustained economic growth. Of course, the business cycle has reared its ugly head twice since the 1990s—first with the technology bubble-burst around 2001 and, more recently, in the credit crunch in 2008. Most observers now agree that although government policy can have a significant impact on the frequency and size of economic downturns, these policies are unlikely to be able to prevent these downturns altogether.

A fifth element of a firm's general environment is **legal and political conditions**. The legal and political dimensions of an organization's general environment are the laws and the legal system's impact on business, together with the general nature of the relationship between government and business. These laws and the relationship between business and government can vary significantly around the world. For example, in Japan, business and the government are generally seen as having a consistently close and cooperative relationship. Indeed, some have observed that one reason that the Japanese economy has been growing so slowly over the past decade has been the government's reluctance to impose economic restructuring that would hurt the performance of some Japanese firms—especially the largest Japanese banks. In the United States, however, the quality of the relationship between business and the government tends to vary over time. In some administrations, rigorous antitrust regulation and tough environmental standards—both seen as inconsistent with the interests of business—dominate. In other administrations, antitrust regulation is less rigorous and the imposition of environmental standards is delayed, suggesting a more business-friendly perspective.

A final attribute of a firm's general environment is **specific international events**. These include events such as civil wars, political coups, terrorism, wars between countries, famines, and country or regional economic recessions. All of these specific events can have an enormous impact on the ability of a firm's strategies to generate competitive advantage.

Of course, one of the most important of these specific events to have occurred over the past several decades was the terrorist attacks on New York City and Washington, D.C., on September 11, 2001. Beyond the tragic loss of life, these attacks had important business implications as well. For example, it took more than five years for airline demand to return to pre–September 11 levels. Insurance companies had to pay out billions of dollars in unanticipated claims as a result of the attacks. Defense contractors saw demand for their products soar as the United States and some of its allies began waging war in Afghanistan and then Iraq.

A firm's general environment defines the broad contextual background within which it operates. Understanding this general environment can help a firm identify some of the threats and opportunities it faces. However, this general environment often has an impact on a firm's threats and opportunities through its impact on a firm's more local environment. Thus, while analyzing a firm's general environment is an important step in any application of the strategic management process, this general analysis must be accompanied by an analysis of a firm's more local environment if the threats and opportunities facing a firm are to be fully understood. The next section discusses specific tools for analyzing a firm's local environment and the theoretical perspectives from which these tools have been derived.

Objective 2.2 Describe how the structure-conduct-performance (S-C-P) model suggests that industry structure can influence a firm's competitive choices.

The Structure-Conduct-Performance Model of Firm Performance

In the 1930s, a group of economists began developing an approach for understanding the relationship among a firm's environment, behavior, and performance. The original objective of this work was to describe conditions under which competition in an industry would *not* develop. Understanding when competition was not developing in an industry assisted government regulators in identifying industries where competition-enhancing regulations should be implemented.[8]

Ethics and Strategy

Is a Firm Gaining a Competitive Advantage Good for Society?

One of the basic tenets of economic theory is that society is better off when industries are very competitive. Industries are very competitive when there are large numbers of firms operating in an industry, when the products and services that these firms sell are similar to each other, and when it is not very costly for firms to enter into or exit these industries. Indeed, as is described in more detail in the Strategy in Depth feature, these industries are said to be **perfectly competitive**.

The reasons that society is better off when industries are perfectly competitive are well known. In such industries, firms must constantly strive to keep their costs low, keep their quality high, and, when appropriate, innovate if they are to even survive. Low costs, high quality, and appropriate innovation are generally consistent with the interests of a firm's customers and, thus, consistent with society's overall welfare.

Indeed, concern for **social welfare**, or the overall good of society, is the primary reason the S-C-P model was developed. This model was to be used to identify industries where perfect competition was not occurring and, thus, where social welfare was not being maximized. With these industries identified, the government could then engage in activities to increase the competitiveness of these industries, thereby increasing social welfare.

Strategic management scholars turned the S-C-P model upside down by using it to describe industries where firms could gain competitive advantages and attain above-average performance. However, some have asked that if strategic management is all about creating and exploiting competitive imperfections in industries, is strategic management also all about reducing the overall good of society for advantages to be gained by a few firms? It is not surprising that individuals who are more interested in improving society than improving the performance of a few firms question the moral legitimacy of the field of strategic management.

However, there is another view about strategic management and social welfare. The S-C-P model assumes that any competitive advantages a firm has in an industry must hurt society. The alternative view is that at least some of the competitive advantages exist because a firm addresses customer needs more effectively than its competitors. From this perspective, competitive advantages are not bad for social welfare; they are actually good for social welfare.

Of course, both perspectives can be true. For example, a firm such as Microsoft has engaged in activities that at least some courts have concluded are inconsistent with social welfare. However, Microsoft also sells applications software that is routinely ranked among the best in the industry, an action that is consistent with meeting customer needs in ways that maximize social welfare.[9]

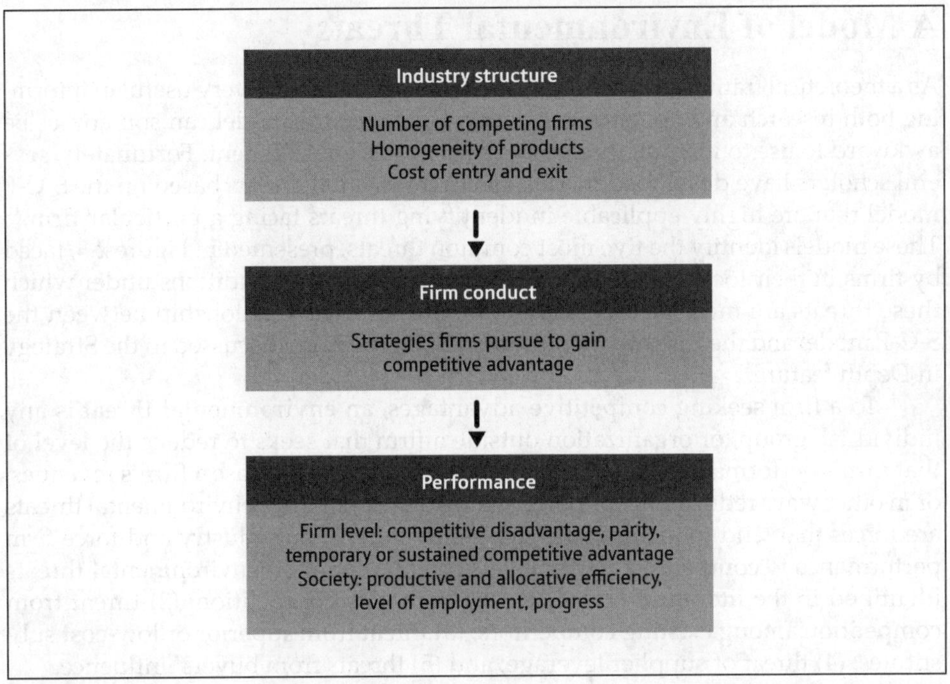

Figure 2.2 The Structure-Conduct-Performance Model

The theoretical framework that developed out of this effort became known as the **structure-conduct-performance (S-C-P) model**; it is summarized in Figure 2.2. The term **structure** in this model refers to industry structure, measured by such factors as the number of competitors in an industry, the heterogeneity of products in an industry, the cost of entry and exit in an industry, and so forth. **Conduct** refers to the strategies that firms in an industry implement. **Performance** in the S-C-P model has two meanings: (1) the performance of individual firms; and (2) the performance of the economy as a whole. Although both definitions of performance in the S-C-P model are important, as suggested in Chapter 1, the strategic management process is much more focused on the performance of individual firms than on the performance of the economy as a whole. That said, the relationship between these two types of performance can sometimes be complex, as described in the Ethics and Strategy feature.

The logic that links industry structure to conduct and performance is well known. Attributes of the industry structure within which a firm operates define the range of options and constraints facing a firm. In some industries, firms have very few options and face many constraints. In general, firms in these industries can only gain competitive parity. In this setting, industry structure completely determines both firm conduct and long-run firm performance.

However, in other, less competitive industries, firms face fewer constraints and a greater range of conduct options. Some of these options may enable them to obtain competitive advantages. However, even when firms have more conduct options, industry structure still constrains the range of options. Moreover, as will be shown in more detail later in this chapter, industry structure also has an impact on how long firms can expect to maintain their competitive advantages in the face of increased competition.

Objective 2.3 Describe the five environmental threats and indicators of when each of these threats will enhance or reduce the attractiveness of an industry.

A Model of Environmental Threats

As a theoretical framework, the S-C-P model has proven to be very useful in informing both research and government policy. However, the model can sometimes be awkward to use to identify threats in a firm's local environment. Fortunately, several scholars have developed models of environmental threats based on the S-C-P model that are highly applicable in identifying threats facing a particular firm.[10] These models identify the five most common threats, presented in Figure 2.3, faced by firms in their local competitive environments and the conditions under which these threats are more or less likely to be present. The relationship between the S-C-P model and the framework presented in Figure 2.3 is discussed in the Strategy in Depth feature.

To a firm seeking competitive advantages, an **environmental threat** is any individual, group, or organization outside a firm that seeks to reduce the level of that firm's performance. Threats increase a firm's costs, decrease a firm's revenues, or in other ways reduce a firm's performance. In S-C-P terms, environmental threats are forces that tend to increase the competitiveness of an industry and force firm performance to competitive parity level. The five common environmental threats identified in the literature are: (1) threat from new competition; (2) threat from competition among existing competitors; (3) threat from superior or low-cost substitutes; (4) threat of supplier leverage; and (5) threats from buyers' influence.

Threat from New Competition

The first environmental threat identified in Figure 2.3 is the threat of new competitors. **New competitors** are firms that have either recently started operating in an industry or that threaten to begin operations in an industry soon. In the music streaming industry, Apple, Google, and Amazon are new competitors.

According to the S-C-P model, new competitors are motivated to enter into an industry either by the superior profits that some incumbent firms in that industry are currently earning, or the profits that firms in this industry may earn some time in the future. Firms seeking these high profits enter the industry, thereby increasing the level of industry competition and reducing the performance of incumbent firms. With the absence of any barriers, entry will continue as long as any firms

Figure 2.3 Environmental Threats and the Profit Potential of Industries

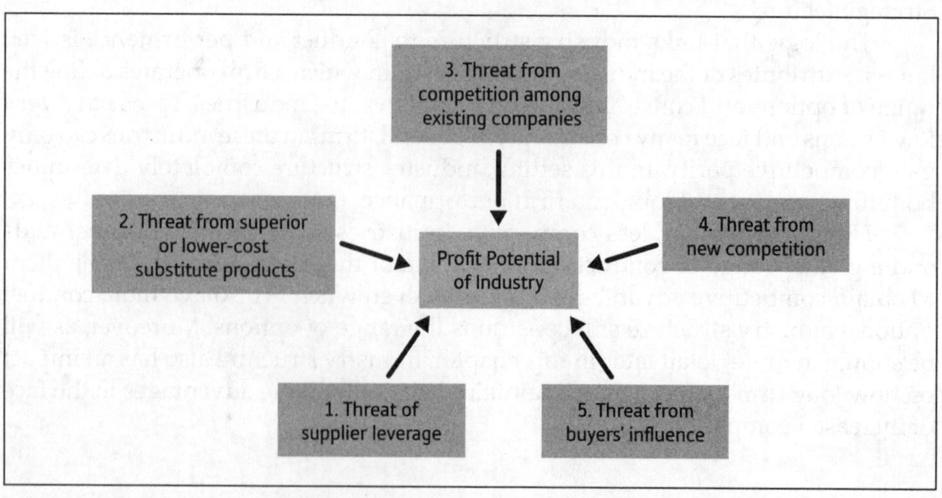

Strategy in Depth

Environmental Threats and the S-C-P Model

The relationship between environmental threats and the S-C-P model turns on the relationship between these threats and the nature of competition in an industry. When all five threats are very high, competition in an industry begins to approach what economists call **perfect competition**. When all five threats are very low, competition in an industry begins to approach what economists call a **monopoly**. Between perfect competition and monopoly, economists have identified two other types of competition in an industry—**monopolistic competition** *and* **oligopoly**—where the five threats identified in the literature are moderately high. These four types of competition, and the expected performance of firms in these different industries, are summarized in the nearby table.

Industries are **perfectly competitive** when there are large numbers of competing firms, the products being sold are homogeneous with respect to cost and product attributes, and entry and exit costs are very low. An example of a perfectly competitive industry is the spot market for crude oil. Firms in perfectly competitive industries can expect to earn only competitive parity.

In **monopolistically competitive industries**, there are large numbers of competing firms and low-cost entry into and exit from the industry. However, unlike the case of perfect competition, products in these industries are not homogeneous with respect to costs or product attributes. Examples of monopolistically competitive industries include toothpaste, shampoo, golf balls, and automobiles. Firms in such industries can earn competitive advantages.

Oligopolies are characterized by a small number of competing firms, by homogeneous products, and by high entry and exit costs. Examples of oligopolistic industries include the U.S. automobile and steel industries in the 1950s and the U.S. breakfast cereal market today. Currently, the top four producers of breakfast cereal account for about 90 percent of the breakfast cereal sold in the United States. Firms in such industries can earn competitive advantages.

Finally, **monopolistic industries** consist of only a single firm. Entry into this type of industry is very costly. There are few examples of purely monopolistic industries. Historically, for example, the U.S. Post Office had a monopoly on home mail delivery. However, this monopoly has been challenged in small-package delivery by FedEx, in larger-package delivery by UPS, and in mail delivery by e-mail. Monopolists can generate competitive advantages—although they are sometimes managed very inefficiently.[11]

Types of Competition and Expected Firm Performance

Type of Competition	Attributes	Examples	Expected Firm Performance
Perfect competition	Large number of firms Homogeneous products Low-cost entry and exit	Stock market Crude oil	Competitive parity
Monopolistic competition	Large number of firms Heterogeneous products Low-cost entry and exit	Toothpaste Shampoo Golf balls Automobiles	Competitive advantage
Oligopoly	Small number of firms Homogenous products Costly entry and exit	U.S. steel and autos in the 1950s U.S. breakfast cereal	Competitive advantage
Monopoly	One firm Costly entry	Home mail delivery	Competitive advantage

TABLE 2.1 Possible Barriers to Entry into an Industry

1. Economies of scale
2. Product differentiation
3. Cost advantages independent of scale
4. Government regulation of entry

in the industry are earning competitive advantages, and entry will cease when all incumbent firms are earning competitive parity.

The extent to which new competitors act as a threat to an incumbent firm's performance depends on the cost of entry. If the cost of entry into an industry is greater than the potential profits a new competitor could obtain by entering, then entry will not be forthcoming, and new competitors are not a threat to incumbent firms. However, if the cost of entry is lower than the return from entry, entry will occur until the profits derived from entry are less than the costs of entry.

The threat of new competitors depends on the cost of entry, and the cost of entry, in turn, depends on the existence and "height" of barriers to entry. **Barriers to entry** are attributes of an industry's structure that increase the cost of entry. The greater the cost of entry, the greater the height of these barriers. When there are significant barriers to entry, potential new competitors will not enter into an industry even if incumbent firms are earning competitive advantages.

Four important barriers to entry have been identified in the S-C-P and strategy literatures. These four barriers, listed in Table 2.1, are: (1) economies of scale; (2) product differentiation; (3) cost advantages independent of scale; and (4) government regulation of entry.[12]

Economies of Scale as a Barrier to Entry

Economies of scale exist in an industry when a firm's costs fall as a function of its volume of production. **Diseconomies of scale** exist when a firm's costs rise as a function of its volume of production. The relationship among economies of scale, diseconomies of scale, and a firm's volume of production is summarized in Figure 2.4. As a firm's volume of production increases, its costs begin to fall. This is a manifestation of economies of scale. However, at some point, a firm's volume

Figure 2.4 Economies of Scale and the Cost of Production

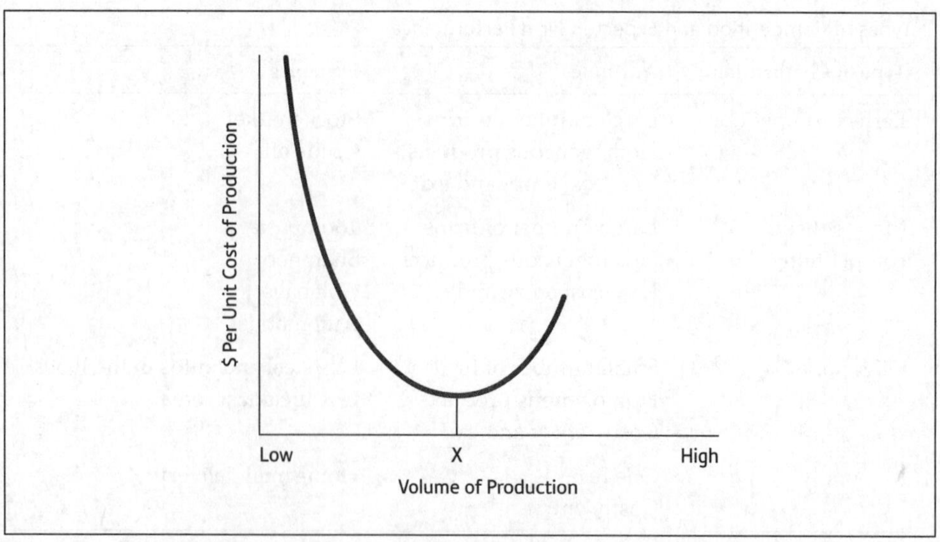

of production becomes too large and its costs begin to rise. This is a manifestation of diseconomies of scale. For economies of scale to act as a barrier to entry, the relationship between the volume of production and firm costs must have the shape of the line in Figure 2.4. This curve suggests that any deviation, positive or negative, from an optimal level of production (point X in Figure 2.4) will lead a firm to experience much higher costs of production.

To see how economies of scale can act as a barrier to entry, consider the following scenario. Imagine an industry with the following attributes: The industry has five incumbent firms (each firm has only one plant); the optimal level of production in each of these plants is 4,000 units (X = 4,000 units); total demand for the output of this industry is fixed at 22,000 units; the economies-of-scale curve is as depicted in Figure 2.4; and products in this industry are very homogeneous. Total demand in this industry (22,000 units) is greater than total supply (5 × 4,000 units = 20,000). Everyone knows that when demand is greater than supply, prices go up. This means that the five incumbent firms in this industry will have high levels of profit. The S-C-P model suggests that, absent barriers, these superior profits should motivate entry.

However, look at the entry decision from the point of view of potential new competitors. Certainly, incumbent firms are earning superior profits, but potential entrants face an unsavory choice. On the one hand, new competitors could enter the industry with an optimally efficient plant and produce 4,000 units. However, this form of entry will lead industry supply to rise to 24,000 units (20,000 + 4,000). Suddenly, supply will be greater than demand (24,000 > 22,000), and all the firms in the industry, including the new entrant, will earn negative profits. On the other hand, the new competitor might enter the industry with a plant of smaller-than-optimal size (e.g., 1,000 units). This kind of entry leaves total industry demand larger than industry supply (22,000 > 21,000). However, the new competitor faces a serious cost disadvantage in this case because it does not produce at the low-cost position on the economies-of-scale curve. Faced with these bleak alternatives, the potential entrant simply does not enter even though incumbent firms are earning positive profits.

Of course, potential new competitors have other options besides entering at the efficient scale and losing money or entering at an inefficient scale and losing money. For example, potential entrants can attempt to expand the total size of the market (i.e., increase total demand from 22,000 to 24,000 units or more) and enter at the optimal size. Potential entrants can also attempt to develop new production technology, shift the economies-of-scale curve to the left (thereby reducing the optimal plant size), and enter. Or potential new competitors may try to make their products seem very special to their customers, enabling them to charge higher prices to offset higher production costs associated with a smaller-than-optimal plant.[13]

Any of these actions may enable a firm to enter an industry. However, these actions are costly. If the cost of engaging in these "barrier-busting" activities is greater than the return from entry, entry will not occur, even if incumbent firms are earning positive profits.

Historically, economies of scale acted as a barrier to entry into the worldwide steel market. To fully exploit economies of scale, traditional steel plants had to be very large. If new entrants into the steel market had built these efficient and large steel-manufacturing plants, they would have had the effect of increasing the steel supply over the demand for steel, and the outcome would have been reduced profits for both new entrants and incumbent firms. This discouraged new entry.

However, in the 1970s, the development of alternative mini-mill technology shifted the economies-of-scale curve to the left by making smaller plants very efficient in addressing some segments of the steel market. This shift had the effect of decreasing barriers to entry into the steel industry. Recent entrants, including Nucor Steel and Chaparral Steel, now have significant cost advantages over firms still using outdated, less efficient production technology.[14]

Product Differentiation as a Barrier to Entry

Product differentiation means that incumbent firms possess brand identification and customer loyalty that potential new competitors do not. Brand identification and customer loyalty serve as entry barriers because new competitors not only have to absorb the standard costs associated with starting production in a new industry; they also have to absorb the costs associated with overcoming incumbent firms' differentiation advantages. If the cost of overcoming these advantages is greater than the potential return from entering an industry, entry will not occur, even if incumbent firms are earning positive profits.

Numerous examples exist of industries in which product differentiation tends to act as a barrier to entry. In the brewing industry, for example, substantial investments by Budweiser, Miller, and Coors (among other incumbent firms) in advertising (will we ever forget the Budweiser frogs?) and brand recognition have made large-scale entry into the U.S. brewing industry very costly.[15] Indeed, rather than attempting to enter the U.S. market, InBev, a large brewer headquartered in Belgium, decided to purchase Anheuser Busch.[16]

E. & J. Gallo Winery, a U.S. winemaker, faced product differentiation barriers to entry in its efforts to sell Gallo wine in the French market. The market for wine in France is huge—the French consume 16.1 gallons of wine per person per year, for a total consumption of more than 400 million cases of wine, whereas U.S. consumers drink only 1.8 gallons of wine per person per year, for a total consumption of less than 200 million cases. Despite this difference, intense loyalties to local French vineyards have made it very difficult for Gallo to break into the huge French market—a market where American wines are still given as "gag gifts" and only American theme restaurants carry U.S. wines on their menus. Gallo is attempting to overcome this product differentiation advantage of French wineries by emphasizing its California roots—roots that many French consider to be exotic—and downplaying the fact that it is a U.S. company; corporate origins that are less attractive to many French consumers.[17]

Cost Advantages Independent of Scale as Barriers to Entry

In addition to the barriers that have been cited, incumbent firms may have a whole range of cost advantages, independent of economies of scale, compared to new competitors. These cost advantages can act to deter entry because new competitors will find themselves at a cost disadvantage vis-à-vis incumbent firms with these cost advantages. New competitors can engage in activities to overcome the cost advantages of incumbent firms, but as the cost of overcoming them increases, the economic profit potential from entry is reduced. In some settings, incumbent firms enjoying cost advantages, independent of scale, can earn superior profits and still not be threatened by new entry because the cost of overcoming those advantages can be prohibitive.

Examples of these cost advantages, independent of scale, are presented in Table 2.2; they include: (1) proprietary technology; (2) managerial know-how; (3) favorable access to raw materials; and (4) learning-curve cost advantages.

TABLE 2.2 Sources of Cost Advantage, Independent of Scale, That Can Act as Barriers to Entry

Proprietary technology When incumbent firms have secret or patented technology that reduces their costs below the costs of potential entrants, potential new competitors must develop substitute technologies to compete. The cost of developing this technology can act as a barrier to entry.

Managerial know-how When incumbent firms have taken-for-granted knowledge, skills, and information that take years to develop and that is not possessed by potential new competitors. The cost of developing this know-how can act as a barrier to entry.

Favorable access to raw materials When incumbent firms have low-cost access to critical raw materials not enjoyed by potential new competitors. The cost of gaining similar access can act as a barrier to entry.

Learning-curve cost advantages When the cumulative volume of production of incumbent firms gives them cost advantages not enjoyed by potential new competitors. These cost disadvantages of potential entrants can act as a barrier to entry.

Proprietary Technology In some industries, **proprietary (i.e., secret or patented) technology** gives incumbent firms important cost advantages over potential entrants. To enter these industries, potential new competitors must develop their own substitute technologies or run the risks of copying another firm's patented technologies. Both of these activities can be costly. Numerous firms in a wide variety of industries have discovered the sometimes-substantial economic costs are associated with violating another firm's patented proprietary technology. Indeed, the number of patent infringement suits continues to increase, especially in industries—such as consumer electronics—where products apply technologies developed by many different companies. In the past few years, Intertrust has sued Apple, Yahoo! has sued Facebook, Google has sued BT, Boston University has sued Apple, Nokia has sued HTC, Samsung has sued Apple, and Apple has sued Samsung.[18] In 2015, a total of 5,830 patent infringement suits were filed in the United States, down from 6,114 in 2013, but up 15 percent from 2014.[19]

Managerial Know-How Even more important than technology per se as a barrier to entry is the managerial know-how built up by incumbent firms over their history.[20] **Managerial know-how** is the oft-taken for granted knowledge and information that are needed to compete in an industry on a day-to-day basis.[21] Know-how includes information that it has taken years, sometimes decades, for a firm to accumulate that enables it to interact with customers and suppliers, to be innovative and creative, to manufacture quality products, and so forth. Typically, new entrants will not have access to this know-how, and it will often be costly for them to build it quickly.

One industry where this kind of know-how is a very important barrier to entry is the pharmaceutical industry. Success in this industry depends on having high-quality research and development skills. The development of world-class research skills—the science behind new medicines—and development skills—knowing how to take drugs through the regulatory and sales process—takes decades to accumulate. New competitors face enormous cost disadvantages for decades as they attempt to develop these abilities, and thus entry into the pharmaceutical industry by integrated research and development firms has been quite limited.[22]

Favorable Access to Raw Materials Incumbent firms may also have cost advantages, compared to new entrants, based on favorable access to raw materials. If, for example, only a few sources of high-quality iron ore are available in a specific geographic region, steel firms that have access to these sources may have a cost advantage over those that must ship their ore in from distant sources.[23]

Learning-Curve Cost Advantages It has been shown that in certain industries (such as airplane manufacturing) the cost of production falls with the cumulative volume of production. Over time, as incumbent firms gain experience in manufacturing, their costs fall below those of potential entrants. Potential new competitors, in this context, must endure substantially higher costs while they gain experience, and thus they may not enter the industry despite the superior profits being earned by incumbent firms.These learning-curve economies are discussed in more detail in Chapter 4.

Government Policy as a Barrier to Entry

Governments, for their own reasons, may decide to increase the cost of entry into an industry. This occurs most frequently when a firm operates as a government-regulated monopoly. In this setting, the government has concluded that it is in a better position to ensure that specific products or services are made available to the population at reasonable prices than competitive market forces. Industries such as electric power generation and elementary and secondary education have been (and, to some extent, continue to be) protected from new competitors by government restrictions on entry.

Threat from Existing Competitors

New competitors are an important threat to the ability of firms to maintain or improve their level of performance, but they are not the only threat in a firm's environment. A second environmental threat comes from the intensity of competition among a firm's current direct competitors. Spotify, Deezer, Pandora, and Rhapsody are all direct competitors in the music streaming industry.

Direct competition threatens firms by reducing their economic profits. High levels of direct competition are indicated by such actions as frequent price cutting by firms in an industry (e.g., price discounts in the airline industry), frequent introduction of new products by firms in an industry (e.g., continuous product introductions in consumer electronics), intense advertising campaigns (e.g., Pepsi versus Coke advertising), and rapid competitive actions and reactions in an industry (e.g., competing airlines quickly matching the discounts of other airlines).

Some of the attributes of an industry that are likely to generate high levels of direct competition are listed in Table 2.3. First, direct competition tends to be high when there are numerous firms in an industry. Such is the case in the Windows PC manufacturing industry. While HP, Dell, Lenovo, Aer, and Asus collectively make 60% of the PCs sold in the world, hundreds of smaller firms also compete in this market. The result of this competition has been that PC retail prices have continued to fall, to an average low in 2014 of $544.30. As striking, the profits that these firms generate on these sales have fallen even faster, down to just $14.87 per unit sold in 2014. This is a retail margin of only 2.7 percent.[24]

TABLE 2.3 Attributes of an Industry That Increase the Threat of Direct Competition

1. Large number of competing firms that are roughly the same size
2. Slow industry growth
3. Lack of product differentiation
4. Capacity added in large increments

Second, direct competition tends to be high when industry growth is slow. When industry growth is slow, firms seeking to increase their sales must often acquire market share from established competitors. This tends to increase competition. Intense price rivalry emerged in the U.S. fast-food industry—with 99-cent Whoppers at Burger King and "dollar menus" at Wendy's and McDonald's—when the growth in this industry declined.[25]

Third, direct competition tends to be high when firms are unable to differentiate their products in an industry. When product differentiation is not a viable strategic option, firms are often forced to compete only on the basis of price. Intense price competition is typical of high-competition industries. In the airline industry, for example, intense competition on longer routes—such as between Los Angeles and New York and Los Angeles and Chicago—has kept prices on these routes down. These routes have relatively few product differentiation options. However, by creating hub-and-spoke systems, certain airlines (American, United, Delta) have been able to develop regions of the United States where they are the dominant carrier. These hub-and-spoke systems enable airlines to partially differentiate their products geographically, thus reducing the level of competition in segments of this industry.[26]

Finally, direct competition tends to be high when production capacity is added in large increments. If, in order to obtain economies of scale, production capacity must be added in large increments, an industry is likely to experience periods of oversupply after new capacity comes online. This overcapacity often leads to price cuts. Much of the growing rivalry in the commercial jet industry between Boeing and AirBus can be traced to the large manufacturing capacity additions made by AirBus when it entered the industry.[27]

Threat of Substitute Products

A third environmental threat is the threat of substitute products. The products or services provided by a firm's direct competitors meet approximately the same customer needs in the same ways as the products or services provided by the firm itself. **Substitutes** meet approximately the same customer needs, but do so in different ways. Substitutes for music streaming include music downloads (from Apple iTunes and other online stores) and physical music sales.

Substitutes place a ceiling on the prices firms in an industry can charge and on the profits firms in an industry can earn. In the extreme, substitutes can ultimately replace an industry's products and services. This happens when a substitute is clearly superior to previous products. Examples include electronic calculators as substitutes for slide rules and mechanical calculators, electronic watch movements as substitutes for pin–lever mechanical watch movements, and compact discs as substitutes for long-playing (LP) records (although some audiophiles continue to argue for the sonic superiority of LPs).

Substitutes are playing an increasingly important role in reducing the profit potential in a variety of industries. For example, in the legal profession private mediation and arbitration services are becoming viable substitutes for lawyers. Computerized texts are becoming viable substitutes for printed books in the publishing industry. Television news programs, especially services such as CNN and Fox News, are very threatening substitutes for weekly newsmagazines, including *Time* and *Newsweek*. In Europe, so-called superstores are threatening smaller food shops. Minor league baseball teams are partial substitutes for major league teams. Cable television is a substitute for broadcast television. Groups of "big box" retailers are substitutes for traditional shopping centers. Private mail delivery systems (such as those in the Netherlands and Australia) are substitutes for government postal services. Home financial planning software is a partial substitute for professional financial planners.[28]

Threat of Supplier Leverage

A fourth environmental threat is supplier leverage. **Suppliers** make a wide variety of raw materials, labor, and other critical assets available to firms. Suppliers can threaten the performance of firms in an industry by increasing the price of their supplies or by reducing the quality of those supplies. Any profits that were being earned in an industry can be transferred to suppliers in this way. In music streaming, the three major record labels—to a large extent—and well known recording artists—to a lesser extent—have significant supplier leverage.

Some supplier attributes that can lead to high levels of threat are listed in Table 2.4. First, suppliers are a greater threat if the *suppliers'* industry is dominated by a small number of firms. In this setting, a firm has little choice but to purchase supplies from these firms. These few firms thus have enormous flexibility to charge high prices, to reduce quality, or in other ways to squeeze the profits of the firms in the industry to which they sell. Much of Microsoft's power in the software industry reflects its dominance in the operating system market, where Windows remains the de facto standard for most personal computers. For now, at least, if a company wants to sell personal computers, it is going to need to interact with Microsoft.

Conversely, when a firm has the option of purchasing from a large number of suppliers, suppliers have less leverage to threaten a firm's profits. For example, as the number of lawyers in the United States has increased over the years (up 40 percent since 1981, currently more than 1 million), lawyers and law firms have been forced to begin competing for work. Some corporate clients have forced law firms to reduce their hourly fees and to handle repetitive simple legal tasks for low flat fees.[29]

Second, suppliers are a greater threat when what they supply is unique or highly differentiated. There is only one LeBron James. As a basketball player, as a spokesperson, and as a celebrity, his unique status gives him enormous bargaining power as a supplier and enables him to extract some of the economic profit that would otherwise have been earned by the teams he plays for (either the Cleveland Cavaliers or the Miami Heat) and Nike. In the same way, Intel's unique ability to develop, manufacture, and sell microprocessors gives it significant bargaining power as a supplier in the personal computer industry.

The uniqueness of suppliers can operate in almost any industry. For example, in the highly competitive world of television talk shows, some guests, as suppliers, can gain surprising fame for their unique characteristics. For example, one woman was a guest on eight talk shows. Her claim to fame: She was the tenth wife of a gay, con-man bigamist.

Third, suppliers are a greater threat to firms in an industry when suppliers are *not* threatened by substitutes. When there are no effective substitutes, suppliers can take advantage of their position to extract economic profits from firms they

TABLE 2.4 Indicators of the Threat of Supplier Leverage in an Industry

1. Suppliers' industry is dominated by small number of firms.
2. Suppliers sell unique or highly differentiated products.
3. Suppliers are *not* threatened by substitutes.
4. Suppliers threaten forward vertical integration.
5. Firms are *not* important customers for suppliers.

supply. Both Intel (in microprocessors) and Microsoft (in PC operating systems) have been accused of exploiting their unique product positions to extract profits from customers.

When there are substitutes for supplies, supplier power is checked. In the food container industry, for example, metal cans are threatened by plastic containers as substitutes. In order to continue to sell to can manufacturers, steel and aluminum companies have had to keep their prices lower than would otherwise have been the case. In this way, the potential power of the meal companies has been checked by the existence of plastic as a substitute product.[30]

Fourth, suppliers are a greater threat to firms when they can credibly threaten to enter into and begin competing in a firm's industry. This is called **forward vertical integration**; in this situation, suppliers cease to be suppliers only and become suppliers *and* direct competitors. This is what happened when Jay Z started a more "artist friendly" streaming company, Tidal.

The threat of forward vertical integration is partially a function of barriers to entry into an industry. When an industry has high barriers to entry, suppliers face significant costs of forward vertical integration, and thus forward integration is not as serious a threat to the profits of incumbent firms. Vertical integration is discussed in more detail in Chapter 8.

Finally, suppliers are a threat to firms when firms are *not* an important part of suppliers' business. Steel companies, for example, are not too concerned with losing the business of a sculptor or of a small construction company. However, they are very concerned about losing the business of the major can manufacturers, major white-goods manufacturers (i.e., manufacturers of refrigerators, washing machines, dryers, and so forth), and automobile companies. Steel companies, as suppliers, are likely to be very accommodating and willing to reduce prices and increase quality for can manufacturers, white-goods manufacturers, and auto companies. Smaller, "less important" customers, however, are likely to be subject to greater price increases, lower-quality service, and lower-quality products.

Threat from Buyers' Influence

The final environmental threat is buyers. **Buyers** purchase a firm's products or services. Whereas powerful suppliers act to increase a firm's costs, powerful buyers act to decrease a firm's revenues. In music streaming, consumers are the ultimate buyer. Some of the important indicators of the threat of buyers are listed in Table 2.5.

First, if a firm has only one buyer or a small number of buyers, these buyers can be very threatening. Firms that sell a significant amount of their output to the U.S. Department of Defense recognize the influence of this buyer on their operations. Reductions in defense spending have forced defense companies to try even harder to reduce costs and increase quality to satisfy government demands. All these actions reduce the economic profits of these defense-oriented companies.[31] Firms that sell to large retail chains have also found it difficult to maintain high

TABLE 2.5 Indicators of the Threat of Buyers' Influence in an Industry

1. Number of buyers is small.
2. Products sold to buyers are undifferentiated and standard.
3. Products sold to buyers are a significant percentage of a buyer's final costs.
4. Buyers are *not* earning significant economic profits.
5. Buyers threaten backward vertical integration.

levels of profitability. Powerful retail firms—such as Wal-Mart and Home Depot—can make significant and complex logistical and other demands on their suppliers, and if suppliers fail to meet these demands, buyers can "fire" their suppliers. These demands can have the effect of reducing the profits of suppliers.

Second, if the products or services that are being sold to buyers are standard and not differentiated, then the threat of buyers can be greater. For example, farmers sell a very standard product. It is very difficult to differentiate products such as wheat, corn, or tomatoes (although this can be done to some extent through the development of new strains of crops, the timing of harvests, and so forth). In general, wholesale grocers and food brokers can always find alternative suppliers of basic food products. These numerous alternative suppliers increase the threat of buyers and force farmers to keep their prices and profits low. If any one farmer attempts to raise prices, wholesale grocers and food brokers simply purchase their supplies from some other farmer.

Third, buyers are likely to be more of a threat when the supplies they purchase are a significant portion of the costs of their final products. In this context, buyers are likely to be very concerned about the costs of their supplies and constantly on the lookout for cheaper alternatives. For example, in the canned food industry, the cost of the can itself can constitute up to 40 percent of a product's final price. Not surprisingly, firms such as Campbell Soup Company are very concerned about keeping the price of the cans they purchase as low as possible.[32]

Fourth, buyers are likely to be more of a threat when they are *not* earning significant economic profits. In these circumstances, buyers are likely to be very sensitive to costs and insist on the lowest possible cost and the highest possible quality from suppliers. This effect can be exacerbated when the profits suppliers earn are greater than the profits buyers earn. In this setting, a buyer would have a strong incentive to enter into its supplier's business to capture some of the economic profits being earned by the supplier. This strategy of **backward vertical integration** is discussed in more detail in Chapter 8.

Finally, buyers are more of a threat to firms in an industry when they have the ability to vertically integrate backward. In this case, buyers become both buyers and direct competitors and lock in a certain percentage of an industry's sales. The extent to which buyers represent a threat to vertically integrate, in turn, depends on the barriers to entry that are not in place in an industry. If there are significant barriers to entry, buyers may not be able to engage in backward vertical integration, and their threat to firms is reduced.

Environmental Threats and Average Industry Performance

These five environmental threats have three important implications for managers seeking to choose and implement strategies. First, they describe the most common sources of local environmental threat in industries. Second, they can be used to characterize the overall level of threat in an industry. Finally, as is shown in Table 2.6, because the overall level of threat in an industry is, according to S-C-P logic, related to the average level of performance of a firm in an industry, they can also be used to anticipate the average level of performance of firms in an industry.

Of course, it will rarely be the case that all five threats in an industry will be equally threatening at the same time. This can sometimes complicate the anticipation of the average level of firm performance in an industry. Consider, for example, the four industries in Table 2.6. It is easy to anticipate the average level of performance of firms in the first two industries: In Industry I, this performance will be low; in Industry II, this performance will be high; however, in Industries III and

TABLE 2.6 Estimating the Level of Average Performance in an Industry

	Industry I	Industry II	Industry III	Industry IV
Threat of new competitors	High	Low	High	Low
Threat of direct competition	High	Low	Low	High
Threat of superior or low cost product substitutes	High	Low	High	Low
Threat of supplier leverage	High	Low	Low	High
Threat of buyers; influence	High	Low	High	Low
Expected average firm performance	Low	High	Mixed	Mixed

IV it is somewhat more complicated. In these mixed situations, the real question to ask in anticipating the average performance of firms in an industry is, "Are one or more threats in this industry powerful enough to appropriate most of the profits that firms in this industry might generate?" If the answer to this question is yes, then the anticipated average level of performance will be low. If the answer is no, then the anticipated performance will be high.

Even more fundamentally, this type of analysis can be used only to anticipate the average level of firm performance in an industry. This is acceptable if a firm's industry is the primary determinant of its overall performance. However, as described in the Research Made Relevant feature, research suggests that the industry a firm operates in is far from the only determinant of its performance.

Another Environmental Force: Complements

Objective 2.4 Discuss the role of complements in analyzing competition within an industry.

Professors Adam Brandenburger and Barry Nalebuff have suggested that another force needs to be added to the analysis of the profit potential of industries.[33] These authors distinguish between competitors and what they call a firm's *complementors.* If you were the chief executive officer of a firm, the following is how you could tell the difference between your competitors and your complementors: Another firm is a **competitor** if your customers value your product less when they have the other firm's product than when they have your product alone. Direct competitors, new competitors, and substitutes are all examples of competitors. In contrast, another firm is a **complementor** if your customers value your product more when they have this other firm's product than when they have your product alone. In the music streaming industry, smart phones are complements to music streaming services.

Consider, as another example, the relationship between producers of television programming and cable television companies. The value of these firms' products partially depends on the existence of one another. Television producers need outlets for their programming. The growth in the number of channels on cable television provides more of these outlets and thus increases the value of these production firms. Cable television companies can continue to add channels, but those channels need content. So, the value of cable television companies depends partly on the existence of television production firms. Because the value of program-producing companies is greater when cable television firms exist and because the value of cable television companies is greater when program-producing companies exist, these types of firms are complements.

Brandenburger and Nalebuff go on to argue that an important difference between complementors and competitors is that a firm's complementors help to increase the size of a firm's market, whereas a firm's competitors divide this market among a set of firms. Based on this logic, these authors suggest that, although it is usually the case that a firm will want to discourage the entry of competitors into its market, it will usually want to encourage the entry of complementors. Returning to the television producers/cable television example, television producers will actually want cable television companies to grow and prosper and constantly add new channels, and cable television firms will want television show producers to grow and constantly create new and innovative programming. If the growth of either of these businesses slows, it hurts the growth of the other.

Of course, the same firm can be a complementor for one firm and a competitor for another. For example, the invention of satellite television and increased popularity of DirecTV and the Dish Network represent a competitive challenge to cable television companies. That is, DirecTV and, say, Cox Communications are competitors. However, DirecTV and television production companies are complementors to each other. In deciding whether to encourage the entry of new complementors, a firm has to weigh the extra value these new complementors will create against the competitive impact of this entry on a firm's current complementors.

It is also the case that a single firm can be both a competitor and a complementor to the same firm. This is very common in industries where it is important to create technological standards. For example, until a standard format for HD video on DVDs was set—through Blu-Ray Disc technology—sales of HD DVD players and HD movies on DVDs would not grow. Once this standard was set, growth of products consistent with the Blu-Ray Disc standard took off.[34]

To develop technology standards, firms must be willing to cooperate. This cooperation means that, with respect to the technology standard, these firms are complementors. And, indeed, when these firms act as complementors, their actions have the effect of increasing the total size of the market. However, once these firms cooperate to establish standards, they begin to compete to try to obtain as much of the market they jointly created as possible. In this sense, these firms are also competitors.

Understanding when firms in an industry should behave as complementors and when they should behave as competitors is sometimes very difficult. It is even more difficult for a firm that has interacted with other firms in its industry as a competitor to change its organizational structure, formal and informal control systems, and compensation policy and start interacting with these firms as a complementor, at least for some purposes. Learning to manage what Brandenburger and Nalebuff call the "Jekyll and Hyde" dilemma associated with competitors and complementors can distinguish excellent from average firms.

Objective 2.5 Describe four generic industry structures and specific strategic opportunities in those industries.

Industry Structure and Environmental Opportunities

Identifying environmental threats is only half the task in accomplishing an external analysis. Such an analysis must also identify opportunities. Fortunately, the same S-C-P logic that made it possible to develop tools for the analysis of environmental threats can also be used to develop tools for the analysis of environmental

Research Made Relevant

For some time now, scholars have been interested in the relative impact of the attributes of the industry within which a firm operates and the attributes of the firm itself on its performance. The first work in this area was published by Richard Schmalansee. Using a single year's worth of data, Schmalansee estimated the variance in the performance of firms that was attributable to the industries within which firms operated versus other sources of performance variance. Schmalansee's conclusion was that approximately 20 percent of the variance in firm performance was explained by the industry within which a firm operated—a conclusion consistent with the S-C-P model and its emphasis on industry as a primary determinant of a firm's performance.

The Impact of Industry and Firm Characteristics on Firm Performance

Richard Rumelt identified some weaknesses in Schmalansee's research. Most important of these was that Schmalansee had only one year's worth of data with which to examine the effects of industry and firm attributes on firm performance. Rumelt was able to use four years' worth of data, which allowed him to distinguish between stable and transient industry and firm effects on firm performance. Rumelt's results were consistent with Schmalansee's in one sense: Rumelt also found that about 16 percent of the variance in firm performance was due to industry effects, versus Schmalansee's 20 percent. However, only about half of this industry effect was stable. The rest represented year-to-year fluctuations in the business conditions in an industry. This result is broadly inconsistent with the S-C-P model.

Rumelt also examined the impact of firm attributes on firm performance and found that more than 80 percent of the variance in firm performance was due to these firm attributes, but that more than half of this 80 percent (46.38 percent) was due to stable firm effects. The importance of stable firm differences in explaining differences in firm performance is also inconsistent with the S-C-P framework. These results are consistent with another model of firm performance called the *resource-based view*, which will be described in Chapter 3.

Since Rumelt's research, efforts to identify the factors that explain variance in firm performance have accelerated. At least nine articles addressing this issue have been published in the literature. One of the most recent of these suggests that, while the impact of the industry and the corporation on business unit performance can vary across industries and across corporations, overall, business unit effects are larger than either corporate or industry effects.[35]

opportunities. However, instead of identifying the threats that are common in most industries, opportunity analysis begins by identifying several generic industry structures and then describing the strategic opportunities that are available in each of these different kinds of industries.[36]

Of course, there are many different generic industry structures. However, four are very common and will be the focus of opportunity analysis in this part of the book: (1) fragmented industries; (2) emerging industries; (3) mature industries; and (4) declining industries. The kinds of opportunities typically associated with these industry structures are presented in Table 2.7.

Two additional generic industry structures—network industries and "empty core" industries—though less common than the other generic industry structures described in this chapter, can still be important. These types of industries, along with the kinds of opportunities that can exist in them, are discussed in the second Strategy in Depth feature.

TABLE 2.7 Industry Structure and Environmental Opportunities

Industry Structure	Opportunities
Fragmented industry	Consolidation
Emerging industry	First-mover advantages
Mature industry	Product refinement
	Investment in service quality
	Process innovation
Declining industry	Leadership
	Niche
	Harvest
	Divestment

Strategy in Depth

Network and Empty Core Industries

Network industries exist when the value of a product or service that is being sold depends, to a great extent, on the number of these products or services being sold. For example, a telephone is not a very valuable product if only a few people own a telephone. It only becomes valuable once it is widely diffused. Because of the relationship between the value of a product or service and the number of products or services sold, network industries are also sometimes called **increasing returns industries**.

Of course, these increasing returns can be important in the other generic industry structures discussed in this chapter. For example, increasing returns can be an important source of first mover advantages in emerging industries. However, when the primary determinant of a product or services value is the number of these products or services sold, the industry within which these products or services are sold is called a network industry.

Network industries are particularly important in the digital age. For example, as the number of people who use a particular piece of software—either an operating system like Windows, a PC application like Word, or an app like WhatsApp—increases, the number of people who can communicate and work together with this software also increases. This increases the value of this software.

The primary opportunity in a network industry is a particular strong form of first mover advantage. If a firm is an early mover in a network industry and builds large market share quickly it may obtain an almost unassailable advantage. These strategies are sometimes called **winner take all** strategies. In these settings, dominant firms can maintain their advantage simply because new entrants, in the beginning, simply cannot provide customers with the same network advantages as incumbent firms. Obviously, these dynamics have made network industries interesting to anti-trust regulators in a variety of countries.

Empty Core Industries exist when four conditions are present: (1) capacity in this industry is added in large increments, relative to demand; (2) there are large unavoidable sunk costs associated with adding this extra capacity; (3) demand fluctuates in difficult to predict ways; and (4) there is limited product differentiation. The name "empty core' comes from the particular game theoretic model that is used to describe competition in this industry, and refers to the fact that in these settings there is no stable profit making equilibrium.

Consider, for example, competition on a particular airline route. Capacity in this route is not added one seat at a time, it is added one airplane at a time. Once access to an airplane for a route is acquired—usually through a lease—it has costs associated with it—like lease payments—that exist whether the plane is flying or not. These are unavoidable fixed costs. Also, demand on a particular route can fluctuate, often in difficult to predict ways. Finally, despite years of efforts trying to convince consumers otherwise, most of us believe that one airline's service is not much different than another airline's service—so there is little product differentiation.

In this setting, imagine that demand falls below supply. Because capacity on this route is added in large increments, an airline company will have some difficulty reducing the supply of airline seats for a route until supply falls low enough. With airplanes flying half empty, an airline company might be tempted to ground airplanes. But the company has to pay the leases on these planes whether they fly or not. And raising prices by offering "superior service" on an airline doesn't seem likely to be successful. In these settings, the profit maximizing decision might be to fly a half empty airplane, and lose $10,000, instead of not flying and losing $30,000. This condition—when a firm's profit maximizing decision generates economic losses—is called **cut throat competition**. If left unchecked, it will lead to bankruptcy—something that has plagued the U.S. airline industry for 50 years.

As dismal as cut throat competition sounds, there are opportunities in empty core industries. First, firms in this type of industry can change technologies so that capacity does not have to be added in large increments. Airlines do this by having the option to fly smaller jets, including Boeing 737s and various regional jets.

Second, firms in these settings can try to make demand more predictable so that they will only add that capacity that needs to be added. Airlines do this through **demand management**; they increase or decrease prices on a route, depending on historical patterns of travel on that route, to try to make sure that supply and demand balance. This is why a ticket may cost $200 one day and $800 the next.

Third, firms can find alternative bases of product differentiation which can enable them to increase their prices. Airlines do this by creating de facto geographic monopolies around their hub and spoke systems. In general, flying from hubs is more expensive then flying from non-hubs, because airlines in hubs have some degree of monopoly power. Thus, flying American Airlines from Dallas, Texas (an American Airlines hub) to Orlando, Florida is generally more expensive than flying American Airlines from Wichita, Kansa (a non-hub airport) to Dallas and then on to Orlando.

Fourth, firms in these industries can try to collude—by explicitly cooperating to reduce competition and keep prices above the cut throat level. This strategy is discussed in the Cooperating to Reduce Competition feature. U.S. airlines have engaged in collusion in the past.—something that has also attracted the interest of anti-trust agencies in several countries.

Finally, if none of these strategies work, firms in empty core industries can seek government regulations to keep prices above a cut throat level. At various times, U.S. airlines have explored the possibility of becoming re-regulated in an effort to restore their profitability.

Airlines are not the only industry that can have the features of an empty core. International shipping—where huge container ships carry goods across the oceans—coal fired power generation, traditional steel manufacturing, and nuclear power generation can all have empty core attributes.[37]

Opportunities in Fragmented Industries: Consolidation

Fragmented industries are industries in which a large number of small- or medium-sized firms operate and no small set of firms has dominant market share or creates dominant technologies. Many service industries, including small retail stores and commercial printing, to name just a few, are fragmented industries.

Industries can be fragmented for a wide variety of reasons. For example, the fragmented industry may have few barriers to entry, thereby encouraging numerous small firms to enter. The industry may have few, if any, economies of scale, and even some important diseconomies of scale, thus encouraging firms to remain small. Also, close local control over enterprises in an industry may be necessary—for example, local high end restaurants—to ensure quality and to minimize losses from theft.

The major opportunity facing firms in fragmented industries is the implementation of strategies that begin to consolidate the industry into a smaller number of firms. Firms that are successful in implementing this **consolidation strategy** can become industry leaders and obtain benefits from this kind of effort, if they exist.

Consolidation can occur in several ways. For example, an incumbent firm may discover new economies of scale in an industry. In the highly-fragmented funeral home industry, Service Corporation International (SCI) found that the development of a chain of funeral homes gave it advantages in acquiring key supplies (coffins) and in the allocation of scarce resources (morticians and hearses). By acquiring numerous previously independent funeral homes, SCI was able to substantially reduce its costs and gain higher levels of economic performance.[38]

Incumbent firms sometimes adopt new ownership structures to help consolidate an industry. Kampgrounds of America (KOA) used franchise agreements with local operators to provide camping facilities to travelers in the fragmented private campgrounds industry. KOA provided local operators with professional training, technical skills, and access to its brand-name reputation. Local operators, in return, provided KOA with local managers who are intensely interested in the financial and operational success of their campgrounds. Similar franchise agreements have been instrumental in the consolidation of other fragmented industries, including fast food (McDonald's), muffler repair (Midas), and motels (La Quinta, Holiday Inn, Howard Johnson's).[39]

The benefits of implementing a consolidation strategy in a fragmented industry turn on the advantages larger firms in such industries gain from their larger market share. As will be discussed in Chapter 4, firms with large market share can have important cost advantages. Large market share can also help a firm differentiate its products (see Chapter 5) and give a firm some power of setting prices in an industry.

Opportunities in Emerging Industries: First-Mover Advantages

Emerging industries are newly created or newly re-created industries formed by technological innovations, changes in demand, the emergence of new customer needs, and so forth. Over the past 30 years, the world economy has been flooded by emerging industries, including the microprocessor industry, the personal computer industry, the medical imaging industry, and the biotechnology industry, to name a few. Firms in emerging industries face a unique set of opportunities, the exploitation of which can be a source of superior performance for some time for some firms.

The opportunities that face firms in emerging industries fall into the general category of first-mover advantages. **First-mover advantages** are advantages that come to firms that make important strategic and technological decisions early in the development of an industry. In emerging industries, many of the rules of the game and standard operating procedures for competing and succeeding have yet to be established. First-moving firms can sometimes help establish the rules of the game and create an industry's structure in ways that are uniquely beneficial to them. In general, first-mover advantages can arise from three primary sources: (1) technological leadership; (2) preemption of strategically valuable assets; and (3) the creation of customer-switching costs.[40]

First-Mover Advantages and Technological Leadership

Firms that make early investments in particular technologies in an industry are implementing a **technological leadership strategy**. Such strategies can generate two advantages in emerging industries. First, firms that have implemented these strategies may obtain a low-cost position based on their greater cumulative volume of production with a particular technology. These cost advantages have had important competitive implications in such diverse industries as the manufacture of titanium dioxide by DuPont and Procter & Gamble's competitive advantage in disposable diapers.[41]

Second, firms that make early investments in a technology may obtain patent protections that enhance their performance.[42] Xerox's patents on the xerography process and General Electric's patent on Edison's original lightbulb design were important for these firms' success when these two industries were emerging.[43] However, although there are some exceptions (e.g., the pharmaceutical industry and specialty chemicals), patents, per se, seem to provide relatively small profit opportunities for first-moving firms in most emerging industries. One group of researchers found that imitators can duplicate first movers' patent-based advantages for about 65 percent of the first mover's costs.[44] These researchers also found that 60 percent of all patents are imitated within four years of being granted—without legally violating patent rights obtained by first movers. As we will discuss in detail in Chapter 3, patents are rarely a source of sustained competitive advantage for firms, even in emerging industries.

First-Mover Advantages and Preemption of Strategically Valuable Assets

First movers that invest only in technology usually do not obtain sustained competitive advantages. However, first movers that move to tie up strategically valuable resources in an industry before their full value is widely understood can gain sustained competitive advantages. **Strategically valuable assets** are resources required to successfully compete in an industry. Firms that are able to acquire these resources have, in effect, erected formidable barriers to imitation in an industry. Some strategically valuable assets that can be acquired in this way include access to raw materials, particularly favorable geographic locations, and particularly valuable product market positions.

When an oil company such as Royal Dutch Shell acquires leases with greater development potential than was expected by its competition, the company is gaining access to raw materials in a way that is likely to make it difficult for other firms to gain access to these same raw materials. When Wal-Mart opens stores in medium-sized cities before the arrival of its competition, Wal-Mart is making it difficult for the competition to enter into this market. And when breakfast cereal companies expand their product lines to include all possible combinations of wheat, oats, bran, corn, and sugar, they, too, are using a first-mover advantage in supermarket shelf space to deter entry.[45]

First-Mover Advantages and Creating Customer-Switching Costs

Firms can also gain first-mover advantages in an emerging industry by creating customer-switching costs. **Customer-switching costs** exist when customers make investments in order to use a firm's particular products or services. These investments tie customers to a particular firm and make it more difficult for customers to begin purchasing from other firms.[46] Such switching costs are important factors in industries as diverse as applications software for personal computers, prescription pharmaceuticals, and groceries.[47]

In applications software for personal computers, users make significant investments to learn how to use a particular software package. Once computer users have learned how to operate particular software, they are unlikely to switch to new software, even if that new software system is superior to what they currently use. Such a switch would require learning the new software and determining how it is similar to and different from the old software. For these reasons, some computer users will continue to use outdated software, even though new software performs much better.

Similar switching costs can exist in some segments of the prescription pharmaceutical industry. Once medical doctors become familiar with a particular drug, its applications, and side effects, they are sometimes reluctant to change to a new drug, even if that new drug promises to be more effective than the older, more familiar one. Trying the new drug requires learning about its properties and side effects. Even if the new drug has received government approvals, its use requires doctors to be willing to "experiment" with the health of their patients. Given these issues, many physicians are unwilling to rapidly adopt new drug therapies. This is one reason that pharmaceutical firms spend so much time and money using their sales forces to educate their physician customers. This kind of education is necessary if a doctor is going to be willing to switch from an old drug to a new one.

Customer-switching costs can even play a role in the grocery store industry. Each grocery store has a particular layout of products. Once customers learn where different products in a particular store are located, they are not likely to change stores because they would then have to relearn the location of products. Many customers want to avoid the time and frustration associated with wandering around a new store looking for some obscure product. Indeed, the cost of switching stores may be large enough to enable some grocery stores to charge higher prices than would be the case without customer-switching costs.

First-Mover Disadvantages

Of course, the advantages of first moving in emerging industries must be balanced against the risks associated with exploiting this opportunity. Emerging industries are characterized by a great deal of uncertainty. When first-moving firms are making critical strategic decisions, it may not be at all clear what the right decisions are. In such highly uncertain settings, a reasonable strategic alternative to first moving may be retaining flexibility. Where first-moving firms attempt to resolve the uncertainty they face by making decisions early and then trying to influence the evolution of an emerging industry, they use flexibility to resolve this uncertainty by delaying decisions until the economically correct path is clear and then moving quickly to take advantage of that path. These issues will be discussed in detail in Chapter 6.

Opportunities in Mature Industries: Product Refinement, Service, and Process Innovation

Emerging industries are often formed by the creation of new products or technologies that radically alter the rules of the game in an industry. However, over time, as these new ways of doing business become widely understood, as technologies diffuse through competitors, and as the rate of innovation in new products and technologies drops, an industry begins to enter the mature phase of its development. As described in the Strategy in the Emerging Enterprise feature, this change in the nature of a firm's industry can be difficult to recognize and can create both strategic and operational problems for a firm.

Common characteristics of **mature industries** include: (1) slowing growth in total industry demand; (2) the development of experienced repeat customers; (3) a slowdown in increases in production capacity; (4) a slowdown in the introduction of new products or services; (5) an increase in the amount of international competition; and (6) an overall reduction in the profitability of firms in the industry.[48]

The fast-food industry in the United States has matured over the last several years. In the 1960s, the United States had only three large national fast-food chains: McDonald's, Burger King, and Dairy Queen. Through the 1980s, all three of these chains grew rapidly, although the rate of growth at McDonald's outstripped the growth rate of the other two firms. During this time period, however, other fast-food chains also entered the market. These included some national chains, such as Kentucky Fried Chicken, Wendy's, and Taco Bell, and some strong regional chains, such as Jack in the Box, In-N-Out Burger, and Five Guys Hamburgers. By the early 1990s, growth in this industry had slowed considerably. McDonald's announced that it was having difficulty finding locations for new McDonald's that did not impinge on the sales of already existing McDonald's. Except for non-U.S. operations, where competition in the fast-food industry is not as mature, the profitability of most U.S. fast-food companies did not grow as much in the 1990s as it did in the 1960s through the 1980s. Indeed, by the mid 2000's, many fast food chains were struggling to increase their profitability.[49]

Opportunities for firms in mature industries typically shift from the development of new technologies and products in an emerging industry to a greater emphasis on refining a firm's current products, an emphasis on increasing the quality of service, and a focus on reducing manufacturing costs and increased quality through process innovations.

Refining Current Products

In mature industries, such as home detergents, motor oil, and kitchen appliances, few, if any, major technological breakthroughs are likely. However, this does not mean that innovation is not occurring in these industries. Innovation in these industries focuses on extending and improving current products and technologies. In home detergents, innovation recently has focused on changes in packaging and on selling more highly concentrated detergents in small packets that are thrown into washing machines. In motor oil, packaging changes (from fiber foil cans to plastic containers), additives that keep oil cleaner longer, and oil formulated to operate in four-cylinder engines are recent examples of this kind of innovation. In kitchen appliances, recent improvements include the availability of refrigerators with crushed ice and water through the door, commercial-grade stoves for home use, and dishwashers that automatically adjust the cleaning cycle depending on how dirty the dishes are.[50] In fast foods, firms like McDonald's and Wendy's have introduced healthy, more adult-oriented food to complement their kid-friendly hamburger-heavy menus. This movement has helped restore the profitability of these firms.

Emphasis on Service

When firms in an industry have only limited ability to invest in radical new technologies and products, efforts to differentiate products often turn toward the quality of customer service. A firm that is able to develop a reputation for high-quality customer service may be able to obtain superior performance even though its products are not highly differentiated.

This emphasis on service has become very important in a wide variety of industries. For example, in the restaurant industry, one of the major reasons for slower growth in the fast-food segment has been growth in the so-called "fast casual dining" segment. This segment includes restaurants such as Panera Bread, Chipotle, and Café Rio—where customers still order and collect food from a counter, but where the both the quality of the food and its presentation is perceived as higher than what is the case in the fast food segment. Moreover, where fast food restaurants are designed to appeal to children—many McDonald's have playgrounds located next to the restaurant—many fast casual dining restaurants have more comfortable seating, are decorated with muted tones and comfortable chairs, fire places that provide warmth and ambience on cold winter nights, and relaxing background music. Combining the speed and convenience of fast food with the food quality and ambience of casual dining (e.g., Applebee's and Chili's), fast casual dining is the fastest growing segment of the restaurant industry.[51]

Process Innovation

A firm's **processes** are the activities it engages in to design, produce, and sell its products or services. **Process innovation**, then, is a firm's effort to refine and improve its current processes. Several authors have studied the relationship between process innovation, product innovation, and the maturity of an industry.[52] This work suggests that, in the early stages of industry development, product innovation is very important. However, over time product innovation becomes less important, and process innovations designed to reduce manufacturing costs, increase product quality, and streamline management become more important. In mature industries, firms can often gain an advantage by manufacturing the same product as competitors, but at a lower cost. Alternatively, firms can manufacture a product that is perceived to be of higher quality and do so at a competitive cost. Process innovations facilitate both the reduction of costs and the increase in quality.

The role of process innovation in more mature industries is perhaps best exemplified by the improvement in quality in U.S. automobiles. In the 1980s, Japanese firms such as Nissan, Toyota, and Honda sold cars that were of significantly higher quality than those produced by U.S. firms General Motors, Ford, and Chrysler. In the face of that competitive disadvantage, the U.S. firms engaged in numerous process reforms to improve the quality of their cars. In the 1980s, U.S. manufacturers were cited for car body panels that did not fit well, bumpers that were hung crookedly on cars, and the wrong engines being placed in cars. Today, the differences in quality between newly manufactured U.S. and Japanese automobiles are very small. Indeed, one well-known judge of initial manufacturing quality—J. D. Powers—now focuses on items such as the quality of a car's cup holders and the maximum distance at which a car's keyless entry system still works to establish quality rankings. For many U.S. manufacturers, the really significant quality issues of the 1980s are virtually gone.[53]

Opportunities in Declining Industries: Leadership, Niche, Harvest, and Divestment

A **declining industry** is an industry that has experienced an absolute decline in unit sales over a sustained period of time.[54] Obviously, firms in a declining industry face more threats than opportunities. Rivalry in a declining industry is likely to be very high, as is the threat of buyers, suppliers, and substitutes. However, even though threats are significant, firms do have opportunities they can exploit. The major strategic opportunities that firms in this kind of industry face are leadership, niche, harvest, and divestment.

Market Leadership

An industry in decline is often characterized by overcapacity in manufacturing, distribution, and so forth. Reduced demand often means that firms in a declining industry will have to endure a significant **shakeout period** until overcapacity is reduced and capacity is brought in line with demand. After the shakeout, a smaller number of lean and focused firms may enjoy a relatively benign environment with few threats and several opportunities. If the industry structure that is likely to exist after a shakeout is quite attractive, firms in an industry before the shakeout may have an incentive to weather the storm of decline—to survive until the situation improves to the point that they can begin to earn higher profits.

If a firm has decided to wait out the storm of decline in hopes of better environmental conditions in the future, it should consider various steps to increase its chances of survival. Most important of these is that a firm must establish itself as a **market leader** in the pre-shakeout industry, most typically by becoming the firm with the largest market share in that industry. The purpose of becoming a market leader is *not* to facilitate tacit collusion or to obtain lower costs from economies of scale (see Chapter 4). Rather, in a declining industry the leader's objective should be to try to facilitate the exit of firms that are not likely to survive a shakeout, thereby obtaining a more favorable competitive environment as quickly as possible.

Market leaders in declining industries can facilitate exit in a variety of ways, including purchasing and then deemphasizing competitors' product lines, purchasing and retiring competitors' manufacturing capacity, manufacturing spare parts for competitors' product lines, and sending unambiguous signals of their intention to stay in an industry and remain a dominant firm. For example, overcapacity problems in the European petrochemical industry were partially resolved when Imperial Chemical Industries (ICI) traded its polyethylene plants to British Petroleum for BP's polyvinylchloride (PVC) plants. In this case, both firms were able to close some excess capacity in specific markets (polyethylene and PVC), while sending clear signals of their intention to remain in these markets.[55]

Market Niche

A firm in a declining industry following a leadership strategy attempts to facilitate exit by other firms, but a firm following a **niche strategy** in a declining industry reduces its scope of operations and focuses on narrow segments of the declining industry. If only a few firms choose a particular niche, then these firms may have a favorable competitive setting, even though the industry as a whole is facing shrinking demand.

Two industries where this niche strategy has emerged are analog photography and analogue music recording (i.e., vinyl records). Both photography and music recording are overwhelmingly dominated by digital formats. But analog devices in these markets have not completely disappeared. For example, at least two firms—a Kodak spinoff called Alaris and an entrepreneurial startup called Lomography—continue to manufacture photographic film for professional and amateur photographers. These photographers are entranced by the quality, beauty, and tonal depth possible with film-based photos, and are convinced that these elements cannot be easily replicated by digital photography. Vinyl records—LPs, EPs, and even 45s, are seeing a resurgence in demand. Some audiophiles believe that the tonal quality of recordings on vinyl is superior to the tonal quality of CDs. In fact, vinyl record sales increased 23.9% in 2015, although they still make up less than 8% of physical album sales in the U.S., and less than 5% in the U.K. But retail firms like Urban Outfitters and Barnes and Noble have seen enough potential in this niche market, and have recently begun selling vinyl records.[56]

Harvest

Leadership and niche strategies, though differing along several dimensions, have one attribute in common: Firms that implement these strategies intend to remain in the industry despite its decline. Firms pursuing a **harvest strategy** in a declining industry do not expect to remain in the industry over the long term. Instead, they engage in a long, systematic, phased withdrawal, extracting as much value as possible during the withdrawal period.

The extraction of value during the implementation of a harvest strategy presumes that there is some value to harvest. Thus, firms that implement this strategy must ordinarily have enjoyed at least some profits at some time in their history, before the industry began declining. Firms can implement a harvest strategy by reducing the range of products they sell, reducing their distribution network, eliminating less profitable customers, reducing product quality, reducing service quality, deferring maintenance and equipment repair, and so forth. In the end, after a period of harvesting in a declining industry, firms can either sell their operations (to a market leader) or simply cease operations.

In principle, the harvest opportunity sounds simple, but in practice it presents some significant management challenges. The movement toward a harvest strategy often means that some of the characteristics of a business that have long been a source of pride to managers may have to be abandoned. Thus, where prior to harvest a firm may have specialized in high-quality service, quality products, and excellent customer value, during the harvest period service quality may fall, product quality may deteriorate, and prices may rise. These changes may be difficult for managers to accept, and higher turnover may be the result. It is also difficult to hire quality managers into a harvesting business because such individuals are likely to seek greater opportunities elsewhere.

For these reasons, few firms explicitly announce a harvest strategy. However, examples can be found. GE seemed to follow a harvest strategy in the electric turbine business. Also, United States Steel and the International Steel Group seemed to follow this strategy in certain segments of the steel market.[57]

Divestment

The final opportunity facing firms in a declining industry is divestment. Like a harvest strategy, the objective of **divestment** is to extract a firm from a declining industry. However, unlike harvest, divestment occurs quickly, often soon after a pattern of decline has been established. Firms without established competitive advantages may find divestment a superior option to harvest because they have few competitive advantages they can exploit through harvesting.

In the 1980s, GE used this rapid divestment approach to virtually abandon the consumer electronics business. Total demand in this business was more or less stable during the 1980s, but competition (mainly from Asian manufacturers) increased substantially. Rather than remain in this business, GE sold most of its consumer electronics operations and used the capital to enter into the medical imaging industry, where this firm has found an environment more conducive to superior performance.[58]

In the defense business, divestment was the stated strategy of General Dynamics, at least in some of its business segments. General Dynamics' managers recognized early on that the changing defense industry could not support all the incumbent firms. When General Dynamics concluded that it could not remain a leader in some of its businesses, it decided to divest those and concentrate on a few remaining businesses. Since 1991, General Dynamics has sold businesses worth more than $2.83 billion, including its missile systems business, its Cessna aircraft division, and its tactical aircraft division (maker of the very successful F-16 aircraft and partner in the development of the next generation of fighter aircraft, the F-22). These divestitures created significant value for General Dynamics' shareholders: its stock went from $25 per share before divestment to a high of $110 per share after divestment. During this time period, General Dynamics' stock provided a total return to stockholders of 555 percent.[59]

Of course, not all divestments are caused by industry decline. Sometimes firms divest certain operations to focus their efforts on remaining operations, sometimes they divest to raise capital, and sometimes they divest to simplify operations. These types of divestments reflect a firm's diversification strategy and are explored in detail in Chapter 8.

Summary

The strategic management process requires that a firm engage in an analysis of threats and opportunities in its competitive environment before a strategic choice can be made. This analysis begins with an understanding of the firm's general environment. This general environment has six components: technological change, demographic trends, cultural trends, economic climate, legal and political conditions, and specific international events. Although some of these components of the general environment can affect a firm directly, more frequently they affect a firm through their impact on its local environment.

The S-C-P model can be used to develop tools for analyzing threats in a firm's competitive environment. The most influential of these tools focuses on five environmental threats to the profitability of firms in an industry. The five threats are: threat from new competitors, threat from existing direct competitors, threat from superior or low cost substitutes, threat of supplier leverage, and the threat from buyers' influence. The threat of new competition depends on the existence and "height" of barriers to entry. Common barriers to entry include economies of scale, product differentiation, cost advantages independent of scale, and government regulation. The threat of current direct competitors depends on the number and competitiveness of firms in an industry. This threat is high in an industry when there are large numbers of competing firms, competing firms are roughly the same size and have the same influence, growth in an industry is slow, there is no product differentiation, and productive capacity is added in large increments. The threat of superior substitutes depends on how close substitute products and services are—in performance and cost—to products and services in an industry. Whereas direct competitors meet the same customer needs in approximately the same way, substitutes meet the same customer needs, but do so in very different ways. The threat of supplier leverage in an industry depends on the number and distinctiveness of the products suppliers provide to an industry. The threat of supplier leverage increases when a supplier's industry is dominated by a few firms, when suppliers sell unique or highly differentiated products, when suppliers are not threatened by substitutes, when suppliers threaten forward vertical integration, and when firms are not important customers for suppliers. Finally, the threat of buyers' influence depends on the number and size of an industry's customers. The threat of buyers' influence is greater when the number of buyers is small, products sold to buyers are undifferentiated and standard, products sold to buyers are a significant percentage of a buyer's final costs, buyers are not earning significant profits, and buyers threaten backward vertical integration. Taken together, the level of these threats in an industry can be used to determine the expected average performance of firms in an industry.

One additional force in a firm's environment is complementors. Where competitors compete with a firm to divide profits in a market, complementors increase the total size of the market. If you are a CEO of a firm, you know that another firm is a complementor when the value of your products to your customers is higher in combination with this other firm's products than when customers use your products alone. Where firms have strong incentives to reduce the entry of competitors, they can sometimes have strong incentives to increase the entry of complementors.

The S-C-P model can also be used to develop tools for analyzing strategic opportunities in an industry. This is done by identifying generic industry structures and the strategic opportunities available in these different kinds of industries. Four common industry structures are fragmented industries, emerging industries, mature industries, and declining industries. The primary opportunity in fragmented industries is consolidation. In emerging industries, the most important opportunity is first-mover advantages from technological leadership, preemption of strategically valuable assets, or creation of customer-switching costs. In mature industries, the primary opportunities are product refinement, service, and process innovation. In declining industries, opportunities include market leadership, niche, harvest, and divestment.

Challenge Questions

2.1. Your former college roommate calls you and asks to borrow $10,000 so that he can open a pizza restaurant in his hometown. In justifying this request, he argues that there must be significant demand for pizza and other fast food in his hometown because there are lots of such restaurants already there, and three or four new ones are opening each month. He also argues that demand for convenience food will continue to increase, and he points to the large number of firms that now sell frozen dinners in grocery stores. What are the risks involved in choosing to lend him money?

2.2. One potential threat in an industry is buyers' influence. Yet unless buyers are satisfied, they are likely to look for satisfaction elsewhere. Can the fact that buyers can be threats be reconciled with the need to satisfy buyers?

2.3. Government policies can have a significant impact on the average profitability of firms in an industry. Government, however, is not included as a potential threat. Should the model be expanded to include government? Why or why not?

2.4. If an industry has large numbers of complementors, does that make it more attractive or less attractive or does it have no impact on the industry's attractiveness? Justify your answer.

2.5. Opportunities analysis seems to suggest that strategic opportunities are available in almost any industry, including declining ones. If that is true, is it fair to say that there is really no such thing as an unattractive industry?

2.6. If there is really no such thing as an unattractive industry, what implications does this have for the applicability of environmental threat analysis?

2.7. Describe an industry that has no opportunities.

2.8. Describe when the evolution of industry structure from an emerging industry to a mature industry to a declining industry is inevitable.

Problem Set

2.9. Perform an analysis of the profit potential on the following two industries:

The Pharmaceutical Industry

The pharmaceutical industry consists of firms that develop, patent, and sell drugs. Although this industry does not have significant production economies of scale, it does have important know how efficiencies in research and development. Product differentiation exists as well because firms often sell branded products. Firms compete in research and development. However, once a product is developed and patented, competition is significantly reduced. Recently, the increased availability of generic, nonbranded drugs has threatened the profitability of some drug lines. Once an effective drug is developed, few, if any, alternatives to that drug usually are available, at least until the drug goes off patent. Most drugs are manufactured with commodity chemicals that are available from numerous suppliers. Major final customers include doctors and patients. Recently, increased costs have led the federal government and insurance companies to pressure drug companies to reduce their prices.

The Pharmaceutical Distribution Industry

The pharmaceutical distribution industry consists of firms that buy drugs from pharmaceutical firms and then sell and distribute those drugs to retail drug stores, hospitals, and to hundreds of thousands of other outlets where drugs are sold to consumers. Because the marginal cost of pushing another drug through a firm's established distribution network is almost zero, there are substantial economies of scale in this industry. Historically, there were over 350 pharmaceutical distribution firms. Through a series of acquisitions, this industry is currently dominated by three firms with over 95 percent of the total market share. Competition among these firms can be fierce—firms have sometimes set their prices below their marginal costs to retain contacts with pharmaceutical firms (on the supply side) and consolidating retail drug stores (on the demand side). Despite the high cost of some pharmaceuticals, they are often a less costly alternative to surgery and more invasive procedures often performed in hospitals.

2.10. Perform an opportunities analysis on the following industries:

(a) The U.S. airline industry
(b) The U.S. beer industry
(c) The U.S. property and casualty insurance industry
(d) The worldwide portable digital media (e.g., flash drives) industry
(e) The worldwide small-package overnight delivery industry

2.11. For each of the following firms, identify at least two competitors (rivals, new entrants, or substitutes) and two complementors.

(a) Ford Motor Company
(b) Microsoft
(c) Dell
(d) Boeing
(e) McDonald's

Writing Assignments

2.12. Describe a situation where a single firm can be both a competitor and a complementor to the same firm.

2.13. Under what conditions can firms gain first-mover advantages in an emerging industry?

CASE STUDY | Jet Airways' Quest for Revival: A Strategic Analysis of the Aviation Industry

The Resurgence

Jet Airways stands at the precipice of a new era, poised for a bold comeback in 2024, under the Jalan-Kalrock Consortium (JKC). This piece of narrative traces the airline's ascent since its commencement in 1993 by its founder, Naresh Goyal, venturing through a couple of decades in aviation dominance, to its grounding in 2019, followed by the subsequent revival efforts. This case study not only chronicles Jet Airways' saga but also sheds light on the broader dynamics and external pressures of the aviation sector, emphasizing the strategic imperatives for the airline's successful comeback.

Evolving Dynamics of the Indian Aviation Sector

The global aviation landscape has witnessed significant shifts, propelled by technological progress, evolving regulatory landscapes, and changing consumer preferences. Post-1990s liberalization, India's aviation market emerged as a global growth leader, driven by economic expansion and increased connectivity demands. Despite such growth, airlines confront ongoing challenges—fluctuating fuel costs, regulatory hurdles, intense competitive rivalry, and more recently, the catastrophic impacts of the COVID-19 pandemic. These elements collectively shape the operational and strategic outlook for airlines, underlining the complex environment in which Jet Airways plans its re-entry.

Jet Airways—Past take-off and landing

Foundational Years and Vision: Launched with boundless ambition, Jet Airways quickly distinguished itself as a premium full-service carrier, celebrated for its exemplary service and expansive route network. However, the airline's journey was marred by financial distress in the late 2010s, caused by increased competition, soaring operational costs, and strategic misalignments, leading to its operational halt in 2019.

Ownership Transition and Revival Efforts: The transition of ownership to JKC marks a pivotal chapter in Jet Airways' history. The consortium's revival plan, infused with substantial capital, aims to rejuvenate the airline, reflecting a significant commitment to reclaiming Jet Airways' position in the aviation market.

Market and Financial Landscape

The Indian aviation arena is predominantly ruled by low-cost carriers, with IndiGo at the forefront. This market scenario is marked by a high sensitivity to pricing among passengers, emphasizing the criticality of cost efficiency and operational agility for airlines. Jet Airways' financial turmoil, characterized by hefty debts and operational inefficiencies, highlights the urgency for a strategic transformation focused on sustainability and market reclamation.

Strategic Blueprint for Revival

Navigating the External Environment: Jet Airways' revival strategy is intricately linked to its external environment, requiring meticulous regulatory compliance, astute market positioning, stringent cost control, and strategic fleet and network planning. The overarching goal is to identify and exploit a unique market position that leverages service quality while ensuring cost competitiveness.

Funding Strategy and Vision for the Future: The consortium's investment strategy is geared towards stabilizing operations, addressing financial liabilities, and setting the stage for growth. Jet Airways aspires to expand its domestic and international presence, targeting a strategic market share increase in a burgeoning aviation sector.

Confronting the Challenges Ahead

The path to revival is laden with obstacles—stiff competition from established carriers, operational and logistical hurdles post-grounding, brand loyalty restoration, and adaptation to market volatilities. These challenges necessitate a balanced approach, combining strategic foresight with operational excellence.

Towards a New Horizon

Jet Airways 2.0's endeavor to soar the skies again is not merely a revival story but a testament to strategic resilience in the face of industry adversities. This journey underscores the importance of adaptability, strategic clarity, and the relentless pursuit of excellence. As Jet Airways manoeuvres through these turbulent times, its comeback offers profound insights into overcoming obstacles, strategic planning, and the dynamics of the aviation industry's ever-evolving landscape. The airline's quest for resurgence is a narrative of rebirth, resilience, and unwavering commitment to reclaiming its sky-high legacy.

Questions:

1. Considering the intense competition in the Indian aviation market, especially from low-cost carriers, how should Jet Airways 2.0 position itself to ensure a successful re-entry? Should it return as a full-service carrier, adopt a low-cost model, or pursue a hybrid approach to differentiate itself from competitors?
2. What operational strategies should Jet Airways implement to manage its cost structure effectively and enhance operational efficiency in the post-COVID-19 aviation landscape?
3. In the wake of its operational suspension and subsequent revival, what measures should Jet Airways take to rebuild brand loyalty and trust among its customer base? How can the airline leverage digital transformation to enhance customer experience and engagement?

References

Directorate General of Civil Aviation (DGCA). (n.d.). *Civil Aviation Requirements*. Accessed from https://dgca.gov.in/digigov-portal on March 10, 2024.

International Air Transport Association (IATA). (2021). *IATA Economics*. Retrieved from https://www.iata.org/en/publications/economics/

CAPA - Centre for Aviation. (n.d.). *India Aviation Industry News*. Retrieved from https://centreforaviation.com/news/region/india

Agnihotri, A., & Bhattacharya, S. (2023). *Jet Airways: Turnaround of an Indian Full-Service Airline as It Emerges From Bankruptcy?*. SAGE Publications: SAGE Business Cases Originals.

Bonelli, Marco I. (2023). *Beyond Financial Ratios: A Novel Approach to Bankruptcy Predictions for Indian Firms*. Indian Journal of Finance, Forthcoming (March 30, 2023). Available at SSRN: https://ssrn.com/abstract=4496001 or http://dx.doi.org/10.2139/ssrn.4496001

End Notes

1 See (2003). *The big book of business quotations.* New York: Basic Books, p. 209.

2 See Weintraub, A. (2004). "Repairing the engines of life." *BusinessWeek*, May 24, 2004, pp. 99+ for a discussion of recent developments in biotechnology research and the business challenges they have created.

3 The data reported here are from an EY (formerly Ernst and Young) survey of 1,200 managers and non-managers across a variety of industries, reported in 2013. See V. Giong (2013) "Here are the Strengths and Weaknesses of Millennials, Gen X, and Boomers," *Business Insiders*, September 9, 2013, retrieved November 7, 2016.

4 These results are described in a report prepared by Oracle for its banking customers. This report can be found at: www.oracle.com/US/industries/financialservices/gen-y-survey-report/65297.pdf retrieved November 7, 2016

5 Census.Gov

6 See E. Bryan "Hola: P & G Seeks Latino Shoppers," *The Wall Street Journal*, September 15, 2011, retrieved on November 7, 2016

7 These and other cultural differences are described in Rugman, A., and R. Hodgetts. (1995). *International business.* New York: McGraw-Hill.

8 Early contributors to the structure-conduct-performance model include Mason, E. S. (1939). "Price and production policies of large scale enterprises." *American Economic Review*, 29, pp. 61–74; and Bain, J. S. (1956). *Barriers to new competition.* Cambridge, MA: Harvard University Press. The major developments in this framework are summarized in Bain, J. S. (1968). *Industrial organization.* New York: John Wiley & Sons, Inc.; and Scherer, F. M. (1980). *Industrial market structure and economic performance.* Boston: Houghton Mifflin. The links between this framework and work in strategic management are discussed by Porter, M. E. (1981a). "The contribution of industrial organization to strategic management." *Academy of Management Review*, 6, pp. 609–620; and Barney, J. B. (1986c). "Types of competition and the theory of strategy: Toward an integrative framework." *Academy of Management Review*, 1, pp. 791–800.

9 J. B. Barney (1986). "Types of competition and the theory of strategy." *Academy of Management Review*, 11, pp. 791–800; H. Demsetz (1973). "Industry structure, market rivalry, and public policy." *Journal of Law and Economics*, 16, pp. 1–9; M. Porter (1981). "The contribution of industrial organization to strategic management." *Academy of Management Review*, 6, pp. 609–620.

10 See, for example, Porter, M. E. (1979). "How competitive forces shape strategy." *Harvard Business Review*, March–April, pp. 137–156; and Porter, M. E. (1980). *Competitive strategy.* New York: Free Press.

11 J. Barney (2007). *Gaining and sustaining competitive advantage*, 3rd ed. Upper Saddle River, NJ: Pearson Higher Education.

12 These barriers were originally proposed by Bain, J. S. (1968). *Industrial organization.* New York: John Wiley & Sons, Inc. It is actually possible to estimate the "height" of barriers to entry in an industry by comparing the cost of entry into an industry with barriers and the cost of entry into that industry if barriers did not exist. The difference between these costs is the "height" of the barriers to entry.

13 Another alternative would be for a firm to own and operate more than one plant. If there are economies of scope in this industry, a firm might be able to enter and earn above-normal profits. An economy of scope exists when the value of operating in two businesses simultaneously is greater than the value of operating in these two businesses separately. The concept of economy of scope is explored in more detail in Part 3 of this book.

14 See Ghemawat, P., and H. J. Stander III. (1992). "Nucor at a crossroads." Harvard Business School Case No. 9-793-039.

15 See Montgomery, C. A., and B. Wernerfelt. (1991). "Sources of superior performance: Market share versus industry effects in the U.S. brewing industry." *Management Science*, 37, pp. 954–959.

16 Sorkin, A. R., and M. Merced. (2008). "Brewer bids $46 billion for Anheuser-Busch." *New York Times*, June 12. http://www.nytimes.com/2008/06/12/business/worldbusiness/12beer.html?_r=0

17 Stecklow, S. (1999). "Gallo woos French, but don't expect Bordeaux by the jug." *The Wall Street Journal*, March 26, pp. A1+.

18 Wingfield, N. (2013). "Intertrust sues Apple over patent violations." Bcts.blogs. NYTimes.com, March 20; Swisler, K. (2012). "Yahoo sues Facebook for patent infringement." Allthings.com, March 12; Fingas, J. (2013). "Google countersues BT." www.engadget.com, February 13; "Boston University sues Apple for patent infringement." (2013). www.macworld.com, July 3; "Nokia taking HTC to court over patent violations." (2013). www.mobilemg.com, May 25;Dobie, A. (2013). "Apple looks to add Sony Galaxy 54 to patent infringement suit."www.androidcentral.com, May 14; "Bad Apple." (2013). www.catholic.org, June 5.

19 See S. Brachmen. "2015 Litigation Trends," ipwatchdog.com, January 8, 2016. Retrieved November 7, 2016.

20 See Kogut, B., and U. Zander. (1992). "Knowledge of the firm, combinative capabilities, and the replication of technology." *Organization Science*, 3, pp. 383–397; and Dierickx, I., and K. Cool. (1989). "Asset stock accumulation and sustainability of competitive advantage." *Management Science*, 35, pp. 1504–1511. Both emphasize the importance of know-how as a barrier to entry into an industry. More generally, intangible resources are seen as particularly important sources of sustained competitive advantage. This will be discussed in more detail in Chapter 3.

21 See Polanyi, M. (1962). *Personal knowledge: Towards a post-critical philosophy.* London: Routledge & Kegan Paul; and Itami, H. (1987). *Mobilizing invisible assets.* Cambridge, MA: Harvard University Press.

22 See Henderson, R., and I. Cockburn. (1994). "Measuring competence: Exploring firm effects in pharmaceutical research." *Strategic Management Journal*, 15, pp. 361–374. Entry by pharmaceutical firms specializing just in research has been more common than entry by integrated research and development firms.

23 See Scherer, F. M. (1980). *Industrial market structure and economic performance.* Boston: Houghton Mifflin.

24 See Z. Epstein. "You Won't Believe How Little Windows PC Makers Earn for Each PC Sold," bgr.com, January 10, 2014. Retrieved on November 7, 2016.

25 Chartier, John. (2002). "Burger battles." CNN/Money, http://money.cnn.com, December 11.

26 See Ghemawat, P., and A. McGahan. (1995). "The U.S. airline industry in 1995." Harvard Business School Case No. 9-795-113.

27 Labich, K. (1992). "Airbus takes off." *Fortune*, June 1, pp. 102–108.

28 See Pollock, E. J. (1993). "Mediation firms alter the legal landscape." *The Wall Street Journal*, March 22, p. B1; Cox, M. (1993). "Electronic campus: Technology threatens to shatter the world of college textbooks." *The Wall Street Journal*, June 1, p. A1; Reilly, P. M. (1993). "At a crossroads: The instant-new age leaves *Time* magazine searching for a mission." *The Wall Street Journal*, May 12, p. A1; Rohwedder, C. (1993). "Europe's smaller food shops face finis." *The Wall Street Journal*, May 12, p. B1; Fatsis, S. (1995). "Major leagues keep minors at a distance." *The Wall Street Journal*, November 8, pp. B1+; Norton, E., and G. Stem. (1995). "Steel and aluminum vie over every ounce in a car's construction." *The Wall Street Journal*, May 9, pp. A1+; Paré, T. P. (1995). "Why the banks lined up against Gates." *Fortune*, May 29, p. 18 "Hitting the mail on the head." *The Economist*, April 30, 1994, pp. 69–70; Pacelle, M. (1996). "'Big Boxes' by discounters are booming." *The Wall Street Journal*, January 17, p. A2; and Pope, K., and L. Cauley. (1998). "In battle for TV ads, cable is now the enemy." *The Wall Street Journal*, May 6, pp. B1+.

29 Tully, S. (1992). "How to cut those #$%* legal costs." *Fortune*, September 21, pp. 119–124.

30 See DeWitt, W. (1997). "Crown Cork & Seal/Carnaud Metalbox." Harvard Business School Case No. 9-296-019.

31 Perry, N. J. (1993). "What's next for the defense industry." *Fortune*, February 22, pp. 94–100.

32 See "Crown Cork and Seal in 1989." Harvard Business School Case No. 5-395-224.

33 See Brandenburger, A., and B. Nalebuff. (1996). *Co-opetition.* New York: Doubleday.

34 See R. Lawler (April 16, 2009) "Analyst: '09 Blue Ray sales Double Those of '08" *Engagent.AOL.* Retrieved November 8, 2016.

35 R. P. Rumelt (1991). "How much does industry matter?" *Strategic Management Journal*, 12, pp. 167–185; R. Schmalansee (1985). "Do markets differ much?" *American Economic Review*, 75, pp. 341–351; V. F. Misangyi, H. Elms, T. Greckhamer, and J. A. Lepine (2006). "A new perspective on a fundamental debate: A multilevel approach to industry, corporate, and business unit effects." *Strategic Management Journal*, 27(6), pp. 571–590.

36 This approach to studying opportunities was also first suggested in Porter, M. E. (1980). *Competitive strategy.* New York: Free Press.

37 K. Conner (1995) "Obtaining Strategic Advantage from Being Imitated," *Management Science*, 41, 209–225; M. Mandel (2000) "Anti-trust in the Digital Age," *Businessweek*, May 15, 51; L. Tesler (1978) *Economic Theory and the Core.* Chicago: Chicago; W. Sjostrom (1989) "Collusion in Ocean Shipping," Journal of Political Economy, 97, 1160–1179; A. McWilliams (1990) "Rethinking Horizontal Market Restrictions: In Defense of Cooperation in Empty Core Markets," *Quarterly Review of Economics and Business*, 30, 3–14

38 Jacob, R. (1992). "Service Corp. International: Acquisitions done the right way." *Fortune*, November 16, p. 96.

39 Porter, M. E. (1980). *Competitive strategy.* New York: Free Press.

40 For the definitive discussion of first-mover advantages, see Lieberman, M., and C. Montgomery. (1988). "First-mover advantages." *Strategic Management Journal*, 9, pp. 41–58.

41 See Ghemawat, P. (1991). *Commitment.* New York: Free Press.

42 See Gilbert, R. J., and D. M. Newbery. (1982). "Preemptive patenting and the persistence of monopoly." *American Economic Review*, 72(3), pp. 514–526.

43 See Bresnahan, T. F. (1985). "Post-entry competition in the plain paper copier market." *American Economic Review*, 85, pp. 15–19, for a discussion of Xerox's patents; and Bright, A. A. (1949). *The electric lamp industry.* New York: Macmillan, for a discussion of General Electric's patents.

44 See Mansfield, E., M. Schwartz, and S. Wagner. (1981). "Imitation costs and patents: An empirical study." *Economic Journal*, 91, pp. 907–918.

45 See Main, O. W. (1955). *The Canadian nickel industry.* Toronto: University of Toronto Press, for a discussion of asset preemption in the oil and gas industry; Ghemawat, P. (1986). "Wal-Mart store's discount operations." Harvard Business School Case No. 9-387-018, for Wal-Mart's preemption strategy; Schmalansee, R. (1978). "Entry deterrence in the ready-to-eat breakfast cereal industry." *Bell Journal of Economics*, 9(2), pp. 305–327; and Robinson, W. T., and C. Fornell. (1985). "Sources of market pioneer advantages in consumer goods industries." *Journal of Marketing Research*, 22(3), pp. 305–307, for a discussion of preemption in the breakfast cereal industry. In this latter case, the preempted valuable asset is shelf space in grocery stores.

46 Klemperer, P. (1986). "Markets with consumer switching costs." Doctoral thesis, Graduate School of Business, Stanford University; and Wernerfelt, B. (1986). "A special case of dynamic pricing policy." *Management Science*, 32, pp. 1562–1566.

47 See Gross, N. (1995). "The technology paradox." *BusinessWeek*, March 6, pp. 691–719; Bond, R. S., and D. F. Lean. (1977). *Sales, promotion, and product differentiation in two prescription drug markets.* Washington, D.C.: U.S. Federal Trade Commission; Montgomery, D. B. (1975). "New product distribution: An analysis of supermarket buyer decision." *Journal of Marketing Research*, 12, pp. 255–264; Ries, A., and J. Trout. (1986). *Marketing warfare.* New York: McGraw-Hill; and Davidson, J. H. (1976). "Why most new consumer brands fail." *Harvard Business Review*, 54, March–April, pp. 117–122, for a discussion of switching costs in these industries.

48 Porter, M. E. (1980). *Competitive strategy.* New York: Free Press.

49 Gibson, R. (1991). "McDonald's insiders increase their sales of company's stock." *The Wall Street Journal*, June 14, p. A1; and Chartier, J. (2002). "Burger battles." CNN/Money, http://money.cnn.com, December 11. McDonald's lost money for only one quarter. It has since repositioned itself with nice upscale fast foods and has returned to profitability.

50 Descriptions of these product refinements can be found in Demetrakakes, P. (1994). "Household-chemical makers concentrate on downsizing." *Packaging*, 39(1), p. 41 Reda, S. (1995). "Motor oil: Hands-on approach." *Stores*, 77(5), pp. 48–49; and Quinn, J. (1995). "KitchenAid." *Incentive*, 169(5), pp. 46–47.

51 See "Fast Casual is the Fastest Growing Foodservice Segment Globally," *qsrmagazine.com*, April 20, 2016. Retrieved November 9, 2016.

52 See Hayes, R. H., and S. G. Wheelwright. (1979). "The dynamics of process-product life cycles." *Harvard Business Review*, March–April, p. 127.

53 See www.jdpowers.com. The exception to this conclusion about U.S. car manufactures seems to be Fiat Chrysler. See J. Stoll (June 17, 2015) "Fiat Chrysler Brands Get Poor Ratings in Quality Study," *Wall Street Journal.* Retrieved November 9, 2016.

54 See Porter, M. E. (1980). *Competitive strategy.* New York: Free Press; and Harrigan, K. R. (1980). *Strategies for declining businesses.* Lexington, MA: Lexington Books.

55 See Aguilar, F. J., J. L. Bower, and B. Gomes-Casseres. (1985). "Restructuring European petrochemicals: Imperial Chemical Industries, P.L.C." Harvard Business School Case No. 9-385-203.

56 See Harrigan, K. R. (1980). *Strategies for declining businesses.* Lexington, MA: Lexington Books. For the photographic film industry, see petapixel.com/film-photography-making-strong-comeback (Accessed January 5, 2017); www.lomography.com; and www.kodakalaris.com. For vinyl records, see DigitalMusicNews/2017/01/03/vinyl-record-sales-1991 (accessed January 5, 2017).

57 See Klebnikov, P. (1991). "The powerhouse." *Forbes*, September 2, pp. 46–52; and Rosenbloom, R. S., and C. Christensen. (1990). "Continuous casting investments at USX corporation." Harvard Business School Case No. 9-391-121.

58 Finn, E. A. (1987). "General Eclectic." *Forbes*, March 23, pp. 74–80.

59 See Smith, L. (1993). "Can defense pain be turned to gain?" *Fortune*, February 8, pp. 84–96; Perry, N. J. (1993). "What's next for the defense industry?" *Fortune*, February 22, pp. 94–100; and Dial, J., and K. J. Murphy. (1995). "Incentive, downsizing, and value creation at General Dynamics." *Journal of Financial Economics*, 37, pp. 261–314.

CHAPTER

3 Evaluating a Firm's Internal Capabilities

LEARNING OBJECTIVES

After reading this chapter, you should be able to:

3.1 Describe the resource-based view and how it differs from the S-C-P model.

3.2 Describe the VRIO framework and how it relates to the resource-based view.

3.3 Be able to apply the VRIO framework to identify the competitive implications of a firm's resources and capabilities.

3.4 Discuss important implications of the resource-based view, including:

a. How value chain analysis can be used to identify a firm's valuable resources and capabilities.

b. The kinds of resources and capabilities that are likely to be costly to imitate.

c. How a firm uses its structure, formal and informal control processes, and compensation policy to exploit its resources.

Biocon's Biopharmaceutical Breakthroughs

Biocon, a pioneering biopharmaceutical firm headquartered in Bangalore, India, is distinguished by its commitment to affordability and quality in healthcare. Founded in 1978 by Kiran Mazumdar-Shaw, the company has grown to become a global leader in biotechnology, earning Mazumdar-Shaw international recognition as India's "biotech queen" and featuring her on Forbes' list of "The World's 100 Most Powerful Women." Biocon's journey reflects innovation, strategic partnerships, and a relentless pursuit of global healthcare improvement.

Biocon's market and financial analysis reveal a company in robust health. With a revenue of $1.4 billion in 2023 and a market capitalization of $3.9 billion, Biocon showcases a strong financial performance amidst challenges. The acquisition of Viatris' biosimilar assets in 2022 for $3.34 billion further signifies Biocon's strategic investments to strengthen its market position and expand its global footprint. The employer value proposition at Biocon is centered around—innovation, diversity, and inclusivity—fostering a culture where over 3,400 employees are encouraged to innovate and contribute to the company's mission. The leadership under Mazumdar-Shaw and other key figures like Christiane Hamacher and Siddharth Mittal has been pivotal in steering the company through its growth phases, ensuring Biocon remains at the forefront of biotechnological innovation.

In recent developments during 2023 and 2024, Biocon has continued to demonstrate its prowess in the biopharmaceutical industry through significant strategic and operational advancements. One of the major highlights is the completion of the integration of the acquired biosimilars business from Viatris in North America by Biocon Biologics, a subsidiary of Biocon Ltd. This move, completed effective September 1st, 2023, marks a significant step in Biocon Biologics' aim to strengthen its leadership position in the global biosimilars market. The integration enables Biocon Biologics to lead commercial operations in the United States and Canada, expanding the availability of high-quality biosimilars for diseases such as diabetes, cancer, and autoimmune disorders, along with introducing products in new therapeutic areas like ophthalmology. Biocon Biologics now boasts a portfolio of in-market and in-development biosimilars across multiple therapies, including notable 'firsts' in the industry like the approval of bTrastuzumab and bPegfilgrastim, as well as interchangeable bGlargine in the United States.

Furthermore, Biocon Biologics has been recognized as an Asia IP Elite for 2023, underscoring its commitment to innovation and excellence in the field of intellectual property. This accolade reflects Biocon's dedication to advancing healthcare and transforming lives through affordable access to high-quality biosimilars worldwide. These achievements underscore Biocon's strategic focus on expanding its global footprint, enhancing its R&D capabilities, and maintaining a competitive edge in the global biopharmaceutical industry. Through these endeavors, Biocon continues to fulfill its mission of addressing unmet medical needs and improving healthcare outcomes across the globe.

Looking ahead, Biocon's future direction involves strengthening its biosimilar portfolio, expanding its global presence, and navigating regulatory landscapes efficiently. The challenges it faces, including intense competition, regulatory hurdles, and the need for continuous innovation, are significant. Yet, Biocon's track record of strategic partnerships, like the recent collaboration with Serum Institute of India to commercialize vaccines and biological drugs, places it in a favourable position to address these challenges and leverage opportunities in the global biopharmaceutical sector. Biocon is a testament to the power of vision, strategic planning, and innovation in transforming healthcare. With its focus on making healthcare accessible and affordable, Biocon not only contributes significantly to the biopharmaceutical industry but also sets a benchmark for companies striving to make a global impact on healthcare.

REFERENCES

Biocon. (n.d.). Financial Fact Sheet. *Biocon - Global Biopharmaceutical Company.* Accessed from https://www.biocon.com on February 5, 2024.

GlobalData. (n.d.). *Biocon Ltd Company Profile – Overview.* Accessed from https://www.globaldata.com on February 5, 2024.

Biocon Biologics Ltd. (2023). *Biocon Biologics Continues to Expand Global Footprint, Completes Integration of Viatris Biosimilars' Business In North America Ahead of Schedule.* Biocon PR Newswire (September 6, 2023). Accessed from https://www.biocon.com on February 5, 2024.

HrNxt.com News Desk (2023). *Biocon Biologics recognized as an Asia IP Elite for 2023.* HrNxt.com (December 15, 2023). Accessed from https://hrnxt.com on February 5, 2024.

Biocon has been extremely successful, first in the biopharma industry and later in related markets. What, if anything, about Biocon's resources and capabilities make it likely that this firm will be able to continue its success? The ideas presented in this chapter help answer this question.

Objective 3.1 Describe the resource-based view and how it differs from the S-C-P model.

The Resource-Based View of the Firm

In Chapter 2, we saw that it was possible to take some theoretical models developed in economics—specifically the structure-conduct-performance (S-C-P) model—and apply them to develop tools for analyzing a firm's external threats and opportunities. The same is true for analyzing a firm's internal strengths and weaknesses. However, whereas the tools described in Chapter 2 were based on the S-C-P model, the tools described in this chapter are based on the resource-based view (RBV) of the firm. The RBV is a model of firm performance that focuses on the resources and capabilities controlled by a firm as sources of competitive advantage.[1]

What Are Resources and Capabilities?

Resources in the RBV are defined as the tangible and intangible assets that a firm controls that it can use to conceive and implement its strategies. Examples of resources include a firm's factories (a tangible asset), its products (a tangible asset), its reputation among customers (an intangible asset), and teamwork among its managers (an intangible asset). Google's tangible assets include its Web site and associated software. Its intangible assets include its brand name and reputation in the search engine business.

Capabilities are a subset of a firm's resources and are defined as the tangible and intangible assets that enable a firm to take full advantage of the other resources it controls. That is, capabilities alone do not enable a firm to conceive and implement its strategies, but they enable a firm to use other resources to conceive and implement such strategies. Examples of capabilities might include a firm's marketing skills and teamwork and cooperation among its managers. At Google, the cooperation among software developers and marketing people that made it possible for Google to dominate the search engine business is an example of a capability.

A firm's resources and capabilities can be classified into four broad categories: financial resources, physical resources, individual resources, and organizational resources. **Financial resources** include all the money, from whatever source, that firms use to conceive and implement strategies. These financial resources include cash from entrepreneurs, equity holders, bondholders, and banks. **Retained earnings**, or the profit that a firm made earlier in its history and invests in itself, are also an important type of financial resource.

Physical resources include all the physical technology used in a firm. This includes a firm's plant and equipment, its geographic location, and its access to raw materials. Specific examples of plant and equipment that are part of a firm's physical resources are a firm's computer hardware and software technology, robots used in manufacturing, and automated warehouses. Geographic location, as a type of physical resource, is important for firms as diverse as Wal-Mart (with its operations in rural markets generating, on average, higher returns than its operations in more competitive urban markets) and L. L. Bean (a catalogue retail firm that believes that its rural Maine location helps its employees identify with the outdoor lifestyle of many of its customers).[2]

Human resources include the training, experience, judgment, intelligence, relationships, and insight of *individual* managers and workers in a firm.[3] The importance of the human resources of well-known entrepreneurs such as Bill Gates (Microsoft) and Steve Jobs (formerly at Apple) is broadly understood. However, valuable human resources are not limited to just entrepreneurs or senior managers. Each employee at a firm like Southwest Airlines is essential for the overall success of the firm. Whether it is the willingness of the gate agent to joke with the harried traveler, or a baggage handler hustling to get a passenger's bag into a plane, or even a pilot's decision to fly in a way that saves fuel—all of these human resources are part of the resource base that has enabled Southwest to gain advantages in the very competitive U.S. airline industry.[4]

Whereas human resources are an attribute of single individuals, **organizational resources** are an attribute of groups of individuals. Organizational resources include a firm's formal reporting structure; its formal and informal planning, controlling, and coordinating systems; its culture and reputation; and informal relations among groups within a firm and between a firm and those in its environment. At Southwest Airlines, relationships among individual resources are an important organizational resource. For example, it is not unusual to see the pilots at Southwest helping to load the bags on an airplane to ensure that the plane leaves on time. This kind of cooperation and dedication shows up in an intense loyalty between Southwest employees and the firm—a loyalty that manifests itself in low employee turnover and high employee productivity, even though more than 80 percent of Southwest's workforce is unionized.

Critical Assumptions of the Resource-Based View

The RBV rests on two fundamental assumptions about the resources and capabilities that firms may control. First, different firms may possess different bundles of resources and capabilities, even if they are competing in the same industry. This is the assumption of firm **resource heterogeneity**. Resource heterogeneity implies that for a given business activity, some firms may be more skilled in accomplishing this activity than other firms. In manufacturing, for example, Toyota continues to be more skilled than, say, Fiat Chrysler. In product design, Apple continues to be more skilled than, say, IBM. In motorcycles, Harley Davidson's reputation for big, bad, and loud rides separates it from its competitors.

Second, some of these resource and capability differences among firms may be long lasting because it may be very costly for firms without certain resources and capabilities to develop or acquire them. This is the assumption of **resource immobility**. For example, Toyota has had its advantage in manufacturing over Fiat and Chrysler, as separate, and now merged, firms for at least 30 years. Apple has had product design advantages over IBM since Apple was founded in the 1980s. And Harley's product reputation has remained distinctive for several decades. It is not that Toyota's, Apple's, and Harley Davidson's competitors are unaware of their disadvantages. Indeed, some of these firms—notably IBM and many Japanese motorcycle firms—have made progress in addressing their disadvantages. However, despite these efforts, Toyota, Apple, and Harley Davidson continue to enjoy advantages over their competition.

Taken together, these two assumptions make it possible to explain why some firms outperform other firms, even if these firms are all competing in the same industry. If a firm possesses valuable resources and capabilities that few other firms possess and if these other firms find it too costly to imitate these resources and capabilities, the firm that possesses these tangible and intangible assets can gain a sustained competitive advantage. The economic logic that underlies the RBV is described in more detail in the Strategy in Depth feature.

Strategy in Depth

Ricardian Economics and the Resource-Based View

The theoretical roots of the resource-based view can be traced to research done by David Ricardo in 1817. Interestingly, Ricardo was not even studying the profitability of firms; he was interested in the economic consequences of owning more or less fertile farm land.

Unlike many other inputs into the production process, the total supply of land is relatively fixed and cannot be significantly increased in response to higher demand and prices. Such inputs are said to be **inelastic in supply** because their quantity of supply is fixed and does not respond to price increases. In these settings, it is possible for those who own higher-quality inputs to gain competitive advantages.

Ricardo's argument concerning land as a productive input is summarized in Figure 3.1. Imagine that there are many parcels of land suitable for growing wheat. Also, suppose that the fertility of these different parcels varies from high-fertility (low costs of production) to low-fertility (high costs of production). It seems obvious that when the market price for wheat is low, it will only pay farmers with the most fertile land to grow wheat. Only these farmers will have costs low enough to make money when the market price for wheat is low. As the market price for wheat increases, then farmers with progressively less fertile land will be able to use it to grow wheat. These observations lead to the market supply curve in panel A of Figure 3.1: As prices (P) go up, supply (S) also goes up. At some point on this supply curve, supply will equal demand (D). This point determines the market price for wheat, given supply and demand. This price is called P^* in the figure.

Now consider the situation facing two different kinds of farmers. Ricardo assumed that both these farmers follow traditional economic logic by producing a quantity (q) such that their marginal cost (MC) equals their marginal revenue (MR); that is, they produce enough wheat so that the cost of producing the last bushel of wheat equals the revenue they will get from selling that last bushel. However, this decision for the farm with less fertile land (in panel B of the

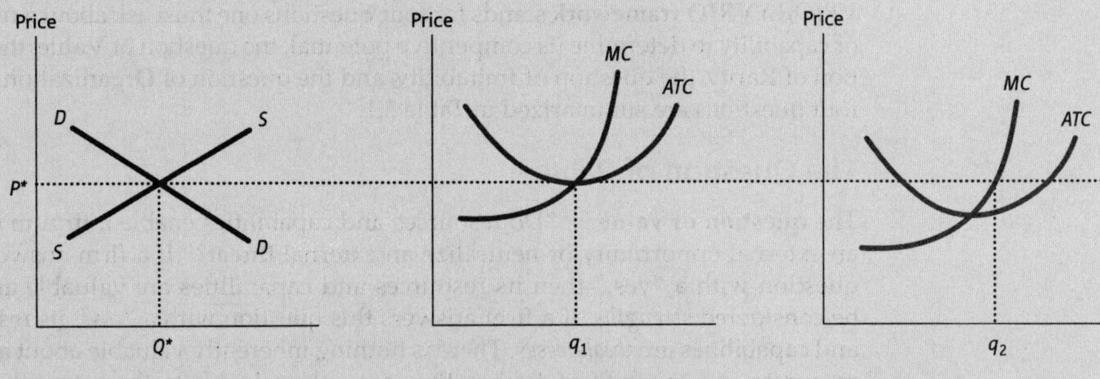

A. Market supply and demand, market quantity (Q^*) and market-determined price (P^*)

B. Performance of firm with less fertile land (higher average total cost – *ATC*)

C. Performance of firm with more fertile land (lower average total cost – *ATC*)

MC = marginal costs, *ATC* = average total costs, *Q* = aggregate quantity produced in the industry, *q* = quantity produced by each firm in the industry

Figure 3.1 The Economics of Land with Different Levels of Fertility

figure) generates revenues that exactly equal the average total cost (*ATC*) of the only capital this farmer is assumed to employ, the cost of his land. In contrast, the farmer with more fertile land (in panel C of the figure) has an average total cost (*ATC*) less than the market-determined price and thus can earn an above-normal economic profit. This is because at the market-determined price, P^*, *MC* equals *ATC* for the farmer with less fertile land, whereas *MC* is greater than *ATC* for the farmer with more fertile land.

In traditional economic analysis, the profit earned by the farmer with more fertile land should lead other farmers to enter this market, that is, to obtain some land and produce wheat. However, all the land that can be used to produce wheat in a way that generates at least a normal return given the market price P^* is already in production. In particular, no more very fertile land is available, and fertile land (by assumption) cannot be created. This is what is meant by land being inelastic in supply. Thus, the farmer with more fertile land and lower production costs has a sustained competitive advantage over those farmers with less fertile land and higher production costs. Therefore, the farmer with the more fertile land can earn an above-normal economic profit.

Of course, at least two events can threaten this sustained competitive advantage. First, market demand may shift down and to the left. This would force farmers with less fertile land to cease production and would also reduce the profit of those with more fertile land. If demand shifted far enough, this profit might disappear altogether.

Second, farmers with less fertile land may discover low-cost ways of increasing their land's fertility, thereby reducing the competitive advantage of farmers with more fertile land. For example, farmers with less fertile land may be able to use inexpensive fertilizers to increase their land's fertility. The existence of such low-cost fertilizers suggests that, although *land* may be in fixed supply, *fertility* may not be. If enough farmers can increase the fertility of their land, then the profits originally earned by the farmers with the more fertile land will disappear.

Of course, what the RBV does is recognize that land is not the only productive input that is inelastic in supply and that farmers are not the only firms that benefit from having such resources at their disposal.[5]

The VRIO Framework

Objective 3.2 Describe the VRIO framework and how it relates to the resource-based view.

Armed with the RBV, it is possible to develop a set of tools for analyzing all the different resources and capabilities a firm might possess and the potential of each of these to generate competitive advantages. In this way, it will be possible to identify a firm's internal strengths and its internal weaknesses. The primary tool for accomplishing this internal analysis is called the VRIO framework.[6] The acronym, *VRIO*, in **VRIO framework** stands for four questions one must ask about a resource or capability to determine its competitive potential: the question of **V**alue, the question of **R**arity, the question of **I**mitability, and the question of **O**rganization. These four questions are summarized in Table 3.1.

The Question of Value

The **question of value** is: "Do resources and capabilities enable a firm to exploit an external opportunity or neutralize an external threat?" If a firm answers this question with a "yes," then its resources and capabilities are valuable and can be considered *strengths*. If a firm answers this question with a "no," its resources and capabilities are *weaknesses*. There is nothing inherently valuable about a firm's resources and capabilities. Rather, they are only valuable to the extent that they enable a firm to enhance its competitive position. Sometimes, the same resources and capabilities can be strengths in one market and weaknesses in another.

Valuable Resources and Firm Performance

Sometimes it is difficult to know for sure whether a firm's resources and capabilities really enable it to exploit its external opportunities or neutralize its external threats. Sometimes, this requires detailed operational information that may not be readily available. Other times, the full impact of a firm's resources and capabilities on its external opportunities and threats may not be known for some time.

One way to track the impact of a firm's resources and capabilities on its opportunities and threats is to examine the impact of using these resources and capabilities on a firm's revenues and costs. In general, firms that use their resources and capabilities to exploit opportunities or neutralize threats will see an increase in their net revenues, or a decrease in their net costs, or both, compared to the situation in which they were not using these resources and capabilities to exploit opportunities or neutralize threats. That is, the value of these resources and capabilities will generally manifest itself in either higher revenues or lower costs or both, once a firm starts using them to exploit opportunities or neutralize threats.

Applying the Question of Value

For many firms, the answer to the question of value has been "yes." That is, many firms have resources and capabilities that are used to exploit opportunities and neutralize threats, and the use of these resources and capabilities enables these firms to increase their net revenues or decrease their net costs. For example, historically, Sony had a great deal of experience in designing, manufacturing, and selling miniaturized electronic technology. Sony used these resources and capabilities to exploit opportunities, including video games, digital cameras, computers and peripherals, handheld computers, home video and audio, portable audio,

TABLE 3.1 Questions Needed to Conduct a Resource-Based Analysis of a Firm's Internal Strengths and Weaknesses

1. **The Question of Value.** Does a resource enable a firm to exploit an environmental opportunity and/or neutralize an environmental threat?
2. **The Question of Rarity.** Is a resource currently controlled by only a small number of competing firms?
3. **The Question of Imitability.** Do firms without a resource face a cost disadvantage in obtaining or developing it?
4. **The Question of Organization.** Are a firm's other policies and procedures organized to support the exploitation of its valuable, rare, and costly-to-imitate resources?

and car audio. 3M has used its resources and capabilities in substrates, coatings, and adhesives, along with an organizational culture that rewards risk-taking and creativity, to exploit opportunities in office products, including invisible tape and Post-It notes. Sony's and 3M's resources and capabilities—including their specific technological skills and their creative organizational cultures—have made it possible for these firms to respond to, and even create, new opportunities.[7]

Unfortunately, for other firms the answer to the question of value appears to be "no." For example, in 2008 Arby's bought Wendy's for $2.34 billion. Efforts to improve each other's fast food operations failed, and Wendy's sold Arby's in 2011. Also, in 2008, Bank of America purchased Countrywide—a mortgage company—for $2.5 billion. Caught up in the financial collapse of 2008, Countrywide ultimately cost Bank of America $40 billion. In 2005, eBay purchased Skype for $2.6 billion; in 2009, eBay sold Skype for $1.9 billion—an impressive destruction of $700 million in value in four years. And in 2000, AOL bought Time Warner for $160 billion—an effort to create a new kind of media company. Time Warner wrote off $90 billion of the AOL acquisition in 2002 and completely separated itself from AOL in 2009. In all these cases, firms looking to enhance and exploit the value of their resources and capabilities apparently failed.[8]

Using Value Chain Analysis to Identify Potentially Valuable Resources and Capabilities

One way to identify potentially valuable resources and capabilities controlled by a firm is to study that firm's value chain. A firm's **value chain** is the set of business activities in which it engages to develop, produce, and market its products or services. Each step in a firm's value chain requires the application and integration of different resources and capabilities. Because different firms may make different choices about which value chain activities they will engage in, they can end up developing different sets of resources and capabilities. This can be the case even if these firms are all operating in the same industry. These choices can have implications for a firm's strategies, and, as described in the Ethics and Strategy feature, they can also have implications for society more generally.

Ethics and Strategy

Strategic management adopts the perspective of a firm's owners in discussing how to gain and sustain competitive advantages. Even when adopting a stakeholder perspective (see the Ethics and Strategy feature in Chapter 1), how a firm can improve its performance and increase the wealth of its owners still takes center stage.

However, an exclusive focus on the performance of a firm and the wealth of its owners can sometimes have broader effects—on society and on the environment—that are not fully recognized. Economists call these broader effects "externalities" because they are external to the core issue in economics and strategic management of how firms can maximize their performance. They are external to this issue because firms generally do not bear the full costs of the externalities their profit-maximizing behavior creates.

Externalities and the Broader Consequences of Profit Maximization

Externalities can take many forms. The most obvious of these has to do with pollution and the environment. If, for example, in the process of maximizing its performance a firm engages in activities that pollute the environment, the impact of that

(Continued)

pollution is an externality. Such pollution reduces our quality of life and hurts the environment, but the firm creating this pollution often does not bear the full costs of doing so.

Other externalities have to do with a firm's impact on the public's health. For example, when tobacco companies maximize their profits by selling tobacco to children, they are also creating a public health externality. Getting children hooked on tobacco early on might be good for the bottom line of a tobacco company, but it increases the chances of these children developing lung cancer, emphysema, heart disease, and the other ailments associated with tobacco. Obviously, these individuals absorb most of the adverse consequences of these diseases, but society suffers as well from the high health care costs that are engendered.

Put differently, while adopting a simple profit-maximizing perspective in choosing and implementing strategies can have positive impacts for a firm, its owners, and its stakeholders, it can also have negative consequences for society as a whole. Two broad solutions to this problem of externalities have been proposed. First, governments can take on the responsibility of directly monitoring and regulating the behavior of firms in areas where these kinds of externalities are likely to develop. Second, governments can use lawsuits and regulations to ensure that firms directly bear more of the costs of any externalities their behavior might generate. Once these externalities are "internalized," it is then a matter of self-interest for firms not to engage in activities that generate negative externalities.

Consider, for example, the oil industry. Figure 3.2 provides a simplified list of all the business activities that must be completed if crude oil is to be turned into consumer products, such as gasoline. These activities include exploring for crude oil, drilling for crude oil, pumping crude oil, shipping crude oil, buying crude oil, refining crude oil, selling refined products to distributors, shipping refined products, and selling refined products to final customers.

Different firms may make different choices about which of these stages in the oil industry they want to operate. Thus, the firms in the oil industry may have very different resources and capabilities. For example, exploring for crude oil is very expensive and requires substantial financial resources. It also requires access to land (a physical resource), the application of substantial scientific and technical knowledge (individual resources), and an organizational commitment to risk-taking and exploration (organizational resources). Firms that operate in this stage

Figure 3.2 A Simplified Value Chain of Activities of Oil-Based Refined Products such as Gasoline and Motor Oil

Exploring for crude oil
↓
Drilling for crude oil
↓
Pumping crude oil
↓
Shipping crude oil
↓
Buying crude oil
↓
Refining crude oil
↓
Selling refined products to distributors
↓
Shipping refined products
↓
Selling refined products to final customers

of the oil business are likely to have very different resources and capabilities than those that, for example, sell refined oil products to final customers. To be successful in the retail stage of this industry, a firm needs retail outlets (such as stores and gas stations), which are costly to build and require both financial and physical resources. These outlets, in turn, need to be staffed by salespeople—individual resources—and marketing these products to customers through advertisements and other means can require a commitment to creativity—an organizational resource.

However, even firms that operate in the same set of value chain activities in an industry may approach these activities very differently and therefore may develop very different resources and capabilities associated with these activities. For example, two firms may sell refined oil products to final customers. However, one of these firms may sell only through retail outlets it owns, whereas the second may sell only through retail outlets it does not own. The first firm's financial and physical resources are likely to be very different from the second firm's, although these two firms may have similar individual and organizational resources.

Consumers can sometimes also help internalize the externalities generated by a firm's behavior by adjusting their consumption patterns to buy products or services only from companies that do not generate negative externalities. Consumers can even be more proactive and let firms know which of their strategies are particularly troubling. For example, many consumers united to boycott firms with operations in South Africa when South Africa was still implementing a policy of apartheid. Ultimately, this pressure not only changed the strategies of many firms; it also helped change South Africa's domestic policies. More recently, consumer pressures on pharmaceutical companies forced these firms to make their AIDS drugs more accessible in less developed countries in Africa; similar pressures forced Nike to adjust the wages and working conditions of the individuals who manufacture Nike's shoes. To the extent that sufficient demand for "socially responsible firms" exists in the marketplace, it may make profit-maximizing sense for a firm to engage in socially responsible behavior by reducing the extent to which its actions generate negative externalities.[9]

Studying a firm's value chain forces us to think about firm resources and capabilities in a disaggregated way. Although it is possible to characterize a firm's resources and capabilities more broadly, it is usually more helpful to think about how each of the activities a firm engages in affects its financial, physical, individual, and organizational resources. With this understanding, it is possible to begin to recognize potential sources of competitive advantage for a firm in a much more detailed way.

Because this type of analysis can be so helpful in identifying the financial, physical, individual, and organizational resources and capabilities controlled by a firm, several generic value chains for identifying them have been developed. One of these, proposed by the management-consulting firm McKinsey and Company, is presented in Figure 3.3.[10] This relatively simple model suggests that the creation of value almost always involves six distinct activities: technology development, product design, manufacturing, marketing, distribution, and service. Firms can develop distinctive capabilities in any one or any combination of these activities.

The Question of Rarity

Understanding the value of a firm's resources and capabilities is an important first consideration in understanding a firm's internal strengths and weaknesses. However, if a particular resource or capability is controlled by numerous competing firms, then that resource is unlikely to be a source of competitive advantage for any

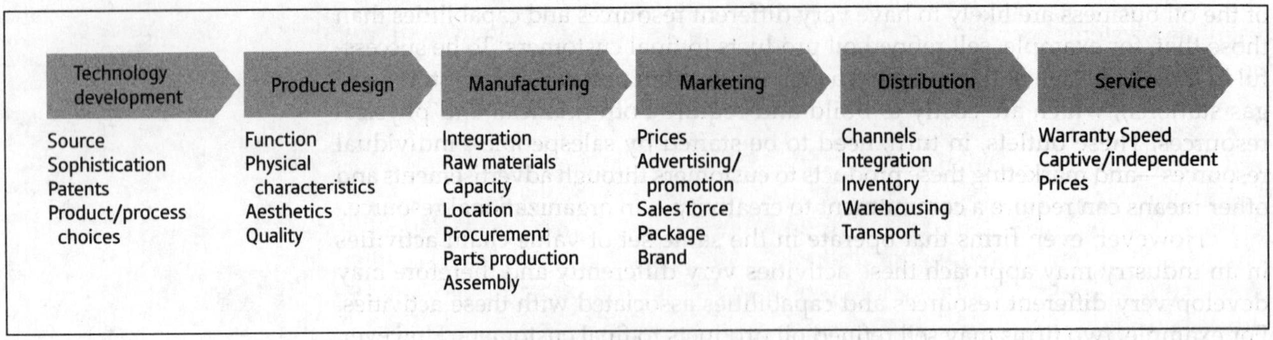

Figure 3.3 The Generic Value Chain Developed by McKinsey and Company

one of them. Instead, valuable but common (i.e., not rare) resources and capabilities are sources of competitive parity. Only when a resource is not controlled by numerous other firms is it likely to be a source of competitive advantage. These observations lead to the **question of rarity**: "How many competing firms already possess particular valuable resources and capabilities?"

Consider, for example, competition among television sports channels. All the major networks and many local channels broadcast sports, but these sports programs are generally part of a diversified program offering that includes game shows, day time dramas, news programs, situation comedies, police and medical dramas, and so forth. Until 1998, there were no all-sports channels on broadcast television or on cable. Enter ESPN—the entertainment and sports network. First conceived of as a channel for broadcasting sports events originating from Connecticut, ESPN grew to cover a broad range of sports and to include some of the most important sporting events in the world—including NFL and college football playoff games. From 1998 to the late 2000s, ESPN (and all its affiliated channels) was the only television outlet committed completely to sports. This unique commitment led ESPN to develop a very strong brand name and to become a very valuable television property. Ultimately, it was purchased by Disney (who also owned ABC). During this period, ESPN's brand and unique commitment to televised sports was valuable and rare, and thus a source of at least a temporary competitive advantage.[11]

However, things have begun to change. First, several sports specialty channels—channels that show one sport only—have begun to arrive on cable and satellite. These include MLB Network (for professional baseball), the NFL Network (for professional football), the Golf Channel, and the Tennis Chanel. Even more importantly, other broadcasters—including NBC, CBS, and Fox—have begun their own 24 hour sports channels—complete with their own nightly review of sports news that directly compete with ESPN's venerable SportsCenter. While ESPN still has the best-known brand in televised sport—a brand leveraged by ABC in its sports broadcasts with the tag line "ESPN on ABC,"—and most of the premiere events, some observers are beginning to wonder how rare ESPN's commitment to sports still is.[12]

Of course, not all of a firm's resources and capabilities have to be valuable and rare. Indeed, most firms have a resource base that is composed primarily of valuable but common resources and capabilities. These resources cannot be sources of even temporary competitive advantage, but are essential if a firm is to gain competitive parity. Under conditions of competitive parity, although no one firm gains a competitive advantage, firms do increase their probability of survival.

Consider, for example, a telephone system as a resource or capability. Because telephone systems are widely available and because virtually all organizations have access to telephone systems, these systems are not rare and thus are not a source of competitive advantage. However, firms that do not possess a telephone system are likely to give their competitors an important advantage and place themselves at a competitive disadvantage.

How rare a valuable resource or capability must be to have the potential for generating a competitive advantage varies from situation to situation. It is not difficult to see that, if a firm's valuable resources and capabilities are absolutely unique among a set of current and potential competitors, they can generate a competitive advantage. However, it may be possible for a small number of firms in an industry to possess a particular valuable resource or capability and still obtain a competitive advantage. In general, as long as the number of firms that possess a particular valuable resource or capability is less than the number of firms needed to generate perfect competition dynamics in an industry, that resource or capability can be considered rare and a potential source of competitive advantage.

The Question of Imitability

Firms with valuable and rare resources are often strategic innovators because they can conceive and engage in strategies that other firms cannot because they lack the relevant resources and capabilities. These firms may gain the first-mover advantages discussed in Chapter 2.

Valuable and rare organizational resources, however, can be sources of sustained competitive advantage only if firms that do not possess them face a cost disadvantage in obtaining or developing them, compared to firms that already possess them. These kinds of resources are **imperfectly imitable.**[13] These observations lead to the **question of imitability**: "Do firms without a resource or capability face a cost disadvantage in obtaining or developing it compared to firms that already possess it?"

Imagine an industry with five essentially identical firms. Each of these firms manufactures the same products, uses the same raw materials, and sells the products to the same customers through the same distribution channels. It is not hard to see that firms in this kind of industry will have normal economic performance. Now, suppose that one of these firms, for whatever reason, discovers or develops a heretofore unrecognized valuable resource and uses that resource either to exploit an external opportunity or to neutralize an external threat. Obviously, this firm will gain a competitive advantage over the others.

This firm's competitors can respond to this competitive advantage in at least two ways. First, they can ignore the success of this one firm and continue as before. This action, of course, will put them at a competitive disadvantage. Second, these firms can attempt to understand why this one firm can be successful and then duplicate its resources to implement a similar strategy. If competitors have no cost disadvantages in acquiring or developing the needed resources, then this imitative approach will generate competitive parity in the industry.

Sometimes, however, for reasons that will be discussed later, competing firms may face an important cost disadvantage in duplicating a successful firm's valuable resources. If this is the case, this one innovative firm may gain a sustained competitive advantage—an advantage that is not competed away through strategic imitation. Firms that possess and exploit costly-to-imitate, rare, and valuable resources in choosing and implementing their strategies may enjoy a period of sustained competitive advantage.[14]

For example, as noted earlier, other sports networks have observed the success of ESPN and are beginning to develop their own sports networks. Many of the resources and capabilities that have made ESPN successful are imitable—including its access to satellites for broadcasting—and thus are not a source of sustained competitive advantage. ESPN's brand, on the other hand, may be costlier for these firms to imitate, and thus may be a source of sustained competitive advantage.

Forms of Imitation: Direct Duplication and Substitution

In general, imitation occurs in one of two ways: **direct duplication** or **substitution**. Imitating firms can attempt to directly duplicate the resources possessed by the firm with a competitive advantage. Thus, NBC creating its own 24-hour sports channel can be thought of as an effort to directly duplicate ESPN's resources and capabilities. If the cost of this direct duplication is too high, then a firm with these resources and capabilities may obtain a sustained competitive advantage. If this cost is not too high, then any competitive advantages in this setting will be temporary.

Imitating firms can also attempt to substitute other resources for a costly-to-imitate resource possessed by a firm with a competitive advantage. Specialty sports channels—the MLB Network, the NFL Network, the Golf Channel, and the Tennis Channel—are potential substitutes for ESPN diversified sports offering. In this sense, these specialty channel's commitment to deep coverage of a single sport is a potential substitute for ESPN's broad commitment to many different sports. If substitute resources exist and if imitating firms do not face a cost disadvantage in obtaining them, then the competitive advantage of other firms will be temporary. However, if these resources have no substitutes or if the cost of acquiring these substitutes is greater than the cost of obtaining the original resources, then competitive advantages can be sustained.

Why Might It Be Costly to Imitate Another Firm's Resources or Capabilities?

A number of authors have studied why it might be costly for one firm to imitate the resources and capabilities of another. Four sources of costly imitation have been noted.[15] They are summarized in Table 3.2 and discussed in the following text.

Unique Historical Conditions It may be the case that a firm could acquire or develop its resources and capabilities in a low-cost manner because of its unique historical conditions. The ability of firms to acquire, develop, and use resources often depends on their place in time and space. Once time and history pass, firms that do not have space-and-time-dependent resources face a significant cost disadvantage in obtaining and developing them because doing so would require them to re-create history.[16]

ESPN's early commitment to 24-hour sports programing is an example of these unique historical conditions. Before ESPN, no one thought that there would be demand for 24-hour sports. For many years, ESPN was alone in this market. This enabled ESPN to develop the capabilities and routines needed to present 24-hour sports in a way that was appealing to consumers. This, in turn, helped ESPN create a brand that others may find costly to imitate.

Unique historical circumstances can give a firm a sustained competitive advantage in at least two ways. First, it may be that a particular firm was the first in an industry to recognize and exploit an opportunity, and being first gave the firm one or more of the first-mover advantages discussed in Chapter 2. Thus, although in principle other firms in an industry could have exploited an opportunity, that only one firm did so makes it costlier for other firms to imitate the original firm.

TABLE 3.2 Sources of Costly Imitation

Unique Historical Conditions When a firm gains low-cost access to resources because of its place in time and space, other firms may find these resources to be costly to imitate. Both first-mover advantages and path dependence can create unique historical conditions.

Causal Ambiguity When competitors cannot tell, for sure, what enables a firm to gain an advantage, that advantage may be costly to imitate. Sources of causal ambiguity include when competitive advantages are based on "taken-for-granted" resources and capabilities, when multiple non-testable hypotheses exist about why a firm has a competitive advantage, and when a firm's advantages are based on complex sets of interrelated capabilities.

Social Complexity When the resources and capabilities a firm uses to gain a competitive advantage involve interpersonal relationships, trust, culture, and other social resources that are costly to imitate in the short term.

Patents Only a source of sustained competitive advantage in a few industries, including pharmaceuticals and specialty chemicals.

A second way that history can have an impact on a firm builds on the concept of **path dependence.**[17] A process is said to be path dependent when events early in the evolution of a process have significant effects on subsequent events. In the evolution of competitive advantage, path dependence suggests that a firm may gain a competitive advantage in the current period based on the acquisition and development of resources in earlier periods. In these earlier periods, it is often not clear what the full future value of particular resources will be. Because of this uncertainty, firms can acquire or develop these resources for less than what will turn out to be their full value. However, once the full value of these resources is revealed, other firms seeking to acquire or develop these resources will need to pay their full known value, which (in general) will be greater than the costs incurred by the firm that acquired or developed these resources in some earlier period. The cost of acquiring both duplicate and substitute resources would rise once their full value became known.

Consider, for example, a firm that purchased land for ranching some time ago and discovered a rich supply of oil on this land in the current period. The difference between the value of this land as a supplier of oil (high) and the value of this land for ranching (low) is a source of competitive advantage for this firm. Moreover, other firms attempting to acquire this or adjacent land will now have to pay for the full value of the land in its use as a supply of oil (high) and thus will be at a cost disadvantage compared to the firm that acquired it some time ago for ranching.

Causal Ambiguity A second reason why a firm's resources and capabilities may be costly to imitate is that imitating firms may not understand the relationship between the resources and capabilities controlled by a firm and that firm's competitive advantage. In other words, the relationship between firm resources and capabilities and competitive advantage may be **causally ambiguous**.

At first, it seems unlikely that causal ambiguity about the sources of competitive advantage for a firm would ever exist. Managers in a firm seem likely to understand the sources of their own competitive advantage. If managers in one firm understand the relationship between resources and competitive advantage, then it seems likely that managers in other firms would also be able to discover these relationships and thus would have a clear understanding of which resources and capabilities they should duplicate or seek substitutes for. If there are no other sources of cost disadvantage for imitating firms, imitation should lead to competitive parity and normal economic performance.[18]

However, it is not always the case that managers in a particular firm will fully understand the relationship between the resources and capabilities they control and competitive advantage. This lack of understanding could occur for at least three reasons. First, it may be that the resources and capabilities that generate competitive advantage are so taken for granted, so much a part of the day-to-day experience of managers in a firm, that these managers are unaware of them.[19] Organizational resources and capabilities such as teamwork among top managers, organizational culture, relationships among other employees, and relationships with customers and suppliers may be almost "invisible" to managers in a firm.[20] If managers in firms that have such capabilities do not understand their relationship to competitive advantage, managers in other firms face significant challenges in understanding which resources they should imitate.

Second, managers may have multiple hypotheses about which resources and capabilities enable their firm to gain a competitive advantage, but they may be unable to evaluate which of these resources and capabilities, alone or in combination, actually create the competitive advantage. For example, if one asks successful entrepreneurs what enabled them to be successful, they are likely to reply with several hypotheses, such as, "hard work, willingness to take risks, and a high-quality top management team." However, if one asks what happened to unsuccessful entrepreneurs, they, too, are likely to suggest that their firms were characterized by, "hard work, willingness to take risks, and a high-quality top management team." It may be the case that, "hard work, willingness to take risks, and a high-quality top management team" are important resources and capabilities for entrepreneurial firm success, but other factors may also play a role. Without rigorous experiments, it is difficult to establish which of these resources have a causal relationship with competitive advantage and which do not.

Finally, it may be that not just a few resources and capabilities enable a firm to gain a competitive advantage, but that literally thousands of these organizational attributes, bundled together, generate these advantages. When the resources and capabilities that generate competitive advantage are complex networks of relationships between individuals, groups, and technology, imitation can be costly.

Whenever the sources of competitive advantage are widely diffused across people, locations, and processes in a firm, those sources will be costly to imitate. Perhaps the best example of such a resource is knowledge itself. To the extent that valuable knowledge about a firm's products, processes, customers, and so on is widely diffused throughout an organization, competitors will have difficulty imitating that knowledge, and it can be a source of sustained competitive advantage.[21]

Social Complexity A third reason that a firm's resources and capabilities may be costly to imitate is that they may be socially complex phenomena, beyond the ability of firms to systematically manage and influence. When competitive advantages are based on such complex social phenomena, the ability of other firms to imitate these resources and capabilities, either through direct duplication or substitution, is significantly constrained. Efforts to influence these kinds of phenomena are likely to be much more costly than they would be if these phenomena developed in a natural way over time in a firm.[22]

A wide variety of firm resources and capabilities may be **socially complex**. Examples include the interpersonal relations among managers in a firm, a firm's culture, and a firm's reputation among suppliers and customers.[23] Notice that in most of these cases it is possible to specify how these socially complex resources add value to a firm. Thus, there is little or no causal ambiguity surrounding the link between these firm resources and capabilities and competitive advantage. However, understanding that an organizational culture with certain attributes or quality relations among managers can improve a firm's efficiency and effectiveness does not necessarily imply that firms lacking these attributes can engage in systematic efforts to create them or that low-cost substitutes for them exist. For the time being, such social engineering may be beyond the abilities of most firms. At the very least, such social engineering is likely to be much more costly than it would be if socially complex resources evolved naturally within a firm.[24]

It is interesting to note that firms seeking to imitate complex physical technology often do not face the cost disadvantages of imitating complex social phenomena. A great deal of physical technology (machine tools, robots, and so forth) can be purchased in supply markets. Even when a firm develops its own unique physical technology, reverse engineering tends to diffuse this technology among competing firms in a low-cost manner. Indeed, the costs of imitating a successful physical technology are often lower than the costs of developing a new technology.[25]

Although physical technology is usually not costly to imitate, the application of this technology in a firm is likely to call for a wide variety of socially complex organizational resources and capabilities. These organizational resources may be costly to imitate, and if they are valuable and rare, the combination of physical and socially complex resources may be a source of sustained competitive advantage. The importance of socially complex resources and capabilities for firm performance has been studied in detail in the field of strategic human resource management, as described in the Research Made Relevant feature.

Patents At first glance, it might appear that a firm's patents would make it very costly for competitors to imitate its products.[26] Patents do have this effect in some industries. For example, patents in the pharmaceutical and specialty chemical industry effectively foreclose other firms from marketing the same products until a firm's patents expire. As suggested in Chapter 2, patents can raise the cost of imitation in a variety of other industries as well.

However, from another point of view a firm's patents may decrease, rather than increase, the costs of imitation. When a firm files for patent protection, it is forced to reveal a significant amount of information about its product. Governments require this information to ensure that the technology in question is patentable. By obtaining a patent, a firm may provide important information to competitors about how to imitate its technology.

Moreover, most technological developments in an industry are diffused throughout firms in that industry in a relatively brief period, even if the technology in question is patented, because patented technology is not immune from low-cost imitation. Patents may restrict direct duplication for a time, but they may actually increase the chances of substitution by functionally equivalent technologies.[27]

The Question of Organization

A firm's potential for competitive advantage depends on the value, rarity, and imitability of its resources and capabilities. However, to fully realize this potential, a firm must be organized to exploit its resources and capabilities. These observations lead to the **question of organization**: "Is a firm organized to exploit the full competitive potential of its resources and capabilities?"

Numerous components of a firm's organization are relevant to the question of organization, including its formal reporting structure, its formal and informal management control systems, and its compensation policies. A firm's **formal reporting structure** is a description of whom in the organization reports to whom; it is often embodied in a firm's **organizational chart**. **Management control systems** include a range of formal and informal mechanisms to ensure that managers are behaving in ways consistent with a firm's strategies. **Formal management controls** include a firm's budgeting and reporting activities that keep people higher up in a firm's organizational chart informed about the actions taken by people lower down in a firm's organizational chart. **Informal management controls** might include a firm's culture and the willingness of employees to monitor each other's behavior. **Compensation policies** are the ways that firms pay employees. Such policies create incentives for employees to behave in certain ways.

Research Made Relevant

Most empirical tests of the RBV have focused on the extent to which history, causal ambiguity, and social complexity have an impact on the ability of firms to gain and sustain competitive advantages. Among the most important of these tests has been research that examines the extent to which human resource practices that are likely to generate socially complex resources and capabilities are related to firm performance. This area of research is known as *strategic human resources management*.

The first of these tests was conducted as part of a larger study of efficient low-cost manufacturing in the worldwide automobile industry. A group of researchers from Massachusetts Institute of Technology developed rigorous measures of the cost and quality of more than 70 manufacturing plants that assembled mid-size sedans around the world. They discovered that at the time of their study only six of these plants had simultaneous low costs and high-quality manufacturing—a position that obviously would give these plants a competitive advantage in the marketplace.

Strategic Human Resource Management Research

In trying to understand what distinguished these six plants from the others in the sample, the researchers found that, not surprisingly, these six plants had the most modern and up-to-date manufacturing technology. However, so did many of the less effective plants. What distinguished these effective plants was not their manufacturing technology, per se, but their human resource (HR) practices. These six plants all implemented a bundle of such practices that included participative decision making, quality circles, and an emphasis on team production. One of the results of these efforts—and another distinguishing feature of these six plants—was a high level of employee loyalty and commitment to a plant, as well as the belief that plant managers would treat employees fairly. These socially complex resources and capabilities are the types of resources that the RBV suggests should be sources of sustained competitive advantage.

Later work has followed up on this approach and has examined the impact of HR practices on firm performance outside the manufacturing arena. Using a variety of measures of firm performance and several different measures of HR practices, the results of this research continue to be very consistent with RBV logic. That is, firms that can use HR practices to develop socially complex human and organizational resources are able to gain competitive advantages over firms that do not engage in such practices.[28]

These components of a firm's organization are often called **complementary resources and capabilities** because they have limited ability to generate competitive advantage in isolation. However, in combination with other resources and capabilities they can enable a firm to realize its full potential for competitive advantage.[29]

For example, it has already been suggested that ESPN may have enjoyed a competitive advantage in sports programming for many years. However, if ESPN's management had not taken advantage of these opportunities by expanding its sports coverage, ensuring that the best sporting events are on ESPN, and adding new and exciting competitions (e.g., the ESPN X-Games that broadcast "extreme sports"), then its potential for competitive advantage would not have been fully realized. Of course, the reason that ESPN has done all these things is because it has an appropriate organizational structure, management controls, and employee compensation policies. By themselves, these attributes of ESPN's organization could not be a source of competitive advantage; however, they were essential for ESPN to realize its full competitive advantage potential.

Having an appropriate organization in place has enabled ESPN to realize the full competitive advantage potential of its other resources and capabilities. Having an inappropriate organization in place prevented Sony from exploiting its valuable, rare, and costly-to-imitate resources and capabilities.

Earlier in this chapter, it was suggested that Sony had unusual experience in designing and building a wide variety of consumer electronics products. In the process of building this giant consumer electronics company, managers at Sony developed and acquired two substantial businesses: Sony Consumer Electronics and Sony Records.

Among the many products developed by the Consumer Electronics business was an early MP3 player (i.e., a portable device that played music and other digital media from a hard drive). The key to MP3 technology was compression—taking analog signals and storing them in a way that they did not take up disproportionate space on the hard drive. Without compression, you could only store a few songs on an MP3 player; with compression, you can store thousands. Sony was a leader in compression technology.

Of course, to be effective, MP3 players must have content to play. Here, the Sony Records Division should have been very helpful to the Consumer Electronics Division: Records had recording contracts with many famous artists, and Consumer Products had the MP3 player (along with compression technology) to play that music.

So, why does Apple—with iPods, iTunes, iPhones, and iPads—dominate the portable music listening market? Apple had no advantages. It was late to the MP3 market (although it did introduce an MP3 player with a particularly elegant interface), it did not own any content, and it had a limited online presence.

One explanation of Apple's success is Sony's failure—despite having the potential to dominate this market, despite its history of dominating similar markets in the past (e.g., the Sony Walkman portable tape player), Sony could not find a way for its two divisions—Consumer Electronics and Music—to cooperate. Put differently, Sony's failure was a failure in organization. The engineers in the Consumer Electronics business could never find a way to work with the artists in the music business.

Of course, Apple had to do a great deal more to take advantage of the opportunity that Sony's organization failure had created for them. Nevertheless, despite its potential, Sony failed to gain or sustain any significant competitive advantages in this lucrative MP3 market.[30]

Objective 3.3 Be able to apply the VRIO framework to identify the competitive implications of a firm's resources and capabilities.

Applying the VRIO Framework

The questions of value, rarity, imitability, and organization can be brought together into a single framework to understand the return potential associated with exploiting any of a firm's resources or capabilities. This is done in Table 3.3. The relationship of the VRIO framework to strengths and weaknesses is presented in Table 3.4.

If a resource or capability controlled by a firm is not valuable, it will not enable a firm to choose or implement strategies that exploit environmental opportunities or neutralize environmental threats. Organizing to exploit this resource will increase a firm's costs or decrease its revenues. These types of resources are weaknesses. Firms must fix these weaknesses or avoid using them when choosing and implementing strategies. If firms do exploit these kinds of resources and capabilities, they can expect to put themselves at a competitive disadvantage compared to those that either do not possess these nonvaluable resources or do not use them in conceiving and implementing strategies.

If a resource or capability is valuable but not rare, exploitation of this resource in conceiving and implementing strategies will generate competitive parity. Exploiting these types of resources will generally not create competitive advantages, but failure to exploit them can put a firm at a competitive disadvantage. In this sense, valuable-but-not-rare resources can be thought of as organizational strengths.

If a resource or capability is valuable and rare but not costly to imitate, exploiting this resource will generate a temporary competitive advantage for a firm. A firm that exploits this kind of resource is, in an important sense, gaining a first-mover advantage because it is the first firm that can exploit a particular resource. However, once competing firms observe this competitive advantage, they will be able to acquire or develop the resources needed to implement this strategy through direct duplication or substitution at no cost disadvantage, compared to the first-moving firm. Over time, any competitive advantage that the first mover obtained would be competed away as other firms imitate the resources needed to compete. Consequently, this type of resource or capability can be thought of as an organizational strength and as a **distinctive competence**.

If a resource or capability is valuable, rare, and costly to imitate, exploiting it will generate a sustained competitive advantage. In this case, competing firms face a significant cost disadvantage in imitating a successful firm's resources and capabilities. As suggested earlier, this competitive advantage may reflect the unique history of the successful firm, causal ambiguity about which resources to imitate, the socially complex nature of these resources and capabilities, or any patent

TABLE 3.3 The VRIO Framework

Is a resource or capability

Valuable?	Rare?	Costly to imitate?	Exploited by organization?	Competitive implications
No	—	—	No	Competitive disadvantage
Yes	No	—	↑	Competitive parity
Yes	Yes	No	↓	Temporary competitive advantage
Yes	Yes	Yes	Yes	Sustained competitive advantage

TABLE 3.4 The Relationship Between the VRIO Framework and Organizational Strengths and Weaknesses

Is a resource or capability				
Valuable?	**Rare?**	**Costly to imitate?**	**Exploited by organization?**	**Strength or weakness**
No	—	—	No	Weakness
Yes	No	—	↑	Strength
Yes	Yes	No	↓	Strength and distinctive competence
Yes	Yes	Yes	Yes	Strength and sustainable distinctive competence

advantages a firm might possess. In any case, attempts to compete away the advantages of firms that exploit these resources will not generate competitive advantage, or even competitive parity, for imitating firms. Even if these firms can acquire or develop the resources or capabilities in question, the very high costs of doing so would put them at a competitive disadvantage. These kinds of resources and capabilities are organizational strengths and **sustainable distinctive competencies**.

The question of organization operates as an adjustment factor in the VRIO framework. For example, if a firm has a valuable, rare, and costly-to-imitate resource and capability but fails to organize itself to take full advantage of this resource, some of its potential competitive advantage could be lost (this is the Sony example). Extremely poor organization, in this case, could actually lead a firm that has the potential for competitive advantage to gain only competitive parity or competitive disadvantages.

Applying the VRIO Framework to Southwest Airlines

To examine how the VRIO framework can be applied in analyzing real strategic situations, consider the competitive position of Southwest Airlines. Southwest Airlines has been the only consistently profitable airline in the United States over the past 30 years. While many U.S. airlines have gone in and out of bankruptcy, Southwest has remained profitable. How could it gain this competitive advantage?

Potential sources of this competitive advantage fall into two big categories: operational choices Southwest has made and Southwest's approach to managing its people. On the operational side, Southwest has chosen to fly only a single type of aircraft (Boeing 737), only flies into smaller airports, has avoided complicated hub-and-spoke route systems, and, instead, flies a point-to-point system. On the people-management side, despite being highly unionized, Southwest has been able to develop a sense of commitment and loyalty among its employees. It is not unusual to see Southwest employees go well beyond their narrowly defined job responsibilities, helping out in whatever way is necessary to get a plane off the ground safely and on time. Which of these—operational choices or Southwest's approach to managing its people—is more likely to be a source of sustained competitive advantage?

Southwest's Operational Choices and Competitive Advantage

Consider first Southwest's operational choices. First, do these operational choices reduce Southwest's costs or increase the willingness of its customers to pay—that is, are these operational choices valuable? It can be shown that most of Southwest's operational choices have the effect of reducing its costs. For example, by flying only one type of airliner, Southwest can reduce the cost of training its maintenance staff, reduce its spare parts inventory, and reduce the time its planes are being repaired. By flying into smaller airports, Southwest reduces the fees it would otherwise have to pay to land at larger airports. Its point-to-point system of routes avoids the costs associated with establishing large hub-and-spoke systems. Overall, these operational choices are valuable.

Second, are these operational choices rare? For most of its history, Southwest's operational choices have been rare. Only recently have large incumbent airlines and smaller new entrants begun to implement similar operational choices.

Third, are these operational choices costly to imitate? Several incumbent airline firms have set up subsidiaries designed to emulate most of Southwest's operational choices. For example, Continental created the Continental Lite division, United created the Ted division, and Delta created the Song division. All of these divisions chose a single type of airplane to fly, flew into smaller airports, adopted a point-to-point route structure, and so forth.

In addition to these incumbent airlines, many new entrants into the airline industry—both in the United States and elsewhere—have adopted similar operational choices as Southwest. In the United States, these new entrants include AirTran Airlines (recently purchased by Southwest), Allegiant Airlines, JetBlue, Skybus Airlines (now bankrupt), Spirit Airlines, and Virgin American Airlines.

Thus, while Southwest's operational choices are valuable and have been rare, they are apparently not costly to imitate. This is not surprising because these operational choices have few of the attributes of resources or capabilities that are costly to imitate. They do not derive from a firm's unique history, they are not path dependent, they are not causally ambiguous, and they are not socially complex.

Finally, is Southwest organized to fully exploit its operational choices? Most observers agree that Southwest's structure, management controls, and compensation policies are consistent with its operational choices.

Taken together, this analysis of Southwest's operational choices suggests that they are valuable, have been rare, but are not costly to imitate. While Southwest is organized to exploit these opportunities, they are likely to be only a source of temporary competitive advantage for Southwest.

Southwest's People-Management and Competitive Advantage

A similar VRIO analysis can be conducted for Southwest's approach to people management. First, is this approach valuable; that is, does it reduce Southwest's costs or increase the willingness of its customers to pay?

Employee commitment and loyalty at Southwest is one explanation of why Southwest can get higher levels of employee productivity than most other U.S. airlines. This increased productivity shows up in numerous ways. For example, the average turnaround time for Southwest flights is around 18 minutes. The average turnaround time for the average U.S. airline is 45 minutes. Southwest Airline employees are simply more effective in unloading and loading luggage, fueling, and catering their airplanes than employees in other airlines. This means that Southwest Airlines airplanes are on the ground for less time and in the air more time than its competitors. Of course, an airplane is only making money if it is in the air. This seemingly simple idea is worth hundreds of millions of dollars in lower costs to Southwest.

Have such loyalty and teamwork been rare in the U.S. airline industry? Over the past 15 years, the U.S. airline industry has been wracked by employment strife. Many airlines have had to cut employment, reduce wages, and in other ways strain their relationship with their employees. Overall, in comparison to incumbent airlines, the relationship that Southwest enjoys with its employees has been rare.

Is this relationship costly to imitate? Certainly, relationships between an airline and its employees have many of the attributes that should make them costly to imitate. They emerge over time; they are path dependent, causally ambiguous, and socially complex. It is reasonable to expect that incumbent airlines, airlines that already have strained relationships with their employees, would have difficulty imitating the relationship Southwest enjoys with its employees. Thus, in comparison to incumbent airlines, Southwest's approach to managing its people is probably valuable, rare, and costly to imitate. Assuming it is organized appropriately (and this seems to be the case), this would mean that—relative to incumbent airlines—Southwest has a sustained competitive advantage.

The situation may be somewhat different for new entrants into the U.S. airline industry. These airlines may not have a history of strained employee relationships. As new firms, they may be able to develop more valuable employee relationships from the very beginning. This suggests that, relative to new entrants, Southwest's approach to people management may be valuable and rare, but not costly to imitate. Again, assuming Southwest is organized appropriately, relative to new entrants into the U.S. airline industry, Southwest's people-management capabilities may be a source of only a temporary competitive advantage.

Imitation and Competitive Dynamics in an Industry

Objective 3.4 Discuss important implications of the resource-based view, including:

a. How value chain analysis can be used to identify a firm's valuable resources and capabilities.
b. The kinds of resources and capabilities that are likely to be costly to imitate.
c. How a firm uses its structure, formal and informal control processes, and compensation policy to exploit its resources.

Suppose a firm in an industry has conducted an analysis of its resources and capabilities, concludes that it possesses some valuable, rare, and costly-to-imitate resources and capabilities, and uses these to choose a strategy that it implements with the appropriate organizational structure, formal and informal management controls, and compensation policies. The RBV suggests that this firm will gain a competitive advantage even if it is operating in what an environmental threat analysis (see Chapter 2) would suggest is a very unattractive industry. Examples of firms that have competitive advantages in unattractive industries include Southwest Airlines, Nucor Steel, and Wal-Mart, to name a few.

Given that a particular firm in an industry has a competitive advantage, how should other firms respond? Decisions made by other firms given the strategic choices of a particular firm define the nature of the **competitive dynamics** that exist in an industry. In general, other firms in an industry can respond to the advantages of a competitor in one of three ways. First, they can choose to limit their response. For example, when Wal-Mart entered the discount grocery market with the creation of Super Walmarts, some competitors (e.g., Safeway) ignored Wal-Mart's moves and continued as before. Other competitors (e.g., Kroger) modified some of their tactics, including, for example, selling more prepared foods and more specialty foods than before. Finally, other firms fundamentally altered their strategies (e.g., Target began building stores that also sold discount groceries).

Not Responding to Another Firm's Competitive Advantage

A firm might not respond to another firm's competitive advantage for at least three reasons. First, this firm might have its own competitive advantage. By responding to another firm's competitive advantage, it might destroy, or at least compromise, its own sources of competitive advantage. For example, digital timekeeping has made accurate watches available to most consumers at reasonable prices. A firm such as Casio has a competitive advantage in this market because of its miniaturization and electronic capabilities. Indeed, Casio's market share and performance in the watch business continue to climb although demand for watches, overall, has gone down. How should Rolex—a manufacturer of very expensive, non-electronic watches—respond to Casio? Rolex's decision has been: *Not at all.* Rolex appeals to a very different market segment than Casio. Should Rolex change its strategies—even if it replaced its mechanical self-winding design with the technologically superior digital design—it could easily compromise its competitive advantage in its own niche market.[31] In general, when a firm already possesses its own sources of competitive advantage, it will not respond to different sources of competitive advantage controlled by another firm.

Second, a firm may not respond to another firm's competitive advantage because it does not have the resources and capabilities to do so. A firm with insufficient or inappropriate resources and capabilities—be they physical, financial, human, or organizational—typically will not be able to imitate a successful firm's resources either through direct duplication or substitution. This may very well be the case with American Airlines and Southwest Airlines. It may simply be beyond the ability of American to imitate Southwest's managerial resources and capabilities. In this setting, American Airlines is likely to find itself at a sustained competitive disadvantage.[32]

Finally, a firm may not respond to the advantages of a competitor because it is trying to reduce the level of rivalry in an industry. Any actions a firm takes that have the effect of reducing the level of rivalry in an industry and that also do not require firms in an industry to directly communicate or negotiate with each other can be thought of as **tacit collusion**. This strategy will be discussed in detail in Chapter 7.

Changing Tactics in Response to Another Firm's Competitive Advantage

Tactics are the specific actions a firm takes to implement its strategies. Examples of tactics include decisions firms make about various attributes of their products—including size, shape, color, and price—specific advertising approaches adopted by a firm, and specific sales and marketing efforts. Generally, firms change their tactics much more frequently than they change their strategies.[33]

When competing firms are pursuing approximately the same strategies, the competitive advantages that any one firm might enjoy at a given point in time are most likely due to the tactics that that firm is pursuing. In this setting, it is not unusual for competing firms to change their tactics by imitating the tactics of the firm with an advantage to reduce that firm's advantage. Although changing one's tactics in this manner will only generate competitive parity, this is usually better than the competitive disadvantage these firms were experiencing.

Several industries provide excellent examples of these kinds of tactical interactions. In consumer goods, for example, if one company increases its sales by adding a "lemon scent" to laundry detergent, then lemon scents start showing up in everyone's laundry detergent. If Coke starts selling a soft drink with half the sugar and half the carbs of regular Coke, can Pepsi's low-sugar/low-carb product be far behind? And when Delta Airlines cuts it airfares, can American and United be far behind? Not surprisingly, these kinds of tactical changes, because they initially may be valuable and rare, are seldom costly to imitate and thus are typically only sources of temporary competitive advantage.

Sometimes, rather than simply imitating the tactics of a firm with a competitive advantage, a firm at a disadvantage may "leapfrog" its competitors by developing an entirely new set of tactics. Procter & Gamble engaged in this strategy when it introduced its laundry detergent, Tide, in a new, concentrated formula. This new formulation required new manufacturing and packaging equipment—the smaller box could not be filled in the current manufacturing lines in the industry—which meant that Tide's competitors had to take more time in imitating the concentrated laundry detergent tactic than other tactics pursued in this industry. Nevertheless, within just a few weeks other firms in this market were introducing their own versions of concentrated laundry detergent.

Indeed, some firms can become so skilled at innovating new products and other tactics that this innovative capability can be a source of sustained competitive advantage. Consider, for example, Sony during its heydays. Most observers agree that Sony possessed some special management and innovation skills that enabled it to conceive, design, and manufacture high-quality miniaturized consumer electronics. However, virtually every time Sony brought out a new miniaturized product several of its competitors quickly duplicated that product through reverse engineering, thereby reducing Sony's technological advantage. In what way can Sony's socially complex miniaturization resources and capabilities be a source of sustained competitive advantage when most of Sony's products were quickly imitated through direct duplication?

After Sony introduced each new product, it experienced a rapid increase in profits attributable to the new product's unique features. This increase, however, leads other firms to reverse-engineer the Sony product and introduce their own versions. Increased competition resulted in a reduction in the profits associated with a new product. Thus, at the level of individual products, Sony apparently enjoys only temporary competitive advantages. However, looking at the total returns earned by Sony across all of its new products over time makes clear the source of Sony's sustained competitive advantage. By exploiting its resources and capabilities in miniaturization, Sony was able to constantly introduce new and exciting personal electronics products. No single product generated a sustained competitive advantage, but, over time, across several such product introductions, Sony's resource and capability advantages led to sustained competitive advantages.[34]

Changing Strategies in Response to Another Firm's Competitive Advantage

Finally, firms sometimes respond to another firm's competitive advantage by changing their strategies. Obviously, this does not occur very often, and it typically only occurs when another firm's strategies usurp a firm's competitive advantage. In this setting, a firm will not be able to gain even competitive parity if it maintains its strategy, even if it implements that strategy very effectively.

Changes in consumer tastes, in population demographics, and in the laws that govern a business can all have the effect of rendering what once was a valuable strategy as valueless. However, the most frequent impact is changes in technology.

For example, no matter how well made a mechanical calculator is, it is simply inferior to an electronic calculator. No matter how efficient the telegraph was in its day, it is an inferior technology to the telephone. And no matter how quickly one's fingers can move the beads on an abacus, an electronic cash register is a better way of keeping track of sales and making change in a store.

When firms change their strategies, they must proceed through the entire strategic management process, as described in Chapter 1. However, these firms will often have difficulty abandoning their traditional strategies. For most firms, their strategy helps define what they do and who they are. Changing its strategy often requires a firm to change its identity and its purposes. These are difficult changes to make, and many firms wait to change their strategy until absolutely forced to do so by disastrous financial results. By then, these firms not only have to change their strategy—with all that implies—they must do so in the face of significant financial pressures.

The ability of virtually all strategies to generate competitive advantages typically expires, sooner or later. In general, it is much better for a firm to change its strategy before that strategy is no longer viable. In this way, a firm can make a planned move to a new strategy that maintains whatever resources and capabilities it still possesses while it develops the new resources and capabilities it will need to compete in the future.

Implications of the Resource-Based View

The RBV and the VRIO framework can be applied to individual firms to understand whether these firms will gain competitive advantages, how sustainable these competitive advantages are likely to be, and what the sources of these competitive advantages are. In this way, the RBV and the VRIO framework can be understood as important complements to the threats and opportunities analyses described in Chapter 2.

However, beyond what these frameworks can say about the competitive performance of a particular firm, the RBV has some broader implications for managers seeking to gain competitive advantages. Some of these broader implications are listed in Table 3.5 and discussed in the following section.

Where Does the Responsibility for Competitive Advantage in a Firm Reside?

First, the RBV suggests that competitive advantages can be found in several of the different resources and capabilities controlled by the firm. These resources and capabilities are not limited to those that are controlled directly by a firm's senior managers. Thus, the responsibility for creating, nurturing, and exploiting valuable, rare, and costly-to-imitate resources and capabilities for competitive advantage is not restricted to senior managers, but falls on every employee in a firm. Therefore, employees should go beyond defining their jobs in functional terms and instead define their jobs in competitive and economic terms.

Consider a simple example. In a recent visit to a very successful automobile manufacturing plant, the plant manager was asked to describe his job responsibilities. He said, "My job is to manage this plant in order to help the firm make and sell the best cars in the world." In response to a similar question, the person in charge

TABLE 3.5 Broader Implications of the Resource-Based View

1. The responsibility for competitive advantage in a firm:
   Competitive advantage is every employee's responsibility.
2. Competitive parity and competitive advantage:
   If all a firm does is what its competition does, it can gain only competitive parity. In gaining competitive advantage, it is better for a firm to exploit its own valuable, rare, and costly-to-imitate resources than to imitate the valuable and rare resources of a competitor.
3. Difficult to implement strategies:
   If the cost of strategy implementation is less than the value of strategy implementation, the relative cost of implementing a strategy is more important for competitive advantage than the absolute cost of implementing a strategy.
   Firms can systematically overestimate and underestimate their uniqueness.
4. Socially complex resources:
   Not only can employee empowerment, organizational culture, and teamwork be valuable, they can also be sources of sustained competitive advantage.
5. The role of the organization:
   Organization should support the use of valuable, rare, and costly-to-imitate resources. If conflicts between these attributes of a firm arise, change the organization.

of the manufacturing line said, "My job is to manage this manufacturing line in order to help the firm make and sell the best cars in the world." A janitor was also asked to describe his job responsibilities. Although he had not been present in the two earlier interviews, the janitor responded, "My job is to keep this facility clean in order to help the firm make and sell the best cars in the world."

Which of these three employees is most likely to be a source of sustained competitive advantage for this firm? Certainly, the plant manager and the manufacturing line manager *should* define their jobs in terms of helping the firm make and sell the best cars in the world. However, it is unlikely that their responses to this question would be any different than the responses of other senior managers at other manufacturing plants around the world. Put differently, although the definition of these two managers' jobs in terms of enabling the firm to make and sell the best cars in the world is valuable, it is unlikely to be rare, and thus it is likely to be a source of competitive parity, not competitive advantage. However, a janitor who defines her job as helping the firm make and sell the best cars in the world instead of simply to clean the facility is, most would agree, quite unusual. Because it is rare, it might be a source of at least a temporary competitive advantage.[35]

The value created by one janitor defining her job in competitive terms rather than functional terms is not huge, but suppose that all the employees in this plant defined their jobs in these terms. Suddenly, the value that might be created could be substantial. Moreover, the organizational culture and tradition in a firm that would lead employees to define their jobs in this way are likely to be costly for other firms to imitate. Thus, if this approach to defining job responsibilities is broadly diffused in a particular plant, it seems likely to be valuable, rare, and costly to imitate and thus a source of sustained competitive advantage, assuming the firm is organized to take advantage of this unusual resource.

In the end, it is clear that competitive advantage is too important to remain the sole property of senior management. To the extent that employees throughout an organization are empowered to develop and exploit valuable, rare, and costly-to-imitate resources and capabilities in the accomplishment of their job responsibilities, a firm may actually be able to gain sustained competitive advantages.

Competitive Parity and Competitive Advantage

Second, the RBV suggests that, if all a firm does is create value in the same way as its competitors, the best performance it can ever expect to gain is competitive parity. To do better than competitive parity, firms must engage in valuable and rare activities. They must do things to create economic value that other firms have not even thought of, let alone implemented.

This is especially critical for firms that find themselves at a competitive disadvantage. Such a firm certainly should examine its more successful competition, understand what has made this competition so successful, and, where imitation has a very low cost, imitate the successful actions of its competitors. In this sense, benchmarking a firm's performance against the performance of its competitors can be extremely important.

However, if this is all that a firm does, it can only expect to gain competitive parity. Gaining competitive advantage depends on a firm discovering its own unique resources and capabilities and how they can be used in choosing and implementing strategies. For a firm seeking competitive advantage, it is better to be excellent in how it develops and exploits its own unique resources and capabilities than it is to be excellent in how it imitates the resources and capabilities of other firms.

This does not imply that firms must always be first movers to gain competitive advantages. Some firms develop valuable, rare, and costly-to-imitate resources and capabilities in being efficient second movers—that is, in rapidly imitating and improving on the product and technological innovations of other firms. Rather than suggesting that firms must always be first movers, the RBV suggests that, to gain competitive advantages, firms must implement strategies that rely on valuable, rare, and costly-to-imitate resources and capabilities, whatever those strategies or resources might be.

Difficult-to-Implement Strategies

Third, as firms contemplate different strategic options, they often ask how difficult and costly it will be to implement different strategies. If the cost of implementing a strategy is less than the value that a strategy creates, the RBV suggests that the critical question facing firms is not, "Is a strategy easy to implement or not?" but rather, "Is this strategy easier for us to implement than it is for our competitors to implement?" Firms that already possess the valuable, rare, and costly-to-imitate resources needed to implement a strategy will, in general, find it easier (i.e., less costly) to implement a strategy than firms that first must develop the required resources and then implement the proposed strategy. For firms that already possess a resource, strategy implementation can be natural and swift.

In understanding the relative costs of implementing a strategy, firms can make two errors. First, they can overestimate the uniqueness of the resources they control. Although every firm's history is unique and no two management teams are exactly the same, this does not always mean that a firm's resources and capabilities will be rare. Firms with similar histories operating in similar industries will often develop similar capabilities. If a firm overestimates the rarity of its resources and capabilities, it can overestimate its ability to generate competitive advantages.

For example, when asked what their most critical sources of competitive advantage are, many firms will cite the quality of their top management team, the quality of their technology, and their commitment to excellence in all that they do. When pushed about their competitors, these same firms will admit that they too have high-quality top management teams, high-quality technology, and a commitment to excellence in all that they do. Although these three attributes can be sources of competitive parity, they cannot be sources of competitive advantage.

Second, firms can sometimes underestimate their uniqueness and thus underestimate the extent to which the strategies they pursue can be sources of sustained competitive advantage. When firms possess valuable, rare, and costly-to-imitate resources, strategy implementation can be relatively easy. In this context, it seems reasonable to expect that other firms will be able to quickly imitate this "easy-to-implement" strategy. Of course, this is not the case if these resources controlled by a firm are, in fact, rare and costly to imitate.

In general, firms must take great care not to overestimate or underestimate their uniqueness. An accurate assessment of the value, rarity, and imitability of a firm's resources is necessary to develop an accurate understanding of the relative costs of implementing a firm's strategies and, thus, the ability of those strategies to generate competitive advantages. Often, firms must employ outside assistance in helping them describe the rarity and imitability of their resources, even though managers in firms will generally be much more familiar with the resources controlled by a firm than outsiders. However, outsiders can provide a measure of objectivity in evaluating the uniqueness of a firm.

Socially Complex Resources

Over the past several decades, much has been written about the importance of employee empowerment, organizational culture, and teamwork for firm performance. Most of this work suggests that firms that empower employees, that have an enabling culture, and that encourage teamwork will, on average, make better strategic choices and implement them more efficiently than firms without these organizational attributes. Using the language of the RBV, most of this work has suggested that employee empowerment, organizational culture, and teamwork, at least in some settings, are economically valuable.[36]

Resource-based logic acknowledges the importance of the value of these organizational attributes. However, it also suggests that these socially complex resources and capabilities can be rare and costly to imitate—and it is these attributes that make it possible for socially complex resources and capabilities to be sources of sustained competitive advantage. Put differently, the RBV actually extends and broadens traditional analyses of the socially complex attributes of firms. Not only can these attributes be valuable, but they can also be rare and costly to imitate and, thus, sources of sustained competitive advantage.

The Role of Organization

Finally, resource-based logic suggests that an organization's structure, control systems, and compensation policies should support and enable a firm's efforts to fully exploit the valuable, rare, and costly-to-imitate resources and capabilities it controls. These attributes of organization, by themselves, are usually not sources of sustained competitive advantage.

These observations suggest that if there is a conflict between the resources a firm controls and that firm's organization, the organization should be changed. However, it is often the case that once a firm's structure, control systems, and compensation policies are put in place they tend to remain, regardless of whether they are consistent with a firm's underlying resources and capabilities. In such settings, a firm will not be able to realize the full competitive potential of its underlying resource base. To the extent that a firm's resources and capabilities are continuously evolving, its organizational structure, control systems, and compensation policies must also evolve. For these attributes of organization to evolve, managers must be aware of their link with a firm's resources and capabilities and of organizational alternatives.

Summary

The RBV is an economic theory that suggests that firm performance is a function of the types of resources and capabilities controlled by firms. Resources are the tangible and intangible assets a firm uses to conceive and implement its strategies. Capabilities are a subset of resources that enable a firm to take advantage of its other resources. Resources and capabilities can be categorized into financial, physical, human, and organizational resources categories.

The RBV makes two assumptions about resources and capabilities: the assumption of resource heterogeneity (that some resources and capabilities may be heterogeneously distributed across competing firms) and the assumption of resource immobility (that this heterogeneity may be long lasting). These two assumptions can be used to describe conditions under which firms will gain competitive advantages by exploiting their resources.

A tool for analyzing a firm's internal strengths and weaknesses can be derived from the RBV. Called the VRIO framework, this tool asks four questions about a firm's resources and capabilities to evaluate their competitive potential. These questions are the question of value, the question of rarity, the question of imitability, and the question of organization.

A firm's resources and capabilities are valuable when they enable it to exploit external opportunities or neutralize external threats. Such valuable resources and capabilities are a firm's strengths. Resources and capabilities that are not valuable are a firm's weaknesses. Using valuable resources to exploit external opportunities or neutralize external threats will have the effect of increasing a firm's net revenues or decreasing its net costs.

One way to identify a firm's valuable resources and capabilities is by examining its value chain. A firm's value chain is the list of business activities it engages in to develop, produce, and sell its products or services. Different stages in this value chain require different resources and capabilities, and differences in value chain choices across firms can lead to important differences among the resources and capabilities controlled by different companies. A generic value chain has been developed by McKinsey and Company.

Valuable and common (i.e., not rare) resources and capabilities can be a source of competitive parity. Failure to invest in such resources can create a competitive disadvantage for a firm. Valuable and rare resources can be a source of at least a temporary competitive advantage. There are fewer firms able to control such a resource and still exploit it as a source of at least temporary competitive advantage than there are firms that will generate perfect competition dynamics in an industry.

Valuable, rare, and costly-to-imitate resources and capabilities can be a source of sustained competitive advantage. Imitation can occur through direct duplication or through substitution. A firm's resources and capabilities may be costly to imitate for at least four reasons: unique historical circumstances, causal ambiguity, socially complex resources and capabilities, and patents.

To take full advantage of the potential of its resources and capabilities, a firm must be appropriately organized. A firm's organization consists of its formal reporting structure, its formal and informal control processes, and its compensation policy. These are complementary resources in that they are rarely sources of competitive advantage on their own.

The VRIO framework can be used to identify the competitive implications of a firm's resources and capabilities—whether they are a source of competitive disadvantage, competitive parity, temporary competitive advantage, or sustained competitive advantage—and the extent to which these resources and capabilities are strengths or weaknesses.

When a firm faces a competitor that has a sustained competitive advantage, the firm's options are to not respond, to change its tactics, or to change its strategies. A firm may choose not to respond in this setting for at least three reasons. First, a response might weaken its own sources of sustained competitive advantage. Second, a firm may not have the resources required to respond. Third, a firm may be trying to create or maintain tacit cooperation within an industry.

The RBV has a series of broader managerial implications as well. For example, resource-based logic suggests that competitive advantage is every employee's responsibility. It also suggests that if all a firm does is what its competition does, it can gain only competitive parity, and that in gaining competitive advantage it is better for a firm to exploit its own valuable, rare, and costly-to-imitate resources than to imitate the valuable and rare resources of a competitor. Also, resource-based logic implies that if the cost of strategy implementation is less than the value of strategy implementation, the relative cost of implementing a strategy is more important for competitive advantage than the absolute cost of implementing a strategy. It also implies that firms can systematically overestimate and underestimate their uniqueness. Regarding a firm's resources and capabilities, resource-based logic suggests that not only can employee empowerment, organizational culture, and teamwork be valuable; they can also be sources of sustained competitive advantage. Also, if conflicts arise between a firm's valuable, rare, and costly-to-imitate resources and its organization, the organization should be changed.

Challenge Questions

3.1. Explain which of the following approaches to strategy formulation is more likely to generate economic profits: (a) evaluating external opportunities and threats and then developing resources and capabilities to exploit these opportunities and neutralize these threats; or (b) evaluating internal resources and capabilities and then searching for industries where they can be exploited?

3.2. Which firm will have a higher level of economic performance: (a) a firm with valuable, rare, and costly-to-imitate resources and capabilities operating in a very attractive industry; or (b) a firm with valuable, rare, and costly-to-imitate resources and capabilities operating in a very unattractive industry? Assume both these firms are appropriately organized. Explain your answer.

3.3. Considering which is more critical to sustaining human life—water or diamonds—why do firms that provide water to customers generally earn lower economic performance than firms that provide diamonds?

3.4. Why would a firm currently experiencing competitive parity be able to gain sustained competitive advantages by studying another firm that is currently experiencing sustained competitive advantages?

3.5. Your former college roommate calls you and asks to borrow $10,000 so that he can open a pizza restaurant in his hometown. He acknowledges that there is a high degree of direct competition in this market, that the cost of entry is low, and that there are numerous substitutes for pizza, but he believes that his pizza restaurant will have some sustained competitive advantages. For example, he is going to have sawdust on his floor, a variety of imported beers, and a late-night delivery service. What are the risks in lending him the money?

3.6. Recently, Boeing did not respond to Airbus's announcement of the development of a super-jumbo aircraft, the A380. Assuming this aircraft will give Airbus a competitive advantage in the segment of the airliner business that supplies airplanes for long international flights, why do you think that Boeing might not have responded?

3.7. Between the following two firms, which one is more likely to be successful in exploiting its sources of sustained competitive advantage in its home market than in a highly competitive, nondomestic market: (a) a firm from a less competitive home country; or (b) a firm from a more competitive home country? Why?

Problem Set

3.8. Apply the VRIO framework in the following settings. Will the actions described be a source of competitive disadvantage, parity, temporary advantage, or sustained competitive advantage? Explain your answers.

(a) Procter & Gamble introduces new, smaller packaging for its Tide laundry detergent.
(b) American Airlines announces a 5 percent across-the-board reduction in airfares.
(c) The Korean automobile firm Hyundai announces a 10-year, 100,000-mile warranty on its cars.
(d) Microsoft makes it easier to transfer data and information from Microsoft Word to Microsoft Excel.
(e) Merck can coordinate the work of its chemists and biologists in the development of new drugs.
(f) Ford patents a new kind of brake pad for its cars.
(g) Ashland Chemical, a specialty chemical company, patents a new chemical.
(h) The New York Yankees sign All-Star pitcher Randy Johnson to a long-term contract.
(i) Michael Dell uses the money he has made from Dell to purchase the Dallas Cowboys football team.
(j) Ted Turner uses the money he has made from his broadcasting empire to purchase the Atlanta Braves baseball team.

3.9. Identify three firms you might want to work for. Using the VRIO framework, evaluate the extent to which the resources and capabilities of these firms give them the potential to realize competitive disadvantages, parity, temporary advantages, or sustained advantages. What implications, if any, does this analysis have for the company you might want to work for?

3.10. You have been assigned to estimate the present value of a potential construction project for your company. How would you use the VRIO framework to construct the cash-flow analysis that is a part of any present-value calculation?

Writing Assignments

3.11. Give an example of how you would apply value chain analysis to identify a firm's valuable resources and capabilities.

3.12. What is required for a firm to gain a sustained competitive advantage from a resource considered rare?

CASE STUDY| Strategic Shifts at L&T: Bridging Engineering with IT Innovation

Larsen & Toubro (L&T), established in 1938 by Henning Holck-Larsen and Søren Kristian Toubro, has evolved from a representative of Danish manufacturers to a colossal Indian multinational conglomerate. L&T's journey from its inception during the challenging times of World War II to becoming an illustration of engineering, construction, and technological prowess is a testament to its founders' vision and resilience. Engaging in a myriad of sectors, including heavy engineering, construction, manufacturing, technology, IT, and financial services, L&T has cemented its position as a leader in each of its operational domains.

In a strategic move to amplify its IT capabilities, Larsen & Toubro (L&T) acquired a dominant stake in Mindtree in 2019, marking a notable foray into the tech sector through a rare hostile takeover in India. By securing 60.06 percent of Mindtree, L&T aimed to leverage Mindtree's digital and IT expertise, thereby enriching its portfolio and reinforcing its market position. This acquisition highlighted L&T's commitment to diversification and innovation, strategically positioning it at the forefront of technological advancements and competitive advantage in the global arena. The company's strategic growth, underlined by its ability to secure and execute large-scale international projects, reflects its global competitiveness and innovative edge. Noteworthy initiatives, like the major debottlenecking project in Saudi Arabia and the turnkey contract for an 1800 MWac Solar Photovoltaic Plant in Dubai, UAE, in 2024, exemplify L&T's engineering excellence and its role as a pivotal player in the global energy sector. These projects not only expand L&T's international footprint but also demonstrate its commitment to leveraging technological advancements for sustainable development. L&T's financial accomplishments in 2023, with a revenue surge to $23.4 billion and a net income growth of 20.8 percent, indicate its robust operational efficiency and strategic acumen.

This financial strength supports L&T's market position and lays a solid foundation for future ventures and expansions. The company's workforce, standing at 49,039 employees, benefits from a culture that prioritizes meritocracy, integrity, and continuous learning, making L&T a desirable workplace within the engineering and construction industry.

The firm's forward-looking approach is marked by an emphasis on digital transformation and innovation, aiming to redefine industry standards and address the evolving needs of its global clientele. L&T's investment in technology and R&D is geared towards enhancing its product and service offerings, thereby ensuring its businesses are well-equipped to navigate the complexities of a rapidly changing world. Facing challenges such as international market dynamics, operational risks, and technological disruptions, L&T remains steadfast in its commitment to innovation, sustainability, and global expansion. Its strategic partnerships, such as joint ventures and collaborations across various sectors, are crucial in this endeavour, providing L&T with a competitive edge and a diversified business model capable of weathering economic fluctuations and capitalizing on emerging market opportunities.

As L&T looks to the future, its focus on sustainability, smart infrastructure, and digitalization is poised to drive growth, enhance operational efficiencies, and contribute to global efforts against climate change. The conglomerate's strategy encompasses a holistic approach to business, prioritizing environmental stewardship, social responsibility, and corporate governance, in line with its vision to build a better, more sustainable future. Larsen & Toubro's legacy, built on a foundation of excellence, innovation, and integrity, continues to thrive as it navigates the challenges and opportunities of the 21st century. Its comprehensive portfolio, strategic initiatives, and unwavering commitment to quality and sustainability ensure L&T's continued growth and leadership in the global marketplace.

Questions

1. How does L&T's acquisition strategy, particularly its acquisition of Mindtree, contribute to its overall strategic management approach?
2. In what ways L&T can leverage technological advancements and strategic partnerships to maintain its competitive edge and drive growth in the global marketplace?
3. Does L&T's focus on sustainability, smart infrastructure, and digitalization align with its long-term strategic objectives and vision for the future?

References

GlobalData. (n.d.). *Larsen & Toubro Ltd Company Profile – Overview.* Accessed from https://www.globaldata.com on February 5, 2024.

Larsen & Toubro. (n.d.). *About L&T Group.* L&T Corporate. Accessed from https://www.larsentoubro.com on February 5, 2024.

Naib, S., & Singh, S. (2019). *Mindtree: hostile takeover bid by Larsen and Toubro.* Emerald Emerging Markets Case Studies, 9(3), 1-33. Emerald Publishing, the UK.

Rasiwala, F., & Rajni, J. (2023). *High or Low Risk: Investor's Dilemma on Cost of Equity.* SAGE Publications: SAGE Business Cases Originals.

Larsen & Toubro Limited. (n.d.). *Home page.* Accessed from https://www.globaldata.com on February 5, 2024.

End Notes

1 The term *the resource-based view* was coined by Wernerfelt, B. (1984). "A resource-based view of the firm." *Strategic Management Journal*, 5, pp. 171–180. Some important early contributors to this theory include Rumelt, R. P. (1984). "Toward a strategic theory of the firm." In R. Lamb (ed.), *Competitive strategic management* (pp. 556–570). Upper Saddle River, NJ: Prentice Hall; and Barney, J. B. (1986). "Strategic factor markets: Expectations, luck and business strategy." *Management Science*, 32, pp. 1512–1514. A second wave of important early resource-based theoretical work includes Barney, J. B. (1991). "Firm resources and sustained competitive advantage." *Journal of Management*, 7, pp. 49–64; Dierickx, I., and K. Cool. (1989). "Asset stock accumulation and sustainability of competitive advantage." *Management Science*, 35, pp. 1504–1511; Conner, K. R. (1991). "A historical comparison of resource-based theory and five schools of thought within industrial organization economics: Do we have a new theory of the firm?" *Journal of Management*, 17(1), pp. 121–154; and Peteraf, M. A. (1993). "The cornerstones of competitive advantage: A resource-based view." *Strategic Management Journal*, 14, pp. 179–191. A review of much of this early theoretical literature can be found in Mahoney, J. T., and J. R. Pandian. (1992). "The resource-based view within the conversation of strategic management." *Strategic Management Journal*, 13, pp. 363–380. The theoretical perspective has also spawned a growing body of empirical work, including Brush, T. H., and K. W. Artz. (1999). "Toward a contingent resource-based theory." *Strategic Management Journal*, 20, pp. 223–250; Marcus, A., and D. Geffen. (1998). "The dialectics of competency acquisition." *Strategic Management Journal*, 19, pp. 1145–1168; Brush, T. H., P. Bromiley, and M. Hendrickx. (1999). "The relative influence of industry and corporation on business segment performance." *Strategic Management Journal*, 20, pp. 519–547; Yeoh, P.-L., and K. Roth. (1999). "An empirical analysis of sustained advantage in the U.S. pharmaceutical industry." *Strategic Management Journal*, 20, pp. 637–653; Roberts, P. (1999). "Product innovation, product-market competition and persistent profitability in the U.S. pharmaceutical industry." *Strategic Management Journal*, 20, pp. 655–670; Gulati, R. (1999). "Network location and learning." *Strategic Management Journal*, 20, pp. 397–420; Lorenzoni, G., and A. Lipparini. (1999). "The leveraging of interfirm relationships as a distinctive organizational capability." *Strategic Management Journal*, 20, pp. 317–338; Majumdar, S. (1998). "On the utilization of resources." *Strategic Management Journal*, 19(9), pp. 809–831; Makadok, R. (1997). "Do inter-firm differences in capabilities affect strategic pricing dynamics?" *Academy of Management Proceedings '97*, pp. 30–34; Silverman, B. S., J. A. Nickerson, and J. Freeman. (1997). "Profitability, transactional alignment, and organizational mortality in the U.S. trucking industry." *Strategic Management Journal*, 18 (Summer special issue), pp. 31–52; Powell, T. C., and A. Dent-Micallef. (1997). "Information technology as competitive advantage." *Strategic Management Journal*, 18(5), pp. 375–405; Miller, D., and J. Shamsie. (1996). "The Resource-based view of the firm in two environments." *Academy of Management Journal*, 39(3), pp. 519–543; and Maijoor, S., and A. Van Witteloostuijn. (1996). "An empirical test of the resource-based theory." *Strategic Management Journal*, 17, pp. 549–569; Barnett, W. P., H. R. Greve, and D. Y. Park. (1994). "An evolutionary model of organizational performance." *Strategic Management Journal*, 15 (Winter special issue), pp. 11–28; Levinthal, D., and J. Myatt. (1994). "Co-evolution of capabilities and industry: The evolution of mutual fund processing." *Strategic Management Journal*, 17, pp. 45–62; Henderson, R., and I. Cockburn. (1994). "Measuring competence? Exploring firm effects in pharmaceutical research." *Strategic Management Journal*, 15, pp. 63–84; Pisano, G. P. (1994). "Knowledge, integration, and the locus of learning: An empirical analysis of process development." *Strategic Management Journal*, 15, pp. 85–100; and Zajac, E. J., and J. D. Westphal. (1994). "The costs and benefits of managerial incentives and monitoring in large U.S. corporations: When is more not better?" *Strategic Management Journal*, 15, pp. 121–142.

2 Ghemawat, P. (1986). "Wal-Mart stores' discount operations." Harvard Business School Case No. 9-387-018, on Wal-Mart; Kupfer, A. (1991). "The champion of cheap clones." *Fortune*, September 23, pp. 115–120; and Holder, D. (1989). "L. L. Bean, Inc.—1974." Harvard Business School Case No. 9-676-014, on L. L. Bean. Some of Wal-Mart's more recent moves, especially its international acquisitions, are described in Laing, J. R. (1999). "Blimey! Wal-Mart." *Barron's*, 79, p. 14. L. L. Bean's lethargic performance in the 1990s, together with its turnaround plan, is described in Symonds, W. (1998). "Paddling harder at L. L. Bean." *BusinessWeek*, December 7, p. 72.

3 For an early discussion of the importance of human capital in firms, see Becker, G. S. (1964). *Human capital*. New York: Columbia University Press.

4 Heskett, J. L., and R. H. Hallowell. (1993). "Southwest Airlines: 1993 (A)." Harvard Business School Case No. 9-695-023.

5 D. Ricardo (1817). *Principles of political economy and taxation*. London: J. Murray.

6 See Barney, J. (1991). "Firm resources and sustained competitive advantage." *Journal of Management*, 17, pp. 99–120.

7 See Schlender, B. R. (1992). "How Sony keeps the magic going." *Fortune*, February 24, pp. 75–84; and (1999). "The weakling kicks back." *The Economist*, July 3, p. 46, for a discussion of Sony. See Krogh, L., J. Praeger, D. Sorenson, and J. Tomlinson. (1988). "How 3M evaluates its R&D programs." *Research Technology Management*, 31, pp. 10–14.

8 Anders, G. (2002). "AOL's true believers." *Fast Company*, July pp. 96+; Karnitschnig, M. (2006). "That's all, folks: After years of pushing synergy, Time Warner, Inc. says enough." *The Wall Street Journal*, June 2, A1+; www.cnbc.com/2009/12/29/top-ten-best-(andworst)-mergers-of-all-time (accessed January 6, 2017).

9 "AIDS in Africa." *British Medical Journal*, June 1, p. 456 J. S. Friedman (2003). "Paying for apartheid." *Nation*, June 6, pp. 7+; L. Lee (2000). "Can Nike still do it?" *BusinessWeek*, February 21, pp. 121+.

10 See Grant, R. M. (1991). *Contemporary strategy analysis*. Cambridge, MA: Basil Blackwell.

11 See Miller, J. and Shales, T. (2011) *ESPN: These guys have all the fun*. NY: Little Brown.

12 See Steinberg, D. (2013). "ESPN strives to maintain its lead as competition heats up." Variety.com/2013/tv/news. Accessed January 6, 2017. ESPN is also challenged by recent trends in "unbundling" cable channels. Currently, ESPN receives fees from cable users, whether those users watch ESPN or not. Unbundling and "cord cutting" would enable consumers to pay for only that content they actually watch. These changes led ESPN, in 2015, to reduce its overall workforce by 4%. See sportsbusinessdaily.com/Journal/Issues/2015/10/26/Media/ESPN. Accessed January 9, 2017.

13 Lipman, S., and R. Rumelt. (1982). "Uncertain imitability: An analysis of interfirm differences in efficiency under competition." *Bell Journal of Economics*, 13, pp. 418–438; Barney, J. B. (1986). "Strategic factor markets: Expectations, luck and business strategy." *Management Science*, 32, pp. 1512–1514; and Barney, J. B. (1986). "Organizational culture: Can it be a source of sustained competitive advantage?" *Academy of Management Review*, 11, pp. 656–665.

14 Note that the definition of sustained competitive advantage presented here, though different, is consistent with the definition given in Chapter 1. In particular, a firm that enjoys a competitive advantage for a long period of time (the Chapter 1 definition) does not have its advantage competed away through imitation (the Chapter 3 definition).

15 These explanations of costly imitation were first developed by Dierickx, I., and K. Cool. (1989). "Asset stock accumulation and sustainability of competitive advantage." *Management Science*, 35, pp. 1504–1511; Barney, J. B. (1991). "Firm resources and sustained competitive advantage." *Journal of Management*, 7, pp. 49–64; Mahoney, J. T., and J. R. Pandian. (1992). "The resource-based view within the conversation of strategic management." *Strategic Management Journal*, 13, pp. 363–380; and Peteraf, M. A. (1993). "The cornerstones of competitive advantage: A resource-based view." *Strategic Management Journal*, 14, pp. 179–191.

16 Dierickx, I., and K. Cool. (1989). "Asset stock accumulation and sustainability of competitive advantage." *Management Science*, 35, pp. 1504–1511. In economics, the role of history in determining competitive outcomes was first examined by Arthur, W. B. (1989). "Competing technologies, increasing returns, and lock-in by historical events." *Economic Journal*, 99, pp. 116–131.

17 This term was first suggested by Arthur, W. B. (1989). "Competing technologies, increasing returns, and lock-in by historical events." *Economic Journal*, 99, pp. 116–131. A good example of path dependence is the development of Silicon Valley and the important role that Stanford University and a few early firms played in creating the network of organizations that has since become the center of much of the electronics business. See Alley, J. (1997). "The heart of Silicon Valley." *Fortune*, July 7, pp. 86+.

18 Reed, R., and R. J. DeFillippi. (1990). "Causal ambiguity, barriers to imitation, and sustainable competitive advantage." *Academy of*

Management Review, 15(1), pp. 88–102, suggest that causal ambiguity about the sources of a firm's competitive advantage need only exist among a firm's competitors for it to be a source of sustained competitive advantage. Managers in a firm, they argue, may fully understand the sources of their advantage. However, in a world where employees freely and frequently move from firm to firm, such special insights into the sources of a firm's competitive advantage would not remain proprietary for very long. For this reason, for causal ambiguity to be a source of sustained competitive advantage, both the firm trying to gain such an advantage and those trying to imitate it must face similar levels of causal ambiguity. Indeed, Wal-Mart sued Amazon for trying to steal some of its secrets by hiring employees away from Wal-Mart. See Nelson, E. (1998). "Wal-Mart accuses Amazon.com of stealing its secrets in lawsuit." *The Wall Street Journal*, October 19, p. B10. For a discussion of how difficult it is to maintain secrets, especially in a world of the World Wide Web, see Farnham, A. (1997). "How safe are your secrets?" *Fortune*, September 8, pp. 114+. The international dimensions of the challenges associated with maintaining secrets are discussed in Robinson, E. (1998). "China spies target corporate America." *Fortune*, March 30, pp. 118+.

19 Itami, H. (1987). *Mobilizing invisible assets*. Cambridge, MA: Harvard University Press.

20 See Barney, J. B., and B. Tyler. (1990). "The attributes of top management teams and sustained competitive advantage." In M. Lawless and L. Gomez-Mejia (eds.), *Managing the high technology firm* (pp. 33–48). Greenwich, CT: JAI Press, on teamwork in top management teams; Barney, J. B. (1986). "Organizational culture: Can it be a source of sustained competitive advantage?" *Academy of Management Review*, 11, pp. 656–665, on organizational culture; Henderson, R. M., and I. Cockburn. (1994). "Measuring competence? Exploring firm effects in pharmaceutical research." *Strategic Management Journal*, 15, pp. 63–84, on relationships among employees; and Dyer, J. H., and H. Singh. (1998). "The relational view: Cooperative strategy and sources of interorganizational competitive advantage." *Academy of Management Review*, 23(4), pp. 660–679, on relationships with suppliers and customers.

21 For a discussion of knowledge as a source of competitive advantage in the popular business press, see Stewart, T. (1995). "Getting real about brain power." *Fortune*, November 27, pp. 201+; Stewart, T. (1995). "Mapping corporate knowledge." *Fortune*, October 30, pp. 209+. For the academic version of this same issue, see Simonin, B. L. (1999). "Ambiguity and the process of knowledge transfer in strategic alliances." *Strategic Management Journal*, 20(7), pp. 595–623; Spender, J. C. (1996). "Making knowledge the basis of a dynamic theory of the firm." *Strategic Management Journal*, 17 (Winter special issue), pp. 109–122; Hatfield, D. D., J. P. Liebeskind, and T. C. Opler. (1996). "The effects of corporate restructuring on aggregate industry specialization." *Strategic Management Journal*, 17, pp. 55–72; and Grant, R. M. (1996). "Toward a knowledge-based theory of the firm." *Strategic Management Journal*, 17 (Winter special issue), pp. 109–122.

22 Porras, J., and P. O. Berg. (1978). "The impact of organizational development." *Academy of Management Review*, 3, pp. 249–266, have done one of the few empirical studies on whether systematic efforts to change socially complex resources are effective. They found that such efforts are usually not effective. Although this study is getting older, it is unlikely that current change methods will be any more effective than the methods examined by these authors.

23 See Hambrick, D. (1987). "Top management teams: Key to strategic success." *California Management Review*, 30, pp. 88–108, on top management teams; Barney, J. B. (1986). "Organizational culture: Can it be a source of sustained competitive advantage?" *Academy of Management Review*, 11, pp. 656–665, on culture; Porter, M. E. (1980). *Competitive strategy*. New York: Free Press; and Klein, B., and K. Leffler. (1981). "The role of market forces in assuring contractual performance." *Journal of Political Economy*, 89, pp. 615–641, on relations with customers.

24 See Harris, L. C., and E. Ogbonna. (1999). "Developing a market oriented culture: A critical evaluation." *Journal of Management Studies*, 36(2), pp. 177–196.

25 Lieberman, M. B. (1987). "The learning curve, diffusion, and competitive strategy." *Strategic Management Journal*, 8, pp. 441–452, has a very good analysis of the cost of imitation in the chemical industry. See also Lieberman, M. B., and D. B. Montgomery. (1988). "First-mover advantages." *Strategic Management Journal*, 9, pp. 41–58.

26 Rumelt, R. P. (1984). "Toward a strategic theory of the firm." In R. Lamb (ed.), *Competitive strategic management* (pp. 556–570). Upper Saddle River, NJ: Prentice Hall, among others, cites patents as a source of costly imitation.

27 Significant debate surrounds the patentability of different kinds of products. For example, although typefaces are not patentable (and cannot be copyrighted), the process for displaying typefaces may be. See Thurm, S. (1998). "Copy this typeface? Court ruling counsels caution." *The Wall Street Journal*, July 15, pp. B1+.

28 J. P. Womack, D. I. Jones, and D. Roos (1990). *The machine that changed the world*. New York: Rawson; M. Huselid (1995). "The impact of human resource management practices on turnover, productivity, and corporate financial performance." *Academy of Management Journal*, 38, pp. 635–672; J. B. Barney and P. Wright (1998). "On becoming a strategic partner." *Human Resource Management*, 37, pp. 31–46.

29 For an insightful discussion of these complementary resources, see Amit, R., and P. J. H. Schoemaker. (1993). "Strategic assets and organizational rent." *Strategic Management Journal*, 14(1), pp. 33–45.

30 See H. Tabuchi (2012) How the tech parade passed Sony by. April 15, 2012. *New York Times*. http://www.nytimes.com/2012/04/15/technology/how-sony-fell-behindinthetechparade. Accessed January 27, 2014.

31 (2004). "Casio." *Marketing*, May 6, p. 95 Weisul, K. (2003). "When time is money—and art." *BusinessWeek*, July 21, p. 86.

32 That said, there have been some "cracks" in Southwest's capabilities armor lately. For example, in 2016, negotiation between Southwest and its unions became very heated. Union officials called for the resignations of Southwest's CEO. Southwest's board declined to do so. (Colmetsch, C. "Southwest's Board Tells Union CEO Not Going Anywhere," www.bloomburg.com, August 6, 2016). Whether this is an early indicator that Southwest's core people management strengths are being lost is not yet known. However, Southwest's stumbling would give other US airlines some hope.

33 This aspect of the competitive dynamics in an industry is discussed in Smith, K. G., C. M. Grimm, and M. J. Gannon. (1992). *Dynamics of competitive strategy*. Newberry Park, CA: Sage.

34 Schlender, B. R. (1992). "How Sony keeps the magic going." *Fortune*, February 24, pp. 75–84.

35 Personal communication.

36 See, for example, Peters, T., and R. Waterman. (1982). *In search of excellence*. New York: Harper Collins; Collins, J., and J. Porras. (1994). *Built to last*. New York: Harper Business; Collins, J. (2001). *Good to great*. New York: Harper Collins; and Bennis, W. G., and R. Townsend. (2006). *Reinventing leadership*. New York: Harper Collins.

Part 1

CASES

Case 1-1: Walmart Stores, Inc.

In November of 2013, Doug McMillon had just been named the CEO of Walmart Stores, Inc. effective February 1, 2014. McMillon had unique preparation for the job. He had held senior executive positions in Walmart's domestic operations and had presided over both the company's international operations and Sam's Club, Walmart's discount club chain. McMillon would likely need to draw upon his diverse experiences to successfully lead the company in the face of mounting challenges.

As recently as 1979, Walmart had been a regional retailer little known outside the South with 229 discount stores compared to the industry leader Kmart's 1,891 stores. In less than 25 years, Walmart had risen to become the largest U.S. corporation in sales. With more than $469 billion in revenues (see Exhibits 1 and 2), Walmart had far eclipsed not only Kmart but all retail competitors. Yet another measure of Walmart's dominance was that it accounted for approximately 45 percent of general merchandise, 30 percent of health and beauty aids, and 29 percent of non-food grocery sales[1] in the United States. *Forbes* put Walmart's success into perspective:

> *. . . all that's left for Walmart is mop-up. It already sells more toys than Toys "R" Us, more clothes than the Gap and Limited combined, and more food than Kroger. If it were its own economy, Walmart Stores would rank 30th in the world, right behind Saudi Arabia. Growing at 11 percent a year, Walmart would hit half a trillion dollars in sales by early in the next decade.*[2]

Despite its remarkable record of success, though, Walmart was not without challenges. Many

Exhibit 1 Walmart Stores, Inc., Income Statement, 2009–2013

In millions of USD (except for per share items)	2013	2012	2011	2010
Revenue	469,162.00	446,950.00	421,849.00	408,085.00
Total Revenue	469,162.00	446,950.00	421,849.00	408,085.00
Cost of Revenue, Total	352,488.00	335,127.00	314,946.00	304,106.00
Gross Profit	116,674.00	111,823.00	106,903.00	103,979.00
Selling/General/Admin. Expenses, Total	88,873.00	85,265.00	81,361.00	79,717.00
Unusual Expense (Income)	—	—	—	260
Total Operating Expense	441,361.00	420,392.00	396,307.00	384,083.00
Operating Income	27,801.00	26,558.00	25,542.00	24,002.00
Income Before Tax	25,737.00	24,398.00	23,538.00	22,118.00
Income After Tax	17,756.00	16,454.00	15,959.00	14,962.00
Minority Interest	−757	−688	−604	−513
Net Income Before Extra Items	16,999.00	15,766.00	15,355.00	14,449.00
Net Income	16,999.00	15,699.00	16,389.00	14,370.00
Income Available to Common Excl. Extra Items	16,999.00	15,766.00	15,355.00	14,449.00
Income Available to Common Incl. Extra Items	16,999.00	15,699.00	16,389.00	14,370.00
Diluted Weighted Average Shares	3,389.00	3,474.00	3,670.00	3,877.00
Diluted EPS Excluding Extraordinary Items	5.02	4.54	4.18	3.73
Dividends per Share—Common Stock Primary Issue	1.59	1.46	1.21	1.09
Diluted Normalized EPS	5.02	4.54	4.18	3.77

Exhibit 2 Walmart Stores, Inc., Balance Sheet

In millions of USD (except for per share items)	2013	2012	2011	2010
Cash and Equivalents	7,066.00	6,003.00	6,891.00	7,907.00
Cash and Short-Term Investments	7,066.00	6,003.00	6,891.00	7,907.00
Accounts Receivable—Trade, Net	6,768.00	5,937.00	5,089.00	4,144.00
Total Receivables, Net	6,768.00	5,937.00	5,089.00	4,144.00
Total Inventory	43,803.00	40,714.00	36,437.00	32,713.00
Prepaid Expenses	1,588.00	1,774.00	2,960.00	3,128.00
Other Current Assets, Total	715	547	635	140
Total Current Assets	59,940.00	54,975.00	52,012.00	48,032.00
Property/Plant/Equipment, Total—Gross	171,724.00	160,938.00	154,489.00	143,517.00
Accumulated Depreciation, Total	−55,043.00	−48,614.00	−46,611.00	−41,210.00
Goodwill, Net	20,497.00	20,651.00	16,763.00	16,126.00
Other Long-Term Assets, Total	5,987.00	5,456.00	4,129.00	3,942.00
Total Assets	203,105.00	193,406.00	180,782.00	170,407.00
Accounts Payable	38,080.00	36,608.00	33,676.00	30,451.00
Accrued Expenses	18,808.00	18,180.00	18,701.00	18,734.00
Notes Payable/Short-Term Debt	6,805.00	4,047.00	1,031.00	523.00
Current Port. of LT Debt/Capital Leases	5,914.00	2,301.00	4,991.00	4,396.00
Other Current Liabilities, Total	2,211.00	1,164.00	204.00	1,439.00
Total Current Liabilities	71,818.00	62,300.00	58,603.00	55,543.00
Long-Term Debt	38,394.00	44,070.00	40,692.00	33,231.00
Capital Lease Obligations	3,023.00	3,009.00	3,150.00	3,170.00
Total Long-Term Debt	41,417.00	47,079.00	43,842.00	36,401.00
Total Debt	54,136.00	53,427.00	49,864.00	41,320.00
Deferred Income Tax	7,613.00	7,862.00	6,682.00	5,508.00
Minority Interest	5,914.00	4,850.00	3,113.00	2,487.00
Total Liabilities	126,762.00	122,091.00	112,240.00	99,939.00
Common Stock, Total	332	342	352	378
Additional Paid-In Capital	3,620.00	3,692.00	3,577.00	3,803.00
Retained Earnings (Accumulated Deficit)	72,978.00	68,691.00	63,967.00	66,357.00
Other Equity, Total	−587	−1,410.00	586	−147
Total Equity	76,343.00	71,315.00	68,542.00	70,468.00
Total Liabilities and Shareholders' Equity	203,105.00	193,406.00	180,782.00	170,407.00
Total Common Shares Outstanding	3,314.00	3,418.00	3,516.00	3,786.00

observers believed that the company would find it increasingly difficult to sustain its remarkable record of growth (see Exhibit 3). Walmart faced a maturing market in its core business that would not likely see the growth rates it had previously enjoyed. Growth in same-store sales had declined in multiple quarters in the previous year. Many investors believed that Walmart had reached a point of saturation with its stores. Supercenters had provided significant growth for Walmart, but it was not clear how long they could deliver the company's customary growth rates. The

Exhibit 3 Walmart Sales Growth by Segment, 2011–2013 (in millions USD)

	2013			2012			2011	
	Net Sales	**Percent of Total**	**Percent Change**	**Net Sales**	**Percent of Total**	**Percent Change**	**Net Sales**	**Percent of Total**
Walmart U.S.	$274,490	58.9%	3.9%	$264,186	59.5%	1.5%	$260,261	62.1%
Walmart International	$135,201	29.0%	7.4%	$125,873	28.4%	15.2%	$125,873	26.1%
Sam's Club	$56,423	12.1%	4.9%	$3,795	12.1%	8.8%	$53,795	11.8%

company added new stores at a prodigious rate, but the new stores often cannibalized sales from nearby Walmart stores. Walmart faced problems in other business areas as well. The Walmart-owned Sam's Club warehouse stores had not measured up to Costco, their leading competitor. International operations were another challenge for Walmart. Faced with slowing growth domestically, it had tried to capitalize on international opportunities. These international efforts, however, had met with only mixed success at best.

Walmart was also a target for critics who attacked its record on social issues.[3] Walmart had been blamed for pushing production from the United States to low-wage overseas producers. Some claimed that Walmart had almost single-handedly depressed wage growth in the U.S. economy. For many, Walmart had become a symbol of capitalism that had run out of control. Indeed, *Time* magazine asked, "Will Walmart Steal Christmas?"[4] Much of the criticism directed at Walmart did not go beyond angry rhetoric. In many cases, however, Walmart had faced stiff community opposition to building new stores.

With such challenges, some investment analysts questioned whether it was even possible for a company like Walmart, with more than $469 billion in sales, to sustain its accustomed high growth rates. To do so, Walmart would have to address a number of challenges such as maturing markets, competition in discount retailing from both traditional competitors and specialty retailers, aggressive efforts by competitors to imitate Walmart's products and processes, international expansion, and increasing competition from online retailers. Indeed, some believed that Walmart would need to find new business if it were to continue its historic success.

The Discount Retail Industry

General retailing in the United States evolved dramatically during the 20th century. Before 1950, general retailing most often took the form of Main Street department stores. These stores typically sold a wide variety of general merchandise. Department stores were also different from other retailers in that they emphasized service and credit. Before World War II, few stores allowed customers to take goods directly from shelves. Instead, sales clerks served customers at store counters. Not until the 1950s did self-help department stores begin to spread. Discount retail stores also began to emerge in the late 1950s. Discount retailers emphasized low prices and generally offered less service, credit, and return privileges. Their growth was spawned by the repeal of fair trade laws in many states. Many states had passed such laws during the Depression to protect local grocers from chains such as the Atlantic & Pacific Company. The laws fixed prices so that local merchants could not be undercut on price. The repeal of these laws freed discounters to offer prices below the manufacturer's suggested retail price.

Among discount retailers, there were both general and specialty chains. General chains carried a wide assortment of hard and soft goods. Specialty retailers, on the other hand, focused on a fairly narrow range of goods such as office products or sporting goods. Specialty discount retailers such as Office Depot, Home Depot, Staples, Best Buy, and Lowe's began to enjoy widespread success in the 1980s. One result of the emergence of both general and specialty discount retailers was the decline of some of the best-known traditional retailers. Moderate-priced general retailers such as Sears and JC Penney had seen their market share decline in response to the rise of discount stores.

Value in the industry was not precisely defined, but involved price, service, quality, and convenience. One example of this value orientation was in apparel. Consumers who once shunned the private-label clothing lines found in discount stores as a source of stigma were increasingly buying labels offered by Kmart, Target, and Walmart. According to one estimate, discount stores were enjoying double-digit growth in apparel while clothing sales in department stores had decreased since the 1990s.

Another aspect of consumers' concern for value involved price. Retail consumers were less reliant on established brand names in a wide variety of goods and showed a greater willingness to purchase the private-label brands of firms such as JC Penney, Sears, Kmart, and Walmart. Convenience had also taken on greater importance for customers. As demographics shifted to include more working mothers and longer workweeks, many American workers placed a greater emphasis on fast, efficient shopping trips. More consumers desired "one-stop shopping," where a broad range of goods were available in one store to minimize the time they spent shopping. This trend accelerated in the previous decade with the spread of supercenters. Supercenters, which combined traditional discount retail stores with supermarkets under one roof, grew to more than $100 billion in sales by 2001 and blurred some of the traditional lines in retailing.

Larger firms had an advantage in discount retailing. Large size enabled firms to spread their overhead costs over more stores. Larger firms were also able to distribute their advertising costs over a broader base. Perhaps the greatest advantage of size, however, was in relationships with suppliers. Increased size led to savings in negotiating price reductions, but it also helped in other important ways. Suppliers were more likely to engage in arrangements with large store chains such as cooperative advertising and electronic data interchange (EDI) links.

The Internet posed an increasing threat to discount retailers as more people became comfortable with shopping online. Internet shopping was appealing because of the convenience and selection available, but perhaps the most attractive aspect was the competitive pricing. Some Internet retailers were able to offer steep discounts because of lower overhead costs. Additionally, customers were able to quickly compare prices between different Internet retailers. Most, if not all, major retailers sold goods via the Internet.

Large discount retailers such as Walmart derived considerable purchasing clout with suppliers because of their immense size. Even many of the company's largest suppliers gained a high proportion of their sales from Walmart (see Exhibit 4). Suppliers with more than $1 billion in sales such as Newell, Fruit of the Loom, Sunbeam, and Fieldcrest Cannon received more than 15 percent of their sales from Walmart. Many of these large manufacturers also sold a substantial proportion of their output to Kmart, Target, and other discount retailers. Walmart's purchasing clout was considerable, though, even compared to other large retailers. For example, Walmart accounted for more than 24 percent of Dial's sales, and it was estimated that it would have to double sales to its next seven largest customers to replace the sales made to Walmart.[5] Frequently, smaller manufacturers were even more reliant on the large discount retailers such as Walmart. For example, Walmart accounted for as much as 50 percent of revenues for many smaller suppliers.

Exhibit 4 Proportion of Sales That Suppliers Receive from Walmart

Company	Walmart Share of Sales
Rayovac	26%
Dial	24
Hasbro	17
Procter & Gamble	17
Newell Rubbermaid	15
Gillette	12
Fruit of the Loom	10
H.J. Heinz	10
Kimberly-Clark	10
Kraft	10

Source: Hopkins, J. (2003). "Wal-Mart's influence grows." *USA Today*, Jan. 21.

Private-label goods offered by discount stores had become much more important in recent years and presented new challenges in supplier relationships. Managing private labels required a high level of coordination between designers and manufacturers (who were often foreign). Investment in systems that could track production and inventory was also necessary.

Technology investments in sophisticated inventory management systems, state-of-the-art distribution centers, and other aspects of logistics were seen as critically important for all discount retailers. Discount retailers were spending large sums of money on computer and telecommunications technology in order to lower their costs in these areas. The widespread use of Universal Product Codes (UPCs.) allowed retailers to more accurately track inventories for shopkeeping units (SKUs) and better match inventory to demand. Discount retailers also used EDI to shorten the distribution cycle. EDI involved the electronic transmission of sales and inventory data from the registers and computers of discounters directly to suppliers' computers. Often, replenishment of inventories was triggered without human intervention. Thus, EDI removed the need for several intermediate steps in procurement such as data entry by the discounter, ordering by purchasers, data entry by the supplier, and even some production scheduling by supplier managers. Walmart was also pushing the adoption of radio frequency identification (RFID), a new technology for tracking and identifying products. RFID promised to eliminate the need for employees to scan UPC codes and would also dramatically reduce shrinkage, another term for shoplifting and employee pilferage. The implementation of RFID had not materialized in the way Walmart had envisioned and, by 2013, was still evolving in ways not forecasted by the company.

Another important aspect of managing inventory was accurate forecasting. Having the right quantity of products in the correct stores was essential to success. Stories of retailers having an abundance of snow sleds in Florida stores while stores in other areas with heavy snowfall had none were common examples of the challenges in managing inventory. Discounters used variables such as past store sales, the presence of competition, variation in seasonal demand, and year-to-year calendar changes to arrive at their forecasts.

Point-of-sale (POS) scanning enabled retailers to gain information for any purchase on the dollar amount of the purchase, category of merchandise, color, vendor, and SKU number. POS scanning, while valuable in managing inventory, was also seen as a potentially significant marketing tool. Databases of such information offered retailers the potential to "micromarket" to their customers. Upscale department stores had used the POS database marketing more extensively than discounters. Walmart, however, had used such information extensively. For example, POS data showed that customers who purchased children's videos typically bought more than one. Based on this finding, Walmart emphasized placing other children's videos near displays of hot-selling videos.

Competitors

Competition in discount retailing came from both general and specialty discount stores. Among the general discount retailers, Walmart was the largest, followed by Target and Kmart. Kmart had approximately 10 times more sales than the next largest retailers, Dollar General and ShopKo. The most formidable specialty discount retailers included office supply chains such as Office Depot with more than $10 billion in sales, Staples with approximately $24 billion, Toys "R" Us with more than $11 billion, and Best Buy in electronics with approximately $45 billion. In warehouse clubs, Costco and Sam's Club dominated. Costco was the leader with more than $99 billion in sales, followed by Sam's Club with $56 billion in revenue. BJ's Wholesale Club followed far behind with around $11 billion in sales before being acquired by a private equity firm in 2011.

Once, Walmart's largest competitor, Kmart, had experienced a long slide in performance. Kmart operated approximately 1,300 stores, about the same number it had had three years previously. Traditionally, Kmart's discount philosophy had differed from Walmart's. Kmart discount centers sought to price close to, but not necessarily lower than, Walmart's everyday low prices (EDLP). More emphasis was placed on sale items at Kmart. Pricing strategy revolved around several key items that were advertised in Kmart's 73 million advertising circulars distributed in newspapers each Sunday. These items were priced sharply lower than competitors' prices. The effective implementation of this strategy had been impeded by Kmart's difficulty in keeping shelves stocked with sale items and by Walmart's willingness to match Kmart's sale prices. An attempt to imitate Walmart's everyday low pricing strategy failed to deliver sales growth; at the same time, it squeezed margins, so Kmart returned to its traditional pricing strategy in 2003.

Kmart sought to follow Walmart's pattern in many of its activities. The company expressed a commitment to building a strong culture that emphasized performance, teamwork, and respect for individuals who, borrowing from Walmart, were referred to as associates. Establishing such a culture was particularly challenging in the midst of workforce reductions that had taken Kmart from 373,000 employees in 1990 to 307,000 at the end of 1995, and then an even more precipitous drop to 158,000 in 2004.

Target, Walmart's other large national competitor, was owned by Target Corporation, formerly Dayton Hudson Corporation, based in Minneapolis, Minnesota. In 2013, Target operated 1,763 stores, which was an increase of only 11 stores from three years earlier. This accounted for $65.4 billion in sales and $2.5 billion in profits. Target was considered an "upscale discounter." The median income of Target shoppers, at $64,000, was considerably higher than its two main competitors, and 50 percent of its customers had completed college.[7] Target attracted a more affluent clientele through a more trendy and upscale product mix and through a store ambience that differed from most discounters in aspects such as wider aisles and brighter lighting. The company also emphasized design much more in its products and had partnered with a number of designers to develop products across a broad range of apparel and housewares. Target had also introduced a proprietary credit card, the Target Guest Card, to differentiate it from other discounters. The conventional wisdom in the industry suggested that pricing at Target was generally not as low as Walmart but was lower than middle-market department stores such as JC Penney and Mervyn's. As with Walmart and Kmart, supercenters were also high on Target's list of strategic priorities. The supercenters, named Super Targets, had opened in many cities, and the company planned to aggressively grow in this area. Promotions were an important part of Target's marketing approach. Each week, more than 100 million Target advertising circulars were distributed in Sunday newspapers. Holiday promotions were also emphasized at Target. Like Kmart, Target had traditionally focused much of its effort on metropolitan areas. Enticed by the growth of large cities relative to suburbs, Target introduced a new downsized format in Chicago in 2012 and planned several other such stores dubbed City for San Francisco, Seattle, and other large cities. Target's philanthropic activities were well known. Each year, the company gave five percent of its pre-tax earnings to not-for-profit organizations—St. Jude Children's Research Hospital and local schools were perhaps Target's highest philanthropic priorities.

While Target had been an increasingly formidable competitor, many believed that the greatest competitive threat to Walmart came from a firm with no bricks and mortar stores: Amazon.com. Amazon began in 1994 as an online bookseller. Before long, Amazon offered other media products such as music CDs, movies (VHS and DVD), software, and video games. By 2013, with sales of $61 billion (in contrast, Walmart's online sales were $7.7 billion), Amazon emphasized price, selection, and convenience and sold a wide diversity of products including perhaps anything that could be purchased at a traditional discount retailer along with a seemingly inexhaustible array of products that could be purchased at the most specialized retailers. In the typical Amazon model, customers selected and purchased items online. Through technology, the company then located the product in large warehouses known as fulfillment centers. The product was then processed and sent to the customer via a third party such as UPS or FedEx. Amazon had invested heavily in its fulfillment capability. By 2013, it had about 35 large fulfillment centers spread throughout the United States with another 25 in Europe and 13 in Asia. For a flat annual fee of $79, customers could receive free two-day shipping and discounted one-day shipping rates on eligible products. Additionally, the company had made very visible moves into technology with its own line of Kindle readers and tablets. Its Prime Instant Video, with over 38,000 movies and TV episodes, competed against online firms such as Netflix and Hulu in the online distribution of media content.

Amazon also hosted a large number of third-party sellers. Customers could view products sold by these sellers, purchase the product through Amazon, and then the seller would ship to the customer. Amazon had begun giving these third-party sellers the option of warehousing their inventory in Amazon's fulfillment network.

Amazon could claim multiple advantages over bricks and mortar retailers. The firm did not have to deal with the extensive overhead involved with traditional stores. Its selection of products was vastly wider than that available in any traditional store. Yet another advantage for Amazon was that customers did not have to pay a state sales tax on many products purchased. For many shoppers, the convenience of shopping online was appealing. Like Walmart, Amazon employed an everyday low pricing strategy. There were some disadvantages to online shopping. Customers typically had to pay shipping costs and wait for products to be shipped. Amazon Prime negated the cost problem and limited the wait time as well. Online sales of consumer products were growing by as much as 20 percent a year. Brick and mortar stores such as Walmart, Best Buy, Macy's, and others were trying to close the online gap with Amazon by embracing what some described as omni-channel fulfillment or ship-from-store. In the omni-channel model, retailers would route the fulfillment of online orders through retail stores near the customer. Though promising, the omni-channel model required sophisticated technology to locate products and reliable execution from local stores in fulfilling orders, a capability generally found more in warehouses than retail outlets.

Amazon's performance offered some indication of the rapid growth in the online sale of consumer products. The company went from $24.5 billion in sales in 2009 to $34.2 billion in 2010, to $48 billion in 2011, to $61 billion in 2012. Amazon was renowned for its long-term perspective. It had clearly traded short-term profits in favor of investing in technology and infrastructure intended to help it achieve dominance in online retailing. Walmart had not been blind to the rise and importance of online retailing generally and, more specifically, the threat from Amazon. From the early days of online commerce, it had sought to build a strong position in online commerce yet lagged dramatically behind Amazon in 2013.

Walmart's History

Walmart was started in 1962 by Sam Walton. The discount retail industry was then in its infancy. Of the four new ventures in discount retailing started that year, Walmart seemed the least likely to succeed. Most Walmart stores were in northwestern Arkansas and adjacent areas of Oklahoma, Missouri, and Kansas. Walton had started his retailing career with Ben Franklin in small towns because his wife Helen did not want to live in any city with a population of more than 10,000 people. He had chosen northwestern Arkansas as a base because it allowed him to take advantage of the quail-hunting season in four states. Walmart was, in Sam Walton's words, "underfinanced and undercapitalized"[8] in the beginning. Nevertheless, Walton sought to grow Walmart as fast as he could, because he feared new competitors would preempt growth opportunities if Walmart did not open stores in new towns. After five years, Walmart had 19 stores and sales of $9 million. In contrast, Kmart had 250 stores and $800 million in sales.

Walton retained many of the practices regarding customer service and satisfaction that he had learned in the variety stores business. The central focus of Walmart, however, was on price. Walton sought to make Walmart the low-priced provider of any product it sold. As Walton said,

> *What we were obsessed with was keeping our prices below everybody else's. Our dedication to that idea was total. Everybody worked like crazy to keep the expenses down. We didn't have systems. We didn't have ordering programs. We didn't have a basic merchandise assortment. We certainly didn't have any sort of computers. In fact, when I look at it today, I realize that so much of what we did in the beginning was really poorly done. But we managed to sell our merchandise as low as we possibly could and that kept us right-side up for the first ten years .... The idea was simple: when customers thought of Walmart, they should think of low prices and satisfaction guaranteed. They could be pretty sure they wouldn't find it any cheaper anywhere else, and if they didn't like it, they could bring it back.*[9]

The other problem that plagued Walmart in its early years was finding a way to keep its costs down. Large vendors were reluctant to call on Walmart and, when they did do business with the company, they would dictate the price and quantity of what they sold. Walton described the situation, "I don't mind saying that we were the victims of a good bit of arrogance from a lot of vendors in those days. They didn't need us, and they acted that way."[10] Another problem that contributed to high costs was distribution. Distributors did not service Walmart with the same care that they did its larger competitors. Walton saw that "the only alternative was to build our own warehouse so we could buy in volume at attractive prices and store the merchandise."[11]

Walmart increased from 32 stores in 1970 to 859 stores 15 years later. For much of that time, Walmart retained its small-town focus. More than half its stores were in towns with populations of less than 25,000. Because of its small-town operations, Walmart was not highly visible to many others in the retail industry. By 1985, though, that had changed. *Forbes* named Sam Walton the richest man in America. Furthermore, Walmart had begun to expand from its small-town base in the South and had established a strong presence in several large cities. By the 1990s, it had spread throughout the United States in both large cities and small towns.

Walmart in 2013

By the beginning of 2013, Walmart's activities had spread beyond its historical roots in domestic discount centers. The number of domestic discount centers had declined to 561 from a high of 1,995 in 1996. Many discount centers had been converted to supercenters, which had increased to 3,158 stores. Walmart Supercenters combined full-line supermarkets and discount centers into one store. Walmart also operated 620 Sam's Clubs, which were warehouse membership clubs. In 1999, Walmart opened its first Neighborhood Markets, which were supermarkets, and it expanded to 286 in operation by 2013.

Operations

From its beginning, Walmart had focused on EDLP. EDLP saved on advertising costs and on labor costs because employees did not have to rearrange stock before and after sales. The company changed its traditional slogan, "Always the Lowest Price," in the 1990s to "Always Low Prices. *Always*." In late 2007, Walmart changed its tagline to "Save Money, Live Better." Despite the changes in slogan, however, Walmart continued to price goods lower than its competitors (see Exhibit 5). When faced with a decline in profits in the late 1990s, Walmart considered raising margins.[12] Instead of pricing 7 to 8 percent below competitors, some managers believed that pricing only about 6 percent below would raise gross margins without jeopardizing sales. Some managers and board members, however, were skeptical that price hikes would work at Walmart. They reasoned that Walmart's culture and identity were so closely attached to low prices that broad price increases would clash with the company's bedrock beliefs. Another concern was that competitors might seize any opportunity to narrow the gap with Walmart. While the reason was unclear, it appeared that some narrowing on price was occurring by 2008. One study showed that the price gap between Walmart and Kroger had shrunk to 7.5 percent in 2007 from 15 percent a few years earlier.[13] Some analysts worried that many shoppers would switch to other retailers as the gap narrowed.

Walmart's low prices were at least partly due to its aggressive use of technology. Walmart had pioneered the use of technology in retail operations for many years and still possessed significant advantages over its competitors. It was the leader in forging EDI links with suppliers. Its Retail Link technology gave over 3,200 vendors POS data and authorization to replace inventory for more than 3,000 stores.[14] Competitors had responded to Walmart's advantage in logistics and EDI by forming cooperative exchanges, but despite their efforts, a large gap remained between Walmart and its competitors.[15] As a result, Walmart possessed a substantial advantage in information about supply and demand, which reduced both the number of items that were either overstocked or out of stock.

Technology was only one area where Walmart exploited advantages through its relationships with suppliers. Walmart's clout was clearly evident in the payment terms it had with its suppliers. Suppliers frequently offered

Exhibit 5 Comparison of Prices at Walmart, Kmart, and Target, Nov. 2013

In millions USD Item	Walmart	Kmart	Target
Oral B Pulsar ProHealth Toothbrush	5.97	6.19	4.74
Crest ProHealth Toothpaste 6 oz.	3.62	3.99	3.79
Pantene Pro V 2-in-1 25.4 oz	5.88	7.79	5.29
Head & Shoulders Classic 14.2 oz	4.72	5.49	4.89
Edge Shave Gel 7 oz	2.27	2.79	1.89
Schick Extreme 3 8 pk	9.97	11.99	9.99
Gillette Mach 3 Disposable 3 pk	6.12	6.99	5.59
1-a-Day Women's Vitamins 100 tab	6.87	8.49	6.89
1-a-Day Energy Vitamins 50 tab	7.87	8.49	6.89
Bausch & Lomb ReNu	6.97	8.29	6.19
Advil Liquigel 40 tablets	6.48	7.29	5.34
Prestone Extended Life Antifreeze 1 gal	—	14.49	9.04
Penzoil Motor Oil 5W-30 1 qt	3.57	3.49	3.29
Armour All Glass Wipes 25	4.24	4.29	4.24
TopFlite D2 Straight Golf Balls 15	14.95	15.99	14.99
Perfect Pullup	—	99.99	99.99
Colemand Quickbed Queen	19.88	24.99	24.99
Crayola Colored Pencils 12 ct	1.88	2.59	1.99
Scott Double-Sided Tape	2.97	3.19	2.99

Some prices are sale prices.

two percent discounts to customers who paid their bills within 15 days. Walmart typically paid its bills at close to 30 days from the time of purchase but still usually received a two percent discount on the gross amount of an invoice rather than the net amount.[16] Several suppliers had attributed performance problems to Walmart's actions. Rubbermaid, for example, experienced higher raw materials costs in the 1990s that Walmart did not allow it to pass along in the form of higher prices. At the same time, Walmart gave more shelf space to Rubbermaid's lower-cost competitors. As a result, Rubbermaid's profits dropped by 30 percent and it was forced to cut its workforce by more than 1,000 employees.[17] Besides pushing for low prices, the large discounters also required suppliers to pick up an increasing amount of inventory and merchandising costs. Walmart required large suppliers such as Procter & Gamble to place large contingents of employees at its Bentonville, Arkansas, headquarters in order to service its account.

Although several companies such as Rubbermaid and the pickle vendor Vlasic had experienced dramatic downfalls largely through being squeezed by Walmart, other companies suggested that their relationship with Walmart had made them much more efficient.[18] Some critics suggested, however, that these extreme efficiency pressures had driven many suppliers to move production from the United States to nations such as China that had much lower wages. Walmart set standards for all of its suppliers in areas such as child labor and safety. A 2001 audit, however, revealed that as many as one-third of Walmart's international suppliers were in "serious violation" of the standards.[19] Walmart pursued steps to help suppliers address the violations, but it was unclear how successful these efforts were.

A *Fast Company* article on Walmart interviewed several former suppliers of the company and concluded, "To a person, all those interviewed credit Walmart with a fundamental integrity in its dealings that's unusual in the world of consumer goods, retailing, and groceries. Walmart does not cheat its suppliers, it keeps its word, it pays its bills briskly. 'They are tough people but very honest; they treat you honestly,' says Peter Campanella, a former Corning manager."[20]

At the heart of Walmart's success was its distribution system. To a large extent, it had been born out of the necessity of servicing so many stores in small towns while trying to maintain low prices. Walmart used distribution centers to achieve efficiencies in logistics. Initially, distribution centers were large facilities—the first were 72,000 square feet—that served 80 to 100 Walmart stores within a 250-mile radius. Newer distribution centers were considerably larger than the early ones and in some cases served a wider geographical radius. Walmart had far more distribution centers than any of its competitors. Cross-docking was a particularly important practice of these centers.[21] In cross-docking, goods were delivered to distribution centers and often simply loaded from one dock to another or even from one truck to another without ever sitting in inventory. Cross-docking reduced Walmart's cost of sales by 2 to 3 percent compared to competitors. Cross-docking was receiving a great deal of attention among retailers with most attempting to implement it for a greater proportion of goods. It was extremely difficult to manage, however, because of the close coordination and timing required between the store, manufacturer, and warehouse. As one supplier noted, "Everyone from the forklift driver on up to me, the CEO, knew we had to deliver on time. Not 10 minutes late. And not 45 minutes early, either . . . . The message came through clearly: you have this 30-second delivery window. Either you're there or you're out."[22] Because of the close coordination needed, cross-docking required an information system that effectively linked stores, warehouses, and manufacturers. Most major retailers were finding it difficult to duplicate Walmart's success at cross-docking.

Walmart's focus on logistics manifested itself in other ways. Before 2006, the company essentially employed two distribution networks, one for general merchandise and one for groceries. The company created High Velocity Distribution Centers in 2006 that distributed both grocery and general merchandise goods that needed more frequent replenishment. Walmart's logistics system also included a fleet of more than 2,000 company-owned trucks. It was able to routinely ship goods from distribution centers to stores within 48 hours of receiving an order. Store shelves were replenished twice a week on average in contrast to the industry average of once every two weeks.[23]

Walmart stores typically included many departments in areas such as soft goods, domestics, hard goods, stationery and candy, pharmaceuticals, records and electronics, sporting goods, toys, shoes, and jewelry. The selection of products varied from one region to another. Department managers and in some cases associates (or employees) had the authority to change prices in response to competitors. This was in stark contrast to the traditional practice of many chains where prices were centrally set at a company's headquarters. Walmart's use of technology was particularly useful in determining the mix of goods in each store. The company used historical selling data and complex models that included many variables such as local demographics to decide what items should be placed in each store.

Unlike many of its competitors, Walmart had no regional offices until 2006. Instead, regional vice presidents maintained their offices at company headquarters in Bentonville, Arkansas. The absence of regional offices was estimated to save Walmart as much as one percent of sales. Regional managers visited stores from Monday to Thursday of each week. Each Saturday at 7:30 A.M., regional vice presidents and a few hundred other managers and employees met with the firm's top managers to discuss the previous week's results and discuss different directions for the next week. Regional managers then conveyed information from the meeting to managers in the field via the videoconferencing links that were present in each store. In 2006, Walmart shifted this policy by requiring many of its 27 regional managers to live in the areas they supervised.

Aside from Walmart's impact on suppliers, it was frequently criticized for its employment practices, which critics characterized as being low in both wages and benefits. Charles Fishman acknowledged that Walmart saved customers $30 billion on groceries alone and possibly as much as $150 billion overall when its effect on competitor pricing was considered, but he estimated that while Walmart created 125,000 jobs in 2005, it destroyed 127,500.[24] Others agreed that Walmart's employment and supplier practices resulted in negative externalities on employees, communities, and taxpayers. Harvard professor Pankaj Ghemawat responded to Fishman by calculating that—based on Fishman's numbers—Walmart created customer savings ranging from $12 million to $60 million for each job lost.[25] He also argued that, because Walmart operated more heavily in lower-income areas of the poorest one-third of the United States, low-income customers were much more likely to benefit from Walmart's lower prices. Another criticism of Walmart was that it consistently drove small local retailers out of business when it introduced new stores in small towns and that employees in such rural areas were increasingly at the mercy of Walmart, essentially redistributing wealth from these areas to Bentonville. Jack and Suzy Welch defended Walmart by pointing out that employees in these areas were better off after a Walmart opened:

> *In most small towns the storeowner drove the best car, lived in the fanciest house, and belonged to the country club. Meanwhile, employees weren't exactly sharing the wealth. They rarely had life insurance or health benefits and certainly did not receive much in the way of training or big salaries. And few of these storeowners had plans for growth or expansion. . . a killer for employees seeking life-changing careers.*[26]

Sam's Club

A notable exception to Walmart's dominance in discount retailing was in the warehouse club segment. Despite significant efforts by Walmart's Sam's Club, Costco was the established leader. Sam's Club had almost exactly the same number of stores as Costco—620 to 622—yet, Costco still reported almost twice the sales—$105 billion versus $54 billion for Sam's. Costco stores averaged considerably more revenue per store than Sam's Club (see Exhibit 6).

To the casual observer, Costco and Sam's Clubs appeared to be very similar. Both charged small membership fees, and both were "warehouse" stores that sold goods from pallets. The goods were often packaged or bundled into larger quantities than typical retailers offered. Beneath these similarities, however, were important differences. Costco focused on more upscale small business owners and consumers while Sam's, following Walmart's pattern, had positioned itself more to the mass middle market. Relative to Costco, Sam's was also concentrated more in smaller cities.

Consistent with its more upscale strategy, Costco stocked more luxury and premium-branded items than Sam's Club had traditionally done. This changed somewhat when Sam's began to stock more high-end merchandise after the 1990s, but some questioned whether or not its typical customers demanded such items. Despite the focus on pricier goods, Costco still focused intensely on managing costs and keeping prices down. Costco set a goal of 10 percent margins and capped markups at 14 percent (compared with the usual 40 percent markup by department stores). Managers were discouraged from exceeding the margin goals.

Some analysts claimed that Sam's Club's lackluster performance was a result of a copycat strategy. Costco was the first of the two competitors to sell fresh meat, produce, and gasoline and to introduce a premium private label for many goods. In each case, Sam's followed suit two to four years later.

> *"By looking at what Costco did and trying to emulate it, Sam's didn't carve out its own unique strategy," says Michael Clayman, editor of the trade newsletter Warehouse Club Focus. And at least one of the "me too" moves made things worse. Soon after Costco and Price Club merged in 1993, Sam's bulked up by purchasing Pace warehouse clubs from Kmart. Many of the 91 stores were marginal operations in marginal locations. Analysts say that Sam's Club management became distracted as it tried to integrate the Pace stores into its system.*[27]

To close the gap against Costco, Walmart in 2003 started to integrate the activities of Sam's Club and Walmart more. Buyers for the two coordinated their efforts to get better prices from suppliers.

Culture

Perhaps the most distinctive aspect of Walmart was its culture. To a large extent, Walmart's culture was an extension of Sam Walton's philosophy and was rooted in the early

Exhibit 6 Costco Versus Sam's Club

	Costco	Sam's Club
Year founded	1983	1983
U.S. revenues	$99.1 billion	$56.4 billion
Number of stores	622	620
Presidents (or equivalents, since founding)	2	12
Membership cardholders	70.2 million	47 million
Members' average salary	$77,000/$74,000/$96,000	N.A.
Annual membership fees	$55	$40
Average sales per square foot	$814 (2009)	$586 (2009)
Average sales per store	$168.8 million	$87.1 million
Starting hourly wage	$11.50	N.A.
Employee turnover per year	17% (2006)	44% (Walmart, 2006)
Private label (as % of sales)	Approximately 20%	Approximately 10%

experiences and practices of Walmart. The Walmart culture emphasized values such as thriftiness, hard work, innovation, and continuous improvement. As Walton wrote,

> *Because wherever we've been, we've always tried to instill in our folks the idea that we at Walmart have our own way of doing things. It may be different and it may take some folks a while to adjust to it at first. But it's straight and honest and basically pretty simple to figure it out if you want to. And whether or not other folks want to accommodate us, we pretty much stick to what we believe in because it's proven to be very, very successful.*[28]

Walmart's thriftiness was consistent with its obsession with controlling costs. One observer joked that, "the Walmart folks stay at Mo 3, where they don't even leave the light on for you."[29] This was not, however, far from the truth. Walton told of early buying trips to New York where several Walmart managers shared the same hotel room and walked everywhere they went rather than use taxis. One of the early managers described how these early trips taught managers to work hard and keep costs low:

> *From the very beginning, Sam was always trying to instill in us that you just didn't go to New York and roll with the flow. We always walked everywhere. We never took cabs. And Sam had an equation for the trips: expenses should never exceed one percent of our purchases, so we would all crowd in these little hotel rooms somewhere down around Madison Square Garden. . . . We never finished up until about twelve-thirty at night, and we'd all go out for a beer except Mr. Walton. He'd say, "I'll meet you at breakfast at six o'clock." And we'd say, "Mr. Walton, there's no reason to meet that early. We can't even get into the buildings that early." And he'd just say, "We'll find something to do."*[30]

The roots of Walmart's emphasis on innovation and continuous improvement can also be seen in Walton's example.

Walton emphasized always looking for ways to improve. Walmart managers were encouraged to critique their own operations. Managers met regularly to discuss their store operations. Lessons learned in one store were quickly spread to other stores. Walmart managers also carefully analyzed the activities of their competitors and tried to borrow practices that worked well. Walton stressed the importance of observing what other firms did well rather than what they did wrong. Another way in which Walmart had focused on improvement from its earliest days was in information and measurement. Long before Walmart had any computers, Walton would personally enter measures on several variables for each store into a ledger he carried with him. Information technology enabled Walmart to extend this emphasis on information and measurement.

International Operations

Walmart's entry into the international retail arena had been somewhat recent. As late as 1992, Walmart's entire international operations consisted of only 162,535 square feet of retail space in Mexico. By 2013, however, international sales contributed nearly 30 percent of the company's sales. With growth rates of 7.4 percent in sales and 8.3 percent in operating income, Walmart's international growth exceeded that of its domestic operations. Although it was the company's fastest-growing division—going from about $59 billion in sales in 2006 to more than $135 billion in 2013—Walmart's performance in international markets had been mixed, or as *Forbes* put it, "Overseas, Walmart has won some—and lost a lot."[31] Only a few years earlier, more than 80 percent of Walmart's international revenue came from only three countries: Canada, Mexico, and the United Kingdom.

Walmart had tried a variety of approaches and faced a diverse set of challenges in the different countries it entered. Entry into international markets had ranged from greenfield development to franchising, joint ventures, and acquisitions. Each country that Walmart had entered had presented new and unique challenges. In China, Walmart had to deal with a backward supply chain. In Japan, it had to negotiate an environment that was hostile to large chains and protective of its small retailers. Strong foreign competitors were the problem in Brazil and Argentina. Labor unions had plagued Walmart's entry into Germany along with unforeseen difficulties in integrating acquisitions. Mistakes in choosing store locations had hampered the company in South Korea and Hong Kong.

Walmart approached international operations with much the same philosophy it had used in the United States. "We're still very young at this, we're still learning,"[32] stated John Menzer, former chief executive of Walmart International. Menzer's approach was to have country presidents make decisions. His thinking was that it would facilitate the faster implementation of decisions. Each country president made decisions regarding his or her own sourcing, merchandising, and real estate. Menzer concluded, "Over time all you really have is speed. I think that's our most important asset."[33]

In most countries, entrenched competitors responded vigorously to Walmart's entry. For example, Tesco, the United Kingdom's biggest grocer, responded by opening supercenters. In China, Lianhua, and Huilan, the two largest retailers, merged in 2003 into one state-owned entity named the Bailan Group. Walmart was also not alone among major international retailers in seeking new growth in South America and Asia. One international competitor, the French retailer Carrefour, was already the leading retailer in Brazil and Argentina. Carrefour expanded into China in the late 1990s with a hypermarket in Shanghai. In Asia, Makro, a Dutch wholesale club retailer, was the regional leader. Both of the European firms were viewed as able, experienced competitors. The Japanese retailer, Yaohan, moved its headquarters from Tokyo to Hong Kong with the aim of becoming the world's largest retailer. Helped by the close relationship between Chairman Kazuo Wada and Mao's successor Deng Xiaoping, Yaohan was the first foreign retail firm to receive a license to operate in China and planned to open more than 1,000 stores there. Like Walmart, these international firms were motivated to expand internationally by slowing down growth in their own domestic markets. Some analysts feared that the pace of expansion by these major retailers was faster than the rate of growth in the market and could result in a price war. Like Walmart, these competitors had also found difficulty in moving into international markets and adapting to local differences. Both Carrefour and Makro had experienced visible failures in their international efforts. Folkert Schukken, chairman of Makro, noted this challenge, "We have trouble selling the same toilet paper in Belgium and Holland." The chairman of Carrefour, Daniel Bernard, agreed, "If people think that going international is a solution to their problems at home, they will learn by spilling their blood. Global retailing demands a huge investment and gives no guarantee of a return."[34]

Walmart sought aggressive growth in its international operations. The company added 497 units during 2013. Walmart's early activities in a country typically involved acquisitions, but it had emphasized organic growth more in recent years.

Looking Ahead

Walmart CEO Doug McMillon faced the daunting challenge of achieving the company's accustomed growth rates despite its enormous size. A five percent organic growth rate would require the firm to add the equivalent of a firm ranking 129th in the *Fortune* 500 each year. To put that into perspective, the company's growth in revenues would need to nearly equal the total sales of Nike and exceed the sales of companies as large as Xerox and Kimberly Clark. What strategic priorities would allow Walmart to achieve that amount of growth? Or would the company need to adjust its aspirations?

End Notes

1 Standard and Poor's Industry Surveys. *Retailing*, February 1998.
2 Upbin, B. "Wall-to-wall Wal-Mart." *Forbes*, April 12, 2004.
3 Nordlinger, J. (2004). "The new colossus: Wal-Mart is America's store, and the world's and its enemies are sadly behind." *National Review*, April 19, 2004.
4 Ibid.
5 Fishman, C. (2003). "The Wal-Mart you don't know." *Fast Company*, December 2003.
6 Berner, R. (2004). "The next Warren Buffett?" *BusinessWeek*, November 22, 2004.
7 Standard and Poor's Industry Surveys. (1998). *Retailing: General*, February 5, 1998.
8 Walton, S. (with J. Huey). (1993). *Sam Walton: Made in America*. New York: Doubleday, p. 63.
9 Ibid., pp. 64–65. 10. Ibid., p. 66.
10 Ibid., p. 66.
11 (1982). *Forbes*, August 16, p. 43.
12 Pulliam, S. (1996). "Wal-Mart considers raising prices, drawing praise from analysts, but concern from board." *Wall Street Journal*, March 8, 1996, p. C2.
13 Bianco, A. (2007). "Wal-Mart's midlife crisis." *BusinessWeek*, April 30, 2007.
14 Standard and Poor 's Industry Surveys. (1998). *Retailing: General*, February 5, 1998.
15 Useem, J. (2003). "America's most admired companies." *Fortune*, February 18, 2003.
16 Schifrin, M. (1996). "The big squeeze." *Forbes*, March 11, 1996.
17 Ibid.
18 Fishman, C. (2003). "The Wal-Mart you don't know." *Fast Company*, December 2003.
19 Walmart website.
20 Fishman, C. (2003). "The Wal-Mart you don't know." *Fast Company*, December 2003, p. 73.
21 Stalk, G., P. Evans, and L. E. Schulman. (1992). "Competing on capabilities: The new rules of corporate strategy." *Harvard Business Review*, March/April 1992, pp. 57–58.
22 Fishman, C. (2003). "The Wal-Mart you don't know." *Fast Company*, December 2003, p. 73.

23 Stalk G., P. Evans, and L. E. Schulman. (1992). "Competing on capabilities: The new rules of corporate strategy." *Harvard Business Review*, March/April 1992, pp. 57–58.
24 Fishman, C. (2006). "Wal-Mart and the decent society: Who knew that shopping was so important." *Academy of Management Perspectives*, August 2006.
25 Ghemawat, P. (2006). "Business, society, and the 'Wal-Mart effect." *Academy of Management Perspectives*, August 2006.
26 Welch, J., and S. Welch. (2006). "What's right about Wal-Mart." *BusinessWeek*, May 1, 2006, p. 112.
27 Helyar, J. (2003). "The only company Wal-Mart fears." *Fortune*, November 24, 2003, p. 158.
28 Walton, S. (with J. Huey). (1993). *Sam Walton: Made in America*. New York: Doubleday, p. 85.
29 Loeb, M. (1994). "Editor's desk: The secret of two successes." *Fortune*, May 2, 1994.
30 Walton, S. (with J. Huey). (1993). *Sam Walton: Made in America*. New York: Doubleday, p. 84.
31 Upbin, B. (2004). "Wall-to-wall Wal-Mart." *Forbes*, April 12, 2004.
32 Ibid.
33 Ibid.
34 Rapoport, C. (1995). "Retailers go global." *Fortune*, February 20, 1995.

Case 1-2: Harlequin Enterprises: The Mira Decision*[1]

IVEY | Ivey Publishing

Richard Ivey School of Business
The University of Western Ontario

During June 1993, Harlequin management was deciding whether or not to launch MIRA, a new line of single-title women's fiction novels. With the increased popularity of single-title women's fiction, Harlequin's leading position as the world's largest romance publisher was being threatened. While Harlequin was the dominant and very profitable producer of series romance novels, research indicated that many customers were reading as many single-title romance and women's fiction books as series romances. Facing a steady loss of share in a growing total women's fiction market, Harlequin convened a task force in December 1992 to study the possibility of relaunching a single-title women's fiction program. Donna Hayes, vice-president of direct marketing, stated:

> *Industry trends reveal that demand for single-title women's fiction continues to grow while demand for series romance remains stable. Our strengths lie in series romance . . . by any account, launching MIRA (single-title) will still be a challenge for us. How do we successfully launch a single-title women's fiction program?*

Tentatively named "MIRA," Harlequin's proposed single-title program would focus exclusively on women's fiction. Management hoped MIRA's launch would provide the opportunity to continue Harlequin's history of strong revenue growth.

Hayes, leader of the MIRA team, knew this was a significant decision for Harlequin. Several years earlier an attempt at single-title publishing—Worldwide Library—had failed. Before going to her executive group for approval, Hayes thought about the decisions the company faced if it wished to enter single-title women's fiction publishing: What were the growth and profitability implications if Harlequin broadened its scope from series romance to single-title women's fiction? What fundamental changes would have to be made to Harlequin's current business model? Did the company have the necessary resources and capabilities to succeed in this new arena? If the company proceeds, how should it go about launching MIRA?

The Publishing Industry[2]

Apart from educational material, traditional single-title book publishing was typically a high-risk venture. Each book was a new product with all the risks attendant on any new product introduction. The risks varied with the author's reputation, the subject matter, and thus the predictability of the market's response. Among the numerous decisions facing the publisher were selecting manuscripts out of the thousands submitted each year, deciding how many copies to print, and deciding how to promote the book.

Insiders judged one key to success in publishing was the creative genius needed to identify good young authors among the hundreds of would-be writers, and then publish and develop them through their careers. Years ago, Sol Stein of Stein and Day Publishers had commented, "Most successful publishers are creative editors at heart and contribute more than risk capital and marketing expertise to the books they publish. If a publisher does not add value to what he publishes, he's a printer, not a publisher."

Traditional single-title publishers allowed distributors 50 percent margins (from which the retailer's margin would come).[3] Some other typical costs included royalty payments of more than 12 percent, warehouse and handling costs of 4 percent, and selling expenses at 5.5 percent. Advertising generally required 6 percent and printing costs[4] required another 12 percent. The remainder was earnings before indirect overhead. Typically, indirect overhead accounted for

---

* Ken Mark prepared this case under the supervision of Professors Rod White and Mary Crossan solely to provide material for class discussion. The authors do not intend to illustrate either effective or ineffective handling of a managerial situation. The authors may have disguised certain names and other identifying information to protect confidentiality.

two percent of the retail price of a book. Because of author advances, pre-publication, promotion, and fixed costs of printing, break-even volumes were significant. And if the publisher failed to sell enough books, the losses could be substantial. Harlequin's core business, series romance fiction, was significantly different from traditional single-title publishing.

Harlequin Enterprises Limited

The word *romance* and the name Harlequin had become synonymous over the last half-century. Founded in 1949, Harlequin began applying its revolutionary approach to publishing—a packaged, consumer-goods strategy—in 1968 shortly after acquiring the publishing business of U.K.-based Mills & Boon. Each book was part of an identifiable product line, consistently delivering the expected benefit to the consumer. With a growth rate of 25 percent per year during the 1970s, Harlequin became the world's largest publisher of women's series romance fiction. It was during this time that Torstar, a newspaper publisher, acquired all of Harlequin Enterprises Ltd.

Over the years, many book publishers had attempted to enter Harlequin's segment of the industry. All had eventually withdrawn. Only once had Harlequin's dominance in series romance fiction been seriously challenged. The "romance wars" began in 1980 when Harlequin took over U.S. distribution of its series products from Simon & Schuster (S&S), a large single-title publisher with established paperback distribution. Subsequently, S&S began publishing series romance fiction under the Silhouette imprint. After several years, a truce was negotiated between Harlequin and S&S. Harlequin acquired Silhouette, S&S's series romance business, and S&S got a 20-year deal as Harlequin's sole U.S. distributor for series fiction.

During the late 1980s and early 1990s, growth in the series market slowed. Harlequin was able to maintain revenues by publishing longer and more expensive series products and generally raising prices. However, as shown in Table 1, global unit volume was no longer growing.

Harlequin's Target Market and Products

Harlequin books were sold in more than 100 international markets in more than 23 languages around the world. Along with romance fiction, Harlequin participated in the series mystery and male action-adventure markets under its Worldwide Library and Gold Eagle imprints. Harlequin had an estimated 20 million readers in North America and 50 million readers around the world.

With a median age of 41, the Harlequin's romance series reader was likely to be married, well-educated, and working outside the home. More than half of Harlequin readers spent at least three hours reading per week. Harlequin series readers were brand loyal; a survey indicated four out of five readers would continue to buy Harlequin books in the next year. Larry Heisey, Harlequin's former chief executive officer and chairman, expanded on the value of Harlequin's products; "I think our books are so popular because they provide relaxation and escape . . . . We get many letters from people who tell us how much these books mean to them."

While Harlequin had advertised its series product on television, current marketing efforts centered on print media. Harlequin advertised in leading women's magazines such as *Cosmopolitan*, *Glamour*, *Redbook*, and *Good Housekeeping*, and general interest magazines such as *People*. The print advertisement usually featured one of Harlequin's series products and also promoted the company's brands.

Romance Series Product: Well Defined and Consistent

Under the Harlequin and Silhouette brands, Harlequin published 13 different series with 64 titles each month. Each series was distinctly positioned, featuring a particular genre (e.g., historical romances) or level of explicitness. Isabel Swift, editorial director of Silhouette, described the different types of series books published by Harlequin:

> *Our different lines deliver different promises to our readers. For example, Harlequin Temptation's tagline is sassy, sexy, and seductive, promising that each*

Table 1 Total Unit Sales (in $000s)

Year	1988	1989	1990	1991	1992	1993
Operating Revenue	344,574	326,539	348,358	357,013	417,884	443,825
Operating Profit	48,142	56,217	57,769	52,385	61,842	62,589
Total Unit Sales	202	191	196	193	205	199

story will deliver a sexy, fun, contemporary romance between one man and one woman, whereas the Silhouette Romance title, in comparison, is a tender read within a framework of more traditional values.

Overall, the product portfolio offered a wide variety of stories to capture readers' interests. For the positioning of Harlequin's series, see Exhibit 1. Sold in more than a dozen countries. Harlequin had the ability to publish series books worldwide. The average retail price of a Harlequin series novel was $4.40,[5] significantly less than the $7 retail price for the typical single-title paperback novel, and much less than the $15 to $25 for longer, hardcover titles by best-selling authors.

Harlequin's series romance product was fundamentally different from that of traditional single-title publishers: content, length, artwork size, basic formats, and print were all well-defined to ensure a consistent product. Each book was not a new product, but rather an addition to a clearly defined product line. Unlike single-title books, Harlequin's series products had a common format. They measured 105 millimeters by 168 millimeters and fit neatly into specially

Exhibit 1 Harlequin/Silhouette Series Positioning Scales

Source: Company files.

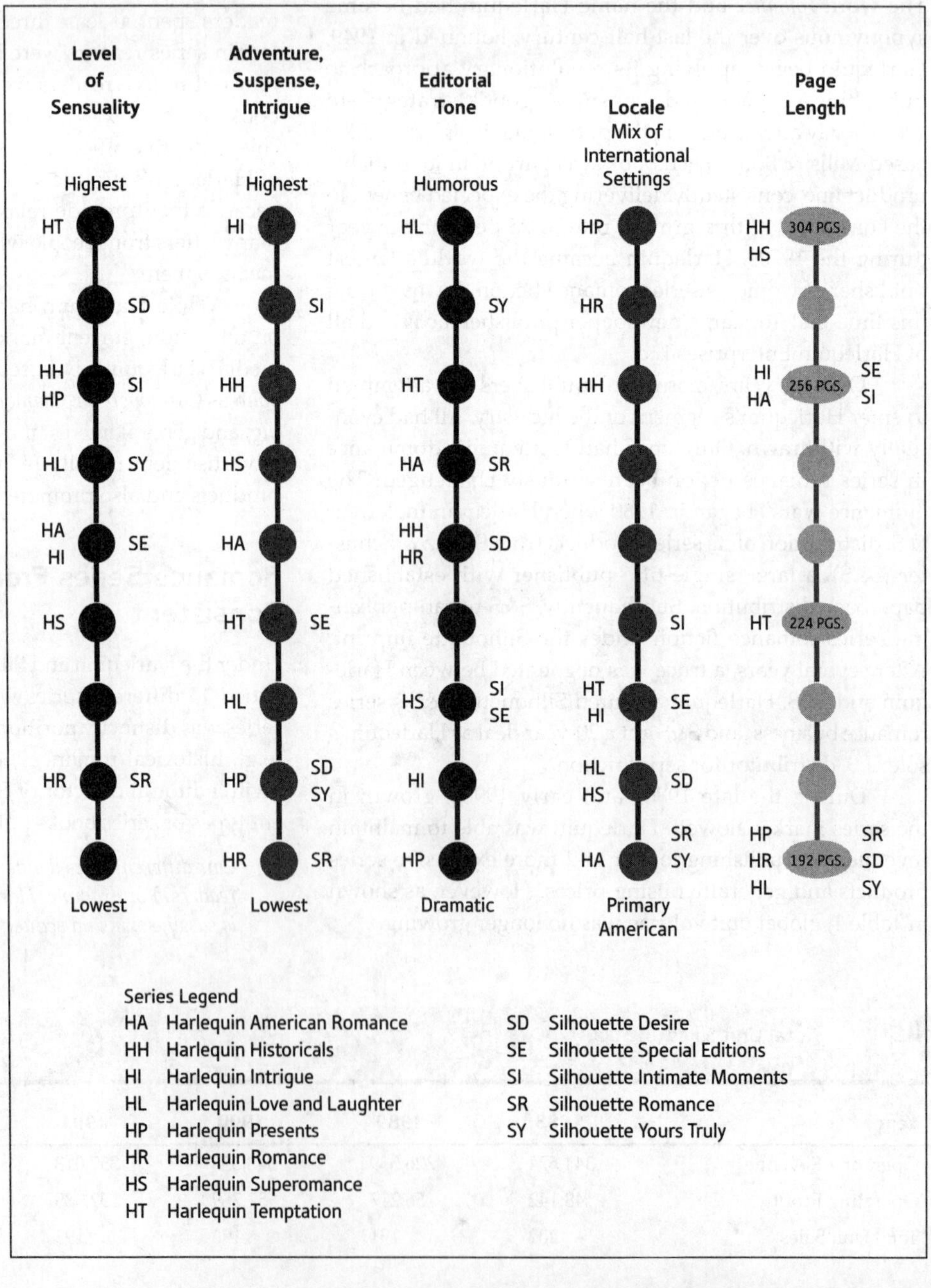

designed racks located primarily in supermarkets and drugstores. Most product lines were 192 to 256 pages in length; some were up to 304 pages in length. Cover designs differed slightly by product line and country, but the look and feel was similar (see Exhibit 2).

Harlequin provided prospective series romance authors with plot, style, and book length guidelines. However, crafting the stories still demanded skill and work. As David Galloway, chief executive officer of Torstar, Harlequin's parent company, and the former head of Harlequin observed:

> *The books are quite simply good stories. If they weren't, we wouldn't be getting the repeat purchases we do. A lot of writers think they can dash off a Harlequin, but they can't. We've had submissions from Ph.D.'s in English who can certainly write but they can't tell a story.*

To ensure a consistent product emerged, Harlequin's editors assessed many elements, including plot, story line, main character(s), setting, percentage of romance in the plot, level of realism, level of fantasy, sensuality, social and/or individual problems, happy ending, and reading impact. Even though many different authors contributed to series romance, Harlequin's editors ensured a consistent finished product, satisfying the needs of their loyal series romance readers. The consequences of this uniformity were significant. The reader was buying a Harlequin novel, and advertising promoted the Harlequin brands rather than a particular book or author.

Bookstores were not the primary channel for series romance novels. Most retail purchases were made at supermarkets or drugstores and increasingly mass merchandisers

Exhibit 2 Typical Harlequin Series Romance Products

Source: Company files.

like Walmart. But many avid Harlequin readers got the product delivered to their home every month through Harlequin's direct mail service. The standardized size and format made warehousing and distribution more efficient. In addition, the product's consistency enabled standing order distribution to retail. As Pam Laycock, director of new product development, explained:

> *A major contributor to our success as a series publisher is our standing order distribution. Each series is distributed to a retail location in a predetermined configuration—for example in a series where we publish four titles per month, a retailer may take six copies per title and this level of distribution is generally agreed upon and maintained for the entire year. This approach enables us to more accurately predict monthly print quantities and achieve significant print cost effectiveness.*

Orders (and sales) for conventional single-title books were not as predictable. Another significant difference was that series romance books were part of Harlequin's standing order distribution plan. And more like magazines, they were displayed on retail shelves for four weeks. Harlequin's distributors then removed and returned any unsold books, and replaced them with the next month's offerings. By comparison, single-title books were typically displayed at retail from 6 to 12 months or more.

Harlequin's series romance business did not generate or even encourage best-sellers. "Best-sellers (in series romance) would ruin our system," a Harlequin insider stated. "Our objective is consistency in volume. We have no winners and no losers." Unsold books could be returned to the publisher for credit. A consequence of Harlequin's even and predictable sales was that order regulation and returns could be more easily optimized to maximize the contribution to profits.

A comparison of Harlequin's series business model and the operations of traditional "one-off" publishers is presented in Exhibit 3.

With a consistent quality product, standing orders, predictable retail traffic patterns, and the ability to produce and deliver books at low costs, Harlequin had achieved great success. Harlequin's series romance business had consistently earned a return on sales of 15 percent. As shown in Exhibit 4, this figure compared favorably with larger traditional publishers.

Loriana Sacilotto, director of retail marketing, explained why Harlequin outperformed other traditional single-title publishers:

> *There are a variety of reasons why other publishers do not achieve the same margins we enjoy. The main reason is that they are broad in their publishing focus whereas we focus on women's fiction. They don't have the same reader recognition, trust and relationships. We invest in it.*

Harlequin Business System

The Global Author/Editor Team Harlequin had established a strong level of reader trust and brand equity by consistently delivering quality content. Editors in three acquisition centers in Toronto, New York, and London were responsible for working closely with 1,300-plus authors to

Exhibit 3 Comparing Harlequin's Series Business Model and a Traditional Publisher's

	Harlequin Series	Single-Title Publisher
Editorial	Emphasizes consistency within established guidelines	Requires separate judgment on potential consumer demand for each manuscript
Rights	Uses standardized contract	Can be a complex process, involving subrights, hard/soft deals, advances, and tying up authors for future books
Author Management	Less dependent on specific authors	Vulnerable to key authors changing publisher
Production	Uses consistent format with focus on efficiency	Emphasizes package, size, and format—cost control secondary
Marketing	Builds the imprint/series	Builds each title/author
Distribution	Supermarkets, drugstores, mass merchandisers, big-box bookstores.	Bookstores (all types)
	Large direct mail	Book clubs and mass merchandisers
Selling	Emphasizes servicing, rack placement, and order regulation	Cover, in-store placement, critical reviews, special promotional tactics (e.g., author signings)
Order Regulation/ Information Systems	Utilizes very sophisticated shipping and returns handling procedures	Historically has not received much attention, and hence, is not as sophisticated

Exhibit 4 Comparison of Harlequin's Performance with Traditional Publishers—1993 (in millions of dollars)

	Harlequin[a]	Simon and Schuster[b]	Harper/Avon[c]
Sales Revenue	417.8	1,929.0	1,210.4
Operating Profit	61.8	218.4	160.8
Identifiable Assets	319.2	2,875.8	2,528.0
R.O.S.	14.8%	11.3%	13.2%
R.O.I.A.	19.4%	7.6%	6.4%

[a]Canadian dollars
[b]U.S. dollars (Cdn$1.20 = US$1)
[c]Australian dollars (Cdn$0.80 = AUD$1)

develop and publish more than 1,000 new titles annually. In addition to the work of its regular writers, Harlequin received approximately 30,000 unsolicited manuscripts per year. Typically, about 100 of these were accepted in any given year.

Series authors received royalties of 13 percent of retail book price. Harlequin's typical series authors had more than 100,000 of each of their books distributed worldwide.

Harlequin's series romance product focused solely on front-list sales. In the publishing world, *front-list* sales refers to the first print runs of a book supporting its initial market launch. *Back-list* refers to books reprinted and reissued years after the book's initial run (often to support an author's subsequent books). Harlequin's series romance novels—unlike a traditional publisher's single-title books—were not available on back-list. However, Harlequin retained these rights.

Printing was a highly competitive business and Harlequin subcontracted its requirements. Costs per series book were typically $0.44 per book compared to the competitors' average costs of $0.88 per single-title soft cover book.

Distribution, Selling, and Promotion With its standing orders, Harlequin's distribution costs per book were $0.18, with selling expenses at an average of $0.09 per book. Because it was the dominant player in series romance, Harlequin had relatively low advertising and promotion costs—about $0.22 per book.

In Canada, Harlequin had its own distribution. Elsewhere in the world, independent distributors were employed. In the United States, Pocketbooks, the sales division of Simon & Schuster, a large traditional publisher, handled Harlequin's series romance books. Supermarkets, drugstores, discount department stores, and mass merchandisers accounted for 70 percent of North American retail sales. Specialty big-box bookstores like Barnes and Noble and other chains and independent bookstores accounted for the remainder of retail sales. Globally, Harlequin's products were in over 250,000 retail outlets. Eighty thousand of these outlets were in North America; almost 50,000 of these were supermarkets and drugstores. Harlequin's series products were in 70 percent of supermarkets, but only 55 percent of bookstores. In Europe, kiosks and tobacconists accounted for the largest proportion of retail outlets.

The direct channel handled direct-to-reader book sales. Harlequin's "Reader Service" book club was an important source of sales and profits. Investing in advertising to acquire readers, this direct mail operation offered frequent Harlequin readers the possibility of purchasing every book the company published, delivered right to their doorstep. In the United States, six books were sold through the book club for every 10 sold at retail. Furthermore, a book sold through the book club yielded Harlequin the full cover price, whereas a book sold at retail netted the company approximately half the retail price, and required advertising, distribution costs, and the acceptance of returns from retailers.

Rise of Single-Title Romance

The proliferation of titles and authors during the "Romance Wars" had resulted in the emergence of single-titles as a significant factor in the women's romance fiction market. Exhibit 5 provides the sales breakdown for romance novels.

In an attempt to capitalize on readers' growing appetite for single-titles, Harlequin launched Worldwide Library in 1986, its first single-title publishing program. This move also gave Harlequin's more accomplished series authors another outlet. Laycock commented:

> *Several authors who began their writing careers with Harlequin writing series romance wanted broader opportunities—opportunities that they saw in the single-title women's fiction publishing arena. Prior to the launch of Worldwide Library, Harlequin didn't have publishing opportunities to meet the desires of these authors. As a result, authors would seek out competitive publishers to support their single-title works.*

Exhibit 5 Romance Novel Sales in North America (millions of units)

	1985	1986	1987	1988	1989	1990
Harlequin series romance	77	79	80	82	83	85
Other romance series publishers	12	12	13	13	14	14
Single-title romance books by other publishers	72	79	86	94	102	112
Total romance books	**161**	**170**	**179**	**189**	**199**	**211**

Exhibit 6 Range of Worldwide Titles (1987)

Book Title	Type/Genre	Unit Sales Data	Harlequin Series Author?
Longest Pleasure	Romance	304,000	Yes
Quarantine	Horror	62,000	No
Eve of Regression	Psychological Thriller	55,000	No
War Moon	Suspense	72,000	No
Illusion	Psychological Suspense	35,000	No
Dream Escape	Romance	297,000	Yes
Alien Planet	Science Fiction	71,000	No

Exhibit 7 Monthly Single-Title Romance Output Analysis North American Market

Single-Title Romance by Category	1985	1989	1991
Contemporary	2	6	12
Historical	22	37	43
Regency	6	8	17
Total	**30**	**51**	**72**
By Publisher			
Zebra (Kensington Publishing)	5	15	21
Bantam/Dell	2	2	8
Diamond	0	0	4
Harper Paperbacks	0	0	3
Avon	4	5	6
Jove	2	2	4
Leisure Books	3	3	5
NAL/Signet	6	7	8
Pocket Books (Simon and Schuster)	1	6	3
Ballantine/Fawcett, Onyx, SMP	4	7	7
Warner Books/Popular Library	3	4	3
Total	**30**	**51**	**72**

Source: Company files.

By 1988, Worldwide was shut down as a result of several problems. "Worldwide could never decide if it was a romance program, a women's fiction program, or a general fiction program," a Harlequin insider commented. Exhibit 6 illustrates a list of typical titles published at Worldwide.

With the shutdown of Worldwide Library, popular authors moved to other publishers. As shown in Exhibit 7, other publishers continued to exploit the popularity of single-title romance novels.

Eager to find ways to grow its publishing business, Harlequin's management reexamined the publishing market. A broader analysis revealed that although Harlequin's series romance had captured well over 80 percent of the North American series romance market by 1990, Harlequin's estimated share of the North American *women's fiction* market was only about five percent. Table 2 provides a breakdown of the women's fiction market.

There was substantial overlap in the readership of series romance fiction and other fiction. Mark Mailman, vice president of market research and analysis, added:

> *One compelling reason to get into single-title publishing is that when we look at our research on customers, they're reading 20 Harlequin books and 20 single-title books from other publishers. We have an opportunity to take a greater share of that market.*

Table 2 North American Women's Fiction Market Size Estimate, 1993 (as a percentage of overall segment sizes in US$ millions)

	General Fiction	Romance	Mystery	Sci-Fi	Total Fiction
Total Segment Size	2,222	1,220	353	476	4,271
Estimated Women's Fiction Share of Segment	60%	100%	60%	38%	69%

Harlequin's Single-Title Task Force

Faced with slow or no growth in series romance, a Harlequin task force convened in 1992 to study the feasibility of launching a new women's fiction single-title program. To begin, they examined why Worldwide had failed and concluded that overall lack of success was attributable to: editorial parameters that were too broad; less than optimal North American retail distribution; very few Worldwide titles distributed through the direct-to-reader channel; global support for the program was not timely and universal; and the selection of authors and titles was unsuccessful. The task force report stated:

> *In the past few years, sell-through efficiencies in the supermarket channels are not as great as the sell-through efficiencies in both mass merchandisers and bookstores. The more efficient retailer knew that the consumer was spending her discretionary reading dollar to buy a diversity of romantic reads, including those that had previously been thought of as mainstream.*
>
> *Since a single-title strategy requires a single-title solicitation from the sales force and more expensive single-title packaging, two of Harlequin's strategic lynchpins of our earlier decades have to be rethought (for single-title): standing order program and same format production. However, Harlequin can still capitalize on its global base and its ability to distribute widely to points of purchase that women visit on a regular basis.*

MIRA Launch Decision

The task force was preparing its recommendation for MIRA, Harlequin's proposed women's fiction single-title program. The addition of single titles would make a welcome contribution to overhead costs. Currently, indirect overhead costs per series novel were $0.09 per book. Because infrastructure was already in place, it was estimated that MIRA novels would not incur additional indirect overhead costs. Printing costs for single-titles were expected to be $0.71 per book (350 pages on average). Estimated advertising and promotional costs for new single-titles were six percent of (the higher) retail price.

Author Management

In the single-title market, authors were categorized into three groups, based on their sales potential: brand new, mid-list, and best-seller (see Exhibit 8). Depending on the author group royalties, sales, and promotional support varied. Best-selling authors were expected to sell more than a million books. Publishers were known to sign established authors for up to a five-book contract with large multimillion dollar advances. It had not been determined whether MIRA should follow suit. In addition to author advances, typical royalties per MIRA-type book were estimated to be 13 percent of the $6.75 retail price.

Exhibit 8 General Industry Contract Terms for Fiction Category by Author Group

	Brand-New Author	Mid-List Author	Best-Selling Author
Advance	$10,000 to $30,000	$80,000 to $200,000	$1 million to $5 million
Royalties	5% to 13%	8% to 15%	10% to 17%
Overseas Publishing Schedule	Within 18 months	Within 12 months	Simultaneous
Overseas Publishing Markets	Major markets	All markets	All markets
Minimum Distribution	30,000 to 80,000	100,000 to 400,000	>1 million
Promotional Support per book	Possibly some support (up to $50,000)	Support ($100,000)	Very strong support (more than $300,000)

Sources: Industry sources and casewriter estimates.

A Different Format

Women's fiction books were expected to have many differences from well-defined series romance books. Unlike series romance, topics would cover a broader range of segments including general fiction, science fiction, and mystery. Women's fiction books would be longer in length: 100,000 to 400,000 words compared with a series romance book length of 75,000 words. Naturally, book sizes would be bigger in terms of page length: from 250 to 400 pages versus a norm of 192 to 304 pages for series romance.

Distribution

Harlequin had a strong distribution network for its series romances through supermarkets, drugstores, and discount department stores. Single-title women's fiction novels required more mainstream distribution focusing on retail bookstores. In addition, standing order distribution, a hallmark of Harlequin's series romance business model, would have to be abandoned in favor of relying on orders generated by the distributor's sales force for single-titles.

Success in the United States would be key for MIRA, and in this market, Harlequin relied upon Simon and Schuster's sales force. Since S&S was a major single-title publisher, Harlequin did not know how much support MIRA would be afforded. Harlequin was considering offering better margins to the distributors than those it offered for series romance distribution. Expenses for single-title distribution were expected to be $0.27 per book.

MIRA books would rely more heavily upon distribution through bookstores when distributed through the same channels as the series product. Retailers would be encouraged to shelve MIRA books separately from the series offering. The more intensive selling effort for single titles would require four percent of the single title retail price. The new single-title program planned to offer $3.38 in margin to the distribution channel for single-title books (50 percent of the typical retail price of $6.75) versus $2.42 for series books (45 percent of the $4.40 suggested retail price).

Acquiring Single-Title Rights

Harlequin subsidiaries in some countries were already buying rights to publish single titles. By launching MIRA Harlequin could negotiate better global-author deals. The task force report added, "By acquiring mainstream titles through a central acquiring office, the collective clout of Harlequin could create the likelihood of better-selling mainstream titles marketed by all countries in the global enterprise."

Harlequin's author and editor relationships remained strong, so much so that many series authors were enthusiastic about maintaining a long-term relationship with a trusted editor as they pursued their break-out mainstream book. With MIRA, these authors could remain loyal to Harlequin.

How Best to Proceed

There were many issues to be resolved prior to any launch of MIRA. Most pressing was the question of whether Harlequin had the resources and capabilities to succeed in its new women's fiction segment. Certainly there were elements of its series business model that could be transferred to the broader women's fiction market. But what were the gaps? What else did Harlequin need?

Hayes had several options if MIRA was launched. Several established best-selling authors had begun their writing careers with Harlequin and had moved on to writing single-title books. These authors had established reputations. Harlequin could approach one or more of these authors to sign with MIRA/Harlequin. Such an arrangement would involve a multi-book contract and substantial advances. While risky, this approach would ensure that MIRA's launch attracted attention.

A different, seemingly less risky alternative was to tap into Harlequin's extensive back-list collection and reissue a selection of novels by current best-selling authors currently signed with rival single-title publishers. The physical size of the book and page length could be extended to 250 pages from 192 by adjusting format. In addition, a new, MIRA-branded cover could be produced to repackage the books. Coincident with the launch of this back-list, Harlequin's editors would cultivate and develop existing series authors, encouraging them to write single-title books for MIRA.

Returning to the strategic dilemma that Harlequin faced, Swift commented on the challenge of successfully launching MIRA:

> *Our biggest challenge is the requirement to publish on a title-by-title basis. Every new book will have to stand on its own, with its own cover, a new marketing plan and possibly even an author tour. Can we as a company develop the flexibility to remain nimble? How patient should we be in waiting for success? Given Worldwide's poor results, how should we approach this challenge?*

End Notes

1. To protect confidentiality, all financial information within this case study has been disguised.
2. This section is adapted from the Richard Ivey School of Business case # 9A87M002. Harlequin Enterprises Limited—1979, Peter Killing.
3. All amounts are a percentage of the suggested retail price.
4. Numbers are for the typical paperback. Hardcover books cost more to produce, but as a percentage of its higher retail price, printing costs were roughly the same proportion.
5. All amounts in Canadian dollars unless otherwise specified.

PART

2 BUSINESS-LEVEL STRATEGIES

CHAPTER

4 Cost Leadership

LEARNING OBJECTIVES

After reading this chapter, you should be able to:

4.1 Define business level strategies.

4.2 Define cost leadership as a business level strategy and identify six reasons firms can differ in their costs.

4.3 Describe how cost leadership can create economic value for a firm.

4.4 Identify the bases of cost leadership that are more likely to be rare and costly to imitate and those that area less likely to be rare and costly to imitate.

4.5 Explain how firms use a functional organizational structure, formal and informal management controls, and compensation policies to implement cost leadership strategies.

DMart's Winning Formula: Everyday Low Pricing

In the dynamic retail industry of India, dominated by various strategic groups employing tactics from product differentiation to cost leadership, DMart emerges as a distinctive player under the visionary leadership of Radhakishan Damani. Launched in 2002, DMart has charted an unparalleled path of growth and profitability, distinguishing itself through an unwavering commitment to providing high-value products at low costs, targeting primarily the middle and lower-middle-class consumer base. This approach has enabled DMart to not only satisfy its vast customer base but also to maintain a favorable stance with investors, ensuring a consistent growth trajectory that defies the typical retail sector's boom-and-bust cycles.

At the core of DMart's strategy lies a meticulously crafted cost structure, characterized by operating expenses below 7 percent which is significantly lower than the 10 percent or higher incurred by its peers. This efficiency allows DMart to offer prices approximately 3 percent lower than competitors without compromising on margins. The company's strategic store ownership, rather than leasing, marks a pivotal aspect of its operational model. By investing in real estate in low-profile areas where costs are comparatively lower and focusing on store sizes that optimize operational efficiency, DMart transforms its stores from mere retail spaces into strategic assets that contribute to its low-cost model. DMart's inventory strategy, emphasizing fast-moving SKUs to ensure high inventory turnover and minimize stockpiling, alongside a cluster expansion strategy that deepens its presence in existing markets before entering new ones, further reinforces its position as a cost leader. This approach not only enhances supply chain efficiency but also translates into direct cost savings for customers. Additionally,

DMart's minimal expenditure on marketing and advertising, relying instead on the strength of its value proposition and word-of-mouth, ensures operational costs are kept in check, enabling the maintenance of low-price offerings.

The challenge of replicating DMart's successful strategy lies in the necessity of a similarly lean cost structure, which competitors often overlook. DMart's success is underpinned by a complex interplay of strategic asset ownership, inventory management, and market positioning—a nuanced approach focusing on long-term sustainability over short-term market capture. As DMart continues to thrive in the Indian retail landscape, leveraging its unique strengths to maintain a strong connection with its customer base and drive sustainable growth, it sets a benchmark for cost leadership in the retail industry. The company's strategic focus on low prices, efficient supply chain management, and customer-centric approach significantly contribute to its success, offering valuable insights for new entrants in the retail sector. DMart's journey from a single store in Mumbai to a dominant player in the Indian retail market exemplifies strategic foresight, operational excellence, and an unwavering commitment to delivering value to customers. By meticulously managing its cost structure and prioritizing efficiency in every aspect of its operations, DMart has established a retail model that is both profitable and sustainable, marking a significant achievement in cost leadership within the retail industry.

In 2023, DMart, operated by Avenue Supermarts Ltd, persisted in its commitment to a cost-leadership strategy, emphasizing its ability to provide a wide range of products, including groceries and general merchandise, at prices well below their maximum retail price (MRP). This strategy, termed Everyday Low Cost & Price (EDLC/LP), is designed to draw a significant customer base to its stores, thereby generating substantial sales volumes. Despite the success of this strategy in fostering consistent revenue and profit growth, industry analysts have highlighted the necessity for DMart to expand its focus beyond the conventional business model to stay competitive, especially in light of the burgeoning e-commerce sector. Although DMart's e-commerce branch, DMart Ready, has shown growth, it still accounts for a minor fraction of the company's overall revenue. This situation highlights the critical balance retail companies like DMart must maintain between cost leadership and strategic flexibility to adapt to evolving consumer preferences and market trends.

REFERENCE

Bansal, R., & Kar, S. K. (2021). *Departmental stores in India: financial performance analysis*. Emerald Emerging Markets Case Studies, 11(3), 1-28.

Harihar, K. (2021). *The success of DMart lies in EDLP Strategy. How?* The Strategy Story (2021, March 31). Accessed from https://thestrategystory.com on March 12, 2024.

Mittal, A., Jain, A., & Dhingra, T. (2021). *DMart an ace in India's retail space*. Emerald Emerging Markets Case Studies, 11(1), 1-20.

Pradhan, S., & Bhatkal, S. (2021). *DMart: driving growth in a changed business environment*. Emerald Emerging Markets Case Studies, 11(3), 1-31.

Venkateswaran, K.R. (2022). *Secret behind DMart's Everyday Low-Price strategy.* LinkedIn Pulse (2022, December 13). Accessed from https://www.linkedin.com on March 12, 2024.

Avenue Supermarts Ltd. (2023.). *Investor relationship*. Accessed from https://www.dmartindia.com on March 12, 2024.

DMart has been able to grow in an industry that has historically been dominated by multiple players including Reliance Mart, Vishal Megamart and Big Bazaar. It did this by keeping its costs low and providing consumers access to products at prices considerably lower than its competitors. This is a classic example of a low-cost strategy.

Objective 4.1 Define business level strategies.

What is Business-Level Strategy?

Part 1 of this book introduced the basic tools required to conduct a strategic analysis: tools for analyzing external threats and opportunities (in Chapter 2) and tools for analyzing internal strengths and weaknesses (in Chapter 3). Once these two analyses have been completed, it is possible to begin making strategic choices. As explained in Chapter 1, strategic choices fall into two large categories: business strategies and corporate strategies. **Business-level strategies** are actions firms take to gain competitive advantages in a single market or industry. **Corporate-level strategies** are actions firms take to gain competitive advantages by operating in multiple markets or industries simultaneously.

The business-level strategies discussed in this book are cost leadership (this chapter), product differentiation (Chapter 5), flexibility (Chapter 6), and collusion (Chapter 7). The importance of these business-level strategies is so widely recognized that they are often called **generic business strategies**.

Objective 4.2 Define cost leadership as a business level strategy and identify six reasons firms can differ in their costs.

What is Cost Leadership?

A firm that chooses a **cost leadership business strategy** focuses on gaining advantages by reducing its costs to below those of all its competitors. This does not mean that this firm abandons other business or corporate strategies. Indeed, a single-minded focus on *just* reducing costs can lead a firm to make low-cost products that no one wants to buy. Recall that Warby Parker focuses on keeping its costs (and prices) low, but that it does not abandon the effort to sell stylish eyeglasses to consumers. That said, a firm pursuing a cost leadership strategy focuses much of its effort on keeping its costs low.

Numerous firms besides Warby Parker have pursued cost leadership strategies. Ryanair follows this strategy in the airline industry, Timex and Casio in the watch industry, and BIC in the disposable pen and razor market. All these firms advertise their products. However, these advertisements tend to emphasize

TABLE 4.1 Important Sources of Cost Advantages for Firms

1. Size differences and economies of scale
2. Size differences and diseconomies of scale
3. Experience differences and learning-curve economies
4. Differential low-cost access to productive inputs
5. Technological advantages independent of scale
6. Policy choices

reliability and low prices—the kinds of product attributes that are usually emphasized by firms pursuing cost leadership strategies.

In automobiles, Fiat has implemented a cost leadership strategy with its emphasis on low-priced cars for basic transportation. Like Ryanair, Timex, Casio, and BIC, Fiat spends a significant amount of money advertising its products, but its advertisements tend to emphasize its sporty, sexy styling and low price. Fiat has positioned its cars as fun and inexpensive, not a high-performance sports car or a luxurious status symbol. Fiat's ability to sell these fun and inexpensive automobiles depends on its design choices (keep it simple) and its low manufacturing costs.[1]

Sources of Cost Advantages

An individual firm may have a cost advantage over its competitors for several reasons. Cost advantages are possible even when competing firms produce similar products. Some of the most important of these sources of cost advantage are listed in Table 4.1 and discussed in this section.

Size Differences and Economies of Scale

One of the most widely cited sources of cost advantages for a firm is its size. When there are significant economies of scale in manufacturing, marketing, distribution, service, or other functions of a business, larger firms (up to some point) can have a cost advantage over smaller firms.

The concept of economies of scale was first defined in Chapter 2. **Economies of scale** are said to exist when the increase in firm size (measured in terms of

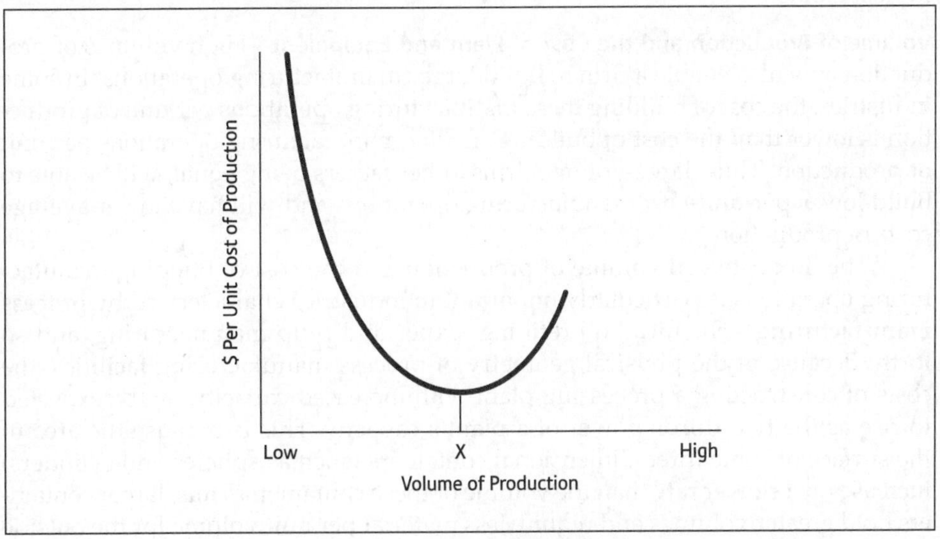

Figure 4.1 Economies of Scale

TABLE 4.2 Why Higher Volumes of Production in a Firm Can Lead to Lower Costs

With higher production volume . . .
1. Firms can use specialized machines
2. Firms can build larger plants
3. Firms can increase employee specialization
4. Firms can spread overhead costs across more units produced

. . . which can lower per-unit production costs.

volume of production) is associated with lower costs (measured in terms of average costs per unit of production), as depicted in Figure 4.1. As the volume of production in a firm increases, the average cost per unit decreases until some optimal volume of production (point X) is reached, after which the average costs per unit of production begins to rise because of **diseconomies of scale** (a concept discussed in more detail later in this chapter).

If the relationship between volume of production and average costs per unit of production depicted in Figure 4.1 holds, and if a firm in an industry has the largest volume of production (but not greater than the optimal level, X), then that firm will have a cost advantage in that industry. Increasing the volume of production can reduce a firm's costs for several reasons. Some of the most important of these reasons are summarized in Table 4.2 and discussed in the following text.

Volume of Production and Specialized Machines When a firm has high levels of production, it is often able to purchase and use specialized manufacturing tools that cannot be kept in operation in small firms. Manufacturing managers at BIC Corporation, for example, have emphasized this important advantage of high volumes of production. A former director of manufacturing at BIC once observed:

> *We are in the automation business. Because of our large volume, one tenth of 1 cent in savings turns out to be enormous. . . . One advantage of the high-volume business is that you can get the best equipment and amortize it entirely over a short period of time (4 to 5 months). I'm always looking for new equipment. If I see a cost-savings machine, I can buy it. I'm not constrained by money.*[2]

Only firms with BIC's level of production in the pen industry can reduce their costs in this manner.

Volume of Production and the Cost of Plant and Equipment High volumes of production may also enable a firm to build larger manufacturing operations. In some industries, the cost of building these manufacturing operations per unit of production is lower than the cost of building smaller manufacturing operations per unit of production. Thus, large-volume firms, other factors being equal, will be able to build lower-per-unit-cost manufacturing operations and will have lower average costs of production.

The link between volume of production and the cost of building manufacturing operations is particularly important in industries characterized by **process manufacturing**—chemical, oil refining, paper and pulp manufacturing, and so forth. Because of the physical geometry of process manufacturing facilities, the costs of constructing a processing plant with increased capacity can be expected to rise as the two-thirds power of a plant's capacity. This is because the area of the surface of some three-dimensional containers (such as spheres and cylinders) increases at a slower rate than the volume of these containers. Thus, larger containers hold greater volumes and require less material per unit volume for the outside skins of these containers. Up to some point, increases in capacity come at a less-than-proportionate rise in the cost of building this capacity.[3]

For example, it might cost a firm \$100 to build a plant with a capacity of 1,000 units, for a per-unit average cost of \$0.01. But, if the "two-thirds rule" applies, it might cost a firm \$465 to build a plant with a capacity of 10,000 units ($465 = 10{,}000^{2/3}$), for a per-unit average cost of \$0.0046. The difference between \$0.01 per unit and \$0.0046 per unit represents a cost advantage for a large firm.

Volume of Production and Employee Specialization High volumes of production are also associated with high levels of employee specialization. As workers specialize in accomplishing a narrow task, they can become more and more efficient at this task, thereby reducing their firm's costs. This reasoning applies both in specialized manufacturing tasks (such as the highly specialized manufacturing functions in an assembly line) and in specialized management functions (such as the highly specialized managerial functions of accounting, finance, and sales).

Smaller firms often do not possess the volume of production needed to justify this level of employee specialization. With smaller volumes of production, highly specialized employees may not have enough work to keep them busy an entire workday. This low volume of production is one reason why smaller firms often have employees that perform multiple business functions and often use outside contract employees and part-time workers to accomplish highly specialized functions, such as accounting, taxes, and human resource management.

Volume of Production and Overhead Costs A firm with high volumes of production has the luxury of spreading its overhead costs over more units and thereby reducing the overhead costs per unit. Suppose, in a particular industry, that the operation of a variety of accounting, control, and research and development functions, regardless of a firm's size, is \$100,000. Clearly, a firm that manufactures 1,000 units is imposing a cost of \$100 per unit to cover overhead expenses. However, a firm that manufactures 10,000 units is imposing a cost of \$10 per unit to cover overhead. Again, the larger-volume firm's average per-unit costs are lower than the small-volume firm's average per-unit cost.

Size Differences and Diseconomies of Scale

Just as economies of scale can generate cost advantages for larger firms, important diseconomies of scale can actually increase costs if firms grow too large. As Figure 4.1 shows, if the volume of production rises beyond some optimal point (point X in the figure), this can actually lead to an increase in per-unit costs. If other firms in an industry have grown beyond the optimal firm size, a smaller firm (with a level of production closer to the optimal) may obtain a cost advantage even when all firms in the industry are producing very similar products. Some important sources of diseconomies of scale for a firm are listed in Table 4.3 and discussed in this section. Also, who the economies of scale curve in an industry can be used to determine the optimal level of production is described in the Strategy in Depth feature.

TABLE 4.3 Major Sources of Diseconomies of Scale

When the volume of production gets too large . . .

1. Physical limits to efficient size
2. Managerial diseconomies
3. Worker de-motivation
4. Distance to markets and suppliers

. . . can increase per-unit costs.

Strategy in Depth

Determining the Optimal Level of Production in an Industry

Figure 4.1 implies that in industries characterized by both economies of scale and diseconomies of scale, that there will be an optimal level of production. Firms that produce less than this level will see their costs rise; firms that produce more than this level will see their costs rise. As presented in the figure, this optimal level of production appears to be very narrow. Of course, in real life, a modest range of production levels may all be consistent with low cost production. Nevertheless, to the extent that economies and diseconomies exist, production below or above this range will lead to higher costs.

Given the importance of this inflection point in the economies of scale curve, determining the value of X can sometimes be important. This can be done empirically by, first, gathering data from firms in an industry about their total costs and their cost drivers. For simplicity, assume that there are only three important cost drivers in an industry: the quantity produced (Q), labor wages (w) and capital (r). A very general cost function that allows for the possibility of both economies and diseconomies of scale is called a **translog cost function**. This function can be written as:

$$\text{Log } TC = b_0 + b_1\log Q + b_2\log w + b_3\log r + b_4(\log Q)^2 + b_5(\log w)^2 + b_6(\log r)^2 + b_7(\log w)(\log r) + b_8(\log w)(\log Q) + b_9(\log r)(\log Q)$$

At first, this looks like a very difficult equation. In fact, it can be estimated using relatively simple regression techniques, and the resulting coefficients can be used to determine the optimal level of production.

To use a very simple example, suppose this functional form was estimated on a sample of firms, the coefficients were transformed out of their log form, and the only statistically significant coefficients were $b_0 = 200$, and $b_4 = 5$. This cost function could then be written as:

$$TC = 200 + 5Q^2$$

Average costs for this equation can be obtained by dividing both sides of this equation by Q:

$$AC = 200/Q + 5Q$$

Some simple calculations show that average costs for firms in this industry fall as Q goes from 1 (AC = 205) to 6 (AC = 63.3) and then begin to rise when Q goes to 7 (AC = 63.57). So, in this simple example, X = 6.[5]

Physical Limits to Efficient Size Applying the two-thirds rule to the construction of manufacturing facilities seems to imply, for some industries at least, that larger is always better. However, there are some important physical limitations to the size of some manufacturing processes. Engineers have found, for example, that cement kilns develop unstable internal aerodynamics at capacities of above 7 million barrels per year. Others have suggested that scaling up nuclear reactors from small installations to huge facilities generates forces and physical processes that, though undetectable in smaller facilities, can become significant in larger operations. These physical limitations on manufacturing processes reflect the underlying physics and engineering in a manufacturing process and suggest when the cost curve in Figure 4.1 will begin to rise.[4]

Managerial Diseconomies Although the underlying physics and engineering in a manufacturing process have an important impact on a firm's costs, managerial diseconomies are perhaps an even more important cause of these cost increases. As a firm increases in size, it often increases in complexity, and the ability of managers to control and operate it efficiently becomes limited.

One well-known example of a manufacturing plant that grew too large and thus became inefficient is Crown, Cork and Seal's can-manufacturing plant in Philadelphia.

Through the early part of this century, this Philadelphia facility handled as many as 75 different can-manufacturing lines. The most efficient plants in the industry, however, were running from 10 to 15 lines simultaneously. The huge Philadelphia facility was simply too large to operate efficiently and was characterized by large numbers of breakdowns, a high percentage of idle lines, and poor-quality products.[6]

Worker De-Motivation A third source of diseconomies of scale depends on the relationship between firm size, employee specialization, and employee motivation. It has already been suggested that one of the advantages of increased volumes of production is that it allows workers to specialize in smaller and more narrowly defined production tasks. With specialization, workers become more and more efficient at the particular task facing them.

However, a significant stream of research suggests that these types of very specialized jobs can be unmotivating for employees. Based on motivational theories taken from social psychology, this work suggests that as workers are removed further from the complete product that is the result of a manufacturing process, the role that a worker's job plays in the overall manufacturing process becomes more and more obscure. As workers become mere, "cogs in a manufacturing machine," worker motivation wanes, and productivity and quality can both suffer.[7]

Distance to Markets and Suppliers A final source of diseconomies of scale can be the distance between a large manufacturing facility and where the goods in question are to be sold or where essential raw materials are purchased. Any reductions in cost attributable to the exploitation of economies of scale in manufacturing may be more than offset by large transportation costs associated with moving supplies and products to and from the manufacturing facility. Firms that build highly efficient plants without recognizing these significant transportation costs may put themselves at a competitive disadvantage compared to firms with slightly less-efficient plants that are located closer to suppliers and key markets.

Experience Differences and Learning-Curve Economies

A third possible source of cost advantages for firms in a particular business depends on their different cumulative levels of production. In some circumstances, firms with the greatest experience in manufacturing a product or service will have the

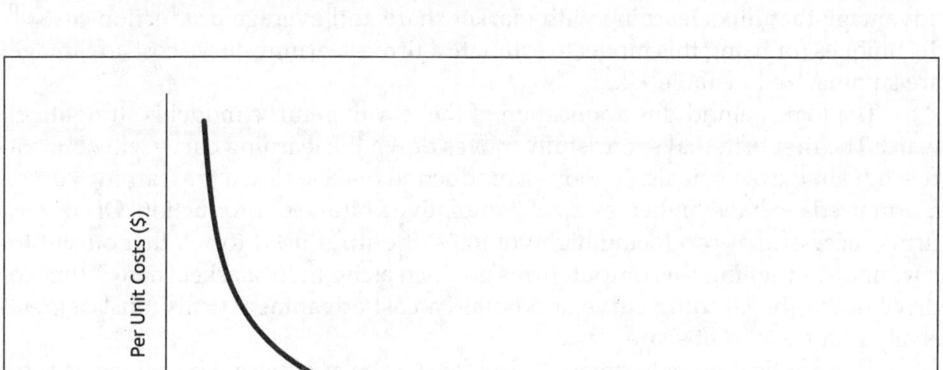

Figure 4.2 The Learning Curve and the Cost of Production

lowest costs in an industry and thus will have a cost-based advantage. The link between cumulative volumes of production and cost has been formalized in the concept of the **learning curve**. The relationship between cumulative volumes of production and per-unit costs is graphically represented in Figure 4.2.

The Learning Curve and Economies of Scale As depicted in Figure 4.2, the learning curve is very similar to the concept of economies of scale. However, there are two important differences. First, whereas economies of scale focus on the relationship between the volume of production at a given point in time and average unit costs, the learning curve focuses on the relationship between the *cumulative* volume of production—that is, how much a firm has produced over time—and average unit costs. Second, where diseconomies of scale are presumed to exist if a firm gets too large, there is no corresponding increase in costs in the learning-curve model as the cumulative volume of production grows. Rather, costs continue to fall until they approach the lowest technologically possible cost.

The Learning Curve and Cost Advantages The learning-curve model is based on the empirical observation that the costs of producing a unit of output fall as the cumulative volume of output increases. This relationship was first observed in the construction of aircraft before World War II. Research showed that the labor costs per aircraft fell by 20 percent each time the cumulative volume of production doubled.[8] A similar pattern has been observed in numerous industries, including the manufacture of ships, computers, spacecraft, and semiconductors. In all these cases, increases in cumulative production have been associated with detailed learning about how to make production as efficient as possible.

However, learning-curve cost advantages are not restricted to manufacturing. Learning can be associated with any business function, from purchasing raw materials to distribution and service. Service industries can also experience important learning effects. The learning curve applies whenever the cost of accomplishing a business activity falls as a function of the cumulative number of times a firm has engaged in that activity.[9] Thus, for example, as Warby Parker's sales have increased, it is likely that their costs for engaging in certain critical business functions has also fallen.

The Learning Curve and Competitive Advantage The learning-curve model summarized in Figure 4.2 has been used to develop a model of cost-based competitive advantage that links learning with market share and average production costs.[10] Techniques for using this model to estimate a firm's learning curve cost advantage are summarized in Table 4.4.

The logic behind this application of the learning-curve model is straightforward: The first firm that successfully moves down the learning curve will obtain a cost advantage over rivals. To move a production process down the learning curve, a firm needs to have higher levels of cumulative volume of production. Of course, firms successful at producing high volumes of output need to sell that output to customers. In selling this output, firms are increasing their market share. Thus, to drive down the learning curve and obtain a cost advantage, firms must aggressively acquire market share.

This application of learning-curve logic has been criticized by a wide variety of authors.[11] Two criticisms are particularly salient. First, although the acquisition of market share is likely to allow a firm to reduce its production costs, the acquisition of share itself is expensive. Indeed, as described in the Research Made Relevant feature, sometimes the cost of acquiring share may rise to equal its value—and thus not be a source of economic profits.

TABLE 4.4 Applying the Learning Curve to Estimate the Costs of Two Firms Selling the Same Product

In this simple example, Firm A has produced 6 products and Firm B has produced just one product. The question is: What is Firm A's cost of its sixth product compared to Firm B's cost of its first product?

Basics: The learning curve in Figure 4.2 can be expressed, in equation form, as:

$$y = ax^{-\beta}$$

Where a is the amount of time a firm spent producing its first unit, x is the total number of units produced, β is a coefficient that describes the rate of learning in producing a product, and y is the average time to produce all x units. The coefficient β depends on the effect on production costs from doubling production. For example, if it takes 20 minutes to produce 6 items and 16 minutes to produce 12 items—note, production has doubled—the rate of learning is 80% (16/20 = .80). The coefficient β is .3219 for an 80% learning curve, .1520 for a 90% learning curve, .0740 for a 95% learning curve, and so forth.

Step One: Identify the learning curve equation for a particular product. Assuming an 80% learning curve and that it takes 45 minutes to produce the first product, this curve is:

$$y = (45)(x)^{-.3219}$$

Step Two: It will take Firm B 45 minutes to produce its first product

Step Three: What is the average time it takes Firm A to produce 6 products?

$$y = (45)(6)^{-.3129} \quad y = 25.3 \text{ minutes}$$

Step Four: What is the total time it takes Firm A to produce 6 products?

$$151.8 \text{ minutes} = (6)(25.3)$$

Step Five: What is the average time it takes Firm A to produce 5 products?

$$y = (45)(5)^{-.3129} \quad y = 26.8 \text{ minutes}$$

Step Six: What is the total time it takes Firm A to produce 5 products?

$$134 \text{ minutes} = (5)(26.8)$$

Step Seven: What is the time it takes for Firm A to produce just its sixth product?

(total time for 6 products − total time for five products) = 151.8 − 134 = 16.8

Thus, while it takes Firm A only 16.8 minutes to produce its 6th product, it takes Firm B 45 minutes to produce its first product. This gives Firm A a substantial cost advantage over Firm B.

The second major criticism of this application of the learning-curve model is that there is, in this logic, no room for any other business or corporate strategies. In other words, this application of the learning curve implicitly assumes that firms can compete only on the basis of their low costs and that other strategies are not possible. Most industries, however, are characterized by opportunities for at least some of these other strategies, and thus this strict application of the learning-curve model can be misleading.[12]

These criticisms aside, it is still the case that in many industries firms with larger cumulative levels of production, other things being equal, will have lower average production costs. Thus, experience in all the facets of production can be a source of cost advantage even if the single-minded pursuit of market share to obtain these cost reductions may not give a firm above normal economic returns.

Research Made Relevant

Research on the relationship between market share and firm performance has continued over many decades. Early work identified market share as the primary determinant of firm performance. Indeed, one particularly influential article identified market share as being *the key* to firm profitability.

This initial conclusion about the relationship between market share and firm performance was based on the observed positive correlation between these two variables. That is, firms with large market share tend to be highly profitable; firms with low market share tend to be less profitable. The logical conclusion of this empirical finding seems to be that if a firm wants to increase its profitability, it should increase its market share.

Not so fast. It turns out that the relationship between market share and firm profits is not that simple. Consider the following scenario: Suppose that 10 companies all conclude that the key to their profitability is gaining market share. To acquire share from each other, each firm will probably increase its advertising and other marketing expenses as well as reduce its prices. This has the effect of putting a price on the market share that a firm seeks to acquire—that is, these competing firms are creating what might be called a "market-for-market share." And because there are 10 firms competing for share in this market, this market is likely to be highly competitive. Returns to acquiring share in such competitive markets for market share should fall to a normal economic level.

How Valuable Is Market Share—Really?

All this analysis suggests that although there may be a cross-sectional positive correlation between market share and firm performance—that is, at a given point in time, market share and firm performance may be positively correlated—this correlation may not be positive over time, as firms seek to increase their market share. Several papers have examined this hypothesis. Two of the most influential of these papers—by Dick Rumelt and Robin Wensley and by Cynthia Montgomery and Birger Wernerfelt—have shown that markets for market share often do emerge in industries, that these markets are often very competitive, and that acquiring market share in these competitive markets does not improve a firm's economic performance. Indeed, in their study of the consolidation of the beer industry Montgomery and Wernerfelt showed that firms such as Anheuser-Busch and Miller paid so much for the market share they acquired that it actually reduced their profitability.

The general consensus in the literature now seems to be that large market share is an outcome of a competitive process within an industry, not an appropriate objective of firm managers, per se. Thus, firms with particularly valuable strategies will naturally attract more customers, which, in turn, suggests that they will often have higher market share. That is, a firm's valuable strategies generate both high levels of firm performance and large market share. This, in turn, explains the positive correlation between market share and firm performance.[13]

Differential Low-Cost Access to Productive Inputs

Besides economies of scale, diseconomies of scale, and learning-curve cost advantages, differential low-cost access to productive inputs may create cost differences among firms producing similar products in an industry. **Productive inputs** are any supplies used by a firm in conducting its business activities; they include, among other things, labor, capital, land, and raw materials. A firm that has differential low-cost access to one or more of these factors is likely to have lower economic costs compared to rivals.

Consider, for example, an oil company with fields in Saudi Arabia compared to an oil company with fields in the North Sea. The cost of obtaining crude oil for the first firm is considerably less than the cost of obtaining crude oil for the second. North Sea drilling involves the construction of giant offshore drilling platforms, housing workers on floating cities, and transporting oil across an often-stormy sea. Drilling in Saudi Arabia requires only the simplest drilling technologies because the oil is found relatively close to the surface.

Of course, to create a cost advantage, the cost of acquiring low-cost productive inputs must be less than the cost savings generated by these factors. For example, even though it may be much less costly to drill for oil in Saudi Arabia than in the North Sea, if it is very expensive to purchase the rights to drill in Saudi Arabia compared to the costs of the rights to drill in the North Sea, the potential cost advantages of drilling in Saudi Arabia can be lost. As with all sources of cost advantages, firms must be careful to weigh the cost of acquiring that advantage against the value of that advantage for the firm.

Differential access to raw materials such as oil, coal, and copper ore can be important determinants of a cost advantage. However, differential access to other productive inputs can be just as important. For example, it may be easier (i.e., less costly) to recruit highly trained electronics engineers for firms located near where these engineers receive their schooling than for firms located some distance away. This lower cost of recruiting is a partial explanation of the development of geographic technology centers such as Silicon Valley in California, Route 128 in Massachusetts, and the Research Triangle in North Carolina. In all three cases, firms are located physically close to several universities that train the engineers that are the lifeblood of high-technology companies. The search for low-cost labor can create ethical dilemmas, as described in the Ethics and Strategy feature.

Technological Advantages Independent of Scale

Another possible source of cost advantage in an industry may be the different technologies that firms employ to manage their business. It has already been suggested that larger firms may have technology-based cost advantages that reflect their ability to exploit economies of scale (e.g., the two-thirds rule).

Traditionally, discussion of technology-based cost advantages has focused on the machines, computers, and other physical tools that firms use to manage their business. Clearly, in some industries, these physical technology differences between firms can create important cost differences—even when the firms in question are approximately the same size in terms of volume of production. In the steel industry, for example, technological advances can substantially reduce the cost of producing steel. Firms with the latest steel-manufacturing technology will typically enjoy some cost advantage compared to similar-sized firms that do not have the latest technology. The same applies in the manufacturing of semiconductors, automobiles, consumer electronics, and a wide variety of other products.[14]

These physical technology cost advantages apply in service firms as well as in manufacturing firms. For example, early in its history Charles Schwab, a leading discount brokerage, purchased a computer system that enabled it to complete customer transactions more rapidly and at a lower cost than its rivals.[15] Kaiser-Permanente, the largest HMO in the United States, has invested in information technology that doctors can use to avoid incorrect diagnoses and procedures that can adversely affect a patient's health. By avoiding these medical mistakes, Kaiser-Permanente can substantially reduce its costs of providing medical service.[16]

However, the concept of technology can be easily broadened to include not just the physical tools that firms use to manage their business, but any processes within a firm used in this way. This concept of firm technology includes not only the

Ethics and Strategy

The Race to the Bottom

One of the most important productive inputs in almost all companies is labor. Getting differential low-cost access to labor can give a firm a cost advantage.

This search for low labor costs has led some firms to engage in an international "race to the bottom." It is well known that the wage rates of most U.S. and Western European workers are much higher than the wage rates of workers in other, less developed parts of the world. While a firm might have to pay its employees $20 per hour (in wages and benefits) to make sneakers and basketball shoes in the United States, that same firm may only have to pay an employee in the Philippines or Malaysia or China $1.00 per day to make the same sneakers and basketball shoes—shoes the firm might be able to sell for $250 a pair in the United States and Europe. Thus, many firms look to overseas manufacturing to keep their labor cost low.

But this search for low labor cost has some important unintended consequences. First, the location of the lowest cost labor rates in the world changes over time. It used to be that Mexico had the lowest labor rates, then Korea and the Philippines, then Malaysia, then China, now Vietnam. As the infrastructures of each of these countries evolve to the point that they can support worldwide manufacturing, firms abandon their relationships with firms in prior countries in search of still lower costs in new countries. The only way former "low-cost centers" can compete is to drive their costs even lower.

This sometimes leads to a second unintended consequence of the "race to the bottom": horrendous working conditions and low wages in these low-cost manufacturing settings. Employees earning $1 for working a 10-hour day, six days a week may look good on the corporate bottom line, but many observers are deeply concerned about the moral and ethical issues associated with this strategy. Indeed, several companies—including Nike and Kmart—have been forced to increase the wages and improve the working conditions of many of their overseas employees.

An even more horrific result of this "race to the bottom" has been the reemergence of what amounts to slavery in some Western European countries and some parts of the United States. In search of the promise of a better life, illegal immigrants are sometimes brought to Western European countries or the United States and forced to work in illegal, underground factories. These illegal immigrants are sometimes forced to work as many as 20 hours a day, for little or no pay—supposedly to "pay off" the price of bringing them out of their less developed countries. And because of their illegal status and language barriers, they often do not feel empowered to go to the local authorities.

Of course, the people who create and manage these facilities are criminals and deserve contempt. But what about the companies that purchase the services of these illegal and immoral manufacturing operations? Aren't they also culpable, both legally and morally?[18]

technological hardware of companies—the machines and robots—but also the **technological software** of firms—things such as the quality of relations between labor and management, an organization's culture, and the quality of managerial controls. All these characteristics of a firm can have an impact on a firm's economic costs.[17]

Policy Choices

Thus far, this discussion has focused on reasons why a firm can gain a cost advantage despite producing products that are similar to competing firms' products. When firms produce essentially the same outputs, differences in economies of scale, learning curve advantages, differential access to productive inputs, and differences in technology can all create cost advantages (and disadvantages) for them.

However, firms can also make choices about the kinds of products and services they will sell—choices that have an impact on their relative cost position. These choices are called **policy choices**.

In general, firms that are attempting to implement a cost leadership strategy will choose to produce relatively simple standardized products that sell for relatively low prices compared to the products and prices firms pursuing other business or corporate strategies choose. These kinds of products often tend to have high volumes of sales, which (if significant economies of scale exist) tend to reduce costs even further.

These kinds of choices in product and pricing tend to have a very broad impact on a cost leader's operations. In these firms, the task of reducing costs is not delegated to a single function or a special task force within the firm, but is the responsibility of every manager and employee. Cost reduction sometimes becomes the central objective of the firm. Indeed, in this setting management must be constantly alert to cost-cutting efforts that reduce the ability of the firm to meet customers' needs. However, it may have ethical implications as well—as described in the Ethics and Strategy feature.

The Value of Cost Leadership

Objective 4.3 Describe how cost leadership can create economic value for a firm.

There is little doubt that cost differences can exist among firms, even when those firms are selling very similar products. Policy choices about the kinds of products firms in an industry choose to produce can also create important cost differences. But under what conditions will these kinds of cost advantages actually create value for a firm?

Cost Leadership and Environmental Threats

It was suggested in Chapter 3 that one way to tell if a resource or capability—such as the ability of a firm to have a cost advantage—actually creates value for a firm is by whether that resource or capability enables a firm to neutralize its external threats or exploit its external opportunities. The ability of a cost leadership position to neutralize external threats will be examined here. The ability of such a position to enable a firm to exploit opportunities will be left as an exercise. The specific economic consequences of cost leadership are discussed in the Strategy in Depth feature.

A cost leadership competitive strategy helps reduce the threat of new entrants by creating cost-based barriers to entry. Recall that many of the barriers to entry cited in Chapter 2, including economies of scale and cost advantages independent of scale, assume that incumbent firms have lower costs than potential entrants. If an incumbent firm is a cost leader, for any of the reasons just listed, then new entrants may have to invest heavily to reduce their costs prior to entry. Often, new entrants will enter using another business strategy (e.g., product differentiation) rather than attempting to compete on costs.

Firms with a low-cost position also reduce the threat of rivalry. The threat of rivalry is reduced through pricing strategies that low-cost firms can engage in and through their relative impact on the performance of a low-cost firm and its higher-cost rivals.

As suggested in Chapter 2, substitutes become a threat to a firm when their cost and performance, relative to a firm's current products or services, become more attractive to customers. Thus, when the price of crude oil goes up, substitutes for crude oil become more attractive. When the cost and performance of electronic calculators improve, demand for mechanical adding machines disappears.

In this situation, cost leaders can keep their products and services attractive relative to substitutes. While high-cost firms may have to charge high prices to cover their costs, thus making substitutes more attractive, cost leaders can keep their prices low and still earn normal or above-normal economic profits.

Suppliers can become a threat to a firm by charging higher prices for the goods or services they supply or by reducing the quality of those goods or services. However, when a supplier sells to a cost leader, that firm has greater flexibility in absorbing higher-cost supplies than does a high-cost firm. Higher supply costs may destroy any above-normal profits for high-cost firms but still allow a cost leader firm to earn an above-normal profit.

Cost leadership based on large volumes of production and economies of scale can also reduce the threat of suppliers. Large volumes of production imply large purchases of raw materials and other supplies. Suppliers are not likely to jeopardize these sales by threatening their customers. Indeed, as was suggested earlier, buyers are often able to use their purchasing volume to extract volume discounts from suppliers.

Cost leadership can also reduce the threat of buyers. Powerful buyers are a threat to firms when they insist on low prices or higher quality and service from their suppliers. Lower prices threaten firm revenues; higher quality can increase a firm's costs. Cost leaders can have their revenues reduced by buyer threats and

Strategy in Depth

The Economics of Cost Leadership

Another way to demonstrate that cost leadership can be a source of economic value is to directly examine the economic profits generated by a firm with a cost advantage operating in an otherwise very competitive industry. This is done in Figure 4.3.

The firms depicted in this figure are **price takers**—that is, the price of the products or services they sell is determined by market conditions and not by individual decisions of firms. This implies that there is effectively no product differentiation in this market and that no one firm's sales constitute a large percentage of this market.

The price of goods or services in this type of market (P^*) is determined by aggregate industry supply and demand. This industry price determines the demand facing an individual firm in this market. Because these firms are price takers, the demand facing an individual firm is horizontal—that is, firm decisions about levels of output have a negligible impact on overall industry supply and thus a negligible impact on the market-determined price. A firm in this setting maximizes its economic performance by producing a quantity of output (Q) so that marginal revenue equals marginal cost (MC). The ability of firms to earn economic profits in this setting depends upon the relationship between the market-determined price (P^*) and the average total cost (ATC) of a firm at the quantity it chooses to produce.

Firms in the market depicted in Figure 4.3 fall into two categories. All but one firm have the average-total-cost curve ATC_2 and marginal-cost curve MC_2. However, one firm in this industry has the average-total-cost curve ATC_1 and marginal-cost curve MC_1. Notice that ATC_1 is less than ATC_2 at the performance-maximizing quantities produced by these two kinds of firms (Q_1 and Q_2, respectively). In this particular example, firms with common average-total-cost curves are earning zero economic profits, while the low-cost firm is earning an economic profit (equal to the shaded area in the figure). A variety of other examples could also be constructed: The cost leader firm could be earning zero economic profits, while other firms in the market are incurring economic losses; the cost leader firm could be earning substantial economic profits, while other firms are earning smaller economic profits; the cost leader firm could be incurring small economic losses, while the other firms are incurring substantial economic losses; and so forth. However, in all these examples the cost leader's economic performance is greater than the economic performance of other firms in the industry. Thus, cost leadership can have an important impact on a firm's economic performance.

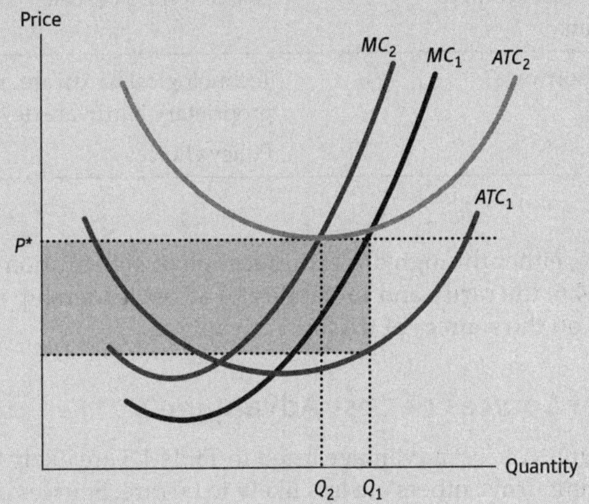

Figure 4.3 Cost Leadership and Economic Performance

still have normal or above-normal performance. These firms can also absorb the greater costs of increased quality or service and still have a cost advantage over their competition.

Buyers can also be a threat through backward vertical integration. Being a cost leader deters backward vertical integration by buyers because a buyer that vertically integrates backward will often not have costs as low as an incumbent cost leader. Rather than vertically integrating backward and increasing its cost of supplies, powerful buyers usually prefer to continue purchasing from their low-cost suppliers.

Finally, if cost leadership is based on large volumes of production, then the threat of buyers may be reduced because buyers may depend on just a few firms for the goods or services they purchase. This dependence reduces the willingness of buyers to threaten a selling firm.

Cost Leadership and Sustained Competitive Advantage

Objective 4.4 Identify the bases of cost leadership that are more likely to be rare and costly to imitate and those that area less likely to be rare and costly to imitate.

Given that cost leadership can be valuable, an important question becomes: "Under what conditions will firms implementing this business strategy be able to maintain that leadership to obtain a sustained competitive advantage?" If cost leadership strategies can be implemented by numerous firms in an industry or if no firms face a cost disadvantage in imitating a cost leadership strategy, then being a cost leader will not generate a sustained competitive advantage for a firm. As suggested in Chapter 3, the ability of a valuable cost leadership competitive strategy to generate a sustained competitive advantage depends on that strategy being rare and

TABLE 4.5 The Rarity of Sources of Cost Advantage

Likely-to-be-rare sources of cost advantage	Less-likely-to-be-rare sources of cost advantage
Learning-curve economies of scale (especially in emerging businesses)	Economies of scale (except when efficient plant size approximately equals total industry demand)
Differential low-cost access to productive inputs	Diseconomies of scale
Technological "software"	Technological hardware (unless a firm has proprietary hardware development skills)
	Policy choices

costly to imitate, either through direct duplication or substitution. As suggested in Tables 4.5 and 4.6, the rarity and imitability of a cost leadership strategy depend, at least in part, on the sources of that cost advantage.

The Rarity of Sources of Cost Advantage

Some of the sources of cost advantage listed in Table 4.5 are likely to be rare among a set of competing firms; others are less likely to be rare. Sources of cost advantage that are likely to be rare include learning-curve economies (at least in emerging industries), differential low-cost access to productive inputs, and technological "software." The remaining sources of cost advantage are less likely to be rare.

Rare Sources of Cost Advantage

Early in the evolution of an industry, substantial differences in the cumulative volume of production of different firms are not unusual. Indeed, this was one of the major benefits associated with first-mover advantages, discussed in Chapter 2. These differences in cumulative volume of production, in combination with substantial learning-curve economies, suggest that, in some settings, learning-curve advantages may be rare and thus a source of at least temporary competitive advantage.

The definition of differential access to productive inputs implies that this access is often rare. Certainly, if large numbers of competing firms have this same access, then it cannot be a source of competitive advantage.

Technological software is also likely to be rare among a set of competing firms. These software attributes represent each firm's path through history. If these histories are unique, then the technological software they create may also be rare. Of course, if several competing firms experience similar paths through history, the technological software in these firms is less likely to be rare.

Less Rare Sources of Cost Advantage

When the efficient size of a firm or plant is significantly smaller than the total size of an industry, there will usually be numerous efficient firms or plants in that industry, and a cost leadership strategy based on economies of scale will not be rare. For example, if the efficient firm or plant size in an industry is 500 units, and the total size of the industry (measured in units produced) is 500,000 units, then there are likely to be numerous efficient firms or plants in this industry, and economies of scale are not likely to give any one firm a cost-based competitive advantage.

Cost advantages based on diseconomies of scale are also not likely to be rare. It is unusual for numerous firms to adopt levels of production more than optimal levels. If only a few firms are too large in this sense, then several competing firms in an industry that are *not* too large will have cost advantages over the firms that are too large. However, because several firms will enjoy these cost advantages, they are not rare.

One important exception to this generalization may be when changes in technology significantly reduce the most efficient scale of an operation. Given such changes in technology, several firms may be inefficiently large. If a small number of firms happen to be sized appropriately, then the cost advantages these firms obtain in this way may be rare. Such changes in technology have made large integrated steel producers "too big" relative to smaller mini-mills. Thus, mini-mills have a cost advantage over larger integrated steel firms.

Technological hardware is also not likely to be rare, especially if it is developed by suppliers and sold on the open market. However, if a firm has proprietary technology development skills, it may possess rare technological hardware that creates cost advantages.

Finally, policy choices by themselves are not likely to be a rare source of cost advantage, particularly if the product or service attributes in question are easy to observe and describe.

The Imitability of Sources of Cost Advantage

Even when a particular source of cost advantage is rare, it must be costly to imitate in order to be a source of sustained competitive advantage. Both direct duplication and substitution, as forms of imitation, are important. Again, as is shown in Table 4.6, the imitability of a cost advantage depends, at least in part, on the source of that advantage.

Easy-to-Duplicate Sources of Cost Advantage

In general, economies of scale and diseconomies of scale are relatively easy-to-duplicate bases of cost leadership. As can be seen in Table 4.6, these sources of cost advantage do not build on history, uncertainty, or socially complex resources and capabilities and thus are not protected from duplication for these reasons.

TABLE 4.6 Direct Duplication of Cost Leadership

		Basis for costly duplication		
	Source of Cost Advantage	**History**	**Uncertainty**	**Social Complexity**
Low-cost duplication possible	1. Economies of scale	—	—	—
	2. Diseconomies of scale	—	—	—
May be costly to duplicate	3. Learning-curve economies	*	—	—
	4. Technological "hardware"	—	*	*
	5. Policy choices	*	—	—
Usually costly to duplicate	6. Differential low-cost access to productive inputs	***	—	**
	7. Technological "software"	***	**	***

— = not a source of costly imitation, * = somewhat likely to be a source of costly imitation, ** = likely to be a source of costly imitation, *** = very likely to be a source of costly imitation

For example, if a small number of firms obtain a cost advantage based on economies of scale and if the relationship between production scale and costs is widely understood among competing firms, then firms at a cost disadvantage will rapidly adjust their production to exploit these economies of scale. This can be done by either growing a firm's current operations to the point that the firm exploits economies or by combining previously separate operations to obtain these economies. Both actions enable a firm at a cost disadvantage to begin using specialized machines, reduce the cost of plant and equipment, increase employee specialization, and spread overhead costs more effectively.

Indeed, perhaps the only time economies of scale are not subject to low-cost duplication is when the efficient size of operations is a significant percentage of total demand in an industry. Of course, this is the situation described in Chapter 2's discussion of economies of scale as a barrier to entry. For example, as suggested earlier, BIC Corporation, with its dominant market share in the disposable pen market, has apparently been able to gain and retain an important cost advantage in that market based on economies of scale. BIC's ability to retain this advantage reflects the fact that the optimal plant size in the disposable pen market is a significant percentage of the pen market, and thus economies of scale act as a barrier to entry in that market.

Like economies of scale, in many settings diseconomies of scale will not be a source of sustained competitive advantage for firms that have *not* grown too large. In the short run, firms experiencing significant diseconomies can shrink the size of their operations to become more efficient. In the long run, firms that fail to adjust their size will earn below-normal economic performance and cease operations.

Although in many ways reducing the size of operations to improve efficiency seems like a simple problem for managers in firms or plants, in practice it is often a difficult change to implement. Because of uncertainty, managers in a firm or plant that is too large may not understand that diseconomies of scale have increased their costs. Sometimes, managers conclude that the problem is that employees are not working hard enough, that problems in production can be fixed, and so forth. These firms or plants may continue their inefficient operations for some time, despite costs that are higher than the industry average.[19]

Other psychological processes can also delay the abandonment of operations that are too large. One of these phenomena is known as **escalation of commitment**. Sometimes, managers committed to an incorrect (cost-increasing or revenue-reducing) course of action *increase* their commitment to this action as its limitations become manifest. For example, a manager who believes that the optimal firm size in an industry is larger than the actual optimal size may remain committed to large operations despite costs that are higher than the industry average.[20]

For all these reasons, firms suffering from diseconomies of scale must often turn to outside managers to assist in reducing costs. Outsiders bring a fresh view to the organization's problems and are not committed to the practices that generated the problems in the first place.[21]

Bases of Cost Leadership That May Be Costly to Duplicate

Although cost advantages based on learning-curve economies are rare (especially in emerging industries), they are usually not costly to duplicate. As suggested in Chapter 2, for learning-curve cost advantages to be a source of sustained competitive advantage the learning obtained by a firm must be proprietary. Most recent empirical work suggests that in most industries learning is not proprietary and thus can be rapidly duplicated as competing firms move down the learning curve by increasing their cumulative volume of production.[22]

However, the fact that learning is not costly to duplicate in *most* industries does not mean it is never costly to duplicate. In some industries, the ability of firms to learn from their production experience may vary significantly. For example, some firms treat production errors as failures and systematically punish employees who make those errors. These firms effectively reduce risk-taking among their production employees and thus reduce the chances of learning how to improve their production process. Alternatively, other firms treat production errors as opportunities to learn how to improve their production process. These firms are likely to move rapidly down the learning curve and retain cost advantages, despite the cumulative volume of production of competing firms. These different responses to production errors reflect the organizational cultures of these different firms. Because organizational cultures are socially complex, they can be very costly to duplicate.[23]

Because technological hardware can usually be purchased across supply markets, it is also not likely to be difficult to duplicate. Sometimes, however, technological hardware can be proprietary or closely bundled with other unique, costly-to-duplicate resources controlled by a firm. In this case, technological hardware *can* be costly to duplicate.

It is unusual, but not impossible, for policy choices, per se, to be a source of sustained competitive cost advantages for a firm. As suggested earlier, if the policies in question focus on easy to observe and easy to describe product characteristics, then duplication is likely, and cost advantages based on policy choices will be temporary. However, if policy choices reflect complex decision processes within a firm, teamwork among different parts of the design and manufacturing process, or any of the software commitments discussed previously, then policy choices can be a source of sustained competitive advantage, if only a few firms have the ability to make these choices.

Indeed, most of the successful firms that operate in unattractive industries make policy choices that are costly to imitate because they reflect historical, causally ambiguous, and socially complex firm processes. Thus, for example, Wal-Mart's supply chain management strategy—a policy with clear low-cost implications—actually reflects Wal-Mart's unique history, its socially complex relations with suppliers, and its unique organizational culture. And Ryanair's low-price pricing strategy—a strategy that reflects its low-cost position—is possible because of the kind of airplane fleet Ryanair has built over time, the commitment of its employees to Ryanair's success, a charismatic founder, and its unique organizational culture. Because these policies reflect costly-to-imitate attributes of these firms, they can be sources of sustained competitive advantage.

However, for these and other firms, it is not these policy choices, per se, that create sustainable cost leadership advantages. Rather, it is how these policies flow from the historical, causally ambiguous, and socially complex processes within a firm that makes them costly to duplicate. This has been the case for the Oakland A's baseball team, as described in the Strategy in the Emerging Enterprise feature.

Costly-to-Duplicate Sources of Cost Advantage

Differential access to low-cost productive inputs and technological software is usually a costly-to-duplicate basis of cost leadership. This is because these inputs often build on historical, uncertain, and socially complex resources and capabilities. As suggested earlier, differential access to productive inputs often depends on the location of a firm. Moreover, to be a source of economic profits, this valuable location must be obtained before its full value is widely understood. Both these attributes of differential access to productive inputs suggest that if, in fact, it is rare, it will often be costly to duplicate. First, some locations are unique and cannot be duplicated. For example, most private golf clubs would like to own courses with the spectacular beauty of Pebble Beach in Monterey, California, but there is only one Pebble Beach—a course that runs parallel to some of the most beautiful oceanfront scenery in the world. Although "scenery" is an important factor of production in running and managing a golf course, the re-creation of Pebble Beach's scenery at some other location is simply beyond our technology.

Second, even if a location is not unique, once its value is revealed, acquisition of that location is not likely to generate economic profits. Thus, for example, although being in Silicon Valley provides access to some important low-cost productive inputs for electronics firms, firms that moved to this location after its value was revealed have substantially higher costs than firms that moved there before its full value was revealed. These higher costs effectively reduce the economic profit that otherwise could have been generated. Referring to the discussion in Chapter 3, these arguments suggest that gaining differential access to productive inputs in a way that generates economic profits may reflect a firm's unique path through history.

Technological software is also likely to be difficult to duplicate and often can be a source of sustained competitive advantage. As suggested in Chapter 3, the values, beliefs, culture, and teamwork that constitute this software are socially complex and may be immune from competitive duplication. Firms with cost advantages rooted in these socially complex resources incorporate cost savings in every aspect of their organization; they constantly focus on improving the quality and cost of their operations, and they have employees who are firmly committed to, and understand, what it takes to be a cost leader. Other firms may talk about low costs; these firms live cost leadership. Ryanair, Dell, Wal-Mart, and Southwest are all examples of such firms. If there are few firms in an industry with these kinds of beliefs and commitments, then they can gain a sustained competitive advantage from their cost advantage.

Substitutes for Sources of Cost Advantage

In an important sense, all the sources of cost advantage listed in this chapter are at least partial substitutes for each other. Thus, for example, one firm may reduce its cost through exploiting economies of scale in large-scale production, and a competing firm may reduce its costs through exploiting learning-curve economies and large cumulative volume of production. If these different activities have similar effects on a firm's cost position and if they are equally costly to implement, then they are strategic substitutes for each other.

Because of the substitute effects of different sources of cost advantage, it is not unusual for firms pursuing cost leadership to simultaneously pursue *all* the cost-reduction activities discussed in this chapter. Implementation Implementation of this *bundle* of cost-reducing activities may have few substitutes. If duplicating this bundle of activities is also rare and difficult, then a firm may be able to gain a sustained competitive advantage from doing so.

Several of the other strategies discussed in later chapters can also have the effect of reducing a firm's costs and thus may be substitutes for the sources of cost reduction discussed in this chapter. For example, one common motivation for firms implementing strategic alliance strategies is to exploit economies of scale in combination with other firms. Thus, a strategic alliance that reduces a firm's costs may be a substitute for a firm exploiting economies of scale on its own to reduce its costs. As is discussed in more detail in Chapter 8, many of the strategic alliances among aluminum mining and smelting companies are motivated by realizing economies of scale and cost reduction. Also, corporate diversification strategies often enable firms to exploit economies of scale across different businesses within which they operate. In this setting, each of these businesses—treated separately—may have scale disadvantages, but collectively their scale creates the same low-cost position as that of an individual firm that fully exploits economies of scale to reduce costs in a single business (see Chapter 9).

Organizing to Implement Cost Leadership

Objective 4.5 Explain how firms use a functional organizational structure, formal and informal management controls, and compensation policies to implement cost leadership strategies.

As with all strategies, firms seeking to implement cost leadership strategies must adopt an organizational structure, management controls, and compensation policies that reinforce this strategy. Some key issues associated with using these organizing tools to implement cost leadership are summarized in Table 4.7.

Organizational Structure in Implementing Cost Leadership

As suggested in Table 4.7, firms implementing cost leadership strategies will generally adopt what is known as a **functional organizational structure**.[24] An example of a functional organizational structure is presented in Figure 4.4. Indeed, this functional organizational structure is the structure used to implement all business-level strategies a firm might pursue, although this structure is modified when used to implement these different strategies.

In a functional structure, each of the major business functions is managed by a **functional manager**. For example, if manufacturing, marketing, finance, accounting, and sales are all included within a functional organization, then a manufacturing manager leads that function, a marketing manager leads that function, a finance manager leads that function, and so forth. In a functional organizational structure, all these functional managers report to one person. This person has many different titles—including *president, CEO, chair,* or *founder*. However, for purposes of this discussion, this person will be called the **chief executive officer (CEO)**.

The CEO in a functional organization has a unique status. Everyone else in this company is a functional specialist. The manufacturing people manufacture, the

TABLE 4.7 Organizing to Realize the Full Potential of Cost Leadership Strategies

Organization structure: Functional structure with
1. Few layers in the reporting structure
2. Simple reporting relationships
3. Small corporate staff
4. Focus on narrow range of business functions

Management control systems
1. Tight cost control systems
2. Quantitative cost goals
3. Close supervision of labor, raw material, inventory, and other costs
4. A cost leadership philosophy

Compensation policies
1. Reward for cost reduction
2. Incentives for all employees to be involved in cost reduction

Figure 4.4 An Example of the U-form Organizational Structure

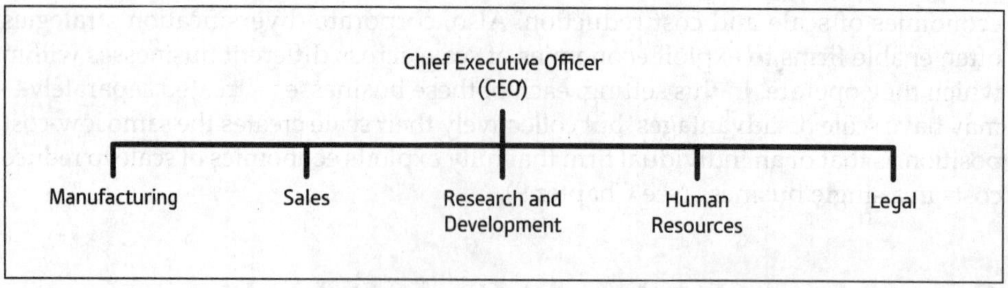

marketing people market, the finance people finance, and so forth. Indeed, only one person in the functional organization must have a multifunctional perspective: the CEO. This role is so important that sometimes the functional organization is called a **U-form structure**, where the "U" stands for "unitary"—because there is only one person in this organization that has a broad, multifunctional corporate perspective.

When used to implement a cost leadership strategy, this U-form structure is kept as simple as possible. As suggested in Table 4.7, firms implementing cost leadership strategies will have relatively few layers in their reporting structure. Complicated reporting structures, including **matrix structures** where one employee reports to two or more people, are usually avoided.[25] Corporate staff in these organizations is kept small. Such firms do not operate in a wide range of business functions, but instead operate only in those few business functions where they have valuable, rare, and costly-to-imitate resources and capabilities.

One excellent example of a firm pursuing a cost leadership strategy is Nucor Steel. A leader in the mini-mill industry, Nucor has only five layers in its reporting structure, compared to 12 to 15 in its major higher-cost competitors. Most operating decisions at Nucor are delegated to plant managers, who have full profit-and-loss responsibility for their operations. Corporate staff at Nucor is small and focuses its efforts on accounting for revenues and costs and on exploring new manufacturing processes to further reduce Nucor's operating expenses and expand its business opportunities. Nucor's former president Ken Iverson believed that Nucor does only two things well: build plants efficiently and run them effectively. Thus, Nucor focuses its efforts in these areas and subcontracts many of its other business functions, including the purchase of its raw materials, to outside vendors.[26]

Responsibilities of the CEO in a Functional Organization

The CEO in a U-form organization has two basic responsibilities: (1) to formulate the strategy of the firm; and (2) to coordinate the activities of the functional specialists in the firm to facilitate the implementation of this strategy. In the special case of a cost leadership strategy, the CEO must decide on which bases such a strategy should be founded—including any of those listed in Table 4.1—and then coordinate functions within a firm to make sure that the economic potential of this strategy is fully realized.

Strategy Formulation The CEO in a U-form organization engages in strategy formulation by applying the strategic management process described in Chapter 1. A CEO establishes the firm's mission and associated objectives, evaluates environmental threats and opportunities, understands the firm's strengths and weaknesses, and then chooses one or more of the business and corporate strategies discussed in this book. In the case of a cost leadership strategy, the application of the strategic management process must lead a CEO to conclude that the best chance for achieving a firm's mission is for that firm to adopt a cost leadership business-level strategy.

Although the responsibility for strategy formulation in a U-form organization ultimately rests with the CEO, this individual needs to draw on the insights, analysis, and involvement of functional managers throughout the firm. CEOs who fail to involve functional managers in strategy formulation run several risks. First, strategic choices made in isolation from functional managers may be made without complete information. Second, limiting the involvement of functional managers in strategy formulation can limit their understanding of, and commitment to, the chosen strategy. This can severely limit their ability, and willingness, to implement any strategy—including cost leadership—that is chosen.[27]

Coordinating Functions for Strategy Implementation Even the best-formulated strategy is competitively irrelevant if it is not implemented. And the only way that strategies can be effectively implemented is if all the functions within a firm are aligned in a way consistent with this strategy.

For example, compare two firms pursuing a cost leadership strategy. All but one of the first firm's functions—marketing—are aligned with this cost leadership strategy. All of the second firm's functions—including marketing—are aligned with this cost leadership strategy. Because marketing is not aligned with the first firm's cost leadership strategy, this firm is likely to advertise products that it does not sell. That is, this firm might advertise its products based on their style and performance, but sell products that are reliable (but not stylish) and inexpensive (but not high performers). A firm that markets products it does not actually sell is likely to disappoint its customers. In contrast, the second firm that has all its functions—including marketing—aligned with its chosen strategy is more likely to advertise products it actually sells and thus is less likely to disappoint its customers. In the long run, it seems reasonable to expect this second firm to outperform the first, at least with respect to implementing a cost leadership strategy.

Of course, alignment is required of all a firm's functional areas, not just marketing. Also, misalignment can emerge in any of a firm's functional areas. Some common misalignments between a firm's cost leadership strategy and its functional activities are listed in Table 4.8.

TABLE 4.8 Common Misalignments Between Business Functions and a Cost Leadership Strategy

	When Function Is *Aligned* with Cost Leadership Strategies	When Function Is *Misaligned* with Cost Leadership Strategies
Manufacturing	Lean, low cost, good quality	Inefficient, high cost, poor quality
Marketing	Emphasize value, reliability, and price	Emphasize style and performance
Research and Development	Focus on product extensions and process improvements	Focus on radical new technologies and products
Finance	Focus on low cost and stable financial structure	Focus on nontraditional financial instruments
Accounting	Collect cost data and adopt conservative accounting principles	Collect no-cost data and adopt very aggressive accounting principles
Sales	Focus on value, reliability, and low price	Focus on style and performance and high price

Management Controls in Implementing Cost Leadership

As suggested in Table 4.7, cost leadership firms are typically characterized by very tight cost-control systems; frequent and detailed cost-control reports; an emphasis on quantitative cost goals and targets; and close supervision of labor, raw materials, inventory, and other costs. Again, Nucor Steel is an example of a cost leadership firm that has implemented these kinds of control systems. At Nucor, groups of employees are given weekly cost and productivity improvement goals. Groups that meet or exceed these goals receive extra compensation. Plant managers are held responsible for cost and profit performance. A plant manager who does not meet corporate performance expectations cannot expect a long career at Nucor. Similar group-oriented cost-reduction systems are in place at some of Nucor's major competitors, including Chaparral Steel.[28]

Less formal management control systems also drive a cost-reduction philosophy at cost leadership firms. For example, although Wal-Mart is one of the most successful retail operations in the world, its Arkansas headquarters is plain and simple. Indeed, some have suggested that Wal-Mart's headquarters looks like a warehouse. Its style of interior decoration was once described as "early bus station." Wal-Mart even involves its customers in reducing costs by asking them to "help keep your costs low" by returning shopping carts to the designated areas in Wal-Mart's parking lots.[29]

Compensation Policies and Implementing Cost Leadership Strategies

As suggested in Table 4.7 compensation in cost leadership firms is usually tied directly to cost-reducing efforts. Such firms often provide incentives for employees to work together to reduce costs and increase or maintain quality, and they expect *every* employee to take responsibility for both costs and quality. For example, an important expense for retail stores like Wal-Mart is "shrinkage"—a nice way of saying people steal stuff. About half the shrinkage in most stores comes from employees stealing their own companies' products.

Wal-Mart used to have a serious problem with shrinkage. Among other solutions (including hiring "greeters" whose real job is to discourage shoplifters), Wal-Mart developed a compensation scheme that took half the cost savings created by reduced shrinkage and shared it with employees in the form of a bonus. With this incentive in place, Wal-Mart's shrinkage problems dropped significantly.

Summary

Firms producing essentially the same products can have different costs for several reasons. Some of the most important of these are: (1) size differences and economies of scale; (2) size differences and diseconomies of scale; (3) experience differences and learning-curve economies; (4) differential access to productive inputs; and (5) technological advantages independent of scale. In addition, firms competing in the same industry can make policy choices about the kinds of products and services to sell that can have an important impact on their relative cost position. Cost leadership in an industry can be valuable by assisting a firm in reducing the threat of each of the five environmental threats in an industry outlined in Chapter 2.

Each of the sources of cost advantage discussed in this chapter can be a source of sustained competitive advantage if it is rare and costly to imitate. Overall, learning-curve economies, differential access to productive inputs, and technological "software" are more likely to be rare than other sources of cost advantage. Differential access to productive inputs and technological "software" is more likely to be costly to imitate—either through direct duplication or through substitution—than the other sources of cost advantage. Thus, differential access to productive inputs and technological "software" will often be more likely to be a source of sustained competitive advantage than cost advantages based on other sources.

Of course, to realize the full potential of these competitive advantages, a firm must be organized appropriately. Organizing to implement a strategy always involves a firm's organizational structure, its management control systems, and its compensation policies. The organizational structure used to implement cost leadership—and other business strategies—is called a *functional,* or *U-form,* structure. The CEO is the only person in this structure who has a corporate perspective. The CEO has two responsibilities: to formulate a firm's strategy and to implement it by coordinating functions within a firm. Ensuring that a firm's functions are aligned with its strategy is essential to successful strategy implementation.

When used to implement a cost leadership strategy, the U-form structure generally has few layers, simple reporting relationships, and a small corporate staff. It focuses on a narrow range of business functions. The management control systems used to implement these strategies generally include tight cost controls; quantitative cost goals; close supervision of labor, raw materials, inventory, and other costs; and a cost leadership culture and mentality. Finally, compensation policies in these firms typically reward cost reduction and provide incentives for everyone in the organization to be part of the cost-reduction effort.

Challenge Questions

4.1. Ryanair, Wal-Mart, Timex, Casio, and Hyundai are all OFTEN cited as examples of firms pursuing cost leadership strategies, but these firms make substantial investments in advertising, which seems more likely to be associated with a product differentiation strategy. Are these firms really pursuing a cost leadership strategy, or are they pursuing a product differentiation strategy by emphasizing their lower costs?

4.2. When economies of scale exist, firms with large volumes of production will have lower costs than those with smaller volumes of production. The realization of these economies of scale, however, is far from automatic. What actions can firms take to ensure that they realize whatever economies of scale are created by their volume of production?

4.3. Firms engage in an activity called "forward pricing" when they establish, during the early stages of the learning curve, a price for their products that is lower than their actual costs, in anticipation of lower costs later on, after significant learning has occurred. Under what conditions, if any, does forward pricing make sense?

4.4. When firms do engage in "forward pricing" what risks, if any, do they face?

4.5. One way of thinking about organizing to implement cost leadership strategies is that firms pursuing this strategy should be highly centralized, have high levels of direct supervision, and keep employee wages to an absolute minimum. Another approach is to decentralize decision-making authority—to ensure that individuals who know the most about reducing costs make decisions about how to reduce costs. This, in turn, would imply less direct supervision and somewhat higher levels of employee wages. Why is this?

4.6. Which of the two approaches used to implement cost leadership strategies seems more reasonable?

4.7. Under what conditions would the two different approaches for implementing cost leadership strategies make more or less sense?

Problem Set

4.8. The economies of scale curve in Figure 4.1 can be represented algebraically in the following equation:

$$\text{Average costs} = a + bQ + cQ^2$$

where Q is the quantity produced by a firm and a, b, and c are coefficients that are estimated from industry data. For example, it has been shown that the economies of scale curve for United States savings and loans is:

$$\text{Average costs} = 2.38 - .615A + .54A^2$$

where A is a savings and loan's total assets. Using this equation, what is the optimal size of a savings and loan? (Hint: Plug in different values of A and calculate average costs. The lowest possible average cost is the optimal size for a savings and loan.)

4.9. The learning curve depicted in Figure 4.2 can be represented algebraically by the following equation:

$$\text{Average time to produce } x \text{ units} = ax^{-\beta}$$

where x is the total number of units produced by a firm in its history, a is the amount of time it took a firm to produce its first unit, and β is a coefficient that describes the rate of learning in a firm.

Suppose it takes a team of workers 45 hours to assemble its first product ($a = 45$) and 40.5 hours to assemble the second. When a firm doubles its production (in this case, from one to two units) and cuts its production time (in this case, from 45 hours to 40.5 hours), learning is said to have occurred (in this case, a 40.5/45, or 90 percent, learning curve). The β for a 90 percent learning curve is 0.3219. Thus, this firm's learning curve is:

$$\text{Average time to produce } x \text{ units} = 45x^{-0.3219}$$

What is the average amount of time it will take this firm to produce six products? (Hint: Simply plug "6" in for x in the equation and solve.) What is the total time it took this firm to produce these six products? (Hint: Simply multiply the number of units produced, 6, by the average time it will take to produce these six products.) What is the average time it will take this firm to produce five products? What is the total time it will take this firm to produce five products? So, what is the total time it will take this firm to produce its sixth product? (Hint: Subtract the total time needed to produce five products from the total time needed to produce six products.)

Suppose a new firm is going to start producing these same products. Assuming this new firm does not learn anything from established firms, what will its cost disadvantage be when it assembles its first product? (Hint: Compare the costs of the experienced firm's sixth product with the cost of the new firm's first product.)

Writing Assignments

4.10. What are the implications and considerations for a small business that chooses a cost leadership business strategy?

4.11. Discuss the impact of a cost leadership strategy on environmental threats.

CASE STUDY | Zerodha Way: Trading reimagined

Founded by brother-duo, Nithin Kamath and Nikhil Kamath, Zerodha commenced operations on 15 August 2010, with a path-breaking goal to dismantle all barriers that traders and investors face in India in terms of cost, support, and technology. The name Zerodha is a derivative from the words Zero and *Rodha* (the Sanskrit word for barrier). The company got the early-mover advantage being the first in the discount broking space, offering reduced commission or low brokerage on the transactions to ideally attract the investors to use this platform. With a client base of more than 5 million, Zerodha is the largest stockbroker in terms of clients with a team of over 1,300 employees.

Zerodha - Startup Launch

Nitin Kamath has been trading in the Indian stock market since the age of 17 and in a very short span, he acquired more clients through referrals, and subsequently became a sub-broker with Reliance Money (RMoney) upon its launch. At Reliance Money, Nitin was one of the most successful sub-brokers, breaking volumes of more than 1,000 sub-brokers at once. "But as a trader, I was still finding something missing with the way RMoney was working, not really what a trader requires. That is when we decided to start Zerodha," added Nithin.

At the initial stage of commencing operations, Zerodha opened 3,000 accounts. The focus on building a community for the traders helped Zerodh. Discount broking model stemmed from the fact that retail investors were often clueless about what stocks should be bought or sold, and lacked research-based guidance and training on trading in stock markets. To counter this challenge, Zerodha launched its learning module which became immensely popular. It ran Trading Q&A, an active forum where traders and investors were able to discuss stock ideas.

Zerodha leverages technology to differentiate itself from the rest in the market. Its flagship trading platform, Kite—available on web and as mobile app—accounts for more than 10 percent of all retail trading turnover in the country. Zerodha eventually launched 'Coin'—an online platform to buy mut ual funds directly.

Cost Leadership

Zerodha's strategy is offer low-cost products the industry. Cost leadership strategy takes place through experience, investment in production facilities, conservation and careful monitoring on the total operating costs. Pursuing a strategy of cost leadership will benefit Zerodha more by leveraging increased managerial control over the costs, refrain from incurring too many expenses from innovation or marketing, and cut prices when selling their products. Zerodha build online trading momentum through cost savings by providing free software, investment information, as well as any form of reward. Although Zerodha's revenue model is not straightforward, the company is arguably one of the most used trading networks in India. Traders across the nation use this platform for investment and trading. The company charges ₹20 or 0.03 percent, whichever is lower, for each Futures & Options and intraday equity trade. Since a large volume of transactions takes place on the platform, it generates revenue. Zerodha's strategy based on differentiation, product R&D, reputation and brand-building, and strong traders and customer networks, provides the firm with a more durable advantages enabling sustainable performance over time.

Product Differentiation

This strategy requires the development of unique and unmatched services by relying on customer loyalty to the brand. A company can offer high quality, performance, or unique features, each of which can justify higher prices. Brokers' primary historical role is to match orders—they bring buyers and sellers of stock together by using the services of dealers on an exchange or in an over-the-counter market. Technological advancement over the past decade has changed the cost structure of the brokerage industry. Conventionally, securities companies establish their customer relationships through direct interactions (e.g., face-to-face or telephonic) between securities brokers and their clients. Customers contact with their brokers spontaneously with huge trading amount.

Zerodha has invested significantly in its technical infrastructure and network configuration to ensure the stability and security of its online trading platform. The business model of Zerodha works on a 'low margin and high-volume model. Zerodha charges a very minimal amount to the traders for transactions because of which the trading volume is generally high. This fee collection of smaller amounts from a larger number of clients leads to good revenue generation for Zerodha. Also, another factor helping high-profit margins for the company is the low operational costs because of its online structure. The fee of online trading is 40 percent less than the conventional way and this is the major reason to attract customers to go online.

Other than this, the company charges a only ₹300 annually for account maintenance. The company has seen a rapid increase in its user base in the past few years. It contributes to more than 2 percent of investors in the stock exchange from its platform that would eventually increase the revenue. Zerodha made headlines when it earned itself a $1 billion valuation, without having ever gone out to raise money from investors. And now, the company is valued at a whopping $3 billion in the Hurun Global Unicorn List of 2020. The Zerodha way is IT-centric to relational-centric, everyone (all customers) to effective exploring segmented customers, "value of customer" to "value to customer", and enriched information to enriched investors.

Business Strategies, Financial Leverage and Performance

Zerodha is the lowest-cost producer in its industry (i.e., a cost leadership strategy) or competing by providing unique products in terms of quality, physical characteristics, or product related services (i.e., a product differentiation strategy). The essence of a firm's business strategy is its ability to deliberately choose a set of activities which will deliver a unique mix of values to its customers. In 2011, Zerodha initiated Rainmatter, an early-stage fund with a corpus of ₹50 crore. By keeping the ticket size lower than $1 million per investment, the fund has focused on minimizing risk but focus on funding start-ups in the field of new technology and new product development. Some notable investments of Rainmatter are in start-ups like Digio, Learnapp, Finception, Smallcase, Sensibull and Quicko. So far. Rainmatter has made 11 investments of which 7 are lead investments, the most recent investment being made on January 28, 2021, when GrowFix raised $2 million.

True Beacon and Mutual Fund AMC

In 2019, Zerodha started True Beacon—the Alternative Investment Fund (AIF)—focused on giving returns in volatile markets through their defensive investment strategy. The $2 million minimum investment fund has been able to generate a return of 26.6 percent in its first year. In 2020, Zerodha has applied for a license to establish a Mutual Fund AMC in India.

Algorithmic Trading and Its Benefits

Streak, an extension to Kite—Zerodha's exchange approved trading platform—is a start-up as part of Rainmatter. In conventional trading, brokers' professional know-how, goodwill, morality, and a company's overall image are the ingredients in building customers' trustworthiness and sustainable relationships. Algorithmic trading is the use of a computer program with a defined set of criteria to carry through trades. The criteria for the system typically includes timing, price, or quantity. Algorithmic trading makes use of complex formulas, combined with mathematical models and human oversight, to make decisions to buy or sell financial securities on an exchange. In theory, the use of algorithmic trading can generate trades and profit at higher frequencies than a human trader can. Algorithmic trading (also known as algo trading) offers high-profit opportunities and streamlines trades, as it removes any possible human variables.

Algo trading can be used in mid to long-term investments like mutual funds, insurance companies, and pension funds. It provides investors with many benefits including anonymity, efficiency, reduced trading costs and risks, lower commissions, and full control of the order. Algo trading has recently become one of the biggest areas of research and investment for Dalal Street.

Financials of Zerodha

Zerodha's financial year 2022 (FY22) showcases a narrative of robust growth and operational efficiency, making it a standout case in the fintech and stock broking sectors.

Revenue and Profitability Growth

In FY22, Zerodha's revenue from operations surged by 82 percent, climbing to ₹4,964 crore from ₹2,729 crore in the preceding fiscal year (FY21). This significant growth underscores the company's expanding market presence and its ability to leverage opportunities in a vibrant stock market environment. Furthermore, the profit after tax (PAT) saw an impressive increase of 86 percent, reaching ₹2,094 crore, up from ₹1,122 crore in FY21. These figures highlight Zerodha's success in enhancing its profitability alongside revenue growth.

Revenue Streams

The breakdown of Zerodha's revenue reveals a diversified portfolio of income sources. The company's earnings are primarily derived from brokerage fees, sale of premium tech products like Kite, Connect, API, user onboarding collections, and exchange transaction charges. In FY22, these collections witnessed an 83.3 percent jump to ₹4,129 crore from ₹2,252.5 crore in FY21, indicating a strong demand for Zerodha's services and products.

Operational Expenses

Zerodha's operational expenses in FY22 totalled ₹2,164 crore, marking a 71.7 percent increase from ₹1,260 crore in FY21. A significant portion of these expenses was attributed to exchange transaction shares, which accounted for 62 percent of the overall costs and rose by 82.3 percent to ₹1,342 crore. Employee benefits, another major expense category, constituted over 21 percent of the total expenditure, surging 45.3 percent to ₹459 crore, which included ₹77.5 crore of share-based payments to employees.

Year-on-Year Comparison and Efficiency Metrics

A year-on-year comparison reveals the scale of Zerodha's growth, with net cash flows from operations reported at ₹2,851 crore. The company's EBITDA margin improved by 231 basis points to 56.78 percent, showcasing enhanced operational efficiency. Remarkably, Zerodha managed to keep its cost-to-income ratio low, spending just ₹0.44 to earn a rupee of operating revenue. This metric is a testament to the company's prudent cost management and operational efficiency.

Zerodha's financial performance in FY22 illustrates a trajectory of sustained growth, profitability, and operational excellence. The company not only expanded its revenue streams and managed its expenditures effectively but also demonstrated remarkable efficiency in converting operational activities into profitability. Zerodha's ability to navigate the dynamic financial services landscape, coupled with its strategic investments in technology and human resources, positions it as a leading player in India's fintech sector. This case study not only sheds light on Zerodha's financial achievements but also offers valuable insights into the strategies that have propelled it to the forefront of financial innovation and service excellence.

Startup Challenges

Certain challenges faced by Zerodha are technical glitches on the platform because of heavy trading which leads to decreasing customer satisfaction. The customer support mechanism of Zerodha is not that efficient as compared to other top brokers in India. Important fact materials like daily reports, quarterly result analysis, news alerts, etc. are not provided by this platform unlike some of the other top brokers.

What Next!

Porter (1980) introduced a framework positing that firms that choose to implement strategies based on either differentiation or cost leadership may enjoy superior performance. Cost leadership based primarily on operational efficiencies, however, is easily imitable and the superior performance achieved through competitors over time. This was exemplified when ICICI Securities, the market leader, was dethroned despite having nearly 8.47 lakh active clients and conducting around 2–3 million trades every day. Zerodha faces some cut-throat competition in the market such as discount broker Upstox. Zerodha also faces serious competition from full-service brokers which are huge and popular amongst traders such as HDFC Securities, Kotak Securities, Motilal Oswal, etc. Zerodha is the largest retail brokerage firm across the world, consistently adding 50,000 to 75,000 accounts every month. Current focus of the company is traders, and the upcoming goals for Zerodha is the aim to add 5–10 million new investors to the Indian stock market with the aid of the platform. Scaling requires delivering new benefits to its corporate strategy, and linking of its structure, system & processes (SSP) with its businesses and resources becomes challenging.

Questions:

1. What resources and capabilities are essential for firms to remain competitive in the stock broking industry?
2. What key competencies have contributed to Zerodha's success in the stock broking market?
3. Considering Zerodha's current market position and industry trends, what strategic direction should the Kamath brothers pursue: further expansion within the existing segment, targeting new market segments, or diversification into unrelated business areas?

References

Palekar, P., Mahapatra, G. P., & Patankar, P. (2023). *Start-Up to Scale-Up: The Changing Entrepreneurs' Competencies.* In Business Cases in Organisation Behaviour and HRM: Perspectives from India (pp. 157-172). Singapore: Springer Nature Singapore.

Kuchi, S., & Gupta, S. (2023, December). *How Successful Online Platforms Create Value?* In International Working Conference on Transfer and Diffusion of IT (pp. 278-289). Cham: Springer Nature Switzerland.

Babu, A., Mathews, A., & Chinmaya, A. M. (2023). *Dave Berkus Method.* In A Practical Guide for Startup Valuation: An Analytic Approach (pp. 209–222). Cham: Springer Nature Switzerland.

Jitesh Kumar Meena and Rohitash Kumar Banyal, *The Complexity Analysis of Stock Market Price and Investment*, In: Satyasai Jagannath Nanda and Rajendra Prasad Yadav (eds), Data Science and Intelligent Computing Techniques, SCRS, India, 2023, pp. 185-195. https://doi.org/10.56155/978-81-955020-2-8-16

Sanchita, K., & Gupta, S. (2023). *Strategies for Value Reconfiguration in Online Platforms*. California Management Review, 66(1), 72-95.

End Notes

1 Kiley, D. (2011). "Fiat headed back to U.S. after 27 years." http://autos.aol.com/article/fiat-500-coming-to-america/ Accessed Aug 21, 2013.

2 Christensen, C. R., N. A. Berg, and M. S. Salter. (1980). *Policy formulation and administration: A casebook of senior management problems in business*, 8th ed. Homewood, IL: Irwin, p. 163.

3 Scherer, F. M. (1980). *Industrial market structure and economic performance*. Boston: Houghton Mifflin; Moore, F. T. (1959). "Economies of scale: Some statistical evidence." *Quarterly Journal of Economics*, 73, pp. 232–245; and Lau, L. J., and S. Tamura. (1972). "Economies of scale, technical progress, and the nonhomothetic leontief production function." *Journal of Political Economy*, 80, pp. 1167–1187.

4 Scherer, F. M. (1980). *Industrial market structure and economic performance*. Boston: Houghton Mifflin; and Perrow, C. (1984). *Normal accidents: Living with high-risk technologies*. New York: Basic Books.

5 See D. Besanko and R. Braeutigam (2014) Microeconomics. 5th edition. NY: Wiley, pg. 320–321; Jay Barney (2011) Gaining and Sustaining Competitive Advantage. 4th edition. NY: Person, pg. 154–155.

6 Hamermesh, R. G., and R. S. Rosenbloom. (1989). "Crown Cork and Seal Co., Inc." Harvard Business School Case No. 9-388-096.

7 See Hackman, J. R., and G. R. Oldham. (1980). *Work redesign*. Reading, MA: Addison-Wesley.

8 This relationship was first noticed in 1925 by the commander of Wright-Patterson Air Force Base in Dayton, Ohio.

9 Learning curves have been estimated for numerous industries. Boston Consulting Group. (1970). "Perspectives on experience." Boston: BCG, presents learning curves for over 20 industries while Lieberman, M. (1984). "The learning curve and pricing in the chemical processing industries." *Rand Journal of Economics*, 15, pp. 213–228, estimates learning curves for 37 chemical products.

10 See Henderson, B. (1974). *The experience curve reviewed III—How does it work?* Boston: Boston Consulting Group; and Boston Consulting Group. (1970). "Perspectives on experience." Boston: BCG.

11 Hall, G., and S. Howell. (1985). "The experience curve from the economist's perspective." *Strategic Management Journal*, 6, pp. 197–212.

12 Hill, C. W. L. (1988). "Differentiation versus low-cost or differentiation and low-cost: A contingency framework." *Academy of Management Review*, 13(3), pp. 401–412.

13 R. D. Buzzell, B. T. Gale, and R. M. Sultan (1975). "Market share—the key to profitability." *Harvard Business Review*, 53, pp. 97–106; R. Rumelt and R. Wensley (1981). "In search of the market share effect." *Proceedings of the Academy of Management Meetings, 1981*, pp. 2–6; C. Montgomery and B. Wernerfelt (1991). "Sources of superior performance: Market share versus industry effects in the U.S. brewing industry." *Management Science*, 37, pp. 954–959.

14 See Ghemawat, P., and H. J. Stander III. (1992). "Nucor at a crossroads." Harvard Business School Case No. 9-793-039 on technology in steel manufacturing and cost advantages; Shaffer, R. A. (1995). "Intel as conquistador." *Forbes*, February 27, p. 130 on technology in semiconductor manufacturing and cost advantages; Monteverde, K., and D. Teece. (1982). "Supplier switching costs and vertical integration in the automobile industry." *Rand Journal of Economics*, 13(1), pp. 206–213; and McCormick, J., and N. Stone. (1990). "From national champion to global competitor: An interview with Thomson's Alain Gomez." *Harvard Business Review*, May/June, pp. 126–135 on technology in consumer electronic manufacturing and cost advantages.

15 Schultz, E. (1989). "Climbing high with discount brokers." *Fortune*, Fall (special issue), pp. 219–223.

16 Schonfeld, E. (1998). "Can computers cure health care?" *Fortune*, March 30, pp. 111+.

17 Ibid.

18 R. DeGeorge (2000). "Ethics in international business—A contradiction in terms?" *Business Credit*, 102, pp. 50+; G. Edmondson, K. Carlisle, I. Resch, K. Nickel Anhalt, and H. Dawley (2000). "Workers in bondage." *BusinessWeek*, November 27, pp. 146+; D. Winter (2000). "Facing globalization." *Ward's Auto World*, 36, pp.

19 See Meyer, M. W., and L. B. Zucker. (1989). *Permanently failing organizations*. Newbury Park, CA: Sage.

20 Staw, B. M. (1981). "The escalation of commitment to a course of action." *Academy of Management Review*, 6, pp. 577–587.

21 Hesterly, W. S. (1989). *Top management succession as a determinant of firm performance and de-escalation: An agency problem*. Unpublished doctoral dissertation, University of California, Los Angeles.

22 Barney, J. B. (1986). "Organizational culture: Can it be a source of sustained competitive advantage?" *Academy of Management Review*, 11, pp. 656–665.

23 See Spence, A. M. (1981). "The learning curve and competition." *Bell Journal of Economics*, 12, pp. 49–70, on why learning needs to be proprietary; Mansfield, E. (1985). "How rapidly does new industrial technology leak out?" *Journal of Industrial Economics*, 34(2), pp. 217–223; Lieberman, M. B. (1982). *The learning-curve, pricing and market structure in the chemical processing industries*. Unpublished doctoral dissertation, Harvard University; Lieberman, M. B. (1987). "The learning curve, diffusion, and competitive strategy." *Strategic Management Journal*, 8, pp. 441–452, on why it usually is not proprietary.

24 Williamson, O. (1975). *Markets and hierarchies*. New York: Free Press.

25 Davis, S. M., and P. R. Lawrence. (1977). *Matrix*. Reading, MA: Addison-Wesley.

26 See Ghemawat, P., and H. J. Stander III. (1992). "Nucor at a crossroads." Harvard Business School Case No. 9-793-039.

27 See Floyd, S. W., and B. Woldridge. (1992). "Middle management involvement in strategy and its association with strategic type: A research note." *Strategic Management Journal*, 13, pp. 153–167.

28 Ibid.

29 Walton, S. (1992). *Sam Walton, Made in America: My story*. New York: Doubleday.

CHAPTER

5 Product Differentiation

LEARNING OBJECTIVES

After reading this chapter, you should be able to:

5.1 Define product differentiation, describe 11 bases of product differentiation, and how these bases of product differentiation can be grouped into three categories.

5.2 Describe how product differentiation can create economic value.

5.3 Describe:

a. Those bases of product differentiation that are not likely to be costly to duplicate, those that may be costly to duplicate, and those that will often be costly to duplicate.

b. The main substitutes for product differentiation strategies.

5.4 Describe how organizational structure, control processes, and compensation policies can be used to implement product differentiation strategies.

5.5 Discuss whether it is possible for a firm to implement cost leadership and product differentiation strategies simultaneously.

Strategic Diversification: Royal Enfield's Route to Global Leadership

Royal Enfield, a brand under Eicher Motors Limited, has etched a unique position in the global motorcycle market through its strategic focus on product differentiation. Founded initially in England to manufacture bicycles, Royal Enfield expanded its product line to include motorcycles in 1901, targeting the Indian market in 1949. The brand's deep historical roots and classic design aesthetics have been pivotal in its differentiation strategy, appealing to a segment of consumers looking for more than just a mode of transportation; they seek an extension of their personality and lifestyle.

At a point, when Royal Enfield was facing downtrends, the revival of the company was significantly led by Siddhartha Lal, who, after taking over as COO of the Eicher group in 2004, divested 13 businesses to focus primarily on Royal Enfield and trucks. Lal's strategy was rooted in leveraging the brand's heritage while modernizing its offerings to cater to contemporary needs without compromising the motorcycles' iconic design and character. This approach has successfully transformed Royal Enfield from a struggling brand into a global name synonymous with quality, tradition, and rugged charm

Royal Enfield's strategic emphasis on product differentiation has significantly strengthened its financial performance, marking 2023 as a year of substantial growth and global sales achievements. The company's focused approach to leveraging its historic brand identity, coupled with the introduction of varied motorcycle models tailored to diverse consumer preferences, has enabled Royal Enfield to achieve a new sales record. In 2023, Royal Enfield's global sales surged by 16.2 percent, reaching a remarkable total of 0.92 million units. This growth was not confined to the Indian market alone but was also evident in significant sales increases across North America (17.1 percent) and Latin America (27.0 percent), highlighting the brand's expanding international footprint and its success in penetrating markets with distinct consumer dynamics.

The journey of Royal Enfield from a traditional motorcycle manufacturer to a global powerhouse underscores the impact of strategic product differentiation. By maintaining its classic design appeal while integrating modern engineering and technology, Royal Enfield has catered to both its loyal customer base and new segments looking for unique riding experiences. This strategy not only revitalized the brand but also positioned it as a lifestyle product, appealing to consumers' desire for motorcycles that offer more than just transportation but also a sense of identity and adventure. The financial implications of Royal Enfield's strategic choices have been profound. By 2023, the brand's commitment to maintaining a blend of heritage and innovation within its product lineup contributed to its record-breaking sales figures. Additionally, Royal Enfield's approach to pricing, which strategically positions its motorcycles as premium yet accessible, has allowed the brand to capture a significant share of the market, competing effectively against both lower-priced models and higher-end global brands. The success of models like the Classic 350, Himalayan, and the Interceptor 650 exemplifies how Royal Enfield has successfully leveraged product differentiation to drive financial growth.

Looking ahead, Royal Enfield faces the challenge of sustaining its growth momentum amid evolving consumer preferences and increasing competition. The brand's future direction will likely involve further innovation in product development, expansion into new geographic markets, and continued emphasis on building a strong brand identity that resonates with consumers worldwide. As Royal Enfield navigates these challenges, its ability to adapt and innovate while staying true to its heritage will be critical in maintaining its competitive edge and financial success.

REFERENCES

Carandbike. (2023). Two-Wheeler Sales October 2023: *Royal Enfield Registers 3 Per Cent Overall Growth*. News (, October 2023). Accessed from https://www.carandbike.com on March 25, 2024.

Chaudhary, P. (2021). *Royal Enfield: Preserving and leveraging legacy appeal while revamping brand imagery*. Journal of Brand Strategy, 10(3), 243-258.

MotorCyclesData. (2024, January 7). *Royal Enfield 2023. Global Sales Hit New All-Time Record*. Accessed from https://www.motorcyclesdata.com on March 25, 2024.

Royal Enfield uses its historic brand identity and classic design aesthetics to help implement its product differentiation strategy. As successful as this effort is, this is only one of many ways that firms can try to differentiate their products.

Objective 5.1 Define product differentiation, describe 11 bases of product differentiation, and how these bases of product differentiation can be grouped into three categories.

What is Product Differentiation?

Warby Parker exemplifies a firm pursuing a cost leadership strategy, Victoria's Secret exemplifies a firm pursuing a product differentiation strategy. **Product differentiation** is a business strategy where firms attempt to gain a competitive advantage by increasing the perceived value of their products or services relative to the perceived value of other firms' products or services. These other firms can be rivals or firms that provide substitute products or services. By increasing the perceived value of its products or services, a firm will be able to charge a higher price than it would otherwise. This higher price can increase a firm's revenues and generate competitive advantages.

A firm's attempts to create differences in the relative perceived value of its products or services often are often made by altering the objective properties of those products or services. Rolex attempts to differentiate its watches from Timex and Casio watches by manufacturing them with solid gold cases. Mercedes attempts to differentiate its cars from Fiat's cars through sophisticated engineering and high performance. Victoria's Secret attempts to differentiate its shopping experience from Wal-Mart, and other retailers, through the merchandise it sells and the way it sells it.

Although firms often alter the objective properties of their products or services to implement a product differentiation strategy, the existence of product differentiation, in the end, is *always* a matter of customer perception. Products sold by two different firms may be very similar, but if customers believe the first is more valuable than the second, then the first product has a differentiation advantage.

In the world of "craft" or "microbrewery" beers, for example, the consumers' image of how a beer was brewed was sometimes very different from how it was actually brewed. Boston Beer Company, for example, sells Samuel Adams Beer. Customers could tour the Boston Beer Company, where they saw a small row of fermenting tanks and two 10-barrel kettles being tended by a brewmaster wearing rubber boots. However, through much of its history Samuel Adams Beer was not actually brewed in this small factory. Instead, it was brewed—in 200-barrel steel tanks—in Cincinnati, Ohio, by the Hudepohl-Schoenling Brewing Company, a contract brewing firm that also manufactured Hudy Bold Beer and Little Kings Cream Ale. Maui Beer Company's Aloha Lager brand was brewed in Portland, Oregon, and Pete's Wicked Ale (a craft beer that claims it is brewed "one batch at a time. Carefully.") was brewed in batches of 400 barrels each by Stroh Brewery Company, makers of Old Milwaukee Beer. However, as long as consumers believed that there were important differences between these "craft" beers and more traditional brews—despite many of their common manufacturing methods—the more willing they were to pay more for a craft beer. This willingness to pay more suggests that an important "perceptual" basis of product differentiation exists for these craft beers.[1] If products or services are *perceived* as being different in a way that is valued by consumers, then product differentiation exists.

Just as perceptions can create product differentiation between products that are essentially identical, the lack of perceived differences between products with very different characteristics can prevent product differentiation. For example, consumers with an untrained palate may not be able to distinguish between two different wines, even though expert wine tasters would be very much aware of their differences. Those who are not aware of these differences, even if they exist, will not be willing to pay more for one wine over the other. In this sense, for these consumers at least, these two wines, though different, are not differentiated.

Product differentiation is always a matter of customer perceptions, but firms can take a variety of actions to influence these perceptions. These actions can be thought of as different bases of product differentiation.

Bases of Product Differentiation

A large number of authors, drawing on both theory and empirical research, have developed lists of ways firms can differentiate their products or services.[2] Some of these are listed in Table 5.1. Although the purpose of all these bases of product differentiation is to create the perception that a firm's products or services are unusually valuable, different bases of product differentiation attempt to accomplish this objective in different ways. For example, the first four bases of product differentiation listed in Table 5.1 attempt to create this perception by focusing directly on the attributes of the products or services a firm sells. The second three attempt to create this perception by developing a relationship between a firm and its customers. The last five attempts to create this perception through linkages within and between firms. Of course, these bases of product differentiation are not mutually exclusive. Indeed, firms will often attempt to differentiate their products or services along multiple dimensions simultaneously. An empirical method for identifying ways that firms have differentiated their products is discussed in the Research Made Relevant feature.

Focusing on the Attributes of a Firm's Products or Services

The first group of bases of product differentiation identified in Table 5.1 focuses on the attributes of a firm's products or services.

TABLE 5.1 Ways Firms Can Differentiate Their Products

To differentiate its products, a firm can focus directly on the attributes of its products or services:

1. Product features
2. Product complexity
3. Timing of product introduction
4. Location

or on relationships between itself and its customers:

5. Product customization
6. Consumer marketing
7. Product reputation

or on linkages within or between firms:

8. Linkages among functions within a firm
9. Linkages with other firms
10. Product mix
11. Distribution channels
12. Service and support

Sources: M. E. Porter (1980). *Competitive strategy*. New York: Free Press; R. E. Caves and P. Williamson (1985). "What is product differentiation, really?" *Journal of Industrial Economics*, 34, pp. 113–132.

Product Features The most obvious way that firms can try to differentiate their products is by altering the features of the products they sell. One industry in which firms are constantly modifying product features to attempt to differentiate their products is the automobile industry. For example, at the 2017 Detroit Auto Show, General Motors introduced a new feature on certain versions of its Cadillac CTS called "V2V"—this is a vehicle to vehicle communication system that will enable cars to gather data from other cars about traffic and road conditions ahead. Bentley introduced a new 48-volt electric system in one of its high-end SUVs—to provide more power than the typical 12 volt systems in most cars, but without the risks that are sometimes associated with the 300 volt systems of electric vehicles. And Volvo, BMW, and Toyota all introduced models with e-axles—typically a rear axle driven by an electric motor that can supplement or even replace power from the front axle driven by a gasoline engine. This hybrid design is less complex than having both gas and electric power delivered through the same axle. All these—and many more—changes in the attributes of automobiles are examples of firms trying to differentiate their products by altering product features.[3]

Product Complexity Product complexity can be thought of as a special case of altering a product's features to create product differentiation. In a given industry, product complexity can vary significantly. The BIC "crystal pen," for example, has only a handful of parts, whereas a Cross or a Mont Blanc pen has many more parts. To the extent that these differences in product complexity convince consumers that the products of some firms are more valuable than the products of other firms, product complexity can be a basis of product differentiation.

Timing of Product Introduction Introducing a product at the right time can also help create product differentiation. As suggested in Chapter 2, in some industry settings (e.g., in emerging industries) *the* critical issue is to be a first mover—to introduce a new product before all other firms. Being first in emerging industries can enable a firm to set important technological standards, preempt strategically valuable assets, and develop customer-switching costs. These first-mover advantages can create a perception among customers that the products or services of the first-moving firm are somehow more valuable than the products or services of other firms.[4]

Timing-based product differentiation, however, does not depend only on being a first mover. Sometimes, a firm can be a later mover in an industry but introduce products or services at just the right time and thereby gain a competitive advantage. This can happen when the ultimate success of a product or service depends on the availability of complementary products or technologies. For example, the domination of Microsoft's MS-DOS operating system, and thus ultimately the domination of Windows, was only possible because IBM introduced its version of the personal computer. Without the IBM PC, it would have been difficult for any operating system—including MS-DOS—to have such a large market presence.[5]

Location The physical location of a firm can also be a source of product differentiation.[6] Consider, for example, Disney's operations in Orlando, Florida. Beginning with The Magic Kingdom and EPCOT Center, Disney built a world-class destination resort in Orlando. Over the years, Disney has added numerous attractions to its core entertainment activities, including Disney Studios, more than 11,000 Disney-owned hotel rooms, a $100 million sports center, an automobile racing track, an after-hours entertainment district, and, most recently, a $1 billion theme park called "The Animal Kingdom"—all in and around Orlando. Now, families can travel from around the world to Orlando, knowing that in a single location they can enjoy a full range of Disney adventures.[7]

Research Made Relevant

Discovering the Bases of Product Differentiation

Of all the possible bases of product differentiation that might exist in a particular market, how does one pinpoint those that have actually been used? Research in strategic management and marketing has shown that the bases of product differentiation can be identified using multiple regression analysis to estimate what are called **hedonic prices**. A hedonic price is that part of the price of a product or service that is attributable to a particular characteristic of that product or service.

The logic behind hedonic prices is straightforward. If customers are willing to spend more for a product with a particular attribute than they are willing to spend for that same product without that attribute, then that attribute differentiates the first product from the second. That is, this attribute is a basis of product differentiation in this market.

Consider, for example, the price of used cars. The market price of a used car can be determined using a variety of used car buying guides. These guides typically establish the base price of a used car. This base price typically includes product features that are common to almost all cars—a radio, a standard engine, a heater/defroster. Because these product attributes are common to virtually all cars, they are not a basis for product differentiation.

However, in addition to these common features, the base price of an automobile is adjusted based on some less common features—a high-end stereo system, a larger engine, air-conditioning. How much the base price of the car is adjusted when these features are added—$300 for a high-end stereo, $500 for a larger engine, $200 for air-conditioning—are the hedonic prices of these product attributes. These product attributes differentiate well-equipped cars from less-well-equipped cars and, because consumers are willing to pay more for well-equipped cars, can be thought of as bases of product differentiation in this market.

Multiple regression techniques are used to estimate these hedonic prices in the following way. For our simple car example, the following regression equation is estimated:

$$Price = a_1 + b_1(Stereo) + b_2(Engine) + b_3(AC)$$

where *Price* is the retail price of cars, *Stereo* is a variable describing whether a car has a high-end stereo, *Engine* is a variable describing whether a car has a large engine, and *AC* is a variable describing whether a car has air-conditioning. If the hedonic prices for these features are those suggested earlier, the results of running this regression analysis would be:

$$Price = \$7{,}800 + \$300(Stereo) + \$500(Engine) + \$200(AC)$$

where $7,800 is the base price of this type of used car.[8]

Focusing on the Relationship Between a Firm and Its Customers

The second group of bases of product differentiation identified in Table 5.1 focuses on relationships between a firm and its customers.

Product Customization Products can also be differentiated by the extent to which they are customized for particular customer applications. Product customization is an important basis for product differentiation in a wide variety of industries, from enterprise software to bicycles.

Enterprise software is software that is designed to support all of a firm's critical business functions, including human resources, payroll, customer service, sales, quality control, and so forth. Major competitors in this industry include Oracle and SAP. However, although these firms sell basic software packages, most firms find it necessary to customize these basic packages to meet their specific business needs. The ability to build complex software packages that can also be customized to meet the specific needs of a particular customer is an important basis of product differentiation in this marketplace.

In the bicycle industry, consumers can spend as little as $50 on a bicycle, and as much as—well, almost as much as they want on a bicycle, easily more than $15,000. High-end bicycles use, of course, the very best components, such as brakes and gears. But what distinguishes these bicycles is their feel when they are ridden. High-end bike frames are built from special steel, carbon fiber, and even titanium. The geometry of the frame can also be customized to a rider's height, weight, torso length, inseam, and so forth. Once a serious rider becomes accustomed to a particular bicycle, it is very difficult for that rider to switch to alternative suppliers.

Consumer Marketing Differential emphasis on consumer marketing has been a basis for product differentiation in a wide variety of industries. Through advertising and other consumer marketing efforts, firms attempt to alter the perceptions of current and potential customers, whether specific attributes of a firm's products or services are actually altered.

For example, in the soft drink industry, Mountain Dew—a product of PepsiCo—was originally marketed as a fruity, lightly carbonated drink that tasted, "as light as a morning dew in the mountains." However, beginning in the late 1990s Mountain Dew's marketing efforts changed dramatically. "As light as a morning dew in the mountains" became, "Do the Dew," and Mountain Dew focused its marketing efforts on young, mostly male, extreme-sports–oriented consumers. Young men riding snowboards, roller blades, mountain bikes, and skateboards—mostly upside down—became central to most Mountain Dew commercials. Mountain Dew became a sponsor of a wide variety of extreme sports contests and an important sponsor of the X Games on ESPN. Note that this radical repositioning of Mountain Dew depended entirely on changes in consumer marketing. The features of the underlying product were not changed.

Reputation Perhaps the most important relationship between a firm and its customers depends on a firm's reputation in its marketplace. Indeed, a firm's **reputation** is no more than a socially complex relationship between a firm and its customers. Once developed, a firm's reputation can last a long time, even if the basis for that reputation no longer exists.[9]

A firm that has tried to exploit its reputation for cutting-edge entertainment is MTV, a division of Viacom, Inc. Although several well-known video artists—including Madonna—have had their videos banned from MTV, it has still been able to develop a reputation for risk-taking on television. MTV believes that its viewers have come to expect the unexpected in MTV programming. One of the first efforts to exploit, and reinforce, this reputation for risk-taking was *Beavis and Butthead*, an animated series starring two teenage boys with serious social and emotional development problems. More recently, MTV exploited its reputation by inventing an entirely new genre of television—"reality TV"—through its *Real World* and *Road Rules* programs. Not only were these shows cheap to produce, they built on MTV's reputation for providing entertainment that is a little risky, a little sexy, and a little controversial. Indeed, MTV has been so successful in providing this kind of entertainment that it had to form an entirely new cable station—MTV 2—to actually show music videos.[10]

Focusing on Links Within and Between Firms

The third group of bases of product differentiation identified in Table 5.1 focuses on links within and between firms.

Linkages Between Functions A less obvious but still important way in which a firm can attempt to differentiate its products is through linking different functions within the firm. For example, research in the pharmaceutical industry suggests that firms vary in the extent to which they can integrate different scientific specialties—such as genetics, biology, chemistry, and pharmacology—to develop new drugs. Firms that can form effective multi-disciplinary teams to explore new drug categories have what some have called an **architectural competence**, that is, the ability to use organizational structure to facilitate coordination among scientific disciplines to conduct research. Firms that have this competence can more effectively pursue product differentiation strategies—by introducing new and powerful drugs—than those that do not have this competence. And in the pharmaceutical industry, where firms that introduce such drugs can experience very large positive returns, the ability to coordinate across functions is an important source of competitive advantage.[11]

Links with Other Firms Another basis of product differentiation is linkages with other firms. Here, instead of differentiating products or services based on linkages between functions within a single firm or linkages between different products, differentiation is based on explicit linkages between one firm's products and the products or services of other firms.

This form of product differentiation has increased in popularity over the past several years. For example, with the growth in popularity of stock car racing in the United States, more and more corporations are looking to link their products or services with famous names and cars in NASCAR. Firms such as Burger King, McDonald's Target, Taco Bell, GEICO, Farmers Insurance, Lowe's, FedEx, 5-Hour Energy, and Miller Lite have all been major sponsors of NASCAR teams. In one year, the Coca-Cola Corporation filled orders for more than 200,000 NASCAR-themed vending machines. Visa struggled to keep up with demand for its NASCAR affinity cards, and more than 1 million NASCAR Barbies were sold by Mattel—generating revenues of about $50 million. The conditions under which cooperative strategic alliances create value and are sources of sustained competitive advantage are discussed in detail in Chapter 11.

Product Mix One of the outcomes of links among functions within a firm and links between firms can be changes in the mix of products a firm brings to the market. This mix of products or services can be a source of product differentiation, especially when: (1) those products or services are technologically linked; or (2) when a single set of customers purchase several of a firm's products or services.

For example, technological interconnectivity is an extremely important selling point in the information technology business and, thus, an important basis of potential product differentiation. However, seamless interconnectivity—where Company A's computers talk to Company B's computers across Company C's data line merging a database created by Company D's software with a database created by Company E's software to be used in a calling center that operates with Company F's technology—has been extremely difficult to realize. For this reason, some information technology firms try to realize the goal of interconnectivity by adjusting their product mix, that is, by selling a bundle of products whose interconnectivity they can control and guarantee to customers. This goal of selling a bundle of interconnected technologies can influence a firm's research and development, strategic alliance, and merger and acquisition strategies because all these activities can influence the set of products a firm brings to market.

Shopping malls are an example of the second kind of linkage among a mix of products—where products have a common set of customers. Many customers prefer to go to one location, to shop at several stores at once, rather than travel to a series of locations to shop. This one-stop shopping reduces travel time and helps turn shopping into a social experience. Mall development companies have recognized that the value of several stores brought together in a particular location is greater than the value of those stores if they were isolated, and they have invested to help create this mix of retail shopping opportunities.[12]

Distribution Channels Linkages within and between firms can also have an impact on how a firm chooses to distribute its products, and distribution channels can be a basis of product differentiation. For example, in the soft drink industry, Coca-Cola, PepsiCo, and 7-Up all distribute their drinks through a network of independent and company-owned bottlers. These firms manufacture key ingredients for their soft drinks and ship these ingredients to local bottlers, who add carbonated water, package the drinks in bottles or cans, and distribute the final product to soft drink outlets in each geographic area. Each local bottler has exclusive rights to distribute a particular brand in a geographic location.

Canada Dry has adopted a completely different distribution network. Instead of relying on local bottlers, Canada Dry packages its soft drinks in several locations and then ships them directly to wholesale grocers, who distribute the product to local grocery stores, convenience stores, and other retail outlets.

One of the consequences of these alternative distribution strategies is that Canada Dry has a relatively strong presence in grocery stores but a relatively small presence in soft drink vending machines. The vending machine market is dominated by Coca-Cola and PepsiCo. These two firms have local distributors that maintain and stock vending machines. Canada Dry has no local distributors and can get its products into vending machines only when they are purchased by local Coca-Cola or Pepsi distributors. These local distributors are likely to purchase and stock Canada Dry products such as Canada Dry ginger ale, but they are contractually prohibited from purchasing Canada Dry's various cola products.[13]

Service and Support Finally, products have been differentiated by the level of service and support associated with them. For example, some personal computer firms have very low levels of service provided by independent service dealers. Others have outsourced service and support functions to overseas companies, often in India. On the other hand, some firms continue to staff support centers with highly qualified individuals, thereby providing a high level of support.[14]

Product Differentiation and Creativity

The bases of product differentiation listed in Table 5.1 indicate a broad range of ways in which firms can differentiate their products and services. In the end, however, any effort to list all possible ways to differentiate products and services is doomed to failure. Product differentiation is ultimately an expression of the creativity of individuals and groups within firms. It is limited only by the opportunities that exist, or that can be created, in a particular industry and by the willingness and ability of firms to creatively explore ways to take advantage of those opportunities. It is not unreasonable to expect that the day some academic researcher claims to have developed the definitive list of bases of product differentiation, some creative engineer, marketing specialist, or manager will think of yet another way to differentiate his or her product.

The Value of Product Differentiation

Objective 5.2 Describe how product differentiation can create economic value.

In order to have the potential for generating competitive advantages, the bases of product differentiation upon which a firm competes must be valuable. The market conditions under which product differentiation can be valuable are discussed in the Strategy in Depth feature. More generally, to be valuable, bases of product differentiation must enable a firm to neutralize its threats and/or exploit its opportunities.

Product Differentiation and Environmental Threats

Successful product differentiation helps a firm respond to each of the environmental threats identified. For example, product differentiation helps reduce the threat of new entry by forcing potential entrants to an industry to absorb not only the standard costs of beginning business, but also the additional costs associated with overcoming incumbent firms' product differentiation advantages. The relationship between product differentiation and new entry has already been discussed in Chapter 2.

Product differentiation reduces the threat of rivalry because each firm in an industry attempts to carve out its own unique product niche. Rivalry is not reduced to zero because these products still compete with one another for a common set of customers, but it is somewhat attenuated because the customers each firm seeks are different. For example, both a Rolls-Royce and a Fiat satisfy the same basic consumer need—transportation—but it is unlikely that potential customers of Rolls-Royce will also be interested in purchasing a Fiat or vice versa.

Product differentiation also helps firms reduce the threat of substitutes by making a firm's current products appear more attractive than substitute products. For example, fresh food can be thought of as a substitute for frozen processed foods. To make its frozen processed foods more attractive than fresh foods, products such as Stouffer's and Swanson are marketed heavily through television advertisements, newspaper ads, point-of-purchase displays, and coupons.

Product differentiation can also reduce the threat of powerful suppliers. Powerful suppliers can raise the prices of the products or services they provide. Often, these increased supply costs must be passed on to a firm's customers in the form of higher prices if a firm's profit margin is not to deteriorate. A firm without a highly differentiated product may find it difficult to pass its increased costs on to customers because these customers will have numerous other ways to purchase similar products or services from a firm's competitors. However, a firm with a highly differentiated product may have loyal customers or customers who are unable to purchase similar products or services from other firms. These types of customers are more likely to accept increased prices. Thus, a powerful supplier may be able to raise its prices, but, up to some point, these increases will not reduce the profitability of a firm selling a highly differentiated product.

Finally, product differentiation can reduce the threat of powerful buyers. When a firm sells a highly differentiated product, it enjoys a "quasi-monopoly" in that segment of the market. Buyers interested in purchasing this particular product must buy it from a particular firm. Any potential buyer power is reduced by the ability of a firm to withhold highly valued products or services from a buyer.

Strategy in Depth

The two classic treatments of the relationship between product differentiation and firm value, developed independently and published at approximately the same time, are by Edward Chamberlin and Joan Robinson.

Both Chamberlin and Robinson examine product differentiation and firm performance relative to perfect competition. As explained in Chapter 2, under perfect competition, it is assumed that there are numerous firms in an industry, each controlling a small proportion of the market, and the products or services sold by these firms are assumed to be identical. Under these conditions, firms face a horizontal demand curve (because they have no control over the price of the products they sell), and they maximize their economic performance by producing and selling output such that marginal revenue equals marginal costs. The maximum economic performance a firm in a perfectly competitive market can obtain, assuming no cost differences across firms, is normal economic performance.

When firms sell differentiated products, they gain some ability to adjust their prices. A firm can sell its output at very high prices and produce relatively smaller amounts of output, or it can sell its output at very low prices and produce relatively greater amounts of output. These trade-offs between price and quantity produced suggest that firms selling differentiated products face a downward-sloping demand curve, rather than the horizontal demand curve for firms in a perfectly competitive market. Firms selling differentiated products and facing a downward-sloping demand curve are in an industry structure described by Chamberlin as

The Economics of Product Differentiation

monopolistic competition. It is as if, within the market niche defined by a firm's differentiated product, a firm possesses a monopoly.

Firms in monopolistically competitive markets still maximize their economic profit by producing and selling a quantity of products such that marginal revenue equals marginal cost. The price that firms can charge at this optimal point depends on the demand they face for their differentiated product. If demand is large, then the price that can be charged is greater; if demand is low, then the price that can be charged is lower. However, if a firm's average total cost is below the price it can charge (i.e., if average total cost is less than the demand-determined price), then a firm selling a differentiated product can earn an above-normal economic profit.

Consider the example presented in Figure 5.1. Several curves are relevant in this figure. First, note that a firm in this industry faces downward-sloping demand (*D*). This means that the industry is not perfectly competitive and that a firm has some control over the prices it will charge for its products. Also, the marginal-revenue curve (*MR*) is downward sloping and everywhere lower than the demand curve. Marginal revenue is downward sloping because to sell additional levels of output of a single product, a firm must be willing to lower its price. The marginal-revenue curve is lower than the demand curve because this lower price applies to all the products sold by a firm, not just to any additional products the firm sells. The marginal-cost curve (*MC*) is upward sloping, indicating that to produce additional outputs a firm must accept additional costs. The average-total-cost curve (*ATC*) can have a variety of shapes, depending on the economies of scale, the cost of productive inputs, and other cost phenomena described in Chapter 4.

These four curves (demand, marginal revenue, marginal cost, and average total cost) can be used to determine the level of economic profit for a firm under monopolistic competition. To maximize profit, the firm produces an amount (Q_e) such that marginal costs equal marginal revenues. To determine the price of a firm's output at this level of production, a vertical line is drawn from the point where marginal costs equal marginal revenues. This line will intersect with the demand curve. Where this vertical line intersects demand, a horizontal line is drawn to the vertical (price) axis to determine the price a firm can charge. In the figure, this price is P_e. At the point P_e, average total cost is less than the price. The total revenue obtained by the firm in this situation (price × quantity) is indicated by the shaded area in the figure. The economic profit portion of this total revenue is indicated by the crosshatched section of the shaded portion of the figure. Because this crosshatched section is above average total costs in the figure, it represents a competitive advantage. If this section was below average total costs, it would represent a competitive disadvantage.

Chamberlin and Robinson go on to discuss the impact of entry into the market niche defined by a firm's differentiated product. As discussed in Chapter 2, a basic assumption of S-C-P models is that the existence of above-normal economic performance motivates entry into an industry or into a market niche within an industry. In monopolistically competitive industries, such entry means that the demand curve facing incumbent firms shifts downward and to the left. This implies that an incumbent firm's customers will buy less of its output if it maintains its prices or (equivalently) that a firm must lower its prices to maintain its current volume of sales. In the long run, entry into this market niche can lead to a situation where the price of goods or services sold when a firm produces output such that marginal cost equals marginal revenue is exactly equal to that firm's average total cost. At this point, a firm earns zero economic profits even if it still sells a differentiated product.[15]

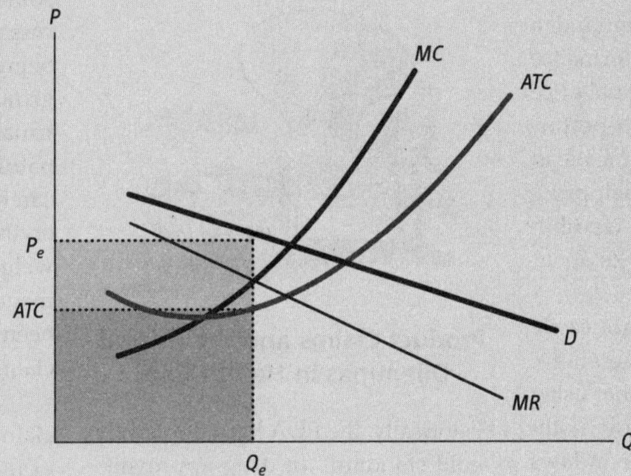

Figure 5.1 Product Differentiation and Firm Performance: The Analysis of Monopolistic Competition

Product Differentiation and Environmental Opportunities

Product differentiation can also help a firm take advantage of environmental opportunities. For example, in fragmented industries firms can use product differentiation strategies to help consolidate a market. In the office-paper industry, Xerox has used its brand name to become the leading seller of paper for office copy machines and printers. Arguing that its paper is specially manufactured to avoid jamming in its own copy machines, Xerox was able to brand what had been a commodity product and facilitate the consolidation of what had been a very fragmented industry.[16]

The role of product differentiation in emerging industries was discussed in Chapter 2. By being a first mover in these industries, firms can gain product differentiation advantages based on perceived technological leadership, preemption of strategically valuable assets, and buyer loyalty due to high switching costs.

In mature industries, product differentiation efforts often switch from attempts to introduce radically new technologies to product refinement as a basis of product differentiation. For example, in the mature retail gasoline market firms attempt to differentiate their products by selling slightly modified gasoline (cleaner-burning gasoline, gasoline that cleans fuel injectors, and so forth) and by altering the product mix (linking gasoline sales with convenience stores). In mature markets, it is sometimes difficult to find ways to actually refine a product or service. In such settings, firms can sometimes be tempted to exaggerate the extent to which they have refined and improved their products or services. The implications of these exaggerations are discussed in the Ethics and Strategy feature.

Product differentiation can also be an important strategic option in a declining industry. Product-differentiating firms may be able to become leaders in this kind of industry (based on their reputation, unique product attributes, or some

Ethics and Strategy

One of the most common ways to try to differentiate a product is to make claims about that product's performance. In general, high-performance products command a price premium over low-performance products. However, the potential price advantages enjoyed by high-performance products can sometimes lead firms to make claims about their products that, at the least, strain credibility and, at the most, simply lie about what their products can do.

Some of these claims are easily dismissed as harmless exaggerations. Few people actually believe that using a particular type of whitening toothpaste is going to make your in-laws like you or that not wearing a particular type of deodorant is going to cause patrons in a bar to collapse when you lift your arms in victory after a foosball game. These exaggerations are harmless and present few ethical challenges.

However, in the field of health care, exaggerated product performance claims can have serious consequences. This can happen when a patient takes a medication with exaggerated performance claims instead of a medication with more modest, although accurate, performance claims. A history of false medical performance claims in the United States led to the formation of the Food and Drug Administration (FDA), a federal regulatory agency charged with evaluating the efficacy of drugs before they are marketed.

Product Claims and the Ethical Dilemmas in Health Care

Historically, the FDA has adopted the "gold standard" of drug approval—not only must a drug demonstrate that it does what it claims, it must also demonstrate that it does not do any significant harm to the patient. Patients can be confident that drugs that pass the FDA approval process meet the highest standards in the world.

However, this "gold standard" of approval creates important ethical dilemmas—mostly stemming from the time it takes a drug to pass the FDA approval process. This process can take between five and seven years. During FDA trials, patients who might otherwise benefit from a drug are not allowed to use it because it has not yet received FDA approval. Thus, although the FDA approval process may work very well for people who may need a drug sometime in the future, it works less well for those who need a drug right now.

A growing suspicion among some consumers that the FDA process may prevent effective drugs from being marketed has helped feed the growth of alternative treatments—usually based on some herbal or more natural formula. Such treatments are careful to note that their claims—everything from regrowing hair to losing weight to enhancing athletic performance to quitting smoking—have not been tested by the FDA. And yet these claims are still made.

Some of these performance claims seem at least reasonable. For example, it is now widely accepted that ephedra does behave as an amphetamine and thus is likely to enhance strength and athletic performance. Others—including those that claim that a mixture of herbs can actually increase the size of male genitals—seem far-fetched, at best. Indeed, a recent analysis of herbal treatments making this claim found no ingredients that could have this effect, but did find an unacceptably high concentration of bacteria from animal feces that can cause serious stomach disorders. Firms that sell products based on exaggerated and unsubstantiated claims face their own ethical dilemmas. And, without the FDA to ensure product safety and efficacy, the adage caveat emptor—let the buyer beware—seems like good advice.[17]

other product differentiation basis). Alternatively, highly differentiated firms may be able to discover a viable market niche that will enable them to survive despite the overall decline in the market.

Finally, the decision to implement a product differentiation strategy can have a significant impact on how a firm acts in a global industry. For example, several firms in the retail clothing industry with important product differentiation advantages in their home markets are beginning to enter the United States retail clothing market. These firms include Sweden's H & M Hennes & Mauritz AB, with its emphasis on "cheap chic"; the Dutch firm Mexx; the Spanish company Zara; and the French sportswear company Lacoste.[18]

Product Differentiation and Sustained Competitive Advantage

Objective 5.3 Describe:

a. Those bases of product differentiation that are not likely to be costly to duplicate, those that may be costly to duplicate, and those that will often be costly to duplicate.
b. The main substitutes for product differentiation strategies.

Product differentiation strategies add value by enabling firms to charge prices for their products or services that are greater than their average total cost. Firms that implement this strategy successfully can reduce a variety of environmental threats and exploit a variety of environmental opportunities. However, as discussed in Chapter 3, the ability of a strategy to add value to a firm must be linked with rare and costly-to-imitate organizational strengths in order to generate a sustained competitive advantage. Each of the bases of product differentiation listed earlier in this chapter varies with respect to how likely it is to be rare and costly to imitate.

Rare Bases for Product Differentiation

The concept of product differentiation generally assumes that the number of firms that have been able to differentiate their products in a particular way is, at some point in time, smaller than the number of firms needed to generate perfect competition dynamics. Indeed, the reason that highly differentiated firms can charge a price for their product that is greater than average total cost is because these firms are using a basis for product differentiation that few competing firms are also using.

Ultimately, the rarity of a product differentiation strategy depends on the ability of individual firms to be creative in finding new ways to differentiate their products. As suggested earlier, highly creative firms will be able to discover or create new ways to do this. These kinds of firms will always be one step ahead of the competition because rival firms will often be trying to imitate these firms' last product differentiation moves while creative firms are working on their next one.

The Imitability of Product Differentiation

Valuable and rare bases of product differentiation must be costly to imitate if they are to be sources of sustained competitive advantage. Both direct duplication and substitution, as approaches to imitation, are important in understanding the ability of product differentiation to generate competitive advantages.

Direct Duplication of Product Differentiation

As discussed in Chapter 4, firms that successfully implement a cost leadership strategy can choose whether they want to reveal this strategic choice to their competition by adjusting their prices. If they keep their prices high—despite their cost advantages—the existence of those cost advantages may not be revealed to competitors. Of course, other firms—such as Wal-Mart—that are confident that their cost advantages cannot be duplicated at low cost are willing to reveal their cost advantage through charging lower prices for their products or services.

Firms pursuing product differentiation strategies usually do not have this option. More often than not, the act of selling a highly differentiated product or service reveals the basis upon which a firm is trying to differentiate its products.

In fact, most firms go to great lengths to let their customers know how they are differentiating their products, and in the process of informing potential customers they also inform their competitors. Indeed, if competitors are not sure how a firm is differentiating its product, all they need to do is purchase that product themselves. Their own experience with the product—its features and other attributes—will tell them all they need to know about this firm's product differentiation strategy.

Knowing how a firm is differentiating its products, however, does not necessarily mean that competitors will be able to duplicate the strategy at low cost. The ability to duplicate a valuable and rare product differentiation strategy depends on the basis upon which a firm is differentiating its products. As suggested in Table 5.2, some bases of product differentiation—including the use of product features—are almost always easy to duplicate. Others—including product mix, links with other firms, product customization, product complexity, and consumer marketing—can sometimes be costly to duplicate. Finally, still other bases of product differentiation—including links between functions, timing, location, reputation, distribution channels, and service and support—are usually costly to duplicate.

How costly it is to duplicate a particular basis of product differentiation depends on the kinds of resources and capabilities that basis uses. When those resources and capabilities are acquired in unique historical settings, when there is some uncertainty about how to build these resources and capabilities, or when these resources and capabilities are socially complex in nature, then product differentiation strategies that exploit these kinds of resources and capabilities will be costly to imitate. These strategies can be a source of sustained competitive advantage for a firm. However, when a product differentiation strategy exploits resources and capabilities that do not possess these attributes, then those strategies are likely to be less costly to duplicate and, even if they are valuable and rare, will only be sources of temporary competitive advantage.

TABLE 5.2 Bases of Product Differentiation and the Cost of Duplication

	History	Uncertainty	Social Complexity
Low-cost duplication usually possible			
1. Product features	—	—	—
May be costly to duplicate			
2. Product mix	*	*	*
3. Links with other firms	*	—	**
4. Product customization	*	—	**
5. Product complexity	*	—	*
6. Consumer marketing	—	**	—
Usually costly to duplicate			
7. Links between functions	*	*	**
8. Timing	***	*	—
9. Location	***	—	—
10. Reputation	***	**	***
11. Distribution channels	**	*	**
12. Service and support	*	*	**

— = Not likely to be a source of costly duplication, * = Somewhat likely to be a source of costly duplication, ** = Likely to be a source of costly duplication, *** = Very likely to be a source of costly duplication

Bases of Product Differentiation That Are Easy to Duplicate The one basis of product differentiation in Table 5.2 that is identified as almost always being easy to duplicate is product features. The irony is that product features are by far the most popular way for firms to try to differentiate their products. Rarely do product features, by themselves, enable a firm to gain sustained competitive advantages from a product differentiation strategy.

For example, virtually every one of the product features used in the automobile industry to differentiate the products of different automobile companies has been duplicated. Chrysler's "cab forward" design has been incorporated into the design of many manufacturers. The curved, sporty styling of the Audi has surfaced in cars manufactured by Lexus and General Motors. GM's "On Star" system has been duplicated by Mercedes. Mercedes' crumple-zone technology has become the industry standard, as has GM's uni-body construction method. Indeed, only the Mazda Miata, Nissan 370Z, and Porsche 911 have remained unduplicated—and this has little to do with the product features of these cars and much more to do with their reputation.

The only time product features, per se, can be a source of sustained competitive advantage for a firm is when those features are protected by patents. However, as was discussed in Chapters 2 and 3, even patents provide only limited protection from direct duplication, except in very unusual settings.

Although product features, by themselves, are usually not a source of sustained competitive advantage, they can be a source of a temporary competitive advantage. During the period when a firm has a temporary competitive advantage from implementing a product differentiation strategy based on product features, it may be able to attract new customers. Once these customers try the product, they may discover other features of a firm's products that make them attractive. If these other features are costly to duplicate, then they can be a source of sustained competitive advantage, even though the features that originally attracted a customer to a firm's products will often be rapidly duplicated by competitors.

Bases of Product Differentiation That May Be Costly to Duplicate Some bases of product differentiation may be costly to duplicate, at least in some circumstances. The first of these, listed in Table 5.2, is product mix.

Duplicating the features of another firm's products is usually not difficult. However, if that firm brings a series of products to market, if each of these products has unique features, and most important, if the products are highly integrated with each other, then this mix of products may be costly to duplicate. Certainly, the technological integration of the mix of information technology products sold by IBM and other firms has been relatively difficult to duplicate for firms that do not manufacture all these products themselves.

However, when this basis of a product mix advantage is a common customer, then duplication is often less difficult. Thus, although having a mall that brings several stores together in a single place is a source of competitive advantage over stand-alone stores, it is not a competitive advantage over other malls that provide the same service. Because there continue to be opportunities to build such malls, the fact that malls make it easier for a common set of customers to shop does not give any one mall a sustained competitive advantage.

Links with other firms may also be costly to duplicate, especially when those links depend on socially complex relationships. The extent to which interfirm links can provide sources of sustained competitive advantage is discussed in more detail in Chapter 11.

In the same way, product customization and product complexity are often easy-to-duplicate bases of product differentiation. However, sometimes the ability of a firm to customize its products for one of its customers depends on the close relationships it has developed with those customers. Product customization of this sort depends on the willingness of a firm to share often-proprietary details about its operations, products, research and development, or other characteristics with a supplying firm. Willingness to share this kind of information, in turn, depends on the ability of each firm to trust and rely on the other. The firm opening its operations to a supplier must trust that that supplier will not make this information broadly available to competing firms. The firm supplying customized products must trust that its customer will not take unfair advantage of it. If two firms have developed these kinds of socially complex relationships, and few other firms have them, then links with other firms will be costly to duplicate and a source of sustained competitive advantage.

The product customization seen in both enterprise software and in high-end customized bicycles has these socially complex features. In a real sense, when these products are purchased, a relationship with a supplier is being established—a relationship that is likely to last a long period. Once this relationship is established, partners are likely to be unwilling to abandon it, unless, of course, a party to the exchange tries to take unfair advantage of another party to that exchange. This possibility is discussed in detail in Chapter 11.

Finally, consumer marketing, though a very common form of product differentiation, is often easy to duplicate. Thus, whereas Mountain Dew has established itself as the "extreme games" drink, other drinks, including Gatorade, have also begun to tap into this market segment. Of course, every once in a while, an advertising campaign or slogan, a point-of-purchase display, or some other attribute of a consumer marketing campaign will unexpectedly catch on and create greater-than-expected product awareness. In beer, marketing campaigns such as "Tastes great, less filling," "Why ask why?," the "Budweiser Frogs," and "What's Up?" have had these unusual effects. If a firm, in relation with its various consumer marketing agencies, is systematically able to develop these superior consumer marketing campaigns, then it may be able to obtain a sustained competitive advantage. However, if such campaigns are unpredictable and largely a matter of a firm's good luck, they cannot be expected to be a source of sustained competitive advantage.

Bases of Product Differentiation That Are Usually Costly to Duplicate The remaining bases of product differentiation listed in Table 5.2 are usually costly to duplicate. Firms that differentiate their products on these bases may be able to obtain sustained competitive advantages.

Linkages across functions within a single firm are usually a costly-to-duplicate basis of product differentiation. Whereas linkages with other firms can be either easy or costly to duplicate, depending on the nature of the relationship that exists between firms, linkages across functions within a single firm usually require socially complex, trusting relations. There are numerous built-in conflicts between functions and divisions within a single firm. Organizations that have a history and culture that support cooperative relations among conflicting divisions may be able to set aside functional and divisional conflicts to cooperate in delivering a differentiated product to the market. However, firms with a history of conflict across functional and divisional boundaries face a significant, and costly, challenge in altering these socially complex, historical patterns.

Indeed, the research on architectural competence in pharmaceutical firms suggests that not only do some firms possess this competence, but that other firms do not. Moreover, despite the significant advantages that accrue to firms with this competence, firms without this competence have, on average, been unable to develop it. All this suggests that such a competence, if it is also rare, is likely to be costly to duplicate and thus a source of sustained competitive advantage.

Timing is also a difficult-to-duplicate basis of product differentiation. As suggested in Chapter 3, it is difficult (if not impossible) to recreate a firm's unique history. If that history endows a firm with special resources and capabilities it can use to differentiate its products, this product differentiation strategy can be a source of sustained competitive advantage. Rivals of a firm with such a timing-based product differentiation advantage may need to seek alternative ways to differentiate their products. Thus, it is not surprising that universities that compete with the oldest universities in the country find alternative ways to differentiate themselves—through their size, the quality of their extramural sports, their diversity—rather than relying on their age.

Location is often a difficult-to-duplicate basis of product differentiation. This is especially the case when a firm's location is unique. For example, research on the hotel preferences of business travelers suggests that location is a major determinant of the decision to stay in a hotel. Hotels that are convenient to both major transportation and commercial centers in a city are preferred, other things being equal, to hotels in other types of locations. Indeed, location has been shown to be a more important decision criterion for business travelers than price. If only a few hotels in a city have these prime locations and if no further hotel development is possible, then hotels with these locations can gain sustained competitive advantages.

Of all the bases of product differentiation listed in this chapter, perhaps none is more difficult to duplicate than a firm's reputation. As suggested earlier, a firm's reputation is a socially complex relationship between a firm and its customers, based on years of experience, commitment, and trust. Reputations are not built quickly, nor can they be bought and sold. Rather, they can only be developed over time by consistent investment in the relationship between a firm and its customers. A firm with a positive reputation can enjoy a significant competitive advantage, whereas a firm with a negative reputation, or no reputation, may have to invest significant amounts over long periods of time to match the differentiated firm.

Distribution channels can also be a costly-to-duplicate basis of product differentiation, for at least two reasons. First, relations between a firm and its distribution channels are often socially complex and thus costly to duplicate. Second, the supply of distribution channels may be limited. Firms that already have access to these channels may be able to use them, but firms that do not have such access may be forced to create their own or develop new channels. Creating new channels or developing entirely new means of distribution can be difficult and costly undertakings.[19] These costs are one of the primary motivations underlying many international joint ventures (see Chapter 11).

Finally, level of service and support can be a costly-to-duplicate basis of product differentiation. In most industries, it is usually not too costly to provide a minimum level of service and support. In home electronics, this minimum level of service can be provided by a network of independent electronic repair shops. In automobiles, this level of service can be provided by service facilities associated with dealerships. In fast foods, this level of service can be provided by a minimum level of employee training.

However, moving beyond this minimum level of service and support can be difficult for at least two reasons. First, increasing the quality of service and support may involve substantial amounts of costly training. McDonald's has created a sophisticated training facility (Hamburger University) to maintain its unusually high level of service in fast foods. General Electric has invested heavily in training for service and support over the past several years. Many Japanese automakers spent millions on training employees to help support auto dealerships before they opened United States manufacturing facilities.[20]

More important than the direct costs of the training needed to provide high-quality service and support, these bases of product differentiation often reflect the attitude of a firm and its employees toward customers. In many firms throughout the world, the customer has become "the bad guy." This is, in many ways, understandable. Employees tend to interact with their customers less frequently than they interact with other employees. When they do interact with customers, they are often the recipients of complaints directed at the firm. In these settings, hostility toward the customer can develop. Such hostility is, of course, inconsistent with a product differentiation strategy based on customer service and support.

In the end, high levels of customer service and support are based on socially complex relations between firms and customers. Firms that have conflicts with their customers may face some difficulty duplicating the high levels of service and support provided by competing firms.

Substitutes for Product Differentiation

The bases of product differentiation outlined in this chapter vary in how rare they are likely to be and in how difficult they are to duplicate. However, the ability of the bases of product differentiation to generate a sustained competitive advantage also depends on whether low-cost substitutes exist.

Substitutes for bases of product differentiation can take two forms. First, many of the bases of product differentiation listed in Table 5.1 can be partial substitutes for each other. For example, product features, product customization, and product complexity are all very similar bases of product differentiation and thus can act as substitutes for each other. A particular firm may try to develop a competitive advantage by differentiating its products on the basis of product customization only to find that its customization advantages are reduced as another firm alters the features of its products. In a similar way, linkages between functions, linkages between firms, and product mix, as bases of product differentiation, can also be substitutes for each other. IBM links its sales, service, and consulting functions to differentiate itself in the computer market. Other computer firms, however, may develop close relationships with computer service companies and consulting firms to close this product differentiation advantage. Given that different bases of product differentiation are often partial substitutes for each other, it is not surprising that firms pursue these multiple bases of product differentiation simultaneously.

Second, other strategies discussed throughout this book can be substitutes for many of the bases of product differentiation listed in Table 5.1. One firm may try to gain a competitive advantage through adjusting its product mix, and another firm may substitute strategic alliances to create the same type of product differentiation. For example, Southwest Airlines' continued emphasis on friendly, on-time, low-cost service and United Airlines' emphasis on its links to Lufthansa and other worldwide airlines through the Star Alliance can both be seen as product differentiation efforts that are at least partial substitutes.[21]

In contrast, some of the other bases of product differentiation discussed in this chapter have few obvious close substitutes. These include timing, location, distribution channels, and service and support. To the extent that these bases of product differentiation are also valuable, rare, and difficult to duplicate, they may be sources of sustained competitive advantage.

Organizing to Implement Product Differentiation

Objective 5.4 Describe how organizational structure, control processes, and compensation policies can be used to implement product differentiation strategies.

As was suggested in Chapter 3, the ability to implement a strategy depends on the adjustment of a firm's structure, its management controls, and its compensation policies to be consistent with that strategy. Whereas strategy implementation for firms adopting a cost leadership strategy focuses on reducing a firm's costs and increasing its efficiency, strategy implementation for a firm adopting a product differentiation strategy must focus on innovation, creativity, and product performance. Whereas cost-leading firms are all about customer value, product-differentiating firms are all about style. How the need for style is reflected in a firm's structure, controls, and compensation policies is summarized in Table 5.3.

Organizational Structure and Implementing Product Differentiation

Both cost leadership and product differentiation strategies are implemented using a functional, or U-form, organizational structure. However, whereas the U-form structure used to implement a cost leadership strategy has few layers, simple reporting relationships, a small corporate staff, and a focus on only a few business functions, the U-form structure for a firm implementing a product differentiation strategy can be somewhat more complex. For example, these firms often use temporary cross-divisional *and* cross-functional teams to manage the development and implementation of new, innovative, and highly differentiated products. These teams bring individuals from different businesses and different functional areas together to cooperate on a particular new product or service.

One firm that has used these cross-divisional and cross-functional teams effectively is the British advertising agency WPP. WPP owns several very large

TABLE 5.3 Organizing to Implement Product Differentiation Strategies

Organizational Structure:
1. Cross-divisional/cross-functional product development teams
2. Complex matrix structures
3. Isolated pockets of intense creative efforts: Skunk works

Management Control Systems:
1. Broad decision-making guidelines
2. Managerial freedom within guidelines
3. A policy of experimentation

Compensation Policies:
1. Rewards for risk-taking, not punishment for failures
2. Rewards for creative flair
3. Multidimensional performance measurement

advertising agencies, several public relations firms, several market research companies, and so forth. Each of these businesses operates relatively independently in most areas. However, the corporation has identified a few markets where cross-divisional and cross-functional collaboration is important. One of these is the health care market. To exploit opportunities in the health care market, WPP, the corporation, forms teams of advertising specialists, market research specialists, public relations specialists, and so on, drawn from each of the businesses it owns. The resulting cross-divisional teams are given the responsibility of developing new and highly differentiated approaches to developing marketing strategies for their clients in the health care industry.[22]

The creation of cross-divisional or cross-functional teams often implies that a firm has implemented some form of matrix structure. As suggested in Chapter 4, a **matrix structure** exists when individuals in a firm have two or more "bosses" simultaneously. Thus, for example, if a person from one of WPP's advertising agencies is assigned temporarily to a cross-divisional team, that person has two bosses: the head of the temporary team and the boss back in the advertising agency. Managing two bosses simultaneously can be very challenging, especially when they have conflicting interests. And as we will see in Chapter 8, the interests of these multiple bosses *will* often conflict.

A particularly important form of the cross-divisional or cross-functional team exists when this team is relieved of all other responsibilities in the firm and focuses all its attention on developing a new innovative product or service. The best-known example of this approach to developing a differentiated product occurred at the Lockheed Corporation during the 1950s and 1960s when small groups of engineers were put on very focused teams to develop sophisticated and top-secret military aircraft. These teams would have a section of the Lockheed facility dedicated to their efforts and designated as off-limits to almost all other employees. The joke was that these intensive creative efforts were so engaging that members of these teams actually would forget to shower—hence the name **"skunk works."** Skunk works have been used by numerous firms to focus the creative energy required to develop and introduce highly differentiated products.[23]

Management Controls and Implementing Product Differentiation

The first two management controls helpful for implementing product differentiation listed in Table 5.3—broad decision-making guidelines and managerial freedom within those guidelines—often go together. How some firms have used these kinds of controls to build entirely new markets is described in the Strategy in Depth feature.

Broad decision-making guidelines help bring order to what otherwise might be a chaotic decision-making process. When managers have no constraints in their decision making, they can make decisions that are disconnected from each other and inconsistent with a firm's overall mission and objectives. This results in decisions that are either not implemented or not implemented well.

However, if these decision-making guidelines become too narrow, they can stifle creativity within a firm. As was suggested earlier, a firm's ability to differentiate its products is limited only by its creativity. Thus, decision guidelines must be narrow enough to ensure that the decisions made are consistent with a firm's mission and objectives. Yet these guidelines also must be broad enough so that managerial creativity is not destroyed. In well-managed firms implementing product

Strategy in Depth

So much innovation in both small and large organizations focuses on repositioning a firm's products along established bases of competition—a more fuel-efficient car, a better-cleaning shampoo, a less expensive insurance policy. While these efforts can, for a time, be a source of product differentiation, for reasons discussed in Chapter 3, they are usually not sustainable.

For this reason, two scholars—W. Chan Kim and Renee Mauborgne—began studying firms that did not just reposition their products in well-established competitive markets but, instead, transcended their competition to identify entirely new markets. They called these markets "blue oceans" because they are not crowded with competitors seeking to improve their positions but instead are empty of competitors and give firms the opportunity to grow quickly. For these authors, blue oceans emerge when managers discover that the only way to beat the competition is to stop *trying* to beat the competition.

Examples of companies that have created blue oceans include Cirque du Soleil—a firm that redefined what a circus was to become an international entertainment sensation—and Casella Wines—a firm whose [yellow tail] brand made

Going in Search of Blue Oceans

drinking wine a simple alternative to drinking beer. Both these companies did not try to compete with established firms; they created a new competitive space where these firms were irrelevant.

So, how can a firm create a blue ocean? Kim and Mauborgne suggest that firms begin by understanding the bases of competition that exist within an industry already. In the United States wine industry, for example, Casella identified seven bases of competition: price, an elite image in packaging, consumer marketing, aging quality of wine, vineyard prestige, taste complexity, and a diverse range of wines. With these bases of product differentiation identified, firms should then ask four questions about competition in their industry:

1. Which factors that the industry currently competes on should be *eliminated*?
2. Which factors that the industry currently competes on should be *reduced well below* the industry's standard?
3. Which factors should be *raised well above* the industry's standard?
4. Which factors should be *created* that the industry has never offered?

By applying these four questions to the bases of competition identified by Casella, this firm decided that elite packaging, aging quality wine, vineyard prestige, and taste complexity all complicated the wine drinking experience and could be eliminated. They also created new bases for competition: easy drinking, ease of selection, and fun and adventure. The result was a wine brand—[yellow tail]—that has grown faster than any other wine over the past 10 years.

Some firms have found it difficult to apply these principles to develop blue oceans for their businesses. Nevertheless, by systematically seeking ways to redefine the bases of competition in an industry, some firms have been able to create entirely new markets where competition does not exist.[24]

differentiation strategies, if managerial decisions fall within the broad decision-making guidelines in a firm, managers have the right—in fact, are expected—to make creative decisions.

A firm that has worked hard to reach this balance between chaos and control is 3M. To provide guiding principles that define the range of acceptable decisions at 3M, its senior managers have developed a set of innovating principles. These are presented in Table 5.4 and define the boundaries of innovative chaos at 3M. Within these boundaries, managers and engineers are expected to be creative and innovative in developing highly differentiated products and services.[25]

TABLE 5.4 Guiding Innovative Principles at 3M*

1. **Vision** Declare the importance of innovation; make it part of the company's self-image.

   "Our efforts to encourage and support innovation are proof that we really do intend to achieve our vision of ourselves . . . that we intend to become what we want to be . . . as a business and as creative individuals."

2. **Foresight** Find out where technologies and markets are going. Identify articulated and unarticulated needs of customers.

   "If you are working on a next-generation medical imaging device, you'll probably talk to radiologists, but you might also sit down with people who enhance images from interplanetary space probes."

3. **Stretch goals** Set goals that will make you and the organization stretch to make quantum improvements. Although many projects are pursued, place your biggest bets on those that change the basis of competition and redefine the industry.

   "We have a number of stretch goals at 3M. The first states that we will drive 30 percent of all sales from products introduced in the past 4 years . . . . To establish a sense of urgency, we've recently added another goal, which is that we want 10 percent of our sales to come from products that have been in the market for just 1 year . . . . Innovation is time sensitive . . . you need to move quickly."

4. **Empowerment** Hire good people and trust them, delegate responsibilities, provide slack resources, and get out of the way. Be tolerant of initiative and the mistakes that occur because of that initiative.

   "William McKnight [a former chairman of 3M] came up with one way to institutionalize a tolerance of individual effort. He said that all technical employees could devote 15 percent of their time to a project of their own invention. In other words, they could manage themselves for 15 percent of the time . . . . The number is not so important as the message, which is this: The system has some slack in it. If you have a good idea, and the commitment to squirrel away time to work on it and the raw nerve to skirt your lab manager's expressed desires, then go for it.

   "Put another way, we want to institutionalize a bit of rebellion in our labs. We can't have all our people off totally on their own . . . we do believe in discipline . . . but at the same time 3M management encourages a healthy disrespect for 3M management. This is not the sort of thing we publicize in our annual report, but the stories we tell—with relish—are frequently about 3Mers who have circumvented their supervisors and succeeded.

   "We also recognize that when you let people follow their own lead . . . everyone doesn't wind up at the same place. You can't ask people to have unique visions and march in lockstep. Some people are very precise, detail-oriented people . . . and others are fuzzy thinkers and visionaries . . . and this is exactly what we want."

5. **Communications** Open, extensive exchanges according to ground rules in forums that are present for sharing ideas and where networking is each individual's responsibility. Multiple methods for sharing information are necessary.

   "When innovators communicate with each other, you can leverage their discoveries. This is critically important because it allows companies to get the maximum return on their substantial investments in new technologies. It also acts as a stimulus to further innovation. Indeed, we believe that the ability to combine and transfer technologies is as important as the original discovery of a technology."

6. **Rewards and recognition** Emphasize individual recognition more than monetary rewards through peer recognition and by choice of managerial or technical promotion routes. "Innovation is an intensely human activity."

   "I've laid out six elements of 3M's corporate culture that contribute to a tradition of innovation: vision, foresight, stretch goals, empowerment, communication, and recognition . . . . The list is . . . too orderly. Innovation at 3M is anything but orderly. It is sensible, in that our efforts are directed at reaching our goals, but the organization . . . and the process . . . and sometimes the people can be chaotic. We are managing in chaos, and this is the right way to manage if you want innovation. It's been said that the competition never knows what we are going to come up with next. The fact is, neither do we."

*As expressed by W. Coyne (1996). Building a tradition of innovation. The Fifth U.K. Innovation Lecture, Department of Trade and Industry, London. Cited in Van de Ven et al. (1999), pp. 198–200.

Firms can also facilitate the implementation of a product differentiation strategy by adopting a **policy of experimentation**. Such a policy exists when firms are committed to engaging in several related product differentiation efforts simultaneously. That these product differentiation efforts are related suggests that a firm has some vision about how a particular market is likely to unfold over time. However, that there are several of these product differentiation efforts occurring simultaneously suggests that a firm is not overly committed to a particular narrow vision about how a market is going to evolve. Rather, several different experiments facilitate the exploration of different futures in a marketplace. Indeed, successful experiments can actually help define the future evolution of a marketplace.

Consider, for example, Charles Schwab, the innovative discount broker. In the face of increased competition from full-service and Internet-based brokerage firms, Schwab engaged in a series of experiments to discover the next generation of products it could offer to its customers and the different ways it could differentiate those products. Schwab investigated software for simplifying online mutual fund selection, online futures trading, and online company research. It also formed an exploratory alliance with Goldman Sachs to evaluate the possibility of enabling Schwab customers to trade in initial public offerings. Not all of Schwab's experiments led to the introduction of highly differentiated products. For example, based on some experimental investments, Schwab decided not to enter the credit card market. However, by experimenting with a range of possible product differentiation moves, it could develop a range of new products for the fast-changing financial services industry.[26]

Compensation Policies and Implementing Product Differentiation Strategies

The compensation policies used to implement product differentiation listed in Table 5.3 very much complement the organizational structure and managerial controls listed in that table. For example, a policy of experimentation has little impact on the ability of a firm to implement product differentiation strategies if every time an innovative experiment fails individuals are punished for taking risks. Thus, compensation policies that reward risk-taking and celebrate a creative flair help to enable a firm to implement its product differentiation strategy.

Consider, for example, Nordstrom. Nordstrom is a department store that celebrates the risk-taking and creative flair of its associates as they try to satisfy their customers' needs. The story is often told of a Nordstrom sales associate who allowed a customer to return a set of tires to the store because she wasn't satisfied with them. What makes this story interesting—whether or not it is true—is that Nordstrom doesn't sell tires. But this sales associate felt empowered to make what was obviously a risky decision, and this decision is celebrated within Nordstrom as an example of the kind of service that Nordstrom's customers should expect.

The last compensation policy listed in Table 5.3 is multidimensional performance measurement. In implementing a cost leadership strategy, compensation should focus on providing appropriate incentives for managers and employees to reduce costs. Various forms of cash payments, stock, and stock options can all be tied to the attainment of specific cost goals and thus can be used to create incentives for realizing cost advantages. Similar techniques can be used to create incentives for helping a firm implement its product differentiation advantage. However, because the implementation of a product differentiation strategy generally involves the integration of multiple business functions, often using product development teams, compensation schemes designed to help implement this strategy must generally recognize its multifunctional character.

Thus, rather than focusing only on a single dimension of performance, these firms often examine employee performance along multiple dimensions simultaneously. Examples of such dimensions include not only a product's sales and profitability, but customer satisfaction, an employee's willingness to cooperate with other businesses and functions within a firm, an employee's ability to effectively facilitate cross-divisional and cross-functional teams, and an employee's ability to engage in creative decision making.

Objective 5.5 Discuss whether it is possible for a firm to implement cost leadership and product differentiation strategies simultaneously.

Can Firms Implement Product Differentiation and Cost Leadership Simultaneously?

The arguments developed in Chapter 4 and in this chapter suggest that cost leadership and product differentiation business strategies, under certain conditions, can both create sustained competitive advantages. Given the beneficial impact of both strategies on a firm's competitive position, an important question becomes: Can a single firm simultaneously implement both strategies? After all, if each separately can improve a firm's performance, wouldn't it be better for a firm to implement both?

No: These Strategies Cannot Be Implemented Simultaneously

A quick comparison of the organizational requirements for the successful implementation of cost leadership strategies and product differentiation strategies presented in Table 5.5 summarizes one perspective on the question of whether

TABLE 5.5 The Organizational Requirements for Implementing Cost Leadership and Product Differentiation Strategies

Cost leadership	Organizational structure
Product differentiation	**Organizational structure**
1. Few layers in the reporting structure	1. Cross-divisional/cross-functional product development teams
2. Simple reporting relationships	2. Willingness to explore new structures to exploit new opportunities
3. Small corporate staff	3. Isolated pockets of intense creative efforts
4. Focus on narrow range of business functions	
Management control systems	**Management control systems**
1. Tight cost-control systems	1. Broad decision-making guidelines
2. Quantitative cost goals	2. Managerial freedom within guidelines
3. Close supervision of labor, raw material, inventory, and other costs	3. Policy of experimentation
4. A cost leadership philosophy	
Compensation policies	**Compensation policies**
1. Reward for cost reduction	1. Rewards for risk-taking, not punishment for failures
2. Incentives for all employees to be involved in cost reduction	2. Rewards for creative flair
	3. Multidimensional performance measurement

these strategies can be implemented simultaneously. In this view, the organizational requirements of these strategies are essentially contradictory. Cost leadership requires simple reporting relationships, whereas product differentiation requires cross-divisional/cross-functional linkages. Cost leadership requires intense labor supervision, whereas product differentiation requires less intense supervision of creative employees. Cost leadership -requires rewards for cost reduction, whereas product differentiation requires rewards for creative flair. It is reasonable to ask, "Can a single firm combine these multiple contradictory skills and abilities?"

Some have argued that firms attempting to implement both strategies will end up doing neither well. This logic suggests that there are often only two ways to earn superior economic performance within a single industry: (1) by selling high-priced products and gaining small market share (product differentiation); or (2) by selling low-priced products and gaining large market share (cost leadership). Firms that do not make this choice of strategies (medium price, medium market share) or that attempt to implement both strategies will fail. These firms are said to be "stuck in the middle."[27]

Yes: These Strategies Can Be Implemented Simultaneously

More recent work contradicts assertions about being "stuck in the middle." This work suggests that firms that are successful in both cost leadership and product differentiation can often expect to gain a sustained competitive advantage. This advantage reflects at least two processes.

Differentiation, Market Share, and Low-Cost Leadership

Firms able to successfully differentiate their products and services are likely to see an increase in their volume of sales. This is especially the case if the basis of product differentiation is attractive to many potential customers. Thus, product differentiation can lead to increased volumes of sales. It has already been established (in Chapter 4) that an increased volume of sales can lead to economies of scale, learning, and other forms of cost reduction. So, successful product differentiation can, in turn, lead to cost reductions and a cost leadership position.[28]

This is the situation that best describes McDonald's. McDonald's has traditionally followed a product differentiation strategy, emphasizing cleanliness, consistency, and fun in its fast-food outlets. Over time, McDonald's has used its differentiated product to become the market share leader in the fast-food industry. This market position has enabled it to reduce its costs, so that it is now the cost leader in fast foods as well. Thus, McDonald's level of profitability depends both on its product differentiation strategy and its low-cost strategy. Either one of these two strategies by itself would be difficult to overcome; together they give McDonald's a very costly-to-imitate competitive advantage.[29]

Managing Organizational Contradictions

Product differentiation can lead to high market share and low costs. It may also be the case that some firms develop special skills in managing the contradictions that are part of simultaneously implementing low-cost and product differentiation strategies. Some recent research on automobile manufacturing helps describe these special skills.[30] Traditional thinking in automotive manufacturing was that plants could either reduce manufacturing costs by speeding up the assembly line or increase the quality of the cars they made by slowing the line, emphasizing team-based production, and so forth. In general, it was thought that plants could not simultaneously build low-cost/high-quality (i.e., low-cost *and* highly differentiated) automobiles.

Several researchers have examined this traditional wisdom. They began by developing rigorous measures of the cost and quality performance of automobile plants and then applied these measures to more than 70 auto plants throughout the world that assembled mid-size sedans. What they discovered was six plants in the entire world that had, at the time this research was done, very low costs *and* very high quality.[31]

In examining what made these six plants different from other auto plants, the researchers focused on a broad range of manufacturing policies, management practices, and cultural variables. Three important findings emerged. First, these six plants had the best manufacturing technology hardware available—robots, laser-guided paint machines, and so forth. However, because many of the plants in the study had these same technologies, manufacturing technology by itself was not enough to make these six plants special. In addition, policies and procedures at these plants implemented a range of highly participative, group-oriented management techniques, including participative management, team production, and total quality management. As important, employees in these plants had a sense of loyalty and commitment toward the plant they worked for—a belief that they would be treated fairly by their plant managers.

What this research shows is that firms *can* simultaneously implement cost leadership and product differentiation strategies if they learn how to manage the contradictions inherent in these two strategies. The management of these contradictions, in turn, depends on socially complex relations among employees, between employees and the technology they use, and between employees and the firm for which they work. These relations are not only valuable (because they enable a firm to implement cost leadership and differentiation strategies) but also socially complex and thus likely to be costly to imitate and a source of sustained competitive advantage.

Recently, many scholars have backed away from the original "stuck in the middle" arguments and now suggest that low-cost firms must have competitive levels of product differentiation to survive and that product differentiation firms must have competitive levels of cost to survive.[32] For example, the fashion design company Versace—the ultimate product differentiating firm—has hired a new CEO and controller to help control its costs.[33]

Summary

Product differentiation exists when customers perceive a particular firm's products to be more valuable than other firms' products. Although differentiation can have several bases, it is, in the end, always a matter of customer perception. Bases of product differentiation include: (1) attributes of the products or services a firm sells (including product features, product complexity, the timing of product introduction, and location); (2) relations between a firm and its customers (including product customization, consumer marketing, and reputation); and (3) links within and between firms (including links between functions, links with other firms, a firm's product mix, its distribution system, and its level of service and support). However, in the end, product differentiation is limited only by the creativity of a firm's managers.

Product differentiation is valuable to the extent that it enables a firm to set its prices higher than what it would otherwise be able to. Each of the bases of product differentiation identified can be used to neutralize environmental threats and exploit environmental opportunities. The rarity and imitability of bases of product differentiation vary. Highly imitable bases of product differentiation include product features. Somewhat imitable bases include product mix, links with other firms, product customization, and consumer marketing. Costly-to-imitate bases of product differentiation include linking business functions, timing, location, reputation, service, and support.

The implementation of a product differentiation strategy involves management of organizational structure, management controls, and compensation policies. Structurally, it is not unusual for firms implementing product differentiation strategies to use cross-divisional and cross-functional teams, together with teams that are focused exclusively on a particular product differentiation effort, so-called "skunk works." Managerial controls that provide free managerial decision making within broad decision-making guidelines can be helpful in implementing product differentiation strategies, as is a policy of experimentation. Finally, compensation policies that tolerate risk-taking and a creative flair and that measure employee performance along multiple dimensions simultaneously can also be helpful in implementing product differentiation strategies.

A variety of organizational attributes is required to successfully implement a product differentiation strategy. Some have argued that contradictions between these organizational characteristics and those required to implement a cost leadership strategy mean that firms that attempt to do both will perform poorly. More recent research has noted the relationship between product differentiation, market share, and low costs and has observed that some firms have learned to manage the contradictions between cost leadership and product differentiation.

Challenge Questions

5.1. Although cost leadership is perhaps less relevant for firms pursuing product differentiation, costs are not totally irrelevant. What advice about costs would you give a firm pursuing a product differentiation strategy?

5.2. Product features are often the focus of product differentiation efforts. Yet product features are among the easiest-to-imitate bases of product differentiation and thus among the least likely bases of product differentiation to be a source of sustained competitive advantage. This appears paradoxical. How can you resolve this paradox?

5.3. What are the strengths and weaknesses of using regression analysis and hedonic prices to describe the bases of product differentiation?

5.4. Chamberlin used the term "monopolistic competition" to describe firms pursuing a product differentiation strategy in a competitive industry. However, it is usually the case that firms that operate in monopolies are less efficient and less competitive than those that operate in more competitive settings (see Chapter 3). Why would this same problem exist for firms operating in a "monopolistic competition" context?

5.5. Implementing a product differentiation strategy seems to require just the right mix of control and creativity. How do you know if a firm has the right mix?

5.6. Is it possible to evaluate the mix of control and creativity when implementing a product differentiation strategy before problems associated with being out of balance manifest themselves? If yes, how? If no, why not?

5.7. A firm with a highly differentiated product can increase the volume of its sales. Increased sales volumes can enable a firm to reduce its costs. High volumes with low costs can lead a firm to have very high profits, some of which the firm can use to invest in further differentiating its products. What advice would you give a firm whose competition is enjoying this product differentiation and cost leadership advantage?

Problem Set

5.8. For each of the listed products, describe at least two ways they are differentiated.

(a) Ben & Jerry's ice cream
(b) The Hummer H2
(c) The X-Games
(d) The movies *Animal House* and *Caddyshack*
(e) Frederick's of Hollywood
(f) Taco Bell

5.9. Which, if any, of the bases of product differentiation in the previous question are likely to be sources of sustained competitive advantage? Why?

5.10. Suppose you obtained the following regression results, where the starred (*) coefficients are statistically significant. What could you say about the bases of product differentiation in this market? (Hint: A regression coefficient is statistically significant when it is so large that its effect is very unlikely to have emerged by chance.)

$$\begin{aligned}\text{House Price} = {} & 125{,}000^* + 15{,}000^*(\text{More than three bedrooms}) \\ & + \$18{,}000^*(\text{More than 3,500 square feet}) \\ & + \$150\ (\text{Has plumbing}) + \$180\ (\text{Has lawn}) \\ & + 17{,}000^*(\text{Lot larger than 1/2 acre})\end{aligned}$$

How much would you expect to pay for a four-bedroom, 3,800-square-foot house on a one-acre lot? How much for a four-bedroom, 2,700-square-foot house on a quarter-acre lot? Do these results say anything about the sustainability of competitive advantages in this market?

5.11. Which of the following management controls and compensation policies is consistent with implementing cost leadership? With product differentiation? With both cost leadership and product differentiation? With neither cost leadership nor product differentiation?

(a) Firm-wide stock options
(b) Compensation that rewards each function separately for meeting its own objectives
(c) A detailed financial budget plan
(d) A document that describes, in detail, how the innovation process will unfold in a firm
(e) A policy that reduces the compensation of a manager who introduces a product that fails in the market
(f) A policy that reduces the compensation of a manager who introduces several products that fail in the market
(g) The creation of a purchasing council to discuss how different business units can reduce their costs

5.12. Identify three industries or markets where it is unlikely that firms will be able to simultaneously implement cost leadership and product differentiation. Which firms in this industry are implementing cost leadership strategies? Which are implementing product differentiation strategies? Are any firms "stuck in the middle"? If yes, which ones? If no, why not? Are any firms implementing both cost leadership and product differentiation strategies? If yes, which ones? If no, why not?

Writing Assignments

5.13. How can product differentiation be used to neutralize environmental threats and exploit environmental opportunities?

5.14. How can organizational structure be used to implement product differentiation strategies?

CASE STUDY | Will Paper Boat Sail through the Storm

Hector Beverages Private Limited (HBPL), the company that owns Paper Boat, was started by four friends—Neeraj Kakkar, Suhas Misra, Neeraj Biyani and James Nuttall—as Hector Beverages in Gurugram, Haryana. Prior to the launch of Paper Boat in 2013, Hector Beverages launched 'Frissia', a protein drink, followed by the energy drink 'Tzinga' in 2011. With the launch of Paper Boat, Hector Beverages shifted its focus to the traditional Indian drinks segment. Paper Boat is India's fastest-growing consumer brand, selling 11 different traditional-nostalgic Indian beverages and foods with 48 SKUs in India, Dubai, Malaysia, the UK and the US. HBPL has aptly captured the people's mind with its beautiful tagline 'Drinks and Memories'.

Market Size

India, a country of more than 1.3 billion consumers of food with expected spending of up to \$5 trillion by the year 2025, offers great opportunity for the expansion of the soft drinks' market. Additionally, given that India is among the youngest country in the world according to population age (as was estimated in 2020), this subcontinent poses a vast market, increasing disposable income, younger population (more than 50 per cent of consumers below the age of 30 years) and changing lifestyles, and all of these put together has tremendous implications for domestic and international firms with business interest in soft drinks. According to a 2021 report by Technopak, the Indian packaged juice market was valued at \$200 million (around ₹1,100 crore) with a projection to grow at a CAGR of 15 percent over the next two years.

History

All it took to ideate Paper Boat was a flask of homemade *Aam Panna* (a traditional raw mango drink, ideal for summer) during a midday office meal shared by the co-founders in the initial stages. While brainstorming potential business ventures. The idea of commercially producing traditional Indian beverages, previously absent from the market, resonated strongly with everyone involved.

HBPL started its first production plant in Manesar in 2009, but soon this plant couldn't keep up with increasing demand, as it lacked the facilities for the manufacture of coconut water and sugar cane juice—drinks that the company was looking forward to launch. Hence in 2014, the company set up its second manufacturing plant with much larger capacity in Mysuru, Karnataka. The Mysuru plant has a production capacity of 380 bottles per minute while the Manesar plant has the capacity of only 80 bottles per minute.

Brand

A phrase made famous by Walter Landor can be summarized as, 'Products are produced in the factory, but brands are produced in the minds of the consumer'. This is true beca use at the initial stages of brand differentiation, the costs primarily reflect the additional money spent on production and marketing, which may not necessarily be related to enhancing the quality or essential benefits of the product. Inspired by life experiences and cherished childhood memories, the name 'Paper Boat' was coined. Paper Boat's tagline is 'drinks and memories' evokes a sense of nostalgia and fondness for our early years.

Innovative Products

Paper Boat has been focused on its competencies and expertise on innovative and unique product development. New product development constitutes an important part of paper boat growth strategy. With more than eleven types of ethnic drinks—*Jal Jeera, Aam Panna, Aam Ras, Alphonso Aam,*

Jamun Kala Khatta, Chilli Guava, Nimbu Pani, Kokum, Neer More, Kanji, Sugarcane Juice, Lychee Ras, Apple, and Orange—new product introductions are constantly focused on for meeting consumer's demand ensuring convenience, health, improved taste, and lifestyle changes. Paper Boat also has a range of milk-based beverages like buttermilk, badam milk, and thandai, while launching coconut water in 2018. Apart from these, Paper Boat produces two seasonal drinks associated with Indian festivals—*Panakam* (available during Ram Navami) and *Sherbet-e-Khas* (available during Eid). In 2017, the brand expanded its offering by launching its drinks in one litre Tetra Prisma Aseptic cartons, replacing the 500 ml packs. This move widened the brand's reach to include the multi-serve category. In the year 2015, introduced *Chikki* (a traditional peanuts and jaggery preparation) in seasonal snack segment.

Pricing

Price of any product is the first thing the consumers look for. Products with reasonable price usually attract more customers compared to products with higher price tags. The beverages of Paper Boat are usually available in different pack sizes, basis which the prices of products may vary. Regardless of which product the customer considers, the prices relatively affordable. This pricing strategy has been very effective for the brand resulting in increased sales year after year.

Unique Packaging

Packaging has evolved over time. Considered earlier merely as containers of products, packaging has emerged into a crucial element for marketing strategies, serving as a conveyer of messages to consumers. Classic design elements that are included in any packaging refer to shape, color and graphics. The Paper Boat pouches are made of a four-part laminate. The two outer layers are a blend of proprietary polypropylene and polyethylene which makes the pack with-stand extremes in pressure and heat while at the same time being easy to print upon. The penultimate layer is made of bonded aluminium which keeps any form of moisture and vapor from entering the pack and tampering the goodness of the drink. This layer makes no contact with the drink. The innermost layer is made of virgin, food-grade polypropylene which keeps the content fresh, safe and tasty. The single-serving flexible packages use Doypack—the same packaging that NASA uses for sending beverages with its astronauts. In August 2019, the company collaborated with Tetra Pak and introduced holographic packaging for two of its variants: *Alphonso Aamras* and pomegranate juice. This new packaging is both appealing and easy to hold.

Distribution Strategies

Usually new beverage brands try to convince departmental stores and *kirana* stores to stock their products. Instead of following the regular route Hector Beverages partnered with Indigo airlines for distribution. The Indigo Airlines partnership enabled to get attention of air travellers during their private and captive time. The beautiful and unique packaging with stories on the pack resonated with the consumers as they enjoyed the ethnic drinks. Eventually, the company partnered with modern trade retail stores such as Big Bazaar and Reliance Fresh followed by coffee chains like Barista Lavazza Hotels like Trident and Westin, collaborations with Google, Facebook, LinkedIn.

To increase its reach in Tier II cities, HBPL has teamed up with Indo Nissin Foods to tap the latter's robust pan-India distribution network. So far, Paper Boat is present in over 120,000 outlets in top towns such as Delhi, Mumbai, Hyderabad, Pune, Chennai and few others. Due to its increasing popularity, the brand is now available in more airliners, trains, modern retail stores, and mom & pop stores. It has partnered with major e-commerce platforms such as Amazon and Flipkart to sell few of its products in multipack formats.

Marketing Strategies

Distinguishing itself with age-old recipes of traditional Indian beverages, Paper Boat's key marketing strategy is capturing the nostalgia of innocent childhood memories through the simplicity of its storytelling campaign. Paper Boat's beautifully utilized social media, including Facebook, Twitter, Instagram and YouTube, for sharing captivating stories with its dedicated fan base and use content to interact with the customers. The content narrative primarily reflects its brand philosophy—'Life still is Beautiful'. Every activity depicted—flying kites, running behind cycle-rickshaws, playing indoor games, making paper boats—became a point of conversation.

Competitors

Despite having a truly differentiated product that is difficult to replicate and offered at competitive prices in the same market, Paper Boat faces stiff competition. Firms capable of differentiating their products are more likely to possess specialized capabilities or special resources that give them a sustained advantage. Paper Boat's major competitors are Dabur India, PepsiCo, Coca-Cola, B Natural, and NourishCo. While Dabur India has entered the functional drink market with aam panna, beverage giants Pepsico and Coca-Cola have also ventured into the non-carbonated drinks space. B Natural, an ITC-owned brand, is posing competition for Paper Boat through a wide variety of Indian beverages made without the use of any concentrate. Noursihco, a joint venture between Tata Global Beverages Pvt. Ltd. And Pepsico India Holdings Pvt. Ltd., is poses serious competition to Paper Boat.

Growth Strategy

Paper Boat's journey began with a vision to reintroduce traditional Indian beverages to the modern market. The brand's growth timeline is marked by strategic product launches, focusing on flavors that evoke nostalgia among Indian consumers. Starting with just a few flavors, Paper Boat has expanded its range to include over a dozen traditional drinks. Key milestones include the introduction of innovative packaging solutions, expansion into healthy snacks, and entering new markets both domestically and internationally. This timeline underscores Paper Boat's commitment to innovation, quality, and celebrating India's rich culinary heritage.

In the fiscal year 2023, Paper Boat achieved a significant milestone by crossing the ₹500 crore mark in revenue, a testament to the brand's growing popularity and market penetration. This 56 percent growth in revenue from ₹324 crore in FY22 highlights the successful expansion of its product line and increased consumer acceptance. The revenue boost was primarily driven by sales of its fruit-based drinks and expansion into healthy snacks, indicating a strong consumer preference for healthier, traditional beverage options. This exhibit illustrates Paper Boat's successful financial strategy and consumer-centric approach, despite the competitive landscape of the Indian beverage market.

Paper Boat's innovative approach and rapid growth have attracted significant interest from investors. The brand's funding history is marked by several rounds of investment, totalling over $103.5 million. Notable investors include Sequoia Capital India, Hillhouse Capital Group, Sofina, and most recently, GIC, which led a $50.1 million funding round in 2022. This financial backing has been crucial for Paper Boat in scaling its operations, expanding its product range, and exploring new markets. The consistent investor confidence reflects the brand's strong market potential and commitment to revolutionizing the Indian beverage industry.

Integrating these exhibits into Paper Boat's broader narrative showcases a company on an upward trajectory, fuelled by innovative products that resonate with consumers' tastes and preferences. The growth timeline highlights the strategic moves that have defined Paper Boat's journey, from product innovation to market expansion. The significant increase in FY23 revenue illustrates not only market acceptance but also the effectiveness of Paper Boat's business model in navigating the competitive landscape. Finally, the detailed funding history underscores the confidence investors have in Paper Boat's vision and execution capabilities.

As Paper Boat continues to evolve, its focus on product differentiation, market expansion, and operational excellence will be crucial. The company's ability to balance growth with maintaining the quality and authenticity of its products will determine its long-term success in the rapidly growing Indian beverage market and beyond.

Blue Ocean Strategy

The Blue Ocean approach entails securing uncontested market room and distancing itself from the competition. Customers' usual value/trade-off benchmarks are disrupted by this new demand created among a new target consumer market. The successful implementation of the Blue Ocean Strategy in India's convenience food market, with a special emphasis on Paper Boat, demonstrates that the only way for entrepreneurs to support their businesses in the long run is to focus on creating, raising, reducing, and eliminating variables. The popularity of Paper Boat in the food industry shows that businesses that target uncontested markets could conquer the obstacles of fierce competition.

The company has specifically turned its emphasis to aftermarket share and implemented a penetrative strategy. Paper Boat depends heavily on digital marketing and advertising, and its digital campaigns are as exclusive as the brand. It uses imaginative doodles, animations, and photos to share its brand tale on Instagram, cleverly using two dogs—Hector and Beverages—to add quirkiness to the storytelling. They took a 50 percent share of the market for ethnic flavour beverages, worth ₹2,000 crores.

Conclusion

Paper Boat has disrupted the Indian industry and has risen to the top of the non-alcoholic drinks market. They describe their winning recipe as 'ethnic flavours, fancy packaging, and quirky digital ads focusing on stirring nostalgia through storytelling.' When Paper Boat first arrived in the market, it ushered in a new genre of packaged ethnic-flavoured beverages, and its packaging set it apart from the competition. With so much happening in the industry, Paper Boat founders need to make a decision about the future of Paper Boat financials to make the business more profitable.

Questions

1. How has Paper Boat distinguished itself from competitors in building its business, particularly in terms of product innovation and marketing strategies?
2. Considering Paper Boat's current market presence and product portfolio, what recommendations would you make for its pricing strategy, localization of marketing efforts, and expansion of its product range to enhance market penetration and customer engagement?
3. What are the unique aspects of Paper Boat's value proposition, including its target customer demographic and brand positioning, and how do these elements contribute to its market potential and brand differentiation in the beverage industry?

References

Garg, P., Farooqi, R., Garg, Y., Kala, D., & Singh, S. (2023). *Using Nostalgic Emotions to Revive Indian Ethnic Drinks Market: Competitive Strategy at Paper Boat.* FIIB Business Review, 23197145231176115.

Haq, Z. U. (2023). *How to enter paradise on earth: a case study of Aava.* The CASE Journal, 19(2), 314–327.

Suryavanshi, A. K. S., Bhatt, V., Thomas, S., Patel, R., & Trivedi, T. (2023). *Predicting CRM purchase intention by examining congruence, shopping orientation and mood moderation: Applying congruence theory with SEM-ANN-NCA method.* International Review on Public and Nonprofit Marketing, 1–30.

Kumar S, S. (2022). *Employee Development in the Conceptual Age: Moving from Left to Right to Create a Whole.* NHRD Network Journal, 15(3), 361–369.

Manchanda, D. (2022). *Food packaging design—its concept and application.* In Food Packaging: Materials, Techniques and Environmental Issues (pp. 227–259). Singapore: Springer Nature Singapore.

End Notes

1 See Ono, Y. (1996). "Who really makes that cute little beer? You'd be surprised." *The Wall Street Journal*, April 15, pp. A1+. Since this 1996 article, some of these craft beer companies have changed the way they manufacture the beers to be more consistent with the image they are trying to project.

2 See Porter, M. E. (1980). *Competitive strategy*. New York: Free Press; and Caves, R. E., and P. Williamson. (1985). "What is product differentiation, really?" *Journal of Industrial Organization Economics*, 34, pp. 113–132.

3 www.usatoday.com/story/money/cars/2016/12/12/six-hot-car-technology-trends-watch-2017/95323726/ Accessed January 25, 2017

4 Lieberman, M. B., and D. B. Montgomery. (1988). "First-mover advantages." *Strategic Management Journal*, 9, pp. 41–58.

5 Carroll, P. (1993). *Big blues: The unmaking of IBM*. New York: Crown Publishers.

6 These ideas were first developed in Hotelling, H. (1929). "Stability in competition." *Economic Journal*, 39, pp. 41–57; and Ricardo, D. (1817). *Principles of political economy and taxation*. London: J. Murray.

7 See Gunther, M. (1998). "Disney's call of the wild." *Fortune*, April 13, pp. 120–124.

8 D. Hay and D. Morris (1979). *Industrial economics: Theory and evidence*. Oxford: Oxford University Press; K. Cowling and J. Cubbin (1971). "Price, quality, and advertising competition." *Economica*, 38, pp. 378–394.

9 The idea of reputation is explained in Klein, B., and K. Leffler. (1981). "The role of market forces in assuring contractual performance." *Journal of Political Economy*, 89, pp. 615–641.

10 See Robichaux M. (1995). "It's a book! A T-shirt! A toy! No, just MTV trying to be Disney." *The Wall Street Journal*, February 8, pp. A1+.

11 See Henderson, R., and I. Cockburn. (1994). "Measuring competence? Exploring firm effects in pharmaceutical research." *Strategic Management Journal*, 15, pp. 63–84.

12 Kotler, P. (1986). *Principles of marketing*. Upper Saddle River, NJ: Prentice Hall.

13 Porter, M. E., and R. Wayland. (1991). "Coca-Cola vs. Pepsi-Cola and the soft drink industry." Harvard Business School Case No. 9-391-179.

14 Ghemawat, P. (1993). "Sears, Roebuck and Company: The merchandise group." Harvard Business School Case No. 9-794-039.

15 E. H. Chamberlin (1933). *The economics of monopolistic competition*. Cambridge, MA: MIT Press; J. Robinson (1934). "What is perfect competition?" *Quarterly Journal of Economics*, 49, pp. 104–120.

16 Welsh, J. (1998). "Office-paper firms pursue elusive goal: Brand loyalty." *The Wall Street Journal*, September 21, p. B6.

17 J. Angwin (2003). "Some 'enlargement pills' pack impurities." *The Wall Street Journal*, April 8, p. B1; G. Pisano (1991). "Nucleon, Inc." Harvard Business School Case No. 9-692-041.

18 See White, E., and K. Palmer. (2003). "U.S. retailing 101." *The Wall Street Journal*, August 12, pp. B1+.

19 See Hennart, J. F. (1988). "A transaction cost theory of equity joint ventures." *Strategic Management Journal*, 9, pp. 361–374.

20 Deutsch, C. H. (1991). "How is it done? For a small fee . . . " *New York Times*, October 27, p. 25 and Armstrong, L. (1991). "Services: The customer as 'Honored Guest.'" *BusinessWeek*, October 25, p. 104.

21 See Yoffie, D. (1994). "Swissair's alliances (A)." Harvard Business School Case No. 9-794-152.

22 "WPP—Integrating icons." Harvard Business School Case No. 9-396-249.

23 Orosz, J. J. (2002). "Big funds need a 'Skunk Works' to stir ideas." *Chronicle of Philanthropy*, June 27, p. 47.

24 W. Chan Kim and Renee Mauborgne (2005). *Blue ocean strategy*. Cambridge: Harvard Business School Press.

25 Van de Ven, A., D. Polley, R. Garud, and S. Venkatraman. (1999). *The innovation journey*. New York: Oxford, pp. 198–200.

26 Position, L. L. (1999). "David S. Pottruck." *BusinessWeek*, September 27, EB 51.

27 Porter, M. E. (1980). *Competitive strategy*. New York: Free Press.

28 Hill, C. W. L. (1988). "Differentiation versus low cost or differentiation and low cost: A contingency framework." *Academy of Management Review*, 13(3), pp. 401–412.

29 Gibson, R. (1995). "Food: At McDonald's, new recipes for buns, eggs." *The Wall Street Journal*, June 13, p. B1.

30 Originally discussed in the Research Made Relevant feature in Chapter 3.

31 Womack, J. P., D. I. Jones, and D. Roos. (1990). *The machine that changed the world*. New York: Rawson.

32 Porter, M. E. (1985). *Competitive advantage*. New York: Free Press.

33 Agins, T., and A. Galloni. (2003). "Facing a squeeze, Versace struggles to trim the fat." *The Wall Street Journal*, September 30, pp. A1+.

CHAPTER

6 Flexibility and Real Options

LEARNING OBJECTIVES

After reading this chapter, you should be able to:

6.1 Define strategic flexibility and real options.

6.2 Specify the conditions under which strategic flexibility and real options will be valuable for firms.

6.3 Identify when strategic flexibility and real options can be a source of sustained competitive advantage.

6.4 Identify the organizational challenges associated with implementing strategic flexibility and a real options strategy.

Why Is Netflix called Netflix?

For the first ten years of its existence, everyone had one question about Netflix: Why was Netflix called Netflix? Everyone got the "flix" part of the name—"flix" was slang for movies, and from its founding in 1997, Netflix was in the movie distribution business. Its business model was to take orders for DVD rentals online and then fulfill those orders by delivering DVDs to consumers through the mail. But the "net" had nothing to do with how Netflix distributed its DVDs. A better name for Netflix might have been "Mailflix" or "Letterflix."

In fact, Netflix was very successful at this DVD by mail distribution model. By 2000, it was challenging the leader in the DVD rental business—Blockbuster. Blockbuster had retail stores that consumers would visit to rent DVDs. They would also have to return these DVDs to the same store. Having DVDs delivered through the mail eliminated these two trips and, except for delays while rented DVDs were sent through the mail, was infinitely more convenient than renting DVDs at retail stores.

In the late 1990s, Blockbuster had tried to duplicate Netflix's DVD distribution model. It failed. Apparently, the fulfillment logistics in the DVDs by mail business—though perfected by Netflix—were very difficult for Blockbuster to imitate. Rather than trying to duplicate Netflix, in 2000 Blockbuster tried to buy Netflix for $50 million. The founders of Netflix—Reed Hastings and Marc Randolph—declined the offer. Instead, Netflix continued its operations in the DVD rental business, continuously exceeded customer expectations, built a well-recognized brand in the entertainment industry, developed an understanding of the movie production business, and generally bided its time until it could realize its full objectives.

In 2002, Netflix went public with an IPO that valued the company at over $309 million. Netflix received this valuation—over six times greater than Blockbuster's offer from two years earlier—not because of its DVD rental business, but because its success in the DVD rental business had positioned Netflix to successfully enter the online video streaming market—a market that did not yet exist, but a market that most observers believed could be important in the entertainment industry in the future. The problem was that, in 2002, fast internet services were still not widely available to consumers. Without a fast internet, there could not be online video streaming.

From 2002 to 2007, Netflix invested in the technology needed to run an online video streaming service. During this same time, fast internet services became more widely available. Finally, in 2007 Netflix was true to its name and started an online video streaming service—"flix" were actually being distributed over the "net."

Fast forward another ten years. By 2017, Netflix had over 93 million people who subscribed to its video streaming services. It was available in over 190 countries around the world. In 2016, it introduced 126 original series—more than any other network on television or cable. And despite significant competition from Hulu, Amazon Prime, YouTube, and a variety of other streaming services, Netflix's market value in 2016 was $41.1 billion—a far cry from the $50 million Blockbuster—a company that no longer exists—offered for the firm in 2000.[1]

Could Netflix have entered the video streaming industry in 2007, without a history of successfully competing in the DVD rental business? Maybe, although it is hard to imagine that it would have been able to raise the capital needed to develop online streaming technology without its track record in DVD rentals. But by successfully competing in the DVD rental market, Netflix created the option for it to invest, and ultimately compete in, the online streaming market. Put another way, Neflix's original business strategy created the flexibility that it needed to consider, and then to enter, the online streaming market.

The two business level strategies discussed in this book so far—cost leadership and product differentiation—require both focus and commitment to implement. Firms that implement these strategies are committing to a way of doing business, a way of organizing themselves, and even an organizational culture. Obviously, firms that choose either of these strategies are not likely to change them frequently.

This chapter examines an alternative approach to business level strategy. Instead of focused commitment, this approach focuses on flexibility. Strategic flexibility implies that rather than committing to a single course of action, a firm maintains multiple strategic options simultaneously and delays committing to a particular course of action until uncertainty about the value of that option is reduced. Netflix maintained the option of investing in the online streaming business all the time it was in the DVD through the mail rental business. Once uncertainty about demand for the online streaming business was reduced by the widespread introduction of fast internet, Netflix exercised its option, invested in the required technology, and began online video streaming.

This emphasis on maintaining options that create strategic flexibility can be thought of as a third generic business level strategy, in addition to cost leadership and product differentiation.

Objective 6.1 Define strategic flexibility and real options.

What is Strategic Flexibility?

A firm has **strategic flexibility** when it can choose among several different strategic options.[2] For example, a firm may choose to implement a product differentiation strategy, but not completely commit to a single basis for differentiating its product. Thus, Progressive Insurance seems mostly committed to "Flo" as its primary advertising spokesperson in the U.S. market, but alternative approaches to differentiating its auto insurance products are explored periodically (e.g., the Progressive Insurance "box" as a spokesperson). At some point, Progressive might exercise the option it has created through investing in these advertising alternatives by abandoning "Flo."[3]

Firms may also create flexibility in their cost leadership strategy. This could happen, for example, when it is not clear if the lowest cost position for a firm would be created by outsourcing production to another firm or by bringing that production in-house. To create flexibility, such a firm might outsource some of its production, bring some of its production in-house, and then closely watch the cost of these two. This experiment may lead a firm to commit to one of these approaches to obtaining a cost leadership position.[4] Alternatively, a firm may choose to maintain both forms of production, since the cost of these different approaches might change over time in some unpredictable ways. If one approach to manufacturing becomes much less costly than the other, this firm could transfer some of its production to the low-cost alternative—at least if that alternative remains less costly.

Indeed, since all the strategies examined in this book—both at the business and corporate level—involve choices among alternatives, strategic flexibility can be an important consideration for all of them. If it is not clear which of these alternatives are superior—vertically integrate or not (Chapter 8), diversify or not (Chapters 9 and 10), form an alliance or not (Chapter 11), and acquire or not (Chapter 12)—then strategic flexibility may be an important consideration in implementing these strategies.

Types of Flexibility

For a firm to have strategic flexibility, it must possess **strategic options**. Strategic options exist when firms have the ability, but not the obligation, to invest in a particular strategy. Those familiar with financial options logic will note a parallel between the definition of strategic options and financial options. Indeed, strategic options can be thought of as an example of a real option. A **real option** exists when a firm has the ability, but not the obligation, to invest in real assets of some type. **Real assets** are tangible resources that can have an impact on a firm's production, including land, buildings, raw materials, finished goods inventories, distribution systems, information technology, and so forth.[5]

Of course, strategic flexibility created by a firm having options can take many forms. Some of the most important types of flexibility a firm may have, and examples of actions that create these different types of flexibility, are listed in Table 6.1.[6]

For example, a firm can make strategic choices that enhance its ability to defer additional investment in a strategy until some later period. This is the **option to defer**. An oil and gas company creates this option when it leases land for potential exploration and oil extraction instead of buying it. By leasing the land, this firm defers the decision about whether to fully invest in exploration and extraction on that land until after uncertainty about future oil prices is resolved and until after the production potential of that land is more completely understood. An oil company that buys this land instead of leasing it forgoes the option of not investing in this land in the future and thus is less flexible than the firm that leases the land.

Firms can also make choices that enhance their ability to "grow" an investment in the future, should that option turn out to be valuable. This is the **option to grow**. Thus, for example, a manufacturing firm creates this option by building a plant with a capacity that can be increased at relatively low cost. This can be done by, say, running several smaller manufacturing lines in a single plant simultaneously and bringing them on line as demand increases.

Firms can also make choices that enhance their ability to get smaller and reduce investment in a strategy, should that option turn out to be valuable in the future. This is the **option to contract**. One way to create this option is to use contract and temporary employees instead of full-time employees. In most countries, contract and temporary employees are much less costly to lay off than full-time

TABLE 6.1 Types of Flexibility and Examples of Actions That Can Create Each Type

Type of Flexibility	Example
The option to defer	An oil company leases land for potential exploration instead of buying it.
The option to grow	A firm builds a plant with the ability to add capacity at low cost.
The option to contract	A firm hires contract and temporary employees instead of full-time employees.
The option to shut down and restart	A firm outsources distribution to a firm that distributes the products of many firms instead of outsourcing distribution to a firm that distributes only its production.
The option to abandon	A firm builds a manufacturing plant that employs only general-purpose machinery.
The option to expand	A firm invests to create one product because that investment could lead to the development of other products in the future.

employees. Indeed, in some countries—including Germany and France—full-time employment growth is significantly limited by the costliness of laying off full-time employees. For this reason, firms that employ a high percentage of contract and temporary employees are more flexible than firms that employ only full-time employees.

A firm can also make choices that enhance its ability to shut down and restart a business should this option be valuable in the future. This is the **option to shut down and restart**. Compare, for example, two firms: one outsources its distribution to a company that distributes only its products and a second that outsources its distribution to a company that distributes the products of numerous firms. Suppose that market conditions compel both of these firms to shut down their operations for some period. Which of these two firms is likely to have a lower cost of restarting operations? Because the first firm's distributor was probably unable to distribute anything during this downtime, it may have suffered significantly. Indeed, it may not have even survived this downtime. The second firm's distributor, on the other hand, because it distributes the products of numerous firms, was probably able to survive during this downtime. Upon restart, the second firm can simply reestablish its relationship with its distributor and go on as before. The first firm may have to find an entirely new distributor. Thus, the cost of restarting the business for the second firm is likely to be much lower than the cost of restarting the business for the first firm. In this sense, working with a firm that distributes the products of numerous firms has the effect of increasing the flexibility of a firm to shut down and restart a business should it decide this is necessary to do.

Firms can also make choices that enhance their ability to abandon a particular strategy. This is the **option to abandon**. For example, a firm creates this option if it builds a manufacturing plant that employs only general-purpose machinery. Compared to highly customized manufacturing equipment, general-purpose machinery has significant salvage and resale value. The ability to extract more residual value from an investment in a strategy reduces the cost of abandoning that strategy and thus has the effect of increasing the flexibility of a firm to abandon a strategy should it decide to do so.

Finally, a firm can also make choices that enhance its ability to expand its strategy beyond its current boundaries. This is the **option to expand**. Suppose a pharmaceutical firm does the R&D necessary to create Product A. This firm creates the option to expand if the R&D it invested in to create Product A can, with some additional investment, be used to create Products B and C in the future, should these products turn out to be valuable. A firm that does not invest in the original R&D does not have the flexibility to decide whether to invest to create Products B and C in the future.

This example also shows that the actions a firm takes can create more than one type of flexibility simultaneously. Thus, not only does investing in Product A have the effect of creating the option to expand, it also has the effect of creating the option to defer investment (in Products B and C) until some future date.

Objective 6.2 Specify the conditions under which strategic flexibility and real options will be valuable for firms.

The Value of Strategic Flexibility

Strategic flexibility is most likely to be valuable under conditions of uncertainty. In this context, the concepts of risk and uncertainty need to be distinguished. A decision-making setting is said to be **risky** when the outcome of that decision is not known with certainty, but the possible outcomes associated with that decision, and their probability, are known before a decision is made.[7]

Gambling at a casino is the classic example of a risky decision. When a bet is made, the outcome of the pull of a lever, a throw of the dice, or the turn of a card are not known with certainty. However, all possible outcomes, and their probability, are known at the time a bet is made. With this information, it is possible to calculate the expected return of making a bet with great precision.

Incorporating Risk in Strategic Decision Making

The concept of risk has been implicitly incorporated into much of the discussion of strategy thus far in this book. It began with the discussion of performance in Chapter 1. There it was suggested that one way to characterize a firm's performance is to compare its return to its weighted average cost of capital. One of the major components of a firm's weighted average cost of capital is its cost of equity, and a firm's cost of equity can be estimated using the capital asset pricing model (CAPM). The CAPM, in turn, includes a measure of how a firm's historical returns are correlated with the historical returns of a diversified portfolio of stocks, i.e., β. This coefficient, β, is one measure of the historical riskiness of a firm.

In general, the most common way risk is introduced to strategic analyses is through present value analysis. The **present value** of the cash flows generated by choosing and implementing a particular strategy is equal to the sum of those cash flows, discounted by how risky they are. The riskiness of these cash flows is represented by the discount rate, k, in the following equation:

$$NPVj = \sum_{t=0}^{N} \frac{(NCFj,t)}{(1+k)^t}$$

Where,

NPV_j = net present value of Firm j's cash flows
N = economic life of an investment
$NCF_{j,t}$ = the net cash flow of Firm j and time t
k = the discount rate

If the cash flows generated by choosing and implementing a particular strategy are not risky, then k in this equation is very small, the denominator in this equation gets close to one, and no discounting occurs. If these cash flows are very risky, then the denominator gets larger and significant discounting occurs.

Limitations of Risk Based Decision Making Under Uncertainty

This approach to incorporating risk into strategic analyses does not work under conditions of uncertainty. A decision making setting is said to be **uncertain** when the outcome of that decision is not known with certainty, and the possible outcomes associated with that decision, and their probability, are also not known before a decision is made. Using the casino gambling analogy introduced earlier, under uncertainty it is not possible to calculate the expected return on a bet because you may not even know what game you are playing, or even if you did, the rules of that game might change in unpredictable ways. Using present value analysis does not work under conditions of uncertainty for three reasons.

First, under conditions of uncertainty, cash flow projections are simply unreliable. Consider the following scenario. If General Motors anticipates increased demand for a particular model, it may consider adding a third shift. Assuming that GM has been operating two shifts for some time, and assuming that GM has considerable experience adding shifts in a plant, it seems reasonable to expect that GM's management will have a good sense of the costs of implementing and running a new shift at an established plant as well as the revenues such an increase in production should produce. That is, GM's managers should be able to anticipate the net cash flow that opening a new shift should generate.

However, suppose that instead of adding a new shift producing an already existing model, GM is trying to decide whether or not it should add a shift to build an entirely new product—something that uses new technology in a new way for new customers in ways that are new to both GM and to the world. The net cash flows of such new to GM/new to the world innovation will be very difficult to anticipate. In these uncertain settings, unforeseeable costs and opportunities may affect realized cash flows in ways that could not have been anticipated.

Second, under conditions of uncertainty, the riskiness of the cash flows generated cannot be reliably anticipated. In traditional risk-based logic, the cash flows generated by choosing and implementing different strategies are all assigned into different risk categories. The riskiest cash flows receive the largest discount rates, the least risky cash flows receive the smallest discount rates. But under conditions of uncertainty, one of the things you do not know is how risky a particular cash flow is. One might conclude that in this setting, the prudent thing to do would be to assume cash flows are very risky and move forward in decision making on that basis.[8] However, adopting this assumption, ex ante, may lead firms to not choose and implement strategies that generate high levels of positive cash flow at low risk, ex post.

Finally, the present value approach to incorporating risk into strategic decision making implicitly assumes that decisions about strategies and how they are implemented are made all at once, at the moment a strategic choice is made and implemented. In reality, strategic choices are often made over time, in a staged manner. The first decision in implementing a strategy, for example, may eliminate some of a firm's strategic options while retaining others. In the face of these multiple second stage options, firms need to make additional strategic choices, choices which may decrease—or even increase—a firm's future strategic flexibility. And so it goes throughout the life of a strategy. An approach to strategic decision making that requires that the implications of that strategy through its entire life must be known at the time it is chosen fails to recognize that the world can change in unpredictable ways, and that retaining flexibility in the face of this uncertainty by staging strategic decision making can create enormous value for a firm.

Valuing Flexibility

Thus, while present value approaches do a wonderful job of incorporating risk into strategic decision making, they cannot be applied under conditions of uncertainty. How then can strategic flexibility in these uncertain settings be valued? Two approaches are presented in this chapter. However, both build on the logic for valuing financial options summarized in the **Strategy in Depth** feature.

Strategy in Depth

It has been shown that the value of an option depends on five variables:

1. the value of the underlying financial asset, S (for example, the value of the stock on which a stock option is written);
2. the option's exercise price, X;
3. the time to an option's maturity, T;
4. the variance in the price of the asset on which an option is written, σ^2 (for example, the variance in the price of the stock on which a stock option is written); and
5. the risk-free rate of interest, r_f.

These variables combine to determine an option's value through the following formula:

$$c = SN(d_1) - [Xe^{-r_fT}N(d_2)]$$

where

c = the value of this option
S = the value of the underlying asset
X = exercise price of the option
T = time to maturity
r_f = risk-free rate

$$d_1 = \frac{\ln(S/X) + r_fT}{\sigma\sqrt{T}} + \frac{1}{2}\sigma\sqrt{T}$$

$$d_2 = d_1 - \sigma\sqrt{T}$$

$N(d_1)$ and $N(d_2)$ are the cumulative area of d_1 and d_2, respectively, in a normal distribution. This is known as the **Black-Scholes formula**.

Although this equation can look formidable, its application can be simplified into three steps. First, identify the inputs needed to calculate d_1 and d_2. Second, using a chart of the areas under the normal curve, calculate $N(d_1)$ and $N(d_2)$. Third, calculate the option value.

The Black-Scholes Model for Valuing Financial Options

This is done for an option with the following attributes: (1) the value of the underlying asset, S (for example, the current stock price if this is a stock option), is \$50; (2) the exercise price of this option, X, is \$45; (3) the time to this option's maturity, T, is three months (expressed as a percentage of one year, $T = .25$); (4) the variance in the price of the underlying asset, σ^2, is 20 percent; and (5) the risk-free interest rate, r_f, is 6 percent.[9]

Putting these values into the equation for estimating d_1 and d_2 yields

$$d_1 = \frac{\ln(50/45) + .06(.25)}{\sqrt{.2}\sqrt{.25}} + \frac{1}{2}(\sqrt{.2}\sqrt{.25})$$

$$= .54 + .11$$

$$= .65$$

$$d_2 = d_1 - \sigma\sqrt{2}$$

$$= .65 - (\sqrt{.2}\sqrt{.25}) = .43$$

Substituting these numbers back into equation 6.2 yields

$$c = SN(.65) - Xe^{r_fT}N(.43)$$

$N(d_1)$ and $N(d_2)$ are calculated using the chart of the areas under the normal curve presented in Table 6.2 and available as a built-in option on many calculators. Table 6.2 presents the area under the normal curve between the mean of this distribution and points to the right of this distribution for $d_1 = .65$ and $d_2 = .43$. Thus, the area between the mean of this distribution (0) and .65 standard deviation to the right of this mean (remember, $d_1 = .65$) is approximately .242. The total area under this curve to the left of this mean is .5. Thus, the cumulative (that is, total) area under this curve for $d = .65$ is $.5 + .242 = .742$. Thus, $N(d_1) = .742$. Repeating this procedure yields the result that $N(d_2) = .665$.

Armed with these estimates of $N(d_1)$ and $N(d_2)$, the value of this option can be calculated as

$$c = 50(.742) - [45e^{-.06(.25)}(.665)]$$

$$= 37.10 - 45(.9851)(.665)$$

$$= 37.10 - 28.48$$

$$= 7.62$$

Thus, the value of this option is \$7.62. That is, an investor should be willing to pay up to \$7.62 for the right, but not the obligation, to buy a stock that is currently selling for \$50 for \$45 in three months, given the historical variance in this stock's value and the risk-free interest rate.[10]

TABLE 6.2 Areas under the Standard Normal Distribution Function

D	.00	.01	.02	.03	.04	.05	.06	.07	.08	.09
0.0	.0000	.0040	.0080	.0120	.0160	.0199	.0239	.0279	.0319	.0359
0.1	.0398	.0438	.0478	.0517	.0557	.0596	.0636	.0675	.0714	.0753
0.2	.0793	.0832	.0871	.0910	.0948	.0987	.1026	.1064	.1103	.1141
0.3	.1179	.1217	.1255	.1293	.1331	.1368	.1406	.1443	.1480	.1517
0.4	.1554	.1591	.1628	.1664	.1700	.1736	.1772	.1808	.1844	.1879
0.5	.1915	.1950	.1985	.2019	.2054	.2088	.2123	.2157	.2190	.2224
0.6	.2257	.2291	.2324	.2357	.2389	.2422	.2454	.2486	.2517	.2549
0.7	.2580	.2611	.2642	.2673	.2704	.2734	.2764	.2794	.2823	.2852
0.8	.2881	.2910	.2939	.2967	.2995	.3023	.3051	.3078	.3106	.3133
0.9	.3159	.3186	.3212	.3238	.3264	.3289	.3315	.3340	.3365	.3389
1.0	.3413	.3438	.3461	.3485	.3508	.3531	.3554	.3577	.3599	.3621

Qualitatively Valuing Strategic Flexibility Before discussing how to value strategic flexibility quantitatively, it is helpful to reflect on the implications of the Black Scholes model for valuing financial options for qualitatively valuing real strategic options. Despite its apparent complications, the Black Scholes model for valuing financial options suggests that the value of these options depends on just five factors: the exercise price of an option (X), the cash flows created by exercising an option (S), the time for an option to mature (T), the risk free rate of return (r_f), and variance in the price of the underlying asset (σ^2). As shown in Table 6.3, each of these variables have meaning in understanding the value of strategic flexibility created by a firm's real options.

First, the lower the cost of exercising a real option (X), the greater is the value of that real option. This is because it is more likely for real options with low exercise prices, other things being equal, to be exercised—that is, to be "in the money." Because a real option is exercised only when the value created by that

TABLE 6.3 Characterizing the Value of a Real Option Subjectively

Attribute of a Real Option	Effect on Value of Real Option
Exercise price (X)	The lower the exercise price, the greater is the value of a real option.
Cash flows generated (S)	The higher the cash flows generated by exercising an option, the greater is the value of a real option.
Time to maturity (T)	The longer the time to maturity, the greater is the value of a real option.
Risk-free interest rate (r_f)	The higher the risk-free interest rate, the greater is the value of a real option.
Uncertainty about future cash flows (σ^2)	The greater the uncertainty about future cash flows, the greater is the value of a real option.

option exceeds the cost of exercising the option, a low exercise price suggests a higher probability of being exercised. Conversely, the higher the exercise price of a real option, the lower is that option's value. If a firm must choose between two strategies, one of which has a low cost of implementation sometime in the future and the other a high cost of implementation sometime in the future, this attribute of real options suggests—other things being equal—that the first strategy is preferred over the second.

Second, the higher the cash flows generated by exercising a real option (*S*), the greater is the value of that real option. It is these cash flows that must offset the cost of exercising a real option if a real option is to pay off for a firm. If these cash flows are much larger than the exercise price of a real option, then the value of that real option can be very large. Other things being equal, a strategy that generates large cash flows sometime in the future is preferred over a strategy that generates small cash flows sometime in the future.

Third, the longer the time to maturity (*T*), the more valuable a real option is. Real options are all about the flexibility afforded a firm under conditions of uncertainty. The further into the future a firm can delay its decision, the more flexibility it retains. Of course, in most circumstances, a firm does not have to wait until the maturity date to exercise a real option.[11] Thus, a long maturity date provides a firm with greater flexibility with no real additional costs. If, during this long time to maturity, it becomes appropriate for a firm to exercise its real option, it can almost always do so. If it is only appropriate to exercise a real option on its maturity date, firms can wait to do so. Long maturity dates provide a firm with increased flexibility and consequently are associated with more valuable real options.

Fourth, the higher the risk-free interest rate (r_f), the more valuable the option is. However, because the risk-free rate is usually outside the direct control of managers making strategic choices, its effect on those choices is not as important to strategic decision makers. If the risk-free rate of interest is expected to change (go either up or down), this can influence the value of a real option compared to making an investment without any flexibility components.

Finally, the greater the uncertainty (σ^2), the more valuable a real option is. Intuitively, the relationship between uncertainty and the value of a real option turns on the importance of flexibility in these conditions. When it is not clear what specific strategic actions a firm should take, flexibility is the best strategic choice. Flexibility implies the ability of a firm to keep its options open. Therefore, the ability to retain options is likely to be more valuable as uncertainty about which strategy to pursue increases.

Analytically, the effect of uncertainty on the value of a real option is extremely important. Firms gain economic value from real options when the cash flows generated from exercising those options are greater than the cost of exercising them (that is, when $S > X$). However, the cost of creating this option is fixed and equal to the investment required to create the option to defer, grow, expand, and so forth. The upside potential of a real option depends on the cash flows that exercising that option may create. The downside risk of a real option, on the other hand, is fixed. In this setting, highly uncertain cash flows are preferred over less uncertain cash flows. This is because highly uncertain cash flows have the chance of generating very high returns for a firm, whereas the downside risk associated with gaining access to those cash flows is fixed. Put differently, under high uncertainty the chance of gain is greater and the chance of loss no larger. Therefore, the greater the uncertainty, the more valuable is the real option.

These subjective characteristics of real options can be used by firms to decide when real options analysis is likely to be important (that is, when uncertainty is high). They can also be used to choose among several different real options investments (that is, low exercise prices are preferred over high exercise prices; high cash flows are preferred over low cash flows; long time to maturity is preferred over short time to maturity; and high risk-free interest rates are preferred over low risk-free interest rates). All this can be done whether or not the actual value of a real option is calculated.

Return again to the example of the pharmaceutical firm deciding whether to invest in Product A, given the effect that producing A may have on its ability to create Products B and C. The criteria presented in Table 6.3 can be used to help make the decision about whether to invest in Product A, to have the option of investing in Products B and C in the future, even if it is not possible to value this option in a formal manner. Questions that managers should ask when subjectively valuing the real option value of investing in Product A include: How much additional investment will be required to develop Products B and C? What kinds of cash flows are Products B and C likely to generate? How long can the firm delay its decision to invest in Products B and C? What is the current risk-free rate of return and how is it likely to evolve? How uncertain are the cash flows associated with Products B and C? If the additional investment required to develop Products B and C is small, if the potential cash flows associated with these products is large, if the firm can delay its final decision about whether to invest in Products B and C for a very long time, if the current and future risk-free rates are high, and if the uncertainty associated with the cash flows from Products B and C is large, then the option value associated with investing in Product A is likely to be very large. In this setting, even if Product A does not generate positive net present value as a standalone investment, it may still be wise for a firm to invest in Product A to gain access to the opportunities associated with Products B and C.

Quantitatively Valuing Strategic Flexibility In many circumstances, qualitatively valuing strategic flexibility using the ideas summarized in Table 6.3 will be enough to guide a firm's strategic decision making under uncertainty. However, in some settings, it may be possible, and even advantageous, to quantitatively value a firm's flexibility due to its real options.

An example of one approach to quantitatively valuing strategic flexibility focuses on the hypothetical two stage strategic investment presented in Table 6.4.[12] In year one, a firm would need to invest $135 million to build Phase One of a plant. This Phase One investment generates the cash flow and terminal value presented in Panel A of Table 6.4. The net present value of this Phase One investment, using conventional means and a discount rate of 12 percent, is $14.24 million. Then, in year three, this firm can invest an additional $487 million in Phase Two of this plant. This Phase Two investment generates the cash flow and terminal value presented in Panel B of Table 6.4. The net present value of the Phase Two investment (also using a 12 percent discount rate) is –$41.68 million. The traditional net present value of this entire investment is, as shown in Panel C of Table 6.4: –$30.62. Based on this analysis, this firm should not invest in this plant. For future considerations, the risk-free rate of interest during this entire period is 5.5 percent.

However, this traditional valuation implicitly assumes that the firm must make the decision about whether to invest in Phase One and Phase Two at the same time. It fails to recognize a real option that is embedded in this phased investment:

TABLE 6.4 An Example of Two-Phase Investment Where Discount Rate = 12 Percent; Risk-free Rate = 5.5 Percent

(A) Phase One of the Investment

Year	0	1	2	3	4	5	6
Cash flow	0	10.0	12.0	13.4	14.5	15.1	12.8
Terminal value							185.0
Investment	(135)						
Discount factor	1.0	.893	.797	.712	.636	.567	.507
Present value	(135)	8.93	9.56	12.69	9.22	8.56	100.28
Net present value =	13.24						

(B) Phase Two of the Investment

Year	0	1	2	3	4	5	6
Cash flow	0	0	0	0	26.2	28.3	27.0
Terminal value							510.1
Investment				(487)			
Discount factor	1.0	.893	.797	.712	.636	.567	.507
Present value	0	0	0	(346.7)	16.7	16.1	272.3
Net present value =	(41.68)						

(C) Combined Phase One and Two

Year	0	1	2	3	4	5	6
Cash flow	0	10.0	12.0	13.4	40.7	43.4	38.8
Terminal value							695.1
Investment	(135)			(487)			
Discount factor	1.0	.893	.797	.712	.636	.567	.507
Present value	(135)	8.93	8.56	(337.2)	25.9	24.6	372.6
Net present value =	(30.6)						

the option to delay the decision to invest in Phase Two of this plant for three years. Thus, the valuation question facing this firm is, "Is the value created by this real option sufficient to justify investing in Phase One of the plant, even though traditional valuation techniques suggest that investing in Phase One and Two will not create value for the firm?" As is shown in Table 6.5, this kind of investment can be valued in six steps.

Step One: Recognize Real Options Step One is to recognize any real options associated with an investment. The two-stage investment in this example clearly creates the kind of flexibility enhancing strategy described in this chapter. By investing in this plant in two stages over time, a firm creates for itself the option to defer, the option to grow, and the option to expand—all depending on how the market happens to evolve—compared to what would have been the case if it built the entire plant all at once. Thus, this investment has real options associated with it.

TABLE 6.5 Steps in Valuing a Real Option

Step One: Recognize the real option →	The two-stage investment allows the decision about whether to invest in Phase Two to be deferred for three years. This creates an option to defer, grow, or expand.
Step Two: Describe the real option using financial option parameters →	See Table 6.6.
Step Three: Establish a benchmark →	The NPV of the investment valued as if the decision about Phase Two has to be made at the same time as the decision about Phase One is −\$30.62 million.
Step Four: Calculate option value metrics →	$NPV_q = S/PV(X)$ $= S/\lvert X/(1+r_f)^T\rvert$ $= .775$ $\sigma\sqrt{T} = .4\sqrt{3}$ $= .693$
Step Five: Estimate the value of the option from the Black-Scholes option pricing table →	$(NPV_q, \sigma\sqrt{T}) = (.775, .693)$ $= 19.7$ $.197 \times S =$ present value $.197(\$305.02) = \$60.09$
Step Six: Compare full present value with option value →	Benchmark value = \$30.62 Full present value = *NPV* of Phase One + option value of Phase Two = \$14.24 + \$60.09 = \$74.33

Because \$74.33 > \$30.62, this firm should invest in Phase One, keeping open its option for investing in Phase Two.

Source: Adapted from T. Luehrman, "Investment Opportunities as Real Options: Getting Started on the Numbers," *Harvard Business Review* 76, no. 4 (1998) 51–67; and T. Luehrman, "Strategy as a Portfolio of Real Options," *Harvard Business Review* 76, no. 5 (1998): 89–98.

Step Two: Describe a Real Option Using Financial Option Parameters Step Two in valuing this kind of investment is to describe it in terms of the five parameters that determine the value of a financial option: S, X, T, σ^2, and r_f. This is done by recognizing the correspondence between the five value-determining attributes of a financial option and similar attributes of a real option. The correspondence of the five parameters of the Black-Scholes option pricing model, attributes of real option investments, and attributes of the example are presented in Table 6.6.

Consider first the exercise price of a real option. A financial option's exercise price, X, is analogous to the amount of money that a firm would have to

TABLE 6.6 Correspondence of Value-Determining Parameters of Financial Options to the Attributes of Real Options, Applied to the Example in Table 6.4

Financial Parameter	Real Option Analogy	Value of Real Option Analogy in the Example
Exercise price: X	Amount of money a firm would have to invest if and when it actually exercised a real option	X = $487 million (i.e., the Phase Two investment in year 3 in Table 8.4)
Price of underlying asset: S	Present value of cash flow generated by assets built or acquired if and when a firm exercised its real option	S = $305.02 (i.e., the present value of the cash flows generated by the Phase Two investment in years 4, 5, and 6 plus the present value of the terminal value of this investment)
Time to maturity: T	Length of time a decision to invest can be deferred	T = 3 years
Risk-free interest rate: r_f	Risk-free interest rate	$r_f = 5.5\%$
Variance in the price of the underlying asset: σ^2	Uncertainty in the cash flow associated with the deferred investment	$\sigma^2 = .16$

invest if and when it actually exercised a real option. In the example, X is $487 million, the amount of money that this firm would have to invest in net working capital and fixed assets if it decides to proceed with the Phase Two investment in year three.

The price of the underlying asset in a financial option, S, corresponds to the present value of the cash flows generated by the assets built or acquired if and when a firm exercises its real option. In the example, S is the present value now (at time zero) of the cash flows that the Phase Two addition to the plant is expected to generate in the fourth year onward. As shown in Panel B of Table 8.4, in this case, S equals $305.02 million (16.67 + 16.05 + 272.3 = 305.02).

A financial option's time to maturity, T, is analogous to the length of time a company can defer the decision about whether to exercise a real option. In the example, T is three years. The time value of money for both financial and real options is the risk-free rate of interest (r_f). In the example, this is given as 5.5 percent.

Finally, the variance in the price of the asset underlying financial options, σ^2 corresponds to the uncertainty about the actual cash flows an exercised real option will generate. Of course, the level of uncertainty associated with a real option's cash flow is usually not known when a real option is first created. Indeed, the whole idea behind investing in ways that create real options is to avoid overcommitting to a particular course of action before this uncertainty is reduced. Thus, estimating σ^2 to value a real option can be difficult.

One way to address this problem is to estimate all the Black-Scholes parameters associated with a real option except σ^2. Then, various values of σ^2 can be used to calculate the value of the real option. By examining the relationship between cash flow uncertainty and real option value, managers can decide whether to invest in a real option. For example, if the only way a real option has a significant positive value is if the cash flow uncertainty associated with that option is very high (for example, $\sigma^2 = .8$); risk-averse managers might decide that investing to create this real option is not worthwhile. Alternatively, if a real option is valuable even when the cash flow uncertainty associated with it is quite low (for example, $\sigma^2 = .09$), even risk-averse managers would probably be willing to invest to create this real option. In the example, it is assumed that σ^2 equals .16.

Step Three: Establishing a Benchmark To see if valuing an investment as a real option creates any extra value for a firm, it is necessary to establish a benchmark. This benchmark is simply the present value of an investment valued without recognizing any real options embedded in that investment. As shown in Panel C of Table 6.3, that benchmark figure is −$30.62.

Step Four: Calculate Option Value Metrics Several authors have shown that it is possible to combine the parameters of the Black-Scholes option pricing model into two variables, called option value metrics. These metrics incorporate all the information about the five option valuation parameters, but do so in two numbers.[13] This can significantly simplify the valuation of a financial option.

Similar metrics can be calculated for real options. The first, often called NPVq, is simply the ratio between the present value now of the cash flows that would be generated by the assets built or acquired if and when a real option is exercised and the present value of the amount of money needed to invest in an option if and when it is exercised. From Table 6.5, we know that this ratio is simply:

$$NPV_q = \frac{S}{PV(X)}$$

$$= \frac{S}{X(1 + r_f)^T}$$

For the example, S = $305.02 million and X = $487 million. With a discount rate of 12 percent, NPVq can be calculated as

$$NPV_q = \frac{305.01}{487(1 + .055)^3}$$

$$= .775$$

The second metric has been called cumulative volatility and is

$$\text{cumulative volatility} = \sigma\sqrt{T}$$

Notice that up to this point, the uncertainty associated with the cash flow generated by a real option has been described by the variance in those cash flows (σ^2). However, in calculating cumulative volatility, the standard deviation of those cash flows (σ) is used. Of course, the standard deviation of these cash flows is simply the square root of their variance. Because in the example, $\sigma^2 = .16$, $\sigma = .4$. Because $T = 3$,

$$\text{cumulative volatility} = .4\sqrt{3}$$

$$= .693$$

Step Five: Estimate the Value of the Option from a Black-Scholes Option Pricing Table One of the advantages of using the two option value metrics to parameterize a real option is that it is then possible to use a pre-calculated table to determine the value of a specific option as a percentage of the underlying project's value. That is, these two metrics define a particular option, and this option's value is known to be equal to a percentage of an underlying project's (or assets) value. A Black-Scholes option pricing table, which is included in the appendix at the end of this book, lists this known percentage as a function of these two parameters.

With NPVq = .775 and σ sqrt 3 = .693, the value of the real option in the investment described in a Black-Scholes option pricing table is approximately 18.7 percent of the value of the underlying asset, S. Because S = 305.02 in this case, the value of this option is $60.08.

Step Six: Compare Full Present Value with the Benchmark Value Recall that the benchmark value of this investment, using traditional present value techniques, was −$30.62. The full investment, recognizing the option value inherent in it, is the present value of Phase One of this investment plus the option value of Phase Two of this project, or

$$\text{Present value} = \$14.24 + \$60.09$$
$$= \$74.33$$

Of course, this is much higher than the net present value of −$30.62 calculated using traditional techniques. Apparently, there is significant economic value associated with the real option that is created by investing in Phase One and then delaying the decision about whether to invest in Phase Two of this project for three years. Traditional logic suggests that a firm should not invest in this project. Real options logic suggests that it should.

Whether a firm qualitatively or quantitatively values its strategic flexibility, research—summarized in the Research Made Relevant feature—is beginning to accumulate that suggests that real options thinking can be very important for a firm's success.

Research Made Relevant

Rita McGrath and Ian MacMillan argue that under conditions of uncertainty, managers should invest in a diversified range of projects that parallel many of the real options discussed in this chapter. These projects can be arrayed as in Figure 6.1.

In this figure, **technical uncertainty** refers to the extent to which managers understand the process by which a new product or service will be developed before that process is undertaken. Low technical uncertainty exists when managers know what kinds of skills and other resources they will need to develop a new product or service, the cost of acquiring these skills and resources, how to manage them effectively, and so forth. High technical uncertainty exists when managers do not know these things about a new product or service.

The Value of Real Options Thinking

Market uncertainty, in Figure 6.1, refers to the extent to which managers understand how a new product or service will be received in the market. Low market uncertainty exists when managers know the price at which a product or service is likely to sell, the likely size

FIGURE 6.1
Categorizing Your Register of Opportunities

Source: R. G. McGrath and I. MacMillan, The Entrepreneurial Mindset. (Boston: Harvard Business School Press, 2000).

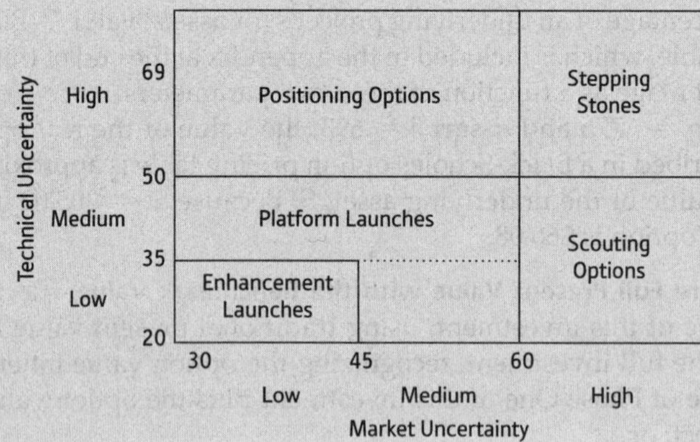

of the market that a new product or service will address, the likely competitive responses to a new product or service, and so forth. High market uncertainty exists when managers do not know these things about a new product or service.

Under conditions of low market uncertainty and low technical uncertainty, investments in new products and services have limited real option value. As suggested in the figure, such new products or services are typically more like simple enhancements of a firm's current products or services. Although such investments may clearly be valuable in traditional present value terms, they have limited value in creating options for a firm.

Under conditions of moderate market uncertainty and moderate technical uncertainty, the value of the real options associated with introducing new products or services increases. In such settings, new product or service offerings may look like the introduction of new technology platforms. Such platforms may be related to a firm's previous products or services, and thus the level of uncertainty in these investments is higher than for single enhancement launches. Moreover, such platform investments may give the firm the opportunity to introduce additional new products or services, but a firm is not required to do so.

Finally, when both market uncertainty and technical uncertainty are high, new investments made by firms typically have substantial real option value. McGrath and MacMillan identify three of these options: **positioning options** (when technical uncertainty is high and market uncertainty is low), **scouting options** (when market uncertainty is high and technical uncertainty is low), and **stepping-stone options** (when both types of uncertainty are high). The definition of these options is summarized in Table 6.7.

TABLE 6.7 Real Options under Technical Uncertainty and Market Uncertainty

Positioning options	Technical uncertainty is high: Take multiple small positions in alternative technologies and wait until technological uncertainty resolves, then invest.
Scouting options	Market uncertainty is high: Put several new offerings in consumer hands to gauge their reactions; once consumer preferences are clear, invest.
Stepping-stone options	Technical uncertainty and market uncertainty are high: Avoid fixing on a particular design or set of features early; fail fast, fail cheap; learn fast, and try again.

Source: R. G. McGrath and I. MacMillan, The *Entrepreneurial Mindset.* (Boston: Harvard Business School Press, 2000).

Positioning options give a firm the opportunity to wait and see what technological standard or standards will emerge in an industry. Such options are created when a firm makes limited investments, through, say, strategic alliances or small acquisitions in several competing technologies.

Creating a positioning option may ensure a firm's survival in the face of technical uncertainty, but such a firm might find itself at least at a temporary competitive disadvantage to a firm that made one technological bet that turned out to be the right bet. This firm will have more experience in the winning technology and may be able to use that experience to gain cost or product differentiation advantages in this market. In this sense, the potential trade-offs between the real options listed in Table 6.1 and other business-level strategies can also exist for the real options listed in Table 6.7.

Per McGrath and MacMillan, scouting options can be thought of as entrepreneurial experiments. They enable a firm to explore new markets with new capabilities, to gauge the size of these markets and the potential value of their new capabilities. However, as with all real options, investments in scouting options need to be kept small. The expectation that a scouting option will generate a positive net present value investment opportunity directly is small. Thus, to keep the costs of building this option low, investments need to be kept small.

However, though it is unlikely that any one scouting option will generate positive economic profit for a firm directly, among all the scouting options in which a firm invests, the probability that at least some of them may generate real profit opportunities directly is higher. Moreover, even if a scouting option does not generate profit opportunities directly, it may generate such opportunities indirectly by suggesting other scouting options that may ultimately generate profit opportunities.

This last possibility—that a scouting option might suggest another scouting option that could lead to creating superior performance for a firm—suggests the final type of option listed in Table 6.7: a stepping-stone option. Stepping-stone options are the classic sequential investments originally discussed in the context of the Black-Scholes evaluation model.

Firms seeking to create and realize the value associated with stepping-stone options must exercise great discipline in identifying decision-making milestones. Examples of such milestones might include, for example, dates by which a decision to invest or not invest in a new plant will be made, conditions under which a decision about whether investments in a new product will be made, and so forth. Without such strong milestones, and the discipline to enforce them, the stepping stones embedded in real options logic can lead down an infinitely long path. Sometimes, firms are so intent on keeping their options open, that they fail to exercise their options. Such firms never actually do anything, although they may have the ability to do something, sometime.

Alternatively, without these milestones and the discipline to enforce them, firms may exercise their options too soon, before the uncertainty that led them to invest in flexibility in the first place is resolved. Such premature execution of options also destroys value.

Only when firms identify clear decision-making milestones with regard to either exercising or abandoning a real option, and then manifest the discipline required to use these milestones, will it be the case that the full value of real options thinking will be realized.

Firms that exclusively adopt a net present value approach to valuing new investments will rarely invest in new products or services beyond enhancement launches—relatively straightforward extensions of their current portfolio. Such investments will often create value for a firm's shareholders, but have limited ability to enable a firm to develop new technologies, resources, and capabilities. That is, such enhancement launches have limited agility to enable a firm to transform itself.

However, if a firm invests in a portfolio of options—some positioning options, some scouting options, and some stepping-stone options—some of these investments may pay off big for the firm. Not only may some of these investments generate direct profits for the firm's stockholders, they may also enable the firm to discover entirely new opportunities that could not otherwise have been anticipated.[14]

Objective 6.3 Identify when strategic flexibility and real options can be a source of sustained competitive advantage.

Strategic Flexibility and Sustained Competitive Advantage

Under conditions of high uncertainty, flexibility is often valuable because it creates real options for firms. However, following the logic presented in Chapter 3, if several competing firms are all contemplating the same uncertain strategic decision and all value the flexibility and options embedded in this decision in the same way, then any actions they take because of this analysis will only be a source of competitive parity. These actions will be valuable, but they will not be rare or costly to imitate. When, if ever, can flexibility be a source of sustained competitive advantage for firms?

Rare and Costly-to-Imitate Flexibility

The concepts of flexibility and real options are closely related to the importance of history and path dependence described as potential sources of sustained competitive advantage in Chapter 3. Firms that are exploring options embedded in real assets that a firm possesses because it happened to be in the right place at the right time in history; or assets that grew up over time in an organization may be able to gain sustained competitive advantages because the options generated by these assets may be rare and costly to imitate. Consider, for example, the parallel between real options and flexibility, on the one hand, and history and path dependence, on the other, in the following example.[15]

Imagine a biotechnology firm deciding about its manufacturing strategy. Two manufacturing tasks must be accomplished for this firm ultimately to be able to bring the product it is developing to the market. The first task is to manufacture product prototypes that can be subjected to certification tests. Assuming the prototypes are certified, this product must then be manufactured for commercial sale. However, suppose that this manufacturing process is very complex, that the only way a firm can learn how to manufacture this product for commercial sale is to have developed its manufacturing skills during the process of manufacturing enough of this product for government tests. Finally, assume that the ultimate market value of this product is very uncertain. How can this firm make a decision about its manufacturing strategy?

As suggested in this chapter, the first step in this process (see Table 6.5) is to recognize that a real option exists in this situation: Under conditions of high uncertainty, the option to delay the decision about whether to build a plant for commercial production is valuable. The option, in this example, is represented in Figure 6.2.

However, notice that the branches on this simple decision tree are not all equally likely to occur. In fact, because of the importance of learning about manufacturing during the certification phase as preparation for commercial manufacturing, if this firm does not build the certification plant, it actually does not have an option to build the commercial plant. Put differently, the decision not to build the test plant is the same as the decision not to build the commercial plant. To retain its flexibility in this uncertain market, this firm must actually build the test plant.

The example in Figure 6.2 shows that, in some circumstances, the ability to create and exercise real options is very path dependent. Only if a firm follows a

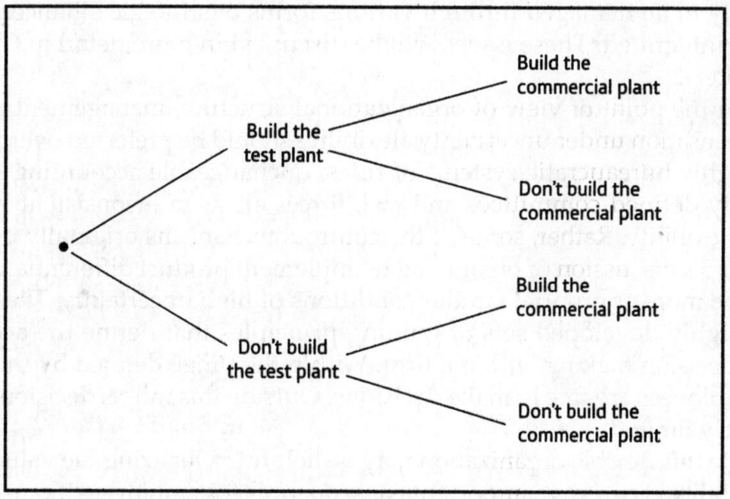

FIGURE 6.2 The Option to Defer Deciding Whether to Build a Commercial Plant

specific path of decisions over time can it retain its flexibility. Once a firm has varied significantly from this specific path, it can be very costly to turn back. A firm that decides not to build the test plant, but then later decides to build the commercial plant, will find itself at a significant competitive disadvantage compared to a firm that builds the test plant in the first place.

All this suggests that when the real options facing a firm are path dependent, and when the ability to do real options analysis is not widely diffused among a set of competing firms, retaining flexibility can actually be a source of sustained competitive advantage for a firm. On the other hand, when real options are not path dependent, or when the ability to do real options analysis is widely diffused among competing firms, this form of analysis is not likely to be a source of competitive advantage for a firm.

Organizing to Implement Strategic Flexibility

Objective 6.4 Identify the organizational challenges associated with implementing strategic flexibility and a real options strategy.

It seems logical to assume that firms seeking to implement a strategy of flexibility under conditions of uncertainty should adopt flexible forms of organization. Although the U-form structure and associated control and compensation policies can provide some flexibility for firms, firms engaging in real options approaches to strategic analysis often need additional flexibility to realize the full potential of this strategy. Thus, while the traditional tools for implementing business-level strategies are used by firms implementing flexibility strategies, these tools are normally augmented with more flexible organizing mechanisms.

As will be described in more detail in Chapter 8, vertically integrating into an exchange is generally less flexible, that is, costlier to change, than using market contracts or strategic alliances to manage an exchange. In particular, when the latter mechanisms are used to manage an uncertain exchange that turns out not to be valuable, these exchanges are simply cancelled, usually at low cost. However, if the type of exchange is brought within the boundaries of the firm, the costs of backing out of it can be much greater. Thus, other things being equal, exchanges characterized by high uncertainty, where flexibility is important, are more likely to be managed through various forms of strategic alliances than be vertically integrated. These issues will be discussed in more detail in Chapter 8 and Chapter 11.

From the point of view of organizational structure, management controls, and compensation under uncertainty, flexibility should be preferred over less flexibility. Highly bureaucratic systems of rules, unchangeable accounting budgets, and rigidly defined committees and task forces all seem inconsistent with this need for flexibility. Rather, some of the control mechanisms originally described in Chapter 5's discussion of organizing to implement product differentiation seem likely to be more appropriate under conditions of high uncertainty. These might include highly developed sets of guiding principles that define the acceptable range of decision making within a firm. Within the range defined by these principles, employees are free to make decisions. Outside this range, decision making is extremely limited.

While this flexible organization may be helpful in realizing the value of strategic flexibility, it can have important consequences for employees. Some of these consequences are described in the **Ethics and Strategy** feature.

Ethics and Strategy Feature

What do these companies have in common? Hewlett-Packard, Microsoft, Proctor and Gamble, Caterpillar, American Express, Cisco, Wal-Mart, Intel, and Bank of America. Obviously, these are some of the best known and most admired companies in the United States. Less obviously, each of these firms has laid of thousands of workers in 2015 and 2016. Hewlett-Packard—a leader in computers and printers—laid off 30,000 employees in 2015; Microsoft laid off 7860 in 2015 and 4700 in 2016; Proctor and Gamble—the packaged goods giant--laid off 6000 in 2015; Caterpillar—the construction equipment firm—laid off 5000 in 2015; American Express 4000 in 2015; Cisco 14,000 in 2016; Wal-Mart 17,500 in 2016; Intel 12,000 in 2016; and Bank of America 8000 in 2016.

Treating Employees as Flexible Assets

It used to be that large and successful firms like these provided secure employment. Not so much anymore. Large firms routinely lay off personnel; so do small firms. Indeed, layoffs are so common these days that you can go online and get samples of letters you can send to employees notifying them that they are being laid off. An entire industry that specializes in laying people off has emerged.

Rather than finding ways to retain employees, more and more companies are treating all their employees as temporary or contract workers. This increases the flexibility of these firms—in ways consistent with the importance of retaining flexibility in uncertain times described in this chapter—but at a real human cost. A broad range of emotional and physical consequences of being laid off have been documented, including anxiety, irritability, anger, fear, an unwillingness to trust (on the emotional side) and fatigue, headaches, weight loss or gain, sleep disorders, and nausea (on the physical side).

All this points to the fact that creating flexibility—especially when it comes to employees—is not costless.[16]

Summary

Firms possess strategic flexibility when they can choose among several strategic alternatives. These alternatives are also called real options. Firms can create many kinds of real options, including the option to defer an investment decision, the option to grow a business sometime in the future, the option to contract a business sometime in the future, and so forth.

While less important under conditions of risk, maintaining flexibility and real options is very important under conditions of uncertainty—where neither all the possible outcomes of a decision, nor their probability are known, ex ante, when a decision is being made. The value of these options can be estimated either qualitatively or quantitatively, although both these approaches build on insights from the Black-Scholes model of option valuation.

Over and above valuing options, options thinking has been shown to help firms manage their portfolio of innovative investments. Depending on the level of technical and market uncertainty, positioning options, scouting options, and stepping stone options can create important forms of strategic flexibility for a firm.

Because some options—especially stepping stone options or options that evolve in a sequence—are embedded in path dependent process, firms that do not use options logic may have difficulty imitating firms that have used this logic. In this way, strategic flexibility and real options may be a source of sustained competitive advantage for a firm.

Finally, organizing for strategic flexibility involves the adoption of flexible organizational structures, management controls, and compensation policies. However, these organizational policies may put significant burdens on some of the resources critical to a firm's success, especially its employees.

Challenge Questions

6.1 In the semi-conductor industry, Moore's law suggests that the power and computational speed of microprocessors will double about every nineteen months. Assuming that Moore's law is correct, is R&D in the microprocessor industry uncertain or risky? Justify your answer.

6.2 Identify a recent acquisition in the business literature. Are there likely to have been any real options associated with this acquisition? If no, why not? What effect, if any, does your analysis have for the price at which this acquisition was completed?

6.3 How are the investment attributes that make it possible to characterize subjectively the value of a real option related to the attractiveness of an industry? For example, when the threat of entry into an industry is high, are real options likely to be more or less valuable? When the level of rivalry in an industry is high, are real options likely to be more or less valuable?

6.4 Over the last few years, several large U.S. technology-based firms have begun to create venture capital funds. Usually, these venture capital funds are not as profitable as independent venture capital funds. In your view, does this mean that the technology-based firms should abandon their venture capital efforts? If appropriate, use real options logic in your analysis.

Problem Set

6.5 Suppose a firm is contemplating investing in a new distribution network to distribute over-the-counter drugs to pharmacies around the world. Also, suppose that the investments and cash flows from creating this distribution network are as depicted in panel A of the following table. Finally, suppose that this distribution network, with some additional investment, could also be used to distribute prescription drugs, and the investments and cash flows of this second investment are as depicted in panel B. Assume that the discount rate for these two investments is 13%.

First, what real options are embedded in the investment in the over-the-counter distribution network? Given the investments and cash flows, what is the exercise price, the value of the underlying asset, and the time to maturity of these options? Assume the risk-free rate of return is 5.5% and the level of uncertainty of the cash flows associated with investing in a prescription drug network is .25. What is the value of creating a new over-the-counter distribution network without considering the possibility of also creating a prescription drug distribution system? What is the value of this real option? Given these numbers, should this firm invest in the over-the-counter distribution network?

(A) Cash Flows from Investing in an Over-the-Counter Drug Distribution Network

Year	0	1	2	3	4	5	6	7	8
Cash Flow	0	7.0	8.5	11.2	11.3	12.0	12.3	12.4	13.0
Terminal Value									87.8
Investment	(72.0)								

(B) Cash Flows from Investing in a Prescription Drug Distribution Network

Year	0	1	2	3	4	5	6	7	8
Cash Flow	0	0	0	0	0	32.4	48.2	65.7	68.4
Terminal Value									428.3
Investment					(275)				

Writing Assignments

6.6. What must be true of flexibility for it to lead to sustained competitive advantage?

6.7. How might organization mechanisms support implementation of a real options strategy?

End Notes

1 Netflix.wikipedia (accessed January 28, 2017); forbes.com/companies/Netflix (accessed, January 29, 2017).
2 Sanchez (1997) "Strategic Flexibility, Firm Organization, and Managerial work in Dynamic Markets: A Strategic Options Perspective," in *Advances in Strategic Management*, Vol. 8
3 Adage.com/article/cmo-strategy/flo-s-progressive-evolution/295734 (accessed April 5, 2017)
4 This strategy has been called "tapered integration." See F. Kessler and R. Stern (1959) "Competition, Contract, and Vertical Integration," Yale Law Journal, 69(1).
5 See R. Brealy and S. Myers (1988) *Principles of Corporate Finance*. 3rd edition. NY: McGraw Hill.
6 See E. Bowman and D. Hurry (1993) "Strategy Through an Options Lens," Academy of Management Review, 18(4): 760–782; R.; B. Kogut (1991) "Joint Ventures and the Option to Expand and Acquire," *Management Science* 37: 19–33.
7 The first author to distinguish between risk and uncertainty was Frank Knight (1921) *Risk, Uncertainty, and Profit*. London: London School of Economics.
8 See I. Gilboa and D. Schmeidler (1989) "Maxmin Expected Utility with Non-Unique Priors," *Journal of Mathematical Economics*, 18(2): 141–153.
9 See T. Copeland and J. Weston (1983) *Financial theory and Corporate Policy*. Reading, MA: Addison-Wesley pages 255–256.
10 See F. Black and M. Scholes (1973) "The Pricing of Options and Corporate Liabilities," *Journal of Political Economy*, 81: 637–658.
11 When firms can exercise an option before its exercise date, that option is called an American Option. Options that can be exercised only on their exercise date are called European Options. Most real options are American options.
12 This approach was first proposed by T. Luehrman (1998) "Investment Opportunities as Real Options: Getting Started with the Numbers," Harvard Business Review, 26: July/August, 51–67.
13 Option metrics are derived in R. Brealy and S. Myers, *Principles of Corporate Finance*, 3rd Ed. NY: McGraw Hill.
14 See R. McGrath and I. MacMillan (2000) *The Entrepreneurial Mindset*. Boston: Harvard Business School Press.
15 The decision tree in this example suggests another approach to valuing real options in the literature. Called the binomial approach, it is described in T. Copeland and P. Tufona, "A Real World Way to Manage Real Options," *Harvard Business Review*, 82(3): 90–99.
16 See fortune.com/2015/10/02/biggest-layoffs-2015; 27wallst.com/special-report/2016/08/19/12-company-laying-of-the–most-workers/5/; www.theatlantice.com/science-agrees-being-laid-off-is-terrible/389447; cardinalatwork.stanford.edu/faculty-staff-help-center/work-related/coping-emotional-impact-layoff

CHAPTER

7 Collusion

LEARNING OBJECTIVES

After reading this chapter, you should be able to:

7.1 Define explicit and tacit collusion and explain why collusion is typically inconsistent with social welfare in an economy.

7.2 Describe how collusion can create economic profits.

7.3 Describe different ways that collusive agreements can fall apart, and how it is possible to use the attributes of an industry to anticipate how sustainable these agreements are likely to be.

7.4 Describe two unique challenges associated with organizing to implement a collusion strategy.

A Gas Station Conundrum

Consider the following scenario. Think of it as a chance to apply all the theories and frameworks discussed in this text so far.

You own and operate a gas station on a busy street corner in your town. There are other gas stations in your city, but they are located over ten miles away. You sell a well-respected brand of gasoline, one that is supported by a national advertising campaign. While you charge a premium for your gas (compared to the other stations in town), your property is clean and well maintained, your self-serve pumps are state of the art, and you run a clean and well-stocked convenience store at your station. The store sells drinks, snack foods, and a few auto supply items, and does so very profitably. According to a recent national survey, your store sells 95% of the top 100 selling items in gas station convenience stores. Even more important, some people say you sell the best hot coffee in town. Two years ago, you added a car washing station behind the store. It too has done well. And you've been the only gas station on this busy corner since you built it five years ago.

Until now.

It began with a rumor that another gas station was going to be built kitty-corner from yours. When the construction began, it was obvious that this rumor was true. About the same size as your station, it was going to sell a different brand of nationally advertised gasoline. The convenience store that was being built was slightly smaller than yours, but as it was stocked, it became clear that it would sell about the same items that your store sold. The new station even had an automatic car wash similar to yours, although a different brand. As the new station got close to opening, you got

to know the new owner. She had a great reputation in town as a business person, and was widely liked and respected. You had every reason to believe that she would run her business very effectively.

Three weeks after the hoopla of her grand opening, something happened that surprised you. Initially, the price of her gasoline—advertised like yours on a sign in front of her station—was the same as yours. You had dropped your price a bit before her grand opening—still higher than the other gas stations in town, but a few cents lower than what it had been—and she matched that price. Until today. Today, she raised the price of her gasoline by five cents per gallon. There was no indication that the wholesale price of gasoline—either yours or hers—had gone up.

How should you respond?

Firms that choose and implement each of the generic business strategies discussed so far—cost leadership, product differentiation, and flexibility—generate economic profits by more efficiently and effectively meeting their customer's needs—by having low costs, by differentiating their products, or by retaining the flexibility to do either of these—than their competitors. In this sense, the economic profits generated by these strategies can be thought of as efficiency profits.

In this chapter, the source of economic profits is not the differential strategic efficiency and effectiveness of a firm. Rather, it is the ability of a group of firms to work together to reduce competition in their market or industry. This strategy is called collusion. Collusion, for example, may lead firms in an industry or market to reduce industry supply below industry demand, thereby increasing prices above a competitive level. These increased prices are the source of economic profits in this chapter. Note that these profits do not require firms to be differentially efficient or effective in meeting customer needs, but only that they collude with other firms to reduce competition. For this reason, these economic profits are called collusion profits.

The gas stations in the opening case are, perhaps, contemplating the implementation of a particular type of collusion, called tacit collusion. The decision by one station to raise the price of gas when there are no obvious reasons to do so—e.g., when the wholesale price of gas has not gone up—may be a signal of an intent to collude—to reduce the level of competition on prices below the competitive level and generate collusion profits. On the other hand, maybe something else is going on. It is difficult to know for sure, and legally, the gas station owners cannot directly discuss their prices. Such explicit collusion is illegal in most developed economies.

So, what would you do if your "competitor," in this situation, raised prices? This chapter will show that there are economic, strategic, legal, and ethical issues associated with making this decision.

Objective 7.1 Define explicit and tacit collusion and explain why collusion is typically inconsistent with social welfare in an economy.

What is Collusion?

Collusion exists when firms in an industry or market cooperate to reduce competition. This cooperation can take a variety of forms including decisions by firms to not compete in the same geographic market (e.g., Coca-Cola's decision to focus on the Western European market and Pepsi's decision to focus on the Russian[1]), decisions to not do research and development in the same technological area (e.g., General Electric's decision to focus on large electric generation turbines and Westinghouse's decision to focus on small electric generation turbines[2]), and decisions to reduce production below a competitive level (e.g., when members of the Organization of Petroleum Exporting Countries [OPEC] agreed to reduce oil shipments in 1973, causing the first U.S. oil crisis[3]). In all these settings, competition is attenuated, prices rise, and firms can gain economic profits.

Of course, not all cooperation among firms is designed to reduce competition in an industry. Thus not all cooperation among firms is collusive. For example, firms may cooperate in strategic alliances to enhance their ability to compete in a market or industry. This form of cooperation is discussed in Chapter 11. However, in this chapter, collusive cooperation is emphasized.

Collusion can take one of two forms, explicit collusion or tacit collusion. **Explicit collusion** exists when firms in an industry directly negotiate agreements about how to reduce competition. Explicit collusion is illegal in most developed countries. To be completely clear: in most developed countries, engaging in explicit collusion can land you in jail. **Tacit collusion**, on the other hand, can be legal. Tacit collusion exists when firms cooperate in reducing competition, but engage in no face-to-face negotiations to do so. When the new gas station owner increased the price of her gasoline she may have been signaling her intention of engaging in tacit collusion without the face to face negotiations that would have constituted illegal explicit collusion.

Whether explicit or implicit, firms that engage in collusion face a number of fundamental ethical challenges. Some of these challenges are discussed in the Ethics and Strategy feature.

Tacit collusion requires firms to signal their willingness to cooperate to reduce competition indirectly. However, these signals can sometimes be difficult to understand and interpret. When this is the case, firms who have much to gain from cooperation may not be able to realize these gains.

Consider the simple, and well known, Prisoner's Dilemma Game example. A payoff matrix for two firms in such a setting is presented in Table 7.1. If the two firms in this situation both choose strategy A—that is, if they cooperate—then they each will earn $3,000. If Firm 1 chooses strategy A, and Firm 2 chooses strategy B—that is, if Firm 2 decides not to cooperate—then Firm 1 will earn $0 while Firm 2 will earn $10,000. In a similar way, if Firm 1 chooses strategy B and Firm 2 chooses strategy A—here Firm 1 is not cooperating—then Firm 1 will earn $10,000 and firm 2 will earn $0. Finally, if neither firm chooses strategy A—both choose to not cooperate—they each earn only $1000.

You don't need to be a sophisticated game theorist to see that both firms are better off if they cooperate ($3,000 each) but that they are each likely to be tempted

Ethics and Strategy Feature

The Ethics of Collusion

It is well established in economic theory that perfectly competitive markets are consistent with social welfare. However, in such markets, firms cannot earn economic profits and so there is little room for strategy or strategic management.

It is also well established that if valuable resources and capabilities are heterogeneously distributed across competing firms in an industry, and those resources and capabilities are immobile, then if firms with resource and capability advantages use those advantages to efficiently and effectively address customer needs, that those actions too are consistent with social welfare. This is true even though firms in these markets may earn economic profits. This is the logic that underlies the resource-based view of strategy and strategic management discussed in Chapter Three of this text.

However, it is also well established that firms with homogeneous resources and capabilities that cooperate to reduce competition below a perfect competition level can generate economic profits (this is discussed in the Strategy in Depth feature in this chapter in detail), but doing so reduces social welfare. In economics, this reduction in social welfare is called a **dead weight loss**. This loss is equal to the economic benefits foregone by consumers who would buy a product if it was priced appropriately, but do not buy it because the collusive price is greater than the benefits they perceive from buying this product.

While there are other sources of dead weight losses (e.g., taxes that subsidize some products but not others), collusion that reduces competition in a market or industry is an important source of these losses. Strategy and strategic management are relevant in these settings, but only to the extent that they reduce competition and thus hurt social welfare. This is the logic that underlies structure-conduct-performance models of strategy presented in Chapter Two of this text.

So while strategy and strategic management is not necessarily inconsistent with social welfare, it can be. Firms that pursue such strategies may be able to generate profits, but may also be subject to anti-trust litigation, government regulation, and other actions that can limit the profits they can generate. Their managers will also have to learn to reconcile their ability to generate economic profits with the fact that these profits come at the expense of the welfare of society generally.[4]

TABLE 7.1 Prisoner's Dilemma Game and Associated Payoff Matrix

		Firm One	
		Strategy A	**Strategy B**
Firm Two	**Strategy A**	Firm one earns $3,000 Firm two earns $3,000	Firm one earns $10,000 Firm two earns $0
	Strategy B	Firm one earns $0 Firm two earns $10,000	Firm one earns $1,000 Firm two earns $1,000

to go for the big payoff (of $10,000), in which case they are both worse off (earning only $1,000 each). Cooperation pays here but may not be realized.

It would be much easier to realize the payoffs from cooperation if Firm 1 and Firm 2 could directly communicate with each other. That way, they could judge each other's intentions, use peer pressure to make sure that agreements to cooperate were actually implemented, form friendships and trust, and so forth. But, such direct communication—at least in the case of collusion where firms are cooperating in an effort to reduce the level of competition in a market or industry—is illegal, and such cooperation may be more difficult to realize.

Despite these challenges, a wide variety of firms have engaged in collusion. Some of it has been explicit, some tacit. For example, in 1990, Major League Baseball owners were found guilty of colluding in the market for baseball free agents. In 1991, MIT and Ivy League schools were found to have colluded by cooperating in the allocation of scholarships to needy applicants. In the early 1990s, U.S. airlines were found guilty of colluding on ticket prices. Archer Daniels Midland (ADM), a large agriculture products firm, was found guilty of colluding with its competitors in 1998. In 2007 and 2008, British Airways and Virgin Air colluded in the charges they added to ticket prices for higher fuel prices. Sainsbury and Asha—two British grocery store chains—colluded on retail milk prices from 2002 to 2003. Four flat glass manufacturing firms from around the world—Asahi, Guardian, Pilkington, and Saint-Gorman—colluded in their pricing from 2004 to 2005. Recently, large appliance manufacturers, tire makers, and credit card companies have each been investigated by the U.S. Department of Justice for possibly collusive activities.[5]

Objective 7.2 Describe how collusion can create economic profits.

The Value of Collusion

One way to understand how collusion can create economic value is to apply the structure-conduct-performance (SCP) model of industry profits first presented in Chapter Two. Recall that this model was originally developed to identify industries where perfect competition dynamics were not unfolding and thus where firms were, on average, earning a rate of return greater than their weighted average cost of capital. Other scholars then used this SCP framework to identify five threats to the profits of firms in an industry: new competitors, existing competitors, substitute products, supplier leverage, and buyer influence.[6] Firms can engage in collusive strategies that reduce the threats associated with each of these elements of competition in an industry.

Colluding to Reduce the Threat of New Competitors

For example, firms can collude to reduce the threats from new competitors by working together to increase the barriers to entry into an industry listed in Tables 7.1 and 7.2. One way this can be done is by incumbent firms cooperating to build very-large-scale production facilities that support their operations but that cannot be expanded to include the operations of new entrants. In such settings, the operating costs of new entrants will be higher than the operating costs of incumbent firms. Oil companies that cooperate to build shared refining capacity can sometimes be examples of such investments.[7] These actions can increase the extent to which economies of scale act as a barrier to entry.

Firms can also develop common technological standards that make it very difficult for new firms to enter an industry. This can be an especially important barrier to entry when only incumbent firms in an industry have the experience and managerial knowhow needed to meet those standards—a situation that is more likely when those standards are set by incumbent firms.[8] This is an example of increasing the extent to which cost advantages independent of scale can act as a barrier to entry.

Firms in an industry can also cooperate in using product differentiation as a barrier to entry. They do this by reducing their emphasis on differentiating their own products and instead focus on differentiating an industry's current products vis a vis potentially new products. Something as simple as an advertising campaign that emphasizes the "home grown" nature of the products made by incumbent firms (e.g., Made in the U.S.A.) can increase the cost of entry by new competitors.

Firms in an industry can even jointly lobby the government to increase the cost of entry into an industry. Rarely will these lobbying efforts be couched in simple terms like, "help us prevent entry to increase our profits." Rather, incumbent firms, collectively, are likely to focus on how entry might destroy domestic jobs, might lead to customer safety risks, might lead to inferior products being sold on the market, might lead to immoral child labor, and so forth. Such joint lobbying efforts can increase the cost of entry into an industry.[9]

Colluding to Reduce the Threat of Current Competitors

By definition, collusion with other firms in an industry involves reducing competition among those firms. On the cost side, collusion can enable firms to avoid costly efforts to reduce their production costs, avoid costly efforts to differentiate their products, and avoid costly efforts to make it easy for customers to buy from them. On the revenue side, these firms can raise prices without the concern that competitors will undercut them on price. Since these firms' costs will be lower than what would be the case without collusion, and since their revenues will be greater than what would be the case without collusion, firms that successfully implement collusion can generally have higher profits than firms operating in more perfectly competitive markets. These general observations are made more precise in the Strategy in Depth feature.

Strategy in Depth

To see how colluding firms can create economic profits, consider the following simple example. Suppose there are two firms in an industry and that they agree to divide everything in this industry down the middle. Each will produce and sell half the input in the industry and each will get 50% of any profits that are generated. Together, these colluding firms face a single downward slopping demand curve. Suppose this curve is described by:

$$P(Q) = 10 - Q$$

where Q is expressed in, say, millions of pounds per year, and P is expressed in dollars per pound. If these firms charge \$8 per pound, together they will sell 2 million pounds in this market; if they charge \$6 per pound, together they will sell 4 million pounds.

How Colluding Firms Generate Economic Profits

Different quantities and their associated prices generate different amounts of total revenue for these two firms. Since total revenue (TR) is price times quantity, total revenue for these two firms is:

$$TR(Q) = P(Q) \times Q$$

$$TR(Q) = (10 - Q)Q$$

$$TR(Q) = 10Q - Q^2$$

If these firms, together, sell 2 million pounds at \$8 per pound, their total revenue together would be \$16 million (10(2) − 4 = 16), or \$8 million each; if they sell 4 million pounds at \$6 per pound, their total revenues together would be \$24 million (10(4) − 16 = 24) or \$12 million each.

(Continued)

Now, suppose each of these firm's total cost of production is given by:

$$TC(Q) = (1/2)Q^2$$

If these firms each produced 1 million pounds, their total costs would each be $500,000. If they each produced 2 million pounds, their total costs each would be $2 million.

As described in Chapter One, a firm's economic profit is simply the difference between its total revenues and its total costs. If together, these firms sell 2 million pounds at $8 per pound, then they would each have revenues of $8 million and total costs of $500,000. Their net profit each would be $7.5 million. If together, these firms sell 4 million pounds at $6 per pound, then they would each have revenues of $12 million and total costs of $2 million. Their net profit each would be $10 million.

This same logic can be generalized to more than two firms. For example, suppose there were four firms in an industry that agreed to divide production and profit among themselves equally. Using the same demand and cost equations as previously, if these firms together produced 4 million pounds, they could sell this output for $6 per pound, and the total industry revenue would be $24 million. The costs of each of these firms would be $500,000, and their profits would be (24/4 − .5) $5.5 million each.

In more competitive settings, these economic profits will induce competitive entry, driving supply in an industry up and prices down. Such entry would continue until there were no longer any economic profits. However, when firms in an industry can cooperate and are protected by high barriers to entry, then collusion can generate economic profits.[10]

Colluding to Reduce Other Competitive Threats

While firms can generate profits by colluding to erect high barriers to entry and through coordinating production and pricing, they can generate such profits by colluding to reduce other competitive threats as well. For example, firms in an industry can collude by agreeing to pay less than what would be the market determined price for certain raw materials (thereby reducing the supplier leverage threats) or by agreeing to limit the number of products they are willing to sell to customers (thereby reducing buyer influence threats).

Of course, these actions may have the effect of increasing the attractiveness of substitutes for the products produced by firms in an industry. Members of OPEC discovered the limits of their ability to collude in reducing the volume of oil they were willing to sell when the increased price of crude oil led a variety of companies to explore alternative sources of energy and consumers to conserve. In this sense, the value of these substitutes put a limit on how much economic profit could be generated by colluding to reduce supply.[11]

Collusion and Sustained Competitive Advantage

Objective 7.3 Describe different ways that collusive agreements can fall apart, and how it is possible to use the attributes of an industry to anticipate how sustainable these agreements are likely to be.

The previous paragraphs suggest that, in principle, collusion can be a source of economic profits. The examples cited suggest that collusion—either explicit or tacit—can exist, for at least some period. However, collusion is often a difficult strategy to maintain over long periods. This is especially true of tacit collusion, where colluding parties do not negotiate their cooperative agreements face to face.

The reason that collusion is a difficult strategy to maintain over time is that while parties to these cooperative agreements often have strong incentives to cooperate—namely, the economic profits they can obtain from doing so—they also have strong incentives to cheat on those cooperative agreements. Recall the Prisoner's Dilemma payoff matrix presented in Table 7.1. While both firms do well if they cooperate—they both earn a $3,000 payoff—one firm actually does better if it does not cooperate while the other firm does cooperate. In this case, the "cheating" non-cooperative firm earned $10,000, and the cooperative firm $0.

Consider, another example. Suppose an industry consists of six firms, all selling undifferentiated products.[12] If five firms stick with an agreement to sell 1,000 widgets for $10 a piece but one firm breaks this agreement and sells 3,000 widgets for $9 apiece, each of the five colluding firms will have revenues of $10,000 (1,000 × $10), but the cheating firm will have revenues of $27,000 (3,000 × $9). Assuming economic costs are constant (at $3 per widget), the five colluding firms will all have economic profits of $7,000 [1,000 × ($10 − $3)], but the cheating firm will have an economic profit of $18,000 [3,000 × ($9 − $3)]. By increasing its output and lowering its price by $1 per widget, the cheating firm is able to increase its economic profit substantially.

Ways Firms Can Cheat on Collusive Agreements

Firms can cheat on their collusive agreements in a wide variety of ways. These different forms of cheating are based on different assumptions about colluding partners' reactions to cheating, and they have different effects on the performance of firms in an industry. Bertrand cheating and Cournot cheating—two of the most important forms of cheating in collusive agreements—and their performance consequences are presented in Table 7.2. These forms of cheating are compared first with fully collusive strategies and then with fully competitive price-taking strategies.

Bertrand Cheating Economist and mathematician Joseph Bertrand examined what happens to profits when colluding firms begin cheating by lowering prices below the cooperative price.[13] In his model, Bertrand makes the (unrealistic) assumption that each time cheating firms adjust their prices, they assume that other firms in the industry will continue cooperating. Bertrand's general conclusion is that, assuming little or no product differentiation among a small number of firms, if one firm decides to cheat on a collusive agreement by reducing its prices, others will as well and, in the long run, firms in this industry will earn no economic profits.

To see how this happens, consider the simple example presented in Table 7.3. In this industry, there are only two firms (a duopoly) and no product differentiation.

TABLE 7.2 Ways Firms Can Cheat on Collusive Agreements, Decision Variables, Behavioral Assumptions, and Equilibrium Performance Implications for Firms in a Duopoly without Product Differentiation

Strategy	Decision Variables	Behavioral Assumptions	Performance Implications
Cooperation	Price/quantity	Both firms maintain agreements	Share monopoly profits
Price taking	Price/quantity	Both firms ignore all interdependence	Normal profits
Bertrand cheating	Price	One firm assumes other firm will maintain price from previous period; no learning across periods	Normal profits
Cournot cheating	Quantity	One firm assumes other firm will maintain quantity from previous period; no learning across periods	Profits fall between shared monopoly and normal profits

TABLE 7.3 Bertrand Cheating in a Duopoly with Homogeneous Products

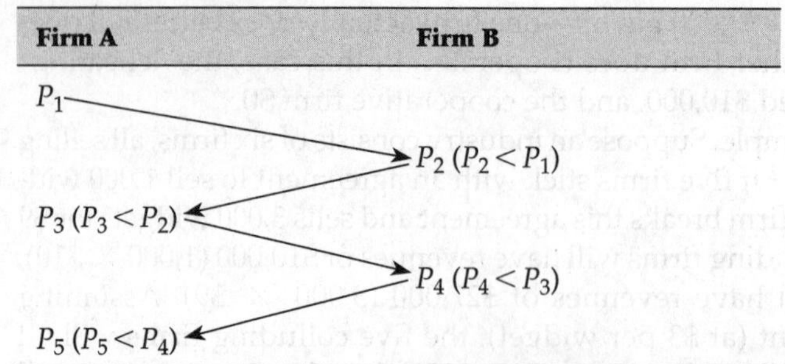

Imagine that Firm A and Firm B have decided to restrict output such that the prices they charge for their products are P_1. Firm B then decides to cheat on this agreement, increases its output, and sets its price equal to P_2. P_2 must be less than P_1, because any new price greater than or equal to P_1 will not increase Firm B's revenues. With the price equal to P_2, all customers switch to Firm B to buy its products. Firm A must respond and sets its new price at P_3 (where $P_3 < P_2$). Customers rapidly switch back to Firm A; Firm B responds, and so forth. This will continue until the prices charged by both firms generate revenues exactly equal to the firms' economic costs, at which point these firms will earn no economic profits.

Cournot Cheating Bertrand's analysis suggests that the superior profits that can be obtained by colluding firms are very fragile—any price reductions by one firm will lead rapidly to zero economic profits for both firms. Antoine-Augustin Cournot took a slightly different approach to analyzing cheating in collusive arrangements.[14] Instead of focusing on reductions in price, Cournot examined the performance consequences if colluding firms cheat by adjusting the quantity of their output and let market forces determine prices.

The performance implications of competing on quantity are examined in Table 7.4 for firms in a duopoly. The table includes information about the economic setting these firms are facing, including information about the industry

TABLE 7.4 Performance Implications of Cournot Cheating in a Duopoly (With Firm A and Firm B) Where: (1) Overall Industry Demand is Given By: $P = 100 - Q$; (2) Where Total Quantity is the Sum of the Production of Firm A and B: $Q = q_1 + q_2$; (3) For Convenience, Where Each Firm's Marginal Cost is Assumed to Equal Zero; and (4) Where Industry Marginal Revenue is Given By: $MR = 100 - 2Q$.

Firm A determines its optimal level of production by assuming Firm B's level of production from the previous period is fixed. In the next period, Firm B adjusts its quantity of production, assuming Firm A's quantity of production from the previous period is fixed, and so forth.[a]

Period	Firm Adjusting Its Quantity of Output, Assuming Other Firm's Output Is Fixed	Level at Which Other Firm's Output Is Assumed to Be Fixed	Optimal Output, Assuming Other Firm's Output Is Fixed	Firm A's Profits	Firm B's Profits
1	A	0	50	2,500	0
2	B	50	25	1,250	625
3	A	25	37.5	1,406	938

Period	Firm Adjusting Its Quantity of Output, Assuming Other Firm's Output Is Fixed	Level at Which Other Firm's Output Is Assumed to Be Fixed	Optimal Output, Assuming Other Firm's Output Is Fixed	Firm A's Profits	Firm B's Profits
4	B	37.5	31.25	1,172	977
5	A	31.25	34.38	1,182	1,074
*	*	*	*	*	*
*	*	*	*	*	*
*	*	*	*	*	*
n	B	33.33	33.33	1,111	1,111

[a] Calculations in the table are done as follows. For example, in period 4, Firm B assumes that Firm A will produce the same quantity of output that it produced in period 3, that is,

$$q_1 = 37.5$$

Firm B then estimates the demand left in the industry by Firm A's decision to produce only 37.5 units,

$$P = 100 - Q$$
$$= 100 - (37.5 + q_2)$$

Firm B then determines its profit-maximizing quantity by setting marginal cost equal to marginal revenue.

$$MC = MR$$
$$0 = 62.5 - 2q_2$$
$$q_2 = 31.25$$

The market price is then calculated.

$$P = 100 - Q$$
$$= 100 - (q_1 + q_2)$$
$$= 100 - (37.5 + 31.25)$$
$$= 31.25$$

At this price, firm revenues for Firms A and B, respectively, can also be calculated.

$$R_A = P \times q_1$$
$$= 31.25 \times 37.5$$
$$= 1{,}172$$
$$R_B = P \times q_2$$
$$= 31.25 \times 31.25$$
$$= 977$$

Because marginal costs in the example are zero, revenue equals profit.

It can be shown that, in the long run, competition in quantity will lead to the situation in which one-third of total industry demand is provided by Firm A, one-third is provided by Firm B, and one-third is not produced, and therefore prices will be higher than a competitive level. Firms that cheat in quantity produced earn economic profits, but these profits are not as large as they would be if firms cooperated completely in making production decisions.

demand curve, marginal revenue, and marginal cost. The intuition behind this table is straightforward. Like Bertrand, Cournot adopts the simplification that Firm A and Firm B will assume that decisions made in a previous period will continue unchanged. Where Bertrand focused on prices, Cournot focused on quantity produced.

Given this assumption, when Firms A and B decide on their own quantity of output, assuming the other firm's quantity is fixed from an earlier decision, they become monopolists over the part of industry demand that is not filled by the other firm. Each of these firms then chooses a profit-maximizing quantity given this unmet demand. However, that quantity choice has an effect on the other firm, which adjusts the demand curve it faces to include demand not met by the first firm and chooses a new profit-maximizing quantity. This new quantity, of course, affects the first firm, which readjusts the demand curve it faces to include demand not met by the other firm, chooses a new profit-maximizing quantity, and so forth. Note that, unlike Bertrand cheating, firms that cheat on collusive agreements through adjusting their quantity of output—Cournot cheating—can still earn some economic profits, although it will not be as large a profit as would be the case if these firms had maintained their collusive agreements.

Other Forms of Cheating The performance results associated with both Bertrand cheating and Cournot cheating depend on assumptions that firms make about how other firms will respond to their own cheating. Both Bertrand and Cournot assume that firms take other firms' prices/outputs in the previous period as fixed, and that firms never learn that other firms adjust their prices/outputs in response to their own decisions. These assumptions seem very unrealistic. In response to these unrealistic assumptions, other models of cheating on collusive arrangements have been developed. Edgeworth, following Bertrand, examined price cheating.[15] However, Edgeworth introduced capacity constraints in his model (based on the observation that firms can change their prices faster than they can change their quantity of output). Because of these capacity constraints, the market share of the firm with a higher price does not go to zero, and firms are able to avoid the perfect competition outcome of pure Bertrand cheating—that is, both firms make positive profits, though not as large as the profits in Cournot cheating.

Stackelberg, following Cournot, focused on quantity decisions but adopted the assumption that one firm (the so-called Stackelberg leader) accurately anticipates how other firms will respond to its output decision, adopts a profit-maximizing quantity, and holds that quantity constant over time.[16] Other firms in this industry (Stackelberg followers) adjust their outputs accordingly. Firms in this kind of industry earn positive economic profits, but these profits are less than the profits earned by firms engaging in pure Cournot cheating.

Other authors have adopted different assumptions about the behavior of rivals. Some authors have examined the profits associated with Bertrand and Cournot cheating when firms sell differentiated products; when there are time lags in discovering that a firm has cheated; when firms interact simultaneously in several markets; when other firms are unable to observe price or quantity cheating; when prices cannot be adjusted quickly; when firms have a reputation for not retaliating against cheaters; and so forth.[17] Generally, long-run profits for firms that cheat on purely collusive agreements in these ways fall somewhere between the perfect competition, zero-economic-profit solution and the perfect cooperation, shared-monopoly-profit solution.

Explicit and Tacit Collusion

Because the performance implications of cheating on collusion depend so critically on the particular assumptions that firms make about how their rivals will respond to cheating, an important question becomes: "How can a firm learn what its rivals' intentions are?" The easiest way to answer this question is for firms to communicate directly with each other about their current price and output decisions and their future price and output decisions. This kind of direct communication will allow firms to judge the likely responses of others and enable them to negotiate price and output strategies that jointly maximize profits. Of course, this form of direct communication and negotiation—explicit collusion—is illegal in most developed economies.

Instead of engaging in direct communication and explicit collusion, colluding firms seeking to choose joint profit-maximizing cooperative strategies must use tacit collusion. Instead of communicating directly, tacitly colluding firms send and interpret signals of intent to cooperate (or intent not to cooperate) sent by potential collusion partners.[18]

Sometimes, signals of intent to collude are very ambiguous. For example, when firms in an industry do not reduce their prices in response to a decrease in demand, they may be sending a signal that they want to collude, or they may be attempting to exploit their product differentiation to maintain high margins. When firms do not reduce their prices in response to reduced supply costs, they may be sending a signal that they want to collude, or they may be individually maximizing their economic performance. In both cases, the organizational intent implied by a firm's behavior is ambiguous at best.

Some recent work in game theory suggests when firms seeking to maintain collusion should send "tough" signals—a signal that they will aggressively respond to cheating—or "soft" signals—a signal that they will not aggressively respond to cheating. These findings are summarized in the Research Made Relevant feature. However, remember that even tacit collusion, with no direct communication between cooperating firms, can be illegal. Firms that consciously make price and output decisions in order to reduce competition may be engaging in what the courts call **conscious parallelism** and thus be subject to antitrust laws and penalties, even if they do not explicitly collude. For this reason, firms contemplating implementing even tacit collusion need to obtain competent legal advice.[19]

Industry Attributes and the Threat of Cheating

Beyond the strategic actions that a firm can take to signal its intentions about cheating on collusive arrangements in an industry discussed in the Research Made Relevant feature, firms can also use a variety of attributes of an industry to estimate the probability of cheating on these agreements. In general, these industry attributes affect the probability that cheating, if it actually occurred in an industry, would be detected. Detected cheating is likely to lead to the competitive responses mentioned earlier in this chapter. Because these competitive outcomes are less attractive than collusive outcomes, if the probability of detecting cheating in a collusive industry is high, the likelihood that cheating in this industry will actually occur is low. On the other hand, if the probability of detecting cheating in a collusive industry is low, the likelihood that cheating in this industry will actually occur is high.

Research Made Relevant

In general, firms can send one of two signals to collusion partners who may cheat on their cooperative agreements: a **tough signal** (that if parties cheat on collusive agreements, the firm sending the signal will decrease prices more or increase output more than would have otherwise been the case) or a **soft signal** (that if parties cheat on collusive agreements, the firm sending the signal will decrease its prices less or increase its output less than would have otherwise been the case). Examples of strategic actions that send a tough signal to colluding partners include investing in a new production process that reduces a firm's marginal cost of production. By reducing its marginal cost, a firm could very easily lower its prices or increase its output should another colluding firm begin cheating. Examples of strategic actions that send a soft signal to a colluding partner include positioning a firm's product so that it does not compete directly with the products of a colluding firm. By positioning its product this way, a firm is suggesting that should its colluding partner cheat, it will simply shift more of its emphasis to the differentially positioned product. In this way, this firm would not have to decrease its prices or increase its output in the market in which it has been colluding with the other firm.

The implications of tough and soft investments for maintaining collusive relationships when price is the primary basis of potential competition among colluding firms, and when quantity is the primary basis of potential competition among colluding firms, are summarized in Table 7.5.[20] When price is likely to be the major basis of competition in an industry, firms should *not* make investments that send a tough signal. Whatever the direct benefits of such investments, their strategic implications are quite negative. Tough investments in this context send a signal that Bertrand cheating is about to unfold. This makes collusive arrangements very difficult to maintain. Instead of making investments that look "tough," firms in this setting should try to look nonaggressive. Some have called this the "puppy-dog ploy." A firm that follows this strategy would not invest in a new production process that reduces marginal costs even if the direct effect of this investment was to enable the firm to implement a cost leadership strategy in order to keep a tacit collusion agreement in place.

Sending Signals to Maintain Collusion

One firm that may have adopted this puppy-dog ploy is Ben & Jerry's Ice Cream, especially since the growth in demand for frozen yogurt. Since its inception, Ben & Jerry's had focused its marketing efforts on selling highly differentiated "premium" ice cream. Most of Ben & Jerry's ice cream flavors include chunks of chocolate, nuts, fruit, or other additives. Beginning in the mid-1990s, demand for premium ice cream began to fall as consumers became more health-conscious. During this same period, demand for frozen yogurt—as a healthy alternative to ice cream—began to rise. Despite the increased popularity of frozen yogurt, Ben & Jerry's did not introduce a line of "premium" frozen yogurt at that time. Partially, the decision not to enter the frozen yogurt market reflected Ben & Jerry's traditional commitment to its ice cream product. However, from a competitive point of view, the decision not to enter the frozen yogurt market at that point was also a decision not to enter into direct competition with frozen yogurt firms. Had Ben & Jerry's entered into this competition, frozen yogurt firms might have felt compelled to enter into the premium ice cream market, and both the frozen yogurt and premium ice cream markets would have become more competitive.[21]

The decision *not* to invest in a tough signal is not the same as the decision to invest in a soft signal. After all, a firm that has decided not to invest in a tough signal could, in principle, decide to make no strategic investments to signal its intentions. In fact, when price is likely to be the basis of competition in an industry, firms should invest proactively in soft signals. These actions have the effect of reassuring collusion partners that price competition is not likely to be forthcoming in the market in which they are cooperating. This strategy has been called the "fat-cat effect" because firms that do this well send a signal that they will not compete aggressively in a market in which they have been colluding, but instead will

TABLE 7.5 Strategic Implications of Soft and Tough Strategies When Collusive Agreements Are Threatened by Cheating on Prices and Quantities

Strategic Logic	Strategic Implication	Strategic Label	Example
When cheating on collusive agreements is likely to focus on prices:			
Investing in a tough strategy is likely to lead other firms to invest in a tough strategy.	Do not invest in tough strategies in order to avoid price competition.	Puppy-dog ploy: Maintaining a nonaggressive stance leads others to be nonaggressive.	Ben & Jerry's delays investing in frozen yogurt.
Investing in a soft strategy is likely to lead other firms not to invest in tough strategies.	Do invest in soft strategies so that competitors will not feel compelled to invest in tough strategies.	Fat-cat effect: Actively investing in ways that others will not find threatening leads others to be non-aggressive.	IKEA invests only in wooden, ready-to- assemble furniture.
When cheating on collusive agreements is likely to focus on quantities:			
Investing in a tough-strategy is likely to lead other firms to invest in a soft strategy.	Do invest in tough strategies so that competitors know you will respond aggressively if they invest in tough strategies.	Top-dog strategy: Aggressive strategic investments threaten massive retaliation if another firm engages in aggressive behavior.	Korean memory chip firms invest in manufacturing capacity to discourage U.S. and Japanese firms from making similar investments.
Investing in a soft strategy is likely to lead other firms to invest in a tough strategy.	Do not invest in soft strategies because they signal your vulnerability to tough strategies pursued by others.	Lean-and-hungry look: Retaining the ability to make aggressive strategic investments has the effect of reducing the incentives of others to make these aggressive investments.	HP spins off its electronic instruments business in order to have the managerial resources necessary to exploit opportunities in the computer and printer industries.

act as a soft fat cat. Firms that follow this strategy try to differentiate their products in ways that do not threaten colluding partners.

Consider, for example, IKEA, the Swedish furniture firm. IKEA has developed a significant market presence in the wooden, ready-to-assemble segment of the furniture industry. Its extensive supply, manufacturing, and distribution capabilities in this segment of the furniture industry give it a significant competitive advantage. It is very likely that IKEA could extend this competitive advantage to the traditional upholstered segments of the furniture industry by modifying the line of products it sells. However, IKEA's large scale entry into the very competitive upholstered segment of the furniture industry could lead firms in the upholstery segment to aggressively enter the wooden, ready-to-assemble segment. And although IKEA's competitive advantage in this segment might remain, its level of profitability would probably fall. Thus, in order to keep competition in the wooden, ready-to-assemble segment of the furniture industry low, IKEA has an incentive not to invest in a significant way in the upholstered segments of the industry. As was the case with Ben & Jerry's delayed entry into the frozen yogurt market, IKEA has an incentive to invest in a puppy-dog ploy with respect to the upholstered furniture market.

However, IKEA has gone beyond simply not investing in the upholstered furniture market. It has aggressively marketed itself in the wooden, ready-to-assemble market. Moreover, it has done so in ways that would be difficult to transfer to most segments of the upholstered furniture market. The reputation of being the lowest-cost, highest-quality, and most convenient supplier of wooden, ready-to-assemble furniture cannot be easily transferred to most types of the

(Continued)

upholstered furniture market. In this sense, marketing investments in positioning IKEA that are specific to the wooden, ready-to-assemble furniture market are not threatening to firms operating in the upholstered furniture market and are examples of the fat-cat effect.[22]

On the other hand, when the primary basis of potential competition in an industry is quantity, then strategic investments that send tough signals can have very positive strategic consequences. In this setting, a firm must convince its collusion partners that if any of them begin to cheat, the consequences will be very negative for all. This has been called a "top-dog strategy." In this setting, firms may invest heavily in, say, manufacturing capacity, even if those investments do not generate positive economic profits directly. However, these investments send a clear signal to colluding firms that has the effect of reducing the likelihood that cheating will actually occur. Because these investments increase the likelihood that collusion will continue, they can have a positive effect on a firm's performance.

Finally, if the basis of competition in an industry is likely to focus on quantity, then making investments that send soft signals to colluding partners may actually increase their aggressiveness, reducing the likelihood that collusion will continue. In this setting, firms that make soft investments look like easy targets for colluding partners that decide to cheat. Rather than making these investments, firms in this setting should retain what has been called a "lean-and-hungry look."

Hewlett-Packard's (HP) decision to spin off its electronic instruments business into a separate company may be, in many ways, an example of a firm that has adopted a lean-and-hungry-look strategy. By focusing all of its efforts on its computer, and especially the printer business, HP assures that it will have all the managerial resources it needs to respond to opportunities in this industry.[23] Firms contemplating entering into this industry, or firms currently in this industry and considering the pursuit of aggressive new technology and product offerings, may think twice before entering into a competitive struggle with the new HP. In this sense, HP's choice to focus its efforts, to become lean and hungry, has had the effect of reducing competition in the computer and printer industry below what would have been the case if it had not spun off its electronics instruments business.

Several attributes of industries have been shown to affect the probability of cheating on collusive agreements. The most important of these are listed in Table 7.6.[24]

Each of these industry attributes can be thought of as helping to define the level of opportunity and threat for pursuing a collusive strategy in an industry.

Small Number of Firms in an Industry Tacit collusion is more likely to be successful if there is a small number of firms in an industry. As suggested earlier, tacit collusion depends on the sending and interpreting of signals of intent to cooperate. Because direct communication about prices and output is forbidden, coordination must be indirect and implicit. Intense monitoring of other firms' behavior helps make this coordination possible. However, as the number of firms in an industry increases, the number of firms whose subtle signals must be monitored and interpreted also increases. Indeed, as the number of firms in an industry increases

TABLE 7.6 Industry Attributes That Facilitate the Development and Maintenance of Tacit Collusion

Small number of firms
Product homogeneity
Cost homogeneity
Price leaders
Industry social structure
High order frequency and small order size
Large inventories and order backlogs
Entry barriers

arithmetically, the number of relationships among those firms that must be monitored and nurtured increases geometrically. As the number of relationships and subtle signals must be interpreted increases, judging the intent of firms sending these signals becomes more problematic (and it is never easy), and maintaining tacit collusion agreements becomes more difficult.

Having a large number of firms in an industry also reduces the effect of any one firm's cheating on the performance of other, still colluding, firms. If there are only two firms in an industry (a duopoly) and one reduces its prices (Bertrand cheating), then the increased sales of the cheating firm will significantly affect (reduce) the sales of the non-cheating firm. To maintain its share, the non-cheating firm must respond to the cheating firm, perhaps by reducing its prices, so that the zero-profit outcome is not far away. Because cheating hurts both firms very much, it is less likely that either firm will want to cheat on a tacit agreement.

However, if there are fifty firms in an industry and one cheats by reducing its prices, that one firm will not have a significant effect on the sales of other firms, and cheating may engender no response. If other firms are not likely to respond to isolated incidents of cheating, cheating is more likely. In the end, if the number of firms in an industry is very small, the interdependence among those firms is, on average, very clear to them, and tacit collusion is more likely. If the number of firms in an industry is large, the interdependence among those firms is less obvious, and tacit collusion is less likely.

Government regulators often use the number of firms competing in an industry as a signal that firms in an industry may decide to pursue collusive business strategies. For example, the charges leveled by a former GE executive that GE and DeBeers were colluding to raise prices in the industrial diamond market were more believable because GE and DeBeers together dominate over 80 percent of this $600 million market. The U.S. Department of Justice filed suit against GE for price-fixing in this market. These charges were dismissed, however, when a federal judge concluded that there was insufficient evidence to bring GE to trial.[25]

Other antitrust actions taken by the U.S. federal government have also been motivated by the small number of competing firms in an industry. These include antitrust suits against IBM (a firm that was dominating the mainframe computer market), AT&T (a firm that dominated the long-distance telephone market), Microsoft (a firm that dominated the personal computer operating systems market), and, most recently, Visa and MasterCard (two firms that dominate the credit card market).

Indeed, the relationship between the number of colluding firms and the ability to implement tacit collusion is so significant that most economists analyze collusion only under conditions of oligopoly. Research on government-sanctioned explicit price-fixing cartels in Western Europe, where (presumably) direct communication between colluding firms can occur, indicates that over 80 percent of these cartels occurred in industries with ten or fewer firms. Thus even when explicit collusion is possible, a small number of firms seem to facilitate the implementation of this cooperative strategy. It is likely that small numbers are even more important for tacit collusion strategies. In general, having a small number of firms in an industry increases the probability that cheating firms will be discovered, and this likelihood reduces the payoffs associated with cheating.

Recent reviews of the empirical relationship between the number of firms competing in a geographic segment of an industry, and prices found that as these geographic segments become more concentrated, prices can rise significantly. In the retail gasoline industry, for example, when the three largest gasoline retailers in a geographic market sell 60 percent of the gasoline in that market, prices are approximately

5 percent higher than when the three largest gasoline retailers sell 50 percent of the gasoline in a market. This is consistent with the effect that a small number of competing firms can have on the ability to implement tacit collusion strategies.[26]

Product Homogeneity Tacit collusion is also more likely when firms produce and sell similar products or services.[27] In general, changes in prices are easier to monitor than are changes in product characteristics or features. A firm may cheat on a tacit collusion strategy by charging the agreed price but providing more features, higher quality, or better service. These efforts at product differentiation are somewhat more difficult to monitor and thus create strong incentives for cheating.

However, if differentiating the products or services of firms in an industry is very costly, potential competition must focus on price reductions, a relatively easy-to-monitor effort at cheating. Once spotted, price reductions (Bertrand cheating) have significant negative consequences for all firms (zero economic profits). Thus, if firms in an industry produce homogeneous products or services, cheating on collusive agreements is more likely to be discovered, and this likelihood reduces the payoffs associated with cheating.

Cost Homogeneity Homogeneity of economic costs enhances the opportunities to implement tacit collusion. When firms have very different costs, their optimal level of output may be very different. This is because, in general, profit-maximizing firms should produce a quantity of products or services such that marginal costs equal marginal revenues. If marginal costs vary significantly among firms, the optimal level of production for these firms will also vary. These differences make it difficult for firms to find a level of output that jointly maximizes profits. In this situation, any tacit collusion agreement is very unstable, because each firm has even stronger incentives to cheat.

Cost heterogeneity is widely cited as one of the major reasons why OPEC, an explicitly colluding cartel, has generally been unable to maintain output and price discipline. Optimal levels of oil production vary sharply across members of OPEC, leading these countries to expand production beyond agreed-to collusive levels.[28]

When cooperating firms have similar economic costs, it may be relatively easy for them to discover an output level that is mutually satisfactory. This facilitates tacit collusion.

Price Leaders

Another industry characteristic that creates opportunities for tacit collusion is the existence of industry price leaders. A **price leader** is a firm that sets "acceptable" industry prices or "acceptable" profit margins in an industry. A price leader is often the firm with the largest market share, which helps create the order and discipline needed to make tacit collusion last over time. Also, a price leader can assist an industry adjusting to higher or lower prices, without jeopardizing an overall cooperative agreement, by defining industry standards for price or margin changes. In general, price leaders can be thought of as Stackelberg leaders.[29]

Through the 1950s and 1960s, GM acted as a price leader in the U.S. automobile market. Each fall, with the introduction of new lines and models, GM publicized the percentage by which it planned to increase the price of its cars. Ford and Chrysler typically followed GM's lead, raising their prices by approximately the same percentage as had been announced by GM. Since the entry of Japanese and German firms as major players in the U.S. automobile industry (and thus the violation of the small-numbers requirement listed earlier), GM no longer plays this price leadership role.[30]

Industry Social Structure

Industry social structure can create opportunities for tacit collusion. **Industry social structure** refers to accepted norms of behavior and competition that often evolve in industries. These norms are usually implicit and constitute what might be called an **industry culture**. Spender calls this collection of expectations and norms an **industry recipe** and emphasizes its pervasive effect on firm behavior.[31] This industry recipe, in an important sense, defines the standard operating procedures, acceptable forms of competition, and norms of behavior for firms in an industry. Violation of these norms and expectations constitutes a major breach of "industrial etiquette."

Several factors may work together to help create an industry social structure. Some industries when they first develop are dominated by one or two firms with very large market shares. Because of this dominance, most managers in the industry receive their training and early experience in these dominant firms. In a sense, the culture within these dominant firms begins to define the culture in the industry as a whole, and expectations about acceptable forms of competition in the industry reflect expectations within the dominant firms. These industry expectations may continue long after dominant firms lose their share leadership.

Managers in firms located in the same geographic area may come into contact at charity functions, private clubs, and in other social settings. These social interactions may lead to the development of mutual expectations concerning acceptable competitive behavior and help create a sense of trustworthiness among firms contemplating collusion. Other social contacts among managers in an industry, including relationships developed at trade association meetings, can also help create an industry recipe.

However they evolve, these social expectations can facilitate tacit collusion by defining some forms of competition as unacceptable. If banned forms of competition would increase rivalry, an industry's culture can make tacit collusion easier to implement.

There is substantial evidence that industry social structure facilitated collusion among the owners of Major League Baseball franchises during the 1980s. Each Major League Baseball franchise in North America is independently owned. However, franchise owners must cooperate in leagues to establish playing schedules, a common set of rules, and other operating standards. While engaging in this legal cooperation, informal agreements not to bid aggressively on free agents were apparently struck. The effect of these agreements was to reduce payments to baseball players from 38 percent of team revenues to just 31 percent of team revenues by 1989.[32] In 1990, an arbitrator found that Major League Baseball owners had behaved collusively and violated their labor agreement with the players' union. The owners were subsequently fined $102.5 million, and players' salaries have risen to over 40 percent of team revenues.

High Order Frequency and Small Order Size

Firms may have incentives to cheat on cooperative agreements when maintaining a collusive agreement has high opportunity costs. Imagine, for example, a firm that has agreed to tacit collusion is seeking a very large contract to supply product to an important customer. Also, suppose that this contract will extend for several years. If this firm obtains this contract, it will have steady and profitable demand for its output for several years. If it does not obtain this contract, its profitability depends on uncertain industry demand and the willingness of other firms in the industry to maintain tacit collusion. Moreover, suppose the opportunity to gain this secure supply contract happens infrequently, once every twenty years. In these settings, firms may be willing to cheat on their collusive agreements to get that secure supply contract.

Numerous industries are characterized by infrequent, large orders. In military aircraft, the failure of a firm to obtain a major contract can have an adverse effect for ten to fifteen years.[33] In commercial aircraft, large orders for one company can have significant effect on another company. It is unlikely that tacit collusion agreements could survive the rivalry created by these infrequent, large orders, even though the number of firms in these industries is quite small.

Large Inventories and Order Backlogs

The ability of firms to produce for inventory and to create order backlogs helps facilitate tacit collusion.[34] Inventory and order backlogs create buffers between a firm and its environment. With these buffers in place, firms do not have to react to every change in market conditions with changes in output and price. Instead of reducing prices when demand drops, firms can produce for inventory and store the products they sell. Instead of increasing prices when demand increases, firms can create an order backlog. These buffers help firms maintain consistency in their output and prices over time, thereby facilitating tacit collusion.

In some industries, inventories may be technologically infeasible, and order backlogs may not satisfy customers. For example, in the fresh fruit business, production for inventory is likely to lead to large spoilage costs. To avoid such costs, firms facing unanticipated reductions in demand, or greater-than-anticipated supply, are likely to have to adjust their prices. These rapid changes in price can have a very destabilizing effect on an industry's price/output structure and make tacit collusion very difficult.

Entry Barriers

Each of the industry attributes listed in Table 7.6 has an effect on the level of opportunity for tacit collusion in an industry. None, however, is more important for this strategy than the existence of barriers to entry. Without barriers to entry, the economic profits associated with tacit collusion create incentives for firms to enter into an industry. New entry into an industry reduces the collusion-enhancing attributes of each of the other industry characteristics listed in Table 7.6. New entry increases the number of firms in the industry. New entry is likely to create both product heterogeneity (as new firms introduce new products) and cost heterogeneity (new firms often have costs different from colluding incumbents). New entrants are likely to ignore price leaders and often are not part of the industry social structure. New entrants are also likely to compete for all orders, small or large, to shrink order backlogs to satisfy customers, and to reduce inventories through stiff price competition. Overall, new entrants can be thought of as loose cannons in otherwise placid and calm industries. To reduce the threat of new entrants, tacitly colluding firms must be protected by barriers to entry.

Rarity and Costly to Imitate Collusion Strategies

At first, it appears that tacit collusion strategies violate the rarity requirement of a sustained competitive advantage first introduced in Chapter 2. After all, rarity seems to imply that a small number of firms in an industry have the resources needed to implement a particular strategy. But for tacit collusion to work, all or certainly the majority of firms in an industry must be involved. In what sense can a strategy implemented by all firms in an industry be considered rare?

The answer to this question depends on the first industry attribute listed in Table 7.6—the small-numbers requirement. From the perspective of firms currently in an industry, the tacit collusion strategy is not rare. However, the development of tacit collusion requires a small number of industry incumbents. So from the point of view of both incumbents *and* potential entrants, the tacit collusion strategy is rare. It is very unlikely that numerous firms, including incumbents and potential entrants, could successfully implement a tacit collusion strategy. Thus, from this broader perspective, tacit collusion must be rare in order to generate economic profits.

Tacit collusion also seems to violate the costly-to-duplicate requirement of sustained competitive advantage. For tacit collusion to work in an industry, incumbent firms that have not joined in the collusion must *not* face a cost disadvantage if they choose to do so. If it is very costly for non-colluding incumbents to begin colluding, then collusion will break down, and the economic profits associated with this strategy will be lost. Therefore, costly-to-duplicate strategies in this context appear to reduce the chance for sustained competitive advantage.

However, including potential entrants in the analysis resolves this apparent contradiction. Because all colluding incumbent firms are implementing the same strategy (tacit collusion), firm-level resources that are costly to duplicate are logically equivalent to industry-level barriers to entry. Industry barriers to entry are essential for the successful implementation of a tacit collusion strategy. Thus, if not only incumbent firms but also potential entrants into an industry are included in an analysis, the VRIO framework developed in Chapter Two can be extended to cooperative tacit collusion strategies. In this context, the small-numbers industry attribute is equivalent to the rarity requirement, and the barrier-to-entry industry attribute is equivalent to the costly-to-duplicate requirement.

Organizing to Implement Tacit Collusion

Objective 7.4 Describe two unique challenges associated with organizing to implement a collusion strategy.

As with all strategies, the return potential of tacit collusion depends on the ability of firms to organize themselves to implement this strategy. However, there are few organizational structures, management controls, or compensation policies that are unique to firms pursuing this strategy. Beyond these general categories, there are two organizational issues that are particularly important and unusual in implementing tacit collusion strategies: maintaining organizational efficiency and organizational self-discipline.

Organizational Efficiency

One of the most significant organizational issues facing tacitly colluding firms concerns the efficiency of their operations. Under competitive conditions, firms are forced to keep their head count and their overhead expenditures low and to cut out strategically unimportant spending. Thus, competitive pressures tend to lead to lean and efficient organizations. Firms that do not meet these criteria either change or are forced out of business by more efficient firms.

Under tacit collusion, competitive pressures toward organizational efficiency are not as pronounced. Indeed, the profits associated with tacit collusion often depend on a firm *not* driving its cost to the lowest possible level, *not* differentiating products as much as possible, and so forth. Such competitive actions are likely to upset tacit collusion, especially if they create cost or product heterogeneity, rivalry, and price competition. In restraining these competitive tendencies, colluding firms may decrease their overall efficiency and effectiveness. This may not be a problem as long as tacit collusion continues, and as long as barriers to entry are in place. However, if collusion breaks down, or if entry occurs, inefficient organizations may be subject to intense competitive pressures.

Given the fragile character of tacit collusion, and the threat of potential entrants, colluding firms would be well advised to maintain an efficient organization—to act *as if* they were facing a competitive environment even though they are not. Of course, maintaining this efficiency is likely to be difficult, given the constraints that tacit collusion places on a firm. Moreover, such efficiency may be costly in the face of current collusion and may reduce (somewhat) a firm's current economic profit. However, if tacit collusion might break down sometime in the future, the ability to move quickly toward a more efficient organization may be worthwhile.

Research on tacitly colluding, explicitly colluding, and monopolistic firms suggests that most of these firms are unable to maintain high levels of organizational efficiency. They tend to become top-heavy with management, highly bureaucratic, risk-averse, overinvested in luxurious office buildings, and so forth. For these reasons, tacit collusion strategies appear to sow the seeds of their own destruction. As tacitly colluding firms become progressively more inefficient in their organization, they become more tempting prey for more efficient new entrants. At some point, the low cost of displacing inefficient incumbent firms may attract new entrants to an industry despite substantial barriers to entry.[35]

Organizational Self-Discipline

The other significant organizational challenge facing colluding firms concerns the maintenance of self-discipline. Once a firm has committed itself to a tacit collusion strategy, its willingness to stick to that strategy will almost certainly be tested. Thus, for example, once GE signaled that it would not engage in price competition in the steam turbine industry, Westinghouse (its major competitor) announced price reductions. In a sense, Westinghouse was testing GE's resolve to stick with its tacit collusion strategy. GE did reduce its prices but gave its customers substantial rebates on previously purchased products. This action indicated that GE would stick by its commitment to price stability. Shortly thereafter, Westinghouse increased its prices to match GE's original prices, and price stability continued in the industry for almost fifteen years.[36]

Because tacitly colluding firms will almost certainly be tested in their resolve to maintain price and output stability, the ability to implement this strategy successfully depends on an unusual level of organizational self-discipline. Only when a tacitly colluding firm knows exactly what it is about and is able to refrain from competitive actions in response to tests by its competitors is this strategy likely to be successful. This self-discipline needs to be reinforced by appropriate management control systems and compensation policies.

Summary

Most of the business strategies discussed so far in this text have focused on how firms can use their valuable and rare resources and capabilities to successfully compete in an industry or market. This chapter examines an alternative approach to gaining economic profits: How firms can collude to reduce competition in a market or industry.

Collusion exists when firms cooperate to reduce competition in an industry, although not all forms of firm cooperation are collusive. Collusion can be explicit—the result of face to face negotiations between firms—or tacit—the result of sending signals of the intent to cooperate to reduce competition. Explicit collusion is illegal in most developed economies. Tacit collusion may be illegal.

Collusion generates economic profits by reducing supply below demand. Collusion can also be used to improve the competitive attributes of an industry by, for example, increasing barriers to entry into an industry and reducing rivalry in an industry.

While there are often strong incentives to collude, once collusive agreements are established, there are also strong reasons to defect from these relationships. "Cheating" on these agreements can take many different forms, and the type of cheating that occurs—Bertrand cheating, Cournot cheating, Stackelberg cheating—has an impact on the profits firms will earn after these arrangements unravel. If firms cheat on price (Bertrand), no firms in an industry will earn any economic profits. If firms cheat on quantity (Cournot), firms can earn some profits in the industry, but they will not be as high as would have been the case if they had continued to collude.

One of the reasons that tacit collusion is so difficult to sustain is that signals about intentions to collude can be ambiguous. Firms can gain some clarity about these signals if they evaluate whether or not a firm's actions will make it more or less likely to retaliate if another firm "cheats" on a collusive agreement. The attributes of an industry—especially the number of firms in an industry and the existence of barriers to entry—can also be used to anticipate how likely it is that collusive arrangements will last.

Organizing to implement collusive strategies presents two unique challenges: How to keep a firm efficient and well managed when it has successfully reduced the threat of competition and how to keep a firm disciplined in implementing a collusion strategy when its commitment to that strategy will almost certainly be tested by other firms.

Challenge Questions

7.1 Firms that engage in Cournot cheating will achieve higher levels of performance than will firms that engage in Bertrand cheating. Why, then, would firms ever engage in Bertrand cheating?

7.2 Both cost homogeneity and product homogeneity enhance the ability of firms in an industry to implement tacit collusion strategies. Under what conditions, if any, would a firm be able to pursue a cost leadership strategy or a product differentiation strategy while simultaneously trying to implement a tacit collusion strategy? Are these strategies mutually exclusive?

7.3 At one level, the requirement that all firms in an industry be involved in a tacit collusion strategy in order for that strategy to be viable seems to contradict the rareness and imitability requirements for sustained competitive advantage, first discussed in Chapter 4. Is it possible to rationalize this apparent contradiction? If yes, how? If no, why not?

7.4 Some have argued that the implementation of a tacit collusion strategy will lead a firm to be relatively inefficient. Others have argued that the implementation of a tacit collusion strategy requires firms to be very efficient at implementing this strategy. Which is it? Do firms implementing a tacit collusion strategy become less efficient or more efficient? Justify your answer.

Problem Set

7.5 The opening case of this chapter poses a specific strategic question. If you owned the established gas station, would you raise your gasoline prices or not? Why?

Writing Assignments

7.6. What is the relationship between industry characteristics and the development of collusion?

7.7. What are the vulnerabilities of firms that organize to implement tacit collusion?

End Notes

1 See npr.org/sections/thesalt/2014/03/10/288570744/what-pepsi-can-teach-us-about-soft-drink-dominance-in Russia. Coca-cola's dominance was so great in Western Europe, in 2005 the EU implemented rules to reduce Coca-Cola's market share. See www.beveragedaily.com/Manufacturers/ED-curbs-Coca-Cola-market-dominance.

2 See Porter. "General Electric vs. Westinghouse in Large Turbine Generators (A)."

3 www.thebalance.com/opec-oil-embargo-causes-and-effects-3365806.

4 See J. Hirshleifer. (1980). Price Theory and its Applications. Upper Saddle River, NJ: Prentice Hall.; H. Demsetz. (1973). "Industry Structure, Market Rivalry, and Public Policy." Journal of Law and Economics 16: 1–9.

5 AN 7 plus: bbc.co.uk/2/hi/business/7132108.stm and mentalfloss.com/article/22843/5-brazen-examples-price-fixing.

6 M. Porter. (1980). *Competitive Strategy*. NY: Free Press.

7 www.jonesday.com/files/Publication/U.S. v Gunnison PDF.

8 J. Anton and D. Yao. (1995). "Standard Setting Consortia, Antitrust, and High Technology Industries;." *Antitrust Law Journal* 64(1): 247–265.

9 G. Grossman and E. Hellpman. (1994). "Protection for Sale." *American Economic Review*, 84: 833–850.

10 D. Besanko and R. Braeutigam. (2014). Microeconomics. 5th ed. NY: Wiley.

11 Recently, this traditional relationship between oil prices and alternative energy has switched. With very low oil prices crude oil producers are investing even more heavily in alternative energy as a substitute for their oil products. See ww.mottmac.com/views/will-the-falling-oil-price-boos-the-renewable-energy-market.

12 This analysis can be generalized to differentiated products. See J. Tirole, *The Theory of Industrial Organization*. (Cambridge, MA: MIT Press, 1988).

13 J. Bertrand. "Théorie mathématique de la richesse sociale." *Journal des Savants* (1883): 499–508.

14 A. Cournot, *Recherches sur les principes mathématiques de la théorie des richesses*. (1838); English edition: N. Bacon, *Researches into the Mathematical Principles of the Theory of Wealth*. (London: Macmillan, 1897). Both Bertrand and Cournot are excellent examples of dead economists.

15 F. Edgeworth. "La teoria pura del monopolio." *Giornale degli Economisti* 40 (1897): 13–31; in English: F. Edgeworth. "The pure theory of monopoly." in *Papers Relating to Political Economy* 1 (1925).

16 H. von Stackelberg. *Marktform und Gleichgewicht*. (Vienna: Julius Springer, 1934).

17 For Bertrand and Cournot cheating when firms sell differentiated products, see R. L. Hall and C. J. Hitch. "Price Theory and Business Behavior." *Oxford Economic Papers* 2. (1939): 1245; P. M. Sweezy. "Demand under Conditions of Oligopoly." *Journal of Political Economy* 45. (1939): 568–573; and H. Hotelling. "Stability in Competition." *Economic Journal* 39. (1929): 41–57. When there are time lags in discovering cheating, see Tirole, *The Theory of Industrial Organization*. When firms interact simultaneously in several markets, see R. D. Bernheim and M. D. Whinston. "Multimarket Contact and Collusive Behavior." *Rand Journal of Economics* 12 (1990): 605–617. When other firms can't observe price or quantity cheating, see E. J. Green and R. H. Porter. "Noncooperative Collusion under Imperfect Price Information." *Econometrica* 52 (1984): 87–100. When prices cannot be adjusted quickly, see E. Maskin and J. Tirole."A Theory of Dynamic Oligopoly." *Econometrica* 56 (1988): 549–600; and J. Eaton and M. Engers. "International Price Competition." (mimeograph, University of Virginia, 1987). When firms have a reputation for not retaliating against cheaters, see A. Ortega-Reichert. "Models for Competitive Bidding under Uncertainty." (dissertation, Stanford University, 1967).

18 See F. M. Scherer. *Industrial Market Structure and Economic Performance*. (Boston: Houghton Mifflin, 1980). Some of these signals of intent to collude are discussed later.

19 See M. E. Porter. "General Electric vs. Westinghouse in Large Turbine Generators (A)." (Harvard Business School Case no. 9-380-128, 1979).

20 This analysis was first developed by D. Fudenberg and J. Tirole, "The Fat Cat Effect, the Puppy Dog Ploy, and the Lean and Hungry Look." *American Economic Review* 74. (1984): 361–366.

21 See J. Theroux and J. M. Hurstak. "Ben & Jerry's Homemade Ice Cream Inc.: Keeping the Mission(s) Alive." (Harvard Business School Case no. 9-392-025, 1993).

22 See *Discount Merchandiser*. "It's the IKEA Way or No Way." 39, no. 1 (1999): 51–53.

23 See E. Nee. "Lew Platt: Why I Dismembered HP." *Fortune*, March 29, 1999, 167–170.

24 Scherer. *Industrial Market Structure and Economic Performance*.

25 See Z. Schiller. "Diamonds and Dirt." *Businessweek*, August 10, 1992, 20–23; Z. Schiller, "This Diamond Case Had Too Many Flaws." *Businessweek*, December 19, 1992, 34; and R. Donoho. "GE Off Hook in Price-Fix case." *Sales and Marketing Management* 147 (1992): 11.

26 Results that link the existence of price-fixing cartels and the number of colluding firms can be found in C. D. Edwards. *Cartelization in Western Europe*. (Washington, DC: U.S. Department of State, Government Printing Office, 1964); G. A. Hay and Kelly. "An Empirical Survey of Price Fixing Conspiracies." *Journal of Law and Economics* 17. (1974): 13–38. Research on the relationship between market concentration and prices is reviewed in L. Weiss, ed., *Concentration and Price*. (Cambridge, MA: MIT Press, 1989); and R. Schmalansee. "Studies of Structure and Performance." in R. Schmalansee and R. Willig, eds., *The Handbook of Industrial Organization*. (Amsterdam: North-Holland, 1989).

27 Scherer. *Industrial Market Structure and Economic Performance*.

28 R. El Mallakh. *OPEC: Twenty Years and Beyond*. (Boulder, CO: Westview Press, 1982).

29 See J. W. Markham. "The Nature and Significance of Price Leadership." *American Economic Review* 41. (1951): 891–905; Scherer. *Industrial Market Structure and Economic Performance*; and von Stackelberg. *Marktform und Gleichgewicht*.

30 L. J. White. *The American Automobile Industry Since 1945*. (Cambridge, MA: Harvard University Press, 1971).

31 J. C. Spender. *Industry Recipes: An Enquiry into the Nature and Sources of Managerial Judgment*. (New York: Blackwell, 1989).

32 A. Berstein. "The Baseball Owners Get Beaned." *Businessweek*. October 15, 1990, p. 122.

33 See E. Schine. "Northrop's Biggest Foe May Have Been Its Past." *Businessweek*. May 6, 1991, pp. 30–31; and J. Cole. "Rising Turbulence: Boeing's Dominance of Aircraft Industry Is Beginning To Erode. *Wall Street Journal*. July 10, 1992, A1.

34 Scherer. *Industrial Market Structure and Economic Performance*.

35 See T. Jankik and A. Makhiga. (2005). "Can Diversification Create Value? Evidence from the Electric Utility Industry." *Financial Management*, 34(1); 61–93 and K. Palmer. (1991). "Diversification by Regulated Monopolies and Incentives for Cost Reducing R&D." *American Economic Review*, 81(2): 266–270.

36 See Porter. "General Electric vs. Westinghouse in Large Turbine Generators (A)."

Case 2–1: McDonald's: Comeback in the U.S. Burger Market?*

McDonald's, one of the world's most iconic brands and companies, faced a crossroad in its comeback path. When Steve Easterbrook was appointed CEO in 2015, the company had lost an astonishing 500,000 U.S. customers in the previous four years. In 2015, for the first time, McDonald's closed more restaurants than it opened. Same-store domestic sales fell 1.3 percent in 2016, and the number of customers visiting McDonald's fell 2.1 percent that year, the fourth straight year for a decline in customers. Reflecting this trend, many younger people had never dined at McDonald's. As indicated by its recent declines in revenue and profit (see Tables 1 and 2), McDonald's faced a variety of challenges. Prices in groceries fell at the same time that the minimum wage was increasing and increasing dramatically in some cities and states. Given that labor was the largest component of cost for restaurant chains, the cost gap between dining out and eating in was at its largest since the 1980s. Efforts to add more products for health-conscious customers such as salads and oatmeal had failed to attract enough new customers to stem the decline. The all-day breakfast menu, introduced in 2015, was a hit, but by 2017, it was losing steam as an engine of growth. A particularly salient threat was the rise of fast, casual burger chains that focused on better-tasting burgers. Chains such as Five Guy's, The Habit Burger Grill, SmashBurger, and In-N-Out among others were expanding at a rapid rate. Such chains typically started as regional enterprises, but each was expanding geographically. Five Guys, particularly, had clearly broken out as a national competitor.

To combat the various threats it faced, McDonald's was implementing digital kiosks for ordering. The company

Table 1 McDonald's Income Statement, 2013-16 (In Millions of USD except for per share items)

	2016	2015	2014	2013
Revenue	24,621.90	25,413.00	27,441.30	28,105.70
Total Revenue	24,621.90	25,413.00	27,441.30	28,105.70
Cost of Revenue, Total	14,417.20	15,623.80	16,985.60	17,203.00
Gross Profit	10,204.70	9,789.20	10,455.70	10,902.70
Selling/General/Admin. Expenses, Total	2,410.50	2,473.20	2,511.40	2,407.40
Research & Development	-	-	-	-
Unusual Expense (Income)	130.50	62.60	9.70	
Total Operating Expense	16,877.40	18,267.50	19,492.10	19,341.40
Operating Income	7,744.50	7,145.50	7,949.20	8,764.30
Other, Net				
Income Before Tax	6,866.00	6,555.70	7,372.00	8,204.50
Income After Tax	4,686.50	4,529.30	4,757.80	5,585.90
Net Income Before Extra Items	4,686.50	4,529.30	4,757.80	5,585.90
Net Income	4,686.50	4,529.30	4,757.80	5,585.90
Preferred Dividends	-	-	-	-
Diluted Weighted Average Shares	861.20	944.60	986.30	1,006.00
Diluted EPS Excluding Extraordinary Items	5.44	4.79	4.82	5.55
Dividends per Share	3.61	3.44	3.28	3.12

* This case was prepared by William Hesterly for the purposes of class discussion.

Table 2 McDonald's Balance Sheet, 2013-16 (In Millions of USD except for per share items)

	2016	2015	2014	2013
Cash & Equivalents	1,223.40	7,685.50	2,077.90	2,798.70
Short Term Investments	144.40	4.50	137.90	16.00
Cash and Short Term Investments	1,367.80	7,690.00	2,215.80	2,814.70
Accounts Receivable - Trade, Net	1,474.10	1,298.70	1,214.40	1,319.80
Total Receivables, Net	1,474.10	1,298.70	1,214.40	1,319.80
Total Inventory	58.90	100.10	110.00	123.70
Prepaid Expenses	388.10	499.20	562.20	763.60
Other Current Assets, Total	1,559.70	55.00	83.10	28.30
Total Current Assets	4,848.60	9,643.00	4,185.50	5,050.10
Property/Plant/Equipment, Total - Gross	34,443.40	37,692.40	39,126.10	40,355.60
Accumulated Depreciation, Total				
Goodwill, Net	2,336.50	2,516.30	2,735.30	2,872.70
Long Term Investments	725.90	792.70	1,004.50	1,209.10
Other Long Term Assets, Total	1,855.30	1,869.10	1,744.60	1,747.10
Total Assets	31,023.90	37,938.70	34,227.40	36,626.30
Accounts Payable	756.00	874.70	860.10	1,086.00
Accrued Expenses	1,402.90	1,583.90	1,382.90	1,432.80
Notes Payable/Short Term Debt	0.00	0.00	0.00	0.00
Current Port. of LT Debt/Capital Leases	77.20	-	-	-
Other Current Liabilities, Total	1,232.20	491.80	504.90	651.20
Total Current Liabilities	3,468.30	2,950.40	2,747.90	3,170.00
Long Term Debt	25,878.50	24,122.10	14,935.70	14,129.80
Total Long Term Debt	25,878.50	24,122.10	14,935.70	14,129.80
Total Debt	25,955.70	24,122.10	14,935.70	14,129.80
Deferred Income Tax	1,817.10	1,704.30	1,624.50	1,647.70
Other Liabilities, Total	2,064.30	2,074.00	2,065.90	1,669.10
Total Liabilities	33,228.20	30,850.80	21,374.00	20,616.60
Common Stock, Total	16.60	16.60	16.60	16.60
Additional Paid-In Capital	6,757.90	6,533.40	6,239.10	5,994.10
Retained Earnings (Accumulated Deficit)	46,222.70	44,594.50	43,294.50	41,751.20
Treasury Stock - Common				
Other Equity, Total				427.60
Total Equity		7,087.90	12,853.40	16,009.70
Total Liabilities & Shareholders' Equity	31,023.90	37,938.70	34,227.40	36,626.30
Total Common Shares Outstanding	819.30	906.80	962.90	990.40

was also experimenting with home delivery and table service. Perhaps most importantly, McDonald's was considering changes in the way it prepared its burgers to improve taste. Such changes had the potential to significantly alter McDonald's strategic position with respect to cost and differentiation. With McDonald's stock price lagging behind both the S&P 500 and Dow Jones Industrial Average, the company needed to figure the right path to a more sustainable turnaround.

McDonald's Model

McDonald's employed the franchise business model for the vast majority of its restaurants. The franchise model was credited with McDonald's sustained growth and global expansion. In many instances, McDonald's acquired and developed prime real estate locations that it then leased back to franchisees. Some observers argued that McDonald's restaurants often enjoyed locational advantages compared to other burger chains. McDonald's set a goal of going from 83% to 95% franchise ownership of its restaurants. This would follow several other chains in what some termed the asset-light business model. Burger King, Carl's Jr., Hardee's, Dunkin Donuts, and Subway were all either 100-percent or nearly - 100-percent franchised owned. The franchise model posed some challenges. Getting franchisees to upgrade locations, adopt new technologies, and change the standard McDonald's menu often took considerable time and effort. Such changes could take several months at a minimum and, in some cases, several years.

Though there was some regional variability such as the McLobster in Maine, McDonald's offered a high degree of standardization in its menu across the U.S. McDonald's offered a breakfast menu, which in 2015, was extended from only morning hours to an all-day offering. McDonald's was best known for its hamburgers, but offered other items including Chicken McNuggets and a variety of sandwiches. McDonald's had emphasized with some success a McCafé line of items such as coffee, latte, shakes and smoothies. From time to time, McDonald's had offered special items for a limited time and had incrementally changed its menu from time to time. Many observers argued that, because of McDonald's immense scale, menu changes often occurred slowly both in formulation and implementation. For example, it did not expect to complete its plan to switch to free range eggs until 2025.

Despite the extent of its franchising, McDonald's was renowned for the uniformity of experience and consistency in quality that it offered customers. McDonald's typically served food within minutes of a customer's order. It was not unusual for customers to receive their food within one minute of ordering. While downtown McDonald's locations in the largest cities were an exception, most U.S. McDonald's locations offered drive-through service. Some estimates put the percentage of revenue from drive-through customers at 70 percent of revenue for the typical McDonald's. McDonald's had optimized its food production over several decades to deliver food of consistent quality with the short waits that customers expected. McDonald's supply chain could procure, process, and deliver frozen beef and potatoes to its stores with both high reliability and scale. This system helped McDonald's both reduce costs and ensure a high degree of consistency. McDonald's hamburgers were generally cooked and then warmed before delivery to a customer. This allowed McDonald's to serve customers much faster than waiting for orders before cooking the burgers.

Trends in Hamburgers

The market for premium burgers made with fresh beef had increased dramatically in the previous decade and was expected to double over the next five years. As recently as 2001, Five Guys had consisted of five stores in the Washington D.C. area. By 2016, it had more than 1,400 locations (see Table 3). Though much smaller than Five Guys, Shake Shack was founded in 2004, and Smashburger in 2007, while The Habit Burger Grill expanded from 23 restaurants in 2007 to 145 by 2016. Even In-N-Out, a California-based chain that had traditionally eschewed growth and geographic expansion, had grown from 89 locations in California and Las Vegas in 1999 to over 300 locations in the western United States and Texas. All of

Table 3 Number of U.S. Locations for McDonald's and Burger Competitors

Restaurant Chain	Number of Locations
McDonald's	14,259
Burger King	7,500
Wendy's	1,440
Carl's Jr./Hardee's	3,450
Jack in the Box	2,954
Five Guys	1,440
SmashBurger	315
Shake Shack	268
The Habit	145
In-N-Out	313

Table 4 McDonald's Versus Select Competitors on Time to Serve

	McDonald's	Five Guys	In N Out	Wendy's	Smashburger	Habit
Time from receiving receipt to hamburger	2:18	6:55	7:49	0:40	7:30	6:52
Drive-through available	Yes	No	Yes	Yes	No	No

Source: Data collected by casewriter's research assistant. The data above is based on one mid-afternoon visit to each of the chains and may not be indicative of overall averages. All of the hamburgers were served within the store rather than by way of drive-through service.

these chains featured menus with significantly fewer items than McDonald's and were, arguably, much more focused on burgers. All featured burgers made from fresh beef that were cooked upon order. This necessarily involved longer wait times (see Table 4). Most did not offer drive-through service. In-N-Out was the exception in that much of its business was drive-through and its hamburgers were not offered at a premium price (see Table 5). In addition to the several fast-growing chains that had emerged, there were many smaller chains that operated in various cities across the U.S. Multiple polls had shown consumers preferred the taste of burgers from chains such as Habit, Smashburger, In-N-Out, Five Guys, and Shake Shack among others to those of McDonald's. Many were limited to specific metropolitan areas while others had a larger geographic footprint. McDonald's also faced competition from its larger traditional competitors such as Burger King, Wendy's, Jack in the Box, as well as Carl's Jr. and its sister chain, Hardee's. Unlike the upstarts in the premium segment, the traditional competitors had not experienced significant growth in previous years. At one point after 2010, Burger King experienced same-store sales declines for 11 consecutive quarters. The number of Wendy's locations had declined from approximately 6,500 to 5,722 in the U.S. since 2011.

McDonald's Strategy

The growth in premium burgers made from fresh beef was not lost on McDonald's as consumer ratings showed the company lagging behind competitors on burger taste (see Tables 5 and 6). The company initially responded by experimenting with the removal of artificial preservatives and replacing margarine with butter among other similar changes. McDonald's then used Dallas as a test market for hamburgers made from fresh beef. The fresh-beef burgers were well-received by customers who rated them higher in taste than McDonald's traditional burgers. McDonald's announced in March 2017 that, by mid-2018, Quarter Pounders would be prepared with fresh beef in a majority of its restaurants. Quarter Pounders would also be cooked when ordered rather than cooked previously and stored in warmers.

Table 5 McDonalds and Select Competitors Price Comparisons

Chain	Lowest Priced Burger	Median Priced Burger	Highest Priced Burger
McDonald's	$ .90	$2.80	$4.85
In-N-Out	2.25	2.55	3.65
The Habit Burger Grill	3.15	4.30	5.85
Five Guys	4.59	6.19	7.79
SmashBurger	5.39	6.69	7.69

Source: Casewriter comparisons in Salt Lake City, Utah, May 2017.

Table 6 Consumer Reports Burger Ratings, 2014

Habit	8.1
SmashBurger	7.9
Culver's	7.7
Steak'n Shake	7.5
Wendy's	6.8
McDonald's	5.8

Source: "McDonald's Knows It's Losing the Burger Battle – Can it Come Back?" *Wall Street Journal*, Oct. 6, 2016 https://www.wsj.com/articles/mcdonalds-knows-its-losing-the-burger-battlecan-it-come-back-1475769684. Accessed May 28, 2017.

A shift to fresh beef was not without risks. Industry insiders suggested that employing fresh beef in burgers could extend the time between the order and the serving of a burger. Using fresh beef would likely increase the cost of burgers. Price sensitive customers might be less inclined to purchase McDonald's burgers. The use of fresh beef increased health risks as well. Fresh beef was much more susceptible to viruses than frozen beef. Chipotle's had still not fully recovered its customer base from problems with bacterial contamination more than two years earlier. A change to fresh beef would also dramatically change McDonald's supply chain and logistics for delivering beef to its stores.

McDonald's announced in March 2017 that it would roll out mobile ordering to all of its U.S. locations. Pizza chains had successfully used mobile ordering for years. In another action that followed long-standing practice by pizza chains, McDonald's also announced that it would dramatically accelerate and scale food delivery. The company had long experimented with delivery and already offered it in markets other than the U.S., particularly Asia and the Middle East. It was not clear how McDonald's planned to rapidly scale delivery, but there was considerable industry speculation that the company might enter an alliance with a delivery service firm such as GrubHub, Inc. McDonald's vast superiority in the number of its restaurants was seen as an advantage in delivery. Many more potential customers lived or worked close to a McDonald's compared to rivals in burgers and fast food generally. In addition to delivery and mobile ordering, the company also planned to spend approximately $1 billion renovating its existing stores.

As part of McDonald's turnaround strategy, the company planned to emphasize the McCafe drinks. In February of 2017, the company announced that McCafe drinks would sell for $2. More generally, McDonald's had placed a global emphasis on serving high quality coffee at a price considerably less than coffee houses.

Most of McDonald's strategic moves—such as the emphases on mobile ordering and store renovation—were seen as either low-risk or catch-up strategies. A shift to fresh beef would potentially have a more profound effect on the company. Would McDonald's traditional price-sensitive customers pay a premium for more costly burgers? Would they tolerate longer waits both in the restaurants and drive-throughs?

Bibliography

"A Closer Look at McDonald's Next 'Big Change'." *Forbes*, March 31, 2017. https://www.forbes.com/sites/greatspeculations/2017/03/31/a-closer-look-at-mcdonalds-next-big-change/#c69c40a57277.

Giammona, Craig. "McDonald's All-Day Breakfast Push No Longer Fueling Growth." *Bloomberg*, January 23, 2017. https://www.bloomberg.com/news/articles/2017-01-23/mcdonald-s-profit-beats-estimates-as-turnaround-gathers-steam.

Jargon, Julie. "McDonald's Knows It's Losing the Burger Battle – Can It Come Back?" *Wall Street Journal*, October 6, 2016. https://www.wsj.com/articles/mcdonalds-knows-its-losing-the-burger-battlecan-it-come-back-1475769684.

Jargon, Julie. "McDonald's, Slow to Industry Trends, Cooks Up Changes." *Wall Street Journal*, January 12, 2017. https://www.wsj.com/articles/mcdonalds-slow-to-industry-trends-cooks-up-changes-1484242650.

La Monica, Paul R. "The Great American McDonald's Comeback May Be Over." *CNN Money*, January 23, 2017. http://money.cnn.com/2017/01/23/investing/mcdonalds-earnings/.

Maynard, Micheline. "With Half A Billion Customers Lost, McDonald's Gambles on Mobile Ordering To Get Them Back." *Forbes*, March 1, 2017. https://www.forbes.com/sites/michelinemaynard/2017/03/01/with-half-a-billion-customers-lost-mcdonalds-gambles-on-mobile-ordering-to-get-them-back/#61c67c6e55e3.

Marks, Tod. "Where to Buy a Better Burger." Consumer Reports, October 28, 2016. http://www.consumerreports.org/food/where-to-buy-a-better-burger/.

"McDonald's Corporation Form 10-K," 2016. http://corporate.mcdonalds.com/content/dam/AboutMcDonalds/Investors/2016%20Annual%20Report.pdf.

Mourdoukoutas, Panos. "How McDonald's Keeps Bouncing Back." Forbes, December 18, 2016. https://www.forbes.com/sites/panosmourdoukoutas/2016/12/18/how-mcdonalds-wins/#7732987865d0.

Patton, Leslie. "McDonald's Sees $100 Billion Delivery Market as Way to Grow." *Bloomberg*. Accessed May 28, 2017. https://www.bloomberg.com/news/articles/2017-03-01/mcdonald-s-sees-100-billion-delivery-market-as-key-to-growth.

Turner, Nick. "McDonald's to Start Using Fresh Beef in 'Watershed Moment'." *Bloomberg*. Accessed May 28, 2017. https://www.bloomberg.com/news/articles/2017-03-30/mcdonald-s-plans-to-use-fresh-beef-nationwide-in-strategic-shift.

Case 2-2: Papa John's International, Inc.: Growth Challenges*

Papa John's International was a classic American success story. Founder John Schnatter had started selling pizza out of a makeshift kitchen in a small lounge in Indiana, and in a little more than a decade had built a business that included more than 4,000 locations. After a slowdown in growth following the 2008 economic crisis, Papa John's had returned to its pre-crisis pattern of opening more than 200 stores per year. Such ambition was not without challenges. The U.S. economy had changed over the two decades that Papa John's had been in business due to an aging population and to the severe economic crisis that faced the nation starting in 2008. The economy had been particularly challenging for firms serving food and drinks. Though clearly profitable (see Exhibit 1), Papa John's had enjoyed relatively incremental growth in the new century. Despite the challenges, the leadership at Papa John's believed that the company had developed some important advantages that could be leveraged for high growth in either the United States or international markets or perhaps even in activities that went beyond pizza. The question facing Papa John's executives was which path would produce rapid but profitable growth.

Exhibit 1 Papa John's, Inc., Income Statement and Balance Sheet, 2009–2012

In millions of USD (except for per share items)	2012	2011	2010	2009
Income Statement				
Revenue	1,342.65	1,217.88	1,126.40	1,078.55
Other Revenue, Total	—	—	—	—
Total Revenue	1,342.65	1,217.88	1,126.40	1,078.55
Cost of Revenue, Total	970.71	892.10	817.29	774.31
Gross Profit	371.94	325.78	309.10	304.24
Selling/General/Admin. Expenses, Total	186.50	160.92	157.13	170.69
Research and Development	—	—	—	—
Depreciation/Amortization	32.80	32.68	32.41	31.45
Interest Expense (Income)—Net Operating	—	—	—	—
Unusual Expense (Income)	0.36	1.75	−5.63	−17.23
Other Operating Expenses, Total	52.48	43.42	38.46	24.12
Total Operating Expense	1,242.85	1,130.87	1,039.65	983.33
Operating Income	99.81	87.02	86.74	95.22
Income Before Tax	98.39	84.79	83.31	84.19
Income After Tax	66.00	58.47	56.06	57.48
Minority Interest	−4.34	−3.73	−3.48	−3.76
Net Income Before Extra Items	61.66	54.73	52.58	53.73
Net Income	61.66	54.73	52.58	53.73
Income Available to Common Excl. Extra Items	61.66	54.73	52.58	53.73
Income Available to Common Incl. Extra Items	61.66	54.73	52.58	53.73
Dilution Adjustment	0	0	0	0.14
Diluted Weighted Average Shares	23.91	25.31	26.47	27.91
Diluted EPS Excluding Extraordinary Items	2.58	2.16	1.99	1.93
Diluted Normalized EPS	2.59	2.21	1.84	1.51

(continued)

*This case is adapted from a report prepared by Rebekah Meier, Wade Okelberry, Odie Washington, Chad Witcher, and J. C. Woelich.

Exhibit 1 Papa John's, Inc., Income Statement and Balance Sheet, 2009–2012 (*continued*)

In millions of USD (except for per share items)	2012	2011	2010	2009
Balance Sheet				
Cash and Equivalents	16.40	18.94	47.83	25.46
Cash and Short-Term Investments	16.40	18.94	47.83	25.46
Accounts Receivable—Trade, Net	44.65	28.17	25.36	22.12
Total Receivables, Net	49.22	32.39	30.09	22.12
Total Inventory	22.18	20.09	17.40	15.58
Prepaid Expenses	12.78	10.21	10.01	8.70
Other Current Assets, Total	18.05	13.19	14.14	12.16
Total Current Assets	118.63	94.82	119.47	84.00
Property/Plant/Equipment, Total—Gross	487.96	445.71	424.69	402.06
Accumulated Depreciation, Total	−291.30	−263.81	−239.32	−214.09
Goodwill, Net	78.96	75.08	74.70	75.07
Long-Term Investments	—	—	—	—
Other Long Term Assets, Total	31.63	27.06	25.34	28.95
Total Assets	438.41	390.38	417.49	393.73
Accounts Payable	32.62	32.97	31.57	26.99
Accrued Expenses	60.53	44.20	42.83	54.24
Notes Payable/Short-Term Debt	—	—	—	—
Other Current liabilities, Total	10.43	3.97	1.79	5.85
Total Current Liabilities	103.58	81.13	76.18	87.08
Long-Term Debt	88.26	51.49	99.02	99.05
Total Long-Term Debt	88.26	51.49	99.02	99.05
Total Debt	88.26	51.49	99.02	99.05
Deferred Income Tax	10.67	6.69	—	—
Minority Interest	18.22	15.03	13.48	8.17
Other Liabilities, Total	36.17	30.39	33.20	22.55
Total Liabilities	256.89	184.74	221.88	216.86
Common Stock, Total	0.37	0.37	0.36	0.36
Additional Paid-In Capital	280.90	262.46	245.38	231.72
Retained Earnings (Accumulated Deficit)	356.46	294.80	240.07	191.21
Treasury Stock—Common	−458.05	−353.83	−291.05	−245.34
Other Equity, Total	1.82	1.85	1.01	1.48
Total Equity	181.51	205.65	195.61	176.87
Total Liabilities and Shareholders' Equity	438.41	390.38	417.49	393.73
Total Common Shares Outstanding	22.24	24.02	25.44	26.93

Firm History and Background

By using fresh dough and superior-quality ingredients, Schnatter believed that he could make a better pizza than others. When Schnatter opened his first Papa John's in 1985, his expectations were not very high. The first Papa John's was a sit-down restaurant. Schnatter learned that he wasn't very good at the sit-down restaurant when he tried to serve too many different items. He paid careful attention to what customers liked and did not like and adjusted his menu accordingly.[1]

The company grew rapidly, opening eight stores during its first year of operation. Papa John's generated revenues of $500,000 in its first year.[2] In January 1986, Papa John's sold its first franchise. The company remained private until the initial public stock offering on June 8, 1993, under the symbol PZZA. Papa John's total revenues for the year ending in December 1992 were close to $50 million, having roughly doubled in size every year since 1986. After going public, the company experienced an accelerated domestic growth in the number of restaurants and opened its first international restaurant in 1998. International growth was aided by the 205-unit acquisition of "Perfect Pizza," the quality leader for pizzas in the United Kingdom.

This domestic and international growth continued unabated until 2001, when it decreased dramatically leading to a 1 percent contraction in domestic growth in 2003. Since 2003, growth has been positive and relatively stable, and Papa John's executives believed that there was significant opportunity for domestic unit growth. Papa John's was among the highest return on invested capital (ROIC) in the restaurant category. While domestic growth was anticipated to be stable, international opportunities were significantly large and promising. Papa John's had 350 domestic restaurants and 1,100 international restaurants that were contractually scheduled to open over the following 10 years.[3] Exhibit 2 shows the historical growth of Papa John's restaurants including projected growth through 2017 and Exhibit 3 reports the current international locations of Papa John's restaurants.

Business Structure

Papa John's had five major reportable segments of its business: domestic restaurants, domestic commissaries, domestic franchises, international operations, and variable interest entities. Domestic restaurants were restaurants that were wholly owned by Papa John's in the contiguous 48 states. Domestic franchises were restaurants in which Papa John's had licensed to franchisees for a franchise fee. These franchisee restaurants, as well as company-owned restaurants, were supported by domestic commissaries that supplied pizza dough, food products, paper products, small wares, and cleaning supplies twice weekly to each restaurant. There were 10 regional commissaries that supported domestic restaurants and franchises.

An important part of Papa John's strategy revolved around the central commissary. It allowed Papa John's to exercise control over the quality and consistency of its products.[4]

The commissary system was frequently cited by industry analysts and company officials as a key factor in the success of Papa John's. The system not only reduced labor costs and reduced waste because the dough was premeasured, but it maintained control over the consistency of the product. The centralized production facility supplied all of the Papa John's stores with the same high-quality ingredients for their pizza. One of the most important aspects of this system is that it allowed Papa John's to start up more stores because it did not require the purchase of additional expensive equipment for each store. Part of the company's strategy was to expand into new markets only after a commissary had been built that could support the growth and geographical expansion of restaurants.[5]

Papa John's was rated number one in customer satisfaction among all pizza chains in the American Customer Satisfaction Index for nine consecutive years from 1999 to 2008. As Schnatter had remarked in a 1997 interview, "We keep it simple, consistent, and focused. We don't keep changing what we are doing."[6] Papa John's president, U.S.A., William Van Epps, echoed this emphasis.

Papa John's core strategy was to sell a high-quality pizza for takeout or delivery. Its focus on using the highest-quality ingredients to produce a high-quality pizza was communicated in its motto; "Better Ingredients. Better Pizza." Schnatter considered it a sign of success when Pizza Hut sued Papa John's over the assertion that it had better ingredients and, therefore, a better pizza. Papa John's was ultimately successful in proving it used fresher ingredients and was, therefore, able to continue using its slogan. Papa John's stated goal was to build the strongest brand loyalty of all pizzerias internationally. Early on, Schnatter also introduced a signature bonus that served to signal the quality of the product: Each pizza was accompanied by a container of the company's special garlic sauce and two pepperoncinis.

Technology, Menu Enhancements, and Company Growth

Papa John's had long strived to be on the cutting edge of the use of technology. The company made ordering pizza even more convenient with the introduction of online ordering in 2001. It was the first pizza company to offer online ordering. Papa John's online sales grew exponentially in the first decade of the 21st century with growth rates of more than 50 percent a year not unusual. In November 2007, Papa John's led the way, once again, by offering text message ordering.[7] More than 20 percent of all Papa John's sales came online or via text. Papa John's was also using both the internet and mobile technologies to make potential customers aware of current promotions and to allow them to easily order a pizza from virtually anywhere.

In October 2006, Papa John's introduced online ordering in Spanish in an attempt to meet growing customer needs and expectations. In 2012, Papa John's became the first pizza chain to offer online ordering in Canada.

Papa John's also extended its menu. In January 2006, Papa John's announced that it was adding dessert pizzas to its carryout and delivery menus. "We created Papa's Sweetreats in direct response to consumer demand," said Catherine Hull, Papa John's vice president of strategy and brand marketing.[8] In July 2008, Papa John's introduced another permanent addition to its menu: Chocolate Pastry Delight.

Menu additions and new ways to order did not signal a change in strategy, according to company executives. Nigel Travis, president and CEO of Papa John's, stated in the company annual report 2007, "our stated strategy from a year ago remains unchanged. We will continue to focus on quality, growing the brand globally, and competing aggressively. It has proven the right course in a challenging economic time and has the opportunity to be even more successful as the economy rebounds." Papa John's targeted restaurants in the international arena as the company's primary source of long-term growth. Papa John's saw its use of innovative marketing, product offerings, and industry-leading technology as a major advantage over its competitors.[9]

Papa John's outlined its company strategy in one annual report as follows; "Our goal is to build the strongest brand loyalty of all pizzerias internationally."

Papa John's strategy for accomplishing this goal centered on five key activities. The first was a commitment to using high quality ingredients in its menu items. The second was operational efficiency from using commissaries and centralizing procurement. A commitment to training and development of its employees and franchise members was the third key activity. Marketing constituted the fourth key to Papa John's strategy. Papa John's marketed nationally through television, print, direct mail, and digital activities. The company also emphasized community-oriented marketing at the restaurant level. Such activities were often directed at schools and sports activities. Building a strong franchise system was the final key element of Papa John's strategy. The company sought to attract franchisees with either restaurant or retail experience and then sought to develop franchisees through a variety of training and development activities.

Cost Management and Operational Support Systems

Papa John's subleased retail locations to franchise owners. Papa John's had lowered the number of corporate-owned stores by about 5 percent in recent years in an effort to lower its lease payments. Leasing building space gave Papa John's the flexibility to move locations quickly with minimal cost, should a profitable location turn bad.

Papa John's also leased the trailers used to distribute ingredients from the commissary centers to the retail locations, typically on an eight-year lease agreement. By leasing the trailers, Papa John's was able to manage its shipping logistics and costs in a structured manner while not being required to maintain the trailers as they aged.

As Papa John's started to grow, Schnatter recognized the importance of sharing his passion for pizza with others in his company. The Operation Support Service and Training (OSST) Center was created and was actively engaged in the training and development of "team" members. In order to instill his passion into his new franchisees and corporate employees, Schnatter had them complete a management training program at the OSST Center when they started with the company. The aim of this training was to help franchise owners be successful and to instill in them a firm understanding of the Papa John's culture. Making franchisees feel like they were in a partnership with Papa John's facilitated a level of buy-in that the company believed was seldom found in restaurant chains.

Throughout Papa John's tremendous growth during its first 10 years of operation, its marketing programs targeted the delivery area of each restaurant, primarily through direct mailings and direct store-to-door couponing.

From its beginning, Papa John's had been active in community affairs, from supporting local sports teams with fundraising opportunities to offering college scholarships. Papa John's had awarded more than $5 million in college scholarships. Papa John's actively supported the National FFA, Cerebral Palsy K.I.D.S. Center, and Children's Miracle Network, to name only a few. Papa John's executives believed that giving back to the community was good business.

Papa John's had entered into numerous marketing partnerships over the years. For example, Papa John's aligned with Coca-Cola to offer only Coke products in its stores. When Papa John's added a pan pizza to its menu, it enlisted the aid of former Miami Dolphins quarterback Dan Marino. At the time, this was the most intensive new product launch ever undertaken by Papa John's. Another combined effort for Papa John's involved coordinating with eBay for a limited edition Superman pan pizza box. In Kentucky, Papa John's and Blockbuster video combined efforts in a "take dinner and a movie online" in which the customer would receive a free 30-day trial of Blockbuster Online with an online pizza purchase at papajohns.com.

By using a combination of internal and external resources, Papa John's was determined to not compete with its competition on price. Focusing on a quality product, active participation in the local communities in which it operated, and product branding enabled Papa John's to hold its own with the other pizza chains. Papa John's had worked to create a product branded in such a way that customers came to expect the very best pizza; and they were willing to pay a premium price. Papa John's was committed to holding firm on the quality and prices of its pizzas.

The Restaurant Industry and Pizza Segment

The restaurant industry had historically been very attractive to entrepreneurs. Most of these new entrants opened single locations. The relatively low capital requirements made the restaurant business very attractive to small-scale entrepreneurs. Some of these businesses succeeded, but there was an intense amount of competition. There were relatively high fixed costs associated with entering into the restaurant business. These factors caused many of the new businesses to fail. However, for the businesses that succeeded, the payback on the investment could be quite high. After sales reached the break-even point, a relatively high percentage of incremental revenues became profit.

Restaurant analysts were generally amazed at how successfully Schnatter built Papa John's. Michael Fineman, a restaurant analyst with Raymond James in St. Petersburg, Florida, stated, "Here's an industry that appears to be mature and saturated, and here comes John Schnatter with his company Papa John's. He has proven to be a fantastic visionary."[10]

Large restaurant chains, like Papa John's, were able to realize economies of scale that made competition extremely difficult for small operators. Some of these advantages included purchasing power in negotiating food and packaging supply contracts, as well as real estate purchasing, location selection, menu development, and marketing.

Papa John's operated in the highly competitive pizza restaurant market, where the cost of entry was relatively low and product differentiation was difficult. Other pizza chains tried to compete in ways other than Papa John's emphasis. Some chains focused on being less expensive or having a broad menu. The meal options available for consumers were increasing both for convenience dining and at-home consumption. The quality of frozen pizza available at grocery stores had improved significantly in recent years. A broader trend was that restaurant and quick-service restaurant dinner occasions were declining, which was significant for pizza restaurants such as Papa John's, which gained 70 percent of its sales from dinner orders. Declining restaurant and quick-service restaurant dining was attributed to an increase in at-home dinner preparation, linked to a decline in the percentage of women in the workforce.[11]

The large number of restaurant types throughout North America made it unlikely that any firm would gain a competitive advantage by offering one style or type of cuisine. The one principle that made Papa John's rare in the restaurant industry was its ongoing passion to offer the perfect pizza. Many companies claimed to place quality at the forefront of their business, but often the commitment to quality went no deeper than public relations and was not a core value.

Papa John's commitment to the highest-quality ingredients created challenges in managing the supply of the foods that went into its pizza. The volatility in the price of cheese had been a major problem for Papa John's. Cheese material costs contribute approximately 35 to 40 percent of Papa John's restaurants' food costs. In order to reduce the cheese price volatility, Papa John's partnered with a third-party entity formed by franchisees, BIBP Commodities, Inc., whose sole purpose was to reduce cheese price volatility to domestic system-wide restaurants. This allowed Papa John's to purchase cheese from BIBP at a fixed quarterly price. Profits and losses from BIBP were then passed on to Papa John's.[12]

Rising costs challenged pizza restaurants in multiple areas. Labor costs, as well as food commodity costs, were rising in the industry. "Although restaurants are experiencing cost increases for labor, utilities, and transportation, perhaps no other factor has prompted restaurants to increase their prices in 2008 more than food commodity cost inflation" (S&P Industry Surveys [2008]). Rising energy costs had a dual impact on Papa John's and its competitors. Food prices of products related to corn were increasing even more rapidly because of corn's use as an alternative fuel. Fluctuating in-store utility costs and delivery driver fuel costs were an ongoing source of concern. In 2007-08, such costs had risen dramatically. Another potential threat of rising costs stemmed from legislation at the federal level as well as many states that mandated a higher minimum wage.

Many companies, including Papa John's, engaged in forward pricing to stabilize food costs. "Forward pricing is a hedging strategy whereby a company negotiates with a supplier to purchase a certain amount of a product at a given price. Some supply contracts, signed by larger chains, can lock in less volatile food products for an entire year. Some of the products subject to the greatest variability, especially dairy products, can be locked in only for shorter periods."[13]

Of the $200-plus-billion restaurant market, the pizza segment currently held 6.7 percent of the market. Pizza Hut, a division of Yum! Brands, Inc., was the leader, followed by Domino's Pizza, Inc., Papa John's International, Inc., and Little Caesars (a division of Ilitch Holdings, Inc.). Each was a large, nationally known pizza provider. These four accounted for 88 percent of the aggregate sales in the pizza chain restaurant segment; each was significantly larger than the #5 chain Chuck E. Cheese's (operated by CEC Entertainment, Inc.).

Papa John's Looking Forward

Schnatter was optimistic about the future of Papa John's. He wanted to see Papa John's get back on the path of opening 200 to 300 stores per year. Over the following five years, he wanted to see Papa John's reach the 4,000-store mark and, long term, he aspired to see 6,000 to 7,000 stores worldwide.[14] Papa John's also sought to reduce the number of company-run stores by turning them into franchising opportunities. At the end of 2012, Papa John's operated 3,204 stores in North America and another 959 internationally. Papa John's owned 20 percent of the North American stores but only 5 percent of the international stores, which were all in China. Franchising more of its current company-run stores offered Papa John's some important benefits. Franchise royalties were based on a percentage of sales and not on a percentage of profits, which allowed Papa John's to ensure a steady stream of revenue even in a difficult operating environment.

Papa John's had several options at its disposal. Among them were international market expansion, increased domestic market penetration, and related diversification (primarily via strategic acquisitions). The case for international expansion was based on the conclusion that the U.S. pizza industry (and quick-serve restaurant industry in general) had matured and that the most significant growth opportunities were beyond U.S. borders. Pizza Hut benefited from a first-mover advantage in several, if not most, attractive international markets. With over 1,000 stores, Pizza Hut operated more stores in China than Papa John's throughout the world. It operated more than 5,200 stores, more than five times the number of Papa John's. Historically, Papa John's international efforts centered in Mexico, Canada, the United Kingdom, the Middle East, and Asia. Some believed that Asian markets would generally favor quality-centered business models due to higher preferences for quality. Another favorable trend in these markets was a growing income base for the local population.

In building its international infrastructure, the company would need to cultivate new relationships and develop new skills. One critical element was the company's ability to continue to partner with local producers in order to maintain tight quality control and keep ingredients fresh. In terms of new skills, Papa John's needed to develop the ability to modify its standard smaller carry-out restaurant blueprint. Looking at the success of firms such as McDonald's or Yum! Brands, Inc.'s Kentucky Fried Chicken, there was persuasive evidence that international customers tended to view their eating-out experience as more of a formal dining event. Thus, the standard Papa John's takeout restaurant model might need to be expanded to accommodate a sit-down dining area for patrons.

In addition to expanding internationally, Papa John's sought to grow and maintain its domestic market share. Traditionally, restaurants did this by adding new menu items or introducing a value selection such as McDonald's dollar menu or Little Caesars' Hot-N-Ready $5 pizza offering. For Papa John's, these strategies presented the risk of overextending its menu and, consequently, reducing its overall brand quality or ability to charge premium prices.

Extending the company's co-branding efforts was another possible avenue for domestic growth. For example, Papa John's partnered with firms such as Nestlé to provide some of its dessert menu offerings. There were a vast number of co-branding opportunities that were, in theory at least, possible.

A third alternative for Papa John's involved diversifying from pizza. For example, Papa John's could develop or acquire an additional restaurant chain under a different brand. Such an approach would allow Papa John's to compete in another restaurant category without fear of diluting its quality brand. Other competitors in the industry had operated chains in multiple categories. McDonald's, for example, had invested in Chipotle Mexican Grill and Boston Market before disposing of its investments in 2006 and 2007, respectively. Yum! Brands, Inc., operated Pizza Hut, Taco Bell, Kentucky Fried Chicken, and A&W. With the growing influence of the Hispanic population and culture in the United States, some believed that a Hispanic/Mexican-themed restaurant would allow the company to benefit from this trend without impairing the Papa John's franchise.

End Notes

1. Interview with John Schnatter, October 2008.
2. (2008) Hoover's Profiles. Papa John's International, Inc.
3. UBS London investor meeting on August 22, 2008.
4. Interview with John Schnatter, October 2008.
5. Hoover's Profiles. Papa John's International, Inc.
6. Walkup, C. (1997). "John Schnatter." *Food Industry*, January.
7. (2007). *Pizza Today*, November 19.
8. (2006). *Pizza Today*, January 17.
9. Papa John's International, Inc., annual report 2007.
10. Walkup, C. (1997). "John Schnatter." *Food Industry*, January.
11. UBS London investor meeting on August 22, 2008.
12. Ibid.
13. *Standard & Poor's Industry Surveys*, September 4, 2008.
14. Interview with John Schnatter, October 2008.

Case 2-3: Torrey Nano, Inc.*

Jack Heiner, the CEO of Torrey Nano, a seven-year-old biotechnology firm, faced an important decision in the spring of 2017. Torrey Nano, based in San Diego, California was a company of 35 employees, most of whom were research scientists. Torrey Nano's pharmaceutical product, codename Nano-4, was almost ready for human testing. The company aspired to be a full-fledged pharmaceutical company. However, like most biotech startups, it had focused on R&D since its founding. Consequently, it had done no manufacturing or marketing. With the impending human testing of Nano-4, however, it faced the decision of whether to build a small-scale pilot plant to manufacture Nano-4 for human trials. Nano-4 was the fourth product that Torrey Nano had developed but the first to advance to human trials. The drug had multiple potential therapeutic applications, but Torrey Nano had focused on diabetes treatment as its first application. The company had three other products in earlier stages of development.

Human testing involved three phases. Phase I, which lasted from 6-12 months, assessed basic human safety (e.g., adverse side effects, etc.). If a product was approved in Phase I, it moved to Phase II where the drug was tested with a small group of patients. Phase II examined the efficacy of a drug in treating a disease and also evaluated whether serious side effects occurred. Phase II usually lasted from one to two years. Products that succeeded in Phases I and II could go on to Phase III. Phase III, which could take two to five years to complete, tested the drug using a large sample of patients. Regulations required that whatever manufacturing processes were used in Phase III must be the same as those used after the drug was approved and marketed commercially.

The manufacturing of drugs based on nanotechnology was considered highly complex and uncertain. Drugs based on nanotechnology were particularly new in 2017 but were generally thought to hold great promise for a wide variety of diseases. Several reports suggested that manufacturing nano-materials was both difficult to replicate and scale. Thus, it was challenging to develop effective processes for manufacturing new nano-drugs. Some nanotechnology drugs, while feasible to make in the small quantities needed for pilot studies, were especially problematic to manufacture on a large scale. Very small differences in processes could lead to failure. Moreover, industry experts reported that firms often had difficulty transferring a manufacturing process from one facility to another. Few young companies had experience manufacturing products of the type of Nano-4. There were, however, a handful of contract manufacturers who had some experience in manufacturing involving nanotechnology. Even for these firms, though, it often required considerable trial and error before mastering the process for a particular drug.

Torrey Nano managers identified five possible scenarios for how they might handle the manufacturing of Nano-4. The five scenarios are listed here with cash flow estimates included in Table 1.

Scenario 1: Torrey Nano builds a pilot plant for Phases I/II and a full-scale plant for Phase III.

Scenario 2: Torrey Nano builds a pilot plant for Phases I/II and licenses out the manufacturing rights for Phase III.

Scenario 3: Contract out manufacturing for Phases I/II, build a full-scale plant in-house for Phase III.

Scenario 4: Contract out manufacturing for Phases I/II and license out manufacturing rights for Phase III.

Scenario 5: Manufacturing in all phases would be done by licensee.

In all five scenarios, Nano-4 would ultimately be distributed and marketed by an established pharmaceutical firm that would serve as Torrey Nano's and/or the eventual manufacturer's, marketing partner. If Nano-4 successfully navigated clinical testing to reach the commercial stage, analysts projected sales ranging from $75 million in 2025 to over $288 million in 2035, the last year of patent protection (see Table 2). As Heiner contemplated his options, it was clear that the scenarios involving in-house manufacturing were costlier, but potentially more lucrative. Both of the first two scenarios required capital investments in 2018 and 2019 to build a pilot plant while scenarios 1 and 3 required large capital outlays to build a full-scale plant in 2020 and 2021 (see Table 3). Cash flow projections suggested that building a full-scale plant would allow Torrey Nano to capture a higher percentage of the revenue stream for Nano-4—$15 million licensing fee from its marketing partner in 2025 upon successful completion of clinical trials and 40 percent of royalties. Licensing the manufacturing rights after Phase II, as required by Scenarios 2 and 4, would yield a lower payout—$10 million licensing fee from the marketing partner and 10 percent royalties.

---

* This case is intended for class discussion only. Torrey Nano is a fictitious company and, while nanotechnology is believed to offer great promise for the future in pharmaceuticals, technical details in the case may not reflect reality.

Table 1 Forecasted Cash Flows for Torrey Nano Investment Scenarios

Phase I/II	Torrey Nano	Torrey Nano	Contractor	Contractor	Licensee
Phase III	**Torrey Nano**	**Licensee**	**Torrey Nano**	**Licensee**	**Licensee**
Year	**Scenario 1**	**Scenario 2**	**Scenario 3**	**Scenario 4**	**Scenario 5**
2018	−5,000	−5,000	0	0	5,000
2019	−3,000	−3,000	−4,000	−4,000	0
2020	−33,000	−3,000	−34,500	−4,500	0
2021	0	0	0	0	0
2022	0	0	0	0	0
2023	0	0	0	0	0
2024	0	0	0	0	0
2025	45,000	17,500	45,000	17,500	3,750
2026	56,000	14,000	56,000	14,000	7,000
2027	70,000	17,500	70,000	17,500	8,750
2028	78,000	19,500	78,000	19,500	9,750
2029	86,000	21,500	86,000	21,500	10,750
2030	90,300	22,575	90,300	22,575	11,288
2031	94,815	23,704	94,815	23,704	11,852
2032	99,556	24,889	99,556	24,889	12,444
2033	104,534	26,133	104,534	26,133	13,067
2034	109,760	27,440	109,760	27,440	13,720
2035	115,248	28,812	115,248	28,812	14,406

Table 2 Projected Sales from Nano-4 (in 000's)

2025	$75,000
2026	$140,000
2027	$175,000
2028	$195,000
2029	$215,000
2030	$225,750
2031	$237,038
2032	$248,889
2033	$261,334
2034	$274,401
2035	$288,121

A pilot plant with sufficient capacity to produce output for Phases I and II involved a $5 million investment in 2018. This investment would cover all expenses including facilities and plant equipment. The company would still incur $1 million in production costs in 2019 and 2020 as well as $2 million in expenses for the clinical trials in those years. A larger-scale plant for Phase III and commercialization would require a $30 million investment in 2020. Torrey Nano had sufficient funds for the Phase I/II investment. The Phase III investment would require another round of venture capital funding. Heiner and Torrey Nano's board, however, were convinced that such funding was highly likely if Nano-4 successfully completed Phase I/II testing. Venture capitalists expected returns of 30%, which a successful pharmaceutical product would insure for a biotech firm such as Torrey Nano.

Table 3 Details for Cash Flows for Each Decision Scenario (in 000's)

	2018	2019	2020	2025	2026-35
Scenario 1					
- Pilot Facility Construction Costs	−5,000				
- Production Costs		−$1,000	−$1,000		
- Clinical Trials		−2,000	−2,000		
- Phase III/Commercial Plant Construction Costs			−30,000		
- Licensing Fee				15,000	40%
- Royalties				40%	
Scenario 2					
- Pilot Facility Construction Costs	−5,000				
- Production Costs		−$1,000	−$1,000		
- Clinical Trials		−2,000	−2,000		
- Licensing Fee				10,000	10%
- Royalties				10%	10%
Scenario 3					
- Contract Production		−2,000	−2,500		
- Phase I/II Clinical Trials		−2,000	−2,000		
- Phase III/Commercial Plant Construction Costs			−30,000		
- Licensing Fee				15,000	
- Royalties				40%	40%
Scenario 4					
- Contract Production		−2,000	−2,500		
- Phase I/II Clinical Trials		−2,000	−2,000		
- Licensing Fee				10,000	10%
- Royalties				10%	10%
Scenario 5					
- Licensing Fee	5,000				
- Royalties					5%

Heiner believed that building a pilot plant (Scenarios 1 and 2) would allow Torrey Nano to develop the foundation for future large-scale manufacturing capabilities. While the company's 35 employees were mostly technically sophisticated research scientists, none had any significant experience in manufacturing. The company did not have any employees with the variety of operations management skills needed for manufacturing. A pilot plant would allow Torrey Nano to hire people and develop organizational capabilities in manufacturing. Building a pilot plant was not without challenges and risks, however. The process challenges involved in producing Nano-4 at even pilot scale were somewhat uncertain and might pose challenging for a firm with early capabilities in manufacturing. Some within the company believed that manufacturing was outside of the company's capabilities and that Torrey Nano should stick to what it did best, which was R&D.

Contract manufacturing (Scenarios 3 and 4) was a second option for Phase I/II. Contracting required little to no capital investment on Torrey Nano's part. Several contract manufacturers had idle capacity, and some had experience with the challenges of scaling nanotechnology. Contracting was expensive. Torrey Nano forecasted paying production costs of $2 million in 2018 and $2.5 million in 2019. The company would also pay $2 million each year for clinical trial expenses. Because of the uncertainties involved in manufacturing a new drug, formulating a contract that was satisfactory to the two firms involved could be a lengthy process. Even with the most well-intentioned efforts, a contract was likely to fail to foresee important contingencies. Such failures in foresight would trigger considerable negotiation between the firms. Contracting also necessitated the sharing of a considerable amount of sensitive proprietary information. Such information could help potential competitors and contractors gain a more advantageous position against Torrey Nano.

Scenario 3 was a compromise between outsourcing and in-house manufacturing. In this scenario, Torrey Nano would contract out the manufacturing for Phases 1 and 2, but vertically integrate for Phase 3 and commercial manufacturing. The costs for Phases I/II were the same as in Scenario 2, but the costs and payout in Phase III and commercialization were identical to those in Scenario I. The appeal of this option is that it would allow Torrey Nano to avoid the significant capital investments involved in developing a pilot plant yet reap the higher royalties (forecasted at 40 percent) that doing manufacturing in-house would yield. Construction on a commercial-scale plant would need to begin as soon as possible after the completion of Phase II trials. The challenge involved in Scenario 3 is that it required Torrey Nano to make the leap to manufacturing on a larger-scale without first developing its capabilities at a smaller scale.

Scenario 4 involved contracting out manufacturing for Phases I/II and then licensing out the manufacturing rights for Phase III and commercialization. In this scenario, Torrey Nano would not need to develop manufacturing capabilities and would not have to incur the $5 million costs of a pilot plant or the $30 million investment associated with Phase III.

Scenario 5 involved entering in a license deal immediately. In this scenario, the licensing partner would bear all the costs and risks involved in manufacturing and regulatory approvals for Phases I, II, and III as well as commercialization. Torrey Nano would receive a $5 million payment and 5 percent royalties from future sales of Nano-4. However, Torrey Nano would forego the opportunity to capture the much higher royalties associated with the other scenarios.

As Heiner reflected on Torrey Nano's scenarios, he realized that they involved important tradeoffs. Some of the scenarios offered a potential stepping stone for the company to realize its aspiration of becoming a stand-alone pharmaceutical firm. Other options increased the company's chance of survival, and would guarantee the company the ability to develop other products. Heiner wondered if other products in the pipeline had as much or more potential than Nano-4. It was difficult to say. What did Heiner's employees want? All were impressive scientists with abundant opportunities at other firms. They gravitated to Torrey Nano because the scientific problems it addressed were both exciting and important. In many cases, though, the scientists were looking to combine interesting science with the opportunity to make their fortunes in the right startup. As Heiner pondered these questions, he realized that the time for analysis was over. He had to decide.

Case 2-4: Collusion in Major League Baseball*

In November 1990, one of Major League Baseball's (MLB) most controversial episodes in its troubled labor relations history concluded with a $290 million settlement. The settlement required teams to pay players $280 million with the Major League Baseball Players Association (MLBPA) governing the distribution of damages to players. How Major League Baseball reached this point is grounded in peculiar history. Baseball historians divide the history of the MLB into distinct eras. These eras represent shifting bargaining power between the players and owners over a 150-year period.

Era 1 1860-1903i

The early days of baseball were characterized by an absence of any institutional structure that limited bargaining by either players or teams. Some star players— termed revolvers— switched teams frequently. In some cases, a player would change teams from one day to the next. Some apocryphal stories claimed that some players switched teams in the middle of a game. Typically, players profited much more than owners did in this era. As a result, both teams and leagues were fragile with many quickly coming into and out of existence. Leagues made some attempts to limit pay, but rival teams and leagues would quickly emerge to bid away the best players. And often, more successful players and owners would simply ignore the rules. Teams that employed revolvers won more games, but often did not make a profit. Teams that did not pay premiums for the best players usually initiated a downward spiral of losing followed by attendance declines, which ultimately led to team dissolution. Indeed, few teams lasted more than two years. Player salaries showed large fluctuations. As new leagues and teams were formed to compete with existing leagues, player salaries went up, but then declined as teams and leagues folded.

Era 2: 1903-1976

Eventually, enough owners realized that unless they cooperated in controlling player wages, that few, if any, teams or leagues would have long-term sustainability. A critical turning point was the formation of the National and American Leagues. In both leagues, the owners vested more centralized authority in the league. This centralization increased dramatically after the 1919 World Series scandal where several players were later convicted of having taken bribes to alter the outcomes of games. Judge Kennesaw Mountain Landis was appointed Commissioner of Baseball and given broad powers over the American and National Leagues as well as all affiliated minor leagues and teams.

The fundamental rule that governed bargaining between players and teams during this era was the reserve cause. The reserve clause was first used in 1879 but by the early 1900s it was universal in Major League contracts. A 1960s version of the reserve clause follows:

> On or before January 15 . . . the Club may tender to the Player a contract for the term of that year by mailing the same to the Player. If prior to the March 1 next succeeding said January 15, the Player and the Club have not agreed upon the terms of such contract, then on or before 10 days after said March 1, the Club shall have the right . . . to renew this contract for the period of one year (Helyar, 1994, p. 36).

The explicit meaning of the reserve clause was that teams could not negotiate or contract with players who were presently under contact with a team or who had previously been under contract to a team within the last year. However, the reserve clause for much of this era was perhaps universally understood to mean that a team could not negotiate or contract with a player whose previous team had not sold or otherwise renounced its rights to employ the player. In other words, most thought that the reserve clause gave a team the exclusive right to employ a player in perpetuity. Thus,

* This case was prepared by William Hesterly for the purposes of class discussion. Much of the case is based on earlier research by William Hesterly and Aya Chacar. Aya S. Chacar and William Hesterly, 2008, "Institutional Settings and Rent Appropriation by Knowledge-based Employees: The Case of Major League Baseball, *Managerial and Decision Economics*, 29:117-136. Aya S. Chacar and William Hesterly, 2004, "Innovation and Value Creation in Major League Baseball." *Business History*, 46, 407-420. This research drew heavily on the historical accounts of the following sources: R.F. Burk, 1994, *Never Just a Game: Players, Owners and American Baseball to 1920.* University of North Carolina Press, Chapel Hill, NC. John Helyar, *Lords of the Realm: The Real History of Baseball.* New York: Ballantine Books. G.E. White, *Creating the National Pastime: Baseball Transforms Itself, 1903-53.* Princeton, NJ: Princeton University Press.

a player unhappy with his present team could not offer his services to other teams. Teams could, however, buy and sell the contracts of players with each other, a practice known as trading players.

There were some early legal challenges to the reserve clause. Several courts split on the constitutionality of the reserve clause, but a Federal Appeals court ruling that it was constitutional was upheld by a 1922 Supreme Court decision. In the decision, Judge Oliver Wendell Holmes famously opined that baseball was exempt from anti-trust laws because "baseball are purely state affairs." Following the Supreme Court decision, there was little to no contesting of the reserve clause for over four decades. With few exceptions, players claimed that the reserve clause was good for them and for baseball more generally. The owners instituted other rules besides the reserve clause that weakened players' bargaining power. Players were not allowed to have agents represent them. Also, contract terms were not public. As a result, many players were told that they ranked much higher in pay on their teams than was actually the case. For example, some players were told that they were among the highest paid players on their teams when they were below the median salary of their teammates. Even some of baseball's greatest stars had little bargaining power. The Philadelphia Athletics tried to cut Jimmie Foxx's salary in 1933 after he achieved baseball's triple crown (the most home runs, highest batting average, and most runs batted in the same year). Lou Gehrig did not receive a pay increase a year later after winning the Triple Crown. Ralph Kiner received a 25% pay cut from the Pittsburgh Pirates in 1953 even though he had led the National League in home runs for seven straight years. Branch Rickey, the president of the Pirates, reportedly told Kiner, "We finished last with you. We can finish last without you." Many players, even stars such as Yogi Berra, held second jobs in the off-season. Few players held out for higher salaries, and when they did, they received little public sympathy.

Remarkably, there were no organized efforts to change the reserve clause and representation rules during this era. The collective actions that players took during this time were centered on inconsequential things such as not requiring the players to purchase their own uniforms. Late in this era, the players did organize more effectively, but their primary goal was to create a pension fund for players.

Era 3: 1977 to the Present

Even though the players' share of baseball's economic pie had been decreasing for decades, the players made little attempt to challenge the owners superior position. A number of catalysts occurred in the 1960s to begin pressure for change. The players hired Marvin Miller, formerly a chief economist for the powerful Steelworkers union. Miller immediately saw what the players had long failed to see. In his view, baseball players were the most oppressed workers that he had seen in the United States. During the 1960s, both the NFL and NBA were challenged by new leagues, the AFL and ABA respectively. Overnight, players were being offered unheard of salaries to jump leagues. This caused both the NFL and the NBA to respond with dramatic salary increases. Seeing their peers in other professional sports receive higher pay led the players to challenge the status quo in baseball's labor relations. The owners' aggressive response to players who spoke out only increased the spread of militancy among players.

Through a series of court cases and arbitrator decisions, the reserve clause was defined to mean that teams did not control a player's rights in perpetuity. An arbitrator ruled in December 1975 that a player became a free agent one year after the expiration of his contract. As a response of the arbitrator's decision, the owners and players reached a series of Collective Bargaining Agreements where players could either enter salary arbitration or free agency (the freedom to sign with any team) after a specified number of years in the Major Leagues. Miller designed a two-tier system of arbitration and free agency with the intent that there would be a limited number of free agents in any given year. His reasoning was that many teams competing for a few free agents would drive the price of free agents much higher than if there were many free agents. The high salaries of free agents would then serve as comparisons for arbitration cases. Thus, the free agency would drive up the salaries of not only free agents but those who went through salary arbitration as well.

Other rule changes further strengthened the players' bargaining position. New rules allowed players to have agent representation. Salary information was made widely available and was available to players and agents in salary negotiations. Average salaries went from $19,000 in 1967 to an average of $371,000 in 1985 (see Table 1 and Figure 1). The minimum salary went from $6,000 to $60,000 during the same period (see Table 1 and Figure 2).

Collusion: 1985-88

The spectacular increase in player salaries was a source of considerable tension for owners. Broadcast revenues generally increased at the same rate as player salaries during this

Table 1 Minimum and Average Salaries in Major League Baseball, 1970-88

Year	Minimum Salary	Percentage Change in Min. Salary	Average Salary	Percentage Change in Avg. Salary
1970	$12,000		$29,303	
1971	$12,750	6.3%	$31,543	7.6%
1972	$13,500	5.9%	$34,092	8.1%
1973	$15,000	11.1%	$36,566	7.3%
1974	$15,000	0.0%	$40,839	11.7%
1975	$16,000	6.7%	$44,676	9.4%
1976	$19,000	18.8%	$51,501	15.3%
1977	$19,000	0.0%	$76,066	47.7%
1978	$21,000	10.5%	$98,876	30.0%
1979	$21,000	0.0%	$113,558	14.8%
1980	$30,000	42.9%	$143,756	26.6%
1981	$32,500	8.3%	$185,651	29.1%
1982	$33,500	3.1%	$241,497	30.1%
1983	$35,000	4.5%	$289,194	19.8%
1984	$40,000	14.3%	$329,408	13.9%
1985	$60,000	50.0%	$371,571	12.8%
1986	$60,000	0.0%	$412,520	11.0%
1987	$62,500	4.2%	$412,454	0.0%
1988	$62,500	0.0%	$438,729	6.4%

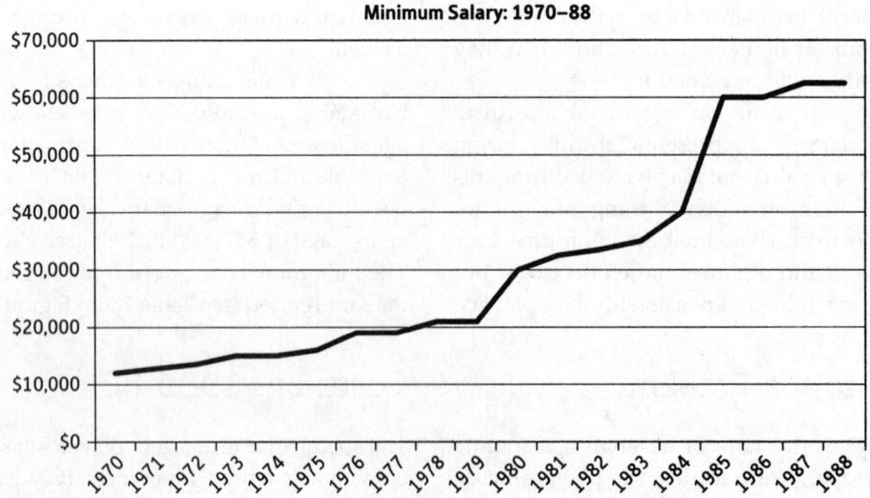

Figure 1

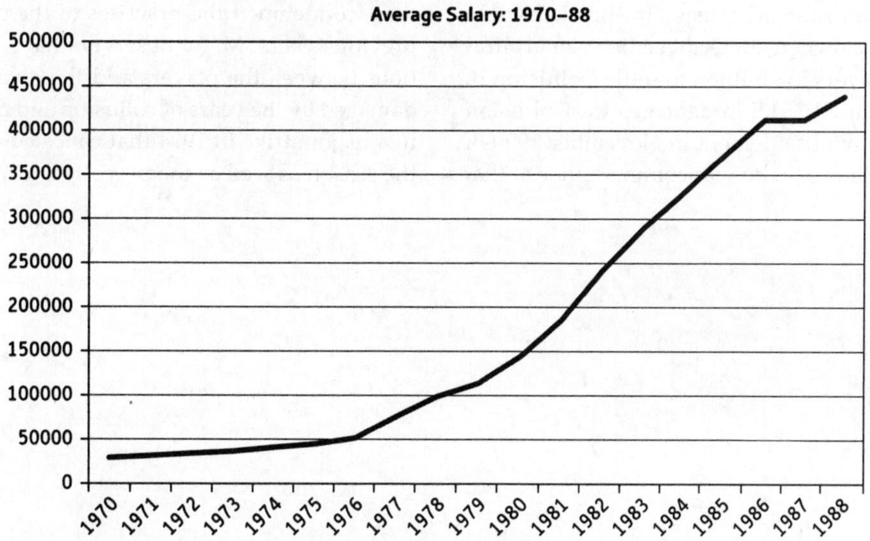

Figure 2

period, but some teams were struggling financially. Some baseball executives were especially concerned that, collectively, teams had over $50 million in financial obligations to players who could no longer play due to injury. Long-term contracts were also a concern. Some team executives claimed that players were less productive after signing such contracts.

These tensions led some baseball executives to urge the need for self-restraint in signing free agents. Baseball's new commissioner, Peter Ueberroth was particularly aggressive in encouraging owners to be more conservative in both signing free agents and signing players to long-term contracts. Though Ueberroth was careful to have attorneys caution owners against collusive behavior, considerable pressure was exerted on teams to not sign free agents. Many teams adopted policies against long-term contracts and signing free agents. In the off season between 1985 and 1986, the free agent market was considerably less friendly to players than in previous years. Even some of baseball's biggest stars found that other teams were not interested in signing them. Remarkably, only four of the 35 free agents that year signed with other teams. Those four players were journeymen who were no longer wanted by their previous team. In February 1986, the players' association filed a grievance that came to be known as Collusion I.

The situation did not improve for free agents between the 1986 and 1987 seasons. The teams began to share with each other their intentions concerning free agents from their teams. For example, a team might share with other teams which of their free agents they intended to re-sign. Players argued that this was a signal to other teams not to offer a contract to that player. As with 1986, only four free agents switched teams in 1987. That year also marked the first time in the free agency era that average player salaries had not increased from one year to the next. The MLBPA responded by filing a second grievance, known as Collusion II.

In September 1987, an arbitrator ruled that, in part because of the precipitous drop in offers of contracts to free agents, the owners had been guilty of collusion between the 1985 and 1986 seasons. However, the arbitrator did not decide on the amount of damages at that time. The owners took this as a signal to offer contracts to more free agents after the 1987 season. Many of these offers merely matched the offers of the player's current team. Other offers for free agents were for less than the player's offer from his current team. Not surprisingly, the players filed a third grievance in January of 1988, termed Collusion III. By this time, however, the owner's coordination was showing some cracks. Some owners pursued desirable free agents out of self-interest and were slow to inform their peers about their intentions and actions. Team profitability had improved also. The ease of economic pressures led some teams to increase their focus on winning, which led to more competition for free agents.

Subsequent arbitrator rulings hastened the breakdown of collusion among the owners. In October 1989, an arbitrator awarded the players $38 million to settle Collusion II. Later arbitrators added $64.5 in damages for Collusion III followed by the final settlement in November 1990 of $280 million. Fay Vincent, who was commissioner at that time, condemned the practices of the owners during the previous years. Many observers have claimed that relations between the players and the owners were severely damaged by the years of collusion and contributed greatly to a major strike in 1994 that canceled the last months of the season as well as the playoffs and World Series.

PART

3 CORPORATE STRATEGIES

CHAPTER

8 Vertical Integration

LEARNING OBJECTIVES

After reading this chapter, you should be able to:

8.1 Define corporate strategy.

8.2 Define vertical integration, forward vertical integration, and backward vertical integration.

8.3 Discuss how vertical integration can create value by:

a. reducing the threat of opportunism;
b. enabling a firm to exploit its valuable, rare, and costly-to-imitate resources and capabilities;
c. enabling a firm to retain its flexibility.

8.4 Describe conditions under which vertical integration can be a source of sustained competitive advantage.

8.5 Describe how the functional organization structure, management controls, and compensation policies are used to implement vertical integration.

JSW Steel's Strategic Mastery

JSW Steel, an integral player in the global steel production market, has demonstrated adeptness in navigating the complexities of the industry through a comprehensive vertical integration strategy. Founded by the Jindals in 1982, the company has grown to become a cornerstone of the steel sector, not only in its home country of India but also on an international scale. The company's vertical integration strategy is meticulously designed to control the entire production process, from raw material acquisition to manufacturing and distribution, allowing JSW Steel to mitigate the volatility of raw material prices and maintain a competitive edge in the market. This strategic approach has been instrumental in the company's ability to expand its operational capacity and maintain financial resilience amidst the cyclical nature of the steel industry.

A pivotal aspect of JSW Steel's strategy is its focus on both greenfield and brownfield capacity expansions, alongside selective inorganic growth opportunities, to bolster its manufacturing capabilities. The company embarked on significant capital expenditure projects, such as the 5 MTPA (million tonnes per annum) Dolvi expansion project, which commenced integrated operations in FY 2021–22 and achieved full ramp-up within a year. Furthermore, JSW Steel has committed to expanding its capacity at Vijayanagar and BPSL (Bhushan Power & Steel Ltd.), aiming to reach a steelmaking capacity of 38.5 MTPA by FY 2024–25, with a long-term vision of achieving 50 MTPA capacity in India by FY 2030–31. Strategic acquisitions and joint ventures have also played a crucial role in JSW Steel's growth narrative. The company's acquisition of ACCIL (Asian Colour Coated Ispat Ltd.) and BPSL, alongside partnerships with international firms like Severfield UK PLC and Marubeni-Itochu Steel, has not only expanded JSW Steel's product portfolio but also enhanced its global footprint and raw material security.

JSW Steel's commitment to sustainability and innovation is evident in its strategic priorities, which include diversification of product profiles, backward integration for raw material security, focus on resource optimization, and prudent financial management. These initiatives underscore the company's dedication to maintaining an optimal capital mix, diversifying its debt profile, and leveraging digital technologies to enhance operational efficiencies. JSW Steel's strategic focus on vertical integration, capacity expansion, strategic acquisitions, and sustainability has positioned it favourably within the global steel production market. The company's ability to adapt and innovate, coupled with its strategic investments, and focus on operational efficiency, will continue to drive its growth and competitiveness in the years to come.

REFERENCES

JSW Steel (2023). *Strategic growth*. Accessed from https://www.jswsteel.in on March 20, 2024.

JSW Steel (2022). *Our strategic priorities.* Accessed from https://www.jswsteel.in on March 20, 2024.

Singh, L. R. (2023). *JSW Steel—Journey with Speed and Innovation*. In Indian Metallurgy: The Platinum Years (pp. 99–103). Singapore: Springer Nature Singapore.

With the decision of vertical integration strategy, the company is able accomplish a specific business function—like controlling the entire production process to mitigate the volatility of raw material prices and maintain a competitive edge—is an example of a decision that determines the level of a firm's vertical integration. This is the case that reflects JSW Steel's focus on sustainability and innovation through strategic vertical integration.

Objective 8.1 Define corporate strategy.

What Is Corporate Strategy?

Vertical integration is the first corporate strategy examined in detail in this book. As suggested in Chapter 1, **business strategy** is a firm's theory of how to gain competitive advantage in a single business or industry. The four business strategies discussed in this book are cost leadership, product differentiation, flexibility, and collusion. **Corporate strategy** is a firm's theory of how to gain competitive advantage by operating in several businesses simultaneously. Decisions about whether to vertically integrate often determine whether a firm is operating in a single business or industry or in multiple businesses or industries. Other corporate strategies discussed in this book include, diversification, strategic alliances, and mergers and acquisitions.

Objective 8.2 Define vertical integration, forward vertical integration, and backward vertical integration.

What Is Vertical Integration?

The concept of a firm's value chain was first introduced in Chapter 3. As a reminder, a **value chain** is that set of activities that must be accomplished to bring a product or service from raw materials to the point that it can be sold to a final customer. A simplified value chain of the oil and gas industry, originally presented in Figure 3.2, is reproduced in Figure 8.1.

A firm's level of **vertical integration** is simply the number of steps in this value chain that a firm accomplishes within its boundaries. Firms that are more vertically integrated accomplish more stages of the value chain within their boundaries than firms that are less vertically integrated. A more sophisticated approach to measuring the degree of a firm's vertical integration is presented in the Strategy in Depth feature.

A firm engages in **backward vertical integration** when it incorporates more stages of the value chain within its boundaries and those stages bring it closer to the beginning of the value chain, that is, closer to gaining access to raw materials. When computer companies developed all their own software, they were engaging in backward vertical integration because these actions are close to the beginning of the value chain. When they began using independent companies operating in India to develop this software, they were less vertically integrated backward.

A firm engages in **forward vertical integration** when it incorporates more stages of the value chain within its boundaries and those stages bring it closer to the end of the value chain; that is, closer to interacting directly with final customers. When companies staffed and operated their own call centers in the United States, they were engaging in forward vertical integration because these activities brought them closer to the ultimate customer. When they started using independent companies in India to staff and operate these centers, they were less vertically integrated forward.

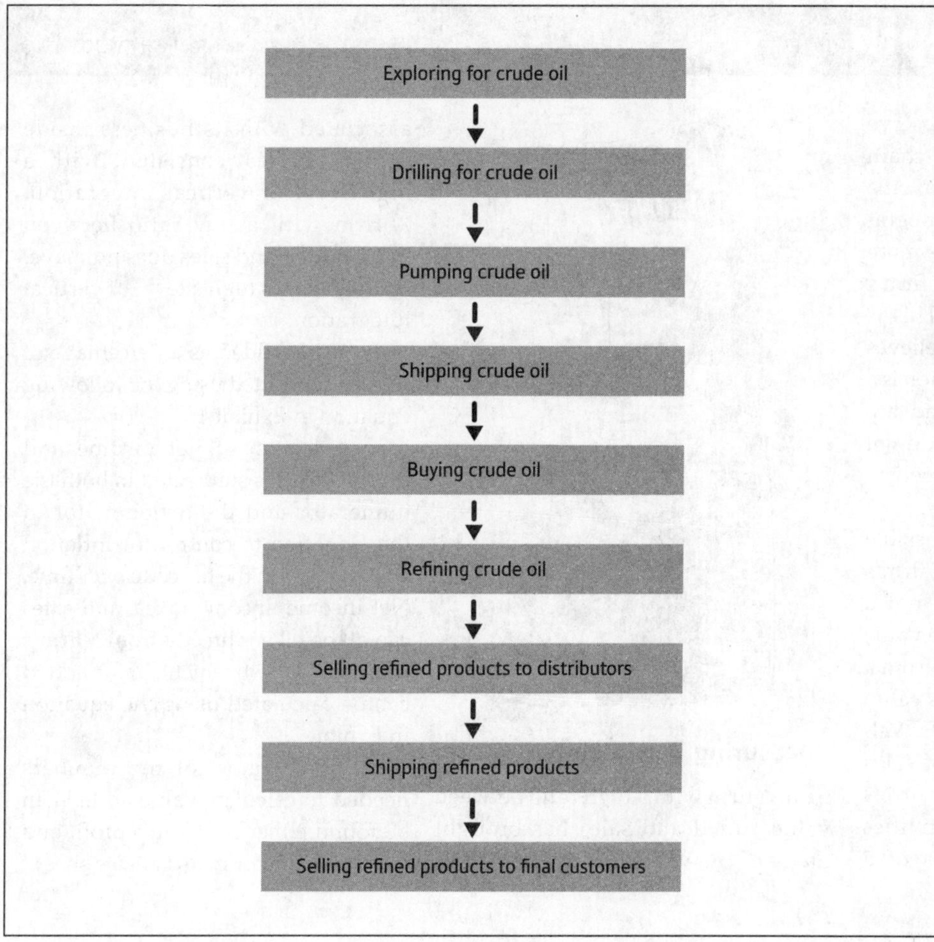

Figure 8.1 A Simplified Value Chain of Activities in the Oil and Gas Industry

Of course, in choosing how to organize its value chain, a firm has more choices than whether to vertically integrate or not vertically integrate. Indeed, between these two extremes a wide range of somewhat vertically integrated options exists. These alternatives include various types of strategic alliances and joint ventures, the primary topic of Chapter 11.

Objective 8.3 Discuss how vertical integration can create value by:

a. reducing the threat of opportunism;
b. enabling a firm to exploit its valuable, rare, and costly-to-imitate resources and capabilities;
c. enabling a firm to retain its flexibility.

The Value of Vertical Integration

The question of vertical integration—which stages of the value chain should be included within a firm's boundaries and why—has been studied by many scholars for almost 100 years. The reason this question has been of such interest was first articulated by Nobel Prize-winning economist Ronald Coase. In a famous article originally published in 1937, Coase asked a simple question: "Given how efficiently markets can be used to organize economic exchanges among thousands, even hundreds of thousands, of separate individuals, why would markets, as a method for managing economic exchanges, ever be replaced by firms? In markets, almost as if by magic, Adam Smith's "invisible hand" coordinates the quantity and quality of goods and services produced with the quantity and

Strategy in Depth

Measuring Vertical Integration

It is sometimes possible to observe which stages of the value chain a firm is engaging in and, thus, the level of that firm's vertical integration. Sometimes, however, it is more difficult to directly observe a firm's level of vertical integration. This is especially true when a firm believes that its level of vertical integration is a potential source of competitive advantage. In this case, the firm would not likely reveal this information freely to competitors.

In this situation, it is possible to get a sense of the degree of a firm's vertical integration—though not a complete list of the steps in the value chain integrated by the firm—from a close examination of the firm's **value added as a percentage of sales.** Valued added as a percentage of sales measures that percentage of a firm's sales that is generated by activities done within the boundaries of a firm. A firm with a high ratio between value added and sales has brought many of the value-creating activities associated with its business inside its boundaries, consistent with a high level of vertical integration. A firm with a low ratio between value added and sales does not have, on average, as high a level of vertical integration.

Value added as a percentage of sales is computed using the following equation in Exhibit 1.

The sum of net income and income taxes is subtracted in both the numerator and the denominator in this equation to control for inflation and changes in the tax code over time. Net income, income taxes, and sales can all be taken directly from a firm's profit and loss statement. Value added can be calculated using the equation in Exhibit 2.

Again, most of the numbers needed to calculate value added can be found either in a firm's profit and loss statement or in its balance sheet.[1]

Exhibit 1

$$\text{vertical integration}_i = \frac{\text{value added}_i - (\text{net income}_i + \text{income taxes}_i)}{\text{sales}_i - (\text{net income}_i + \text{income taxes}_i}$$

where,

$\text{vertical integration}_i$ = the level of vertical integration for firm_i

value added_i = the level of value added for firm_i

net inform_i = the level of net income for firm_i

in come taxes_i = firm_i's income taxes

sales_i = firm_i's sales

Exhibit 2

value added = depreciation + amortization + fixed charges + interest expense + labor and related expenses + pension and retirement expenses + income taxes + net income (after taxes) + rental expense quality of goods and services demanded through the adjustment of prices—all without a centralized controlling authority. However, in firms, centralized bureaucrats monitor and control subordinates who, in turn, battle each other for "turf" and control of inefficient internal "fiefdoms." Why would the "beauty" of the invisible hand ever be replaced by the clumsy "visible hand" of the modern corporation?"[2]

Coase began to answer his own question when he observed that sometimes the cost of using a market to manage an economic exchange must be higher than the cost of using vertical integration and bringing an exchange within the boundary of a firm. Over the years, efforts have focused on identifying the conditions under which this would be the case. The resulting work has described several different situations where vertical integration can either increase a firm's revenues or decrease its costs compared with not vertically integrating, that is, several situations where vertical integration can be valuable. The following sections present three of the most influential of these explanations of when vertical integration can create value for a firm.

Vertical Integration and the Threat of Opportunism

One of the best-known explanations of when vertical integration can be valuable focuses on using vertical integration to reduce the threat of opportunism.[3] **Opportunism** exists when a firm is unfairly exploited in an exchange. Examples of opportunism include when a party to an exchange expects a high level of quality in a product it is purchasing, only to discover it has received a lower level of quality than it expected; when a party to an exchange expects to receive a service by a particular point in time and that service is delivered late (or early); and when a party to an exchange expects to pay a price to complete this exchange and its exchange partner demands a higher price than what was previously agreed.

Obviously, when one of its exchange partners behaves opportunistically, this reduces the economic value of a firm. One way to reduce the threat of opportunism is to bring an exchange within the boundary of a firm, that is, to vertically integrate into this exchange. This way, managers in a firm can monitor and control this exchange instead of relying on the market to manage it. If the exchange that is brought within the boundary of a firm brings a firm closer to its ultimate suppliers, it is an example of backward vertical integration. If the exchange that is brought within the boundary of a firm brings a firm closer to its ultimate customer, it is an example of forward vertical integration.

Of course, firms should only bring market exchanges within their boundaries when the cost of vertical integration is less than the cost of opportunism. If the cost of vertical integration is greater than the cost of opportunism, then firms should not vertically integrate into an exchange. This is the case for both backward and forward vertical integration decisions.

So, when will the threat of opportunism be large enough to warrant vertical integration? Research has shown that the threat of opportunism is greatest when a party to an exchange has made transaction-specific investments. A **transaction-specific investment** is any investment in an exchange that has significantly more value in the current exchange than it does in alternative exchanges. Perhaps the easiest way to understand the concept of a transaction-specific investment is through an example.

Consider the economic exchange between an oil refining company and an oil pipeline building company, which is depicted in Figure 8.2. As can be seen in the figure, this oil refinery is built on the edge of a deep-water bay. Because of this, the refinery has been receiving supplies of crude oil from large tanker ships. However, an oil field exists several miles distant from the refinery, but the only way to transport crude oil from the oil field to the refinery is with trucks—a very expensive way to move crude oil, especially compared to large tankers. But if the oil refining company could find a way to get crude oil from this field cheaply, it would probably make this refinery even more valuable.

Enter the pipeline company. Suppose this pipeline company approaches the refinery and offers to build a pipeline from the oil field to the refinery. In return, all the pipeline company expects is for the refinery to promise to buy a certain number of barrels of crude at an agreed-to price for some period, say, five years, through the pipeline. If reasonable prices can be negotiated, the oil refinery is likely to find this offer attractive, for the cost of crude oil carried by the pipeline is likely to be lower than the cost of crude oil delivered by ship or by truck. Based on this analysis, the refinery and the oil pipeline company are likely to cooperate and the pipeline is likely to be built.

Now, five years go by, and it is time to renegotiate the contract. Which of these two firms has made the largest transaction-specific investments? Remember that a transaction-specific investment is any investment in an exchange that is more valuable in that particular exchange than in alternative exchanges.

What specific investments has the refinery made? Well, how much is this refinery worth if this exchange with the pipeline company is not renewed? Its value would probably drop some because oil through the pipeline is probably cheaper than oil through ships or trucks. So, if the refinery doesn't use the pipeline any

Figure 8.2 The Exchange Between an Oil Refinery and an Oil Pipeline Company

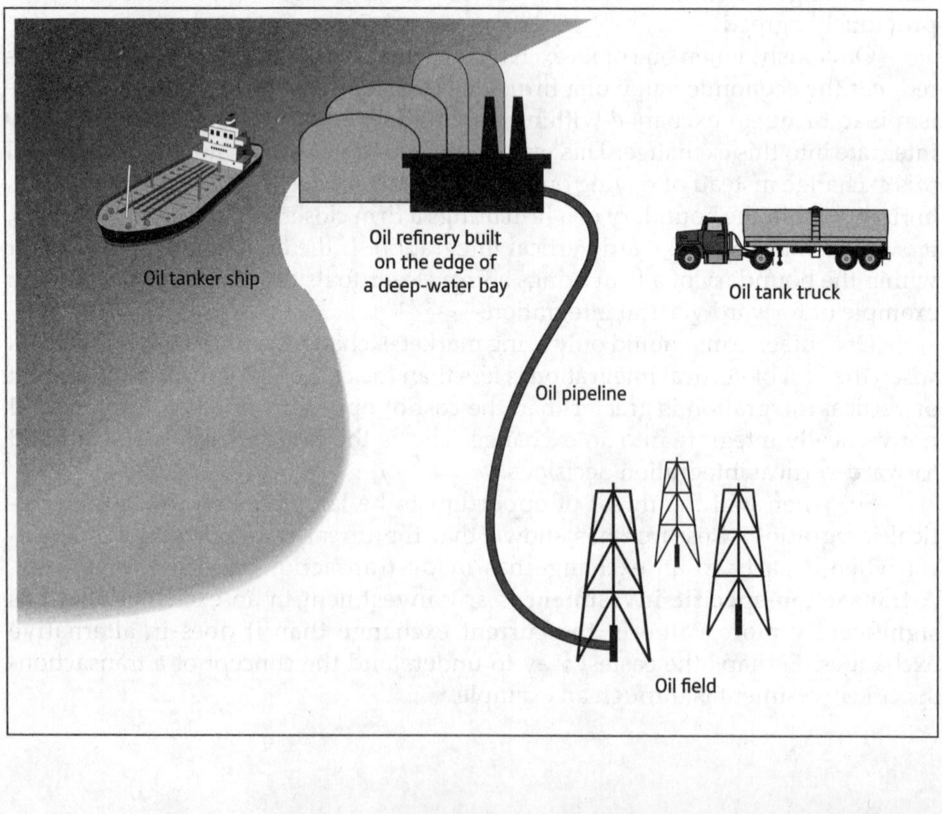

longer, it will have to should use these alternative supplies. This will reduce its value some—say, from $1 million to $900,000. This $100,000 difference is the size of the transaction-specific investment made by the refining company.

However, the transaction-specific investment made by the pipeline firm is probably much larger. Suppose the pipeline is worth $750,000 as long as it is pumping oil to the refinery. But if it is not pumping oil, how much is it worth? Not very much. An oil pipeline that is not pumping oil has limited alternative uses. It has value either as scrap or (perhaps) as the world's largest enclosed water slide. If the value of the pipeline is only $10,000 if it is not pumping oil to the refinery, then the level of transaction-specific investment made by the pipeline firm is substantially larger than that made by the firm that owns the refinery: $750,000 – $10,000 or $740,000, for the pipeline company versus $100,000 for the refining company.

So, which company is at greater risk of opportunism when the contract is renegotiated; the refinery or the pipeline company? Obviously, the pipeline company has more to lose. If it cannot come to an agreement with the oil refining company, it will lose $740,000. If the refinery cannot come to an agreement with the pipeline company, it will lose $100,000. Knowing this, the refining company can squeeze the pipeline company during the renegotiation by insisting on lower prices or more timely deliveries of higher-quality crude oil, and the pipeline company really cannot do much about it.

Of course, managers in the pipeline firm are not stupid. They know that after the first five years of their exchange with the refining company they will be in a very difficult bargaining position. So, in anticipation, they will insist on much higher prices for building the oil pipeline in the first place than would otherwise be the case. This will drive up the cost of building the pipeline, perhaps to the point that it is no longer cheaper than getting crude oil from ships. If this is the case, then the pipeline will not be built, even though if it could be built and the threat of opportunism eliminated, both the refining company and the pipeline company would be better off.

One way to solve this problem is for the oil refining company to buy the oil pipeline company—that is, for the oil refinery to backward vertically integrate.[4] When this happens, the incentive for the oil refinery to exploit the vulnerability of the pipeline company will be reduced. After all, if the refinery business tries to rip off the pipeline business, it only hurts itself because it owns the pipeline business.

This, then, is the essence of opportunism-based explanations of when vertical integration creates value: transaction-specific investments make parties to an exchange vulnerable to opportunism, and vertical integration solves this vulnerability problem. Using language developed in Chapter 2, this approach suggests that vertical integration is valuable when it reduces threats from a firm's powerful suppliers or powerful buyers due to any transaction-specific investments a firm has made.

Vertical Integration and Firm Capabilities

A second approach to vertical integration decisions focuses on a firm's capabilities and its ability to generate sustained competitive advantages.[5] This approach has two broad implications. First, it suggests that firms should vertically integrate into those business activities where they possess valuable, rare, and costly-to-imitate resources and capabilities. This way, firms can appropriate at least some of the profits that using these capabilities to exploit environmental opportunities will create. Second, this approach also suggests that firms should not vertically integrate into business activities where they do not possess the resources necessary to gain competitive advantages. Such vertical integration decisions would not be a source of profits to a firm, because they do not possess any of the valuable, rare, or costly-to-imitate resources needed to gain competitive advantages in these business activities. Indeed, to the extent that some other firms have competitive advantages in these business activities, vertically integrating into them could put a firm at a competitive disadvantage.

This, then, is the essence of the capabilities approach to vertical integration: if a firm possesses valuable, rare, and costly-to-imitate resources in a business activity, it should vertically integrate into that activity; otherwise, no vertical integration. This perspective can sometimes lead to vertical integration decisions that conflict with decisions derived from opportunism-based explanations of vertical integration.

Consider, for example, firms acting as suppliers to Wal-Mart. Wal-Mart has a huge competitive advantage in the discount retail industry. In principle, firms that sell to Wal-Mart could vertically integrate forward into the discount retail market to sell their own products. That is, these firms could begin to compete against Wal-Mart. However, such efforts are not likely to be a source of competitive advantage for these firms. Wal-Mart's resources and capabilities are just too extensive and costly to imitate for most of these suppliers. So, instead of forward vertical integration, most of these firms sell their products through Wal-Mart.

Of course, the problem is that by relying so much on Wal-Mart, these firms are making significant transaction-specific investments. If they stop selling to Wal-Mart, they may go out of business. However, this decision will have a limited impact on Wal-Mart. Wal-Mart can go to any number of suppliers around the world that are willing to replace this failed firm. So, Wal-Mart's suppliers are at risk of opportunism in this exchange, and indeed, it is well-known that Wal-Mart can squeeze its suppliers, in terms of the quality of the products it purchases, the price at which it purchases them, and the way in which these products are delivered.

So, the tension between these two approaches to vertical integration becomes clear. Concerns about opportunism suggest that Wal-Mart's suppliers should vertically integrate forward. Concerns about having a competitive disadvantage if they do vertically integrate forward suggest that Wal-Mart's suppliers should not vertically integrate. So, should they or shouldn't they vertically integrate?

Not many of Wal-Mart's suppliers could resolve this difficult problem. Most do not vertically integrate into the discount retail industry. However, they try to reduce the level of transaction-specific investment they make with Wal-Mart by supplying other discount retailers, both in the United States and abroad. They also try to use their special capabilities to differentiate their products so much that Wal-Mart's customers insist on Wal-Mart selling these products. And these firms constantly search for cheaper ways to make and distribute higher-quality products.

Vertical Integration and Flexibility

A third perspective on vertical integration builds on the concept of flexibility first introduced in Chapter 6. As described in that chapter, **flexibility** refers to how costly it is for a firm to alter its strategic and organizational decisions. Flexibility is high when the cost of changing strategic choices is low; flexibility is low when the cost of changing strategic choices is high.

So, which is less flexible—vertical integration or no vertical integration? Research suggests that, in general, vertically integrating is less flexible than not vertically integrating.[6] This is because once a firm has vertically integrated, it has committed its organizational structure, its management controls, and its compensation policies to a particular vertically integrated way of doing business. Undoing this decision often means changing these aspects of an organization.

Suppose, for example, that a vertically integrated firm decides to get out of a particular business. To do so, the firm must sell or close its factories (actions that can adversely affect both the employees it must lay off and those that remain), alter its supply relationships, hurt customers that have come to rely on it as a partner, and change its internal reporting structure. In contrast, if a non-vertically integrated firm decides to get out of a business, it simply stops. It cancels whatever contracts it might have had in place and ceases operations in that business. The cost of exiting a non-vertically integrated business is generally much lower than the cost of exiting a vertically integrated business.

Of course, flexibility is not always valuable. In fact, as was described in Chapter 6, flexibility is only valuable when the decision-making setting a firm is facing is uncertain. Recall that a decision-making setting is **uncertain** when both the possible outcomes of a decision and their probability cannot be known when a decision is being made. In such settings, less vertical integration is better than more vertical integration. This is because vertically integrating into an exchange is less flexible than not vertically integrating into an exchange. If an exchange turns out not to be valuable, it is usually costlier for firms that have vertically integrated into an exchange to exit that exchange compared with those that have not vertically integrated.

Consider, for example, a pharmaceutical firm making investments in biotechnology. The outcome of biotechnology research is very uncertain. If a pharmaceutical company vertically integrates into a particular type of biotechnology research by hiring particular types of scientists, building an expensive laboratory, and developing the other skills necessary to do this particular type of biotechnology research, it has made a very large investment. Now suppose that this research turns out not to be profitable. This firm has made huge investments that now have little value. As important, it has failed to make investments in other areas of biotechnology that could turn out to be valuable.

A flexibility-based approach to vertical integration suggests that rather than vertically integrating into a business activity whose value is highly uncertain, firms should not vertically integrate but should instead form a strategic alliance to manage this exchange. A strategic alliance is more flexible than vertical integration but still gives a firm enough information about an exchange to estimate its value over time.

An alliance has a second advantage in this setting. The downside risks associated with investing in a strategic alliance are known and fixed. They equal the cost of creating and maintaining the alliance. If an uncertain investment turns out not to be valuable, parties to this alliance know the maximum amount they can lose—an amount equal to the cost of creating and maintaining the alliance. On the other hand, if this exchange turns out to be very valuable, then maintaining an alliance can give a firm access to this huge upside potential. This partially explains why, to the extent that U.S. pharmaceutical firms outsource basic R&D to Indian partners, they do so through joint ventures. These aspects of strategic alliances will be discussed in more detail in Chapter 11.

Each of these explanations of vertical integration has received significant empirical attention in the academic literature. Some of these studies are described in the Research Made Relevant feature.

Applying the Theories to the Management of Call Centers

One of the most common business functions to be outsourced, and even offshored, is a firm's call center activities. So, what do these three theories say about how call centers should be managed: when should they be brought within the boundaries of a firm, and when should they be outsourced? Each of these theories will be discussed in turn.

Transaction-Specific Investments and Managing Call Centers

When applying opportunism-based explanations of vertical integration, start by looking for actual or potential transaction-specific investments that would need to be made to complete an exchange. High levels of such investments suggest the need for vertical integration; low levels of such investments suggest that vertically integrating this exchange is not necessary.

When the call-center approach to providing customer service was first developed in the 1980s, it required substantial levels of transaction-specific investment. First, a great deal of special-purpose equipment had to be purchased. And although this equipment could be used for any call center, it had little value except within a call center. Thus, this equipment was an example of a somewhat specific investment.

More important, to provide service in call centers, call center employees would have to be fully aware of all the problems likely to emerge with the use of

Research Made Relevant

Empirical Tests of Theories of Vertical Integration

Of the three explanations of vertical integration discussed here, opportunism-based explanations are the oldest and thus have received the greatest empirical support. One review of this empirical work, by Professor Joe Mahoney of the University of Illinois, observes that the core assertion of this approach—that high levels of transaction-specific investment lead to higher levels of vertical integration—receives consistent empirical support.

More recent work has begun to examine the trade-offs among these three explanations of vertical integration by examining their effects on vertical integration simultaneously. For example, Professor Tim Folta of Purdue University examined the opportunism and flexibility approaches to vertical integration simultaneously. His results show that the basic assertion of the opportunism approach still holds. However, when he incorporates uncertainty into his empirical analysis, he finds that firms engage in less vertical integration than predicted by opportunism by itself. In other words, firms apparently worry not only about transaction-specific investments when they make vertical integration choices; they also worry about how costly it is to reverse those investments in the face of high uncertainty.

An even more recent study by Michael Leiblein from The Ohio State University and Doug Miller from the University of Illinois examines all three of these explanations of vertical integration simultaneously. These authors studied vertical integration decisions in the semiconductor manufacturing industry and found that all three explanations hold. That is, firms in this industry worry about transaction-specific investment, the capabilities they possess, the capabilities they would like to possess, and the uncertainty of the markets within which they operate when they make vertical integration choices.[7]

a firm's products. This required a firm to study its products very closely and then to train call center employees to be able to respond to any problems customers might have. This training was sometimes very complex and time-consuming and represented substantial transaction-specific investments on the part of call center employees. Only employees that worked full time for a large corporation—where job security was usually high for productive workers—would be willing to make these kinds of specific investments. Thus, vertical integration into call center management made a great deal of sense.

However, as information technology improved, firms found it was possible to train call center employees much faster. Now, all call center employees had to do was follow scripts that were prewritten and preloaded onto their computers. By asking a few scripted questions, call center employees could diagnose most problems. In addition, solutions to those problems were also included on an employee's computer. Only really unusual problems could not be handled by employees working off these computer scripts. Because the level of specific investment required to use these scripts was much lower, employees were willing to work for companies without the job security usually associated with large firms. Indeed, call centers became good part-time and temporary employment opportunities. Because the level of specific investment required to work in these call centers was much lower, not vertically integrating into call center management made a great deal of sense.

Capabilities and Managing Call Centers

In opportunism-based explanations of vertical integration, you start by looking for transaction-specific investments and then make vertical integration decisions based on these investments. In capability-based approaches, you start by looking for valuable, rare, and costly-to-imitate resources and capabilities and then make vertical integration decisions appropriately.

In the early days of call center management, how well a firm operated its call centers could actually be a source of competitive advantage. During this period, the technology was new, and the training required to answer a customer's questions was extensive. Firms that developed special capabilities in managing these processes could gain competitive advantages and thus would vertically integrate into call center management.

However, over time, as more and more call center management suppliers were created and as the technology and training required to staff a call center became more widely available, the ability of a call center to be a source of competitive advantage for a firm dropped. That is, the ability to manage a call center was still valuable, but it was no longer rare or costly to imitate. In this setting, it is not surprising to see firms getting out of the call center management business, outsourcing this business to low-cost specialist firms, and focusing on those business functions where they might be able to gain a sustained competitive advantage.

All of this assumed, of course, that providing high quality on-line service to customers was not a source of competitive advantage. Over the last few years, some firms have found that outsourcing call centers has reduced their ability to address the service needs of some of their customers—particularly those with complicated or unusual problems. To be more effective in providing service to these customers, some firms have actually re-vertically integrated at least some of the call center operations. They do so because they believe providing high quality service can be a source of at least a temporary competitive advantage. A detailed example of Dell Computer re-vertically integrating some of its call center operations will be discussed later in this chapter.[8]

Flexibility and Managing Call Centers

Opportunism logic suggests starting with a search for transaction-specific investments; capabilities logic suggests starting with a search for valuable, rare, and costly-to-imitate resources and capabilities. Flexibility logic suggests starting by looking for sources of uncertainty in an exchange.

One of the biggest uncertainties in providing customer service through call centers is the question of whether the people staffing the phones actually help a firm's customers. This is a particularly troubling concern for firms that are selling complex products that can have numerous types of problems. A variety of technological solutions have been developed to try to address this uncertainty. But, if a firm vertically integrates into the call center management business, it is committing to a particular technological solution. This solution may not work, or it may not work as well as some other solutions.

In the face of this uncertainty, maintaining relationships with several different call-center management companies—each of whom have adopted different technological solutions to the problem of how to use call center employees to assist customers who are using very complex products—gives a firm technological flexibility that it would not otherwise have. Once a superior solution is identified, then a firm no longer needs this flexibility and may choose to vertically integrate into call center management or not, depending on opportunism and capabilities considerations.

Integrating Different Theories of Vertical Integration

At first glance, having three different explanations about how vertical integration can create value seems troubling. After all, won't these explanations sometimes contradict each other?

The answer to this question is yes. We have already seen such a contradiction in the case of opportunism and capabilities explanations of whether Wal-Mart suppliers should forward vertically integrate into the discount retail industry.

However, more often than not, these three explanations are complementary in nature. That is, each approach generally leads to the same conclusion about how a firm should vertically integrate. Moreover, sometimes it is simply easier to apply one of these approaches to evaluate a firm's vertical integration choices than the other two. Having a "tool kit" that includes three explanations of vertical integration enables the analyst to choose the approach that is most likely to be a source of insight in a particular situation.

Even when these explanations make contradictory assertions about vertical integration, having multiple approaches can be helpful. In this context, having multiple explanations can highlight the trade-offs that a firm is making when choosing its vertical integration strategy. Thus, for example, if opportunism-based explanations suggest that vertical integration is necessary because of high transaction-specific investments, capabilities-based explanations caution about the cost of developing the resources and capabilities necessary to vertically integrate and flexibility concerns caution about the risks that committing to vertical integration imply, and the costs and benefits of whatever vertical integration decision is ultimately made can be understood very clearly.

Overall, having three explanations of vertical integration has several advantages for those looking to analyze the vertical integration choices of real firms. Of course, applying these explanations can create important ethical dilemmas for a firm, especially when it becomes clear that a firm needs to become less vertically integrated than it has historically been. Some of these dilemmas are discussed in the Ethics and Strategy feature.

Vertical Integration and Sustained Competitive Advantage

Objective 8.4 Describe conditions under which vertical integration can be a source of sustained competitive advantage.

Of course, for vertical integration to be a source of sustained competitive advantage, not only must it be valuable (because it responds to threats of opportunism; enables a firm to exploit its own or other firms' valuable, rare, and costly-to-imitate resources; or gives a firm flexibility), it must also be rare and costly to imitate, and a firm must be organized to implement it correctly.

The Rarity of Vertical Integration

A firm's vertical integration strategy is rare when few competing firms can create value by vertically integrating in the same way. A firm's vertical integration strategy can be rare because it is one of a small number of competing firms that can vertically integrate efficiently or because it is one of a small number of firms that is able to adopt a non-vertically integrated approach to managing an exchange.

Rare Vertical Integration

A firm may be able to create value through vertical integration, when most of its competitors are not able to, for at least three reasons. Not surprisingly, these reasons parallel the three explanations of vertical integration presented in this chapter.

Rare Transaction-Specific Investment and Vertical Integration First, a firm may have developed a new technology or a new approach to doing business that requires its business partners to make substantial transaction-specific investments. Firms that engage in these activities will find it in their self-interest to vertically integrate, whereas firms that have not engaged in these activities will not find it in their self-interest to vertically integrate. If these activities are rare and costly to imitate, they can be a source of competitive advantage for a vertically integrating firm.

For example, many firms in the computer industry are offshoring some of their key business functions. However, one firm—Dell—brought one of these functions—its technical call center for business customers—back from India and re-vertically integrated it into its business function.[9] The problems faced by corporate customers are typically much more complicated than those faced by individual consumers. Thus, it is much more difficult to provide call center employees with the training they need to address corporate problems. Moreover, because corporate technologies change more rapidly than many consumer technologies, keeping call-center employees up to date on how to service corporate customers is also more complicated than having call center employees provide services to its non-corporate

Ethics and Strategy

Imagine a firm that has successfully operated in a vertically integrated manner for decades. Employees come to work, they know their jobs, they know how to work together effectively, they know where to park. The job is not just the economic center of their lives; it has become the social center as well. Most of their friends work in the same company, in the same function, as they do. The future appears to be much as the past—stable employment and effective work, all aiming toward a comfortable and well-planned retirement. And then the firm adopts a new outsourcing strategy. It changes its vertical integration strategy by becoming less vertically integrated and purchasing services from outside suppliers that it used to obtain internally.

The economics of outsourcing can be compelling. Outsourcing can help firms reduce costs and focus their efforts on those business functions that are central to their competitive advantage. When done well, outsourcing creates value—value that firms can share with their owners, their stockholders.

The Ethics of Outsourcing

Indeed, outsourcing is becoming a trend in business. Some observers predict that by 2015, an additional 3.3 million jobs in the United States will be outsourced, many to operations overseas.

But what of the employees whose jobs are taken away? What of their lifetime of commitment, their steady and reliable work? What of their stable and secure retirement? Outsourcing often devastates lives, even as it creates economic value. Of course, some firms go out of their way to soften the impact of outsourcing on their employees. Those that are near retirement age are often given an opportunity to retire early. Others receive severance payments in recognition of their years of service. Other firms hire "outplacement" companies—firms that specialize in placing suddenly unemployed people in new jobs and new careers.

But all these efforts to soften the blow do not make the blow go away. Many employees assume that they have an implicit contract with the firms they work for. That contract is: "As long as I do my job well, I will have a job." That contract is being replaced with: "As long as a firm wants to employ me, I will have a job." In such a world, it is not surprising that many employees now look first to maintain their employability in their current job—by receiving additional training and experiences that might be valuable at numerous other employers—and are concerned less with what they can do to improve the performance of the firm they work for.[10]

customers. Because Dell needs the people staffing its corporate call centers to make substantial specific investments in its technology and in understanding its customers, it has found it necessary to bring these individuals within the boundaries of the firm and to re-vertically integrate the operation of this particular type of service center.

If Dell, through this vertical integration decision, can satisfy its customers more effectively than its competitors and if the cost of managing this call center is not too high, then this vertical integration decision is both valuable and rare and thus a source of at least a temporary competitive advantage for Dell.

Rare Capabilities and Vertical Integration A firm such as Dell might also conclude that it has unusual skills, either in operating a call center or in providing the training that is needed to staff certain kinds of call centers. If those capabilities are valuable and rare, then vertically integrating into businesses that exploit these capabilities can enable a firm to gain at least a temporary competitive advantage. Indeed, the belief that a firm possesses valuable and rare capabilities is often a justification for rare vertical integration decisions in an industry.

Rare Uncertainty and Vertical Integration Finally, a firm may be able to gain an advantage from vertically integrating when it resolves some uncertainty it faces sooner than its competition. Suppose, for example, that several firms in an industry all begin investing in a very uncertain technology. Flexibility logic suggests that, to the extent possible, these firms will prefer to not vertically integrate into the manufacturing of this technology until its designs and features stabilize and market demand for this technology is well established.

However, imagine that one of these firms can resolve these uncertainties before any other firm. This firm no longer needs to retain the flexibility that is so valuable under conditions of uncertainty. Instead, this firm might be able to, say, design special-purpose machines that can efficiently manufacture this technology. Such machines are not flexible, but they can be very efficient.

Of course, outside vendors would have to make substantial transaction-specific investments to use these machines. Outside vendors may be reluctant to make these investments. In this setting, this firm may find it necessary to vertically integrate to be able to use its machines to produce this technology. Thus, this firm, by resolving uncertainty faster than its competitors, can gain some of the advantages of vertical integration sooner than its competitors. Whereas the competition is still focusing on flexibility in the face of uncertainty, this firm gets to focus on production efficiency in meeting customers' product demands. This can obviously be a source of competitive advantage.

Rare Vertical Dis-Integration

Each of the examples of vertical integration and competitive advantage described so far has focused on a firm's ability to vertically integrate to create competitive advantage. However, firms can also gain competitive advantages through their decisions to vertically dis-integrate, that is, through the decision to outsource an activity that used to be within the boundaries of the firm. Whenever a firm is among the first in its industry to conclude that the level of specific investment required to manage an economic exchange is no longer high, or that a particular exchange is no longer rare or costly to imitate, or that the level of uncertainty about the value of an exchange has increased, it may be among the first in its industry to vertically dis-integrate this exchange. Such activities, to the extent they are valuable, will be rare and, thus, a source of at least a temporary competitive advantage.

The Imitability of Vertical Integration

The extent to which these rare vertical integration decisions can be sources of sustained competitive advantage depends, as always, on the imitability of the rare resources that give a firm at least a temporary competitive advantage. Both direct duplication and substitution can be used to imitate another firm's valuable and rare vertical integration choices.

Direct Duplication of Vertical Integration

Direct duplication occurs when competitors develop or obtain the resources and capabilities that enable another firm to implement a valuable and rare vertical integration strategy. To the extent that these resources and capabilities are path dependent, socially complex, or causally ambiguous, they may be immune from direct duplication and, thus, a source of sustained competitive advantage.

With respect to offshoring business functions, it seems that the very popularity of this strategy suggests that it is highly imitable. Indeed, this strategy is becoming so common that firms that move in the other direction by vertically integrating a call center and managing it in the United States (like Dell) make news.

But the fact that many firms are implementing this strategy does not mean that they are all equally successful in doing so. These differences in performance may reflect some subtle and complex capabilities that some of these outsourcing firms possess but others do not. These are the kinds of resources and capabilities that may be sources of sustained competitive advantage.

Some of the resources that might enable a firm to implement a valuable and rare vertical integration strategy may not be susceptible to direct duplication. These might include a firm's ability to analyze the attributes of its economic exchanges and its ability to conceive and implement vertical integration strategies. Both of these capabilities may be socially complex and path dependent—built up over years of experience.

Substitutes for Vertical Integration

The major substitute for vertical integration—strategic alliances—is the major topic of Chapter 11. An analysis of how strategic alliances can substitute for vertical integration will be delayed until then.

Objective 8.5 Describe how the functional organization structure, management controls, and compensation policies are used to implement vertical integration.

Organizing to Implement Vertical Integration

Organizing to implement vertical integration involves the same organizing tools as implementing any business or corporate strategy: organizational structure, management controls, and compensation policies.

Organizational Structure and Implementing Vertical Integration

The organizational structure that is used to implement the first two business level strategies discussed in this book—cost leadership and product differentiation—is also used to implement a vertical integration strategy. This is the functional, or U-form, structure. Indeed, each of the exchanges included within the boundaries of a firm because vertical integration decisions are incorporated into one of the functions in a functional organizational structure. Decisions about which manufacturing activities to vertically integrate into determine the range and responsibilities of the manufacturing function within a functionally organized firm; decisions about which marketing activities to vertically integrate into determine the range and responsibilities of the marketing function within a functionally organized firm; and so forth. Thus, in an important sense, vertical integration decisions made by a firm determine the structure of a functionally organized firm.

The chief executive officer (CEO) in this vertically integrated, functionally organized firm has the same two responsibilities that were first identified in Chapter 4: strategy formulation and strategy implementation. However, these two responsibilities take on added dimensions when implementing vertical integration decisions. In particular, although the CEO must take the lead in making decisions about whether each individual function should be vertically integrated into a firm, this person must also work to resolve conflicts that naturally arise between vertically integrated functions.

Resolving Functional Conflicts in a Vertically Integrated Firm

From a CEO's perspective, coordinating functional specialists to implement a vertical integration strategy almost always involves conflict resolution. Conflicts among functional managers in a U-form organization are both expected and normal. Indeed, if there is no conflict among certain functional managers in a U-form organization, then some of these managers probably are not doing their jobs. The task facing the CEO is not to pretend this conflict does not exist or to ignore it, but to manage it in a way that facilitates strategy implementation.

Consider, for example, the relationship between manufacturing and sales managers. Typically, manufacturing managers prefer to manufacture a single product with long production runs. Sales managers, however, generally prefer to sell numerous customized products. Manufacturing managers generally do not like large inventories of finished products; sales managers generally prefer large inventories of finished products that facilitate rapid deliveries to customers. If these various interests of manufacturing and sales managers do not, at least sometimes, come into conflict in a vertically integrated U-form organization, then the manufacturing manager is not focusing enough on cost reduction and quality improvement in manufacturing or the sales manager is not focusing enough on meeting customer needs in a timely way or both.

Numerous other conflicts arise among functional managers in a vertically integrated U-form organization. Accountants often focus on maximizing managerial accountability and close analysis of costs; research and development managers may fear that such accounting practices will interfere with innovation and creativity. Finance managers often focus on the relationship between a firm and its external capital markets; human resource managers are more concerned with the relationship between a firm and external labor markets.

In this context, the CEO's job is to help resolve conflicts in ways that facilitate the implementation of the firm's strategy. Functional managers do not have to "like" one another. However, if a firm's vertical integration strategy is correct, the reason that a function has been included within the boundaries of a firm is that this decision creates value for the firm. Allowing functional conflicts to get in the way of taking advantage of each of the functions within a firm's boundaries can destroy this potential value.

Management Controls and Implementing Vertical Integration

Although having the correct organizational structure is important for firms implementing their vertical integration strategies, that structure must be supported by a variety of management control processes. Among the most important of these processes are the budgeting process and the management committee oversight process, which can also help CEOs resolve the functional conflicts that are common within vertically integrated firms.

The Budgeting Process

Budgeting is one of the most important control mechanisms available to CEOs in vertically integrated U-form organizations. Indeed, in most U-form companies, enormous management effort goes into the creation of budgets and the evaluation of performance relative to budgets. Budgets are developed for costs, revenues, and a variety of other activities performed by a firm's functional managers. Often, managerial compensation and promotion opportunities depend on the ability of a manager to meet budget expectations.

Although budgets are an important control tool, they can also have unintended negative consequences. For example, the use of budgets can lead functional managers to overemphasize short-term behavior that is easy to measure and underemphasize longer-term behavior that is more difficult to measure. Thus, for example, the strategically correct thing for a functional manager to do might be to increase expenditures for maintenance and management training, thereby ensuring that the function will have both the technology and the skilled people needed to do the job in the future. An overemphasis on meeting current budget requirements, however, might lead this manager to delay maintenance and training expenditures. By meeting short-term budgetary demands, this manager may be sacrificing the long-term viability of this function, compromising the long-term viability of the firm.

CEOs can do a variety of things to counter the "short-termism" effects of the budgeting process. For example, research suggests that evaluating a functional manager's performance relative to budgets can be an effective control device when: (1) the process used in developing budgets is open and participative; (2) the process reflects the economic reality facing functional managers and the firm; and (3) quantitative evaluations of a functional manager's performance are augmented by qualitative evaluations of that performance. Adopting an open and participative process for setting budgets helps ensure that budget targets are realistic and that functional managers understand and accept them. Including qualitative criteria for evaluation reduces the chances that functional managers will engage in behaviors that are very harmful in the long run but enable them to make budget in the short run.[11]

The Management Committee Oversight Process

In addition to budgets, vertically integrated U-form organizations can use various internal management committees as management control devices. Two particularly common internal management committees are the **executive committee** and the **operations committee** (although these committees have many different names in different organizations).

The executive committee in a U-form organization typically consists of the CEO and two or three key functional senior managers. It normally meets weekly and reviews the performance of the firm on a short-term basis. Functions represented on this committee generally include accounting, legal, and other functions (such as manufacturing or sales) that are most central to the firm's short-term business success. The fundamental purpose of the executive committee is to track the short-term performance of the firm, to note and correct any budget variances for functional managers, and to respond to any crises that might emerge. Obviously, the executive committee can help avoid many functional conflicts in a vertically integrated firm before they arise.

In addition to the executive committee, another group of managers meets regularly to help control the operations of the firm. Often called the *operations committee*, this committee typically meets monthly and usually consists of the CEO and each of the heads of the functional areas included in the firm. The executive committee is a subset of the operations committee.

The primary objective of the operations committee is to track firm performance over time intervals slightly longer than the weekly interval of primary interest to the executive committee and to monitor longer-term strategic investments and activities. Such investments might include plant expansions, the introduction of new products, and the implementation of cost-reduction or quality improvement programs. The operations committee provides a forum in which senior functional managers can come together to share concerns and opportunities and to coordinate efforts to implement strategies. Obviously, the operations committee can help resolve functional conflicts in a vertically integrated firm after they arise.

In addition to these two standing committees, various other committees and task forces can be organized within the U-form organization to manage specific projects and tasks. These additional groups are typically chaired by a member of the executive or operations committee and report to one or both of these standing committees, as warranted.

Compensation in Implementing Vertical Integration Strategies

Organizational structure and management control systems can have an important impact on the ability of a firm to implement its vertical integration strategy. However, a firm's compensation policies can be important as well.

We have already seen how compensation can play a role in implementing cost leadership and product differentiation and how compensation can be tied to budgets to help implement vertical integration. However, the three explanations of vertical integration presented in this chapter have important compensation implications as well. We will first discuss the compensation challenges these three explanations suggest and then discuss ways these challenges can be addressed.

Opportunism-Based Vertical Integration and Compensation Policy

Opportunism-based approaches to vertical integration suggest that employees who make firm-specific investments in their jobs will often be able to create more value for a firm than employees who do not. Firm-specific investments are a type of transaction-specific investment. Whereas transaction-specific investments are investments that have more value in a particular exchange than in alternative exchanges, **firm-specific investments** are investments made by employees that have more value in a particular firm than in alternative firms.[12]

Examples of firm-specific investments include an employee's understanding of a particular firm's culture, his or her personal relationships with others in the firm, and an employee's knowledge about a firm's unique business processes. All this knowledge can be used by an employee to create a great deal of value in a firm. However, this knowledge has almost no value in other firms. The effort to create this knowledge is thus a firm-specific investment.

Despite the value that an employee's firm-specific investments can create, opportunism-based explanations of vertical integration suggest that employees will often be reluctant to make these investments because, once they do, they become vulnerable in their exchange with this firm. For example, an employee who has made very significant firm-specific investments may not be able to quit and go to work for another company, even if he or she is passed over for promotion, does not receive a raise, or is even actively discriminated against. This is because by quitting this firm, this employee loses all the investment he or she made in this particular firm. Because this employee has few employment options other than his or her current firm, this firm can treat this employee badly and the employee can do little about it. Therefore, employees are often reluctant to make firm-specific investments.

But the firm needs its employees to make such investments if it is to realize its full economic potential. Thus, one of the tasks of compensation policy is to create incentives for employees whose firm-specific investments could create great value to actually make those investments.

Capabilities and Compensation

Capability explanations of vertical integration also acknowledge the importance of firm-specific investments in creating value for a firm. Indeed, many of the valuable, rare, and costly-to-imitate resources and capabilities that can exist in a firm are a manifestation of firm-specific investments made by a firm's employees. However, whereas opportunism explanations of vertical integration tend to focus on firm-specific investments made by individual employees, capabilities explanations tend to focus on firm-specific investments made by groups of employees.[13]

In Chapter 3, it was suggested that one of the reasons that a firm's valuable and rare resources may be costly to imitate is that these resources are socially complex in nature. Socially complex resources reflect the teamwork, cooperation, and culture that have evolved within a firm—capabilities that can increase the value of a firm significantly, but capabilities that other firms will often find costly to imitate, at least in the short to medium term. Moreover, these are capabilities that exist because several employees—not just a single employee—have made specific investments in a firm.

From the point of view of designing a compensation policy, capabilities analysis suggests that not only should a firm's compensation policy encourage employees whose firm-specific investments could create value to actually make those investments; it also recognizes that these investments will often be collective in nature—that, for example, until all the members of a critical management team make firm-specific commitments to that team, that team's ability to create and sustain competitive advantages will be significantly limited.

Flexibility and Compensation

Flexibility explanations of vertical integration also have some important implications for compensation. In particular, because the creation of flexibility in a firm depends on employees being willing to engage in activities that have fixed and known downside risks and significant upside potential, it follows that compensation that has fixed and known downside risks and significant upside potential would encourage employees to choose and implement flexible vertical integration strategies.

Compensation Alternatives

Table 8.1 lists several compensation alternatives and how they are related to each of the three explanations of vertical integration discussed in this chapter. Not surprisingly, opportunism-based explanations suggest that compensation that focuses on individual employees and how they can make firm-specific investments will be important for firms implementing their vertical integration

TABLE 8.1 Types of Compensation and Approaches to Making Vertical Integration Decisions

Opportunism explanations	Salary Cash bonuses for individual performance Stock grants for individual performance
Capabilities explanations	Cash bonuses for corporate or group performance Stock grants for corporate or group performance
Flexibility explanations	Stock options for individual, corporate, or group performance

strategies. Such individual compensation includes an employee's salary, cash bonuses based on individual performance, and **stock grants**—or payments to employees in a firm's stock—based on individual performance.

Capabilities explanations of vertical integration suggest that compensation that focuses on groups of employees making firm-specific investments in valuable, rare, and costly-to-imitate resources and capabilities will be particularly important for firms implementing vertical integration strategies. Such collective compensation includes cash bonuses based on a firm's overall performance and stock grants based on a firm's overall performance.

Finally, flexibility logic suggests that compensation that has a fixed and known downside risk and significant upside potential is important for firms implementing vertical integration strategies. **Stock options,** whereby employees are given the right, but not the obligation, to purchase stock at predetermined prices, are a form of compensation that has these characteristics. Stock options can be granted based on an individual employee's performance or the performance of the firm as a whole.

The task facing CEOs looking to implement a vertical integration strategy through compensation policy is to determine what kinds of employee behavior they need to have for this strategy to create sustained competitive advantages and then to use the appropriate compensation policy. Not surprisingly, most CEOs find that all three explanations of vertical integration are important in their decision making. Thus, not surprisingly, many firms adopt compensation policies that feature a mix of the compensation policies listed in Table 6.1. Most firms use both individual and corporate-wide compensation schemes along with salaries, cash bonuses, stock grants, and stock options for employees who have the greatest impact on a firm's overall performance.

Summary

Vertical integration is defined as the number of stages in an industry's value chain that a firm has brought within its boundaries. Forward vertical integration brings a firm closer to its ultimate customer; backward vertical integration brings a firm closer to the sources of its raw materials. In making vertical integration decisions for a particular business activity, firms can choose to be not vertically integrated, somewhat vertically integrated, or vertically integrated.

Vertical integration can create value in three different ways: first, it can reduce opportunistic threats from a firm's buyers and suppliers due to transaction-specific investments the firm may have made. A transaction-specific investment is an investment that has more value in a particular exchange than in any alternative exchanges. Second, vertical integration can create value by enabling a firm to exploit its valuable, rare, and costly-to-imitate resources and capabilities. Firms should vertically integrate into activities in which they enjoy such advantages and should not vertically integrate into other activities. Third, vertical integration typically only creates value under conditions of low uncertainty. Under high uncertainty, vertical integration can commit a firm to a costly-to-reverse course of action and the flexibility of a non-vertically integrated approach may be preferred.

Often, all three approaches to vertical integration will generate similar conclusions. However, even when they suggest different vertical integration strategies, they can still be helpful to management.

The ability of valuable vertical integration strategies to generate a sustained competitive advantage depends on how rare and costly to imitate the strategies are. Vertical integration strategies can be rare in two ways: (1) when a firm is vertically integrated while most competing firms are not vertically integrated; and (2) when a firm is not vertically integrated while most competing firms are. These rare vertical integration strategies are possible when firms vary in the extent to which the strategies they pursue require transaction-specific investments; they vary in the resources and capabilities they control; or they vary in the level of uncertainty they face.

The ability to directly duplicate a firm's vertical integration strategies depends on how costly it is to directly duplicate the resources and capabilities that enable a firm to pursue these strategies. The closest substitute for vertical integration—strategic alliances—is discussed in more detail in Chapter 11.

Organizing to implement vertical integration depends on a firm's organizational structure, its management controls, and its compensation policies. The organizational structure most commonly used to implement vertical integration is the functional, or U-form, organization, which involves cost leadership and product differentiation strategies. In a vertically integrated U-form organization, the CEO must focus not only on deciding which functions to vertically integrate into, but also on how to resolve conflicts that inevitably arise in a functionally organized vertically integrated firm. Two management controls that can be used to help implement vertical integration strategies and resolve these functional conflicts are the budgeting process and management oversight committees.

Each of the three explanations of vertical integration suggests different kinds of compensation policies that a firm looking to implement vertical integration should pursue. Opportunism-based explanations suggest individual-based compensation—including salaries and cash bonus and stock grants based on individual performance; capabilities-based explanations suggest group-based compensation—including cash bonuses and stock grants based on corporate or group performance; and flexibility-based explanations suggest flexible compensation—including stock options based on individual, group, or corporate performance. Because all three approaches to vertical integration are often operating in a firm, it is not surprising that many firms employ all these devices in compensating employees whose actions are likely to have a significant impact on firm performance.

Challenge Questions

8.1. Some firms have engaged in backward vertical integration strategies to appropriate the economic profits that would have been earned by suppliers selling to them. How is this motivation for backward vertical integration related to the opportunism logic for vertical integration described in this chapter? (Hint: Compare the competitive conditions under which firms may earn economic profits to the competitive conditions under which firms will be motivated to avoid opportunism through vertical integration.)

8.2. Recently, a home delivery shaving company, "Harry's Razors" claimed it can sell higher-quality razors at a lower price because it owned the factory that makes the razors. What conditions must hold for this assertion to be true?

8.3. How is buying a car (as opposed to leasing a car) like and unlike vertical integration decisions? Suppose you are about to purchase a used car. What kinds of threats do you face in this purchase and what can you do to protect yourself from the threats in this situation? Suppose you are about to purchase a new car. What kinds of threats do you face in this purchase and what can you do to protect yourself from the threats in this situation?

8.4. What are the competitive implications for firms if they assume that all potential exchange partners cannot be trusted?

8.5. Common conflicts between sales and manufacturing are mentioned in the text. What conflicts might exist between other functional areas? Consider the following pairings: research and development and manufacturing; finance and manufacturing; marketing and sales; and accounting and everyone else?

8.6. What could a CEO do to help resolve the conflicts found between functional areas of the organization?

8.7. Under what conditions would you accept a lower-paying job over a higher-paying one?

8.8. What implications does your accepting a lower-paying job over a higher-paying one have for your potential employer's compensation policy?

Problem Set

8.9. Which of the following two firms is more vertically integrated? How can you tell?

(a) Firm A has included manufacturing, sales, finance, and human resources within its boundaries and has outsourced legal and customer service.

(b) Firm B has included manufacturing, sales, legal, and customer service within its boundaries and has outsourced finance and human resources.

8.10. What is the level of transaction-specific investment for each firm in the following transactions? Who in these transactions is at greater risk of being taken unfair advantage of?

(a) Firm I has built a plant right next door to Firm II. Firm I's plant is worth $5 million if it supplies Firm II. It is worth $200,000 if it does not supply Firm II. Firm II has three alternative suppliers. If it receives supplies from Firm I, it is worth $10 million. If it does not receive supplies from Firm I, it is worth $9.8 million.

(b) Firm A has just purchased a new computer system that is only available from Firm B. Firm A has redesigned its entire production process around this new computer system. The old production process is worth $1 million; the new process is worth $12 million. Firm B has several hundred customers for its new computer system.

(c) Firm Alpha, a fast-food restaurant company, has a contract with Firm Beta, a movie studio. After negotiating with several other potential partners, Firm Alpha agreed to a contract that requires Firm Alpha to pay Firm Beta $5 million per year for the right to use characters from Firm Beta's movies in its packaged meals for children. Demand for children's movies has recently dropped.

(d) Firm I owns and runs a printing press. Firm J uses the services of a printing press. Historically, Firm I has sold its services to many customers. However, it was recently approached by Firm J to become its exclusive supplier of printing-press services. Currently, Firm I is worth $1 million. If it became the sole supplier to Firm J, it would be worth $8 million. To complete this deal, Firm I would have to stop supplying its current customers and modify its machines to meet Firm J's needs. No other firm needs the same services as Firm J. Firm J contacted several other suppliers who said they would be willing to become a sole supplier for Firm J before deciding to propose this arrangement with Firm I.

8.11. In each of the following situations, would you recommend vertical integration or no vertical integration? Explain.

(a) Firm A needs a new and unique technology for its product line. No substitute technologies are available. Should Firm A make this technology or buy it?

(b) Firm I has been selling its products through a distributor for some time. It has become the market share leader. Unfortunately, this distributor has not been able to keep up with the evolving technology and customers are complaining. No alternative distributors are available. Should Firm I keep its current distributor, or should it begin distribution on its own?

(c) Firm Alpha has manufactured its own products for years. Recently, however, one of these products has become more and more like a commodity. Several firms are now able to manufacture this product at the same price and quality as Firm Alpha. However, they do not have Firm Alpha's brand name in the marketplace. Should Firm Alpha continue to manufacture this product, or should it outsource it to one of these other firms?

(d) Firm I is convinced that a certain class of technologies holds real economic potential. However, it does not know, for sure, which particular version of this technology is going to dominate the market. There are eight competing versions of this technology currently, but ultimately only one will dominate the market. Should Firm I invest in all eight of these technologies itself? Should it invest in just one of these technologies? Should it partner with other firms that are investing in these different technologies?

Writing Assignments

8.12. How can vertical integration create value by enabling a firm to retain its flexibility?

8.13. Describe how both direct duplication and substitution can be used to imitate another firm's valuable and rare vertical integration choices.

CASE STUDY | PVR-INOX Integration: Navigating Challenges, Sustaining Growth

PVR Cinemas, under the leadership of Ajay Bijli, has carved a distinctive path in the Indian film exhibition industry through strategic growth and vertical integration. This approach, paralleling JSW Steel's strategy in the steel sector (see Chapter 6 opening vignette), has enabled PVR to become a dominant player in the entertainment landscape. From its inception, PVR focused on expanding its footprint across India, emphasizing quality and viewer experience. This strategy led to a series of acquisitions, including the notable purchase of Cinemax, which significantly increased PVR's screen count and market presence. The strategic acquisitions have not only expanded PVR's direct control over more screens but also enhanced its bargaining power with film distributors and mall owners, consolidating its position in the market.

Expansion Strategy

The merger with INOX Leisure marked a significant turn in PVR's strategy, creating the largest multiplex chain in India. This merger was driven by the need to overcome the challenges posed by the COVID-19 pandemic, which had severely impacted the film exhibition sector. By combining forces, PVR and INOX aim to leverage their collective strength to negotiate better terms with content producers and streamline operations, leading to estimated revenue and cost synergies. PVR's approach to vertical integration extends beyond acquisitions to a focus on enhancing the customer experience. This includes innovations in cinema technology and service offerings, aiming to provide a superior viewing experience that differentiates PVR from its competitors. The company's emphasis on location, developer relationships, and property development reflects a comprehensive strategy that considers the broader ecosystem impacting its business.

The INOX Merger

PVR Cinemas, after its merger with INOX in January 2023, demonstrated significant financial performance improvements in Q1 FY24. The company reported an 11 percent increase in admissions, with 33.9 million patrons visiting their cinemas. This growth was supported by a 3 percent increase in average ticket price and a 9 percent increase in food & beverage spend per head. As a result, ticket sales rose by 15 percent and food & beverage sales by 22 percent. However, the company reported a PAT loss of ₹441 million for the quarter. This period also saw PVR INOX opening 31 ne w screens and exiting 14 underperforming screens, bringing their total to 1,707 screens across 114 cities. This expansion and operational optimization are part of PVR's vertical integration strategy, aimed at enhancing its control over the cinema value chain and improving profitability.

Significant Challenges

Despite the success, the merger between PVR and INOX raises concerns about potential monopolistic tendencies within the sector. However, both companies have expressed their intention to maintain a collaborative relationship with content producers and other industry stakeholders, ensuring a healthy ecosystem for all parties involved. Looking ahead, PVR's strategy will likely continue focusing on expanding its presence, both organically and through further acquisitions, while maintaining a commitment to innovation and customer satisfaction. The challenges ahead include navigating the post-pandemic recovery of the film exhibition industry and addressing concerns related to market dominance. Nonetheless, PVR's strategic moves, underscored by the merger with INOX, position it to lead the sector's revival and growth in the years to come.

Questions

1. What are the potential benefits and risks associated with the merger between PVR and INOX in the context of the film exhibition industry. How can the merged entity effectively address concerns about monopolistic tendencies while maintaining collaborative relationships with content producers and other stakeholders?
2. Analyze PVR's strategic approach to expanding its presence through acquisitions and organic growth. Can PVR navigate the challenges of the post-pandemic while ensuring innovation and customer satisfaction remain central to its strategy?
3. How can PVR effectively address concerns about potential monopolistic tendencies following its merger with INOX, while simultaneously fostering a collaborative environment with content producers and other industry stakeholders to ensure a healthy ecosystem within the film exhibition sector?

References

Pant, K., & Sahay, A. (2022). *PVR Limited at a crossroads*. Emerald Emerging Markets Case Studies, 12(4), 1–28.

Ray Chaudhuri, B., & Dyondi, R. (2024). *Multiplex Industry: A Journey Through the Path of an Industry Lifecycle*. SAGE Publications: SAGE Business Cases Originals.

Chakraborty, E., & Patra, N. (2023). *An Exploratory Study on the Co-Existence of OTT and Multiplexes Post Pandemic*. Mass Communicator: International Journal of Communication Studies, 17(4), 16–22.

End Notes

1 A. Laffer (1969). "Vertical integration by corporations: 1929–1965." *Review of Economics and Statistics*, 51, pp. 91–93; I. Tucker and R. P. Wilder (1977). "Trends in vertical integration in the U.S. manufacturing sector." *Journal of Industrial Economics*, 26, pp. 81–94; K. Harrigan (1986). "Matching vertical integration strategies to competitive conditions." *Strategic Management Journal*, 7, pp. 535–555.

2 Coase, R. (1937). "The nature of the firm." *Economica*, 4, pp. 386–405.

3 This explanation of vertical integration is known as transactions cost economics in the academic literature. See Williamson, O. (1975). *Markets and hierarchies: Analysis and antitrust implications*. New York: Free Press; Williamson, O. (1985). *The economic institutions of capitalism*. New York: Free Press; and Klein, B., R. Crawford, and A. Alchian. (1978). "Vertical integration, appropriable rents, and the competitive contracting process." *Journal of Law and Economics*, 21, pp. 297–326.

4 Another option—forming an alliance between these two firms—is discussed in more detail in Chapter 9.

5 This explanation of vertical integration is known as the capabilities-based theory of the firm in the academic literature. It draws heavily from the resource-based view described in Chapter 3. See Barney, J. B. (1991). "Firm resources and sustained competitive advantage." *Journal of Management*, 17, pp. 99–120; Barney, J. B. (1999). "How a firm's capabilities affect boundary decisions." *Sloan Management Review*, 40(3); and Conner, K. R., and C. K. Prahalad. (1996). "A resource-based theory of the firm: Knowledge versus opportunism." *Organization Science*, 7, pp. 477–501.

6 This explanation of vertical integration is known as real-options theory in the academic literature. See Kogut, B. (1991). "Joint ventures and the option to expand and acquire." *Management Science*, 37, pp. 19–33.

7 J. Mahoney (1992). "The choice of organizational form: Vertical financial ownership versus other methods of vertical integration." *Strategic Management Journal*, 13, pp. 559–584; T. Folta (1998). "Governance and uncertainty: The trade-off between administrative control and commitment." *Strategic Management Journal*, 19, pp. 1007–1028; M. Leiblein and D. Miller (2003). "An empirical examination of transaction-and firm-level influences on the vertical boundaries of the firm." *Strategic Management Journal*, 24(9), pp. 839–859.

8 Witsil, F. (2014). "Call center jobs increase as more return from overseas." *Detroit Free Press*, Aug 4, 2014. https://www.usatoday.com/story/money/business/2014/08/04/call-center-jobs-overseas/13560107/. Accessed 8/31/2017.

9 Kripalani, M., and P. Engardio. (2003). "The rise of India." *BusinessWeek*, December 8, pp. 66+.

10 S. Steele-Carlin (2003). "Outsourcing poised for growth in 2002." FreelanceJobsNews.com, October 20; (2003). "Who wins in off-shoring?" McKinseyQuarterly.com, October 20.

11 See Gupta, A. K. (1987). "SBU strategies, corporate-SBU relations and SBU effectiveness in strategy implementation." *Academy of Management Journal*, 30(3), pp. 477–500.

12 Becker, G. S. (1993). *Human capital: A theoretical and empirical analysis, with special reference to education*. Chicago: University of Chicago Press.

13 Barney, J. B. (1991). "Firm resources and sustained competitive advantage." *Journal of Management*, 17, pp. 99–120.

CHAPTER

9 Corporate Diversification

LEARNING OBJECTIVES

After reading this chapter, you should be able to:

9.1 Define corporate diversification and describe five types of corporate diversification.

9.2 Specify the two conditions that a corporate diversification strategy must meet to create economic value.

a. Define the concept of "economies of scope" and identify nine potential economies of scope a diversified firm might try to exploit.

b. Identify which of these economies of scope a firm's outside equity investors can realize on their own at low cost.

9.3 Specify the circumstances under which a firm's diversification strategy will be a source of sustained competitive advantage.

a. Explain which of the economies of scope identified in this chapter are more likely to be subject to low-cost imitation and which are less likely to be subject to low-cost imitation.

b. Identify two potential substitutes for corporate diversification.

Mahindra Group: Diversified Growth and Global Reach

Mahindra Group's corporate diversification strategy illustrates a comprehensive approach to growth across various sectors, underpinned by a rich history of strategic acquisitions, innovation, and global expansion. Founded in 1945, the group has successfully navigated its expansion from the automotive industry into agriculture, IT, and beyond, showcasing a dynamic adaptation to market changes and opportunities. The group's leadership under Anand Mahindra, as Chairman, and Dr. Anish Shah, as Group CEO and MD, has been pivotal in steering its diversified operations toward sustainable growth and global reach.

Mahindra's diversification spans six business sectors, including three directly related to the automotive industry—automotive, farm equipment, and Mahindra systems, automotive technologies, alongside infrastructure development, telecom & software, and trade & financial services. This diversification strategy has been instrumental in mitigating risks associated with market fluctuations, allowing Mahindra to leverage opportunities across different economic conditions. The success of this strategy is evident in the financial year 2005, when Mahindra saw a significant year-on-year sales growth of 34 percent, driven by robust performances in tractors, three-wheelers, and utility vehicles. Export markets also saw a remarkable 90 percent increase, highlighting the group's expanding global footprint.

The Mahindra Group's financial performance in FY23 showcased significant growth, with a 56 percent increase in Consolidated PAT, reaching ₹10,282 crore, and a 34 percent rise in Consolidated Revenue at ₹1,21,269 crore. This growth is attributed to robust performances across its diversified sectors, including automotive, farm equipment, and financial services. The Group maintained leadership in various segments, notably in SUVs, LCVs, farm equipment, and electric 3-wheelers. Operational efficiencies, strategic capital allocation, and innovative partnerships have been key to achieving these results, positioning Mahindra well for future growth.

The strategic acquisitions and joint ventures have also played a crucial role in Mahindra's diversification. The group's foray into various sectors, including the acquisition of stakes in companies like Jiangling Tractor Company in China and the formation of joint ventures for entering the passenger car and commercial vehicle segments, demonstrate Mahindra's commitment to growth through collaboration and strategic partnerships. These moves have not only expanded Mahindra's product portfolio but also enhanced its manufacturing capabilities and market reach. However, diversification also presents challenges, such as integrating varied business units and maintaining operational efficiency across different sectors. Mahindra's future direction seems to focus on leveraging technology and innovation, emphasizing sustainability and digital transformation as key drivers of growth. The group's commitment to education and community development, through initiatives like Project Nanhi Kali and Mahindra University, further underscores its holistic approach to corporate responsibility and societal contribution.

Mahindra Group's strategic diversification has positioned it as a powerhouse in the global market, with a diversified portfolio that spans critical sectors of the economy. Despite the challenges of managing such a diversified conglomerate, Mahindra's strategic focus on innovation, sustainability, and global expansion continues to drive its success and resilience in the face of changing market dynamics.

REFERENCES

Mahindra Group. (2023). *Annual Report 2022–2023.* Mumbai: Mahindra & Mahindra Ltd. Accessed from https://www.mahindra.com on March 30, 2024.

Shilpa, K. (2023). *Mahindra and Mahindra Financial Services Ltd–A Case Study.* International Journal of Case Studies in Business, IT and Education (IJCSBE), 7(4), 379-391.

Mahindra is one of the most large companies in India: It has diversified operations. Indeed, virtually all the large firms India are diversified, either by product or geographically. Large single-business firms are very unusual. However, like most of these large diversified firms, Mahindra has diversified along some dimensions but not others.

Objective 9.1 Define corporate diversification and describe five types of corporate diversification.

What is Corporate Diversification?

A firm implements a **corporate diversification strategy** when it operates in multiple industries or markets simultaneously. When a firm operates in multiple industries simultaneously, it is said to be implementing a **product diversification strategy**. When a firm operates in multiple geographic markets simultaneously, it is said to be implementing a **geographic market diversification strategy**. When a firm implements both types of diversification simultaneously, it is said to be implementing a **product-market diversification strategy**.

We have already seen glimpses of these diversification strategies in the discussion of vertical integration strategies in Chapter 8. Sometimes, when a firm vertically integrates backward or forward, it begins operations in a new product or geographic market. This happened to computer software firms when they began manning their own call centers. These firms moved from the "computer software development" business to the "call-center management" business when they vertically integrated forward. In this sense, when firms vertically integrate, they may also be implementing a diversification strategy. However, the critical difference between the diversification strategies studied here and vertical integration (discussed in Chapter 8) is that in this chapter, product-market diversification is the primary objective of these strategies, whereas in Chapter 8, such diversification was often a secondary consequence of pursuing a vertical integration strategy.

Types of Corporate Diversification

Firms vary in the extent to which they have diversified the businesses within which they operate. These strategies fall into three broad categories presented in Figure 9.1: **limited corporate diversification**, **related corporate diversification**, or **unrelated corporate diversification**.

Limited Corporate Diversification

A firm has implemented a strategy of **limited corporate diversification** when all or most of its business activities fall within a single industry and geographic market (see Panel A of Figure 9.1). Two kinds of firms are included in this corporate diversification category: **single-business firms** (firms with greater than 95 percent of their total sales in a single-product market) and **dominant-business firms** (firms with between 70 and 95 percent of their total sales in a single-product market).

Differences between single-business and dominant-business firms are represented in Panel A of Figure 9.1. The firm pursuing a single-business corporate diversification strategy engages in only one business, Business A. An example of a single-business firm is the WD-40 Company of San Diego, California. This company manufactures and distributes only one product: the spray lubricant WD-40.

The dominant-business firm pursues two businesses, Business E and a smaller Business F. An example of a dominant-business firm is Donato's Pizza. Donato's Pizza does the vast majority of its business in a single product—pizza—in a single market—the United States. However, Donato's has begun selling non-pizza food products, including sandwiches, and owns a subsidiary that makes a machine that automatically slices and puts pepperoni on pizzas. Not only does Donato's use this machine in its own pizzerias, it also sells this machine to food manufacturers that make frozen pepperoni pizza.

In an important sense, firms pursuing a strategy of limited corporate diversification are not leveraging their resources and capabilities beyond a single product or market. Thus, the analysis of limited corporate diversification is logically equivalent to the analysis of business-level strategies (discussed in Part 2 of this book). Because these kinds of strategies have already been discussed, the remainder of this chapter focuses on corporate strategies that involve higher levels of diversification.

Related Corporate Diversification

As a firm begins to engage in businesses in more than one product or market, it moves away from being a single-business or dominant-business firm and begins to adopt higher levels of corporate diversification. When less than 70 percent of

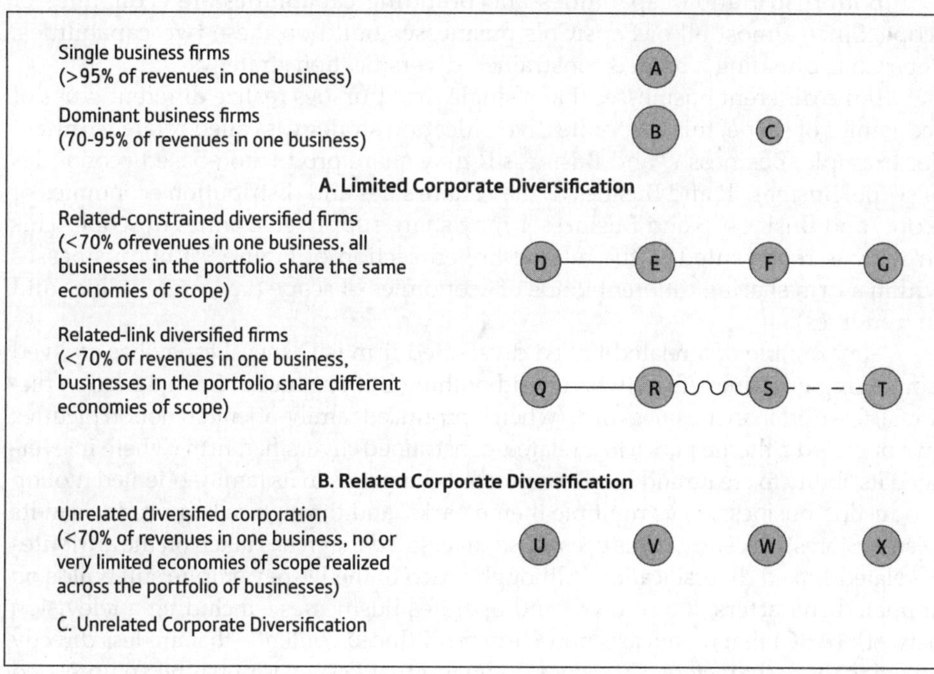

Figure 9.1 Levels and Types of Diversification

a firm's revenue comes from a single-product market and these multiple lines of business share important economies of scope, the firm has implemented a strategy of **related corporate diversification**. An **economy of scope** exists when the value created by several businesses operated together is greater than the value of these businesses operated separately. Potential sources of economies of scope are discussed later in this chapter.

The multiple businesses that a diversified firm pursues can realize economies of scope in at least at least two ways (see Panel B in Figure 9.1). If all the businesses in which a firm operates share the same economies of scope, then this corporate diversification strategy is called **related-constrained.** This strategy is *related* because of the economies of scope that exist among a firm's businesses; it is *constrained* because all (or at least most) of the businesses in a firm's portfolio share the same economies of scope.

PepsiCo is an example of a related-constrained diversified firm. Although PepsiCo operates in multiple businesses around the world, all its businesses focus on providing snack-type products, either food or beverages. This enables PepsiCo to exploit at least two economies of scope across all its businesses: common distribution processes and an emphasis on brands.

Regarding distribution, almost all of PepsiCo's products are sold in similar outlets—grocery stores, convenience stores, sandwich shops, fast food and other restaurants, and so forth. Supplying these different outlets with PepsiCo's products can be a challenge, but this firm has developed a variety of distribution capabilities that it applies to each of its businesses.

Also, PepsiCo uses its ability to build and exploit brands in most of its businesses. Whether it's Pepsi, Doritos, Mountain Dew, or Big Red, PepsiCo is all about building, and then exploiting, brand names. In fact, PepsiCo has 22 brands that each generate well over $1 billion or more in revenues a year.[1]

Both distribution capabilities and branding capabilities are economies of scope. Since almost all of PepsiCo's businesses build on these two capabilities, PepsiCo is pursuing a related constrained diversification strategy.

If the different businesses that a single firm pursues realize different types of economies of scope, this corporate diversification strategy is called **related-linked**. For example, Business Q and Business R may share production-based economies of scope, Business R and Business S may share sales and distribution economies of scope, and Business S and Business T may share supply economies of scope. This strategy is represented in the related-linked section of Figure 9.1 by businesses within a firm sharing different kinds of economies of scope (i.e., straight lines and curved lines).

An example of a related-linked diversified firm is Disney. Disney has evolved from a single-business firm (when it did nothing but produce animated motion pictures), to a dominant business firm (when it produced family-oriented motion pictures and operated a theme park), to a related-constrained diversified firm (where it leveraged its ability to create and market animated characters in its family-oriented motion production business, in its multiple theme parks, and through selling products in its Disney Stores). Recently, it has become so diversified that it has taken on the attributes of related-linked diversification. Although much of the Disney empire still builds on animated characters, it also owns and operates businesses—including a television network (ABC) that broadcasts non-Disney-produced content—that are less directly linked to these characters. This is not to suggest that Disney is pursuing an unrelated diversification strategy. After all, most of its businesses are in the entertainment industry, broadly defined, and share a variety of economies of scope. Rather, this is only to suggest that it is no longer possible to find a single economy of scope—like a Mickey Mouse or a Lion King—that connects all of Disney's business enterprises. In this sense, Disney has become a related-linked diversified firm.[2]

Unrelated Corporate Diversification

Firms that pursue a strategy of related corporate diversification have some type of economy of scope that benefits the different businesses they pursue. However, it is possible for firms to pursue numerous different businesses and for there to be *no* such economies of scope (see Panel C of Figure 9.1). When less than 70 percent of a firm's revenues is generated in a single-product market and when the businesses in a firm's portfolio share few, if any, economies of scope, then that firm is pursuing a strategy of **unrelated corporate diversification**.

As will be discussed shortly, there is little economic justification for firms pursuing multiple businesses that do not share economies of scope. For this reason, there are relatively few examples of such firms in the modern economy—although such diversification has existed in the past.

The Value of Corporate Diversification

Objective 9.2 Specify the two conditions that a corporate diversification strategy must meet to create economic value.

For corporate diversification to be economically valuable, two conditions must hold. First, there must be some valuable economy of scope among the multiple businesses in which a firm is operating. Second, it must be less costly for managers in a firm to realize these economies of scope than for outside equity holders on their own. If outside investors could realize the value of an economy of scope on their own and at low cost, then they would have few incentives to "hire" managers to realize this economy of scope for them. Each of these requirements for corporate diversification to add value for a firm will now be considered.

What Are Valuable Economies of Scope?

As suggested earlier, **economies of scope** exist when the value created by operating several businesses simultaneously is greater than the value of operating these businesses separately. In this definition, the term *scope* refers to the range of businesses in which a diversified firm operates. *Economies* refer to the lower costs or higher revenues associated with operating multiple businesses. Thus, only diversified firms can exploit economies of scope. Economies of scope are valuable to the extent that they do, in fact, increase a firm's revenues or decrease its costs, compared with what would be the case if these economies of scope did not exist, or had the potential to exist but were not exploited.

A wide variety of potentially valuable sources of economies of scope have been identified in the literature. Some of the most important of these are listed in Table 9.1 and discussed in the following text. How valuable economies of scope actually are, on average, has been the subject of a great deal of research, which is summarized in the Research Made Relevant feature.

Diversification to Exploit Shared Activities

In Chapter 3, it was suggested that value-chain analysis can be used to describe the specific business activities of a firm. This same value-chain analysis can also be used to describe the business activities that may be shared across several different businesses within a diversified firm. These **shared activities** are potential sources of operational economies of scope for diversified firms.

Consider, for example, the hypothetical firm presented in Figure 9.2. This diversified firm engages in three businesses: A, B, and C. However, these three businesses share a variety of activities throughout their value chains. For example, all three draw on the same technology development operation. Product design and manufacturing are shared in Businesses A and B and separate for Business C. All

TABLE 9.1 Different Types of Economies of Scope

1. Shared activities as an economy of scope
2. Core competencies as an economy of scope
   - Shared business level competencies
   - Corporate competencies
3. Financial economies of scope
   - Internal capital allocation
   - Risk reduction
   - Tax advantages
4. Anticompetitive economies of scope
   - Multipoint competition
   - Exploiting market power
5. Maximizing management compensation

Research Made Relevant

In 1994, Lang and Stulz published a sensational article that suggested that, on average, when a firm began implementing a corporate diversification strategy, it destroyed about 25 percent of its market value. Lang and Stulz came to this conclusion by comparing the market performance of firms pursuing a corporate diversification strategy with portfolios of firms pursuing a limited diversification strategy. Taken together, the market performance of a portfolio of firms that were pursuing a limited diversification strategy was about 25 percent

How Valuable Are Economies of Scope?

higher than the market performance of a single diversified firm operating in all the businesses included in this portfolio. These results suggested that not only were economies of scope not valuable, but, on average, efforts to realize these economies destroyed economic value. Similar results were published by Comment and Jarrell using different measures of firm performance.

Not surprisingly, these results generated quite a stir. If Lang and Stulz were correct, then diversified firms—no matter what kind of diversification strategy they engaged in—destroyed an enormous amount of economic value. This could lead to a fundamental restructuring of the U.S. economy.

However, several researchers questioned Lang and Stulz's conclusions. Two new findings suggest that, even if there is a 25-percent discount, diversification can still add value. First, Villalonga and others found that firms pursuing diversification strategies were generally performing more poorly before they began diversifying than firms that never pursued diversification strategies. Thus, although it might appear that diversification leads to a significant loss of economic value, that loss of value occurred before these firms began implementing a diversification strategy. Indeed, some more recent research suggests that these relatively poor-performing firms may increase their market value over what would have been the case if they did not diversify.

Second, Miller found that firms that find it in their self-interest to diversify do so in a very predictable pattern. These firms tend to diversify into the most profitable new business first, the second-most profitable business second, and so forth. Not surprisingly, the fiftieth diversification move made by these firms might not generate huge additional profits. However, these profits—it turns out—are still, on average, positive. Because multiple rounds of diversification increase profits at a decreasing rate, the overall average profitability of diversified firms will generally be less than the overall average profitability of firms that do not pursue a diversification strategy—thus, a substantial difference between the market value of non-diversified and diversified firms might exist. However, this discount, per se, does not mean that the diversified firm is destroying economic value. Rather, it may mean only that a diversifying firm is creating value in smaller increments as it continues to diversify.

All the results examine returns to diversification, on average. But returns to diversification depend on the specific resources and capabilities a firm possess and whether those can be used to create value through diversification. So, for example, a firm—like WD-40—that can generate value by remaining focused (i.e., not diversifying) should not diversify at all. A firm that can use shared activities to generate value—like ESPN—should engage in related diversification. Finally, a firm that can use corporate core competencies, without shared activities, to generate value—like Berkshire Hathaway—should engage in unrelated diversification. A recent paper by Mackey, Barney, and Dotson shows that all forms of diversification can create value for firms, and that over 90% of firms choose that form of diversification that creates the most value for their shareholders.[3]

three businesses share a common marketing and service operation. Business A has its own distribution system.

These kinds of shared activities are quite common among both related-constrained and related-linked diversified firms. At Texas Instruments, for example, a variety of electronics businesses share some research and development activities, and many share common manufacturing locations. Procter & Gamble's numerous consumer products businesses often share common manufacturing locations and rely on a common distribution network (through retail grocery stores).[4] Some of the most common shared activities in diversified firms and their location in the value chain are summarized in Table 9.2.

Many of the shared activities listed in Table 9.2 can have the effect of reducing a diversified firm's costs. This is especially the case if these shared activities are subject to economies of scale. For example, if a diversified firm has a purchasing function that is common to several of its different businesses, it can often obtain volume discounts on its purchases that would otherwise not be possible. Also, by manufacturing products that are used as inputs into several of a diversified firm's businesses, the total costs of producing these products can be reduced. A single sales force representing the products or services of several different businesses

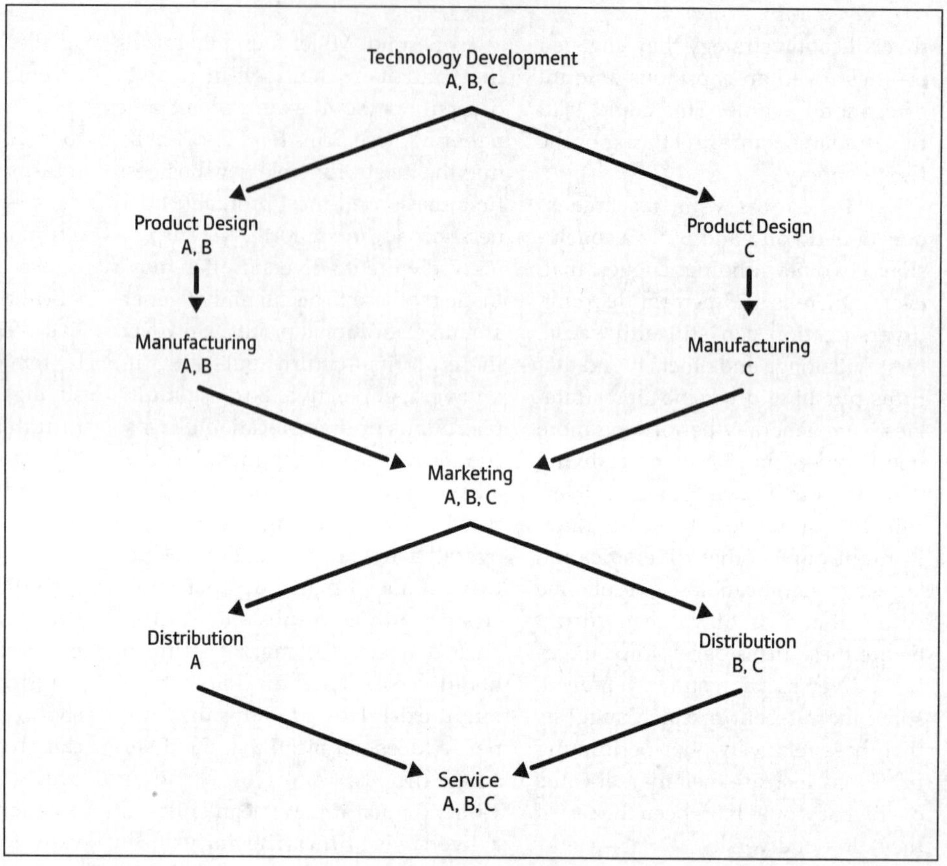

Figure 9.2 A Hypothetical Firm Sharing Activities Among Three Businesses

TABLE 9.2 Possible Shared Activities and Their Place in the Value Chain

Value Chain Activity	Shared Activities
Input activities	Common purchasing
	Common inventory control system
	Common warehousing facilities
	Common inventory delivery system
	Common quality assurance
	Common input requirements system
	Common suppliers
Production activities	Common product components
	Common product components manufacturing
	Common assembly facilities
	Common quality control system
	Common maintenance operation
	Common inventory control system
Warehousing and distribution	Common product delivery system
	Common warehouse facilities
Sales and marketing	Common advertising efforts
	Common promotional activities
	Cross-selling of products
	Common pricing systems

TABLE 9.2 Continued

Value Chain Activity	Shared Activities
	Common marketing departments
	Common distribution channels
	Common sales forces
	Common sales offices
	Common order processing services
Dealer support and service	Common service network
	Common guarantees and warranties
	Common accounts receivable management systems
	Common dealer training
	Common dealer support services

Sources: M. E. Porter (1985). *Competitive advantage.* New York: Free Press; R. P. Rumelt (1974). *Strategy, structure, and economic performance.* Cambridge, MA: Harvard University Press; H. I. Ansoff (1965). *Corporate strategy.* New York: McGraw-Hill.

within a diversified firm can reduce the cost of selling these products or services. Firms such as IBM, HP, and General Motors (GM) have all used shared activities to reduce their costs in these ways.

Failure to exploit shared activities across businesses can lead to out-of-control costs. For example, Kentucky Fried Chicken, when it was a division of PepsiCo, encouraged each of its regional business operations in North America to develop its own quality improvement plan. The result was enormous redundancy and at least three conflicting quality efforts—all leading to higher-than-necessary costs. In a similar way, Levi Strauss's unwillingness to centralize and coordinate order processing led to a situation where six separate order-processing computer systems operated simultaneously. This costly redundancy was ultimately replaced by a single, integrated ordering system shared across the entire corporation.[5]

Shared activities can also increase the revenues in diversified firms' businesses. This can happen in at least two ways. First, it may be that shared product development and sales activities may enable two or more businesses in a diversified firm to offer a bundled set of products to customers. Sometimes, the value of these "product bundles" is greater than the value of each product separately. This additional customer value can generate revenues greater than would have been the case if the businesses were not together and sharing activities in a diversified firm.

These bundles of products are what has led firms like AT&T—initially a provider of mobile telephone services—to acquire first a variety of cable television companies, and more recently, DirectTV—a supplier of satellite television services. Now AT&T customers can watch television programs on any of their devices—TV, tablets, mobile phones—receive a single bill, and interact with a single company. If consumers find these linkages valuable, these shared activities are likely to create value for AT&T's shareholders.[6]

Such product bundles are important in other firms as well. Many grocery stores now sell prepared foods alongside traditional grocery products in the belief that busy customers want access to all kinds of food products in the same location.[7]

Second, shared activities can enhance business revenues by exploiting the strong, positive reputations of some of a firm's businesses in other of its businesses.

For example, if one business has a strong positive reputation for high-quality manufacturing, other businesses sharing this manufacturing activity will gain some of the advantages of this reputation. And, if one business has a strong positive reputation for selling high-performance products, other businesses sharing sales and marketing activities with this business will gain some of the advantages of this reputation. In both cases, businesses that draw on the strong reputation of another business through shared activities with that business will have larger revenues than they would were they operating on their own.

The Limits of Activity Sharing Despite the potential of activity sharing to be the basis of a valuable corporate diversification strategy, this approach has three important limits.[8] First, substantial organizational issues are often associated with a diversified firm's learning how to manage cross-business relationships. Managing these relationships effectively can be very difficult, and failure can lead to excess bureaucracy, inefficiency, and organizational gridlock. These issues are discussed in detail in Chapter 10.

Second, sharing activities may limit the ability of a business to meet its specific customers' needs. For example, if two businesses share manufacturing activities, they may reduce their manufacturing costs. However, to gain these cost advantages, these businesses may need to build products using somewhat standardized components that do not fully meet their individual customers' needs. Businesses that share distribution activities may have lower overall distribution costs but be unable to distribute their products to all their customers. Businesses that share sales activities may have lower overall sales costs but be unable to provide the specialized selling required in each business.

One diversified firm that has struggled with the ability to meet the specialized needs of customers in its different divisions is GM. To exploit economies of scope in the design of new automobiles, GM shared the design process across several automobile divisions. The result over many years was "cookie-cutter" cars where the traditional distinctiveness of several GM divisions, including Oldsmobile and Cadillac, was all but lost.[9]

Third, if one business in a diversified firm has a poor reputation, sharing activities with that business can reduce the quality of the reputation of other businesses in the firm.

Taken together, these limits on activity sharing can more than offset any possible gains. Indeed, over the past decade more and more diversified firms have been abandoning efforts at activity sharing in favor of managing each business's activities independently. For example, ABB, Inc. (a Swiss engineering firm) and CIBA-Geigy (a Swiss chemical firm) have adopted explicit corporate policies that restrict almost all activity sharing across businesses.[10] Other diversified firms, including Nestlé and GE, restrict activity sharing to just one or two activities (such as research and development or management training). However, to the extent that a diversified firm can exploit shared activities while avoiding these problems, shared activities can add value to a firm.

Core Competencies as an Economy of Scope

A second potential economy of scope in a diversified corporation is called a core competence. **Core competence** has been defined by Prahalad and Hamel as, "the collective learning in the organization, especially how to coordinate diverse production skills and integrate multiple streams of technologies."[11] Core competencies are complex sets of resources and capabilities that link different businesses in a diversified firm through managerial and technical know-how, experience, and wisdom.[12]

Shared Business and Transnational Core Competencies At least two types of core competencies have been described in the literature. The first focuses on learning, know-how, and experience that develops in a business within a diversified firm that can then be leveraged in other businesses within that firm. This **shared business level competence** may or may not be accompanied by shared activities. When the business within a diversified firm that develops and then shares this core competence with other businesses in the firm in a non-domestic market, this core competence is the basis of what is called a **transnational strategy**.[13]

One firm that has exploited a transnational core competence as an economy of scope is General Electric in its medical imaging business. Originally, GE entered China to source costly parts for its MRI and related medical imaging machines. Those parts were then shipped out of China and incorporated into imaging products that were sold back into the Chinese market and elsewhere around the world. Unfortunately, the imaging devices that were designed to work in the West were not as reliable in China. In particular, MRI's in the United States are typically used five or six times a day, whereas the same units in China were often used 25 to 30 times a day. GE's imaging machines were not designed to be used that many times a day, and their reliability in China was low.

GE's Chinese division became aware of this problem and began designing a new type of imaging machine that could be used much more frequently each day. Once built, this machine became very popular in the Chinese market. However, what is particularly interesting about this example is that non-Chinese GE business started to sell the Chinese imaging machine outside of China. That is, the competence that GE's Chinese division had developed and incorporated into its imaging technology was valuable in non-Chinese markets serviced by other GE divisions. These other divisions leveraged the Chinese division's competence in a way that generated value for the entire corporation. The Chinese division's products are now among GE's most successful imaging technologies.[14]

Corporate Competencies A second type of core competence is called a **corporate competence**. This kind of competence exists when a firm develops managerial skills, technical knowhow, experience, and wisdom in managing a diversified corporation. This type of competence usually exists at a firm's corporate headquarters, and may or may not be associated with shared activities.

One example of a firm with this corporate competence, with no shared activities, is Berkshire Hathaway. With sales more than $210 billion, Berkshire Hathaway operates in four large segments: insurance; railroads; utilities and energy; and manufacturing, services, and retail. However, its businesses are run through literally hundreds of wholly owned subsidiaries. Some of these subsidiaries are relatively obscure and sell only to other companies, e.g., TTI, a Texas company that distributes components to electronics manufacturing firms. Other subsidiaries are well-known in consumer markets, e.g., GEICO, Fruit of the Loom, Justin Brands, Benjamin Moore, Dairy Queen, RC Wiley, and Helzberg Diamonds to name just a few.

In addition to owning hundreds of businesses outright, Berkshire Hathaway also invests cash from its businesses to take substantial, but not controlling, interests in a variety of other companies, including Mars, American Express, Coca-Cola, Wells Fargo, and IBM.

However, unlike firms that exploit shared activities as an economy of scope, the businesses Berkshire Hathaway owns have very few, if any, shared activities. In fact, perhaps the only thing that all these businesses have in common is that Berkshire Hathaway likes them to generate positive cash flows.

However, that Berkshire Hathaway does not have shared activities does not mean they do not realize economies of scope. Instead of shared activities, Berkshire Hathaway has developed significant skills in managing this type of corporation. Consider how Berkshire Hathaway describes that competence in their 2012 10K report, "Berkshire's operating businesses are managed on an unusually decentralized basis. There are essentially no centralized or integrated business functions (such as sales, marketing, purchasing, legal, or human resources) and there is minimal involvement by Berkshire's corporate headquarters in the day to day business activities of the operating businesses."

In describing Berkshire's operating principles, founder and chair, Warren Buffett, has written, "Although our form is corporate, our attitude is partnership. Charlie Munger (Vice Chair of the Board) and I think of our shareholders as owner-partners, and ourselves as managing partners . . . We do not view the company as the ultimate owner of our business assets but instead view the company as a conduit through which our shareholders own the assets . . . Our long term economic goal is to maximize Berkshire's average annual rate of gain in intrinsic business value on a per-share basis. We do not measure the economic significance or performance of Berkshire by its size; we measure by per-share progress."[15]

Core Competencies and Shared Activities Of course, core competencies and shared activities are not mutually exclusive. Diversified firms can exploit both these kinds of economies of scope at the same time. Danaher Corporation is a firm that exploits both these economies of scope simultaneously. With over $20 billion in sales, Danaher is a widely diversified manufacturing firm that has developed a corporate competence in applying lean manufacturing capabilities to a wide variety of business processes. While most operating decisions in this corporation are delegated to operating divisions, the corporate office trains leaders from all over the corporation in lean manufacturing techniques.[16] Thus, Danaher's commitment to use lean manufacturing processes in all its businesses is an example of a core competence as an economy of scope, and the processes it uses to train employees in its different businesses how to apply these lean manufacturing techniques is an example of a shared activity.

Limits of Core Competencies Just as there are limits to the value of shared activities as sources of economies of scope, so there are limits to core competencies as sources of these economies. The first of these limitations stems from important organizational issues to be discussed in Chapter 11. The way that a diversified firm is organized can either facilitate the exploitation of core competencies or prevent this exploitation from occurring.

A second limitation of core competencies is a result of the intangible nature of these economies of scope. Whereas shared activities are reflected in tangible operations in a diversified firm, core competencies may be reflected only in shared knowledge, experience, and wisdom across businesses. The intangible character of these relationships is emphasized when they are described as a **dominant logic** in a firm, or a common way of thinking about strategy across different businesses.[17]

The intangibility of core competencies can lead diversified firms to make two kinds of errors in managing relatedness. First, intangible core competencies can be illusory inventions by creative managers who link even the most completely unrelated businesses and thereby justify their diversification strategy. A firm that manufactures airplanes and running shoes can rationalize this diversification by claiming to have a core competence in managing transportation businesses. A firm operating in the professional football business and the movie business can rationalize this diversification by claiming to have a core competence in managing entertainment businesses. Such **invented competencies** are not real sources of economies of scope.

Second, a diversified firm's businesses may be linked by a core competence, but this competence may affect these businesses' costs or revenues in a trivial way. Thus, for example, all a firm's businesses may be affected by government actions, but the impact of these actions on costs and revenues in different businesses may be quite small. A firm may have a core competence in managing relationships with the government, but this core competence will not reduce costs or enhance revenues for these businesses very much. Also, each of a diversified firm's businesses may use some advertising. However, if advertising does not have a major impact on revenues for these businesses, core competencies in advertising are not likely to significantly reduce a firm's costs or increase its revenues. In this case, a core competence may be a source of economies of scope, but the value of those economies may be very small.

Diversification to Exploit Financial Economies of Scope

A third class of motivations for diversification focuses on financial advantages associated with diversification. Three financial implications of diversification have been studied: diversification and capital allocation, diversification and risk reduction, and tax advantages of diversification.

Diversification and Capital Allocation Capital can be allocated to businesses in one of two ways. First, businesses operating as independent entities can compete for capital in the external capital market. They do this by providing a sufficiently high return to induce investors to purchase shares of their equity, by having a sufficiently high cash flow to repay principal and interest on debt, and in other ways. Alternatively, a business can be part of a diversified firm. That diversified firm competes in the external capital market and allocates capital among its various businesses. In a sense, diversification creates an **internal capital market** in which businesses in a diversified firm compete for corporate capital.[18]

For an internal capital market to create value for a diversified firm, it must offer some efficiency advantages over an external capital market. It has been suggested that a potential efficiency gain from internal capital markets depends on the greater amount and quality of information that a diversified firm possesses about the businesses it owns, compared with the information that external suppliers of capital possess. Owning a business gives a diversified firm access to detailed and accurate information about the actual performance of the business, its true future prospects, and thus the actual amount and cost of the capital that should be allocated to it. External sources of capital, in contrast, have relatively limited access to information and thus have a limited ability to judge the actual performance and future prospects of a business.

Some have questioned whether a diversified firm, as a source of capital, has more and better information about a business it owns, compared with external sources of capital. After all, independent businesses seeking capital have a strong incentive to provide sufficient information to external suppliers of capital to obtain required funds. However, a firm that owns a business may have at least two informational advantages over external sources of capital.

First, although an independent business has an incentive to provide information to external sources of capital, it also has an incentive to downplay or even not report any negative information about its performance and prospects.[19] Such negative information would raise an independent firm's cost of capital. External sources of capital have limited ability to force a business to reveal all information about its performance and prospects and thus may provide capital at a lower cost than they would if they had full information. Ownership gives a firm the right to compel more complete disclosure, although even here full disclosure is not guaranteed. With this more complete information, a diversified firm can allocate just the right amount of capital, at the appropriate cost, to each business.

Second, an independent business may have an incentive not to reveal all the positive information about its performance and prospects. In Chapter 3, the ability of a firm to earn economic profits was shown to depend on the imitability of its resources and capabilities. An independent business that informs external sources of capital about all of its sources of competitive advantage is also informing its potential competitors about these sources of advantage. This information sharing increases the probability that these sources of advantage will be imitated. Because of the competitive implications of sharing this information, firms may choose not to share it, and external sources of capital may underestimate the true performance and prospects of a business.

A diversified firm, however, may gain access to this additional information about its businesses without revealing it to potential competitors. This information enables the diversified firm to make more informed decisions about how much capital to allocate to a business and about the cost of that capital, compared with the external capital market.[20]

Over time, there should be fewer errors in funding businesses through internal capital markets, compared with funding businesses through external capital markets. Fewer funding errors, over time, suggest a slight capital allocation advantage for a diversified firm, compared with an external capital market. This advantage should be reflected in somewhat higher rates of return on invested capital for the diversified firm, compared with the rates of return on invested capital for external sources of capital.

However, the businesses within a diversified firm do not always gain cost-of-capital advantages by being part of a diversified firm's portfolio. Several authors have argued that because a diversified firm has lower overall risk (see the following discussion), it will have a lower cost of capital, which it can pass along to the businesses within its portfolio. Although the lower risks associated with a diversified firm may lower the firm's cost of capital, the appropriate cost of capital to businesses within the firm depends on the performance and prospects of each of those businesses. The firm's advantages in evaluating its businesses' performances and prospects result in more appropriate capital allocation, not just in lower cost of capital for those businesses. Indeed, a business's cost of capital may be lower than it could have obtained in the external capital market (because the firm can more fully evaluate the positive aspects of that business), or it may be higher than it could have obtained in the external capital market (because the firm can more fully evaluate the negative aspects of that business).

Of course, if these businesses also have lower cost or higher revenue expectations because they are part of a diversified firm, then those cost/revenue advantages will be reflected in the appropriate cost of capital for these businesses. In this sense, any operational economies of scope for businesses in a diversified firm may be recognized by a diversified firm exploiting financial economies of scope.

Limits on Internal Capital Markets Although internal capital allocation has several potential advantages for a diversified firm, this process also has several limits. First, the diversification strategy that a firm pursues can affect the efficiency of this allocation process. A firm that implements a strategy of unrelated diversification, and does not develop a corporate competence, requires managers to evaluate the performance and prospects of numerous very different businesses. This can put a greater strain on the capital allocation skills of its managers.

Second, the increased efficiency of internal capital allocation depends on managers in a diversified firm having better information for capital allocation than the information available to external sources. However, this higher-quality information is not guaranteed. The incentives that can lead managers to exaggerate their performance and prospects to external capital sources can also lead to this behavior within a diversified firm. Indeed, several examples of business managers falsifying performance records to gain access to more internal capital have been reported.[21] Research suggests that capital allocation requests by managers are routinely discounted in diversified firms to correct for these managers' inflated estimates of the performance and prospects of their businesses.[22]

Finally, not only do business managers have an incentive to inflate the performance and prospects of their business in a diversified firm, but managers in charge of capital allocation in these firms may have an incentive to continue investing in a business despite its poor performance and prospects. The reputation and status of these managers often depend on the success of these business investments because often they initially approved them. These managers often continue throwing good money at these businesses in hope that they will someday improve, thereby justifying their original decision. Organizational psychologists call this process **escalation of commitment** and have presented numerous examples of managers becoming irrationally committed to an investment.[23]

Indeed, research on the value of internal capital markets in diversified firms suggests that, on average, the limitations of these markets often outweigh their advantages. For example, even controlling for firm size, excessive investment in poorly performing businesses in a diversified firm reduces the market value of the average diversified firm.[24] However, the fact that many firms do not gain the advantages associated with internal capital markets does not necessarily imply that no firms gain these advantages. If only a few firms can obtain the advantages of internal capital markets while avoiding their limitations, this financial economy of scope may be a source of at least a temporary competitive advantage.

Diversification and Risk Reduction Another possible financial economy of scope for a diversified firm has already been briefly mentioned—the riskiness of the cash flows of diversified firms is lower than the riskiness of the cash flows of undiversified firms. Consider, for example, the riskiness of two businesses operating separately compared with the risk of a diversified firm operating in those same two businesses simultaneously. If both these businesses are very risky on their own and the cash flows from these businesses are not highly correlated over time, then combining these two businesses into a single firm will generate a lower level of overall risk for the diversified firm than for each of these businesses on their own.

This lower level of risk is due to the low correlation between the cash flows associated with these two businesses. If Business I is having a bad year, Business II might be having a good year, and a firm that operates in both of these businesses simultaneously can have moderate levels of performance. In another year, Business II might be off, while Business I is having a good year. Again, the firm operating in both these businesses can have moderate levels of performance. Firms that diversify to reduce risk will have relatively stable returns over time, especially as they diversify into many different businesses with cash flows that are not highly correlated over time.

Tax Advantages of Diversification Another financial economy of scope from diversification stems from possible tax advantages of this corporate strategy. These possible tax advantages reflect one or a combination of two effects. First, a diversified firm can use losses in some of its businesses to offset profits in others, thereby reducing its overall tax liability. Of course, substantial losses in some of its businesses may overwhelm profits in other businesses, forcing businesses that would have remained solvent if they were independent to cease operation. However, if business losses are not too large, a diversified firm's tax liability can be reduced. Empirical research suggests that diversified firms do, sometimes, offset profits in some businesses with losses in others, although the tax savings of these activities are usually small.[25]

Second, because diversification can reduce the riskiness of a firm's cash flows, it can also reduce the probability that a firm will declare bankruptcy. This can increase a firm's debt capacity. This effect on debt capacity is greatest when the cash flows of a diversified firm's businesses are perfectly and negatively correlated. However, even when these cash flows are perfectly and positively correlated, there can still be a (modest) increase in debt capacity.

Debt capacity is particularly important in tax environments where interest payments on debt are tax deductible. In this context, diversified firms can increase their leverage up to their debt capacity and reduce their tax liability accordingly. Of course, if interest payments are not tax deductible or if the marginal corporate tax rate is relatively small, then the tax advantages of diversification can be quite small. Empirical work suggests that diversified firms do have greater debt capacity than undiversified firms.[26]

Diversification to Exploit Anticompetitive Economies of Scope

A third group of motivations for diversification is based on the relationship between diversification strategies and various anticompetitive activities by firms. Two specific examples of these activities are: (1) multipoint competition to facilitate mutual forbearance and tacit collusion; and (2) exploiting market power.

Multipoint Competition Multipoint competition exists when two or more diversified firms simultaneously compete in multiple markets. For example, HP and Dell compete in both the personal computer market and the market for computer printers. Michelin and Goodyear compete in both the U.S. automobile tire market and the European automobile tire market. Disney and AOL/Time Warner compete in both the movie production and book publishing businesses.

Multipoint competition can serve to facilitate a type of tacit collusion called **mutual forbearance**. As suggested in Chapter 7, firms engage in **tacit collusion** when they cooperate to reduce rivalry below the level expected under perfect competition. Consider the situation facing two diversified firms, A and B. These two firms operate in the same businesses, I, II, III, and IV (see Figure 9.3). In this context, any decisions that Firm A might make to compete aggressively in Businesses I and III must consider the possibility that Firm B will respond by competing aggressively in Businesses II and IV and vice versa. The potential loss that each of these firms may experience in some of its businesses must be compared with the potential gain that each might obtain if it exploits competitive advantages in other of its businesses. If the present value of gains does not outweigh the present value of losses from retaliation, then both firms will avoid competitive activity. Refraining from competition is mutual forbearance.[27]

Mutual forbearance because of multipoint competition has occurred in several industries. For example, this form of tacit collusion has been described as existing between Michelin and Goodyear, Maxwell House and Folger's, Caterpillar and John Deere, and BIC and Gillette.[28] Another clear example of such cooperation can be found in the airline industry. For example, America West (now part of American Airlines through its merger with U.S. Air) began service into the Houston Intercontinental Airport with very low introductory fares. Continental Airlines (now part of United Airlines), the dominant firm at Houston Intercontinental, rapidly responded to America West's low Houston fares by reducing the price of its flights from Phoenix, Arizona, to several cities in the United States. Phoenix is the home airport of America West. Within just a few weeks, America West withdrew its low introductory fares in the Houston market, and Continental withdrew its reduced prices in the Phoenix market. The threat of retaliation across markets apparently led America West and Continental to tacitly collude on prices.[29]

Some recent research investigates the conditions under which mutual forbearance strategies are pursued, as well as conditions under which multipoint competition does not lead to mutual forbearance.[30] In general, the value of the threat of retaliation must be substantial for multipoint competition to lead to mutual forbearance. However, not only must the payoffs to mutual forbearance be substantial, but the firms pursuing this strategy must have strong strategic linkages among their diversified businesses. This suggests that firms pursuing mutual forbearance strategies based on multipoint competition are usually pursuing a form of related diversification.[31]

Diversification and Market Power Internal allocations of capital among a diversified firm's businesses may enable it to exploit in some of its businesses the market power advantages it enjoys in other of its businesses. For example, suppose that a firm is earning monopoly profits in a business. This firm can use some of these monopoly profits to subsidize the operations of another of its businesses. This cross-subsidization can take several forms, including **predatory pricing**—that is, setting prices so that they are less than the subsidized business's

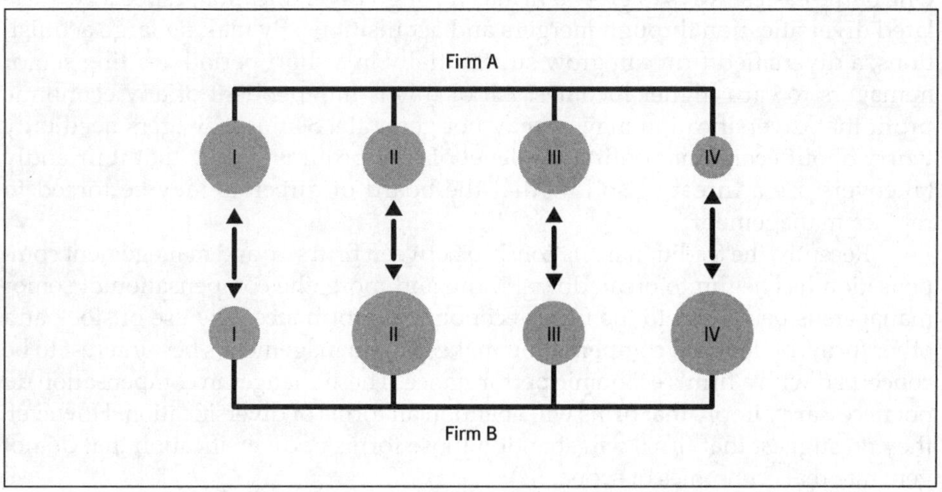

Figure 9.3 Multipoint Competition Between Hypothetical Firms A and B

costs. The effect of this cross-subsidy may be to drive competitors out of the subsidized business and then to obtain monopoly profits in that subsidized business. In a sense, diversification enables a firm to apply its monopoly power in several different businesses. Economists call this a **deep-pockets model** of diversification.[32]

Diversified firms with operations in regulated monopolies have been criticized for this kind of cross-subsidization. For example, most of the regional telephone companies in the United States are engaging in diversification strategies. The consent decree that forced the breakup of the original AT&T expressly forbade cross-subsidies between these regional companies' telephone monopolies and other business activities, under the assumption that such subsidies would give these firms an unfair competitive advantage in their diversified business activities.[33]

Although these market power economies of scope, in principle, may exist, relatively little empirical work documents their existence. Indeed, research on regulated utilities diversifying into nonregulated businesses in the 1980s suggests not that these firms use monopoly profits in their regulated businesses to unfairly subsidize non-regulated businesses, but that non-competition-oriented management skills developed in the regulated businesses tend to make diversification less profitable rather than more profitable.[34] Nevertheless, the potential that large diversified firms have to exercise market power and to behave in socially irresponsible ways has led some observers to call for actions to curtail both the economic and political power of these firms. These issues are discussed in the Ethics and Strategy feature.

Firm Size and Employee Incentives to Diversify

Employees may have incentives to diversify that are independent of any benefits from other sources of economies of scope. This is especially the case for employees in senior management positions and employees with long tenure in a firm. These employee incentives reflect the interest of employees to diversify because of the relationship between firm size and management compensation.

Research over the years demonstrates conclusively that the primary determinant of the compensation of top managers in a firm is not the economic performance of the firm but the size of the firm, usually measured in sales.[35] Thus, managers seeking to maximize their income should attempt to grow their firm. One of the easiest ways to grow a firm is through diversification, especially unrelated diversification through mergers and acquisitions. By making large acquisitions, a diversified firm can grow substantially in a short period, leading senior managers to earn higher incomes. All of this is independent of any economic profit that diversification may or may not generate. Senior managers need only worry about economic profit if the level of that profit is so low that unfriendly takeovers are a threat or so low that the board of directors may be forced to replace management.

Recently, the traditional relationship between firm size and management compensation has begun to break down. More and more, the compensation of senior managers is being tied to the firm's economic performance. The use of stock and other forms of deferred compensation makes it in management's best interest to be concerned with a firm's economic performance. These changes in compensation do not necessarily imply that firms will abandon all forms of diversification. However, they do suggest that firms will abandon those forms of diversification that do not generate real economies of scope.

Can Equity Holders Realize These Economies of Scope on Their Own?

Earlier in this chapter, it was suggested that for a firm's diversification strategies to create value, two conditions must hold. First, these strategies must exploit valuable economies of scope. Potentially valuable economies of scope were presented in Table 9.1 and discussed in the previous section. Second, it must be less costly for managers in a firm to realize these economies of scope than for outside equity holders on their own. If outside equity holders could realize an economy of scope on their own, without a firm's managers, at low cost, why would they want to hire managers to do this for them by investing in a firm and providing capital to managers to exploit an economy of scope?

Table 9.3 summarizes the discussion on the potential value of the different economies of scope listed in Table 9.1. It also suggests which of these economies of scope will be difficult for outside equity investors to exploit on their own and thus which bases of diversification are most likely to create positive returns for a firm's equity holders.

Most of the economies of scope listed in Table 9.3 cannot be realized by equity holders on their own. This is because most of them require activities that equity holders cannot engage in or information that equity holders do not possess. For example, shared activities, core competencies, multipoint competition, and exploiting market power all require the detailed coordination of business activities across multiple businesses in a firm. Although equity holders may own a portfolio of equities, they are not able to coordinate business activities across this portfolio. In a similar way, internal capital allocation requires information about a business's prospects that is simply not available to a firm's outside equity holders. All this suggests reasons why firms may engage in diversification. Some of the potential ethical implications of this diversification are discussed in the Ethics and Strategy feature.

Indeed, the only two economies of scope listed in Table 9.3 that do not have the potential for generating positive returns for a firm's equity holders are diversification to maximize the size of a firm—because firm size, per se, is not valuable—and

TABLE 9.3 The Competitive Implications of Different Economies of Scope

Types of Economy of Scope	Can They Be Valuable	Can They Be Realized by Equity Holders on their Own	Performance Implications
Shared activities	Yes	No	Positive
Core Competencies			
Business Level	Yes	No	Positive
Corporate	Yes	No	Positive
Financial			
Capital Allocation	Yes	No	Positive
Risk Reduction	Yes	Yes	Negative
Tax Savings	Yes	No	Positive
Anti-Competitive			
Multipoint Competition	Yes	No	Positive
Exploiting Market Power	Yes	No	Positive
Management Compensation	No	No	Negative

diversification to reduce risk—because equity holders can do this on their own at very low cost by simply investing in a diversified portfolio of stocks. Indeed, although risk reduction is often a published rationale for many diversification moves, this rationale, by itself, is not directly consistent with the interests of a firm's equity holders. However, some scholars have suggested that this strategy may directly benefit other of a firm's stakeholders and thus indirectly benefit its equity holders. This possibility is discussed in detail in the Strategy in Depth feature.

Ethics and Strategy

Globalization and the Threat of the Multinational Firm

In 1999, a loose coalition of union members, environmentalists, youth, indigenous peoples, human rights activists, small farmers, and displaced workers took to the streets of Seattle, Washington, to protest a meeting of the World Trade Organization (WTO) and to fight against the growing global power of corporations. Government officials and corporate officers alike were confused by these protests. After all, hadn't world trade increased 19 times from 1950 to 1995 ($0.4 trillion to $7.6 trillion in constant 2003 dollars), and hadn't the total economic output of the entire world gone from $6.4 trillion in 1950 to $60.7 trillion in 2005 (again, in constant 2003 dollars)? Why protest a global economic system—a system that was enhancing the level of free trade and facilitating global economic efficiency—that was so clearly improving the economic well-being of the world's population? This 1999 protest turned out to be the first of many such demonstrations, culminating in the Occupy Movement after the financial crisis of 2007 and, in some ways, the election of Donald Trump as President of the United States in 2016. And, still, many business and government leaders remain confused. Empirically, globalization has improved the world economy, so why the controversy?

The message that these events were sending to government and big business was that these aggregate growth numbers masked more truth than they told. Yes, there has been economic growth. But that growth has benefited only a small percentage of the world's population. Most of the population still struggles to survive. The combined net worth of 358 U.S. billionaires in the early 1990s ($760 billion) was equal to the combined net worth of the 2.5 billion poorest people on the earth! 83 percent of the world's total income goes to the richest fifth of the population while the poorest fifth of the world's population receives only 1.4 percent of the world's total income. Currently, 65.3 million people worldwide have had to leave their home countries to find work—and safety—in foreign lands, and approximately 1.4 billion people around the world live on less than $1 a day. Even in relatively affluent societies such as the United States, people find it increasingly difficult to meet their financial obligations. Falling real wages, economic insecurity, and corporate downsizing have led many people to work longer hours, to hold two or more jobs, and to remain underemployed as they have watched their factory jobs being shipped to cost centers overseas.

The causes of this apparent contradiction—global economic growth linked with growing global economic frustration—are numerous and complex. However, one explanation focuses on the growing economic power of the diversified multinational corporation. The size of these institutions can be immense—many international diversified firms are larger than the entire economies of many nations. And these huge institutions, with a single-minded focus on maximizing their performance, can make profit-making decisions that adversely affect their suppliers, their customers, their employees, and the environment, all with relative impunity. Armed with the unspoken mantra that "Greed is good," these corporations can justify almost any action if it increases the wealth of their shareholders.

Of course, even if one accepts this hypothesis—and it is far from being universally accepted—solutions to the growing power of internationally diversified firms are not obvious. The problem is that one way that firms become large and powerful is by being able to meet customer demands effectively. Thus, firm size, per se, is not necessarily an indication that a firm is behaving in ways inconsistent with the public good. Government efforts to restrict the size of firms simply because they are large could easily have the effect of making citizens worse off. However, once firms are large and powerful, they may very well be tempted to exercise that power in ways that benefit themselves at great cost to society.

Whatever the causes and solutions to these problems, protests that began in Seattle in 1999 have at least one clear message: global growth for growth's sake is no longer universally accepted as the correct objective of international economic policy.[36]

Corporate Diversification and Sustained Competitive Advantage

Objective 9.3 Specify the circumstances under which a firm's diversification strategy will be a source of sustained competitive advantage.

Table 9.3 describes those economies of scope that are likely to create real economic value for diversifying firms. However, as we have seen with all the other strategies discussed in this book, the fact that a strategy is valuable does not necessarily imply that it will be a source of sustained competitive advantage. For diversification to be a source of sustained competitive advantage, it must be not only valuable but also rare and costly to imitate, and a firm must be organized to implement this strategy. The rarity and imitability of diversification are discussed in this section; organizational questions are deferred until the next chapter.

The Rarity of Diversification

At first glance, it seems clear that diversification per se is usually not a rare firm strategy. Most large firms have adopted some form of diversification, if only the

Strategy in Depth

Although diversifying to reduce risk generally does not directly benefit outside equity investors in a firm, it can *indirectly* benefit outside equity investors through its impact on the willingness of other stakeholders in a firm to make firm-specific investments. A firm's **stakeholders** include all those groups and individuals who have an interest in how a firm performs. In this sense, a firm's equity investors are one of a firm's stakeholders. Other firm stakeholders include employees, suppliers, and customers.

Firm stakeholders make **firm-specific investments** when the value of the investments they make in a firm is much greater than the value of those same investments would be in other firms. Consider, for example, a firm's employees. An employee with a long tenure in a firm has generally made substantial **firm-specific human capital investments**. These investments include understanding a firm's culture, policies, and procedures; knowing the "right" people to contact to complete a task; and so forth. Such investments have significant value in the firm where they are made. Indeed, such firm-specific knowledge is generally necessary if an employee is to be able to help a firm conceive and implement valuable strategies. However, the

Risk-Reducing Diversification and a Firm's Other Stakeholders

(*Continued*)

specific investments that an employee makes in a firm have almost no value in other firms. If a firm were to cease operations, employees would instantly lose almost all the value of any of the firm-specific investments they had made in that firm.

Suppliers and customers can also make these firm-specific investments. Suppliers make these investments when they customize their products or services to the specific requirements of a customer. They also make firm-specific investments when they forgo opportunities to sell to other firms in order to sell to a particular firm. Customers make firm-specific investments when they customize their operations to fully utilize the products or services of a firm. Also, by developing close relationships with a firm, customers may forgo the opportunity to develop relationships with other firms. These, too, are firm-specific investments made by customers. If a firm were to cease operations, suppliers and customers would instantly lose almost the entire value of the specific investments they have made in this firm.

Although the firm-specific investments made by employees, suppliers, and customers are risky—in the sense that almost their entire value is lost if the firm in which they are made ceases operations—they are extremely important if a firm is going to be able to generate economic profits. As was suggested in Chapter 3, valuable, rare, and costly-to-imitate resources and capabilities are more likely to be a source of sustained competitive advantage than resources and capabilities without these attributes. Firm-specific investments are more likely to have these attributes than non-firm-specific investments. Non-firm-specific investments are investments that can generate value in numerous different firms.

Thus, valuable, rare, and costly-to-imitate firm-specific investments made by a firm's employees, suppliers, and customers can be the source of economic profits. And because a firm's outside equity holders are residual claimants on the cash flows generated by a firm, these economic profits benefit equity holders. Thus, a firm's outside equity holders generally will want a firm's employees, suppliers, and customers to make specific investments in a firm because those investments are likely to be sources of economic wealth for outside equity holders.

However, given the riskiness of firm-specific investments, employees, suppliers, and customers will generally only be willing to make these investments if some of the riskiness associated with making them can be reduced. Outside equity holders have little difficulty managing the risks associated with investing in a firm because they can always create a portfolio of stocks that fully diversifies this risk at very low cost. Therefore, diversification that reduces the riskiness of a firm's cash flows does not generally directly benefit a firm's outside equity holders. However, a firm's employees, suppliers, and customers usually do not have these low-cost diversification opportunities. Employees, for example, are rarely able to make firm-specific human capital investments in a large enough number of different firms to fully diversify the risks associated with making them. And although suppliers and customers can diversify their firm-specific investments to a greater degree than employees—through selling to multiple customers and through buying from multiple suppliers—the cost of this diversification for suppliers and customers is usually greater than the costs that are borne by outside equity holders in diversifying their risk.

Because it is often very costly for a firm's employees, suppliers, and customers to diversify the risks associated with making firm-specific investments on their own, these stakeholders will often prefer that a firm's managers help manage this risk for them. Managers in a firm can do this by diversifying the portfolio of businesses in which a firm operates. If a firm is unwilling to diversify its portfolio of businesses, then that firm's employees, suppliers, and customers will generally be unwilling to make specific investments in that firm. Moreover, because these firm-specific investments can generate economic profits and because economic profits can directly benefit a firm's outside equity holders, equity holders have an indirect incentive to encourage a firm to pursue a diversification strategy, even though that strategy does not directly benefit them.

Put differently, a firm's diversification strategy can be thought of as compensation for the firm-specific investments that a firm's employees, suppliers, and customers make in a firm. Outside equity holders have an incentive to encourage this compensation in return for access to some of the economic profits that these firm-specific investments can generate. In general, the greater the impact of the firm-specific investment made by a firm's employees, suppliers, and customers on the ability of a firm to generate economic profits, the more likely that pursuing a corporate diversification strategy is indirectly consistent with the interests of a firm's outside equity holders. In addition, the more limited the ability of a firm's employees, suppliers, and customers to diversify the risks associated with making firm-specific investments at low cost, the more that corporate diversification is consistent with the interests of outside equity investors.[37]

limited diversification of a dominant-business firm. Even many small and medium-sized firms have adopted different levels of diversification strategy.

However, the rarity of diversification depends not on diversification per se but on how rare the economies of scope associated with that diversification are. If only a few competing firms have exploited an economy of scope, that economy of scope can be rare. If numerous firms have done so, it will be common and not a source of competitive advantage.

The Imitability of Diversification

Both forms of imitation—direct duplication and substitution—are relevant in evaluating the ability of diversification strategies to generate sustained competitive advantages, even if the economies of scope that they create are rare.

Direct Duplication of Diversification

The extent to which a valuable and rare corporate diversification strategy is immune from direct duplication depends on how costly it is for competing firms to realize this same economy of scope. As suggested in Table 9.4, some economies of scope are, in general, costlier to duplicate than others.

Shared activities, risk reduction, tax advantages, and employee compensation as bases for corporate diversification are usually relatively easy to duplicate. Because shared activities are based on tangible assets that a firm exploits across multiple businesses, such as common research and development labs, common sales forces, and common manufacturing, they are usually relatively easy to duplicate. The only duplication issues for shared activities concern developing the cooperative cross-business relationships that often facilitate the use of shared activities—issues discussed in the next chapter. Moreover, because risk reduction, tax advantages, and employee compensation motives for diversifying can be accomplished through any type of diversification, these motives for diversifying tend to be relatively easy to duplicate.

Other economies of scope are much more difficult to duplicate. These difficult-to-duplicate economies of scope include core competencies, internal capital allocation efficiencies, multipoint competition, and exploitation of market power. Because core competencies are more intangible, their direct duplication is often challenging. The realization of capital allocation economies of scope requires very substantial information-processing capabilities. These capabilities are often very difficult to develop. Multipoint competition requires very close coordination between the different businesses in which a firm operates. This kind of coordination is socially complex and thus often immune from direct duplication.[38] Finally, exploitation of market power may be costly to duplicate because it requires that a firm must possess significant market power in one of its lines of business. A firm that does not have this market power advantage would have to obtain it. The cost of doing so, in most situations, would be prohibitive.

TABLE 9.4 Costly Duplication of Economies of Scope

Less Costly-to-Duplicate Economies of Scope	Costly-to-Duplicate Economies of Scope
Shared activities	Core competencies
Risk reduction	Internal capital allocation
Tax advantages	Multipoint competition
Employee compensation	Exploiting market power

Substitutes for Diversification

Two obvious substitutes for diversification exist. First, instead of obtaining cost or revenue advantages from exploiting economies of scope *across* businesses in a diversified firm, a firm may decide to simply grow and develop each of its businesses separately. In this sense, a firm that successfully implements a cost leadership strategy or a product differentiation strategy in a single business can obtain the same cost or revenue advantages it could have obtained by exploiting economies of scope but without having to develop cross-business relations. Growing independent businesses within a diversified firm can be a substitute for exploiting economies of scope in a diversification strategy.

A second substitute for exploiting economies of scope in diversification can be found in strategic alliances. By using a strategic alliance, a firm may be able to gain the economies of scope it could have obtained if it had carefully exploited economies of scope across its businesses. Thus, for example, instead of a firm exploiting research and development economies of scope between two businesses it owns, it could form a strategic alliance with a different firm and form a joint research and development lab. Instead of a firm exploiting sales economies of scope by linking its businesses through a common sales force, it might develop a sales agreement with another firm and obtain cost or revenue advantages in this way.

Summary

Firms implement corporate diversification strategies that range from limited diversification (single-business, dominant-business) to related diversification (related-constrained, related-linked) to unrelated diversification. To be valuable, corporate diversification strategies must reduce costs or increase revenues by exploiting economies of scope that outside equity holders cannot realize on their own at low cost.

Several motivations for implementing diversification strategies exist, including exploiting shared activities, core competencies (shared business level competencies, corporate competencies), financial economies of scope (internal capital allocation, risk reduction, obtaining tax advantages), anti-competitive economies of scope (multipoint competition, market power advantages), and employee incentives to maximize compensation. All these reasons for diversifying, except diversifying to maximize management compensation and (maybe) risk reduction, have the potential to create economic value for a firm. Moreover, a firm's outside equity holders will find it costly to realize all these bases for diversification, except risk reduction. Thus, diversifying to maximize management compensation or diversifying to reduce risk is not consistent with the wealth-maximizing interests of a firm's equity holders.

The ability of a diversification strategy to create sustained competitive advantages depends not only on the value of that strategy, but also on its rarity and imitability. The rarity of a diversification strategy depends on the number of competing firms that are exploiting the same economies of scope through diversification. Imitation can occur either through direct duplication or through substitutes. Costly-to-duplicate economies of scope include core competencies, internal capital allocation, multipoint competition, and exploitation of market power. Other economies of scope are usually less costly to duplicate. Important substitutes for diversification are when relevant economies are obtained through the independent actions of businesses within a firm and when relevant economies are obtained through strategic alliances. This discussion set aside important organizational issues in implementing diversification strategies. These issues are examined in detail in the next chapter.

Challenge Questions

9.1. One simple way to think about relatedness is to look at the products or services a firm manufactures. The more similar these products or services are, the more related is the firm's diversification strategy. Would firms that exploit core competencies in their diversification strategies always produce products or services that are like each other? Why or why not?

9.2. A firm implementing a diversification strategy has just acquired what it claims is a strategically related target firm but announces that it is not going to change this recently acquired firm in any way. Would this type of diversifying acquisition enable the firm to realize any valuable economies of scope that could not be duplicated by outside investors on their own? Why or why not?

9.3. One of the reasons why internal capital markets may be more efficient than external capital markets is that firms may not want to reveal full information about their sources of competitive advantage to external capital markets in order to reduce the threat of competitive imitation. This suggests that external capital markets may systematically undervalue firms with competitive advantages that are subject to imitation. If you agree with this analysis, how could you trade on this information in your own investment activities?

9.4. A firm is owned by members of a single family. Most of the wealth of this family is derived from the operations of this firm, and the family does not want to "go public" with the firm by selling its equity position to outside investors. Will this firm choose to pursue a highly related diversification strategy or a somewhat less related diversification strategy?

9.5. Under what conditions will a related diversification strategy not be a source of competitive advantage for a firm?

Problem Set

9.6. Visit the corporate Web sites for the following firms. How would you characterize the corporate strategies of these companies? Are they following a strategy of limited diversification, related diversification, or unrelated diversification?

(a) ExxonMobil
(b) Google
(c) General Motors
(d) JetBlue
(e) Citigroup
(f) Entertainment Arts
(g) IBM
(h) Dell
(i) Alphabet

9.7. Consider the following list of strategies. In your view, which are examples of potential economies of scope underlying a corporate diversification strategy? For those strategies that are an economy of scope, which economy of scope are they? For those strategies that are not an economy of scope, why aren't they?

(a) The Coca-Cola Corporation replaces its old diet cola drink (Tab) with a new diet cola drink called Diet Coke.
(b) Apple introduces an iPhone with a larger memory.
(c) PepsiCo distributes Lay's Potato Chips to the same stores where it sells Pepsi.
(d) Wal-Mart uses the same distribution system to supply its Wal-Mart stores, its Wal-Mart Supercenters (Wal-Mart stores with grocery stores in them), and its Sam's Clubs.

(e) Head Ski Company introduces a line of tennis rackets.

(f) General Electric borrows money from Bank of America at three percent interest and then makes capital available to its jet engine subsidiary at eight percent interest.

(g) McDonald's acquires Boston Market and Chipotle (two restaurants where many customers sit in the restaurant to eat their meals).

(h) A venture capital firm invests in a firm in the biotechnology industry and a firm in the entertainment industry.

(i) Another venture capital firm invests in two firms in the biotechnology industry.

9.8. Consider the following facts. The standard deviation of the cash flows associated with Business I is 0.8. The larger this standard deviation, the riskier a business's future cash flows are likely to be. The standard deviation of the cash flows associated with Business II is 1.3. That is, Business II is riskier than Business I. Finally, the correlation between the cash flows of these two businesses over time is 0.8. This means that when Business I is up, Business II tends to be down, and vice versa. Suppose one firm owns both businesses.

(a) Assuming that Business I constitutes 40 percent of this firm's revenues and Business II constitutes 60 percent of its revenues, calculate the riskiness of this firm's total revenues using the following equation:

$$sd_{I,II} = \sqrt{w^2 sd_I^2 + (1 - w)^2 sd_{II}^2 + 2w(1 - w)(r_{I,II} sd_I sd_{II})}$$

Where $w = 0.40$; $sd_I = 0.8$, $sd_{II} = 1.3$, and $r_{I,II} = -8$.

(b) Given this result, does it make sense for this firm to own both Business I and Business II? Why or why not?

Writing Assignments

9.9. Not all firms will choose corporate diversification. Describe the benefits and challenges of the alternatives.

9.10. Internal capital markets have several limitations. When a firm is confronted by these limitations, what is it likely to do?

CASE STUDY | Godrej Group's Journey: From Locks to a Diverse Conglomerate

The Godrej Group, an emblem of India's industrial revolution, has charted a remarkable journey since its inception in 1897 by Ardeshir Godrej and Pirojsha Burjorji Godrej. This conglomerate, with its headquarters nestled in Mumbai, Maharashtra, has burgeoned into a diverse empire, straddling various sectors such as consumer goods, real estate, industrial engineering, and more. The conglomerate's diversification strategy, underpinned by innovation and global expansion, has not only fortified its position in the domestic market but also on the international stage.

Financially, the Godrej Group has demonstrated robust performance. In the fiscal year 2023, the conglomerate reported a revenue of ₹33,000 crore ($4.1 billion), showcasing the financial success underlying its diversification strategy. The group's expansive reach, serving customers worldwide and employing around 28,000 people as of 2016, underscores its significant impact on the global economy.

Diversification has been a cornerstone of Godrej's strategy, allowing it to navigate the vicissitudes of market dynamics adeptly. By spreading its interests across different sectors, Godrej has effectively mitigated risks associated with market fluctuations. This strategy has enabled the group to capitalize on opportunities across diverse economic conditions, demonstrating remarkable adaptability and resilience. The group's historical timeline reveals a strategic expansion into sectors beyond its original lock-making business, venturing into agriculture, consumer goods, and more, signifying its dynamic approach to business expansion and innovation. However, diversification presents its own set of challenges, including the integration of diverse business units and maintaining operational efficiency across varied sectors. A discussion highlighted by the chairman of the Godrej Group emphasized the importance of clear and focused accountability in each business unit to create value within a conglomerate. This insight underscores the complexity of managing a diversified business empire and the need for strategic focus and accountability.

Looking forward, the Godrej Group appears poised to continue leveraging technology and innovation, with a keen emphasis on sustainability and digital transformation as key drivers of future growth. Godrej group's commitment to education and community development, evidenced by initiatives like Project Nanhi Kali and its educational institutions, reflects a broader vision of corporate responsibility and societal contribution. The Godrej Group's strategic diversification and robust financial performance exemplify its enduring success and resilience. Despite the challenges inherent in managing a diversified conglomerate, the group's focus on innovation, sustainability, and ethical leadership continues to propel its growth and competitive advantage in the global market.

Questions

1. How has the Godrej Group effectively utilized diversification as a strategic approach to navigate market dynamics and mitigate risks?
2. In what ways has the Godrej Group demonstrated its commitment to innovation, sustainability, and ethical leadership as key drivers of future growth? How do initiatives like Project Nanhi Kali and educational institutions reflect the group's broader vision of corporate responsibility and societal contribution, and how do they contribute to the group's competitive advantage in the global market?
3. How does the group's emphasis on technology and digital transformation position it for future growth, and what strategic considerations should the group prioritize to sustain its competitive edge amidst evolving market trends and challenges?

References

Godrej Group. (2023). *Annual Report 2022–2023*. Mumbai: Godrej Industries Limited. Accessed from https://godrejindustries.com on March 29, 2024

Pattanayak, L., Jena, L. K., & Sahoo, K. (2020). *Leadership at Godrej: a treasured heirloom transformed into a valuable brand.* Vilakshan-XIMB Journal of Management, 17(1/2), 153–171.

Chatterjee, C., & Palanichami, A. (2023). *Godrej Properties Limited: Leading Strategic Transformation in Indian Real Estate Markets.* Indian Institute of Management, Ahmedabad.

End Notes

1 www.pepsico.com/brands Accessed February 14, 2017

2 The Walt Disney Company. (1995). Harvard Business School Case No. 1-388-147.

3 H. P. Lang and R. M. Stulz (1994). "Tobin's *q*, corporate diversification, and firm performance." *Journal of Political Economy*, 102, pp. 1248–1280; R. Comment and G. Jarrell (1995). "Corporate focus and stock returns." *Journal of Financial Economics*, 37, pp. 67–87; D. Miller (2006). "Technological diversity, related diversification, and firm performance." *Strategic Management Journal*, 27(7), pp. 601–620; B. Villalonga (2004). "Does diversification cause the 'diversification discount'?" *Financial Management*, 33(2), pp. 5–28; T. Mackey, J. Barney, and J. Dotson (2017) "Corporate diversification and the value of individual firms: A Bayesian approach. *Strategic Management Journal*, 32(2): pp. 322–341.

4 See Rogers, A. (1992). "It's the execution that counts." *Fortune*, November 30, pp. 80–83; and Porter, M. E. (1981). "Disposable diaper industry in 1974." Harvard Business School Case No. 9-380-175. A more general discussion of the value of shared activities can be found in St. John, C. H., and J. S. Harrison. (1999). "Manufacturing-based relatedness, synergy, and coordination." *Strategic Management Journal*, 20, pp. 129–145.

5 See Fuchsberg, G. (1992). "Decentralized management can have its drawbacks." *The Wall Street Journal*, December 9, p. B1.

6 See about.att.com/story/att-completes-acquisition-of-DirectTV. Accessed February 14, 2017.

7 de Lisser, E. (1993). "Catering to cooking-phobic customers, supermarkets stress carryout." *The Wall Street Journal*, April 5, p. B1.

8 See, for example, Davis, P., R. Robinson, J. Pearce, and S. Park. (1992). "Business unit relatedness and performance: A look at the pulp and paper industry." *Strategic Management Journal*, 13, pp. 349–361.

9 Loomis, C. J. (1993). "Dinosaurs?" *Fortune*, May 3, pp. 36–42.

10 Rapoport, C. (1992). "A tough Swede invades the U.S." *Fortune*, June 29, pp. 776–779.

11 Prahalad, C. K., and G. Hamel. (1990). "The core competence of the organization." *Harvard Business Review*, 90, p. 82.

12 See also Grant, R. M. (1988). "On 'dominant logic' relatedness and the link between diversity and performance." *Strategic Management Journal*, 9, pp. 639–642; Chatterjee, S., and B. Wernerfelt. (1991). "The link between resources and type of diversification: Theory and evidence." *Strategic Management Journal*, 12, pp. 33–48; Constantinos C. Markides, and P. J. Williamson. (1994). "Related diversification, core competencies, and corporate performance." *Strategic Management Journal*, 15, pp. 149–165; Montgomery, C. A., and B. Wernerfelt. (1991). "Sources of superior performance: Market share versus industry effects in the U.S. brewing industry." *Management Science*, 37, pp. 954–959; Liedtka, J. M. (1996). "Collaborating across lines of business for competitive advantage." *Academy of Management Executive*, 10(2), pp. 20–37; and Farjoun, M. (1998). "The independent and joint effects of the skill and physical bases of relatedness in diversification." *Strategic Management Journal*, 19, pp. 611–630.

13 See Bartlett, C.A. and S. Ghoshal (1989) *Managing Across Borders: The Transnational Solution*. Boston, MA: Harvard Business School Press.

14 Presentation by V. P. of Research and Development, General Electric Medical Imaging Chinese Division, SMS Special Conference in Guangzhou, China, December, 2015.

15 *10K report for Berkshire Hathaway*; W. Buffet (2013). "An owner's manual, revised." www.berkshirehathaway.com. Accessed July 26, 2013 and February 14, 2017,

16 Danaher Case, HBS

17 Prahalad, C. K., and R. A. Bettis. (1986). "The dominant logic: A new linkage between diversity and performance." *Strategic Management Journal*, 7(6), pp. 485–501.

18 See Williamson, O. E. (1975). *Markets and hierarchies: Analysis and antitrust implications*. New York: Free Press.

19 Publically traded firms often have to be more forthcoming about both their performance and prospects. However, even among these firms, managers may know more about their firm's performance and prospects than they say in public statements.

20 See Liebeskind, J. P. (1996). "Knowledge, strategy, and the theory of the firm." *Strategic Management Journal*, 17 (Winter Special Edition), pp. 93–107.

21 Perry, L. T., and J. B. Barney. (1981). "Performance lies are hazardous to organizational health." *Organizational Dynamics*, 9(3), pp. 68–80.

22 Bethel, J. E. (1990). *The capital allocation process and managerial mobility: A theoretical and empirical investigation*. Unpublished doctoral dissertation, University of California at Los Angeles.

23 Staw, B. M. (1981). "The escalation of commitment to a course of action." *Academy of Management Review*, 6, pp. 577–587.

24 See Comment, R., and G. Jarrell. (1995). "Corporate focus and stock returns." *Journal of Financial Economics*, 37, pp. 67–87; Berger, P. G., and E. Ofek. (1995). "Diversification's effect on firm value." *Journal of Financial Economics*, 37, pp. 39–65; Maksimovic, V., and G. Phillips. (1999). "Do conglomerate firms allocate resources inefficiently?" Working paper, University of Maryland; Matsusaka, J. G., and V. Nanda. (1998). "Internal capital markets and corporate refocusing." Working paper, University of Southern California; Palia, D. (1998). "Division-level overinvestment and agency conflicts in diversified firms." Working paper, Columbia University; Rajan, R., H. Servaes, and L. Zingales. (1997). "The cost of diversity: The diversification discount and inefficient investment." Working paper, University of Chicago; Scharfstein, D. S. (1997). "The dark side of internal capital markets II: Evidence from diversified conglomerates." NBER [National Bureau of Economic Research]. Working paper; Shin, H. H., and R. M. Stulz. (1998). "Are internal capital markets efficient?" *The Quarterly Journal of Economics*, May, pp. 551–552. But Houston and James (1998) show that internal capital markets can create competitive advantages for firms: Houston, J., and C. James. (1998). "Some evidence that banks use internal capital markets to lower capital costs." *Journal of Applied Corporate Finance*, 11(2), pp. 70–78.

25 Scott, J. H. (1977). "On the theory of conglomerate mergers." *Journal of Finance*, 32, pp. 1235–1250.

26 See Brennan, M. (1979). "The pricing of contingent claims in discrete time models." *Journal of Finance*, 34, pp. 53–68; Cox, J., S. Ross, and M. Rubinstein. (1979). "Option pricing: A simplified approach." *Journal of Financial Economics*, 7, pp. 229–263; Stapleton, R. C. (1982). "Mergers, debt capacity, and the valuation of corporate loans." In M. Keenan and L. J. White. (eds.), *Mergers and acquisitions*. Lexington, MA: D. C. Heath, Chapter 2; and Galai, D., and R. W. Masulis. (1976). "The option pricing model and the risk factor of stock." *Journal of Financial Economics*, 3, pp. 53–82.

27 See Karnani, A., and B. Wernerfelt. (1985). "Multiple point competition." *Strategic Management Journal*, 6, pp. 87–96; Bernheim, R. D., and M. D. Whinston. (1990). "Multimarket contact and collusive behavior." *Rand Journal of Economics*, 12, pp. 605–617; Tirole, J. (1988). *The theory of industrial organization*. Cambridge, MA: MIT Press; Gimeno, J., and C. Y. Woo. (1999). "Multimarket contact, economies of scope, and firm performance." *Academy of Management Journal*, 43(3), pp. 239–259; Korn, H. J., and J. A. C. Baum. (1999). "Chance, imitative, and strategic antecedents to multimarket contact." *Academy of Management Journal*, 42(2), pp. 171–193; Baum, J. A. C., and H. J. Korn. (1999). "Dynamics of dyadic competitive interaction." *Strategic Management Journal*, 20, pp. 251–278; Gimeno, J. (1999). "Reciprocal threats in multimarket rivalry: Staking our 'spheres of influence' in the U.S. airline industry." *Strategic Management Journal*, 20, pp. 101–128; Gimeno, J., and C. Y. Woo. (1996). "Hypercompetition in a multimarket environment: The role of strategic similarity and multimarket contact in competitive de-escalation." *Organization Science*, 7(3), pp. 322–341; Ma, H. (1998). "Mutual forbearance in international business." *Journal of International Management*, 4(2), pp. 129–147; McGrath, R. G., and M.-J. Chen. (1998). "Multimarket maneuvering in uncertain spheres of influence: Resource diversion strategies." *Academy of Management Review*, 23(4), pp. 724–740; Chen, M.-J. (1996). "Competitor analysis and interfirm rivalry: Toward a theoretical integration." *Academy of Management Review*, 21(1), pp. 100–134; Chen, M.-J., and K. Stucker. (1997). "Multinational management and multimarket rivalry: Toward a theoretical development of global competition." *Academy of Management Proceedings 1997*, pp. 2–6; and Young, G., K. G. Smith, and C. M. Grimm. (1997). "Multimarket contact, resource heterogeneity, and rivalrous firm behavior." *Academy of Management Proceedings 1997*, pp. 55–59. This idea was originally proposed by Edwards, C. D. (1955). "Conglomerate bigness as a source of power." In *Business concentration and price policy*. NBER Conference Report. Princeton, NJ: Princeton University Press.

28 See Karnani, A., and B. Wernerfelt. (1985). "Multiple point competition." *Strategic Management Journal*, 6, pp. 87–96.

29 This was documented by Gimeno, J. (1994). "Multipoint competition, market rivalry and firm performance: A test of the mutual forbearance hypothesis in the United States airline industry, 1984–1988." Unpublished doctoral dissertation, Purdue University.

30 The best work in this area has been done by Gimeno, J. (1994). "Multipoint competition, market rivalry and firm performance: A test of the mutual forbearance hypothesis in the United States airline industry, 1984–1988." Unpublished doctoral dissertation, Purdue University. See also Smith, F., and R. Wilson. (1995). "The predictive validity of the Karnani and Wernerfelt model of multipoint competition." *Strategic Management Journal*, 16, pp. 143–160.

31 See M. Sengul and J. Gimeno (2013) "Constrained delegation: Limiting subsidiary's decision rights and resources in firms that compete across multiple industries," *Administrative Science Quarterly*,58(3): 425–471.

32 See Tirole, J. (1988). *The theory of industrial organization.* Cambridge, MA: MIT Press.

33 Carnevale, M. L. (1993). "Ring in the new: Telephone service seems on the brink of huge innovations." *The Wall Street Journal*, February 10, p. A1. SBC acquired the remaining assets of the original AT&T and renamed the newly merged company AT&T.

34 See Russo, M. V. (1992). "Power plays: Regulation, diversification, and backward integration in the electric utility industry." *Strategic Management Journal*, 13, pp. 13–27. Work by Jandik and Makhija (1999) indicates that when a regulated utility diversifies out of a regulated industry, it often earns a more positive return than when an unregulated firm does this. Jandik, T., and A. K. Makhija. (1999). "An empirical examination of the atypical diversification practices of electric utilities: Internal capital markets and regulation." Fisher College of Business, Ohio State University, working paper (September). This work shows that regulators have the effect of making a regulated firm's internal capital market more efficient. Differences between Russo's (1992) findings and Jandik and Makhija's (1999) findings may have to do with when this work was done. Russo's (1992) research may have focused on a time period before regulatory agencies had learned how to improve a firm's internal capital market. However, even though Jandik and Makhija (1999) report positive returns from regulated firms diversifying, these positive returns do not reflect the market power advantages of these firms.

35 Finkelstein, S., and D. C. Hambrick. (1989). "Chief executive compensation: A study of the intersection of markets and political processes." *Strategic Management Journal*, 10, pp. 121–134.

36 D. C. Korten (2001). *When corporations rule the world*, 2nd ed. Bloomfield, CT: Kumarian Press; H. Demsetz (1973). "Industry structure, market rivalry, and public policy." *Journal of Law and Economics*, 16, pp. 1–9; J. Stiglitz (2007). *Making globalization work.* New York: Norton; www.unrefugees.org Accessed February 16, 2017.

37 J. B. Barney (1991). "Firm resources and sustained competitive advantage." *Journal of Management*, 17, pp. 99–120; R. M. Stulz (1996). "Rethinking risk management." *Journal of Applied Corporate Finance*, Fall, pp. 8–24; K. Miller (1998). "Economic exposure and integrated risk management," *Strategic Management Journal*, 33, pp. 756–779; R. Amit and B. Wernerfelt (1990). "Why do firms reduce business risk?" *Academy of Management Journal*, 33, pp. 520–533; H. Wang and J. Barney (2006), "Employee incentives to make firm specific investments: Implications for resource-based theories of diversification." *Academy of Management Review*, 31(2), pp. 466–476.

38 See M. Sengul and J. Gimeno (2013) "Constrained delegation: Limiting subsidiary's decision rights and resources in firms that compete across multiple industries," *Administrative Science Quarterly, 58(3): 425–471.*

CHAPTER 10

Organizing to Implement Corporate Diversification

LEARNING OBJECTIVES

After reading this chapter, you should be able to:

10.1 Describe the multidivisional, or M-form, organizational structure and the roles of the board of directors, institutional investors, the senior executive, corporate staff, division general managers, and shared activity managers in making the M-form structure work.

10.2 Describe how three management control processes—measuring divisional performance, allocating corporate capital, and transferring intermediate products—are used to help implement a corporate diversification strategy.

10.3 Describe the role of management compensation in helping to implement a corporate diversification strategy.

Infosys: Balancing Growth and Governance

Infosys, leading IT services and consulting firm, has navigated its corporate diversification strategy amidst the complexities of agency conflict, a common challenge in such expansive endeavours. Founded in 1981, Infosys has grown significantly, broadening its service offerings beyond its original focus, adapting to market changes, and seizing opportunities across different economic conditions. This evolution is reflected in its strategic initiatives such as Infosys 3.0, aimed at melding transformational consulting with emerging technologies to accelerate long-term growth.

Infosys has navigated its corporate diversification with strategic initiatives, such as Infosys 3.0, aimed at blending transformational consulting with emerging technologies. This approach reflects efforts to mitigate agency conflicts, aligning the interests of various stakeholders while aiming to compete with industry leaders like Accenture and IBM. The company's financial health is robust, as indicated by strong free cash flow and a debt-free balance sheet. Despite facing short-term challenges, such as economic uncertainties affecting consumer spending, Infosys's strategy of winning large deals and investing in digital capabilities positions it for long-term growth. However, navigating agency conflicts and managing the risks associated with competitive pricing and large deals will be crucial for sustaining growth and profitability The firm's focus on building up nearshore America's capacity and capabilities, acquiring consulting capacity in Europe, and investing in intellectual property reflects a strategic response to these challenges, aiming to enhance its global competitiveness and market positioning.

Infosys' commitment to corporate governance and ethical leadership is also evident in its ESG roadmap for 2030, highlighting ambitions in environmental sustainability, social development, and governance excellence. The company aims to serve the preservation of our planet, develop people by shaping a future with meaningful opportunities for all, and lead through core values, emphasizing the interests of all stakeholders. This forward-looking vision is part of Infosys' strategic efforts to mitigate agency conflicts through a commitment to world-class corporate governance, robust compliance, and stakeholder engagement. The company's strategic initiatives, such as the acquisition of Lodestone and investments in nearshore capabilities, demonstrate a clear direction toward balancing growth with operational efficiency and stakeholder alignment. Infosys' journey illustrates the intricate balance between diversification, agency conflict management, and sustainable growth. The company's strategic direction, underpinned by ethical governance and a commitment to innovation and sustainability, positions it well for future challenges and opportunities in the ever-evolving global market.

In 2023, Infosys' international strategy highlights its dedication to sustainability, client engagement, and technological innovation, particularly in cloud computing, through initiatives like Infosys Cobalt. Emphasizing a blend of global talent development and local expertise, Infosys aims to deepen its client relationships across diverse markets, including significant commitments in the U.S. This strategy is further enriched by its ambitious ESG roadmap targeting substantial reductions in greenhouse gas emissions, achieving carbon neutrality, and enhancing digital skills across communities, aiming to empower millions through technology. The focus on ESG initiatives, coupled with strategic partnerships and cloud technology advancements, positions Infosys as a forward-thinking leader in IT services, committed to delivering impactful business outcomes while fostering sustainable and inclusive growth.

REFERENCE

Infosys. (2023). *Annual Report 2022–2023. Infosys Limited*. Retrieved from: https://www.infosys.com on March 30, 2024

Sawhney, M., Poddar, V., & Kruse, K. (2023). *Tapping Into a Digital Brain: AI-Powered Talent Management at Infosys.* Case 5-122-003 (KE1222). Kellogg School of Management.

Mehta, S., & Baskaran, A. (2023). *Upgrading within Global Value Chains and Innovation Capabilities: Lessons from Indian Information Technology Sector.* Institutions and Economies, 113–140.

This chapter is about how large diversified firms—like Infosys—are managed and governed efficiently. The chapter explains how these kinds of firms are managed in a way that is consistent with the interests of their owners—equity holders—as well as the interests of their other stakeholders. The three components of organizing to implement any strategy, which were first identified in Chapter 3—organizational structure, management controls, and compensation policy—are also important in implementing corporate diversification strategies.

Objective 10.1 Describe the multidivisional, or M-form, organizational structure and the roles of the board of directors, institutional investors, the senior executive, corporate staff, division general managers, and shared activity managers in making the M-form structure work.

Organizational Structure and Implementing Corporate Diversification

The most common organizational structure for implementing a corporate diversification strategy is the **M-form**, or **multidivisional**, structure. A typical M-form structure, as it would appear in a firm's annual report, is presented in Figure 10.1. This same structure is redrawn in Figure 10.2 to emphasize the roles and responsibilities of each of the major components of the M-form organization.[1]

In the multidivisional structure, each business that the firm engages in is managed through a **division**. Different firms have different names for these divisions—strategic business units (SBUs), business groups, companies. Whatever their names, the divisions in an M-form organization are true **profit-and-loss centers:** Profits and losses can be calculated at the level of the division in these firms.

Different firms use different criteria for defining the boundaries of profit-and-loss centers. For example, General Electric defines its divisions in terms of the types of products each one manufactures and sells (e.g., aviation, capital, energy management, and health care). Nestlé defines its divisions with reference to the geographic scope of each of its businesses (North America, South America, and so forth). General Motors defines its divisions in terms of the brand names of its products (Cadillac, Chevrolet,

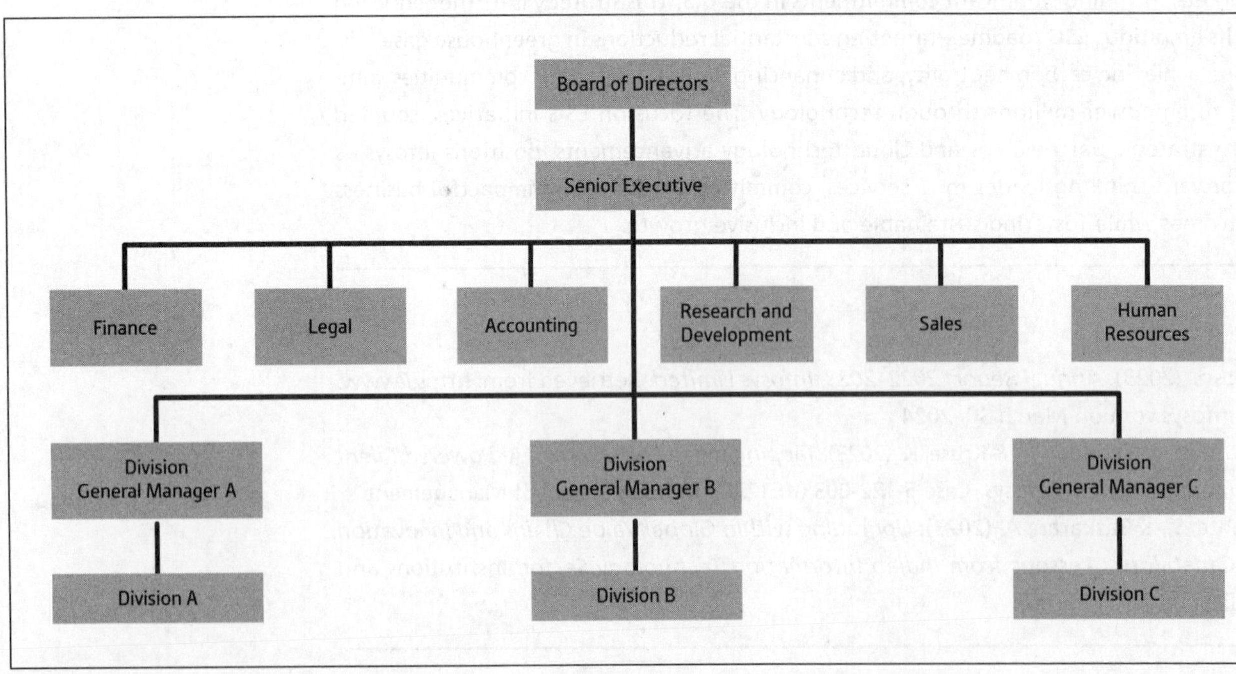

Figure 10.1 An Example of M-Form Organizational Structure as Depicted in a Firm's Annual Report

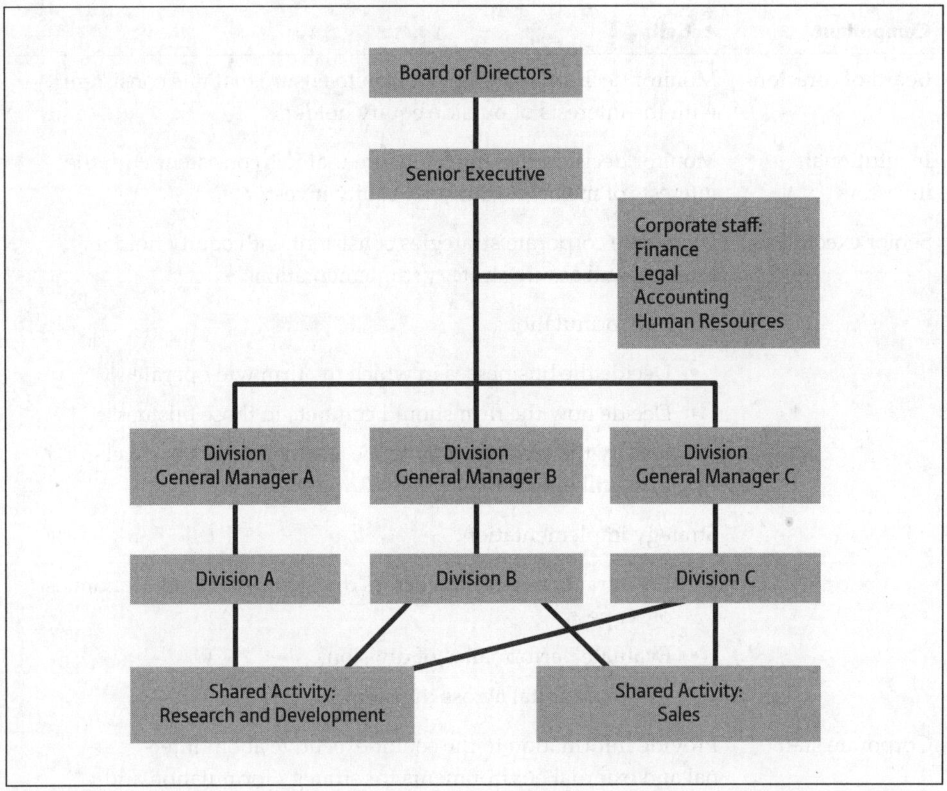

Figure 10.2 An M-Form Structure Redrawn to Emphasize Roles and Responsibilities

and so forth). However they are defined, divisions in an M-form organization should be large enough to represent identifiable business entities but small enough so that each one can be managed effectively by a division general manager. Indeed, each division in an M-form organization typically adopts a U-form structure (see the discussion of the U-form structure in Chapters 4, 5, and 6), and the division general manager takes on the role of a U-form senior executive for his or her division.

In Alphabet, the Google Division is a classic profit and loss center, although some of the businesses within the Google Division, e.g., Android, Google Search, may also be large enough and separate enough as a business to calculate profit and losses for these businesses as well. The Other Bets Division in Alphabet houses businesses that may someday grow large enough to become full profit and loss centers in Alphabet. However, by 2017, none of these businesses had yet reached this scale of operations.

The M-form structure is designed to create checks and balances for managers that increase the probability that a diversified firm will be managed in ways consistent with the interests of its equity holders. The roles of each of the major elements of the M-form structure in accomplishing this objective are summarized in Table 10.1 and discussed in the following text. Some of the conflicts of interest that might emerge between a firm's equity holders and its managers are described in the Strategy in Depth feature.

The Board of Directors

One of the major components of an M-form organization is a firm's **board of directors**. In principle, all the firm's senior managers report to the board. The board's primary responsibility is to monitor decision making in the firm, ensuring that it is consistent with the interests of outside equity holders.

TABLE 10.1 The Roles and Responsibilities of Major Components of the M-Form Structure

Component	Activity
Board of directors	Monitor decision making in a firm to ensure that it is consistent with the interests of outside equity holders
Institutional investors	Monitor decision making to ensure that it is consistent with the interests of major institutional equity investors
Senior executives	Formulate corporate strategies consistent with equity holders' interests and assure strategy implementation Strategy formulation: • Decide the businesses in which the firm will operate • Decide how the firm should compete in those businesses • Specify the economies of scope around which the diversified firm will operate Strategy implementation: • Encourage cooperation across divisions to exploit economies of scope • Evaluate performance of divisions • Allocate capital across divisions
Corporate staff	Provide information to the senior executive about internal and external environments for strategy formulation and implementation
Division general managers	Formulate divisional strategies consistent with corporate strategies and assure strategy implementation Strategy formulation: • Decide how the division will compete in its business, given the corporate strategy Strategy implementation: • Coordinate the decisions and actions of functional managers reporting to the division general manager to implement divisional strategy • Compete for corporate capital allocations • Cooperate with other divisions to exploit corporate economies of scope
Shared activity managers	Support the operations of multiple divisions

A board of directors typically consists of 10 to 15 individuals drawn from a firm's top management group and from individuals outside the firm. A firm's **senior executive** (often identified by the title *president* or *chief executive officer* or *CEO*), its chief financial officer (CFO), and a few other senior managers are usually on the board—although managers on the board are typically outnumbered by outsiders. The firm's senior executive is often, but not always, the **chairman of the board**.

Strategy in Depth

Agency Conflicts Between Managers and Equity Holders

It is often in the self-interest of equity holders to delegate to managers the day-to-day management of their equity investments in a firm. This will be the case when equity investors cannot realize a valuable economy of scope on their own, while managers *can* realize that economy of scope (see Chapter 9).

Several authors have suggested that whenever one party in an exchange delegates decision-making authority to a second party, an **agency relationship** has been created between these parties. The party delegating this decision-making authority is called the **principal**; the party to whom this authority is delegated is called the **agent**. In the context of corporate diversification, an agency relationship exists between a firm's outside equity holders (as principals) and its managers (as agents) to the extent that equity holders delegate the day-to-day management of their investment to those managers.

The agency relationship between equity holders and managers can be very effective if managers make investment decisions that are consistent with equity holders' interests. Thus, if equity holders are interested in maximizing the rate of return on their investment in a firm and if managers make their investment decisions with this objective in mind, then equity holders will have few concerns about delegating the day-to-day management of their investments to managers. However, in numerous situations the interests of a firm's outside equity holders and its managers do not coincide. When parties in an agency relationship differ in their decision-making objectives, **agency problems** arise. Two common agency problems have been identified: investment in managerial perquisites and managerial risk aversion.

Managers may decide to take some of a firm's capital and invest it in **managerial perquisites** that do not add economic value to the firm but do directly benefit those managers. Examples of such investments include lavish offices, fleets of corporate jets, and corporate vacation homes. Dennis Kozlowski, former CEO of Tyco International, is accused of "stealing" $600 million in these kinds of managerial perquisites from his firm. The list of goods and services that Kozlowski lavished on himself and those close to him is truly astounding—a multimillion-dollar birthday party for his wife, a $6,000 wastebasket, a $15,000 umbrella stand, a $144,000 loan to a board member, toga-clad waiters at an event, and so on.

As outrageous as some of these managerial perquisites can be, the second source of agency problems—**managerial risk aversion**—is probably more important in most diversified firms. As discussed in Chapter 9, equity holders can diversify their portfolio of investments at very low cost. Through their diversification efforts, they can eliminate all firm-specific risk in their portfolios. In this setting, equity holders would prefer that managers make riskier rather than less risky investments because the expected return on risky investments is usually greater than the expected return on less risky investments.

Managers, in contrast, have limited ability to diversify their human capital investments in their firm. Some portion of these investments is specific to a particular firm and has limited value in alternative uses. The value of a manager's human capital investment in a firm depends critically on the continued existence of the firm. Thus, managers are *not* indifferent to the riskiness of investment opportunities in a firm. Very risky investments may jeopardize a firm's survival and thus eliminate the value of a manager's human capital investments. These incentives can make managers more risk averse in their decision making than equity holders would like them to be.

One of the purposes of the M-form structure, and indeed of all aspects of organizing to implement corporate diversification, is to reduce these agency problems.[2]

Research Made Relevant

A great deal of research has tried to determine when boards of directors are more or less effective in ensuring that firms are managed in ways consistent with the interests of equity holders. Three issues have received particular attention: (1) the roles of insiders (i.e., managers) and outsiders on the board; (2) whether the board chair and the senior executive should be the same or different people; and (3) whether the board should be active or passive.

With respect to insiders and outsiders on the board, in one way this seems like a simple problem. Because the primary role of the board of directors is to monitor managerial decisions to ensure that they are consistent with the interests of equity holders, it follows that the board should consist primarily of outsiders because they face no conflict of interest in evaluating managerial performance. Obviously, managers, as inside members of the board, face significant conflicts of interest in evaluating their own performance.

Research on outsider members of boards of directors tends to support this point of view. Outside directors, as compared with insiders, tend to focus more on monitoring a firm's economic performance than on other measures of firm performance. Obviously, a firm's economic performance is most relevant to its equity investors. Outside board members are also more likely than inside members to dismiss CEOs for poor performance. Also, outside board members have a stronger incentive than inside members to maintain their reputations as effective monitors. This incentive by itself can lead to more effective monitoring by outside board members. Moreover, the monitoring effectiveness of outside board members seems to be enhanced when they personally own a substantial amount of a firm's equity.

The Effectiveness of Boards of Directors

However, the fact that outside members face fewer conflicts of interest in evaluating managerial performance compared with management insiders on the board does not mean that there is no appropriate role for inside board members. Managers bring something to the board that cannot be easily duplicated by outsiders—detailed information about the decision-making activities inside the firm. This is precisely the information that outsiders need to effectively monitor the activities of a firm, and it is information available to them only if they work closely with insiders (managers). One way to gain access to this information is to include managers as members of the board of directors. Thus, while most research suggests that a board of directors should be composed primarily of outsiders, there is an important role for insiders/managers to play as members of a firm's board.

There is currently some debate about whether the roles of board chair and CEO should be combined or separated and, if separated, what kinds of people should occupy these positions. Some have argued that the roles of CEO and board chair should definitely be separated and that the role of the chair should be filled by an outside (non-managerial) member of the board of directors. These arguments assume that only an outside member of the board can ensure the independent monitoring of managerial decision making. Others have argued that effective monitoring often requires more information than would be available to outsiders, and thus the roles of board chair and CEO should be combined and filled by a firm's senior manager.

Empirical research on this question suggests that whether these roles of CEO and chair should be combined depends on the complexity of the information analysis and monitoring task facing the CEO and board chair. Brian Boyd has found that combining the roles of CEO and chair is positively correlated with firm performance when firms operate in slow-growth and simple competitive environments—environments that do not overtax the cognitive capability of a single individual. This finding suggests that combining these roles does not necessarily increase conflicts between a firm and its equity holders. This research also found that separating the roles of CEO and board chair is positively correlated with firm performance when firms operate in high-growth and very complex environments. In such environments, a single individual cannot fulfill all the responsibilities of both CEO and board chair, and thus the two roles need to be held by separate individuals.

Finally, with respect to active versus passive boards, historically the boards of major firms have been relatively passive and would take dramatic action, such as firing the senior executive, only if a firm's performance was significantly below expectations for long periods of time. However, more recently, boards have become more active proponents of equity holders' interests. This recent surge in board activity reflects a new economic reality: if a board does not become more active in monitoring firm performance, then other monitoring mechanisms will. Consequently, the board of directors has become progressively more influential in representing the interests of a firm's equity holders.

However, board activity can go too far. To the extent that the board begins to operate a business on a day-to-day basis, it goes beyond its capabilities. Boards rarely have sufficient detailed information to manage a firm directly. When it is necessary to change a firm's senior executive, boards will usually not take on the responsibilities of that executive, but rather will rapidly identify a single individual—either an insider or outsider—to take over this position.[3]

The task of managerial board members—including the board chair—is to provide other board members information and insights about critical decisions being made in the firm and the effect those decisions are likely to have on a firm's equity holders. The task of outsiders on the board is to evaluate the past, current, and future performance of the firm and of its senior managers to ensure that the actions taken in the firm are consistent with equity holders' interests.[4]

Boards of directors are typically organized into several subcommittees. An **audit committee** is responsible for ensuring the accuracy of accounting and financial statements. A **finance committee** maintains the relationship between the firm and external capital markets. A **nominating committee** nominates new board members. A **personnel and compensation committee** evaluates and compensates the performance of a firm's senior executive and other senior managers. Often, membership on these standing committees is reserved for external board members. Other standing committees reflect specific issues for a particular firm and are typically open to external and internal board members.[5]

Over the years, a great deal of research has been conducted about the effectiveness of boards of directors in ensuring that a firm's managers make decisions in ways consistent with the interests of its equity holders. Some of this work is summarized in the Research Made Relevant feature.

Institutional Owners

Historically, the typical large diversified firm has had its equity owned in small blocks by millions of individual investors. The exception to this general rule was family-owned or dominated firms, a phenomenon that is relatively more common outside the United States. When a firm's ownership is spread among millions of small investors, it is difficult for any one of these investors to have a large enough ownership position to influence management decisions directly. The only course of action open to such investors if they disagree with management decisions is to sell their stock.

However, the growth of institutional owners has changed the ownership structure of many large diversified firms over the past several years. **Institutional owners** are usually pension funds, mutual funds, insurance companies, or other groups of individual investors that have joined together to manage their investments. In 1970, institutions owned 32 percent of the equity traded in the United States. By 1990, institutions owned 48 percent of this equity. In 2005, they owned

59 percent of all equity traded in the United States and 69 percent of the equity of the 1,000 largest firms in the United States.[6]

Institutional investors can use their investment clout to insist that a firm's management behaves in ways consistent with the interests of equity holders. Observers who assume that institutional investors are interested more in maximizing the short-term value of their portfolios than in the long-term performance of firms in those portfolios fear that such power will force firms to make only short-term investments. Research in the United States and Japan, however, suggests that institutional investors are not unduly myopic. Rather, as suggested earlier, these investors use approximately the same logic equity investors use when evaluating the performance of a firm. For example, one group of researchers examined the impact of institutional ownership on research and development investments in research and development (R&D)-intensive industries. R&D investments tend to be longer term in orientation. If institutional investors are myopic, they should influence firms to invest in relatively less R&D in favor of investments that generate shorter-term profits. This research showed that high levels of institutional ownership did not adversely affect the level of R&D in a firm. These findings are consistent with the notion that institutional investors are not inappropriately concerned with the short term in their monitoring activities.[7]

More generally, other researchers have shown that high levels of institutional ownership lead firms to sell businesses that do not share an economy of scope. This effect of institutional investors is enhanced if, in addition, outside directors on a firm's board have substantial equity investments in the firm. Given the discussion of the value of diversification in Chapter 9, it seems clear that these divestment actions are typically consistent with maximizing the present value of a firm.[8]

The Senior Executive

As suggested in Table 10.1, the senior executive (the president or CEO) in an M-form organization has two responsibilities: strategy formulation and strategy implementation. *Strategy formulation* entails deciding which set of businesses a diversified firm will operate in; *strategy implementation* focuses on encouraging behavior in a firm that is consistent with this strategy. Each of these responsibilities of the senior executive is discussed in turn.

Strategy Formulation

At the broadest level, deciding which businesses a diversified firm should operate in is equivalent to discovering and developing valuable economies of scope among a firm's current and potential businesses. If these economies of scope are also rare and costly to imitate, they can be a source of sustained competitive advantage for a diversified firm.

The senior executive is uniquely positioned to discover, develop, and nurture valuable economies of scope in a diversified firm. Every other manager in this kind of firm either has a divisional point of view (e.g., division general managers and shared activity managers) or is a functional specialist (e.g., corporate staff and functional managers within divisions). Only the senior executive has a truly corporate perspective. However, the senior executive in an M-form organization should involve numerous other divisional and functional managers in strategy formulation to ensure complete and accurate information as input to the process and a broad understanding of and commitment to that strategy once it has been formulated.

Strategy Implementation

As is the case for senior executives in a U-form structure, strategy implementation in an M-form structure almost always involves resolving conflicts among groups of managers. However, instead of simply resolving conflicts between functional managers (as is the case in a U-form), senior executives in M-form organizations must resolve conflicts within and between each of the major managerial components of the M-form structure: corporate staff, division general managers, and shared activity managers. Various corporate staff managers may disagree about the economic relevance of their staff functions, corporate staff may come into conflict with division general managers over various corporate programs and activities, division general managers may disagree with how capital is allocated across divisions, division general managers may come into conflict with shared activity managers about how shared activities should be managed, shared activity managers may disagree with corporate staff about their mutual roles and responsibilities, and so forth.

Obviously, the numerous and often conflicting relationships among groups of managers in an M-form organization can place significant strategy implementation burdens on the senior executive.[9] While resolving these numerous conflicts, however, the senior executive needs to keep in mind the reasons why the firm began pursuing a diversification strategy in the first place: to exploit real economies of scope that outside investors cannot realize on their own. Any strategy implementation decisions that jeopardize the realization of these real economies of scope are inconsistent with the underlying strategic objectives of a diversified firm. These issues are analyzed in detail later in this chapter, in the discussion of management control systems in the M-form organization.

The Office of the President: Board Chair, CEO, and COO

It is often the case that the roles and responsibilities of the senior executive in an M-form organization are greater than can be reasonably managed by a single individual. This is especially likely if a firm is broadly diversified across numerous complex products and markets. In this situation, it is not uncommon for the tasks of the senior executive to be divided among two or three people: the **board chair**, the **chief executive officer (CEO)**, and the **chief operating officer (COO)**. The primary responsibilities of each of these roles in an M-form organization are listed in Table 10.2. Together, these roles are known as the **office of the president**. In general, as the tasks facing the office of the president become more demanding and complex, the more likely it is that the roles and responsibilities of this office will be divided among two or three people.

Corporate Staff

The primary responsibility of **corporate staff** is to provide information about the firm's external and internal environments to the firm's senior executive. This information is vital for both the strategy formulation and the strategy implementation responsibilities of the senior executive. Corporate staff functions that

TABLE 10.2 Responsibilities of Three Different Roles in the Office of the President

Board chair	Supervision of the board of directors in its monitoring role
Chief executive officer	Strategy formulation
Chief operating officer	Strategy implementation

provide information about a firm's external environment include finance, investor relations, legal affairs, regulatory affairs, and corporate advertising. Corporate staff functions that provide information about a firm's internal environment include accounting and corporate human resources. These corporate staff functions report directly to a firm's senior executive and are a conduit of information to that executive.

Corporate and Divisional Staff

Many organizations recreate some corporate staff functions within each division of the organization. This is particularly true for internally oriented corporate staff functions such as accounting and human resources. At the division level, divisional staff managers usually have a direct "solid-line" reporting relationship to their respective corporate staff functional managers and a less formal "dotted-line" reporting relationship to their division general manager. The reporting relationship between the divisional staff manager and the corporate staff manager is the link that enables the corporate staff manager to collect the information that the senior executive requires for strategy formulation and implementation. The senior executive can also use this corporate staff/division staff relationship to communicate corporate policies and procedures to the divisions, although these policies can also be communicated directly by the senior executive to division general managers.

Although divisional staff managers usually have a less formal relationship with their division general managers, in practice division general managers can have an important influence on the activities of divisional staff. After all, divisional staff managers may formally report to corporate staff managers, but they spend most of their time interacting with their division general managers and with the other functional managers who report to their division general managers. These divided loyalties can sometimes affect the timeliness and accuracy of the information transmitted from divisional staff managers to corporate staff managers and thus affect the timeliness and accuracy of the information the senior executive uses for strategy formulation and implementation.

Nowhere are these divided loyalties potentially more problematic than in accounting staff functions. Obviously, it is vitally important for the senior executive in an M-form organization to receive timely and accurate information about divisional performance. If the timeliness and accuracy of that information are inappropriately affected by division general managers, the effectiveness of senior management can be adversely affected. Moreover, in some situations division general managers can have very strong incentives to affect the timeliness and accuracy of divisional performance information, especially if a division general manager's compensation depends on this information or if the capital allocated to a division depends on this information.

Efficient monitoring by the senior executive requires that corporate staff, and especially the accounting corporate staff function, remains organizationally independent of division general managers—thus, the importance of the solid-line relationship between divisional staff managers and corporate staff managers. Nevertheless, the ability of corporate staff to obtain accurate performance information from divisions also depends on close cooperative working relationships between corporate staff, divisional staff, and division general managers—hence, the importance of the dotted-line relationship between divisional staff managers and division general managers. How one maintains the balance between the distance and objectivity needed to evaluate a division's performance on the one hand, and, on the other hand, the cooperation and teamwork needed to gain access to the information required to evaluate a division's performance distinguishes excellent from mediocre corporate staff managers.

Overinvolvement in Managing Division Operations

Over and above the failure to maintain a balance between objectivity and cooperation in evaluating divisional performance, the one sure way that corporate staff can fail in a multidivisional firm is to become too involved in the day-to-day operations of divisions. In an M-form structure, the management of such day-to-day operations is delegated to division general managers and to functional managers who report to division general managers. Corporate staff managers collect and transmit information; they do not manage divisional operations.

One way to ensure that corporate staff does not become too involved in managing the day-to-day operations of divisions is to keep corporate staff small. This is certainly true for some of the best-managed diversified firms in the world including Berkshire Hathaway, with only 24 employees at corporate headquarters, but 288,500 employees worldwide. Only 1.5 percent of Johnson & Johnson's more than 80,000 employees work at the firm's headquarters, and only some of those individuals are members of the corporate staff. Hanson Industries has in its U.S. headquarters 120 people who help manage a diversified firm with $8 billion in revenues. Clayton, Dubilier, and Rice, a management buyout firm, has only 11 headquarters staff members overseeing eight businesses with collective sales of more than $6 billion.[10]

Division General Manager

Division general managers in an M-form organization have primary responsibility for managing a firm's businesses from day to day. Division general managers have full profit-and-loss responsibility and typically have multiple functional managers reporting to them. As general managers, they have both strategy formulation and strategy implementation responsibilities. On the strategy formulation side, division general managers choose strategies for their divisions, within the broader strategic context established by the senior executive of the firm. Many of the analytical tools described in Parts 1 and 2 of this book can be used by division general managers to make these strategy formulation decisions.

The strategy implementation responsibilities of division general managers in an M-form organization parallel the strategy implementation responsibilities of senior executives in U-form organizations. In particular, division general managers must be able to coordinate the activities of often-conflicting functional managers in order to implement a division's strategies.

In addition to their responsibilities as a U-form senior executive, division general managers in an M-form organization have two additional responsibilities: to compete for corporate capital and to cooperate with other divisions to exploit corporate economies of scope. Division general managers compete for corporate capital by promising high rates of return on capital invested by the corporation in their business. In most firms, divisions that have demonstrated the ability to generate high rates of return on earlier capital investments gain access to more capital or to lower-cost capital, compared with divisions that have not demonstrated a history of such performance.

Division general managers cooperate to exploit economies of scope by working with shared activity managers, corporate staff managers, and the senior executive in the firm to isolate, understand, and use the economies of scope around which the diversified firm was originally organized. Division general managers can even become involved in discovering new economies of scope that were not anticipated when the firm's diversification strategy was originally implemented but nevertheless may be both valuable and costly for outside investors to create on their own.

Of course, a careful reader will recognize a fundamental conflict between the last two responsibilities of division general managers in an M-form organization. These managers are required to compete for corporate capital and to cooperate to exploit economies of scope at the same time. Competition is important because it leads division general managers to focus on generating high levels of economic performance from their divisions. If each division is generating high levels of economic performance, then the diversified firm as a whole is likely to do well also. However, cooperation is important to exploit economies of scope that are the economic justification for implementing a diversification strategy in the first place. If divisions do not cooperate in exploiting these economies, there are few, if any, justifications for implementing a corporate diversification strategy, and the diversified firm should be split into multiple independent entities. The need to simultaneously compete and cooperate puts significant managerial burdens on division general managers. It is likely that this ability is both rare and costly to imitate across most diversified firms.[11]

Shared Activity Managers

One of the potential economies of scope identified in Chapter 9 was shared activities. Divisions in an M-form organization exploit this economy of scope when one or more of the stages in their value chains are managed in common. Typical examples of activities shared across two or more divisions in a multidivisional firm include common sales forces, common distribution systems, common manufacturing facilities, and common research and development efforts (also see Table 9.2). The primary responsibility of the individuals who manage shared activities is to support the operations of the divisions that share the activity.

The way in which M-form structure is often depicted in company annual reports (as in Figure 10.1) tends to obscure the operational role of shared activities. In this version of the M-form organizational chart, no distinctions are made between corporate staff functions and shared activity functions. Moreover, it appears that managers of shared activities report directly to a firm's senior executive, just like corporate staff. These ambiguities are resolved by redrawing the M-form organizational chart to emphasize the roles and responsibilities of different units within the M-form (as in Figure 10.2). In this more accurate representation of how an M-form actually functions, corporate staff groups are separated from shared activity managers, and each is shown reporting to its primary "internal customer." That "internal customer" is the senior executive for corporate staff groups and two or more division general managers for shared activity managers.

Shared Activities as Cost Centers

Shared activities are often managed as cost centers in an M-form structure. That is, rather than having profit-and-loss responsibility, **cost centers** are assigned a budget and manage their operations to that budget. When this is the case, shared activity managers do not attempt to create profits when they provide services to the divisions they support. Rather, these services are priced to internal customers in such a way that the shared activity just covers its cost of operating.

Because cost center shared activities do not have to generate profits from their operations, the cost of the services they provide to divisions can be less than the cost of similar services provided either by a division itself or by outside suppliers. If a shared activity is managed as a cost center, and the cost of services from this shared activity is *greater than* the cost of similar services provided by alternative sources, then either this shared activity is not being well managed or it was not a real economy of scope in the first place. However, when the cost of services from a shared activity is *less than* the cost of comparable services provided by a division itself or by an outside supplier, then division general managers have a strong incentive to use the services of shared activities, thereby exploiting an economy of scope that may have been one of the original reasons why a firm implemented a corporate diversification strategy.

Shared Activities as Profit Centers

Some diversified firms are beginning to manage shared activities as profit centers, rather than as cost centers. Moreover, rather than requiring divisions to use the services of shared activities, divisions retain the right to purchase services from internal shared activities or from outside suppliers or to provide services for themselves. In this setting, managers of shared activities are required to compete for their internal customers based on the price and quality of the services they provide.[12]

One firm that has taken this profit-center approach to managing shared activities is ABB, Inc., a Swiss engineering firm. ABB eliminated almost all of its corporate staff and reorganized its remaining staff functions into shared activities. Shared activities in ABB compete to provide services to ABB divisions. Not only do some traditional shared activities—such as research and development and sales—compete for internal customers, but many traditional corporate staff functions—such as human resources, marketing, and finance—do as well. ABB's approach to managing shared activities has resulted in a relatively small corporate staff and in increasingly specialized and customized shared activities.[13]

Of course, the greatest risk associated with treating shared activities as profit centers and letting them compete for divisional customers is that divisions may choose to obtain no services or support from shared activities. Although this course of action may be in the self-interest of each division, it may not be in the best interest of the corporation as a whole if, in fact, shared activities are an important economy of scope around which the diversified firm is organized.

In the end, the task facing the managers of shared activities is the same: to provide such highly customized and high-quality services to divisional customers at a reasonable cost that those internal customers will not want to seek alternative suppliers outside the firm or provide those services themselves. In an M-form organization, the best way to ensure that shared activity economies of scope are realized is for shared activity managers to satisfy their internal customers.

This discussion of the importance of shared activities in realizing some economies of scope in diversified firms does not presume that every diversified firm must use shared activities as an economy of scope. As shown in Table 9.3, there are many economies of scope in a diversified firm that do not rely on shared activities. Indeed, Alphabet is an example of a diversified corporation where one division—the Google Division—uses shared activities as an economy of scope and where another—the Other Bets Division—does not.

Objective 10.2 Describe how three management control processes—measuring divisional performance, allocating corporate capital, and transferring intermediate products—are used to help implement a corporate diversification strategy.

Management Controls and Implementing Corporate Diversification

The M-form structure presented in Figures 10.1 and 10.2 is complex and multifaceted. However, no organizational structure by itself can fully implement a corporate diversification strategy. The M-form structure must be supplemented with a variety of management controls. Three of the most important management controls in an M-form structure—systems for evaluating divisional performance, for allocating capital across divisions, and for transferring intermediate products between divisions—are discussed in this section.[14]

Evaluating Divisional Performance

Because divisions in an M-form structure are profit-and-loss centers, evaluating divisional performance should, in principle, be straightforward: Divisions that are very profitable should be evaluated more positively than divisions that are less profitable. In practice, this seemingly simple task is surprisingly complex. Two problems typically arise: (1) How should division profitability be measured; and (2) How should economy-of-scope linkages between divisions be factored into divisional performance measures.

Measuring Divisional Performance

Divisional performance can be measured in at least two ways. The first focuses on a division's accounting performance; the second on a division's economic performance.

Accounting Measures of Divisional Performance Both accounting and economic measures of performance can be used in measuring the performance of divisions within a diversified firm. Common accounting measures of divisional performance include the return on the assets controlled by a division, the return on a division's sales, and a division's sales growth. These accounting measures of divisional performance are then compared with some standard to see if a division's performance exceeds or falls short of that standard. Diversified firms use three different standards of comparison when evaluating the performance of a division: (1) a hurdle rate that is common across all the different business units in a firm; (2) a division's budgeted level of performance (which may vary by division); and (3) the average level of profitability of firms in a division's industry.

Each of these standards of comparison has its strengths and weaknesses. For example, if a corporation has a single hurdle rate of profitability that all divisions must meet or exceed, there is little ambiguity about the performance objectives of divisions. However, a single standard ignores important differences in performance that might exist across divisions.

Comparing a division's actual performance to its budgeted performance allows the performance expectations of different divisions to vary, but the budgeting process is time-consuming and fraught with political intrigue. One study showed that corporate managers routinely discount the sales projections and capital requests of division managers on the assumption that division managers are trying to "game" the budgeting system.[15] Moreover, division budgets are usually based on a single set of assumptions about how the economy is going to evolve, how competition in a division's industry is going to evolve, and what actions that division is going to take in its industry. When these assumptions no longer hold, budgets are redone—a costly and time-consuming process that has little to do with generating value in a firm.

Finally, although comparing a division's performance with the average level of profitability of firms in a division's industry also allows performance expectations to vary across divisions within a diversified firm, this approach lets other firms determine what is and is not excellent performance for a division within a diversified firm. This approach can also be manipulated—by choosing just the "right" firms with which to compare a division's performance, almost any division can be made to look like it's performing better than its industry average.[16]

No matter what standard of comparison is used to evaluate a division's accounting performance, most accounting measures of divisional performance have a common limitation. All these measures have a short-term bias. This short-term bias reflects the fact that all these measures treat investments in resources and capabilities that have the potential for generating value in the long run as costs during a particular year. To reduce costs in a given year, division managers may sometimes forgo investing in these resources and capabilities, even if they could be a source of sustained competitive advantage for a division in the long run.

Economic Measures of Divisional Performance Given the limitations of accounting measures of divisional performance, several firms have begun adopting economic methods of evaluating this performance. Economic methods build on accounting methods but adjust those methods to incorporate short-term investments that may generate long-term benefits. Economic methods also compare a division's performance with a firm's cost of capital (see Chapter 1). This avoids some of the gaming that can characterize the use of other standards of comparison in applying accounting measures of divisional performance.

Perhaps the most popular of these economically oriented measures of division performance is known as **economic value added (EVA)**.[17] EVA is calculated by subtracting the cost of capital employed in a division from that division's earnings in the following manner:

$$\text{EVA} = \text{adjusted accounting earnings}$$
$$-\ (\text{weighted average cost of capital} \times \text{total capital employed by a division})$$

Several of the terms in the EVA formula require some discussion. For example, the calculation of economic value added begins with a division's "adjusted" accounting earnings. These are a division's traditional accounting earnings, adjusted so that they approximate a division's economic earnings. Several adjustments to a division's accounting statements have been described in the literature. For example, traditional accounting practices require R&D spending to be deducted each year from a division's earnings. This can lead division general managers to under-invest in longer-term R&D efforts. In the EVA measure of divisional performance, R&D spending is added back into a division's performance, and R&D is then treated as an asset and depreciated over some period.

One consulting firm (Stern Stewart) that specializes in implementing EVA-based divisional evaluation systems in multidivisional firms makes up to 40 "adjustments" to a division's standard accounting earnings so that they more closely approximate economic earnings. Many of these adjustments are proprietary to this consulting firm. However, the most important adjustments—such as how R&D should be treated—are broadly known.

The terms in parentheses in the EVA equation reflect the cost of investing in a division. Rather than using some alternative standard of comparison, EVA applies financial theory and multiplies the amount of money invested in a division by a firm's weighted average cost of capital. A firm's weighted average cost of capital is the amount of money a firm could earn if it invested in any of its other divisions. In this sense, a firm's weighted average cost of capital can be thought of as the opportunity cost of investing in a particular division, as opposed to investing in any other division in the firm.

By adjusting a division's earnings and accounting for the cost of investing in a division, EVA is a much more accurate estimate of a division's economic performance than are traditional accounting measures of performance. The number of diversified firms evaluating their divisions with EVA-based measures of divisional performance is impressive and growing. These firms include AT&T, Coca-Cola, Quaker Oats, CSX, Briggs and Stratton, and Allied Signal. At Allied Signal, divisions that do not earn their cost of capital are awarded the infamous "leaky bucket" award. If this performance is not improved, division general managers are replaced. The use of EVA has been touted as the key to creating economic wealth in a diversified corporation.[18]

Economies of Scope and the Ambiguity of Divisional Performance

Whether a firm uses accounting measures to evaluate the performance of a division or uses economic measures of performance such as EVA, divisional performance in a well-managed diversified firm can never be evaluated unambiguously. Consider a simple example.

Suppose that in a particular multidivisional firm there are only two divisions (Division A and Division B) and one shared activity (R&D). Also, suppose that the two divisions are managed as profit-and-loss centers and that the R&D shared activity is managed as a cost center. To support this R&D effort, each division pays $10 million per year and has been doing so for 10 years. Finally, suppose that after 10 years of effort (and investment) the R&D group develops a valuable new technology that perfectly addresses Division A's business needs.

Obviously, no matter how divisional performance is measured, it is likely to be the case that Division A's performance will rise relative to Division B's performance. In this situation, what percentage of Division A's improved performance should be allocated to Division A, what percentage should be allocated to the R&D group, and what percentage should be allocated to Division B?

The managers in each part of this diversified firm can make compelling arguments in their favor. Division general manager A can reasonably argue that without Division A's efforts to exploit the new technology, the full value of the technology would never have been realized. The R&D manager can reasonably argue that, without the R&D effort, there would not have been a technology to exploit in the first place. Finally, division general manager B can reasonably argue that, without the dedicated long-term investment of Division B in R&D, there would have been no new technology and no performance increase for Division A.

That all three of these arguments can be made suggests that, to the extent that a firm exploits real economies of scope in implementing a diversification strategy, it will not be possible to unambiguously evaluate the performance of individual divisions in that firm. The fact that there are economies of scope in a diversified firm means that all the businesses a firm operates in are more valuable bundled together than they would be if kept separate from one another. Efforts to evaluate the performance of these businesses as if they were separate from one another are futile.

One solution to this problem is to force businesses in a diversified firm to operate independently of each other. If each business operates independently, then it will be possible to unambiguously evaluate its performance. Of course, to the extent that this independence is enforced, the diversified firm is unlikely to be able to realize the very economies of scope that were the justification for the diversification strategy in the first place.

Divisional performance ambiguity is bad enough when shared activities are the primary economy of scope that a diversified firm is trying to exploit. This ambiguity increases dramatically when the economy of scope is based on intangible core competencies. In this situation, it is shared learning and experience that justify a firm's diversification efforts. The intangible nature of these economies of scope multiplies the difficulty of the divisional evaluation task.

Even firms that apply rigorous EVA measures of divisional performance are unable to fully resolve these performance ambiguity difficulties. For example, the Coca-Cola division of the Coca-Cola Company has made enormous investments in the Coke brand name over the years, and the Diet Coke division has exploited some of that brand name capital in its own marketing efforts. Of course, it is not clear that all of Diet Coke's success can be attributed to the Coke brand name. After all, Diet Coke has developed its own creative advertising, its own loyal group of customers, and so forth. How much of Diet Coke's success—as measured through that division's economic value added—should be allocated to the Coke brand name (an investment made long before Diet Coke was even conceived), and how much should be allocated to the Diet Coke division's efforts? EVA measures of divisional performance do not resolve ambiguities created when economies of scope exist across divisions.[19]

In the end, the quantitative evaluation of divisional performance—with either accounting or economic measures—must be supplemented by the experience and judgment of senior executives in a diversified firm. Only by evaluating a division's performance numbers in the context of a broader, more subjective evaluation of the division's performance can a true picture of divisional performance be developed.

Allocating Corporate Capital

Another potentially valuable economy of scope outlined in Chapter 7 (besides shared activities and core competencies) is internal capital allocation. In that discussion, it was suggested that for internal capital allocation to be a justification for diversification the information made available to senior executives allocating capital in a diversified firm must be superior, in both amount and quality, to the information available to external sources of capital in the external capital market. Both the quality and the quantity of the information available in an internal capital market depend on the organization of the diversified firm.

One of the primary limitations of internal capital markets is that division general managers have a strong incentive to overstate their division's prospects and understate its problems to gain access to more capital at lower costs. Having an independent corporate accounting function in a diversified firm can help address this problem. However, given the ambiguities inherent in evaluating divisional performance in a well-managed diversified firm, independent corporate accountants do not resolve all these informational problems.

In the face of these challenges, some firms use a process called **zero-based budgeting** to help allocate capital. In zero-based budgeting, corporate executives create a list of all capital allocation requests from divisions in a firm, rank them from "most important" to "least important," and then fund all the projects a firm can afford, given the amount of capital it has available. In principle, no project will receive funding for the future simply because it received funding in the past. Rather, each project must stand on its own merits each year by being included among the important projects the firm can afford to fund.

Although zero-based budgeting has some attractive features, it has some important limitations as well. For example, evaluating and ranking all projects in a diversified firm from "most important" to "least important" is a very difficult task. It requires corporate executives to have a very complete understanding of the strategic role of each of the projects being proposed by a division, as well as an understanding of how these projects will affect the short-term performance of divisions.

In the end, no matter what process firms use to allocate capital, allocating capital inside a firm in a way that is more efficient than could be done by external capital markets requires the use of information that is not available to those external markets. Typically, that information will be intangible, tacit, and complex. Corporate managers looking to realize this economy of scope must find a way to use this kind of information effectively.[20] The difficulty of managing this process effectively may be one of the reasons why internal capital allocation often fails to qualify as a valuable economy of scope in diversified firms.[21]

Transferring Intermediate Products

The existence of economies of scope across multiple divisions in a diversified firm often means that products or services produced in one division are used as inputs for products or services produced by a second division. Such products or services are called **intermediate products or services**. Intermediate products or services can be transferred between any of the units in an M-form organization. This transfer is perhaps most important and problematic when it occurs between profit center divisions.

The transfer of intermediate products or services among divisions is usually managed through a **transfer-pricing system**: One division "sells" its product or service to a second division for a transfer price. Unlike a market price, which is typically determined by market forces of supply and demand, transfer prices are set by a firm's corporate management to accomplish corporate objectives.

Setting Optimal Transfer Prices

From an economic point of view, the rule for establishing the optimal transfer price in a diversified firm is quite simple: the transfer price should be the value of the opportunities forgone when one division's product or service is transferred to another division. Consider the following example. Division A's marginal cost of production is $5 per unit, but Division A can sell all its output to outside customers for $6 per unit. If Division A can sell all its output to outside customers for $6 per unit, the value of the opportunity forgone of transferring a unit of production from Division A to Division B is $6—the amount of money that Division A forgoes by transferring its production to Division B instead of selling it to the market.

However, if Division A is selling all the units it can to external customers for $6 per unit but still has some excess manufacturing capacity, the value of the opportunity forgone in transferring the product from Division A to Division B is only $5 per unit—Division A's marginal cost of production. Because the external market cannot absorb any more of Division A's product at $6 per unit, the value of the opportunity forgone when Division A transfers units of production to Division B is not $6 per unit (Division A can't get that price), but only $5 per unit.[22]

When transfer prices are set equal to opportunity costs, selling divisions will produce output up to the point that the marginal cost of the last unit produced equals the transfer price. Moreover, buying divisions will buy units from other divisions in the firm if the net revenues from doing so just cover the transfer price. These transfer prices will lead profit-maximizing divisions to optimize the diversified firm's profits.

Difficulties in Setting Optimal Transfer Prices

Setting transfer prices equal to opportunity costs sounds simple enough, but it is very difficult to do in real diversified firms. Establishing optimal transfer prices requires information about the value of the opportunities forgone by the "selling" division. This, in turn, requires information about this division's marginal costs, its manufacturing capacity, external demand for its products, and so forth. Much of this information is difficult to obtain. Moreover, it is rarely stable. As market conditions change, demand for a division's products can change, marginal costs can change, and the value of opportunities forgone can change. Also, to the extent that a selling division customizes the products or services it transfers to other divisions in a diversified firm, the value of the opportunities forgone by this selling division become even more difficult to calculate.

Even if this information could be obtained and updated rapidly, division general managers in selling divisions have strong incentives to manipulate the information in ways that increase the perceived value of the opportunities forgone by their division. These division general managers can thus increase the transfer price for the products or services they sell to internal customers and thereby appropriate for their division profits that should have been allocated to buying divisions.

Setting Transfer Prices in Practice

Because it is rarely possible for firms to establish an optimal transfer-pricing scheme, most diversified firms must adopt some form of transfer pricing that attempts to approximate optimal prices. Several of these transfer-pricing schemes are described in Table 10.3. However, no matter what particular scheme a firm uses, the transfer prices it generates will, at times, create inefficiencies and conflicts in a diversified firm. Some of these inefficiencies and conflicts are described in Table 10.4.[23]

The inefficiencies and conflicts created by transfer-pricing schemes that only approximate optimal transfer prices mean that few diversified firms are ever fully satisfied with how they set transfer prices. Indeed, one study found that as the level of resource sharing in a diversified firm increases

TABLE 10.3 Alternative Transfer-Pricing Schemes

Scheme	Description
Exchange autonomy	• Buying and selling division general managers are free to negotiate transfer price without corporate involvement. • Transfer price is set equal to the selling division's price to external customers.
Mandated full cost	• Transfer price is set equal to the selling division's actual cost of production. • Transfer price is set equal to the selling division's standard cost (i.e., the cost of production if the selling division were operating at maximum efficiency).
Mandated market based	• Transfer price is set equal to the market price in the selling division's market.
Dual pricing	• Transfer price for the buying division is set equal to the selling division's actual or standard costs. • Transfer price for the selling division is set equal to the price to external customers or to the market price in the selling division's market.

Source: R. Eccles (1985). *The transfer pricing problem: A theory for practice.* Lexington Books: Lexington, MA. Used with permission of Rowman and Littlefield Publishing Group.

TABLE 10.4 Weaknesses of Alternative Transfer-Pricing Schemes

1. Buying and selling divisions negotiate transfer price.
   - What about the negotiating and haggling costs?
   - The corporation risks not exploiting economies of scope if the right transfer price cannot be negotiated.
2. Transfer price is set equal to the selling division's price to external customers.
   - Which customers? Different selling division customers may get different prices.
   - Shouldn't the volume created by the buying division for a selling division be reflected in a lower transfer price?
   - The selling division doesn't have marketing expenses when selling to another division. Shouldn't that be reflected in a lower transfer price?
3. Transfer price is set equal to the selling division's actual costs.
   - What are those actual costs and who gets to determine them?
   - *All* the selling division's costs or only the costs relevant to the products being purchased by the buying division?
4. Transfer price is set equal to the selling division's standard costs.
   - Standard costs are the costs the selling division would incur if it were running at maximum efficiency. This hypothetical capacity subsidizes the buying division.
5. Transfer price is set equal to the market price.
   - If the product in question is highly differentiated, there is no simple "market price."
   - Shouldn't the volume created by the buying division for a selling division be reflected in a lower transfer price?
   - The selling division doesn't have marketing expenses when selling to a buying division. Shouldn't that be reflected in a lower transfer price?
6. Transfer price is set equal to actual costs for the selling division and to market price for the buying division.
   - This combination of schemes simply combines other problems of setting transfer prices.

(thereby increasing the importance of transfer-pricing mechanisms) the level of job satisfaction for division general managers decreases.[24]

It is not unusual for a diversified firm to change its transfer-pricing mechanisms every few years to find the "right" transfer-pricing mechanism. Economic theory tells us what the "right" transfer-pricing mechanism is: Transfer prices should equal opportunity cost. However, this "correct" transfer-pricing mechanism cannot be implemented in most firms. Firms that continually change their transfer-pricing mechanisms generally find that all these systems have some weaknesses. In deciding which system to use, a firm should be less concerned about finding the right transfer-pricing mechanism and more concerned about choosing a transfer-pricing policy that creates the fewest management problems—or at least the kinds of problems that the firm can manage effectively. Indeed, some scholars have suggested that the search for optimal transfer pricing should be abandoned in favor of treating transfer pricing as a conflict-resolution process. Viewed in this way, transfer pricing highlights differences between divisions and thus makes it possible to begin to resolve those differences in a mutually beneficial way.[25]

Overall, the three management control processes described here—measuring divisional performance, allocating corporate capital, and transferring intermediate products—suggest that the implementation of a corporate diversification strategy requires a great deal of management skill and experience. They also suggest that sometimes diversified firms may find themselves operating businesses that no longer fit with the firm's overall corporate strategy. This can often lead to divesting a business, an important topic in Chapter 12.

Compensation Policies and Implementing Corporate Diversification

Objective 10.3 Describe the role of management compensation in helping to implement a corporate diversification strategy.

A firm's compensation policies constitute a final set of tools for implementing diversification. Traditionally, the compensation of corporate managers in a diversified firm has been only loosely connected to the firm's economic performance. One important study examined the relationship between executive compensation and firm performance and found that differences in CEO cash compensation (salary plus cash bonus) are not very responsive to differences in firm performance.[26] In particular, this study showed that a CEO of a firm whose equity holders lost, collectively, $400 million in a year earned average cash compensation worth $800,000, while a CEO of a firm whose equity holders gained, collectively, $400 million in a year earned average cash compensation worth $1,040,000. Thus, an $800 million difference in the performance of a firm only had, on average, a $204,000 impact on the size of a CEO's salary and cash bonus. Put differently, for every million dollars of improved firm performance, CEOs, on average, get paid an additional $255. After taxes, increasing a firm's performance by a million dollars is roughly equal in value to a good dinner at a nice restaurant.

However, this same study was able to show that if a substantial percentage of a CEO's compensation came in the form of stock and stock options in the firm, changes in compensation would be closely linked with changes in the firm performance. In particular, the $800 million difference in firm performance just described would be associated with a $1.2 million difference in the value of CEO compensation if CEO compensation included stock and stock options in addition to cash compensation. In this setting, an additional million dollars of firm performance increases a CEO's salary by $667.

These, and similar findings reported elsewhere, have led more and more diversified firms to include stock and stock options as part of the compensation package for the CEO. As important, many firms now extend this non-cash compensation to other senior managers in a diversified firm, including division general managers. For example, the top 1,300 managers at General Dynamics receive stock and stock options as part of their compensation package. Moreover, the cash bonuses of these managers also depend on General Dynamics' stock market performance. At Johnson & Johnson, all division general managers receive a five-component compensation package. The level of only one of those components, salary, does not vary with the economic profitability of the business over which a division general manager presides. The level of the other four components—a cash bonus, stock grants, stock options, and a deferred income package—varies with the economic performance of a particular division. Moreover, the value of some of these variable components of compensation also depends on Johnson & Johnson's long-term economic performance.[27]

To the extent that compensation in diversified firms gives managers incentives to make decisions consistent with stockholders' interests, they can be an important part of the process of implementing corporate diversification. However, the sheer size of the compensation paid to some CEOs raises ethical issues for some. These ethical issues are discussed in the Ethics and Strategy feature.

Ethics and Strategy

Do CEOs Get Paid Too Much?

Nothing in business gets as much negative press as CEO salaries. In 2016, for example, Dara Khosrowshahi, CEO of Expedia, was paid $94.6 million; Leslie Moonves, CEO of CBS was paid $56.4 million; Philipe Dauman, CEO of Viacom $54.1 million; and co-CEOS of Oracle, Mark Hurd and Safra Catz, were paid $53.2 million each. Reasonable people ask, "Is anyone worth this much money?"

Indeed, in a 2016 survey conducted in the United States, over 74% survey respondents believed that CEOs in the United States were being paid too much. This was the case even though these respondents thought that CEOSs in the United States earned, on average, $1 million a year. In fact, CEOs of publically traded firms in the United States earned an average of $10.3 million in 2016.

But determining what CEOs "should" be paid is a difficult question. Some firms adopt policies that state that their CEOs cannot make more than some multiple of the lowest-paid employee in a firm. This is how Ben & Jerry's Ice Cream compensated its CEO. However, this policy may have cost its shareholders millions of dollars because it prevented Ben & Jerry's from recruiting a CEO who would have facilitated Ben & Jerry's acquisition by a firm that could effectively leverage the Ben & Jerry's brand.

Many firms delegate the responsibility of determining CEO salary to the compensation committee on the board of directors. The compensation committee often identifies a set of comparable firms (i.e., firms about the same size and in the same industry) as its firm and then calculates the average compensation of CEOs in these firms. Of course, because no firm wants to think that its CEO is in the "bottom half" of its comparable firms, most firms pay their CEOs something over this average—a decision-making process that ensures that, in the long run, CEO pay will continue to rise.

The mix of compensation also makes it difficult to know how much a CEO should get paid. For example, most of the "big bucks" in CEO compensation come not from salary but from bonuses, stock, stock options, and other perquisites. Most of these non-salary forms of compensation depend on the performance of a firm and are designed to align the financial interests of CEOs and a firm's shareholders. This is the case at Berkshire Hathaway, where a key operating principle is that most of the personal wealth of Warren Buffett and his senior management team is held in Berkshire Hathaway stock. In fact, one study showed that, on average, CEO compensation in excess of what would be expected based on a CEO's business experience is positively correlated with a firm's performance.

Of course, correlation is not causation. The question remains open: Does a CEO must receive massive incentive compensation—literally hundreds of millions of dollars over time—just so he (or she) will do his (or her) job: to maximize returns to shareholders? And what are the implications of this compensation for the other employees in a firm—does it encourage their ambitions to seek employment among the senior ranks of a firm, or does it discourage and demoralize them that one person can get paid so much while they get paid so little?[28]

Summary

To be valuable, diversification strategies must exploit valuable economies of scope that cannot be duplicated by outside investors at low cost. However, to realize the value of these economies of scope, firms must organize themselves appropriately. A firm's organizational structure, its management control processes, and its compensation policies are all relevant in implementing a corporate diversification strategy.

The best organizational structure for implementing a diversification leveraging strategy is the multidivisional, or M-form, structure. The M-form structure has several critical components, including the board of directors, institutional investors, the senior executive, corporate staff, division general managers, and shared activity managers.

This organizational structure is supported by a variety of management control processes. Three critical management control processes for firms implementing diversification strategies are: (1) evaluating the performance of divisions; (2) allocating capital across divisions; and (3) transferring intermediate products between divisions. The existence of economies of scope in firms implementing corporate diversification strategies significantly complicates the management of these processes.

Finally, a firm's compensation policies are also important for firms implementing a diversification strategy. Historically, management compensation has been only loosely connected to a firm's economic performance, but recently the increased popularity of using stock and stock options to help compensate managers. Such compensation schemes help reduce conflicts between managers and outside investors, but the absolute level of CEO compensation is still very high, at least in the United States.

Challenge Questions

10.1. Agency theory has been criticized for assuming that managers, left on their own, will behave in ways that reduce the wealth of outside equity holders when, in fact, most managers are highly responsible stewards of the assets they control. This alternative view of managers has been called *stewardship theory*. Why would you agree with this criticism of agency theory?

10.2. Suppose that the concept of the stewardship theory is correct and that most managers, most of the time, behave responsibly and make decisions that maximize the present value of the assets they control. What implications, if any, would this supposition have on organizing to implement diversification strategies?

10.3. The M-form structure enables firms to pursue complex corporate diversification strategies by delegating different management responsibilities to different individuals and groups within a firm. Based on the concept of the M-form structure is there a natural limit to the efficient size of a diversified firm?

10.4. Most observers agree that centrally planned economies fail because it is impossible for bureaucrats in large government hierarchies to coordinate different sectors of an economy as efficiently as market mechanisms do. Many diversified firms, however, are as large as some economies and use private sector hierarchies to coordinate diverse business activities in a firm. Why would you consider these large, private sector hierarchies somehow different from the government hierarchies of centrally planned economies?

10.5. Most observers agree that centrally planned economies fail because it is impossible for bureaucrats in large government hierarchies to coordinate different sectors of an economy as efficiently as market mechanisms do. Many diversified firms, however, are as large as some economies and use private sector hierarchies to coordinate diverse business activities in a firm. If you do not consider these large, private sector hierarchies as different from the government hierarchies of centrally planned economies, then why do they continue to exist?

10.6. Suppose that the optimal transfer price between one business and all other business activities in a firm is the market price. What does this condition say about whether this firm should own this business?

Problem Set

10.7. Which elements of the M-form structure (the board of directors, the office of the CEO, corporate staff, division general managers, shared activity managers) should be involved in the following business activities? If more than one of these groups should be involved, indicate their relative level of involvement (e.g., 20 percent office of the CEO, 10 percent shared activity manager, 70 percent division general manager). Justify your answers.

(a) Determining the compensation of the CEO
(b) Determining the compensation of the corporate vice president of human resources
(c) Determining the compensation of a vice president of human resources in a particular business division
(d) Deciding to sell a business division
(e) Deciding to buy a relatively small firm whose activities are closely related to the activities of one of the firm's current divisions
(f) Deciding to buy a larger firm that is not closely related to the activities of any of a firm's current divisions
(g) Evaluating the performance of the vice president of sales, a manager whose sales staff sells the products of three divisions in the firm
(h) Evaluating the performance of the vice president of sales, a manager whose sales staff sells the products of only one division in the firm
(i) Determining how much money to invest in a corporate R&D function
(j) Deciding how much money to invest in an R&D function that supports the operations of two divisions within the firm
(k) Deciding whether to fire an R&D scientist
(l) Deciding whether to fire the vice president of accounting in a particular division
(m) Deciding whether to fire the corporation's vice president of accounting
(n) Deciding whether to take a firm public by selling stock in the firm to the general public for the first time

10.8. Consider the following facts. Division A in a firm has generated $847,000 of profits on $24 million worth of sales, using $32 million worth of dedicated assets. The cost of capital for this firm is 9 percent, and the firm has invested $7.3 million in this division.

(a) Calculate the Return on Sales (ROS) and Return on Total Assets (ROA) of Division A. If the hurdle rates for ROS and ROA in this firm are, respectively, 0.06 and 0.04, has this division performed well?
(b) Calculate the EVA of Division A (assuming that the reported profits have already been adjusted). Based on this EVA, has this division performed well?
(c) Suppose you were CEO of this firm. How would you choose between ROS/ROA and EVA for evaluating this division?

10.9. Suppose that Division A sells an intermediate product to Division B. Choose one of the ways of determining transfer prices described in this chapter (not setting transfer prices equal to the selling firm's opportunity costs) and show how Division Manager A can use this mechanism to justify a higher transfer price while Division Manager B can use this mechanism to justify a lower transfer price. Repeat this exercise with another approach to setting transfer prices described in the chapter.

Writing Assignments

10.10. How are the roles of senior executives and shared activity managers different in making the M-form structure work?

10.11. What are the implications for a multidivisional firm when the corporate staff become too involved in the day-to-day operations of divisions?

CASE STUDY: OYO – Rise of Sharing Economy

The emergence of peer-to-peer platforms, collectively known as the "sharing economy," has enabled people to collaboratively make use of underutilized inventory through fee-based sharing. Consumers have so far enthusiastically adopted the services offered by firms such as Airbnb, OYO, Ola, Uber, and others. The rapid growth of peer-to-peer platforms has arguably been enabled by two key factors—technology innovations and supply-side flexibility. The confluence of information technology, entrepreneurship, and venture capital has led to the creation of many new ventures, and that is generally good for any economy. Smartphone apps, cloud-based servers, and GPS technology have made various sharing services easy to launch and use. OYO changed its business model from the aggregator to the franchise model and selling their rooms to customers at competitive prices.

History

OYO was the brainchild of Ritesh Agarwal, a 17-year-old teen who launched Oravel Stays in 2012. Fast-forward to 2021, its name has changed to OYO Hotels & Homes, but still the name remains synonymous to hotel rooms. OYO doesn't own hotels; instead, it ties up with various hotels and acquires some rooms to be given out to people who want to avail OYO services. It focuses on standardizing the hotels in the non-branded hospitality sector.

OYO's original business model was similar to Airbnb Inc.'s. OYO Room is an asset-light, branded, digital aggregator of budget hotel rooms suited to Indian market. The company has operations in more than 450,000 listings in almost 5,000 cities across India, the UK, the UAE, Dubai, China, Singapore, Indonesia, and others. OYO delivers on its brand promise by using a 150-point essential checklist features, such as air conditioning and Wi-Fi availability in select rooms within the hotel. OYO typically seeks to onboard 40 percent of the rooms in a partner hotel onto the OYO platform. In the year 2019, valuation of Ritesh Agarwal touched $10 billion making it the second-most valuable start-up in India after Vijay Shekhar Sharma-controlled Paytm (valued at around $16 billion).

In 2018, the company became a 100 percent leased and franchised hotel chain. It recorded global stayed room nights of 75 million in 2018, almost six times more than in 2017, and collected a revenue of $211 million. In 2015, 2016 and 2017, OYO recorded global stayed room nights of 4 million, 6 million, and 13 million, respectively. In 2019, OYO generated a revenue of $951 million and witnessed an increase of $740 million, 4.5 times more than in 2018. Headquartered in Gurugram with 25,000+ employees, OYO employs a dynamic, algorithmically determined pricing model. Hoteliers can decide how much of their inventory they want to offer at that given price. The algorithm seeks to optimize profitability by balancing inventory and cost and taking market demand into account.

Business Model

The sharing economy is gaining increasing interest in management practice, and a major idea behind this phenomenon is that sharing products can be more efficient than individually owning them. Popular examples of the sharing economy address the needs of these customers. First step in reinventing business model is challenging the fundamental assumptions about what it means to be a business, employee, partner, or customer. OYO has reimagined what it means to be in the hospitality industry by disintermediating branding, operations, and quality assurance.

Business Model At Initial Phase: Earlier the company would take some rooms from partner hotels under the branding of OYO. These rooms needed to be maintained by the property owner according to OYO's pre-defined standards. OYO would pay in advance for the rooms. Because of advance payment and bulk booking, OYO got partner hotel rooms at heavy discounts. These rooms were then listed on OYO's platforms which it would sell to customers with some profit margin.

Current Business Model: As an aggregator to hotels, OYO faced standardization of hotels in its earlier business model. Hence, 2018 onwards OYO shifted to franchise-based model. Now, instead of taking rooms from partner hotels, OYO asks partner hotels to operate as an OYO franchise. This means although OYO doesn't own single hotel, it manages the entire hotel as a hospitality servicing company. This allows OYO to standardize all hotels under its brand, thereby giving same user experience to all its customers. Currently, the company earns 90 percent of its revenue from renting out hotel rooms.

The company further divided their hotels and stays under various categories— like OYO Townhouse, Capital O,

OYO Homes, OYO Life—for their growing customer base, who can choose their stay as per their requirement. Furthermore, the company has started subscription service OYO Wizard under which a 'wizard member' can avail exclusive discounts, offers, deals, and cash back advantages. OYO also backed Weddingz.in to form a category called OYO's Weddingz under which OYO partnered with several banquet hall vendors to allow people to book their wedding venues through its easy booking services and within best prices.

Revenue Structure

Commissions from hotels: OYO makes most amount of their revenue from this stream by charging average 22 percent commission charge from property owners. Commission charge varies as per services and features offered.

Room Reservation Fee: When customer is booking the hotel through OYO platforms, OYO charges room reservation fee of around 10–20 percent of room charges. This is also an important revenue stream OYO.

Membership Fees: OYO provides OYO Wizard membership and those who are members of Oyo Wizard are charged by a subscription which starts from ₹499.

Advertising: OYO also charges different companies to place their ads on OYO's app and website. It also generates sizable revenue for the company.

Sponsors and Partnerships: OYO also charges some amount from its sponsors and key partners by promoting their brand name through advertising on their app.

Consulting: OYO charges for its business consulting and data analysis services, it provides to its clients, including hotel, clubs, organizations, etc. It provides these services as it owns an extensive database of locations, hotels, event organizations, users, and their preferences.

Marketing Strategy

The OYO brand exudes charm and warmth of being a go-getter. The company was the first to identify the need for branding the domestic hospitality segment and offer hotel rooms within the price range of ₹999–₹3,000. Before the advent of OYO, the low and mid-budget hotel segment wasn't online and barely well-managed while always falling short of customers' expectations and expected parameters. The key value propositions OYO Hotels & Rooms have to offer are standardization, affordability, and technology. For a customer, an OYO branding means consistent experience, extended to the real-life. An OYO hotel means they get what they have seen on the website or app and paid for. Customer-centric practices, quality amenities at pocket-friendly prices have always been the USP of OYO. Both the app and the website are user-friendly and light for making hassle-free bookings in just a few clicks.

OYO has been aggressively pushing fresh content to lure Tier-II and Tier-III cities. It wanted to reach out to its demographics of young people who are continually using smartphones. The company's digital marketing campaign runs across multiple channels with a focus on personalized customer experience. Its Twitter (now X) account has over 74K followers reflects its robust presence. OYO on Facebook has wide-spread reach with more than one million followers and likes. The company stays active with daily posts and maintains regular customer engagement. Social media presence of the brand is marked by several popular videos, including the ones such as #AurKyaChahiye on YouTube, #OYOnauts, Jai Hind Campaign, and so on. OYO has optimized YouTube to bring forward the 'human' side of doing business with it.

Customer Experience

Unlike Airbnb that only connects travellers with local hosts, OYO takes full responsibility for services of the hotels listed on its platform. The aim of the OYO is to determine which aspects of its operations are the most beneficial to the organization and which can be changed to gain a competitive advantage. When it comes to making successful marketing articulation strategies, the STP approach is extremely useful because it allows marketers to prioritize ideas and then engage with various audiences.

Customers or buyers prefer semi-independent travel, where they pre-book or use vacation packages before arriving at their destination. This package includes a stay in OYO rooms.

Consumers pre-book OYO rooms for a variety of reasons, including value and convenience. This is a positive part of the company's business model.

Segmentation, Targeting, Positioning

OYO has served over 180 million multiple customer segments in 2019. The customer segments of OYO includes adventure, leisure, family, and business travellers.

OYO divides its market segments on the basis of geographic, demographics, psychographics, behavioral, and benefits sought.

Demographic: OYO has tied up with around 2,000 hotels, and rooms are available across 226 Indian cities which make people to find a decent hotel room to stay. Age, income, gender, generation, marital status, family size, occupation, education, ethnicity and religion are including under demographics while psychographics refers to a person's lifestyle, attitude, habits, interests and opinions. With OYO rooms, there are no such restrictions regardless of the demographic and psychographic characteristics listed above, OYO provides rooms to its customers with all of the mentioned amenities.

Behavioral: The usage rate plays the most important behavioral role. Customer satisfaction determines the usage rate of every regular customer. Customers are dissatisfied with a few of the hotels and their standards under OYO, it can cause the company to fall behind in customer loyalty. As a result, OYO provides specific guidelines for hotels in order to better serve its customers.

Benefit Sought: Convenience to find the room is one of the key characteristics for OYO to have. This element can be found all over OYO and is well-served. It is critical to get good value for your money. OYO platforms witness per second 5 customers booking rooms, while 77.5 million is the global app user base.

Targeting

The company caters to any regular, budget-conscious customer by offering rooms at a lower cost than those offered by other hotels. The key attraction is that it provides all necessary facilities for a fraction of the average cost, i.e., ₹4,000. Availability and usability are the most important requirements. OYO services are available 24 hours a day, 7 days a week throughout the year in various cities. The company majorly caters to frequent travellers in categories of backpackers—who on a tight budget, and are willing to compromise on quality—and business executives—who travel often and need technology as well as inexpensive lodging without sacrificing quality.

Positioning

OYO's status is referred to as 'standardized budget hotels,' which is short for aggregators. OYO has established itself in a market that values money. The company offers all of the best services at a low cost which adds value to the brand and brings in more customers on a daily basis. It has positioned itself as a company that cares for its customers. Customers have received several deals or discounts on a daily basis. OYO employs the idea of 'OYO money' in which consumers receive coupons in their wallets which they can then use the next time they check in. This gives OYO an advantage in retaining life-time customers.

Standardized OYO rooms assures that all of its rooms will have the same facilities for the similar amazing experience. OYO offers rooms at affordable rates than other budget player in the market. Superior technology to link all of its roles and provide a seamless and satisfying experience for its customers. In addition, OYO had made good use of social media for advertising, with its large number of followers on Facebook and Twitter (now X).

OYO's Financial Health in FY22

OYO has demonstrated a commendable fiscal turnaround in FY22 following a severe downturn in FY21, which saw the travel and hospitality sectors grappling with the pandemic's impact. The company's strategic approach, described as a 'Virtuous Cycle', allowed it to recover and make significant strides in financial performance. OYO's revenue from operations reflected a healthy increase of 20.7 percent, totaling ₹4,781 crore for FY22, as revealed in the company's financials. This upswing is attributed to OYO's compelling value proposition, which has resonated well with customers in a post-pandemic market.

The company also managed to pare down its losses by a substantial 51 percent, bringing them to ₹1,940 crore for FY22. This was further evidenced in the first quarter of FY23, where OYO sustained its operational revenue at ₹1,459 crore and contained losses to ₹414 crore. A closer look at the company's revenue breakdown shows that the sale of accommodation services and booking commissions were the linchpins of its operating revenue, accounting for approximately 90 percent of OYO's total earnings. These segments saw an uptick of 12.6 percent and 42.3 percent respectively, indicating a resilient demand for Oyo's services.

Further diversification of income streams such as rental and cancellation fees, along with the sale of tours, food and beverages, and other services, collectively grew by 37.5 percent, amounting to ₹465 crore in FY22. On the expenditure side, employee benefits emerged as the largest cost component, forming about 27 percent of the total costs. Despite this, OYO exhibited prudent financial management, with employee benefit costs rising only 7 percent to ₹1,862 crore in FY22, which included ₹680 crore in ESOP expenses. Other notable expenditures such as lease rent and service components of the lease increased modestly by 10.7 percent and 13.7 percent to ₹1,316 crore and ₹1,262 crore respectively. OYO's financial charges, including interests on borrowings, escalated by 32.6 percent to ₹744 crore. The company also incurred ₹546 crore on commissions and brokerage, cumulatively leading to a total cost of ₹6,984 crore for FY22.

The concerted effort in scaling operations and controlling costs resulted in a 51 percent reduction in losses from R ₹3,945 crore in FY21 to ₹1,940 crore in FY22. Cash outflows also witnessed a significant decrease of 62 percent, amounting to ₹922 crore due to stringent austerity measures. Analyzing OYO's unit economics reveals that the company spent ₹1.46 to earn a single rupee of operating revenue in FY22. Notably, the EBITDA margin and Return on Capital Employed (ROCE) witnessed an improvement to a –21.12 percent and –20.67 percent respectively.

While OYO's financial performance has improved markedly in FY22, challenges lie ahead as the company prepares for its IPO. With the precedent of public market responses to earnings misses set by peers' like Paytm and Zomato, OYO's loss of ₹1,940 crore could be a cause for concern. The company's business model—once a disruptive force in hospitality—is gradually aligning with traditional industry practices, potentially affecting its valuation premium.

As OYO advances towards its public listing with plans to raise ₹8,430 crore through primary and secondary share sales, it must navigate a market that may be indifferent to a loss-making hospitality chain. The company's ability to sustain profitability and demonstrate a viable growth model will be critical in securing a favorable market position.

Future Challenges and Opportunities

As OYO steers through the post-pandemic recovery, it faces challenges and opportunities in adapting to changing consumer behaviors and the competitive landscape. Strategic alliances and technological innovation will be pivotal in sustaining its competitive advantage. OYO's agility in responding to market demands and its continued focus on enhancing customer experiences through technology will be crucial for its future success.

This refined case study, enriched with detailed numbers and insights, offers a comprehensive overview of OYO's strategic direction, competitive positioning, and financial performance, highlighting its journey towards becoming a global leader in the hospitality sector.

Questions:

1. How do strategic alliances contribute to Oyo's innovation and market agility, and what are the key factors for building successful collaborations that drive value creation?
2. In the context of Oyo's expansion strategy, how does the company leverage different types of strategic alliances (equity and non-equity) to enhance operational efficiency and competitive positioning in the global market?
3. Considering the challenges and opportunities in strategic alliance management, what best practices can Oyo adopt to ensure the long-term success and sustainability of its partnerships in the rapidly evolving hospitality industry?

References

Simran, S. and Bajj, A. (2023). *OYO Marketing Strategy: How Is OYO Positioning Itself to Dominate the Market?* Startup Talky (October 14, 2023). Accessed from https://startuptalky.com on March 31, 2024.

Parker, B. (2021). *OYO Business Model | How Does Oyo Make Money?* Business Strategy Hub (September 30, 2021). Accessed from https://bstrategyhub.com on March 31, 2024.

Skyram (March 11, 2020). *OYO – Room for Everyone – A Case Study*. Accessed from https://www.skyramtechnologies.com on March 28, 2024.

Sharma, Tripti & Jain, Rohit & Kapoor, Sahil & Gaur, Vijeyta & Roy, Abhishek. (2017). *OYO Rooms: providing affordable hotel stays*. Emerald Emerging Markets Case Studies. 7. 1-26. 10.1108/EEMCS-01-2017-0015.

Lapaas India (2019). *Oyo Business Model (Case Study) How Oyo Works & Earns?* Lapaas (September 9, 2019). Accessed from https://lapaas.com on March 28, 2024.

B Bhalla, R., Rawat, S., Pradhan, S., Sharma, S., & Singh, T., (2024). *OYO: a journey through the hotel chain's first ten years*. In Sage Business Cases. SAGE Publications, Ltd., https://doi.org/10.4135/9781071946299

Kukul, Y., Thakur, K., & Jena, L. K. (2023). *Exploring Crisis Leadership During COVID-19: A Case Study on OYO*. Business Perspectives and Research, 22785337221148812.

Verma, A., & Verma, M. (2023). *OYO-RE-DEFINING BUDGET HOTELS*. Journal of Hospitality Application & Research, 18(1).

End Notes

1 The structure and function of the multidimensional firm were first described by Chandler, A. (1962). *Strategy and structure: Chapters in the history of the industrial enterprise*. Cambridge, MA: MIT Press. The economic logic underlying the multidimensional firm was first described by Williamson, O. E. (1975). *Markets and hierarchies: Analysis and antitrust implications*. New York: Free Press. Empirical examinations of the impact of the M-form or firm performance include Armour, H. O., and D. J. Teece. (1980). "Vertical integration and technological innovation." *Review of Economics and Statistics*, 60, pp. 470–474. There continues to be some debate about the efficiency of the M-form structure. See Freeland, R. F. (1966). "The myth of the M-form? Governance, consent, and organizational change." *American Journal of Sociology*, 102(2), pp. 483–626; and Shanley, M. (1996). "Straw men and M-form myths: Comment on Freeland." *American Journal of Sociology*, 102(2), pp. 527–536.

2 M. C. Jensen and W. H. Meckling (1976). "Theory of the firm: Managerial behavior, agency costs, and ownership structure." *Journal of Financial Economics*, 3, pp. 305–360; J. Useem (2003). "The biggest show." *Fortune*, December 8, pp. 157+; R. Lambert (1986). "Executive effort and selection of risky projects." *Rand Journal of Economics*, 13(2), pp. 369–378.

3 E. Zajac and J. Westphal (1994). "The costs and benefits of managerial incentives and monitoring in large U.S. corporations: When is more not better?" *Strategic Management Journal*, 15, pp. 121–142; P. Rechner and D. Dalton (1991). "CEO duality and organizational performance: A longitudinal analysis." *Strategic Management Journal*, 12, pp. 155–160; S. Finkelstein and R. D'Aveni (1994). "CEO duality as a double-edged sword: How boards of directors balance entrenchment avoidance and unity of command." *Academy of Management Journal*, 37, pp. 1079–1108; B. K. Boyd (1995). "CEO duality and firm performance: A contingency model." *Strategic Management Journal*, 16, pp. 301–312; I. F. Kesner and R. B. Johnson (1990). "An investigation of the relationship between board composition and stockholder suits." *Strategic Management Journal*, 11, pp. 327–336.

4 See Finkelstein, S., and R. D'Aveni. (1994). "CEO duality as a double-edged sword: How boards of directors balance entrenchment avoidance and unity of command." *Academy of Management Journal*, 37, pp. 1079–1108.

5 Kesner, I. F. (1988). "Director's characteristics and committee membership: An investigation of type, occupation, tenure and gender." *Academy of Management Journal*, 31, pp. 66–84; and Zahra, S. A., and J. A. Pearce II. (1989). "Boards of directors and corporate financial performance: A review and integrative model." *Journal of Management*, 15, pp. 291–334.

6 Investor Relations Business. (2000). "Reversal of fortune: Institutional ownership is declining." *Investor Relations Business*, May 1, pp. 8–9; and Federal Reserve Board. (2006). "Flow of funds report." www.corpgov.net.

7 See Hansen, G. S., and C. W. L. Hill. (1991). "Are institutional investors myopic? A time-series study of four technology-driven industries." *Strategic Management Journal*, 12, pp. 1–16.

8 See Bergh, D. (1995). "Size and relatedness of units sold: An agency theory and resource-based perspective." *Strategic Management Journal*, 16, pp. 221–239; and Bethel, J., and J. Liebeskind. (1993). "The effects of ownership structure on corporate restructuring." *Strategic Management Journal*, 14, pp. 15–31.

9 Burdens that are well described by Westley, F., and H. Mintzberg. (1989). "Visionary leadership and strategic management." *Strategic Management Journal*, 10, pp. 17–32.

10 See Dumaine, B. (1992). "Is big still good?" *Fortune*, April 20, pp. 50–60.

11 See Golden, B. (1992). "SBU strategy and performance: The moderating effects of the corporate–SBU relationship." *Strategic Management Journal*, 13, pp. 145–158; Berger, P., and E. Ofek. (1995). "Diversification effect on firm value." *Journal of Financial Economics*, 37, pp. 36–65; Lang, H. P., and R. M. Stulz. (1994). "Tobin's *q*, corporate diversification, and firm performance." *Journal of Political Economy*, 102, pp. 1248–1280; and Rumelt, R. (1991). "How much does industry matter?" *Strategic Management Journal*, 12, pp. 167–185.

12 See Halal, W. (1994). "From hierarchy to enterprise: Internal markets are the new foundation of management." *The Academy of Management Executive*, 8(4), pp. 69–83.

13 Bartlett, C., and S. Ghoshal. (1993). "Beyond the M-form: Toward a managerial theory of the firm." *Strategic Management Journal*, 14, pp. 23–46.

14 See Simons, R. (1994). "How new top managers use control systems as levers of strategic renewal." *Strategic Management Journal*, 15, pp. 169–189.

15 Bethel, J. E. (1990). "The capital allocation process and managerial mobility: A theoretical and empirical investigation." Unpublished doctoral dissertation, UCLA.

16 Some of these are described in Duffy, M. (1989). "ZBB, MBO, PPB, and their effectiveness within the planning/marketing process." *Strategic Management Journal*, 12, pp. 155–160.

17 See Stern, J., B. Stewart, and D. Chew. (1995). "The EVA financial management system." *Journal of Applied Corporate Finance*, 8, pp. 32–46; and Tully, S. (1993). "The real key to creating wealth." *Fortune*, September 20, pp. 38–50.

18 Applications of EVA are described in Tully, S. (1993). "The real key to creating wealth." *Fortune*, September 20, pp. 38–50; Tully, S. (1995). "So, Mr. Bossidy, we know you can cut. Now show us how to grow." *Fortune*, August 21, pp. 70–80; and Tully, S. (1995). "Can EVA deliver profits to the post office?" *Fortune*, July 10, p. 22.

19 A special issue of the *Journal of Applied Corporate Finance* in 1994 addressed many of these issues.

20 See Priem, R. (1990). "Top management team group factors, consensus, and firm performance." *Strategic Management Journal*, 11, pp. 469–478; and Wooldridge, B., and S. Floyd. (1990). "The strategy process, middle management involvement, and organizational performance." *Strategic Management Journal*, 11, pp. 231–241.

21 A point made by Westley, F. (1900). "Middle managers and strategy: Microdynamics of inclusion." *Strategic Management Journal*, 11, pp. 337–351; Lamont, O. (1997). "Cash flow and investment: Evidence from internal capital markets." *The Journal of Finance*, 52(1), pp. 83–109; Shin, H. H., and R. M. Stulz. (1998). "Are internal capital markets efficient?" *Quarterly Journal of Economics*, May, pp. 531–552; and Stein, J. C. (1997). "Internal capital markets and the competition for corporate resources." *The Journal of Finance*, 52(1), pp. 111–133.

22 See Brickley, J., C. Smith, and J. Zimmerman. (1996). *Organizational architecture and managerial economics approach*. Homewood, IL: Irwin; and Eccles, R. (1985). *The transfer pricing problem: A theory for practice*. Lexington, MA: Lexington Books.

23 See Cyert, R., and J. G. March. (1963). *A behavioral theory of the firm*. Upper Saddle River, NJ: Prentice Hall; Swieringa, R. J., and J. H. Waterhouse. (1982). "Organizational views of transfer pricing." *Accounting, Organizations & Society*, 7(2), pp. 149–165; and Eccles, R. (1985). *The transfer pricing problem: A theory for practice*. Lexington, MA: Lexington Books.

24 Gupta, A. K., and V. Govindarajan. (1986). "Resource sharing among SBUs: Strategic antecedents and administrative implications." *Academy of Management Journal*, 29, pp. 695–714.

25 A point made by Swieringa, R. J., and J. H. Waterhouse. (1982). "Organizational views of transfer pricing." *Accounting, Organizations and Society*, 7(2), pp. 149–165.

26 Jensen, M. C., and K. J. Murphy. (1990). "Performance pay and top management incentives." *Journal of Political Economy*, 98, pp. 225–264.

27 See Dial, J., and K. J. Murphy. (1995). "Incentive, downsizing, and value creation at General Dynamics." *Journal of Financial Economics*, 37, pp. 261–314, on General Dynamics' compensation scheme; and Aguilar, F. J., and A. Bhambri. (1983). "Johnson & Johnson (A)." Harvard Business School Case No. 9-384-053, on Johnson & Johnson's compensation scheme.

28 www.equilar.com/reports/38-new-york-times-200-highest-paid-CEOs-2006; www.gsb.stanford.edu/faculty/publications/americans-CEO-pay-2016-public-perception-survey-CEO-compensation. Both accessed March 2, 2017; A. Mackey (2006). "Dynamics in executive labor markets: CEO effects, executive-firm matching, and rent sharing." Dissertation, The Ohio State University.

CHAPTER

11 Strategic Alliances

LEARNING OBJECTIVES

After reading this chapter, you should be able to:

11.1 Define a strategic alliance and give three specific examples of strategic alliances.

11.2 Describe how strategic alliances can create value for firms.

11.3 Describe how adverse selection, moral hazard, and holdup can threaten the ability of alliances to generate value.

11.4 Describe the conditions under which a strategic alliance can be rare and costly to duplicate.

11.5 Describe how contracts, equity investments, firm reputations, joint ventures, and trust can all reduce the threat of cheating in strategic alliances.

From Alliance to Impact: Pfizer and BioNTech's Joint Venture in COVID-19 Vaccine Production

The strategic alliance between Pfizer and BioNTech to develop and distribute the COVID-19 vaccine, known as Comirnaty, represents a landmark case in strategic alliances and sustained competitive advantage. Announced on March 17, 2020, this collaboration aimed to accelerate the development of BioNTech's mRNA-based vaccine candidate, BNT162, to prevent COVID-19 infection. The rapid progression of this partnership builds on a previous 2018 agreement to jointly develop mRNA-based vaccines for influenza, highlighting the strategic foresight and mutual leveraging of expertise and resources from both companies.

This alliance, termed "Project Light Speed" within Pfizer, embarked on one of history's most ambitious vaccine development programs, successfully producing a vaccine within months, a process that traditionally could take years. This effort necessitated seamless collaboration across companies and countries, scaling up manufacturing to meet the goal of producing billions of vaccine doses. Such an endeavour required not only dedication and sacrifice but also innovative logistical solutions, including the development of novel shipping containers to maintain the vaccine's required low temperatures during global distribution.

Financially, the alliance demonstrated a significant impact, with Pfizer and BioNTech committing to supply millions of doses worldwide, including agreements with the

U.S. government for up to 600 million doses and commitments to the COVAX initiative to ensure global access. By the end of 2021, Pfizer aimed to manufacture 3 billion doses of the vaccine, reflecting the scale and ambition of this venture. The strategic alliance between Pfizer and BioNTech leveraged their complementary strengths: BioNTech's innovative mRNA technology and Pfizer's extensive vaccine development, regulatory, and commercialization capabilities. This partnership not only accelerated the vaccine's development and distribution but also positioned both companies at the forefront of the global response to the COVID-19 pandemic, enhancing their competitive advantage in the pharmaceutical and biotechnology sectors.

Looking forward, the Pfizer-BioNTech collaboration sets a new standard for rapid vaccine development and distribution in response to global health crises. The challenges ahead include addressing vaccine hesitancy, adapting to emerging variants, and ensuring equitable access to vaccines worldwide. However, the success of this strategic alliance offers valuable lessons in innovation, agility, and the power of partnership in achieving public health objectives.

REFERENCES

Lewis, L. M., Badkar, A. V., Cirelli, D., Combs, R., & Lerch, T. F. (2023). *The race to develop the Pfizer-BioNTech COVID-19 vaccine: From the pharmaceutical scientists' perspective.* Journal of Pharmaceutical Sciences, 112(3), 6406–47.

Meo, S. A., Bukhari, I. A., Akram, J., Meo, A. S., & Klonoff, D. C. (2021). *COVID-19 vaccines: comparison of biological, pharmacological characteristics and adverse effects of Pfizer/BioNTech and Moderna Vaccines.* European Review for Medical & Pharmacological Sciences, 25(3).

Moghadas, S. M., Vilches, T. N., Zhang, K., Nourbakhsh, S., Sah, P., Fitzpatrick, M. C., & Galvani, A. P. (2021). *Evaluation of COVID-19 vaccination strategies with a delayed second dose.* PLoS biology, 19(4), e3001211.

The use of strategic alliances to manage economic exchanges has grown substantially over the past several years. In the early 1990s, strategic alliances were relatively uncommon, except in a few industries. However, by the late

1990s they had become much more common in a wide variety of industries. Indeed, more than 20,000 alliances were created worldwide in 2000 and 2001. In the computer technology-based industries, more than 2200 alliances were created between 2001 and 2005. This, the complex web of relationships that characterizes the links between Apple and Samsung, is becoming increasingly more common.[2]

Objective 11.1 Define a strategic alliance and give three specific examples of strategic alliances.

What is a Strategic Alliance?

A **strategic alliance** exists whenever two or more independent organizations cooperate in the development, manufacture, or sale of products or services. As suggested in the opening case, alliances can be created for a wide variety of reasons. However, structurally, as shown in Figure 11.1, strategic alliances can be grouped into three broad categories: nonequity alliances, equity alliances, and joint ventures.

In a **nonequity alliance**, cooperating firms agree to work together to develop, manufacture, or sell products or services, but they do not take equity positions in each other or form an independent organizational unit to manage their cooperative efforts. Rather, these cooperative relations are managed using various contracts. **Licensing agreements** (where one firm allows others to use its brand name to sell products), **supply agreements** (where one firm agrees to supply others), and **distribution agreements** (where one firm agrees to distribute the products of others) are examples of nonequity strategic alliances. IBM's alliance with the Chinese firm Inspur International is an example of a non-equity alliance.

In an **equity alliance**, cooperating firms supplement contracts with equity holdings in alliance partners. For example, when GM began importing small cars manufactured by Isuzu, not only did these partners have supply contracts in place, but GM purchased 34.2 percent of Isuzu's stock. Ford had a similar relationship with Mazda, and Chrysler had a similar relationship with Mitsubishi.[3] Equity alliances are also very common in the biotechnology industry. Large pharmaceutical firms such as Pfizer and Merck often own equity positions in several startup biotechnology companies. Wal-Mart's alliance with JD.com is an example of an equity alliance.

Figure 11.1 Types of Strategic Alliances

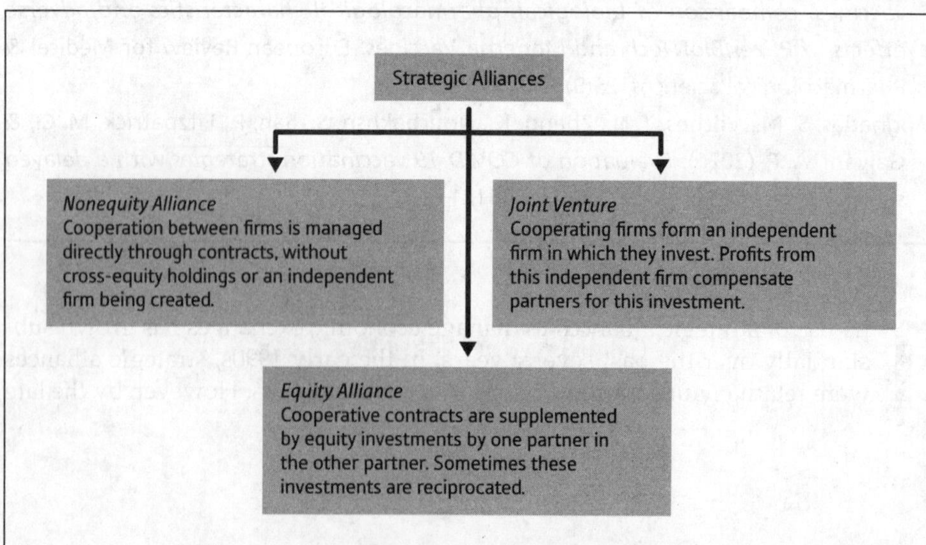

In a **joint venture**, cooperating firms create a legally independent firm in which they invest and from which they share any profits that are created. Some of these joint ventures can be very large. For example, Dow and Corning's joint venture, Dow-Corning, is a *Fortune 500* company on its own. CFM—a joint venture between General Electric and SNECMA (a French aerospace firm)—is one of the world's leading manufacturers of jet engines for commercial aircraft. If you have ever flown on a Boeing 737, then you have placed your life in the hands of this joint venture because it manufactures the engines for virtually all of these aircraft.

How do Strategic Alliances Create Value?

Objective 11.2 Describe how strategic alliances can create value for firms.

Like all the strategies discussed in this book, strategic alliances create value by exploiting opportunities and neutralizing threats facing a firm. Some of the most important opportunities that can be exploited by strategic alliances are listed in Table 11.1. Threats to strategic alliances are discussed later in this chapter.

Strategic Alliance Opportunities

Opportunities associated with strategic alliances fall into three large categories. First, these alliances can be used by a firm to improve the performance of its current operations. Second, alliances can be used to create a competitive environment favorable to superior firm performance. Finally, they can be used to facilitate a firm's entry into or exit from new markets or industries.

Improving Current Operations

Firms can use alliances to improve current operations in at least three ways: to realize economies of scale, to learn from competitors, and to manage risks and share costs.

Realizing Economies of Scale Firms can use strategic alliances to improve their current operations by using alliances to realize economies of scale. The concept of economies of scale was first introduced in Chapter 2. **Economies of scale** exist when the per-unit cost of production falls as the volume of production increases. Thus, for example, although the per-unit cost of producing one BIC pen is very high, the per-unit cost of producing 50 million BIC pens is very low.

TABLE 11.1 Ways Strategic Alliances Can Create Economic Value

Helping firms improve the performance of their current operations

1. Exploiting economies of scale
2. Learning from competitors
3. Managing risk and sharing costs

Creating a competitive environment favorable to superior performance

1. Facilitating the development of technology standards
2. Facilitating tacit collusion

Facilitating low-cost entry into and exit from industries and industry segments

1. Low-cost exit from industries and industry segments
2. Managing uncertainty
3. Low-cost entry into new markets

To realize economies of scale, firms must have a large volume of production, or at least a volume of production large enough so that the cost advantages associated with scale can be realized. Sometimes—as was described in Chapters 2 and 4—a firm can realize these economies of scale by itself; other times, it cannot. When a firm cannot realize the cost savings from economies of scale all by itself, it may join in a strategic alliance with other firms. Jointly, these firms may have sufficient volume to be able to gain the cost advantages of economies of scale.

But why wouldn't a firm be able to realize these economies all by itself? A firm may have to turn to alliance partners to help realize economies of scale for several reasons. For example, if the volume of production required to realize these economies is very large, a single firm might have to dominate an entire industry to obtain these advantages. It is often very difficult for a single firm to obtain such a dominant position in an industry. And even if it does so, it may be subject to anti-monopoly regulation by the government. Also, although a particular part or technology may be very important to several firms, no one firm may generate sufficient demand for this part or technology to realize economies of scale in its development and production. In this setting as well, independent firms may join to form an alliance to realize economies of scale in the development and production of the part or technology.

Learning from Competitors Firms can also use alliances to improve their current operations by learning from their competitors. As suggested in Chapter 3, different firms in an industry may have different resources and capabilities. These resources can give some firms competitive advantages over others. Firms that are at a competitive disadvantage may want to form alliances with the firms that have an advantage to learn about their resources and capabilities.

General Motors formed this kind of alliance with Toyota. In the early 1990s, GM and Toyota jointly invested in a previously closed GM plant in Fremont, California. This joint venture—called NUMMI—was to build compact cars to be distributed through GM's distribution network. But why did GM decide to build these cars in an alliance with Toyota? Obviously, it could have built them in any of its own plants. However, GM was very interested in learning about how Toyota could manufacture high-quality small cars at a profit. Indeed, in the NUMMI plant, Toyota agreed to take total responsibility for the manufacturing process, using former GM employees to install and operate the "lean manufacturing" system that had enabled Toyota to become the quality leader in the small-car segment of the automobile industry. However, Toyota also agreed to let GM managers work in the plant and directly observe how Toyota managed this production process. Since its inception, GM has rotated thousands of its managers from other GM plants through the NUMMI plant so that they can be exposed to Toyota's lean manufacturing methods.

It is clear why GM would want this alliance with Toyota. But why would Toyota want this alliance with GM? Certainly, Toyota was not looking to learn about lean manufacturing, per se. However, because Toyota was contemplating entering the United States by building its own manufacturing facilities, it did need to learn how to implement lean manufacturing in the United States with U.S. employees. Thus, Toyota also had something to learn from this alliance.

When both parties to an alliance are seeking to learn something from that alliance, an interesting dynamic called a **learning race** can evolve. This dynamic is described in more detail in the Strategy in Depth feature. Of course, when an alliance is based on the need for one or more parties to learn from the other, when the parties involved have learned all they can from the alliance, then the alliance is no longer required. Thus, for example, in 2010, the NUMMI alliance between GM and Toyota was closed. Interestingly, the Fremont California plant used by NUMMI was then sold to Tesla.

Strategy in Depth

Winning Learning Races

A learning race exists in a strategic alliance when both parties to that alliance seek to learn from each other but the rate at which these two firms learn varies. In this setting, the first firm to learn what it wants to learn from an alliance has the option to begin to underinvest in, and perhaps even withdraw from, an alliance. In this way, the firm that learns faster can prevent the slower-learning firm from learning all it wanted from an alliance. If, outside of this alliance, these firms are competitors, winning a learning race can create a sustained competitive advantage for the faster-learning firm over the slower-learning firm.

Firms in an alliance may vary in the rate they learn from each other for a variety of reasons. First, they may be looking to learn different things, some of which are easier to learn than others. For example, in the GM/Toyota example, GM wanted to learn about how to use "lean manufacturing" to build high-quality small cars profitably. Toyota wanted to learn how to apply the "lean manufacturing" skills it already possessed in the United States. Which of these is easier to learn—"lean manufacturing" or how to apply "lean manufacturing" in the United States?

An argument can be made that GM's learning task was much more complicated than Toyota's. At the very least, for GM to apply knowledge about "lean manufacturing" gleaned from Toyota, it would have to transfer that knowledge to several of its currently operating plants. Using this knowledge would require these plants to change their current operations—a difficult and time-consuming process. Toyota, however, only had to transfer its knowledge of how to operate a "lean manufacturing" operation in the United States to its other U.S. plants—plants that at the time this alliance was first created had yet to be built. Because GM's learning task was more complicated than Toyota's, it is very likely that Toyota's rate of learning was greater than GM's.

Second, firms may differ in terms of their ability to learn. This ability has been called a firm's **absorptive capacity**. Firms with high levels of absorptive capacity will learn at faster rates than firms with low levels of absorptive capacity, even if these two firms are trying to learn exactly the same things in an alliance. Absorptive capacity has been shown to be an important organizational capability in a wide variety of settings.

Third, firms can engage in activities to try to slow the rate of learning of their alliance partners. For example, although a firm might make its technology available to an alliance partner—thereby fulfilling the alliance agreement—it may not provide all the know-how necessary to exploit this technology. This can slow a partner's learning. Also, a firm might withhold critical employees from an alliance, thereby slowing the learning of an alliance partner. All these actions, to the extent that they slow the rate of a partner's learning without also slowing the rate at which the firm engaging in these activities learns, can help this firm win a learning race.

Although learning race dynamics have been described in a wide variety of settings, they are particularly common in relations between entrepreneurial and large firms. In these alliances, entrepreneurial firms are often looking to learn about all the managerial functions required to bring a product to market, including manufacturing, sales, distribution, and so forth. This is a difficult learning task. Large firms in these alliances often are only looking to learn about the entrepreneurial firm's technology. This is a less difficult learning task. Because the learning task facing entrepreneurial firms is more challenging than that facing their large-firm partners, larger firms in these alliances typically win the learning race. Once these large firms learn what they want from their alliance partners, they often underinvest or even withdraw from these alliances. This is why, in one study, almost 80 percent of the managers in entrepreneurial firms felt unfairly exploited by their large-firm alliance partners.[4]

Cost and Risk Sharing Finally, firms can use alliances to improve their current operations through sharing costs and risks. For example, HBO produces most of its original programs in alliances with independent producers. Most of these alliances are created to share costs and risks. Producing new television shows can be costly. Development and production costs can run into the hundreds of millions of dollars, especially for long and complicated series like HBO's *Game of Thrones*. And, despite audience testing and careful market analyses, the production of these new shows is also very risky. Even supposedly bankable stars and directors can't guarantee a film's success. In 2016, Brad Pitt starred in a movie called *Allied*. Right—you never heard of it. It lost between $75 and $90 million. Mark Whalberg starred in *Deepwater Horizon*—it lost $60 million. And Steven Spielberg directed *The BFG*. It lost $90 to $100 million.[5]

In this context, it is not surprising that HBO decides to not "go it alone" in its production efforts. If HBO was to be the sole producer of its original programming, not only would it have to absorb all the production costs, but it would also bear all the risk if a production turned out not to be successful. Of course, by getting other firms involved in its production efforts, HBO also must share whatever profits a particular production generates. Apparently, HBO has concluded that sharing this upside potential is more than compensated for by sharing the costs and risks of these productions.

Creating a Favorable Competitive Environment

Firms can also use strategic alliances to create a competitive environment that is more conducive to superior performance. This can be done in at least two ways: by facilitating the development of technology standards and by facilitating tacit collusion.

Facilitating Technical Standards Technical standards are important in many industries. Until firms agree on these standards, customers may be unwilling to make purchases that commit them to a particular technology when that technology may not be in production in the future.

Such technological standards are particularly important in what were called **network industries** in Chapter 2. Such industries are characterized by **increasing returns to scale**. Consider, for example, fax machines. How valuable is one fax machine, all by itself? Obviously, not very valuable. Two fax machines that can talk to each other are a little more valuable, three that can talk to each other are still more valuable, and so forth. The value of each individual fax machine depends on the total number of fax machines in operation that can talk to each other. This is what is meant by increasing returns to scale—the value (or returns) on each product increases as the number of these products (or scale) increases.

If there are 100 million fax machines in operation but none of these machines can talk to each other, none of these machines has any value whatsoever—except as a large paperweight. For their full value to be realized, they must be able to talk to each other. And to talk to each other, they must all adopt the same—or at least compatible—communication standards. Therefore, setting technology standards is so important in network industries.

Standards can be set in two ways. First, different firms can introduce different standards, and consumers can decide which they prefer. This is how the standard for high-definition DVDs was set. Initially, two formats competed: HD DVD (supported by Toshiba) and Blu-Ray DVD (supported by the Blu-Ray Disc Association, a group of 50 or so electronics firms and content providers). Both formats had attractive features, but they could not be played on each other's players. Competition between the two formats continued for some time, until firms like Panasonic (in 2004), Samsung (in 2005), Disney (in 2004), and Paramount (in 2005) committed to the Blu-Ray Disc format. By 2008, even Toshiba had to acknowledge the dominance of Blu-Ray Discs. Toshiba released its own Blu-Ray Disc player in 2009.[6]

Of course, the biggest problem with letting customers and competition set technology standards is that customers may end up purchasing technologies that are incompatible with the standard that is ultimately set in the industry. What about all those consumers who purchased HD products? For this reason, customers may be unwilling to invest in a new technology until the standards of that technology are established.

This is where strategic alliances come in. Sometimes, firms form strategic alliances with the sole purpose of evaluating and then choosing a technology standard. With such a standard in place, technologies can be turned into products that customers are likely to be more willing to purchase because they know that they will be compatible with industry standards for at least some period. Thus, in this setting, strategic alliances can be used to create a more favorable competitive environment.

Facilitating Tacit Collusion Another incentive for cooperating in strategic alliances is that such activities may facilitate the development of tacit collusion. As explained in Chapter 7, **collusion** exists when two or more firms in an industry coordinate their strategic choices to reduce competition in an industry. This reduction in competition usually makes it easier for colluding firms to earn high levels of performance. A common example of collusion is when firms cooperate to reduce the quantity of products being produced in an industry to drive prices up. **Explicit collusion** exists when firms directly communicate with each other to coordinate their levels of production, their prices, and so forth. Explicit collusion is illegal in most countries.

Because managers that engage in explicit collusion can end up in jail, most collusion must be tacit in character. **Tacit collusion** exists when firms coordinate their production and pricing decisions not by directly communicating with each other, but by exchanging signals with other firms about their intent to cooperate. Examples of such signals might include public announcements about price increases, public announcements about reductions in a firm's productive output, public announcements about decisions not to pursue a new technology, and so forth.

Sometimes, signals of intent to collude are very ambiguous. For example, when firms in an industry do not reduce their prices in response to a decrease in demand, they may be sending a signal that they want to collude, or they may be attempting to exploit their product differentiation to maintain high margins. When firms do not reduce their prices in response to reduced supply costs, they may be sending a signal that they want to collude, or they may be individually maximizing their economic performance. In both these cases, a firm's intent to collude or not, as implied by its activities, is ambiguous at best.

In this context, strategic alliances can facilitate tacit collusion. Separate firms, even if they are in the same industry, can form strategic alliances. Although communication between these firms cannot legally include sharing information about prices and costs for products or services that are produced outside the alliance, such interaction does help create the social setting within which tacit collusion may develop.[7] As suggested in the Research Made Relevant feature, most early research on strategic alliances focused on their implications for tacit collusion. More recently, research suggests that alliances do not usually facilitate tacit collusion.

Research Made Relevant

Do Strategic Alliances Facilitate Tacit Collusion?

Several authors have concluded that joint ventures, as a form of alliance, do increase the probability of tacit collusion in an industry. As reviewed in books by Scherer and Barney, one study found that joint ventures created two industrial groups, besides U.S. Steel, in the U.S. iron and steel industry in the early 1900s. In this sense, joint ventures in the steel industry were a substitute for U.S. Steel's vertical integration and had the effect of creating an oligopoly in what (without joint ventures) would have been a more competitive market. Other studies found that more than 50 percent of joint venture parents belong to the same industry. After examining 885 joint venture bids for oil and gas leases, yet another study found only 16 instances where joint venture parents competed with one another on another tract in the same sale. These results suggest that joint ventures might encourage subsequent tacit collusion among firms in the same industry.

In a particularly influential study, Pfeffer and Nowak found that joint ventures were most likely in industries of moderate concentration. These authors argued that in highly concentrated industries—where there were only a small number of competing firms—joint ventures were not necessary to create conditions conducive to collusion. In highly fragmented industries, the high levels of industry concentration conducive to tacit collusion could not be created by joint ventures. Only when joint venture activity could effectively create concentrated industries—that is, only when industries were moderately concentrated—were joint ventures likely.

Scherer and Barney also reviewed more recent work that disputes these findings. Joint ventures between firms in the same industry may be valuable for a variety of reasons that have little or nothing to do with collusion. Moreover, by using a lower level of aggregation, several authors have disputed the finding that joint ventures are most likely in moderately concentrated industries. The original study defined industries using very broad industry categories—"the electronics industry," "the automobile industry," and so forth. By defining industries less broadly—"consumer electronics" and "automobile part manufacturers"—subsequent work found that 73 percent of the joint ventures had parent firms coming from different industries. Although joint ventures between firms in the same industry (defined at this lower level of aggregation) may have collusive implications, subsequent work has shown that these kinds of joint ventures are relatively rare.[8]

Facilitating Entry and Exit

A final way that strategic alliances can be used to create value is by facilitating a firm's entry into a new market or industry or its exit from a market or industry. Strategic alliances are particularly valuable in this context when the value of market entry or exit is uncertain.

Facilitating Entry Entry into an industry can require skills, abilities, and products that a potential entrant does not possess. Strategic alliances can help a firm enter a new industry by avoiding the high costs of creating these skills, abilities, and products.

For example, DuPont wanted to enter the electronics industry. However, building the skills and abilities needed to develop competitive products in this industry can be very difficult and costly. Rather than absorb these costs, DuPont developed a strategic alliance (DuPont/Philips Optical) with an established electronics firm, Philips, to distribute some of Philips's products in the United States. In this way, DuPont could enter a new industry (electronics) without having to absorb all the costs of creating electronics resources and abilities from the ground up.

Of course, for this joint venture to succeed, Philips must have had an incentive to cooperate with DuPont. Whereas DuPont was looking to reduce its cost of entry into a new industry, Philips was looking to reduce its cost of continued entry into a new market—the United States. Philips used its alliance with DuPont to sell in the United States the compact discs it already was selling in Europe.[9] The role of alliances in facilitating entry into new geographic markets will be discussed in more detail later in this chapter.

Alliances to facilitate entry into new industries can be valuable even when the skills needed in these industries are not as complex and difficult to learn as skills in the electronics industry. For example, rather than develop their own frozen novelty foods, Welch Foods, Inc., and Leaf, Inc. (maker of Heath candy bars) asked Eskimo Pie to formulate products for this industry. Eskimo Pie developed Welch's frozen grape juice bar and the Heath toffee ice cream bar. These firms then split the profits derived from these products.[10] If the cost of using an alliance to enter a new industry is less than the cost of learning new skills and capabilities, an alliance can be a valuable strategic opportunity.

Facilitating Exit Some firms use strategic alliances as a mechanism to withdraw from industries or industry segments in a low-cost way. Firms are motivated to withdraw from an industry or industry segment when their level of performance in that business is less than expected and when there are few prospects of it improving. When a firm desires to exit an industry or industry segment, often it will need to dispose of the assets it has developed to compete in that industry or industry segment. These assets often include tangible resources and capabilities, such as factories, distribution centers, and product technologies, and intangible resources and capabilities, such as brand name, relationships with suppliers and customers, a loyal and committed workforce, and so forth.

Firms will often have difficulty in obtaining the full economic value of these tangible and intangible assets as they exit an industry or industry segment. This reflects an important information asymmetry that exists between the firms that currently own these assets and firms that may want to purchase these assets. By forming an alliance with a firm that may want to purchase its assets, a firm is giving its partner an opportunity to directly observe how valuable those assets are. If those assets are actually valuable, then this "sneak preview" can lead the assets to be more appropriately priced and thereby facilitate the exit of the firm that is looking to sell its assets. These issues will be discussed in more detail in Chapter 10's discussion of mergers and acquisitions.

One firm that has used strategic alliances to facilitate its exit from an industry or industry segment is Corning. In the late 1980s, Corning entered the medical diagnostics industry. After several years, however, Corning concluded that its resources and capabilities could be more productively used in other businesses. For this reason, it began to extract itself from the medical diagnostics business. However, to ensure that it received the full value of the assets it had created in the medical diagnostics business upon exiting, it formed a strategic alliance with the Swiss specialty chemical company Ciba-Geigy. Ciba-Geigy paid $75 million to purchase half of Corning's medical diagnostics business. A couple of years later, Corning finished exiting from the medical diagnostics business by selling its remaining assets in this industry to Ciba-Geigy. However, whereas Ciba-Geigy had paid $75 million for the first half of Corning's assets, it paid $150 million for the second half. Corning's alliance with Ciba-Geigy had made it possible for Ciba-Geigy to fully value Corning's medical diagnostics capabilities. Any information asymmetry that might have existed was reduced, and Corning could get more of the full value of its assets upon exiting this industry.[11]

Managing Uncertainty Finally, firms may use strategic alliances to manage **uncertainty**. As explained in Chapter 6, under conditions of high uncertainty, firms may not be able to tell at a particular point in time which of several different strategies they should pursue. Firms in this setting have an incentive to retain the flexibility to move quickly into a particular market or industry once the full value of that strategy is revealed. In this sense, strategic alliances enable a firm to maintain a point of entry into a market or industry, without incurring the costs associated with full-scale entry.

Based on this logic, strategic alliances have been analyzed as **real options**.[12] In this sense, a joint venture is an option that a firm buys, under conditions of uncertainty, to retain the ability to move quickly into a market or industry if valuable opportunities present themselves. One way in which firms can move quickly into a market is simply to buy out their partner(s) in the joint venture. Moreover, by investing in a joint venture a firm may gain access to the information it needs to evaluate full-scale entry into a market. In this approach to analyzing strategic alliances, firms that invest in alliances as options will acquire their alliance partners only after the market signals an unexpected increase in value of the venture; that is, only after uncertainty is reduced and the true, positive value of entering a market is known. Empirical findings are consistent with these expectations.[13]

Given these observations, it is not surprising to see firms in new and uncertain environments develop numerous strategic alliances. This is one of the reasons that strategic alliances are so common in the biotechnology industry. Although there is relatively little uncertainty that at least some drugs created through biotechnology will ultimately prove to be very valuable, which specific drugs will turn out to be the most valuable is very uncertain. Rather than investing in a small number of biotechnology drugs on their own, pharmaceutical companies have invested in numerous strategic alliances with small biotechnology firms. Each of these smaller firms represents a particular "bet" about the value of biotechnology in a particular class of drugs. If one of these "bets" turns out to be valuable, then the large pharmaceutical firm that has invested in that firm has the right, but not the obligation, to purchase the rest of this company. In this sense, from the point of view of the pharmaceutical firms, alliances between large pharmaceutical firms and small biotechnology firms can be thought of as real options.

Objective 11.3 Describe how adverse selection, moral hazard, and holdup can threaten the ability of alliances to generate value.

Alliance Threats: Incentives to Cheat on Strategic Alliances

Just as there are incentives to cooperate in strategic alliances, there are also incentives to cheat on these cooperative agreements. Indeed, research shows that as many as one-third of all strategic alliances do not meet the expectations of at least one alliance partner.[14] Although some of these alliance "failures" may be due to firms forming alliances that do not have the potential for creating value, some are also due to parties to an alliance cheating—that is, not cooperating in a way that maximizes the value of the alliance. Cheating can occur in at least the three different ways presented in Table 11.2: adverse selection, moral hazard, and holdup.[15]

TABLE 11.2 Ways to Cheat in Strategic Alliances

- *Adverse selection:* Potential partners misrepresent the value of the skills and abilities they bring to the alliance.
- *Moral hazard:* Partners provide to the alliance skills and abilities of lower quality than they promised.
- *Holdup:* Partners exploit the transaction-specific investments made by others in the alliance.

Adverse Selection

Potential cooperative partners can misrepresent the skills, abilities, and other resources that they will bring to an alliance. This form of cheating, called **adverse selection**, exists when an alliance partner promises to bring to an alliance certain resources that it either does not control or cannot acquire. For example, a local firm engages in adverse selection when it promises to make available to alliance partners a local distribution network that does not currently exist. Firms that engage in adverse selection are not competent alliance partners.

Adverse selection in a strategic alliance is likely only when it is difficult or costly to observe the resources or capabilities that a partner brings to an alliance. If potential partners can easily see that a firm is misrepresenting the resources and capabilities it possesses, they will not create a strategic alliance with that firm. Armed with such understanding, they will seek a different alliance partner, develop the needed skills and resources internally, or perhaps forgo this particular business opportunity.

However, evaluating the veracity of the claims of potential alliance partners is often not easy. The ability to evaluate these claims depends on information that a firm may not possess. To fully evaluate claims about a potential partner's political contacts, for example, a firm needs its own political contacts; to fully evaluate claims about potential partners' market knowledge, a firm needs significant market knowledge. A firm that can completely, and at low cost, evaluate the resources and capabilities of potential alliance partners probably does not really need these partners in a strategic alliance. The fact that a firm is seeking an alliance partner is in some sense an indication that the firm has limited abilities to evaluate potential partners.

In general, the less tangible the resources and capabilities that are to be brought to a strategic alliance, the costlier it will be to estimate their value before an alliance is created, and the more likely it is that adverse selection will occur. Firms considering alliances with partners that bring intangible resources such as "knowledge of local conditions" or "contacts with key political figures" will need to guard against this form of cheating.

Moral Hazard

Partners in an alliance may possess high-quality resources and capabilities of significant value in an alliance but fail to make those resources and capabilities available to alliance partners. This form of cheating is called **moral hazard**. For example, a partner in an engineering strategic alliance may agree to send only its most talented and best-trained engineers to work in the alliance but then actually send less-talented, poorly trained engineers. These less-qualified engineers may not be able to contribute substantially to making the alliance successful, but they may be able to learn a great deal from the highly qualified engineers provided by other alliance partners. In this way, the less-qualified engineers effectively transfer wealth from other alliance partners to their own firm.[16]

The existence of moral hazard in a strategic alliance does not necessarily mean that any of the parties to that alliance are malicious or dishonest. Rather, what often happens is that market conditions change after an alliance is formed, requiring one or more partners to an alliance to change their strategies.

For example, in the early days of the personal computer industry Compaq Computer Corporation relied on a network of independent distributors to sell its computers. However, as competition in the personal computer industry increased, Internet, mail order, and so-called computer superstores became much more valuable distribution networks, and alliances between Compaq and its traditional distributors became strained. Over time, Compaq's traditional distributors were unable to obtain the inventory they wanted in a timely manner. Indeed, to satisfy the needs of large accounts, some traditional distributors actually purchased Compaq computers from local computer superstores and then shipped them to their customers. Compaq's shift from independent dealers to alternative distributors looked like moral hazard—at least from the point of view of the independent dealers. However, from Compaq's perspective, this change simply reflected economic realities in the personal computer industry.[17]

Holdup

Even if alliance partners do not engage in either adverse selection or moral hazard, another form of cheating may evolve. Once a strategic alliance has been created, partner firms may make investments that have value only in the context of that alliance and in no other economic exchanges. These are the transaction-specific investments mentioned in Chapter 8. For example, managers from one alliance partner may have to develop close, trusting relationships with managers from other alliance partners. These close relationships are very valuable in the context of the alliance, but they have limited economic value in other economic exchanges. Also, one partner may have to customize its manufacturing equipment, distribution network, and key organizational policies to cooperate with other partners. These modifications have significant value in the context of the alliance, but they do not help the firm, and may even hurt it, in economic exchanges outside the alliance. As was the case in Chapter 8, whenever an investment's value in its first-best use (in this case, within the alliance) is much greater than its value in its second-best use (in this case, outside the alliance), that investment is said to be **transaction specific**.[18]

When one firm makes more transaction-specific investments in a strategic alliance than partner firms make, that firm may be subject to the form of cheating called **holdup**. Holdup occurs when a firm that has not made significant transaction-specific investments demands returns from an alliance that are higher than the partners agreed to when they created the alliance.

For example, suppose two alliance partners agree to a 50/50 split of the costs and profits associated with an alliance. To make the alliance work, Firm A must customize its production process. Firm B, however, does not have to modify itself to cooperate with Firm A. The value to Firm A of this customized production process, if it is used in the strategic alliance, is $5000. However, outside the alliance, this customized process is only worth $200 (as scrap).

Obviously, Firm A has made a transaction-specific investment in this alliance and Firm B has not. Consequently, Firm A may be subject to holdup by Firm B. In particular, Firm B may threaten to leave the alliance unless Firm A agrees to give Firm B part of the $5000 value that Firm A obtains by using the modified production process in the alliance. Rather than lose all the value that could be generated by its investment, Firm A may be willing to give up some of its $5000 to avoid gaining only $200. Indeed, if Firm B extracts up to the value of Firm A's production process in its next-best use (here, only $200), Firm A will still be better off continuing in this relationship rather than dissolving it. Thus, even though Firm A and Firm B initially agreed on a 50/50 split from this strategic alliance, the agreement may be modified if one party to the alliance makes significant transaction-specific investments. Research on international joint ventures suggests that the existence of transaction-specific investments in these relationships often leads to holdup problems.[19]

Although holdup is a form of cheating in strategic alliances, the threat of holdup can also be a motivation for creating an alliance. Bauxite-smelting companies often join in joint ventures with mining companies to exploit economies of scale in mining. However, these firms have another option: They could choose to operate large and efficient mines by themselves and then sell the excess bauxite (over and above their needs for their own smelters) on the open market. Unfortunately, bauxite is not a homogeneous commodity. Moreover, different kinds of bauxite require different smelting technologies. For one firm to sell its excess bauxite on the market, other smelting firms would have to make enormous investments, the sole purpose of which would be to refine that particular firm's bauxite. These investments would be transaction specific and subject these other smelters to holdup problems.

In this context, a strategic alliance can be thought of as a way of reducing the threat of holdup by creating an explicit management framework for resolving holdup problems. In other words, although holdup problems might still exist in these strategic alliances, the alliance framework may still be a better way in which to manage these problems than attempting to manage them in arm's-length market relationships. Some of the ethical dimensions of adverse selection, moral hazard, and holdup are discussed in the Ethics and Strategy feature.

Ethics and Strategy

When It Comes to Alliances, Do "Cheaters Never Prosper"?

Firms in strategic alliances can cheat on their alliance partners by engaging in adverse selection, moral hazard, or holdup. These three activities all have at least one thing in common—they all involve one alliance partner lying to another. And these lies can often pay off big in the form of the lying firm appropriating more than its "fair share" of the value created in an alliance. Are alliances one place in the economy where the adage "cheaters never prosper" does not hold?

There is little doubt that, in the short run, firms that cheat on their alliance partners can gain some advantages. But research suggests that cheating does not pay in the long run because firms that cheat on their alliance partners will find it difficult to form alliances with new partners and thus have many valuable exchange opportunities foreclosed to them.

One study that examined the long-term return to "cheaters" in strategic alliances analyzed alliances using a simple game called the "Prisoner's Dilemma." In a "Prisoner's Dilemma" game, firms have two options: to continue cooperating in a strategic alliance or to "cheat" on that alliance through adverse selection, moral hazard, or holdup. The payoffs to firms in this game depend on the decisions made by both firms. Recall from Chapter 7, if both firms decide to cooperate, they each get a good size payoff from the alliance (say $3000); if they both decide to

(continued)

cheat on the alliance, they each get a very small payoff (say $1000); and if one decides to cheat while the other decides to cooperate, then the cheating firm gets a very big payoff ($5000) while the cooperating firm gets a very small payoff ($0).

If Firm 1 and Firm 2 in this game are going to engage in only one strategic alliance, then they have a very strong incentive to "cheat." The worst that could happen if they cheat is that they earn a $1000 payoff, but there is a possibility of a $5000 payoff. However, research has shown that if a firm is contemplating engaging in multiple strategic alliances over time, then the optimal strategy is to cooperate in all its alliances. This is true even if all these alliances are not with the same partner firm.

The specific "winning" strategy in repeated "Prisoner Dilemma" games is called a "tit-for-tat" strategy. "Tit-for-tat" means that Firm 1 will cooperate in an alliance if Firm 2 cooperates. However, as soon as Firm 2 cheats on an alliance, Firm 1 cheats as well. "Tit-for-tat" works well in this setting because adopting a cooperative posture in an alliance ensures that, most of the time, the alliance will generate a high payoff (of $3000). However, by immediately responding to cheaters by cheating, the firm implementing a "tit-for-tat" strategy also minimizes the times when it will earn the lowest payoff in the table ($0). So, "tit-for-tat" maximizes the upside potential of an alliance while minimizing its downside.

All this analysis suggests that although cheating on an alliance can give a firm competitive advantage in the short to medium term, in the long run, "cheaters never prosper."[20]

Objective 11.4 Describe the conditions under which a strategic alliance can be rare and costly to duplicate.

Strategic Alliances and Sustained Competitive Advantage

The ability of strategic alliances to be sources of sustained competitive advantage, like all the other strategies discussed in this book, can be analyzed with the VRIO framework developed in Chapter 3. An alliance is economically valuable when it exploits any of the opportunities listed in Table 11.1 but avoids the threats in Table 11.2. In addition, for a strategic alliance to be a source of sustained competitive advantage it must be rare and costly to imitate.

The Rarity of Strategic Alliances

The rarity of strategic alliances does not only depend on the number of competing firms that have already implemented an alliance. It also depends on whether the benefits that firms obtain from their alliances are common across firms competing in an industry.

Consider, for example, the U.S. automobile industry. Over the past several years, strategic alliances have become very common in this industry, especially with Japanese auto firms. General Motors developed an alliance with Toyota that has already been described; Ford developed an alliance with Mazda before it purchased this Japanese firm outright; and Chrysler developed an alliance with Mitsubishi. Given the frequency with which alliances have developed in this industry, it is tempting to conclude that strategic alliances are not rare and thus not a source of competitive advantage.

Closer examination, however, suggests that these alliances may have been created for different reasons. For example, GM and Toyota cooperated only in building a single line of cars, the Chevrolet Nova. General Motors was less interested in learning design skills from Toyota and more interested in learning about manufacturing high-quality small cars profitably. Ford and Mazda, in contrast, worked closely together in designing new cars and had joint manufacturing operations. Indeed, Ford and Mazda worked so closely together that Ford once purchased 33 percent of Mazda's stock. Since 2008, Ford has reduced its investment in Mazda dramatically.

Mitsubishi has acted primarily as a supplier to Chrysler. Indeed, Nissan recently purchased Mitsubishi. Thus, although all three U.S. firms have strategic alliances, the alliances serve different purposes, and therefore each may be rare.[21]

One of the reasons why the benefits that accrue from a particular strategic alliance may be rare is that relatively few firms may have the complementary resources and abilities needed to form an alliance. This is particularly likely when an alliance is formed to enter a new market, especially a new foreign market. In many less-developed economies, only one local firm or very few local firms may exist with the local knowledge, contacts, and distribution network needed to facilitate entry into that market. Moreover, sometimes the government acts to limit the number of these local firms. Although several firms may seek entry into this market, only a very small number will be able to form a strategic alliance with the local entity, and therefore the benefits that accrue to the allied firms will likely be rare.

The Imitability of Strategic Alliances

As discussed in Chapter 3, the resources and capabilities that enable firms to conceive and implement valuable strategies may be imitated in two ways: direct duplication and substitution. Both duplication and substitution are important considerations in analyzing the imitability of strategic alliances.

Direct Duplication of Strategic Alliances

Research suggests that successful strategic alliances are often based on socially complex relations among alliance partners.[22] In this sense, successful strategic alliances often go well beyond simple legal contracts and are characterized by socially complex phenomena such as a trusting relationship between alliance partners, friendship, and even (perhaps) a willingness to suspend narrow self-interest for the longer-term good of the relationship.

Some research has shown that the development of trusting relationships between alliance partners is both difficult and essential to the success of strategic alliances. In one study, the most common reason that alliances failed to meet the expectations of partner firms was the partners' inability to trust one another. Interpersonal communication, tolerance for cultural differences, patience, and willingness to sacrifice short-term profits for longer-term success were all important determinants of the level of trust among alliance partners.[23]

Of course, not all firms in an industry are likely to have the organizational and relationship-building skills required for successful alliance building. If these skills and abilities are rare among a set of competing firms and costly to develop, then firms that can exploit these abilities by creating alliances may gain competitive advantages. Examples of firms that have developed these specialized skills include Corning and Cisco, with several hundred strategic alliances each.[24]

Substitutes for Strategic Alliances

Even if the purpose and objectives of a strategic alliance are valuable and rare and even if the relationships on which an alliance is created are socially complex and costly to imitate, that alliance will still not generate a sustained competitive advantage if low-cost substitutes are available. At least two possible substitutes for strategic alliances exist: "going it alone" and acquisitions.[25]

"Going It Alone" Firms "go it alone" when they attempt to develop all the resources and capabilities they need to exploit market opportunities and neutralize market threats by themselves. Sometimes "going it alone" can create the same—or even more—value than using alliances to exploit opportunities and neutralize threats. In these settings, "going it alone" is a substitute for a strategic alliance. However, in other settings using an alliance can create substantially more value than "going it alone." In these settings, "going it alone" is not a substitute for a strategic alliance.

So, when will firms prefer an alliance over "going it alone?" Not surprisingly, the three explanations of vertical integration, discussed in Chapter 8, are relevant here as well. These three explanations focused on the threat of opportunism, the impact of firm resources and capabilities, and the role of uncertainty. If you need to review these three explanations, they are described in detail in Chapter 8. They are relevant here because "going it alone"—as a potential substitute for a strategic alliance—is an example of vertical integration. The implications of these three explanations for when strategic alliances will be preferred over "going it alone" are summarized in Table 11.3. If any of the conditions listed in Table 11.3 exist, then "going it alone" will not be a substitute for strategic alliances.

Recall from Chapter 8 that opportunism-based explanations of vertical integration suggest that firms will want to vertically integrate an economic exchange when they have made high levels of transaction-specific investment in that exchange. That is, using language developed in this chapter, firms will want to vertically integrate an economic exchange when using an alliance to manage that exchange could subject them to holdup. Extending this logic to strategic alliances suggests that strategic alliances will be preferred over "going it alone" and other alternatives when the level of transaction-specific investment required to complete an exchange is moderate. If the level of this specific investment is low, then market forms of exchange will be preferred; if the level of this specific investment is high, then "going it alone" in a vertically integrated way will be preferred; if the level of this specific investment is moderate, then some sort of strategic alliance will be preferred. Thus, when the level of specific exchange in a transaction is moderate, then "going it alone" is not a substitute for a strategic alliance.

Capabilities-based explanations suggest that an alliance will be preferred over "going it alone" when an exchange partner possesses valuable, rare, and costly-to-imitate resources and capabilities. A firm without these capabilities may find them to be too costly to develop on its own. If a firm must have access to capabilities it cannot develop on its own, it must use an alliance to gain access to those capabilities. In this setting, "going it alone" is not a substitute for a strategic alliance.[26]

Finally, it has already been suggested that, under conditions of high uncertainty, firms may be unwilling to commit to a particular course of action by engaging in an exchange within a firm. In such settings, firms may choose the strategic flexibility associated with alliances. As suggested earlier in this chapter, alliances can be thought of as real options that give a firm the right, but not the obligation, to invest further in an exchange—perhaps by bringing it within the boundaries of a firm—if that exchange turns out to be valuable sometime in

TABLE 11.3 When Alliances Will Be Preferred Over "Going It Alone"

Alliances will be preferred over "going it alone" when:

1. The level of transaction-specific investment required to complete an exchange is moderate.
2. An exchange partner possesses valuable, rare, and costly-to-imitate resources and capabilities.
3. There is great uncertainty about the future value of an exchange.

the future. Thus, under conditions of high uncertainty, "going it alone" is not a substitute for strategic alliances.

Acquisitions The acquisition of other firms can also be a substitute for alliances. In this case, rather than developing a strategic alliance or attempting to develop and exploit the relevant resources by "going it alone," a firm seeking to exploit the opportunities listed in Table 11.1 may simply acquire another firm that already possesses the relevant resources and capabilities. However, such acquisitions have four characteristics that often limit the extent to which they can act as substitutes for strategic alliances. These are summarized in Table 11.4.[27]

First, there may be legal constraints on acquisitions. These are especially likely if firms are seeking advantages by combining with other firms in their own industry. Thus, for example, using acquisitions as a substitute for strategic alliances in the aluminum industry would lead to a very concentrated industry and subject some of these firms to serious antitrust liabilities. These firms have acquisitions foreclosed to them and must look elsewhere to gain advantages from cooperating with their competition.

Second, as has already been suggested, strategic alliances enable a firm to retain its flexibility either to enter or not to enter a new business. Acquisitions limit that flexibility because they represent a strong commitment to engage in a certain business activity. Consequently, under conditions of high uncertainty, firms may choose strategic alliances over acquisitions to exploit opportunities while maintaining the flexibility that alliances create.

Third, firms may choose strategic alliances over acquisitions because of the unwanted organizational baggage that often comes with an acquisition. Sometimes, the value created by combining firms depends on combining particular functions, divisions, or other assets in the firms. A strategic alliance can focus on exploiting the value of combining just those parts of firms that create the most value. Acquisitions, in contrast, generally include the entire organization, both the parts of a firm where value is likely to be created and parts of a firm where value is not likely to be created.

From the point of view of the acquiring firm, parts of a firm that do not create value are essentially unwanted baggage. These parts of the firm may be sold off subsequent to an acquisition. However, this sell-off may be costly and time consuming. If enough baggage exists, firms may determine that an acquisition is not a viable option, even though important economic value could be created between a firm and a potential acquisition target. To gain this value, an alternative approach—a strategic alliance—may be preferred. These issues will be explored in more detail in Chapter 12.

Finally, sometimes a firm's resources and capabilities are valuable because that firm is independent. In this setting, the act of acquiring a firm can actually reduce the value of a firm. When this is the case, any value between two firms is best realized through an alliance, not an acquisition. For example, the international growth of numerous marketing-oriented companies in the 1980s led to strong pressures for advertising agencies to develop global marketing capabilities. During the 1990s, many domestic-only advertising firms acquired non-domestic agencies to

TABLE 11.4 Reasons Why Strategic Alliances May Be More Attractive Than Acquisitions to Realize Exchange Opportunities

Alliances will be preferred to acquisitions when:

1. There are legal constraints on acquisitions.
2. Acquisitions limit a firm's flexibility under conditions of high uncertainty.
3. There is substantial unwanted organizational "baggage" in an acquired firm.
4. The value of a firm's resources and capabilities depends on its independence.

form a few large international advertising agencies. However, one firm that was reluctant to be acquired to be part of an international advertising network was the French advertising company Publicis. Over and above the personal interests of its owners to retain control of the company, Publicis wanted to remain an independent French agency to retain its stable of French and French-speaking clients—including Renault and Nestlé. These firms had indicated that they preferred working with a French advertising agency and that they would look for alternative suppliers if Publicis were acquired by a foreign firm. Because much of the value that Publicis created in a potential acquisition depended on obtaining access to its stable of clients, the act of acquiring Publicis would have had the effect of destroying the very thing that made the acquisition attractive. For this reason, rather than allowing itself to be acquired by foreign advertising agencies, Publicis developed a complex equity strategic alliance and joint venture with a U.S. advertising firm, Foote, Coyne, and Belding. Although, ultimately, this alliance was not successful in providing an international network for either of these two partner firms, an acquisition of Publicis by Foote, Coyne, and Belding would almost certainly have destroyed some of the economic value that Publicis enjoyed as a stand-alone company.

Organizing to Implement Strategic Alliances

Objective 11.5 Describe how contracts, equity investments, firm reputations, joint ventures, and trust can all reduce the threat of cheating in strategic alliances.

One of the most important determinants of the success of strategic alliances is their organization. The primary purpose of organizing a strategic alliance is to enable partners in the alliance to gain all the benefits associated with cooperation while minimizing the probability that cooperating firms will cheat on their cooperative agreements. The organizing skills required in managing alliances are, in many ways, unique. It often takes some time for firms to learn these skills and realize the full potential of their alliances. Therefore, some firms can gain competitive advantages from managing alliances more effectively than their competitors. Indeed, sometimes firms may have to choose alternatives to alliances—including "going it alone" and acquisitions—even when those alternatives are not preferred, simply because they do not have the skills required to organize and manage alliances.

A variety of tools and mechanisms can be used to help realize the value of alliances and minimize the threat of cheating. These include contracts, equity investments, firm reputations, joint ventures, and trust.

Explicit Contracts and Legal Sanctions

One way to avoid cheating in strategic alliances is for the parties to an alliance to anticipate the ways in which cheating may occur (including adverse selection, moral hazard, and holdup) and to write explicit contracts that define legal liability if cheating does occur. Writing these contracts, together with the close monitoring of contractual compliance and the threat of legal sanctions, can reduce the probability of cheating. Earlier in this chapter, such strategic alliances were called nonequity alliances.

However, contracts sometimes fail to anticipate all forms of cheating that might occur in a relationship—and firms may cheat on cooperative agreements in subtle ways that are difficult to evaluate in terms of contractual requirements. Thus, for example, a contract may require parties in a strategic alliance to make available to the alliance certain proprietary technologies or processes. However, it may be very difficult to communicate the subtleties of these technologies or processes to alliance partners. Does this failure in communication represent a clear violation of contractual requirements, or does it represent a good-faith effort by alliance partners? Moreover, how can one partner tell whether it is obtaining all the necessary information about a technology or process when it is unaware of all the information that exists in another firm? Hence, although contracts are an important component of most strategic alliances, they do not resolve all the problems associated with cheating.

Although most contracts associated with strategic alliances are highly customized, these different contracts do have some common features. These common features are described in detail in Table 11.5. In general, firms contemplating a strategic alliance that will be at least partially governed by a contract must include clauses that address the issues presented in Table 11.5.

Equity Investments

The effectiveness of contracts can be enhanced by having partners in an alliance make equity investments in each other. When Firm A buys a substantial equity position in its alliance partner, Firm B, the market value of Firm A now depends,

TABLE 11.5 Common Clauses in Contracts Used to Govern Strategic Alliances

Establishment Issues
Shareholdings: Percentage of JV owned by various partners
Voting rights: Votes held by various partners
Dividend percentage: How profits are to be allocated
Minority protection: How minority owner interests are protected
Board of directors: Initial board and rules for modifying the board
Articles of association: Processes for making decisions
Place of incorporation
Accountants, lawyers, and other advisors
Operating Issues
Performance expectations
Noncompete agreements
Nonsolicitation clauses: Partners cannot recruit employees from each other
Confidentiality clauses
Licensing intellectual property rights: Who owns the intellectual property created by a joint venture?
Liability of the alliance and liability of cooperating partners
Process of changing the contract
Process of resolving disputes
Termination Issues
Preemption rights: If one partner wishes to sell its shares, it must first offer them to the other partner
When one partner can force the other partner to sell its shares to it
When a partner has the right to force another partner to buy its alliance shares
Drag-along rights: When one partner can arrange a sale to an outside firm and force the other partner to sell shares as well
Tag-along rights: When one partner can prevent the sale of the second partner's shares to an outside firm unless that outside firm also buys the first partner's shares
When an initial public offering (IPO) will be pursued
Termination: When the JV can be terminated

Source: Based on E. Campbell and J. Reuer (2001). "Note on the legal negotiation of strategic alliance agreements."

to some extent, on the economic performance of that partner. The incentive of Firm A to cheat Firm B falls, for to do so would be to reduce the economic performance of Firm B and thus the value of Firm A's investment in its partner. These kinds of strategic alliances are called equity alliances.

Many firms use cross-equity investments to help manage their strategic alliances. These arrangements are particularly common in Japan, where a firm's largest equity holders often include several of its key suppliers, including its main banks. These equity investments, because they reduce the threat of cheating in alliances with suppliers, can reduce these firms' supply costs. In turn, not only do firms have equity positions in their suppliers, but suppliers often have substantial equity positions in the firms to which they sell.[28]

Firm Reputations

A third constraint on incentives to cheat in strategic alliances exists in the effect that a reputation for cheating has on a firm's future opportunities. Although it is often difficult to anticipate all the different ways in which an alliance partner may cheat, it is often easier to describe after the fact how an alliance partner has cheated. Information about an alliance partner that has cheated is likely to become widely known. A firm with a reputation as a cheater is not likely to be able to develop strategic alliances with other partners in the future, despite any special resources or capabilities that it might be able to bring to an alliance. In this way, cheating in a current alliance may foreclose opportunities for developing other valuable alliances. For this reason, firms may decide not to cheat in their current alliances.[29]

Substantial evidence suggests that the effect of reputation on future business opportunities is important. Firms go to great lengths to make sure that they do not develop a negative reputation. Nevertheless, this reputational control of cheating in strategic alliances does have several limitations.[30]

First, subtle cheating in a strategic alliance may not become public, and if it does become public, the responsibility for the failure of the strategic alliance may be very ambiguous. In one equity joint venture attempting to perfect the design of a new turbine for power generation, financial troubles made one partner considerably more anxious than the other partner to complete product development. The financially healthy, and thus patient, partner believed that if the alliance required an additional infusion of capital, the financially troubled partner would have to abandon the alliance and would have to sell its part of the alliance at a relatively low price. The patient partner thus encouraged alliance engineers to work slowly and carefully in the guise of developing the technology to reach its full potential. The financially troubled, and thus impatient, partner encouraged alliance engineers to work quickly, perhaps sacrificing some quality to develop the technology sooner. Eventually, the impatient partner ran out of money, sold its share of the alliance to the patient partner at a reduced price, and accused the patient partner of not acting in good faith to facilitate the rapid development of the new technology. The patient partner accused the other firm of pushing the technology too quickly, thereby sacrificing quality and, perhaps, worker safety. In some sense, both firms were cheating on their agreement to develop the new technology cooperatively. However, this cheating was subtle and difficult to spot and had relatively little impact on the reputation of either firm or on the ability of either firm to establish alliances in the future. It is likely that most observers would simply conclude that the patient partner obtained a windfall because of the impatient partner's bad luck.[31]

Second, although one partner to an alliance may be unambiguously cheating on the relationship, one or both firms may not be sufficiently connected into a network with other firms to make this information public. When information about cheating remains private, public reputations are not tarnished and future opportunities are not forgone. This is especially likely to happen if one or both alliance partners operate in less-developed economies where information about partner behavior may not be rapidly diffused to other firms or to other countries.

Finally, the effect of a tarnished reputation, if cheating in an alliance is unambiguous and publicly known, may foreclose future opportunities for a firm, but it does little to address the current losses experienced by the firm that was cheated. Moreover, any of the forms of cheating discussed earlier—adverse selection, moral hazard, or holdup—can result in substantial losses for a firm currently in an alliance. Indeed, the wealth created by cheating in a current alliance may be large enough to make a firm willing to forgo future alliances. In this case, a tarnished reputation may be of minor consequence to a cheating firm.[32]

Joint Ventures

A fourth way to reduce the threat of cheating is for partners in a strategic alliance to invest in a joint venture. Creating a separate legal entity, in which alliance partners invest and from whose profits they earn returns on their investments, reduces some of the risks of cheating in strategic alliances. When a joint venture is created, the ability of partners to earn returns on their investments depends on the economic success of the joint venture. Partners in joint ventures have limited interests in behaving in ways that hurt the performance of the joint venture because such behaviors end up hurting both partners. Moreover, unlike reputational consequences of cheating, cheating in a joint venture does not just foreclose future alliance opportunities; it can hurt the cheating firm in the current period as well.

Given the advantages of joint ventures in controlling cheating, it is not surprising that when the probability of cheating in a cooperative relationship is greatest, a joint venture is usually the preferred form of cooperation. For example, bauxite mining has some clear economies of scale. However, transaction-specific investments would lead to significant holdup problems in selling excess bauxite in the open market, and legal constraints prevent the acquisition of other smelter companies to create an intraorganizational demand for excess bauxite. Holdup problems would continue to exist in any mining strategic alliances that might be created. Nonequity alliances, equity alliances, and reputational effects are not likely to restrain cheating in this situation because the returns on holdup, once transaction-specific investments are in place, can be very large. Thus, most of the strategic alliances created to mine bauxite take the form of joint ventures. Only this form of strategic alliance is likely to create incentives strong enough to significantly reduce the probability of cheating.[33]

Despite these strengths, joint ventures are not able to reduce all cheating in an alliance without cost. Sometimes the value of cheating in a joint venture is sufficiently large that a firm cheats even though doing so hurts the joint venture and forecloses future opportunities. For example, a particular firm may gain access to a technology through a joint venture that would be valuable if used in another of its lines of business. This firm may be tempted to transfer this technology to this other line of business even if it has agreed not to do so and even if doing so would limit the performance of its joint venture. Because the profits earned in this other line of business may have a greater value than the returns that could have been earned in the joint venture and the returns that could have been earned in the future with other strategic alliances, cheating may occur.

Trust

It is sometimes the case that alliance partners rely only on legalistic and narrowly economic approaches to manage their alliance. However, recent work seems to suggest that although successful alliance partners do not ignore legal and economic disincentives to cheating, they strongly support these narrower linkages with a rich set of interpersonal relations and trust. Trust, in combination with contracts, can help reduce the threat of cheating. More important, trust may enable partners to explore exchange opportunities that they could not explore if only legal and economic organizing mechanisms were in place.[34]

At first glance, this argument may seem far-fetched. However, some research offers support for this approach to managing strategic alliances, suggesting that successful alliance partners typically do not specify all the terms and conditions in their relationship in a legal contract and do not specify all possible forms of cheating and their consequences. Moreover, when joint ventures are formed, partners do not always insist on simple 50/50 splits of equity ownership and profit sharing. Rather, successful alliances involve trust, a willingness to be flexible, a willingness to learn, and a willingness to let the alliance develop in ways that the partners could not have anticipated.[35]

Commitment, coordination, and trust are all important determinants of alliance success. Put another way, a strategic alliance is a relationship that evolves over time. Allowing the lawyers and economists to too rigorously define, a priori, the boundaries of that relationship may limit it and stunt its development.[36]

This "trust" approach also has implications for the extent to which strategic alliances may be sources of sustained competitive advantage for firms. The ability to move into strategic alliances in this trusting way may be very valuable over the long run. There is strong reason to believe that this ability is not uniformly distributed across all firms that might have an interest in forming strategic alliances and that this ability may be history-dependent and socially complex and thus costly to imitate. Firms with these skills may be able to gain sustained competitive advantages from their alliance relationships. The observation that just a few firms, including Corning and Cisco, are well-known for their strategic alliance successes is consistent with the observation that these alliance management skills may be valuable, rare, and costly to imitate.

Summary

Strategic alliances exist whenever two or more organizations cooperate in the development, manufacture, or sale of products or services. Strategic alliances can be grouped into three large categories: nonequity alliances, equity alliances, and joint ventures.

Firms join in strategic alliances for three broad reasons: to improve the performance of their current operations, to improve the competitive environment within which they are operating, and to facilitate entry into or exit from markets and industries. Just as there are incentives to cooperate in strategic alliances, there are also incentives to cheat. Cheating generally takes one or a combination of three forms: adverse selection, moral hazard, or holdup.

Strategic alliances can be a source of sustained competitive advantage. The rarity of alliances depends not only on the number of competing firms that have developed an alliance, but also on the benefits that firms gain through their alliances.

Imitation through direct duplication of an alliance may be costly because of the socially complex relations that underlie an alliance; however, imitation through substitution is more likely. Two substitutes for alliances may be "going it alone," where firms develop and exploit the relevant sets of resources and capabilities on their own, and acquisitions. Opportunism, capabilities, and uncertainty all have an impact on when "going it alone" will be a substitute for a strategic alliance. Acquisitions may be a substitute for strategic alliances when there are no legal constraints, strategic flexibility is not an important consideration, when the acquired firm has relatively little unwanted "organizational baggage," and when the value of a firm's resources and capabilities does not depend on its remaining independent. However, when these conditions do not exist, acquisitions are not a substitute for alliances.

The key issue facing firms in organizing their alliances is to facilitate cooperation while avoiding the threat of cheating. Contracts, equity investments, firm reputations, joint ventures, and trust can all reduce the threat of cheating in different contexts.

Challenge Questions

11.1. One reason firms might want to pursue a strategic alliance strategy is to exploit economies of scale. Exploiting economies of scale should reduce a firm's costs. Why would this mean that a firm pursuing an alliance strategy to exploit economies of scale is actually pursuing a cost leadership strategy?

11.2. Consider the joint venture between General Motors and Toyota. GM was interested in learning how to profitably manufacture high-quality small cars from its alliance with Toyota. Toyota was interested in gaining access to GM's U.S. distribution network and in reducing the political liability associated with local content laws. Which of these firms do you think was more likely to accomplish its objectives, and why? What implications, if any, does this alliance have for a possible "learning race?"

11.3. Some researchers have argued that strategic alliances are one way in which firms can help facilitate the development of a tacit collusion strategy. In your view, what are the critical differences between tacit collusion strategies and strategic alliance strategies?

11.4. How can one tell whether two firms are engaging in an alliance to facilitate collusion or are engaging in an alliance for other purposes?

11.5. Some researchers have argued that alliances can be used to help firms evaluate the economic potential of entering a new industry or market. Under what conditions will a firm seeking to evaluate these opportunities need to invest in an alliance to accomplish this evaluation?

11.6. Some researchers have argued that alliances can be used to help firms evaluate the economic potential of entering a new industry or market. Why couldn't such a firm simply hire some smart managers, consultants, and industry experts to evaluate the economic potential of entering a new industry?

11.7. Some researchers have argued that alliances can be used to help firms evaluate the economic potential of entering a new industry or market. What, if anything, about an alliance makes this a better way to evaluate entry opportunities than alternative methods?

11.8. If adverse selection, moral hazard, and holdup are such significant problems for firms pursuing alliance strategies, why do firms even bother with alliances?

11.9. If adverse selection, moral hazard, and holdup are such significant problems for firms pursuing alliance strategies, why don't they instead adopt a "go it alone" strategy to replace strategic alliances?

Problem Set

11.10. Which of the following firms faces the greater threat of "cheating" in the alliances described, and why?

(a) Firm I and Firm II form a strategic alliance. As part of the alliance, Firm I agrees to build a new plant right next to Firm II's primary facility. In return, Firm II promises to buy most of the output of this new plant. Which is at risk, Firm I or Firm II?

(b) Firm A and Firm B form a strategic alliance. As part of the alliance, Firm A promises to begin selling products it already sells around the world in the home country of Firm B. In return, Firm B promises to provide Firm A with crucial contacts in its home country's government. These contacts are essential if Firm A is going to be able to sell in Firm B's home country. Which is at risk, Firm A or Firm B?

(c) Firm 1 and Firm 2 form a strategic alliance. As part of the alliance, Firm 1 promises to provide Firm 2 access to some new and untested technology that Firm 2 will use in its products. In return, Firm 2 will share some of the profits from its sales with Firm 1. Which is at risk, Firm 1 or Firm 2?

11.11. For each of the strategic alliances described in the above question, what actions could be taken to reduce the likelihood that partner firms will "cheat" in these alliances?

11.12. Examine the Web sites of the following strategic alliances and determine which of the sources of value presented in Table 11.1 are present:

(a) Dow-Corning (an alliance between Dow Chemical and Corning)
(b) CFM (an alliance between General Electric and SNECMA)
(c) NCAA (an alliance among colleges and universities in the United States)
(d) Visa (an alliance among banks in the United States)
(e) The alliance among United, Delta, Singapore Airlines, AeroMexico, Alitalia, and Korean Air

Writing Assignments

11.13. How would a firm's reputation reduce the threat of cheating in a strategic alliance?

11.14. How can holdup be considered a form of cheating in strategic alliances and threat of holdup be considered a motivation for creating an alliance?

CASE STUDY | Accelerating India's Digital Transformation: Google and Bharti Airtel

The strategic alliance between Google and Bharti Airtel for cloud solutions is a significant development in India's digital ecosystem. Announced on January 28, 2022, this partnership is part of Google's initiative to invest up to $1 billion through its Google for India Digitization Fund. The collaboration aims to accelerate the growth of India's digital landscape by leveraging the strengths and resources of both giants. Google's commitment includes a $700 million equity investment in Bharti Airtel and an additional $300 million allocated for potential multi-year commercial agreements to foster further technological and infrastructural advancements.

This strategic partnership is set to focus on several key areas, including enhancing affordable access to smartphones across various price ranges and co-creating India-specific network domain use cases for 5G, among other standards. The initiative is designed to address the challenges of affordability, access, and digital inclusion, thus paving the way for a more connected and digitally inclusive India. Furthermore, both companies are committed to exploring and investing in a wide spectrum of areas to create digital solutions tailored to India's unique needs, from expanding cloud ecosystems to accelerating digital transformation for businesses across the nation.

The collaboration between Google and Bharti Airtel is not just about financial investment but also about bringing together their expertise to solve complex problems related to digital access and inclusion. This partnership is expected to utilize multiple research and development sites from both companies, including locations in the United States and Germany, to house activities identified by the collaboration agreement. The deal is subject to necessary regulatory approvals, highlighting the strategic and structured approach both entities are taking to ensure the success and effectiveness of their joint efforts. As part of the first commercial agreement under this partnership, Airtel and Google will work on expanding Airtel's offerings, covering a range of Android-enabled devices to consumers through innovative affordability programs. The long-term vision includes co-creating specific network domain use cases for 5G to enhance network experience and exploring the scaling of Google's network virtualization solutions. This partnership is a testament to the shared vision of both companies to contribute to India's digital transformation journey, ensuring that the benefits of technological advancements are accessible to a wider audience.

The alliance between Google and Bharti Airtel marks a significant milestone in the journey towards a digitally empowered India, highlighting the importance of collaborative efforts in bridging the digital divide and fostering an inclusive digital ecosystem. It exemplifies how strategic partnerships can play a pivotal role in shaping the future of digital infrastructure, access, and services, setting a precedent for future collaborations in the tech industry.

Questions

1. What strategic objectives are Google and Bharti Airtel aiming to achieve through their partnership in cloud solutions, and how do these objectives align with their respective corporate goals and visions?
2. How does the partnership between Google and Bharti Airtel address the challenges of affordability, access, and digital inclusion in India, and what specific measures are outlined to ensure the success of this collaborative effort?
3. What regulatory approvals are necessary for the success of this collaboration, and what steps are both companies taking to navigate regulatory considerations effectively, ensuring compliance and facilitating the implementation of their joint initiatives?

References

Bharti Airtel. (2022, January 28). *Airtel and Google partner to help grow India's digital ecosystem.* Accessed from https://www.airtel.in on March 30, 2024

Bharti Airtel. (n.d.). Press Release 2021–2022: *Airtel and Google partner to help grow India's digital ecosystem.* Accessed from https://www.bharti.com on March 30, 2024

Pandey, S., & Hallur, G. G. (2023, January). *Study of the competition in Indian telecom industry: A 20-year period with Airtel as the case company.* In AIP Conference Proceedings (Vol. 2523, No. 1). AIP Publishing.

End Notes

1 See news.Wal-Mart.com/2016/06/20/Wal-Mart-and-JDcom-announce-strategic-alliance-to-serve-consummers-across-china; www.businessinser.com/r-in-china-us-teach-firms-turn-to-domestic-rivals-for-survival-2015-1; https://bol.bna.com/mcguirewoods-joins-those-creating-alliances-with-chinese-firms; http://techcrunch.com/2016/06/20/Wal-Mart-sells-yihaodian-its-chinese-e-commerce-marketplace-to-alibaba-rival-jd-com. All accessed March 6, 2017.

2 See www.pwc.com/extweb/exccps.nsf/docid; www.addme.com/issue208; McCracken, J. (2006). "Ford doubles reported loss for second quarter." *The Wall Street Journal*, August 3, p. A3; and www.msnbc.msn.com/id/13753688.

3. Badaracco, J. L., and N. Hasegawa. (1988). "General Motors' Asian alliances." Harvard Business School Case No. 9-388-094.

4 S. A. Alvarez and J. B. Barney (2001). "How entrepreneurial firms can benefit from alliances with large partners." *Academy of Management Executive*, 15, pp. 139–148; G. Hamel (1991). "Competition for competence and inter-partner learning within international alliances." *Strategic Management Journal*, 12, pp. 83–103; W. Cohen and D. Levinthal (1990). "Absorptive capacity: A new perspective on learning and innovation." *Administrative Science Quarterly*, 35, pp. 128–152.

5 www.HollywoodReporter.com/lists/2016s-biggest-box-office-bombs. Accessed March 6, 2017.

6 See www.blu-ray.com.

7 See Burgers, W. P., C. W. L. Hill, and W. C. Kim. (1993). "A theory of global strategic alliances: The case of the global auto industry." *Strategic Management Journal*, 14, pp. 419–432.

8 F. M. Scherer (1980). *Industrial market structure and economic performance.* Boston: Houghton Mifflin; J. B. Barney (2006). *Gaining and sustaining competitive advantage*, 3rd ed. Upper Saddle River, NJ: Prentice Hall; J. Pfeffer and P. Nowak (1976). "Patterns of joint venture activity: Implications for anti-trust research." *Antitrust Bulletin*, 21, pp. 315–339.

9 See Freeman, A., and R. Hudson. (1980). "DuPont and Philips plan joint venture to make, market laser disc products." *The Wall Street Journal*, December 22, p. 10.

10 Teitelbaum, R. S. (1992). "Eskimo pie." *Fortune*, June 15, p. 123.

11 Nanda, A., and C. A. Bartlett. (1990). "Corning Incorporated: A network of alliances." Harvard Business School Case No. 9-391-102.

12 See Knight, F. H. (1965). *Risk, uncertainty, and profit.* New York: John Wiley & Sons, Inc., on uncertainty; Kogut, B. (1991). "Joint ventures and the option to expand and acquire." *Management Science*, 37, pp. 19–33; Burgers, W. P., C. W. L. Hill, and W. C. Kim. (1993). "A theory of global strategic alliances: The case of the global auto industry." *Strategic Management Journal*, 14, pp. 419–432; Noldeke, G., and K. M. Schmidt. (1998). "Sequential investments and options to own." *Rand Journal of Economics*, 29(4), pp. 633–653; and Folta, T. B. (1998). "Governance and uncertainty: The tradeoff between administrative control and commitment." *Strategic Management Journal*, 19, pp. 1007–1028.

13 See Kogut, B. (1991). "Joint ventures and the option to expand and acquire." *Management Science*, 37, pp. 19–33; and Balakrishnan, S., and M. Koza. (1993). "Information asymmetry, adverse selection and joint-ventures." *Journal of Economic Behavior & Organization*, 20, pp. 99–117.

14 See, for example, Ernst, D., and J. Bleeke. (1993). *Collaborating to compete: Using strategic alliances and acquisition in the global marketplace.* New York: John Wiley & Sons, Inc.

15 These terms are defined in Barney, J. B., and W. G. Ouchi. (1986). *Organizational economics.* San Francisco: Jossey-Bass; and Holmstrom, B. (1979). "Moral hazard and observability." *Bell Journal of Economics*, 10(1), pp. 74–91. Problems of cheating in economic exchanges in general, and in alliances in particular, are discussed by Gulati, R., and H. Singh. (1998). "The architecture of cooperation: Managing coordination costs and appropriation concerns in strategic alliances." *Administrative Science Quarterly*, 43, pp. 781–814; Williamson, O. E. (1991). "Comparative economic organization: The analysis of discrete structural alternatives." *Administrative Science Quarterly*, 36, pp. 269–296; Osborn, R. N., and C. C. Baughn. (1990). "Forms of interorganizational governance for multinational alliances." *Academy of Management Journal*, 33(3), pp. 503–519; Hagedoorn, J., and R. Narula. (1996). "Choosing organizational modes of strategic technology partnering: International and sectoral differences." *Journal of International Business Studies*, second quarter, pp. 265–284; Hagedorn, J. (1996). "Trends and patterns in strategic technology partnering since the early seventies." *Review of Industrial Organization*, 11, pp. 601–616; Kent, D. H. (1991). "Joint ventures vs. non-joint ventures: An empirical investigation." *Strategic Management Journal*, 12, pp. 387–393; and Shane, S. A. (1998). "Making new franchise systems work." *Strategic Management Journal*, 19, pp. 697–707.

16 Such alliance difficulties are described in Ouchi, W. G. (1984). *The M-form society: How American teamwork can capture the competitive edge.* Reading, MA: Addison-Wesley; and Bresser, R. K. (1988). "Cooperative strategy." *Strategic Management Journal*, 9, pp. 475–492.

17 Pope, K. (1993). "Dealers accuse Compaq of jilting them." *The Wall Street Journal*, February 26, pp. 8, B1+.

18 Williamson, O. E. (1975). *Markets and hierarchies: Analysis and antitrust implications.* New York: Free Press; Klein, B., R. Crawford, and A. Alchian. (1978). "Vertical integration, appropriable rents, and the competitive contracting process." *Journal of Law and Economics*, 21, pp. 297–326.

19 See, for example, Yan, A., and B. Gray. (1994). "Bargaining power, management control, and performance in United States–China joint ventures: A comparative case study." *Academy of Management Journal*, 37, pp. 1478–1517.

20 R. M. Axelrod (1984). *The evolution of cooperation.* New York: Basic Books; D. Ernst and J. Bleeke (1993). *Collaborating to compete.* New York: Wiley.

21 See Badaracco, J. L., and N. Hasegawa. (1988). "General Motors' Asian alliances." Harvard Business School Case No. 9-388-094, on GM and Toyota; Patterson, G. A. (1991). "Mazda hopes to crack Japan's top tier." *The Wall Street Journal*, September 20, pp. B1+; and Williams, M., and M. Kanabayashi. (1993). "Mazda and Ford drop proposal to build cars together in Europe." *The Wall Street Journal*, March 4, p. A14, on Ford and Mazda; and Ennis, P. (1991). "Mitsubishi group wary of deeper ties to Chrysler." *Tokyo Business Today*, 59, July, p. 10, on DaimlerChrysler and Mitsubishi, and www.reuters.com/article/US-mitsubishimotors-nissan-idUSKCN12K0DX accessed March 3, 2017.

22 See, for example, Ernst, D., and J. Bleeke. (1993). *Collaborating to compete: Using strategic alliances and acquisition in the global marketplace.* New York: John Wiley & Sons, Inc.; and Barney, J. B., and M. H. Hansen. (1994). "Trustworthiness as a source of competitive advantage." *Strategic Management Journal*, 15, winter (special issue), pp. 175–190.

23 Ernst, D., and J. Bleeke. (1993). *Collaborating to compete: Using strategic alliances and acquisition in the global marketplace*. New York: John Wiley & Sons, Inc.

24 Bartlett, C., and S. Ghoshal. (1993). "Beyond the M-form: Toward a managerial theory of the firm." *Strategic Management Journal*, 14, pp. 23–46.

25 See Nagarajan, A., and W. Mitchell. (1998). "Evolutionary diffusion: Internal and external methods used to acquire encompassing, complementary, and incremental technological changes in the lithotripsy industry." *Strategic Management Journal*, 19, pp. 1063–1077; Hagedoorn, J., and B. Sadowski. (1999). "The transition from strategic technology alliances to mergers and acquisitions: An exploratory study." *Journal of Management Studies*, 36(1), pp. 87–107; and Newburry, W., and Y. Zeira. (1997). "Generic differences between equity international joint ventures (EIJVs), international acquisitions (IAs) and International Greenfield investments (IGIs): Implications for parent companies." *Journal of World Business*, 32(2), pp. 87–102, on alliance substitutes.

26 Barney, J. B. (1999). "How a firm's capabilities affect boundary decisions." *Sloan Management Review*, 40(3), pp. 137–145.

27 See Hennart, J. F. (1988). "A transaction cost theory of equity joint ventures." *Strategic Management Journal*, 9, pp. 361–374; Kogut, B. (1988). "Joint ventures: Theoretical and empirical perspectives." *Strategic Management Journal*, 9, pp. 319–332; and Barney, J. B. (1999). "How a firm's capabilities affect boundary decisions." *Sloan Management Review*, 40(3), pp. 137–145, for a discussion of these limitations.

28 See Ouchi, W. G. (1984). *The M-form society: How American teamwork can capture the competitive edge*. Reading, MA: Addison-Wesley; and Barney, J. B. (1990). "Profit sharing bonuses and the cost of debt: Business finance and compensation policy in Japanese electronics firms." *Asia Pacific Journal of Management*, 7, pp. 49–64.

29 This is an argument developed by Barney, J. B., and M. H. Hansen. (1994). "Trustworthiness as a source of competitive advantage." *Strategic Management Journal*, 15, winter (special issue), pp. 175–190; Weigelt, K., and C. Camerer. (1988). "Reputation and corporate strategy: A review of recent theory and applications." *Strategic Management Journal*, 9, pp. 443–454; and Granovetter, M. (1985). "Economic action and social structure: The problem of embeddedness." *American Journal of Sociology*, 3, pp. 481–510.

30 See, for example, Eichenseher, J., and D. Shields. (1985). "Reputation and corporate strategy: A review of recent theory and applications." *Strategic Management Journal*, 9, pp. 443–454; Beatty, R., and R. Ritter. (1986). "Investment banking, reputation, and the underpricing of initial public offerings." *Journal of Financial Economics*, 15, pp. 213–232; Kalleberg, A. L., and T. Reve. (1992). "Contracts and commitment: Economic and Sociological Perspectives on Employment Relations." *Human Relations*, 45(9), pp. 1103–1132; Larson, A. (1992). "Network dyads in entrepreneurial settings: A study of the governance of exchange relationships." *Administrative Science Quarterly*, March, pp. 76–104; Stuart, T. E., H. Hoang, and R. C. Hybels. (1999). "Interorganizational endorsements and the performance of entrepreneurial ventures." *Administrative Science Quarterly*, 44, pp. 315–349; Stuart, T. E. (1998). "Network positions and propensities to collaborate: An investigation of strategic alliance formation in a high-technology industry." *Administrative Science Quarterly*, 43(3), pp. 668–698; and Gulati, R. (1998). "Alliances and networks." *Strategic Management Journal*, 19, pp. 293–317.

31 Personal communication, April 8, 1986.

32 This same theoretic approach to firm reputation is discussed in Tirole, J. (1988). *The theory of industrial organization*. Cambridge, MA: MIT Press.

33 Scherer, F. M. (1980). *Industrial market structure and economic performance*. Boston: Houghton Mifflin.

34 See, again, Ernst, D., and J. Bleeke. (1993). *Collaborating to compete: Using strategic alliances and acquisition in the global marketplace*. New York: John Wiley & Sons, Inc.; and Barney, J. B., and M. H. Hansen. (1994). "Trustworthiness as a source of competitive advantage." *Strategic Management Journal*, 15, winter (special issue), pp. 175–190. In fact, there is a great deal of literature on the role of trust in strategic alliances. Some of the most interesting of this work can be found in Holm, D. B., K. Eriksson, and J. Johanson. (1999). "Creating value through mutual commitment to business network relationships." *Strategic Management Journal*, 20, pp. 467–486; Lorenzoni, G., and A. Lipparini. (1999). "The leveraging of interfirm relationships as a distinctive organizational capability: A longitudinal study." *Strategic Management Journal*, 20(4), pp. 317–338; Blois, K. J. (1999). "Trust in business to business relationships: An evaluation of its status." *Journal of Management Studies*, 36(2), pp. 197–215; Chiles, T. H., and J. F. McMackin. (1996). "Integrating variable risk preferences, trust, and transaction cost economics." *Academy of Management Review*, 21(1), pp. 73–99; Larzelere, R. E., and T. L. Huston. (1980). "The dyadic trust scale: Toward understanding interpersonal trust in close relationships." *Journal of Marriage and the Family*, August, pp. 595–604; Butler, J. K., Jr. (1983). "Reciprocity of trust between professionals and their secretaries." *Psychological Reports*, 53, pp. 411–416; Zaheer, A., and N. Venkatraman. (1995). "Relational governance as an interorganizational strategy: An empirical test of the role of trust in economic exchange." *Strategic Management Journal*, 16, pp. 373–392; Butler, J. K., Jr., and R. S. Cantrell. (1984). "A behavioral decision theory approach to modeling dyadic trust in superiors and subordinates." *Psychological Reports*, 55, pp. 19–28; Carney, M. (1998). "The competitiveness of networked production: The role of trust and asset specificity." *Journal of Management Studies*, 35(4), pp. 457–479.

35 Ernst, D., and J. Bleeke. (1993). *Collaborating to compete: Using strategic alliances and acquisition in the global marketplace*. New York: John Wiley & Sons, Inc.

36 See Mohr, J., and R. Spekman. (1994). "Characteristics of partnership success: Partnership attributes, communication behavior, and conflict resolution techniques." *Strategic Management Journal*, 15, pp. 135–152; and Zaheer, A., and N. Venkatraman. (1995). "Relational governance as an interorganizational strategy: An empirical test of the role of trust in economic exchange." *Strategic Management Journal*, 16, pp. 373–392.

CHAPTER

12 Mergers and Acquisitions

LEARNING OBJECTIVES

After reading this chapter, you should be able to:

12.1 Describe different types of mergers and acquisitions.

12.2 Describe how mergers and acquisitions can create economic value:

a. When bidding and target firms share no economies of scope
b. When bidding and target firms share economies of scope
c. Why firms might engage in these strategies even when, on average, they do not create profits for bidding firms.

12.3 Describe three ways that bidding firms might be able to generate economic profits from implementing mergers or acquisitions.

12.4 Describe the major challenges that firms integrating acquisitions are likely to face.

Strategic Merger in Indian Finance: HDFC Ltd and HDFC Bank Unite

The merger between HDFC Ltd. and HDFC Bank, announced on April 4, 2022, and completed by July 1, 2023, is a significant event in the Indian financial sector, aiming to create a financial behemoth by integrating HDFC's housing finance leadership with HDFC Bank's banking excellence. This strategic amalgamation is designed to enhance their service offerings, expanding access to housing finance and banking services across India, and is expected to drive growth through synergies between the two entities. The merger aims to leverage the combined strengths of both entities to create a financial powerhouse capable of offering an unparalleled range of products and services to its customers.

The strategic rationale behind the merger includes several key motivations. Firstly, it enables HDFC Bank to significantly expand its housing loan portfolio, thereby enhancing its position in the retail lending space. Moreover, it allows the merged entity to leverage HDFC Ltd.'s extensive experience and expertise in the housing finance sector to fuel further growth. From a financial standpoint, the merger is anticipated to result in considerable synergies, improving efficiency and profitability for the combined entity. It also aims to address the evolving needs of customers by providing a more comprehensive suite of financial solutions, thereby improving customer experience and satisfaction. However, mergers of such scale often come with their set of challenges and potential agency conflicts. Aligning the interests of stakeholders from both companies, integrating the corporate cultures, systems, and processes, and managing the expectations of employees and customers are critical areas that require careful attention. Additionally, regulatory approvals and maintaining compliance in a complex financial landscape add layers of complexity to the merger process.

The future direction of the merged entity is focused on leveraging technological advancements to drive innovation in financial products and services. It aims to capitalize on the growing digitalization of India's economy to reach more customers and provide more accessible and efficient banking and financial services. Moreover, the merged entity is likely to focus on expanding its reach in underpenetrated markets, thereby contributing to the broader goal of financial inclusion in India. Despite the potential challenges, the merger between HDFC Ltd and HDFC Bank is poised to create a robust platform that can significantly impact India's banking and financial services sector. By combining their strengths, the merged entity is well-positioned to drive growth, enhance shareholder value, and contribute to the economic development of the country.

REFERENCES

HDFC Bank. (2022). *HDFC Limited And HDFC Bank Limited Announce a Transformational Merger.* Accessed from https://www.hdfcbank.com on March 29, 2024.

Tandon, D., & Batra, D. K. (2023). *Merger of Hdfc Ltd & Hdfc Bank: Integration for achieving growth.* JIMS8M The Journal of Indian Management & Strategy, 28(2), 61–64.

Preeti, & Roy, S. (2022). *Operational Performance Modelling of Indian Banks: A Data Envelopment Analysis Approach.* Paradigm, 26(1), 29–49.

Of course, acquisitions are not limited to just the technology sector. In 2016, large non-technology acquisitions included Bayer's purchase of Monsanto for $66 billion (in the agricultural products industry), British American Tobacco's purchase of Reynolds American for $58 billion (in the tobacco industry), Sunoco Logistics acquisition of Energy Transfer Partners for $52 billion (in the oil and gas transportation industry), Shire's purchase of Baxala for $32 billion (in the specialty pharmaceutical industry), Abbott Laboratories purchase of St. Jude Medical (in the medical technology industry) for $30.6 billion, and Johnson Controls acquisition of Tyco International for $16.6 billion. Indeed, mergers and acquisitions are one very common way that a firm can accomplish its vertical integration and diversification objectives.

However, although a firm may be able to accomplish its vertical integration and diversification objectives through mergers or acquisitions, it is sometimes difficult to generate real economic profit from doing so. Indeed, one of the strongest empirical findings in the fields of strategic management and finance is that, on average, the equity holders of target firms in mergers and acquisitions make money while the equity holders of bidding firms in these same mergers and acquisitions usually only "break even."

That mergers and acquisitions often do not generate economic profits for acquiring firms is not the only controversial aspect of this strategic option. Indeed, it may be the case that there are more ethical issues associated with this strategy than any other strategy discussed in this text. These issues are discussed in the Ethics and Strategy feature.

Ethics and Strategy

In the 1987 movie Wall Street—required viewing for every business student, even in the 21st century—corporate raider Gordon Gecko (played by Michael Douglas in rare form) lectures a stockholder's meeting about the morality of unfriendly takeovers. In justifying his approach to investing, Gecko utters the now famous phrase "Greed is good." What he means by this is that his efforts to make money by acquiring the stock of underperforming firms gives firms strong incentives to address their customer's needs as efficiently and effectively as possible. In a sense, Gecko is arguing that "corporate raiders" help make sure that product markets are highly competitive and that—per economic theory—should mean that social welfare is maximized. While his language is harsh, his underlying message is consistent with economic theory.

Is Greed Good?

Or is it?

In the movie, Gecko earns his money by trading on insider information. This is illegal in the United States and many developed countries, and in the end, Gecko goes to jail. But should insider trading be illegal? Some have argued that the primary concern of main street investors, i.e., those who are not focused on trading stocks as their only source of income, is that any information about the value of a firm be revealed to the market. That a few people, with privileged information, earn a profit from making this information public does not mean that main street investors will not also benefit from this information. From this point of view, insider trading should be legal.

Or maybe it should be illegal.

Another way that Gecko makes money in the movie is by breaking up the companies he buys, selling off the parts to the highest bidders. This can have an adverse effect on the stability of the employment in the firms he targets. Indeed, acquisitions often lead to layoffs and corporate downsizing. Some early work suggests that after this downsizing, firm employment recovers and then actually grows. Usually, but not always, these actions increase the wealth of a firm's shareholders. Today, this function in the economy is usually delegated to private equity firms, not corporate raiders. Maybe a firm should focus its efforts only on maximizing the wealth of its shareholders and avoid adding superfluous employees to the payroll in the first place, so that it won't be the object of these kinds of actions.

Or maybe not.

Finally, the dollars that are often associated with acquisitions are so high, one must wonder about the morality of these payments. This is especially the case for intermediaries in these exchanges—the lawyers and investment bankers—and for managers—who see their incomes rise as their firms get larger. It turns out that intermediaries and managers do make quite a bit of money in acquisitions. In the United States, for example, total investment banking fees in acquisitions range between 2.3 and 2.4% of a target's purchase price. However, the vast majority of the value that is created by these strategies is appropriated by shareholders. And who are these shareholders? More and more of them are institutions—like mutual funds and pension funds (see Chapter 10). But these institutions invest the funds they control for smaller investors around the world. So, in this sense, creating value for investors through acquisition strategies is a highly democratic approach to capitalism.

Or maybe it isn't.

The ethical issues surrounding mergers and acquisitions are complex and subtle. Sweeping conclusions that all such strategies are inherently immoral seem just as problematic as sweeping conclusions that they are all justifiable on ethical grounds. The phrase "Greed is good" makes many uncomfortable, but it gives us an opportunity to think much deeper about the ethics of mergers and acquisitions.[1]

What Are Mergers and Acquisitions?

Objective 12.1 Describe different types of mergers and acquisitions.

The terms *mergers* and *acquisitions* are often used interchangeably, even though they are not synonyms. A firm engages in an **acquisition** when it purchases a second firm. The form of this purchase can vary. For example, an acquiring firm can use cash it has generated from its ongoing businesses to purchase a target firm; it can go into debt to purchase a target firm; it can use its own equity to purchase a target firm; or it can use a mix of these mechanisms to purchase a target firm. Also, an acquiring firm can purchase all a target firm's assets; it can purchase a majority of those assets (greater than 51 percent); or it can purchase a **controlling share** of those assets (i.e., enough assets so that the acquiring firm is able to make all the management and strategic decisions in the target firm).

Acquisitions also vary on several other dimensions. For example, **friendly acquisitions** occur when the management of the target firm wants the firm to be acquired. **Unfriendly acquisitions** occur when the management of the target firm does not want the firm to be acquired. Some unfriendly acquisitions are also known as **hostile takeovers**. Some acquisitions are accomplished through direct negotiations between an acquiring firm's managers and the managers of a target firm. This is especially common when a target firm is **privately held** (i.e., when it has not sold shares on the public stock market) or **closely held** (i.e., when it has not sold very many shares on the public stock market). Other acquisitions are accomplished by the acquiring firm publicly announcing that it is willing to purchase the outstanding shares of a potential target for a particular price. This price is normally greater than the current market price of the target firm's shares. The difference between the current market price of a target firm's shares and the price a potential acquirer offers to pay for those shares is known as an **acquisition premium**. This approach to purchasing a firm is called a **tender offer**. Tender offers can be made either with or without the support of the management of the target firm. Obviously, tender offers with the support of the target firm's management are typically friendly in character; those made without the support of the target firm's management are typically unfriendly.

It is usually the case that larger firms—in terms of sales or assets—acquire smaller firms. For example, Google has been larger than all its intended targets, including Motorola Mobile. In contrast, when the assets of two similar-sized firms are combined, this transaction is called a **merger**. Mergers can be accomplished in many of the same ways as acquisitions, that is, using cash or stock to purchase a percentage of another firm's assets. Typically, however, mergers will not be unfriendly. In a merger, one firm purchases some percentage of a second firm's assets while the second firm simultaneously purchases some percentage of the first firm's assets. For example, DaimlerChrysler was created as a merger between Daimler-Benz (the maker of Mercedes-Benz) and Chrysler. Daimler-Benz invested some of its capital in Chrysler, and Chrysler invested some of its capital in Daimler-Benz. More recently, these merged companies split into two firms again. Then, after the financial crisis of 2007, Chrysler merged with Fiat.

Although mergers typically begin as a transaction between equals—that is, between firms of equal size and profitability—they often evolve after a merger such that one firm becomes more dominant in the management of the merged firm than the other. For example, most observers believe that Daimler (the German part of DaimlerChrysler) became more dominant in the management of the combined firm than Chrysler (the American part). And now, most believe that Fiat is more dominant.[2] Put differently, although mergers usually start out as something different from acquisitions, they usually end up looking more like acquisitions than mergers.

Objective 12.2 Describe how mergers and acquisitions can create economic value:

a. When bidding and target firms share no economies of scope
b. When bidding and target firms share economies of scope
c. Why firms might engage in these strategies even when, on average, they do not create profits for bidding firms.

The Value of Mergers and Acquisitions

That merger and acquisition strategies are an important strategic option open to firms pursuing diversification and vertical integration strategies can hardly be disputed. The number of firms that have used merger and acquisition strategies to become diversified over the past few years is staggering. In 2015, there were over 45,000 acquisitions worldwide, and in 2016, the total value of all acquisitions topped $4.5 trillion.[3]

That mergers and acquisitions are common is clear. What is less clear is that they actually generate value for firms implementing these strategies. Two cases will be examined here: mergers and acquisitions between firms where no economies of scope exist and mergers and acquisitions between firms where economies of scope do exist.

Mergers and Acquisitions: No Economies of Scope

Imagine the following scenario: one firm (the target) is the object of an acquisition effort, and 10 firms (the bidders) are interested in making this acquisition. Suppose the **current market value** of the target firm is $10,000—that is, the price of each of this firm's shares times the number of shares outstanding equals $10,000. Also, suppose the current market value of each of the bidding firms is $15,000.[4] Finally, suppose there are no economies of scope between these bidding firms and the target. This means that the value of any one of these bidding firms when combined with the target firm exactly equals the sum of the value of these firms as separate entities. In this example, because the current market value of the target is $10,000 and the current market value of the bidding firms is

$15,000, the value of this target when combined with any of these bidders would be $25,000 ($10,000 + $15,000). Given this information, at what price will this target be acquired, and what are the economic performance implications for bidding and target firms at this price?

In this and all acquisition situations, bidding firms will be willing to pay a price for a target up to the value that the target firm adds to the bidder once it is acquired. This price is simply the difference between the value of the two firms combined (in this case, $25,000) and the value of the bidding firm by itself (in this case, $15,000). Notice that this price does not depend on the value of the target firm acting as an independent business; rather, it depends on the value that the target firm creates when it is combined with the bidding firm. Any price for a target less than this value (i.e., less than $10,000) will be a source of economic profit for a bidding firm; any price equal to this value (i.e., equal to $10,000) will be a source of zero economic profits; and any price greater than this value (i.e., greater than $10,000) will be a source of economic losses for the bidding firm that acquires the target.

It is not hard to see that the price of this acquisition will quickly rise to $10,000 and that at this price the bidding firm that acquires the target will earn zero economic profits. The price of this acquisition will quickly rise to $10,000 because any bid less than $10,000 will generate economic profits for a successful bidder. These potential profits, in turn, will generate entry into the bidding war for a target. Because entry into the acquisition contest is very likely, the price of the acquisition will quickly rise to its value, and economic profits will not be created.

Moreover, at this $10,000 price the target firm's equity holders will also gain zero economic profits. Indeed, for them, all that has occurred is that the market value of the target firm has been capitalized in the form of a cash payment from the bidder to the target. The target was worth $10,000, and that is exactly what these equity holders will receive.

Mergers and Acquisitions: When Economies of Scope Exist

The conclusion that the acquisition of targets when no economies of scope exist will generate only zero economic profits for both the bidding and the target firms is not surprising. It is very consistent with the discussion of the economic consequences of diversification in Chapter 9. There, it was argued that there is no economic justification for a corporate diversification strategy that does not build on some type of economy of scope across the businesses within which a firm operates. So, if there is any hope that mergers and acquisitions will be a source of superior performance for bidding firms, it must be because of some sort of economy of scope between bidding and target firms.

Types of Economies of Scope in Acquisitions

Of course, economies of scope between bidding and target firms can vary dramatically. Three particularly important lists of these potential linkages are discussed here.[5]

The Federal Trade Commission Categories Because mergers and acquisitions can have the effect of increasing (or decreasing) the level of concentration in an industry, the Federal Trade Commission (FTC) is charged with the responsibility of evaluating the competitive implications of proposed mergers or acquisitions. In principle, the FTC will disallow any acquisition involving firms with headquarters in the United States that could have the potential for generating monopoly (or oligopoly) profits in an industry. To help in this regulatory effort, the FTC has developed a typology of mergers and acquisitions (see Table 12.1). Each category in this typology can be thought of as a different way in which a bidding firm and a target firm can be related in a merger or acquisition.

Per the FTC, a firm engages in a **vertical merger** when it vertically integrates, either forward or backward, through its acquisition efforts. Vertical mergers could include a firm purchasing critical suppliers of raw materials (backward vertical integration) or acquiring customers and distribution networks (forward vertical integration). Disney's acquisition of Capital Cities/ABC can be understood as an attempt by Disney to forward vertically integrate into the entertainment distribution industry, and its acquisition of ESPN can be seen as backward vertical integration into the entertainment production business.[6]

A firm engages in a **horizontal merger** when it acquires a former competitor; Adidas's acquisition of Reebok is an example of a horizontal merger, as the number 2 and number 3 sneaker manufacturers in the world combined their efforts. Obviously, the FTC is particularly concerned with the competitive implications of horizontal mergers because these strategies can have the most direct and obvious anti-competitive implications in an industry. For example, the FTC raised antitrust concerns in the $10 billion merger between Oracle and PeopleSoft because these firms, collectively, dominated the enterprise software market. Similar concerns were raised in the $16.4 billion merger between ChevronTexaco and Unocal and the merger between Mobil and Exxon.

The third type of merger identified by the FTC is a **product extension merger**. In a product extension merger, firms acquire complementary products through their merger and acquisition activities. Examples include Google's acquisition of Motorola Mobile.

The fourth type of merger identified by the FTC is a **market extension merger**. Here the primary objective is to gain access to new geographic markets. Examples include SABMiller's acquisition of Bavaria Brewery Company in Columbia, South America.

The final type of merger or acquisition identified by the FTC is a **conglomerate merger**. For the FTC, conglomerate mergers are a residual category. If there are no vertical, horizontal, product extension, or market extension links between firms, the FTC defines the merger or acquisition activity between firms as a conglomerate merger.

Other Types of Strategic Relatedness Although the FTC categories of mergers and acquisitions provide some information about possible motives underlying these corporate strategies, they do not capture the full complexity of the links that might exist between bidding and target firms. Several authors have attempted to develop more complete lists of possible sources of economies of scope between bidding and target firms. One of these lists, developed by Professor Michael Lubatkin, is summarized in Table 12.2. This list includes **technical economies** (in marketing,

TABLE 12.1 Federal Trade Commission Categories of Mergers and Acquisitions

• Vertical merger	A firm acquires former suppliers or customers
• Horizontal merger	A firm acquires a former competitor
• Product extension merger	A firm gains access to complementary products through an acquisition
• Market extension merger	A firm gains access to complementary markets through an acquisition
• Conglomerate merger	There is no strategic relatedness between a bidding and a target firm

TABLE 12.2 Lubatkin's List of Potential Sources of Economies of Scope Between Bidding and Target Firms

Technical economies	Scale economies that occur when the physical processes inside a firm are altered so that the same amounts of input produce a higher quantity of outputs. Sources of technical economies include marketing, production, experience, scheduling, banking, and compensation.
Pecuniary economies	Economies achieved by the ability of firms to dictate prices by exerting market power
Diversification economies	Economies achieved by improving a firm's performance relative to its risk attributes or lowering its risk attributes relative to its performance. Sources of diversification economies include portfolio management and risk reduction.

Source: M. Lubatkin (1983). "Mergers and the performance of the acquiring firm." *Academy of Management Review*, 8, pp. 218–225.

production, and similar forms of relatedness), **pecuniary economies** (market power), and **diversification economies** (in portfolio management and risk reduction) as possible bases of strategic relatedness between bidding and target firms.

A second important list of possible sources of economies of scope between bidding and target firms was developed by Michael Jensen and Richard Ruback after a comprehensive review of empirical research on the economic returns to mergers and acquisitions. This list is summarized in Table 12.3 and includes the following factors as possible sources of economic gains in mergers and acquisitions: potential reductions in production or distribution costs (from economies of scale, vertical integration, reduction in agency costs, and so forth); the realization of financial opportunities (such as gaining access to underutilized tax shields, avoiding bankruptcy costs); the creation of market power; and the ability to eliminate inefficient management in the target firm.

TABLE 12.3 Jensen and Ruback's List of Reasons Why Bidding Firms Might Want to Engage in Merger and Acquisition Strategies

To reduce production or distribution costs:

1. Through economies of scale
2. Through vertical integration
3. Through the adoption of more efficient production or organizational technology
4. Through the increased utilization of the bidder's management team
5. Through a reduction of agency costs by bringing organization-specific assets under common ownership

Financial motivations:

1. To gain access to underutilized tax shields
2. To avoid bankruptcy costs
3. To increase leverage opportunities
4. To gain other tax advantages
5. To gain market power in product markets
6. To eliminate inefficient target management

Source: Reprinted from Jensen, M. C., and R. S. Ruback (1983). "The Market for Corporate Control: The Scientific Evidence." *Journal of Financial Economics*, 11, pp. 5–50. Vol. II.

To be economically valuable, links between bidding and target firms must meet the same criteria as diversification strategies (see Chapter 9). First, these links must build on real economies of scope between bidding and target firms. These economies of scope can reflect either cost savings or revenue enhancements that are created by combining firms. Second, not only must this economy of scope exist, but it must be less costly for the merged firm to realize than for outside equity holders to realize on their own. As is the case with corporate diversification strategies, by investing in a diversified portfolio of stocks, outside equity investors can gain many of the economies associated with a merger or acquisition on their own. Moreover, investors can realize some of these economies of scope at almost zero cost. In this situation, it makes little sense for investors to "hire" managers in firms to realize these economies of scope for them through a merger or acquisition. Rather, firms should pursue merger and acquisition strategies only to obtain valuable economies of scope that outside investors find too costly to create on their own.

Economic Profits in Related Acquisitions

If bidding and target firms are linked by potential economies of scope, then the economic value of these two firms combined is greater than their economic value as separate entities. To see how this changes returns to merger and acquisition strategies, consider the following scenario: as before, there is one target firm and 10 bidding firms. The market value of the target firm as a stand-alone entity is $10,000, and the market value of the bidding firms as stand-alone entities is $15,000. However, unlike the earlier scenario in this chapter, the bidding and target firms are linked by economies of scope. Any of the links between firms identified in Table 12.1, Table 12.2, or Table 12.3 could be the source of these economies of scope. They imply that when any of the bidding firms and the target are combined, the market value of this combined entity will be $32,000—note that $32,000 is greater than the sum of $15,000 and $10,000. At what price will this target firm be acquired, and what are the economic profit implications for bidding and target firms at this price?

As before, bidding firms will be willing to pay a price for a target up to the value that a target firm adds once it is acquired. Thus, the maximum price bidding firms are willing to pay is still the difference between the value of the combined entity (here, $32,000) and the value of a bidding firm on its own (here, $15,000), or $17,000.

As was the case for acquisition without economies of scope, it is not hard to see that the price for actually acquiring the target firm in this scenario will rapidly rise to $17,000 because any bid less than $17,000 has the potential for generating profits for a bidding firm. Suppose that one bidding firm offers $13,000 for the target. For this $13,000, the bidding firm gains access to a target that will generate $17,000 of value once it is acquired. Thus, to this bidding firm, the target is worth $17,000, and a bid of $13,000 will generate $4,000 economic profit. Of course, these potential profits will motivate entry into the competitive bidding process. Entry will continue until the price of this target equals $17,000. Any price greater than $17,000 would mean that a bidding firm is actually losing money on its acquisition.[7]

At this $17,000 price, the successful bidding firm earns zero economic profits. After all, this firm has acquired an asset that will generate $17,000 of value and has paid $17,000 to do so. However, the owners of the target firm will earn an economic profit worth $7,000. As a stand-alone firm, the target is worth $10,000; when combined with a bidding firm, it is worth $17,000. The difference between the value of the target as a stand-alone entity and its value in combination with a bidding firm is the value of the economic profit that can be appropriated by the owners of the target firm.

Thus, the existence of economies of scope between bidding and target firms is not a sufficient condition for the equity holders of bidding firms to earn economic profits from their acquisition strategies. If the economic potential of acquiring a particular target firm is widely known and if several potential bidding firms can all obtain this value by acquiring a target, the equity holders of bidding firms will, at best, earn only zero economic profits from implementing an acquisition strategy. In this setting, a merger or acquisition will create economic value, but this value will be distributed in the form of economic profits to the equity holders of acquired target firms.

Returns to Mergers and Acquisitions: Research Results

The empirical implications of this discussion of returns to bidding and target firms in mergers and acquisitions have been examined in a variety of academic literatures. One study reviewed more than 40 empirical merger and acquisition studies in the finance literature. This study concluded that acquisitions, on average, increased the market value of target firms by about 25 percent and left the market value of bidding firms unchanged. The authors of this report concluded that, "corporate takeovers generate positive gains, . . . target firm equity holders benefit, and, . . . bidding firm equity holders do not lose."[8] The way these studies evaluate the return to acquisition strategies is discussed in the Strategy in Depth feature.

Strategy in Depth

By far, the most popular way to evaluate the performance effects of acquisitions for bidding firms is called **event study analysis**. Rooted in the field of financial economics, event study analysis compares the actual performance of a stock after an acquisition has been announced with the expected performance of that stock if no acquisition had been announced. Any performance greater (or less) than what was expected in a short period of time around when an acquisition is announced is attributed to that acquisition. This **cumulative abnormal return (CAR)** can be positive or negative depending on whether the stock in question performs better or worse than expected without an acquisition.

The CAR created by an acquisition is calculated in several stages. First, the expected performance of a stock, without an acquisition, is estimated with the following regression equation:

$$E(R_{j,t}) = a_j + b_j R_{m,t} + e_{j,t}$$

Evaluating the Performance Effects of Acquisitions

where $E(R_{j,t})$ is the expected return of stock j during time t; a_j is a constant (approximately equal to the rate of return on risk-free equities); b_j is an empirical estimate of the financial parameter β (equal to the covariance between the returns of a particular firm's stock and the average return of all stocks in the market, over time); $R_{m,t}$ is the actual average rate of return of all stocks in the market over time; and $e_{j,t}$ is an error term. The form of this equation is derived from the capital asset pricing model in finance. In this model, $E(R_{j,t})$ is simply the expected performance of a stock, given the historical relationship between that stock and the overall performance of the stock market.

To calculate the unexpected performance of a stock, this expected level of performance is simply subtracted from the actual level of performance for a stock. This is done in the following equation:

$$XR_{j,t} = R_{j,t} - (a_j + b_j R_{m,t})$$

where $R_{j,t}$ is the actual performance of stock j during time t, and $XR_{j,t}$ is the unexpected performance of stock j during time t.

In calculating the CAR for a particular acquisition, it is necessary to sum the unexpected returns ($XR_{j,t}$) for a stock across the t periods when the stock market is responding to news about this acquisition. Most analyses of acquisitions examine the market's reaction one day before an acquisition is formally announced to three days after it is announced. The sum of these unexpected returns over this period is the CAR attributable to this acquisition.

This methodology has been applied to literally thousands of acquisition episodes. For example, when Manulife Financial purchased John Hancock Financial, Manulife's CAR was −10 percent, whereas John Hancock's CAR was 6 percent; when Anthem acquired Wellpoint, Anthem's CAR was −10 percent, and Wellpoint's was 7 percent; when Bank of America acquired FleetBoston Financial, Bank of America's CAR was −9 percent, and FleetBoston's was 24 percent; and when UnitedHealth acquired Mid Atlantic Medical, UnitedHealth's CAR was −4 percent, and Mid Atlantic Medical's was 11 percent.

Although the event study method has been used widely, it does have some important limitations. First, it is based entirely on the capital asset pricing model, and there is some reason to believe that this model is not a particularly good predictor of a firm's expected stock price. Second, it assumes that a firm's equity holders can anticipate all the benefits associated with making an acquisition at the time that acquisition is made. Some scholars have argued that value creation continues long after an acquisition is announced as parties in this exchange discover value-creating opportunities that could not have been anticipated.[9]

Strategy researchers have also attempted to examine in more detail the sources of value creation in mergers and acquisitions and the question of whether these sources of value creation affect whether bidders or targets appropriate this value. For example, two well-known studies examined the impact of the type and degree of strategic relatedness (defined using the FTC typology summarized in Table 12.1) between bidding and target firms on the economic consequences of mergers and acquisitions.[10] These studies found that the more economies of scope existed between bidding and target firms, the more economic value mergers and acquisitions create. However, like the finance studies, this work found that this economic value was appropriated by the owners of the target firm, regardless of the type or degree of economy of scope between the bidding and target firms. Bidding firms—even when they attempt to acquire targets with whom they enjoy valuable economies of scopes—earn, on average, zero economic profits from their merger and acquisition strategies.

Why Are There So Many Mergers and Acquisitions?

Given the overwhelming empirical evidence that most of the economic value created in mergers and acquisitions is appropriated by the owners of the target firm most of the time, an important question becomes: "Why do managers of bidding firms continue to engage in merger and acquisition strategies?" Some possible explanations are summarized in Table 12.4 and discussed in this section.

TABLE 12.4 Possible Motivations to Engage in Mergers and Acquisitions Even Though They Usually Do Not Generate Profits for Bidding Firms

1. To ensure survival
2. Free cash flow
3. Agency problems
4. Managerial hubris
5. The potential for above-normal profits

To Ensure Survival

Even if mergers and acquisitions, on average, generate only zero economic profits for bidding firms, it may be necessary for bidding firms to engage in these activities to ensure their survival. In particular, if all of a bidding firm's competitors have been able to improve their efficiency and effectiveness through a particular type of acquisition, then failing to make such an acquisition may put a firm at a competitive disadvantage. Here the purpose of a merger or acquisition is not to gain competitive advantages, but rather to gain competitive parity.

Many recent mergers among banks in the United States seem to have competitive parity and normal economic profits as an objective. Most bank managers recognize that changing bank regulations, increased competition from nonbanking financial institutions, and soft demand are likely to lead to a consolidation of the U.S. banking industry. To survive in this consolidated industry, many U.S. banks must merge. As the number of banks engaging in mergers and acquisitions goes up, the ability to earn superior profits from those strategies goes down. These lower returns from acquisitions have already reduced the economic value of some of the most aggressive acquiring banks. Despite these lower returns, acquisitions are likely to continue for the foreseeable future, as banks seek survival opportunities in a consolidated industry.[11]

Free Cash Flow

Another reason why firms may continue to invest in merger and acquisition strategies is that these strategies, on average, can be expected to generate at least competitive parity for bidding firms. This zero economic profit may be a more attractive investment for some firms than alternative strategic investments. This is particularly the case for firms that generate free cash flow.[12]

Free cash flow is simply the amount of cash a firm has to invest after all positive net present-value investments in its ongoing businesses have been funded. Free cash flow is created when a firm's ongoing business operations are very profitable but offer few opportunities for additional investment. One firm that seems to have generated a great deal of free cash flow over the past several years is Philip Morris. Philip Morris's retail tobacco operations are extremely profitable. However, regulatory constraints, health concerns, and slowing growth in demand limit investment opportunities in the tobacco industry. Thus, the amount of cash generated by Philip Morris's ongoing tobacco business has probably been larger than the sum of its positive net present-value investments in that business. This difference is free cash flow for Philip Morris.[13]

A firm that generates a great deal of free cash flow must decide what to do with this money. One obvious alternative would be to give it to stockholders in the form of dividends or stock buybacks. However, in some situations (e.g., when stockholders face high marginal tax rates), stockholders may prefer a firm to retain this cash flow and invest it for them. When this is the case, how should a firm invest its free cash flow?

Because (by definition) no positive net present-value investment opportunities in a firm's ongoing business operations are available, firms have only two investment options: to invest their free cash flow in strategies that generate competitive parity or in strategies that generate competitive disadvantages. In this context, merger and acquisition strategies are a viable option because bidding firms, on average, can expect to generate at least competitive parity. Put differently, although mergers and acquisitions may not be a source of superior profits, there are worse things you could do with your free cash flow.

Agency Problems

Another reason why firms might continue to engage in mergers and acquisitions, despite earning only competitive parity from doing so, is that mergers and acquisitions benefit managers directly, independent of any value they may or may not create for a bidding firm's stockholders. As suggested in Chapter 10, these conflicts of interest are a manifestation of agency problems between a firm's managers and its stockholders.

Merger and acquisition strategies can benefit managers—even if they do not directly benefit a bidding firm's equity holders—in at least two ways. First, managers can use mergers and acquisitions to help diversify their human capital investments in their firm. As discussed in Chapter 9, managers have difficulty diversifying their firm-specific human capital investments when a firm operates in a narrow range of businesses. By acquiring firms with cash flows that are not perfectly correlated with the cash flows of a firm's current businesses, managers can reduce the probability of bankruptcy for their firm and thus partially diversify their human capital investments in their firm.

Second, managers can use mergers and acquisitions to quickly increase firm size, measured in either sales or assets. If management compensation is closely linked to firm size, managers who increase firm size can increase their compensation. Of all the ways to increase the size of a firm quickly, growth through mergers and acquisitions is perhaps the easiest. Even if there are no economies of scope between a bidding and a target firm, an acquisition ensures that the bidding firm will grow by the size of the target (measured in either sales or assets). If there are economies of scope between a bidding and a target firm, the size of the bidding firm can grow at an even faster rate, as can the value of management's compensation, even though, on average, acquisitions do not generate wealth for the owners of the bidding firm.

Managerial Hubris

Another reason why managers may choose to continue to invest in mergers and acquisitions, even though, on average, they gain no profits from doing so, is the existence of what has been called **managerial hubris**.[14] This is the unrealistic belief held by managers in bidding firms that they can manage the assets of a target firm more efficiently than the target firm's current management. This notion can lead bidding firms to engage in acquisition strategies even though there may not be positive economic profits from doing so.

The existence of managerial hubris suggests that the economic value of bidding firms will fall once they announce a merger or acquisition strategy. Although managers in bidding firms might truly believe that they can manage a target firm's assets more efficiently than the target firm's managers, investors in the capital markets are much less likely to be caught up in this hubris. In this context, a commitment to a merger or acquisition strategy is a strong signal that a bidding firm's management has deluded itself about its abilities to manage a target firm's assets. Such delusions will certainly adversely affect the economic value of the bidding firm.

Of course, empirical work on mergers and acquisitions discussed earlier in this chapter has concluded that although bidding firms do not obtain profits from their merger and acquisition strategies, they also do not, on average, reduce their economic value from implementing these strategies. This is inconsistent with the "hubris hypothesis." However, the fact that, on average, bidding firms do not lose economic value does not mean that some bidding firms do not lose economic value.

Thus, although it is unlikely that all merger and acquisition strategies are motivated by managerial hubris, it is likely that at least some of them are.[15]

The Potential for Economic Profits

A final reason why managers might continue to pursue merger and acquisition strategies is the potential that these strategies offer for generating profits for at least some bidding firms. The empirical research on returns to bidding firms in mergers and acquisitions is very strong. On average, bidding firms do not gain profits from their merger and acquisition strategies. However, the fact that bidding firms, *on average*, do not earn profits on these strategies does not mean that *all* bidding firms will *always* fail to earn profits. In some situations, bidding firms may be able to gain competitive advantages from merger and acquisition activities. These situations are discussed in the following section.

Mergers and Acquisitions and Sustained Competitive Advantage

Objective 12.3 Describe three ways that bidding firms might be able to generate economic profits from implementing mergers or acquisitions.

We have already seen that the economies of scope that motivate mergers and acquisitions between strategically related bidding and target firms can be valuable. However, the ability of these economies to generate profits and competitive advantages for bidding firms depends not only on their economic value, but also on the competitiveness of the market for corporate control through which these valuable economies are realized. The **market for corporate control** is the market that is created when multiple firms actively seek to acquire one or several firms. Only when the market for corporate control is imperfectly competitive might it be possible for bidding firms to earn profits from implementing a merger or acquisition strategy. To see how the competitiveness of the market for corporate control can affect returns to merger and acquisition strategies, we will consider three scenarios involving bidding and target firms and examine their implications for the managers of these firms.[16]

Valuable, Rare, and Private Economies of Scope

An imperfectly competitive market for corporate control can exist when a target is worth more to one bidder than it is to any other bidders and when no other firms—including bidders and targets—are aware of this additional value. In this setting, the price of a target will rise to reflect public expectations about the value of the target. Once the target is acquired, however, the performance of the special bidder that acquires the target will be greater than generally expected, and this level of performance will generate profits for the equity holders of the bidding firm.

Consider a simple case. Suppose the market value of bidder Firm A combined with target firms is $12,000, whereas the market value of all other bidders combined with targets is $10,000. No other firms (bidders or targets) are aware of Firm A's unique relationship with these targets, but they are aware of the value of all other bidders combined with targets (i.e., $10,000). Suppose also that the market value of all bidding firms, as stand-alone entities, is $7,000. In this setting, Firm A will be willing to pay up to $5,000 to acquire a target ($12,000 – $7,000), and all other bidders will only be willing to pay up to $3,000 to acquire a target ($10,000 – $7,000).

Because publicly available information suggests that acquiring a target is worth $3,000 more than the target's stand-alone price, the price of targets will rapidly rise to this level, ensuring that, if bidding firms, apart from Firm A, acquire a target, they will obtain no profits. If there is only one target in this market for corporate control, then Firm A will be able to bid slightly more than $3,000 (perhaps $3,001) for this target. No other firms will bid higher than Firm A because, from their point of view, the acquisition is simply not worth more than $3,000. At this $3001 price, Firm A will earn a profit of $1,999—Firm A had to spend only $3,001 for a firm that brings $5,000 in value above its stand-alone market price. Alternatively, if there are multiple targets, then several bidding firms, including Firm A, will pay $3,000 for their targets. At this price, these bidding firms will all earn zero economic profits, except for Firm A, which will earn an economic profit equal to $2,000. That is, only Firm A will gain a competitive advantage from acquiring a target in this market.

For Firm A to obtain this profit, the value of Firm A's economy of scope with target firms must be greater than the value of any other bidding firms with that target. This special value will generally reflect unusual resources and capabilities possessed by Firm A—resources and capabilities that are more valuable in combination with target firms than are the resources and capabilities that other bidding firms possess. Put differently, to be a source of economic profits and competitive advantage, Firm A's link with targets must be based on resources and capabilities that are rare among those firms competing in this market for corporate control.

However, not only must Firm A possess valuable and rare links with bidding firms to gain economic profits and competitive advantages from its acquisition strategies, but information about these special economies of scope must not be known by other firms. If other bidding firms know about the additional value associated with acquiring a target, they are likely to try to duplicate this value for themselves. Typically, they would accomplish this by imitating the type of relatedness that exists between Firm A and its targets by developing the resources and capabilities that enabled Firm A to have its valuable economies of scope with targets. Once other bidders developed the resources and capabilities necessary to obtain this more valuable economy of scope, they would be able to enter bidding, thereby increasing the likelihood that the equity holders of successful bidding firms would earn no economic profits.

Target firms must also be unaware of Firm A's special resources and capabilities if Firm A is to obtain competitive advantages from an acquisition. If target firms were aware of this extra value available to Firm A, along with the sources of this value, they could inform other bidding firms. These bidding firms could then adjust their bids to reflect this higher value, and competitive bidding would reduce profits to bidders. Target firms are likely to inform bidding firms in this way because increasing the number of bidders with more valuable economies of scope increases the likelihood that target firms will extract all the economic value created in a merger or acquisition.[17]

Valuable, Rare, and Costly-to-Imitate Economies of Scope

The existence of firms that have valuable, rare, and private economies of scope with targets is not the only way that the market for corporate control can be imperfectly competitive. If other bidders cannot imitate one bidder's valuable and rare economies with targets, then competition in this market for corporate control will be imperfect, and the equity holders of this special bidding firm will earn economic profits. In this case, the existence of valuable and rare economies does not need to be private because other bidding firms cannot imitate these economies, and therefore bids that substantially reduce the profits for the equity holders of the special bidding firm are not forthcoming.

Typically, bidding firms will be unable to imitate one bidder's valuable and rare economies of scope with targets when the strategic relatedness between the special bidder and the targets stems from some rare and costly-to-imitate resources or capabilities controlled by the special bidding firm. Any of the costly-to-imitate resources and capabilities discussed in Chapter 3 could create costly-to-imitate economies of scope between a firm and a target. If, in addition, these economies are valuable and rare, they can be a source of profits to the equity holders of the special bidding firm. This can happen even if all firms in this market for corporate control are aware of the more valuable economies of scope available to this firm and its sources. Although information about this special economy of scope is publicly available, equity holders of special bidding firms will earn a profit when acquisition occurs. The equity holders of target firms will not obtain all this profit because competitive bidding dynamics cannot unfold when the sources of a more valuable economy of scope are costly to imitate.

Of course, it may be possible for a valuable, rare, and costly-to-imitate economy of scope between a bidding and a target firm to also be private. Indeed, it is often the case that those attributes of a firm that are costly to imitate are also difficult to describe and thus can be held as proprietary information. In that case, the analysis of profits associated with valuable, rare, and private economies of scope presented earlier applies.

Unexpected Valuable Economies of Scope Between Bidding and Target Firms

Thus far, this discussion has adopted, for convenience, the strong assumption that the present value of the strategic relatedness between bidders and targets is known with certainty by individual bidders. This is, in principle, possible, but certainly not likely. Most modern acquisitions and mergers are massively complex, involving numerous unknown and complicated relationships between firms. In these settings, unexpected events after an acquisition has been completed may make an acquisition or merger more valuable than bidders and targets anticipated it would be. The price that bidding firms will pay to acquire a target will equal the expected value of the target only when the target is combined with the bidder. The difference between the unexpected value of an acquisition actually obtained by a bidder and the price the bidder paid for the acquisition is a profit for the equity holders of the bidding firm.

Of course, by definition, bidding firms cannot expect to obtain unexpected value from an acquisition. Unexpected value, in this context, is a surprise, a manifestation of a bidding firm's good luck, not its skill in acquiring targets. For example, when the British advertising firm WPP acquired J. Walter Thompson for $550 million, it discovered some property owned by J. Walter Thomson in Tokyo. No one knew of this property when the firm was acquired. It turned out to be worth more than $100 million after taxes, a financial windfall that helped offset the high cost of this acquisition. When asked, Martin Sorrel, president of WPP and the architect of this acquisition, admitted that this $100 million windfall was simply good luck.[18]

Implications for Bidding Firm Managers

The existence of valuable, rare, and private economies of scope between bidding and target firms and of valuable, rare, and costly-to-imitate economies of scope between bidding and target firms suggests that although, on average, most bidding firms do not generate competitive advantages from their acquisition strategies, in some special circumstances it may be possible for them to do so. Thus, the task facing managers in firms contemplating merger and acquisition strategies is to choose strategies that have the greatest likelihood of being able to generate profits for their equity holders. Several important managerial prescriptions can be derived from this discussion. These "rules" for bidding firm managers are summarized in Table 12.5.

Search for Valuable and Rare Economies of Scope

One of the main reasons why bidding firms do not obtain competitive advantages from acquiring strategically related target firms is that several other bidding firms value the target firm in the same way. When multiple bidders all value a target in the same way, competitive bidding is likely. Competitive bidding, in turn, drives out the potential for superior performance. To avoid this problem, bidding firms should seek to acquire targets with which they enjoy valuable and rare linkages.

Operationally, the search for rare economies of scope suggests that managers in bidding firms need to consider not only the value of a target firm when combined with their own company, but also the value of a target firm when combined with other potential bidders. This is important because it is the difference between the value of a particular bidding firm's relationship with a target and the value of other bidding firms' relationships with that target that defines the size of the potential economic profits from an acquisition.

In practice, the search for valuable and rare economies of scope is likely to become a search for valuable and rare resources already controlled by a firm that are synergistically related to a target. For example, if a bidding firm has a unique reputation in its product market and if the target firm's products could benefit by association with that reputation, then the target firm may be more valuable to this particular bidder than to other bidders (firms that do not possess this special reputation). Also, if a particular bidder possesses the largest market share in its industry, the best distribution system, or restricted access to certain key raw materials and if the target firm would benefit from being associated with these valuable and rare resources, then the acquisition of this target may be a source of economic profits.

The search for valuable and rare economies of scope as a basis of mergers and acquisitions tends to rule out certain interfirm linkages as sources of economic profits. For example, most acquisitions can lead to a reduction in overhead costs because much of the corporate overhead associated with the target firm can be eliminated after acquisition. However, the ability to eliminate these overhead costs

TABLE 12.5 Rules for Bidding Firm Managers

1. Search for valuable and rare economies of scope
2. Keep information away from other bidders
3. Keep information away from targets
4. Avoid winning bidding wars
5. Close the deal quickly
6. Operate in "thinly traded" acquisition markets

is not unique to any one bidder, and thus the value created by these reduced costs will usually be captured by the equity holders of the target firm.

Keep Information Away from Other Bidders

One of the keys to earning superior performance in an acquisition strategy is to avoid multiple bidders for a single target. One way to accomplish this is to keep information about the bidding process, and about the sources of economies of scope between a bidder and target that underlie this bidding process, as private as possible. For other firms to become involved in bidding for a target, they must be aware of the value of the economies of scope between themselves and that target. If only one bidding firm knows this information and if this bidding firm can close the deal before the full value of the target is known, then it may gain a competitive advantage from completing this acquisition.

Of course, in many circumstances, keeping all this information private is difficult. Often, it is illegal. For example, when seeking to acquire a publicly traded firm, potential bidders must meet disclosure requirements that effectively reduce the amount of private information a bidder can retain. In these circumstances, unless a bidding firm has some valuable, rare, and costly-to-imitate economy of scope with a target firm, the possibility of economic profits coming from an acquisition is very low. It is not surprising that the research conducted on mergers and acquisitions of firms traded on public stock exchanges governed by the U.S. Securities and Exchange Commission (SEC) disclosure rules suggests that, most of the time, bidding firms do not earn economic profits from implementing their acquisition strategies.

However, not all potential targets are publicly traded. Privately held firms may be acquired in an information environment that can create opportunities for above-normal performance for bidding firms. Moreover, even when acquiring a publicly traded firm, a bidder does not have to release all the information it has about the potential value of that target in combination with itself. Indeed, if some of this value reflects a bidding firm's taken-for-granted "invisible" assets, it may not be possible to communicate this information. In this case, as well, there may be opportunities for competitive advantages for bidding firms.

Keep Information Away from Targets

Not only should bidding firms keep information about the value of their economy of scope with a target away from other bidders, they should also keep this information away from target firms. Suppose that the value of a target firm to a bidding firm is $8,000, but the bidding firm, in an attempt to earn economic profits, has bid only $5,000 for the target. If the target knows that it is actually worth $8,000, it is very likely to hold out for a higher bid. In fact, the target may contact other potential bidding firms and tell them of the opportunity created by the $5,000 bid. As the number of bidders goes up, the possibility of superior economic performance for bidders goes down. Therefore, to keep the possibility of these profits alive, bidding firms must not fully reveal the value of their economies of scope with a target firm. Again, in some circumstances, it is very difficult, or even illegal, to attempt to limit the flow of information to target firms. In these settings, superior economic performance for bidding firms is very unlikely.

Limiting the amount of information that flows to the target firm may have some other consequences as well. For example, it has been shown that a complete sharing of information, insights, and perspectives before an acquisition is completed increases the probability that economies of scope will actually be realized once it is completed.[19] By limiting the flow of information between itself and a target, a bidding firm may actually be increasing the cost of integrating the target into its ongoing business, thereby jeopardizing at least some of the superior economic performance that limiting information flow is designed to create. Bidding firms will need to carefully balance the economic benefits of limiting the information they share with the target firm against the costs that limiting information flow may create.

Avoid Winning Bidding Wars

It should be reasonably clear that if a number of firms bid for the same target, the probability that the firm that successfully acquires the target will gain competitive advantages is very low. Indeed, to ensure that competitive bidding occurs, target firms can actively encourage other bidding firms to enter the bidding process. The implications of these arguments are clear: bidding firms should generally avoid winning a bidding war. To "win" a bidding war, a bidding firm will often have to pay a price at least equal to the full value of the target. Many times, given the emotions of an intense bidding contest, the winning bid may actually be larger than the true value of the target. Completing this type of acquisition will certainly reduce the economic performance of the bidding firm.

The only time it might make sense to "win" a bidding war is when the winning firm possesses a rare and private or a rare and costly-to-imitate economy of scope with a target that is more valuable than the strategic relatedness that exists between any other bidders and that target. In this setting, the winning firm may be able to earn a profit if it can fully realize the value of its relationship with the target.

Close the Deal Quickly

Another rule of thumb for obtaining superior performance from implementing merger and acquisition strategies is to close the deal quickly. All the economic processes that make it difficult for bidding firms to earn economic profits from acquiring a strategically related target take time to unfold. It takes time for other bidders to become aware of the economic value associated with acquiring a target; it takes time for the target to recruit other bidders; information leakage becomes more of a problem over time; and so forth. A bidding firm that begins and ends the bidding process quickly may forestall some of these processes and thereby retain some superior performance for itself.

The admonition to close the deal quickly should not be taken to mean that bidding firms need to make their acquisition decisions quickly. Indeed, the search for valuable and rare economies of scope should be undertaken with great care. There should be little rush in isolating and evaluating acquisition candidates. However, once a target firm has been located and valued, bidding firms have a strong incentive to reduce the period between the first bid and the completion of the deal. The longer this period of negotiation, the less likely it is that the bidding firm will earn economic profits from the acquisition.

Complete Acquisitions in "Thinly Traded" Markets

Finally, an acquisition strategy can be a source of economic profits to bidding firms if these firms implement this corporate strategy in what could be described as "thinly traded markets." In general, a **thinly traded market** is a market where there are only a small number of buyers and sellers, where information about opportunities in this market is not widely known, and where interests besides purely maximizing the value of a firm can be important. In the context of mergers and acquisitions, thinly traded markets are markets where only a few (often only one) firms are implementing acquisition strategies. These unique firms may be the only firms that understand the full value of the acquisition opportunities in this market. Even target firm managers may not fully understand the value of the economic opportunities in these markets, and, if they do, they may have other interests besides maximizing the value of their firm if it becomes the object of a takeover.

In general, thinly traded merger and acquisition markets are highly fragmented. Competition in these markets occurs at the local level, as one small local firm competes with other small local firms for a common group of geographically defined customers. Most of these small firms are privately held. Many are sole proprietorships. Examples of these thinly traded markets have included, at various points in history, the printing industry, the fast-food industry, the used-car industry, the dry-cleaning industry, and the barbershop/hair salon industry.

As was suggested in Chapter 2, the major opportunity in all highly fragmented industries is consolidation. In the context of mergers and acquisitions, consolidation can occur by one firm (or a small number of firms) buying numerous independent firms to realize economies of scope in these industries. Often, these economies of scope reflect economies of scale in these industries—economies of scale that were not realized in a highly fragmented setting. If the number of firms implementing this consolidation strategy is small, then the market for corporate control in these markets will probably be less than perfectly competitive, and opportunities for profits from implementing an acquisition strategy may be possible.

More generally, if a merger or acquisition contest is played out through full-page ads in *The Wall Street Journal*, the ability of bidding firms to gain competitive advantages from their acquisitions is limited. Such highly public acquisitions are likely to lead to very competitive markets for corporate control. Competitive markets for corporate control, in turn, assure that the equity holders of the target firm will appropriate any value that could be created by an acquisition. However, if these contests occur in obscure, out-of-the-way industries, it is more likely that bidding firms will be able to earn profits from their acquisitions.

Service Corporation International: An Example

Empirical research on mergers and acquisitions suggests that it is not easy for bidding firms to earn economic profits from these strategies. However, it may be possible for some bidding firms, some of the time, to do so. One firm that was successful in gaining competitive advantages from its merger and acquisition strategies is Service Corporation International (SCI). Service Corporation International is in the funeral home and cemetery business. It grew from a collection of five funeral homes in 1967 to being the largest owner of cemeteries and funeral homes in the United States today. It did this through an aggressive and, what was until recently, a highly profitable acquisitions program in this historically fragmented industry.

The valuable and rare economy of scope that SCI brought to the funeral home industry is the application of traditional business practices in a highly fragmented and not often professionally managed industry. Service Corporation International–owned funeral homes operate with gross margins approaching 30 percent, nearly three times the gross margins of independently owned funeral homes. Among other things, higher margins reflected savings from centralized purchasing services, centralized embalming and professional services, and the sharing of underutilized resources (including hearses) among funeral homes within geographic regions. Service Corporation International's scale advantages made a particular funeral home more valuable to SCI than to one of SCI's smaller competitors and more valuable than if a particular funeral home was left as a stand-alone business.

Moreover, the funeral homes that SCI targeted for acquisition were, typically, family-owned and lacked heirs to continue the business. Many of the owners or operators of these funeral homes were not fully aware of the value of their operations to SCI (they are morticians more than business managers), nor were they just interested in maximizing the sale price of their funeral homes. Rather, they were often looking to maintain continuity of service in a community, secure employment for their loyal employees, and ensure a comfortable (if not lavish) retirement for themselves. Being acquired by SCI was likely to be the only alternative to closing the funeral home once an owner or operator retired. Extracting less than the full value of the funeral home when selling to SCI often seemed preferable to other alternatives.

Because SCI's acquisition of funeral homes exploited real and valuable economies of scope, this strategy had the potential for generating superior economic performance. Because SCI was, for many years, the only firm implementing this strategy in the funeral home industry, because the funeral homes that SCI acquired were generally not publicly traded, and because the owners or operators of these funeral homes often had interests besides simply maximizing the price of their operations when they sold them, it seems likely that SCI's acquisition strategy generated superior economic performance for many years.

However, information about SCI's acquisition strategy has become widely known. This has led other funeral homes to begin bidding to acquire formerly independent funeral homes. Moreover, independent funeral home owners have become more aware of their full value to SCI. Although SCI's economy of scope with independent funeral homes is still valuable, it is no longer rare, and thus it is no longer a source of economic profits to SCI. Put differently, the imperfectly competitive market for corporate control that SCI exploited for almost 10 years has become more perfectly competitive. Future acquisitions in this market by SCI are not likely to be a source of sustained competitive advantage and economic profit. In response, SCI now focuses on effectively managing its more than 1,800 funeral homes in the United States.[20]

Implications for Target Firm Managers

Although bidding firm managers can do several things to attempt to maximize the probability of earning economic profits from their merger and acquisition strategies, target firm managers can attempt to counter these efforts to ensure that the owners of target firms appropriate whatever value is created by a merger or acquisition. These "rules" for target firm managers are summarized in Table 12.6.

Seek Information from Bidders

One way a bidder can attempt to obtain superior performance from implementing an acquisition strategy is to keep information about the source and value of the strategic relatedness that exists between the bidder and target private. If that relationship is actually worth $12,000, but targets believe it is only worth $8,000, then a target might be willing to settle for a bid of $8,000 and, thereby, forgo the extra $4,000 it could have extracted from the bidder. Once the target knows that its true value to the bidder is $12,000, it is in a much better position to obtain this full value when the acquisition is completed. Therefore, not only should a bidding firm inform itself about the value of a target, target firms must inform themselves about their value to potential bidders. In this way, they can help obtain the full value of their assets.

TABLE 12.6 Rules for Target Firm Managers

1. Seek information from bidders
2. Invite other bidders to join the bidding competition
3. Delay, but do not stop, the acquisition

Invite Other Bidders to Join the Bidding Competition

Once a target firm is fully aware of the nature and value of the economies of scope that exist between it and current bidding firms, it can exploit this information by seeking other firms that may have the same relationship with it and then informing these firms of a potential acquisition opportunity. By inviting other firms into the bidding process, the target firm increases the competitiveness of the market for corporate control, thereby increasing the probability that the value created by an acquisition will be fully captured by the target firm.

Delay, but Do Not Stop, the Acquisition

As suggested earlier, bidding firms have a strong incentive to expedite the acquisition process to prevent other bidders from becoming involved in an acquisition. Of course, the target firm wants other bidding firms to enter the process. To increase the probability of receiving more than one bid, target firms have a strong incentive to delay an acquisition.

The objective, however, should be to delay an acquisition to create a more competitive market for corporate control, not to stop an acquisition. If a valuable economy of scope exists between a bidding firm and a target firm, the merger of these two firms will create economic value. If the market for corporate control within which this merger occurs is competitive, then the equity holders of the target firm will appropriate the full value of this economy of scope. Preventing an acquisition in this setting can be very costly to the equity holders of the target firm.

Target firm managers can engage in a wide variety of activities to delay the completion of an acquisition. Some common responses of target firm management to takeover efforts, along with their economic implications for the equity holders of target firms, are discussed in the Research Made Relevant feature.

Research Made Relevant

The Wealth Effects of Management Responses to Takeover Attempts

Managers in potential target firms can respond to takeover attempts in a variety of ways. As suggested in Table 12.7, some of these responses increase the wealth of target firm shareholders, some have no impact on target firm shareholders, and others decrease the wealth of target firm shareholders.

Management responses that have the effect of reducing the value of target firms include greenmail, standstill agreements, and "poison pills." Each of these is an anti-takeover action that target firm managers can take to reduce the wealth of target firm equity holders. **Greenmail** is a maneuver in which a target firm's management purchases any of the target firm's stock owned by a bidder and does so for a price that is greater than the current market value of that stock. Greenmail effectively ends a bidding firm's effort to acquire a particular target and does so in a way that can greatly reduce the wealth of a target firm's equity holders. Not only do these equity holders not appropriate any economic value that could have been created if an acquisition had been completed, but they must bear the cost of the premium price that management pays to buy its stock back from the bidding firm.

Not surprisingly, target firms that resort to greenmail substantially reduce the economic wealth of their equity holders. One study found that the value of target firms that pay greenmail drops, on average, 1.76

TABLE 12.7 The Wealth Effects of Target Firm Management Responses to Acquisition Efforts

1. Responses that reduce the wealth of target firm equity holders:
   - Greenmail
   - Standstill agreements
   - Poison pills
2. Responses that do not affect the wealth of target firm equity holders:
   - Shark repellents
   - Pac Man defense
   - Crown jewel sale
   - Lawsuits
3. Responses that increase the wealth of target firm equity holders:
   - Search for white knights
   - Creation of bidding auctions
   - Golden parachutes

percent. Another study reported a 2.85 percent drop in the value of such firms. These reductions in value are greater if greenmail leads to the cancellation of a takeover effort. Indeed, this second study found that such episodes led to a 5.50 percent reduction in the value of target firms. These reductions in value as a response to greenmail activities stand in marked contrast to the generally positive market response to efforts by a firm to repurchase its own shares in non-greenmail situations.

Standstill agreements are often negotiated in conjunction with greenmail. A standstill agreement is a contract between a target and a bidding firm wherein the bidding firm agrees not to attempt to take over the target for some period of time. When a target firm negotiates a standstill agreement, it prevents the current acquisition effort from being completed, and it reduces the number of bidders that might become involved in future acquisition efforts. Thus, the equity holders of this target firm forgo any value that could have been created if the current acquisition had occurred, and they also lose some of the value that they could have appropriated in future acquisition episodes by the target's inviting multiple bidders into a market for corporate control.

Standstill agreements, either alone or in conjunction with greenmail, reduce the economic value of a target firm. One study found that standstill agreements that were unaccompanied by stock repurchase agreements reduced the value of a target firm by 4.05 percent. Such agreements, in combination with stock repurchases, reduced the value of a target firm by 4.52 percent.

So-called **poison pills** include any of a variety of actions that target firm managers can take to make the acquisition of the target prohibitively expensive. In one common poison-pill maneuver, a target firm issues rights to its current stockholders indicating that if the firm is acquired in an unfriendly takeover, it will distribute a special cash dividend to stockholders. This cash dividend effectively increases the cost of acquiring the target and can discourage otherwise interested bidding firms from attempting to acquire this target. Another poison-pill tactic substitutes the distribution of additional shares of a target firm's stock, at very low prices, for the special cash dividend. Issuing this low-price stock to current stockholders effectively undermines the value of a bidding firm's equity investment in a target and thus increases the cost of the acquisition. Other poison pills involve granting current stockholders other rights—rights that effectively increase the cost of an unfriendly takeover.

Although poison pills are creative devices that target firms can use to prevent an acquisition, they generally have not been very effective. If a bidding firm and a target firm are strategically related, the value that can be created in an acquisition can be substantial, and most of this value will be appropriated by the stockholders of the target firm. Thus, target firm stockholders have a strong incentive to see that the target firm is acquired, and they are amenable to direct offers made by a bidding firm to them as individual investors; these are called **tender offers**. However, to the extent that poison pills actually do prevent mergers and acquisitions, they are usually bad for the equity holders of target firms.

Target firm management can also engage in a wide variety of actions that have little or no impact on the wealth of a target firm's equity holders. One class of these responses is known as shark repellents. **Shark repellents** include a variety of relatively minor corporate governance changes that, in principle, are supposed to make it somewhat more difficult to acquire a target firm. Common examples of shark repellents include **supermajority voting rules** (which specify that more than 50 percent of the target firm's board of directors must approve a takeover) and state incorporation laws (in some states, incorporation laws make it difficult to acquire a firm incorporated in that state). However, if the value created by an acquisition is sufficiently large, these shark repellents will neither slow an acquisition attempt significantly nor prevent it from being completed.

Another response that does not affect the wealth of target firm equity holders is known as the **Pac Man defense**. Targets using this tactic fend off an acquisition by taking over the firm or firms bidding for them. Just as in the old video game, the hunted becomes the hunter; the target turns the tables on current and potential bidders. It should not be too surprising that the Pac Man defense does not, on average, either hurt or help the stockholders of target firms. In this defense, targets become bidders, and we know from empirical literature that, on average, bidding firms earn only zero economic profits from their acquisition efforts. Thus, one would expect that, on average, the Pac Man defense would generate only zero economic profits for the stockholders of target firms implementing it.

Another ineffective and inconsequential response is called a **crown jewel sale**. The idea behind a crown jewel sale is that sometimes a bidding firm is interested in just a few of the businesses currently being operated by the target firm. These businesses are the target firm's "crown jewels." To prevent an acquisition, the target firm can sell off these crown jewels, either directly to the bidding firm or by setting up a separate company to own and operate these businesses. In this way, the bidding firm is likely to be less interested in acquiring the target.

A final, relatively ineffective defense that most target firm managers pursue is filing lawsuits against bidding firms. Indeed, at least in the United States, the filing of a lawsuit has been almost automatic as soon as an acquisition effort is announced. These suits, however, usually do not delay or stop an acquisition or merger.

Finally, as suggested in Table 12.7, some of the actions that the management of target firms can take to delay (but not stop) an acquisition actually benefit target firm equity holders. The first of these is the search for a **white knight**—another bidding firm that agrees to acquire a particular target in the place of the original bidding firm. Target firm management may prefer to be acquired by some bidding firms over others. For example, it may be that some bidding firms possess much more valuable economies of scope with a target firm than other bidding firms. It may also be that some bidding firms will take a longer-term view in managing a target firm's assets than other bidding firms. In both cases, target firm managers are likely to prefer some bidding firms over others.

Whatever motivation a target firm's management has, inviting a white knight to bid on a target firm has the effect of increasing the number of firms bidding for a target by at least one. If there is currently only one bidder, inviting a white knight into the bidding competition doubles the number of firms bidding for a target. As the number of bidders increases, the competitiveness of the market for corporate control and the likelihood that the equity holders of the target firm will appropriate all the value created by an acquisition also increase. On average, the entrance of a white knight into a competitive bidding contest for a target firm increases the wealth of target firm equity holders by 17 percent.

If adding one firm into the competitive bidding process increases the wealth of target firm equity holders some, then adding more firms to the process is likely to increase this wealth even more. Target firms can accomplish this outcome by creating an **auction** among bidding firms. On average, the creation of an auction among multiple bidders increases the wealth of target firm equity holders by 20 percent.

A third action that the managers of a target firm can take to increase the wealth of their equity holders from an acquisition effort is the institution of **golden parachutes**. A golden parachute is a compensation arrangement between a firm and its senior management team that promises these individuals a substantial cash payment if their firm is acquired and they lose their jobs in the process. These cash payments can appear to be very large, but they are actually quite small in comparison to the total value that can be created if a merger or acquisition is completed. In this sense, golden parachutes are a small price to pay to give a potential target firm's top managers incentives not to stand in the way of completing a takeover of their firm. Put differently, golden parachutes reduce agency problems for the equity holders of a potential target firm by aligning the interests of top managers with the interests of that firm's stockholders. On average, when a firm announces golden parachute compensation packages for its top management team, the value of this potential target firm's equity increases by seven percent.

Overall, substantial evidence suggests that delaying an acquisition long enough to ensure that a competitive market for corporate control emerges can significantly benefit the equity holders of target firms. One study found that when target firms did not delay the completion of an acquisition, their equity holders experienced, on average, a 36 percent increase in the value of their stock once the acquisition was complete. If, however, target firms did delay the completion of the acquisition, this average increase in value jumped to 65 percent.

Of course, target firm managers can delay too long. Delaying too long can create opportunity costs for their firm's equity holders because these individuals do not actually realize the gain from an acquisition until it has been completed. Also, long delays can jeopardize the completion of an acquisition, in which case the equity holders of the target firm do not realize any gains from the acquisition.[21]

Objective 12.4 Describe the major challenges that firms integrating acquisitions are likely to face.

Organizing to Implement a Merger or Acquisition

To realize the full value of any strategic relatedness that exists between a bidding firm and a target firm, the merged organizations must be organized appropriately. The realization of each of the types of strategic relatedness discussed earlier in this chapter requires at least some coordination and integration between the bidding and target firms after an acquisition has occurred. For example, to realize economies of scale from an acquisition, bidding and target firms must coordinate in the combined firm the functions that are sensitive to economies of scale. To realize the value of any technology that a bidding firm acquires from a target firm, the combined firm must use this technology in developing, manufacturing, or selling its products. To exploit underutilized leverage capacity in the target firm, the balance sheets of the bidding and target firms must be merged, and the resulting firm must then seek additional debt funding. To realize the opportunity of replacing the target firm's inefficient management with more efficient management from the bidding firm, these management changes must actually take place.

Post-acquisition coordination and integration is essential if bidding and target firms are to realize the full potential of the strategic relatedness that drove the acquisition in the first place. If a bidding firm decides not to coordinate or integrate any of its business activities with the activities of a target firm, then why was this target firm acquired? Just as corporate diversification requires the active management of linkages among different parts of a firm, mergers and acquisitions (as one way in which corporate diversification strategies can be created) require the active management of linkages between a bidding and a target firm.

Post-Merger Integration and Implementing a Diversification Strategy

Given that most merger and acquisition strategies are used to create corporate diversification strategies, the organizational approaches previously described for implementing diversification are relevant for implementing merger and acquisition strategies as well. Thus, mergers and acquisitions designed to create diversification strategies should be managed through the M-form structure. The management control systems and compensation policies associated with implementing diversification strategies should also be applied in organizing to implement merger and acquisition strategies. In contrast, mergers and acquisitions designed to create vertical integration strategies should be managed through the U-form structure and have management controls and compensation policies consistent with this strategy.

Special Challenges in Post-Merger Integration

Although, in general, organizing to implement merger and acquisition strategies can be seen as a special case of organizing to implement corporate diversification strategies or vertical integration strategies, implementing merger and acquisition strategies can create special problems. Most of these problems reflect the fact that operational, functional, strategic, and cultural differences between bidding and target firms involved in a merger or acquisition are likely to be much greater than these same differences between the different parts of a diversified or vertically integrated business that was not created through acquisition. The reason for this difference is that the firms involved in a merger or acquisition have had a separate existence, separate histories, separate management philosophies, and separate strategies.

Differences between bidding and target firms can manifest themselves in a wide variety of ways. For example, the firms may own and operate different computer systems, different telephone systems, and other conflicting technologies. These firms might have very different human resource policies and practices. One firm might have a very generous retirement and health care program; the other, a less generous program. One firm's compensation system might focus on high salaries; the other firm's compensation system might focus on large cash bonuses and stock options. Also, these firms might have very different relationships with customers. At one firm, customers might be thought of as business partners; in another, the relationship with customers might be more arm's-length in character. Integrating bidding and target firms may require the resolution of numerous differences.

Perhaps the most significant challenge in integrating bidding and target firms has to do with cultural differences.[22] In Chapter 3, it was suggested that it can often be difficult to change a firm's organizational culture. The fact that a firm has been acquired does not mean that the culture in that firm will rapidly change to become more like the culture of the bidding firm; cultural conflicts can last for very long periods of time.

The failures of what some observers believe are some of the worst acquisitions ever have all been attributed to cultural clashes.[23] For example, the merger between Daimler (the maker of Mercedes-Benz) and Chrysler pitted the culture of a German company that focused on luxury vehicles with a midwestern U.S. company that sold lower-prestige cars and Jeeps. The merger became the source of a widely known joke: "How do you pronounce DaimlerChrysler? Daimler. The Chrysler is silent." These two firms split after only a few painful years.

Also, Novell's acquisition of Word Perfect brought together two management teams that refused to cooperate. While Novell and Word Perfect managers fought each other, Microsoft emerged as the dominant firm in the word processing industry with Microsoft Word. After two years, Novell sold Word Perfect for $1 billion less than its purchase price.

Another disastrous acquisition involved the combination of America Online (AOL) and Time Warner. In 2000, before the merger, AOL's shares sold for more than \$75; in 2008, after the merger, they sold for \$15. The problem: the clash between the "new media" AOL culture with the "old media" Time Warner culture.

Sprint's acquisition of Nextel was also a spectacular failure. In 2005, the deal cost Sprint \$35 billion. Within three years, 80 percent of Sprint's investment in Nextel was written off. The culprit, once again, was the clash between the cultures of these two firms—Sprint was a "button-down" bureaucratic culture that could not tolerate Nextel's more freewheeling entrepreneurial culture. The two management teams fought about everything from advertising strategy to cell phone technology. Not surprisingly, in 2012, SprintNextel was purchased by the third-largest Japanese mobile phone company, Softbank, for \$20.1 billion—almost \$15 billion less than Sprint had paid for Nextel seven years earlier.

Finally, HP's acquisition of Compaq reduced the market capitalization of HP by approximately \$13 billion. HP's engineering and consensus-driven culture clashed with Compaq's quick-decision, sales-driven culture. After several years, HP made cultural and leadership changes that have improved the performance of this acquisition, but this integration has been long in coming.

Operational, functional, strategic, and cultural differences between bidding and target firms can all be compounded by the merger and acquisition process—especially if that process was unfriendly. Unfriendly takeovers can generate anger and animosity among the target firm management that is directed toward the management of the bidding firm. Research has shown that top management turnover is much higher in firms that have been taken over compared with firms not subject to takeovers, reflecting one approach to resolving these management conflicts.[24]

The difficulties often associated with organizing to implement a merger and acquisition strategy can be thought of as an additional cost of the acquisition process. Bidding firms, in addition to estimating the value of the strategic relatedness between themselves and a target firm, also need to estimate the cost of organizing to implement an acquisition. The value that a target firm brings to a bidding firm through an acquisition should be discounted by the cost of organizing to implement this strategy. In some circumstances, it may be the case that the cost of organizing to realize the value of strategic relatedness between a bidding firm and a target may be greater than the value of that strategic relatedness, in which case the acquisition should not occur. For this reason, many observers argue that potential economies of scope between bidding and target firms are often not fully realized.

Although organizing to implement mergers and acquisitions can be a source of significant cost, it can also be a source of value and opportunity. Some scholars have suggested that value creation can continue to occur in a merger or acquisition long after the formal acquisition is complete.[25] As bidding and target firms continue to coordinate and integrate their operations, unanticipated opportunities for value creation can be discovered. These sources of value could not have been anticipated at the time a firm was originally acquired (and thus are, at least partially, a manifestation of a bidding firm's good luck), but bidding firms can influence the probability of discovering these unanticipated sources of value by learning to cooperate effectively with target firms while organizing to implement a merger or acquisition strategy.

Summary

Firms can use mergers and acquisitions to create corporate diversification and vertical integration strategies. Mergers or acquisitions between firms with no economies of scope can be expected to generate only competitive parity for both bidders and targets. Thus, firms contemplating merger and acquisition strategies must search for targets where those economies of scope exist.

Several sources of these economies of scope have been discussed in literature. On average, the acquisition of these targets does create economic value, but most of that value is captured by the equity holders of target firms. The equity holders of bidding firms generally gain competitive parity even when bidding firms acquire targets with economies of scope. Empirical research on mergers and acquisitions is consistent with these expectations. On average, acquisitions do create value, but that value is captured by target firms, and acquisitions do not hurt bidding firms.

Given that most mergers and acquisitions generate only zero economic profits for bidding firms, an important question becomes: "Why are there so many mergers and acquisitions?" Explanations include: (1) the desire to ensure firm survival; (2) the existence of free cash flow; (3) agency problems between bidding firm managers and equity holders; (4) managerial hubris; and (5) the possibility that some bidding firms might earn economic profits from implementing merger and acquisition strategies.

To gain competitive advantages and economic profits from mergers or acquisitions, these strategies must be either valuable, rare, and private or valuable, rare, and costly to imitate. In addition, a bidding firm may exploit unanticipated sources of strategic relatedness with a target. These unanticipated sources of relatedness can also be a source of economic profits for a bidding firm. These observations have several implications for the managers of bidding and target firms.

Organizing to implement a merger or acquisition strategy can be seen as a special case of organizing to implement a corporate diversification or vertical integration strategy. However, historical differences between bidding and target firms may make the integration of different parts of a firm created through acquisitions more difficult than if a firm is not created through acquisitions. Cultural differences between bidding and target firms are particularly problematic. Bidding firms need to estimate the cost of organizing to implement a merger or acquisition strategy and discount the value of a target by that cost. However, organizing to implement a merger or acquisition can also be a way that bidding and target firms can discover unanticipated economies of scope.

Challenge Questions

12.1. Consider the following scenario: a firm acquires a strategically related target after successfully fending off four other bidding firms. Under what conditions, if any, can the firm that acquired this target expect to earn an economic profit from doing so?

12.2. Consider this scenario: a firm acquires a strategically related target; there were no other bidding firms. Under what conditions, if any, can the firm that acquired this target expect to earn an economic profit from doing so?

12.3. Some researchers have argued that the existence of free cash flow can lead managers in a firm to make inappropriate acquisition decisions. To avoid these problems, these authors have argued that firms should increase their debt-to-equity ratio and "soak up" free cash flow through interest and principal payments. Is free cash flow a significant problem for many firms?

12.4. What are the strengths and weaknesses of increased leverage as a response to free cash flow problems in a firm?

12.5. The hubris hypothesis suggests that managers continue to engage in acquisitions, even though, on average, they do not generate economic profits, because of the unrealistic belief on the part of these managers that they can manage a target firm's assets more efficiently than that firm's current management. This type of systematic non-rationality usually does not last too long in competitive market conditions. Firms led by managers with these unrealistic beliefs change, are acquired, or go bankrupt in the long run. What are the attributes of the market for corporate control that suggest that managerial hubris could exist in this market, despite its performance-reducing implications for bidding firms?

12.6. The hubris hypothesis suggests that managers continue to engage in acquisitions, even though, on average, they do not generate economic profits, because of the unrealistic belief on the part of these managers that they can manage a target firm's assets more efficiently than that firm's current management. This type of systematic nonrationality usually does not last too long in competitive market conditions. Firms led by managers with these unrealistic beliefs change, are acquired, or go bankrupt in the long run. Can the hubris hypothesis be a legitimate explanation for continuing acquisition activity?

12.7. It has been shown that so-called poison pills rarely prevent a takeover from occurring. In fact, sometimes when a firm announces that it is instituting a poison pill, its stock price goes up. Why?

Problem Set

12.8. For each of the following scenarios, estimate how much value an acquisition will create, how much of that value will be appropriated by each of the bidding firms, and how much of that value will be appropriated by each of the target firms. In each of these scenarios, assume that firms do not face significant capital constraints.

(a) A bidding firm, A, is worth $27,000 as a stand-alone entity. A target firm, B, is worth $12,000 as a stand-alone entity, but $18,000 if it is acquired and integrated with Firm A. Several other firms are interested in acquiring Firm B, and Firm B is also worth $18,000 if it is acquired by these other firms. If Firm A acquired Firm B, would this acquisition create value? If yes, how much? How much of this value would the equity holders of Firm A receive? How much would the equity holders of Firm B receive?

(b) The same scenario as above except that the value of Firm B, if it is acquired by the other firms interested in it, is only $12,000.

(c) The same scenario in part (a), except that the value of Firm B, if it is acquired by the other firms interested in it, is $16,000.

(d) The same scenario as in part (b), except that Firm B contacts several other firms and explains to them how they can create the same value with Firm B that Firm A does.

(e) The same scenario as in part (b), except that Firm B sues Firm A. After suing Firm A, Firm B installs a "supermajority" rule in how its board of directors operates. After putting this new rule in place, Firm B offers to buy back any stock purchased by Firm A for 20 percent above the current market price.

Writing Assignments

12.9. How would a firm's investment in merger and acquisition strategies, on average, be expected to generate at least competitive parity for bidding firms?

CASE STUDY | Asian Paints: All Great Things Start Small

In 1942, during the World War II, paint import was banned in India. Champak Lal Choksey with four of his friends found this 'import ban' as an opportunity and established Asian Paints Limited on February 1, 1942. Initially they set up as a partnership firm with the objective to become the largest decorative paint producer in world. Eventually, the name was changed from Asian Oil and Paint Company Pvt. Ltd. to Asian Paints (India) Pvt. Ltd in 1965. The mission statement of Asian paints is—To be the forerunner of inspiring décor and to actively empower customers to create their dream homes.

Asian paints started as an economy brand and now it has a wide range of products for all type of customers consisting of different income levels. Today the company produces paints for the decorative, automotive, and industrial segments. Apart from these, the company also produces a variety of accessories such as wall primer, wood primer, putty, and strainers, among other things. Asian paints is a leader in the Indian paint industry since its beginning in 1942 with the market share of 39 percent with a group turnover of ₹20,515 crores (US$2.9 billion) registered in 2020.

Growth

Asian Paints operates in 17 countries with 26 paint manufacturing facilities servicing consumers in over 65 countries. While the company's bulk of revenues flow from the paint segment, which accounts for over 96 per cent of the company's total sales, the chemicals division contribute only 3.1 per cent to the company's total revenues. Asian Paints operates mainly in five regions around the world—South Asia, South East Asia, South Pacific, Middle East, and Caribbean. The company has strategically located Indian plants in Bhandup (Maharashtra), Kasna (Uttar Pradesh), and Sriperumbudur (Tamil Nadu), Ankleshwar (Gujarat), Patancheru (Andhra Pradesh), and the latest constructed plant in Rohtak (Haryana).

The company has a state–of–the–art supply chain infrastructure in India that combines all of its manufacturing units, regional distribution centres, outsourced processing centres, and branches using cutting–edge technology. Asian paints boasts an intregrated network of around 35,000 dealers and 18 processing centres, 6 regional distribution centres, 72. In addition, there are 3000 Stock Keeping Units (SKUs) and 80 sales offices.

Currently, the company has 70,000+ shopkeepers across the nation. It has also been strengthening its dealer-network for the past 40 years. Asian Paints has a phenomenal supply chain as it carries out around 2.5–3 lakh deliveries per day and its trucks visit the dealers around 4 times a day.

Market Structure

Indian paint market is oligopolistic with the top 4 players commanding nearly 70 percent of the market share. Considering the nature of the market, Asian Paints has an opportunity to increase its share in the industry segment with its ability to scale up the world-class technology that it can afford.

The paint industry is growing at 10.4 percent CAGR and the market size reached ₹520 bn. Over the years, the decorative paint segment (market share of 75–80 percent) has grown at a CAGR of 11.4 percent against the industrial segment (market share of 20–25 percent) which has grown at a CAGR of 7.9 percent. Within the industry, the organized sector has been commanding 70 percent market share and the balance 30 percent is accounted for by the unorganized sector. Till the first half of the 2010s, the unorganized sector had 35 percent market share, but with demonetization and implementation of GST, the organized players have been able to capture market share from the unorganized players.

Competitors

Asian Paints has acquired market leadership and has been maintaining its position for over 50 years. While Asian Paints is the market leader in the decorative segment, Kansai Nerolac dominates the industrial and automotive segment. Nerolac displaced Jenson & Nicholson in 1967 and became India's first paint manufacturing company to have a high quality research and development, robust supply chain, and a good pricing policy catering to all levels of customer. However, the market share for Nerolac Paints in decorative paint market is relatively low.

Berger Paints holds the second position in the industrial paint sector with a not-so-impressive market share. The company offers comparatively higher discounts compared to retailers for gaining better market share. Among others, ICI Paints is in their finishing business has one of the best quality refinish paint for cars. In decorative paints too, it has delivered good performance. With their industrial paint market presence of almost 2–3 percent, the company is trying to create a footprint in the international markets through its recent strategic mergers.

Coping with Uncertainty

Asian Paints is likely to decrease production, expenditure, and employee compensation as a result of uncertainty. Large capital projects, in particular, the ones with high degree of irreversibility, can be especially vulnerable to high levels of uncertainty. The first market implication is that established risks can be anticipated and mitigated. This can be accomplished either through the purchase of premiums or through the use of more advanced approaches such as financial instruments to protect against these risks. Additionally, Asian Paints tries to improve its readiness for unforeseen risks by simulating future incidents and evaluating the effect on the balance sheet and day-to-day operations.

The COVID-19 Pandemic Impact

In 2020, the outbreak of Coronavirus disease (COVID-19) served as a major constraint on the paints and coatings industry, as supply chains were disrupted by trade restrictions and demand fell due to government lockdowns across the world. Because of the coronavirus outbreak, the paint and coatings industry has been among the one that faced the hardest hit. Due to the lockdown measures, major manufacturers have had to shut down or suspend their ongoing projects and plans. The industry has also been adversely affected by the closure of other supporting industries. Owing to this fact, there has seen a substantial decline in demand and investment. The company's sales have been affected by the lackluster demand induced by the lockdown as well as the prolonged downturn in the automotive industry.

The loss of sales due to the lockdown in March impacted the decorative business segment. Although with the loss of sales, the decorative business segment registered double-digit volume growth for the year 2020. However, industrial business segment under the automotive coatings and industrial coatings continue to be impacted by the downturn in the automotive industry and the overall slowdown in the economy. A complete shutdown of business in the last few days of March 2020 added to the pressure for these segments. As respite, profitability was backed by the fact of benign raw material prices and successful efforts towards cost optimization.

GDP Correlation

Since paint consumption is positively correlated with GDP growth, a slowdown in GDP would have a direct effect on the paint industry. Furthermore, since paint is a discretionary purchase, customers can put their paint needs on hold for a period of time, affecting renovation demand.

Monsoon Vagaries

Monsoon has an impact on demand as well. The trend depicts that there is an increase in agriculture and industrial output when the monsoon is strong. This has a positive effect on people's disposable income, resulting in high demand. However, with poor monsoon, demand suffers, particularly in the decorative paints segment. An extended monsoon will exacerbate the problems of decorative paint makers, especially for the ones with slow sales growth due higher prices and rising interest rates that have dampened demand for new homes. The months of September and October account for nearly 40 percent of the decorative paint manufacturers' total sales. With continuing downpour, consumers prefer not repainting their homes, resulting in a 10–20 percent drop in business.

Volatilities in the infrastructures and construction activities

Rural growth, which had for many years constantly outpaced urban growth, is now losing steam. As a result, companies that were previously focused on expanding their presence in rural areas and developing products for the rural market are now moving their attention to urban areas and developing more urban-centric products (premium margin accretive products). The overall demand for paint companies would be impacted if infrastructure and construction activities slowed. Delays in the auto industry's revival will continue to pose a threat to the demand for industrial paints.

Raw Materials

Raw materials play a much greater role in the paint and coating industry due to the raw material intensive nature of the industry. In addition, minor changes in raw material prices have a significant effect on the profitability and operations of paint manufacturers.

Narrowing Knowledge Gaps to Reduce Uncertainty

Use of analytics: Simple statistical models are often more accurate than more detailed models when dealing with highly complex scenarios. When it comes to social networks and other complex structures, the issue is that a sophisticated model is more likely to match past data well but struggle to predict the future, while a simpler model is less likely to fit past data but more likely to predict various future scenarios.

Keeping the initiative assessment on the inputs rather than the outputs

Even the best attempts to achieve results can be thwarted by randomness, so Asian Paints considers the consistency of the decision to pursue the project when determining its performance. The company not only look at the project's actual result (good or bad), but also consider the consistency of the process that went into its preparation and execution.

Maintain versatility and aim to respond quickly: There's no substitute for being aware of and listening to what's going on and identifying incidents as soon as they happen. As an organization, Asian Paints focusses on "sense and respond," and this approach inspires the people to move rapidly and decisively. The company has a policy that is firm in concept but broad enough to allow for flexibility, keeping in mind that actual outcomes will differ.

Developing a reputation for trust: Asian Paints intends for success, failure, and all in between. The company knows that it will never be alone as long as people believe that Asian Paints is trustworthy. The company focuses on doing the right thing, and hence their clients, staff, and other stakeholders are interested in seeing their business weather whatever storms may arise.

Strategies adopted: In 2023, Asian Paints demonstrated a profound commitment to sustainable growth, substantiated by an impressive financial performance and strategic ESG integration. With a total income of ₹15,585.6 crores bolstered by shareholders' funds of ₹93.8 crores and a manageable debt profile of ₹3,487.6 crores, the company's financial resilience is evident. This economic fortitude is further illustrated by a robust 19.8 percent revenue growth and an EBITDA increase of 25.8 percent, indicating operational efficiency and profitability. However, beyond the numbers, the company's strategic endeavors encapsulate a broader vision.

At the heart of Asian Paints's success is its governance model that pivots on creating value through purpose-driven leadership and material topics such as consumer delight and climate change. Their ESG strategy, underpinned by an investment of ₹77.2 Crores in CSR initiatives, has been pivotal in achieving substantial environmental milestones, including a significant 62.2 percent consumption of renewable electricity and an outstanding water conservation rate of 0.45 KL/KL. This environmental stewardship is not just about compliance but is integral to their business ethos, reflecting in their product offerings ranging from paints to decor, which now command a market presence supported by over 150,000+ retail touchpoints and an influential network of 240,000+ business influencers.

The company's international strategy aligns with its vision to "beautify, preserve, and transform spaces" globally, and is geared towards leveraging these ESG achievements to gain a competitive edge in new markets. The commitment to innovation is a cornerstone of this strategy, with an in-house R&D center spending over ₹83.2 crores on innovation, substantiated by the filing of 25 patents. This focus on scientific rigor and customer passion has led to the launch of 22 new products, setting a precedent for competitors and establishing Asian Paints as a thought leader in the sector. Moreover, the company's operational strategy is characterized by its expansive in-house and outsourced processing centers with a considerable capacity of 1,730,000 KL/annum for decorative paints, showcasing an adeptness at scaling operations to meet market demands. Their operational excellence is further reflected in a commendable decrease in specific hazardous waste disposal by 71 percent, underscoring their commitment to sustainability.

Despite this progress, Asian Paints navigates a landscape rife with uncertainties such as climate change risks and the need for rigorous corporate governance. However, the company views these as opportunities for technological enhancement and digitization, potentially opening new avenues for growth. Their stakeholder ecosystem, enriched by a Net Promoter Score (NPS) of 68 percent and community engagement programs benefiting over 510,000 individuals, stands as a testament to their societal impact. Asian Paints' financial strength, coupled with its strategic ESG and innovation-driven approach, not only underscores its current market leadership but also sets a robust foundation for sustainable international expansion. The year 2023 stands as a pivotal point for the company, marking its transition from a market player to a market leader, poised to capitalize on the interplay between financial robustness, strategic foresight, and dedicated execution of its core values.

Customized service: Painting service matches with a painting specialist who assists in providing healthy and hygienic home painting/sanitization services using genuine and high-quality Asian Paints products. Deliverables with a wide range of options, such as wallpapers, selective colours, and equipment. Use of cutting-edge software and technology such as the 3-D home décor visualization, Internet of

Things (IoT), natural language translation, artificial intelligence (AI), conversational chat bots. Transforming a brick-and-mortar store to a click-and-mortar store Focus on information technology (IT) and how it is used in day-to-day company operations.

Sensitivity Analysis

The effect of reasonably probable changes in market rates on the company's financial results, cash flows, and financial position has been analyzed.

Market Risk: The risk that the fair value of a financial instrument's future cash flows will fluctuate due to market price changes is known as market risk. Interest rate risk, currency risk, and other price risk are the three kinds of market risk. Borrowings, investments, trade payables, trade receivables, loans, and derivative financial instruments are all affected by market risk.

Interest rate risk: Interest rate risk is the risk that a financial instrument's fair value or future cash flows will fluctuate due to changes in market interest rates. Because Asian Paints has a small amount of interest-bearing debt, the risk of market interest rate changes is low.

Foreign Currency risk: Foreign Exchange Risk The risk that the fair value or future cash flows of an exposure will fluctuate due to changes in foreign exchange rates is known as foreign currency risk. Asian Paints policy is to hedge its exposures above predetermined thresholds from recognized liabilities and firm obligations due in the next 20–30 days. It does not engage in any derivative instruments for the purpose of trading or speculation. The company is primarily affected by changes in the US dollar. The sensitivity analysis is based on the company's net unhedged exposure as of the reporting date. Any percentage reflects management's estimate of a reasonable foreign exchange rate change.

Other Price risk: The risk that the fair value of a financial instrument will fluctuate due to changes in market traded price is known as other price risk. Financial assets, such as investments in equity instruments and bonds, pose another source of price risk. Asian Paints is exposed to price risk as a result of its investments in FVTOCI-recognized equity instruments.

Credit Risk: Credit risk is the possibility that a counterparty may fail to meet its contractual obligations, causing the company to lose money. Financial assets such as trading receivables, mutual fund investments, derivative financial instruments, other bank balances, loans, and other receivables are the main sources of credit risk. Only dealing with counterparties with a reasonably high credit rating is a policy adopted by the company. Asian Paints exposure and counterparty credit ratings are constantly monitored, and the total value of transactions is fairly distributed among the counterparties.

Liquidity Risk: The risk that the company will have trouble raising funds to satisfy obligations related to financial instruments that are settled by delivering cash or another financial asset is known as liquidity risk. Liquidity risk arises when a financial asset cannot be sold quickly at a price that is close to its fair value. For managing its short-, medium-, and long-term financing and liquidity management needs, Asian Paints has developed a liquidity risk management framework.

Innovation

Asian paints has a dedicated, strongly motivated, and purpose-driven R&D team, which consistently help to achieve breakthroughs in product innovation to create value for the company's product offerings. Asian Paints continues to make investments in modern instrumentation of analysis and characterization of raw materials and finished products.

Asian Paints is present in all four segments of decorative paints, namely Interior Wall Finishes, Exterior Wall Finishes, Enamels, and Wood Finishes. Colour Worlds (Dealer Tinting Systems), Home Solutions (painting solutions service), Kids World (painting solutions for kid's room), Colour Next (prediction of colour trends through in–depth research), and Royale Play Special Effect Paints were among the many innovative concepts introduced in the Indian paint industry. Innovations in products inclusde anti-bacterial paint and water proofing paints.

Introduction of online tools like Paint Budget Calculator, Colour Catalogue, Colour Visualiser, Paint Selector Hassle-Free Home painting services boosted business growth.

A dozen papers authored by the company's researchers have featured in national and international journals of repute. The company has a comprehensive program of 'Breakthrough Innovation' which created a transformative process, not only in the research and technology operations but across the entire organization. The National Research Development Corporation of Government of India, New Delhi, bestowed the prestigious National Innovation Award 2019 to Asian Paints Ltd. for its patented technology 'Hydroxy-functional Acrylic co-polymer from derivative castor oil for coating applications' for high-performance sustainable coatings.

Future Prospects

Asian Paints is committed to excellence in the industry. The new business environment made the customer stronger and urged the organizations to examine their relationship with their existing and potential customers in future. Capabilities to face the competitors with superior experience and compete for a share in the domestic and international markets. To respond effectively, Asian Paints needed to identify and leverage on their accumulated strengths, learn, catch up, innovate, and be viable in the dynamic business environment. On top of this, Asian Paints is expected to improve profitability, increase revenue growth, and capture and protect larger market share is challenging. In recent strategic moves, Asian Paints has broadened its product offerings and market reach through targeted acquisitions, demonstrating a forward-thinking approach to expansion within the home decor and solutions sector. In 2022, Asian Paints entered into definitive agreements to acquire a 51 percent stake in Harind Chemicals and Pharmaceuticals Private Limited, a move valued at ₹127.5 million. This acquisition not only diversifies Asian Paints' portfolio but also signifies its entry into new business domains, underscoring its ambition to be a comprehensive provider of home decor solutions beyond its traditional paint products. Harind's established presence in the chemicals and pharmaceuticals sector represents a strategic addition to Asian Paints' growing portfolio, offering new avenues for growth and innovation.

Moreover, Asian Paints' acquisition of a majority stake in Weatherseal Fenestration, a company specializing in the manufacturing of uPVC windows and doors, further highlights its commitment to expanding its home improvement and decor solutions. This acquisition, advised by EY, enables Asian Paints to tap into the burgeoning market for premium fenestration products, aligning with consumer trends toward more integrated and stylish home decor solutions. It represents a strategic step for Asian Paints to extend its offerings in the home decor space, moving beyond surface aesthetics to functional and durable home improvements.

The acquisitions are part of Asian Paints' broader strategy to diversify its revenue streams and enhance its product portfolio, reinforcing its position as a leading player in the home decor and improvement sector in India and beyond. By integrating these new business lines, Asian Paints is well-positioned to meet the evolving needs of consumers, leveraging established brand presences and distribution networks to scale up its operations effectively in these new segments.

Questions

1. What are the key factors that contribute to the attractiveness of the paint manufacturing industry, and how does Asian Paints Limited leverage these factors to maintain its competitive edge?
2. Considering the evolving market dynamics, how should Asian Paints Limited adapt its planning approach between forecast-driven and scenario-based planning to sustain its market leadership and drive future growth?
3. Given the current competitive landscape and emerging market trends, can Asian Paints Limited effectively defend its leadership position, and what strategic initiatives should it prioritize to ensure sustained growth and market dominance?

References

Asian Paints Limited. (2022). *Asian Paints Limited entered into definitive agreements to acquire 51 percent stake in Harind Chemicals and Pharmaceuticals Private Limited.* MarketScreener (October 19, 2022). Accessed from https://www.marketscreener.com on March 29, 2024

EY (2022, April 4). *Asian Paints acquires a majority stake in Weatherseal Fenestration.* Accessed from https://www.ey.com on March 29, 2024

Chaudhury, A., & Dawar, V. (2023). *Asian Paints: a valuation dilemma.* Emerald Emerging Markets Case Studies, 13(3), 1–24.

ASIAN Paints website. Available at http://www.asianpaints.com

ICI DULUX Paints website. Available at http://www.icidulux.co.in

End Notes

1 See www.cnbc.com/id/100917279/why-insder-trading-should-be-legal; www.forbes.com/sites/jeffreydorfman/2015/03/22/a-modern-insider-trading-law-would-recognize-the-victims-of-the-current-law/#a9Od4be34b3e; www.investmentbank.com/fees; www.eurofound.europa.eu/observatories/eurowork/articles/impact-of-mergers-and-acquisitions-on-employment-and-labor-relations

2 See Welch, D., and G. Edmondson. (2004). "A shaky automotive *ménage à trois*." *BusinessWeek*, May 10, pp. 40–41.

3 https://imaa-institute.org/merger-and-acquisitions-statistics. Accessed March 6, 2017.

4 Here, and throughout this chapter, it is assumed that capital markets are semi-strong efficient, that is, all publicly available information about the value of a firm's assets is reflected in the market price of those assets. One implication of semi-strong efficiency is that firms will be able to gain access to the capital they need to pursue any strategy that generates positive present value. See Fama, E. F. (1970). "Efficient capital markets: A review of theory and empirical work." *Journal of Finance*, 25, pp. 383–417.

5 See Trautwein, I. (1990). "Merger motives and merger prescriptions." *Strategic Management Journal*, 11, pp. 283–295; and Walter, G., and J. B. Barney. (1990). "Management objectives in mergers and acquisitions." *Strategic Management Journal*, 11, pp. 79–86. The three lists of potential links between bidding and target firms were developed by the Federal Trade Commission; Lubatkin, M. (1983). "Mergers and the performance of the acquiring firm." *Academy of Management Review*, 8, pp. 218–225; and Jensen, M. C., and R. S. Ruback. (1983). "The market for corporate control: The scientific evidence." *Journal of Financial Economics*, 11, pp. 5–50.

6 See Huey, J. (1995). "Eisner explains everything." *Fortune*, April 17, pp. 44–68; and Lefton, T. (1996). "Fitting ABC and ESPN into Disney: Hands in glove." *Brandweek*, 37(18), April 29, pp. 30–40.

7 This is because if the combined firm is worth $32,000 the bidder firm is worth $15,000 on its own. If a bidder pays, say, $20,000 for this target, it will be paying $20,000 for a firm that can only add $17,000 in value. So, a $20,000 bid would lead to a $3000 economic loss.

8 This is Jensen, M. C., and R. S. Ruback. (1983). "The market for corporate control: The scientific evidence." *Journal of Financial Economics*, 11, pp. 5–50.

9 A. Arikan (2004). "Long-term returns to acquisitions: The case of purchasing tangible and intangible assets." Unpublished, Fisher College of Business, Ohio State University; S. J. Brown and J. B. Warner (1985). "Using daily stock returns: The case of event studies." *Journal of Financial Economics*, 14, pp. 3–31; D. Henry, M. Der Hovanseian, and D. Foust (2003). "M&A deals: Show me." *BusinessWeek*, November 10, pp. 38+.

10 See Lubatkin, M. (1987). "Merger strategies and stockholder value." *Strategic Management Journal*, 8, pp. 39–53; and Singh, H., and C. A. Montgomery. (1987). "Corporate acquisition strategies and economic performance." *Strategic Management Journal*, 8, pp. 377–386.

11 See Grant, L. (1995). "Here comes Hugh." *Fortune*, August 21, pp. 43–52; Serwer, A. E. (1995). "Why bank mergers are good for your savings account." *Fortune*, October 2, p. 32 and Deogun, N. (2000). "Europe catches merger fever as global volume sets record." *The Wall Street Journal*, January 3, p. R8.

12 The concept of free cash flow has been emphasized in Jensen, M. C. (1986). "Agency costs of free cash flow, corporate finance, and takeovers." *American Economic Review*, 76, pp. 323–329; and Jensen, M. (1988). "Takeovers: Their causes and consequences." *Journal of Economic Perspectives*, 2, pp. 21–48.

13 See Miles, R. H., and K. S. Cameron. (1982). *Coffin nails and corporate strategies*. Upper Saddle River, NJ: Prentice Hall.

14 Roll, R. (1986). "The hubris hypothesis of corporate takeovers." *Journal of Business*, 59, pp. 205–216.

15 See Dodd, P. (1980). "Merger proposals, managerial discretion and stockholder wealth." *Journal of Financial Economics*, 8, pp. 105–138; Eger, C. E. (1983). "An empirical test of the redistribution effect in pure exchange mergers." *Journal of Financial and Quantitative Analysis*, 18, pp. 547–572; Firth, M. (1980). "Takeovers, shareholder returns, and the theory of the firm." *Quarterly Journal of Economics*, 94, pp. 235–260; Varaiya, N. (1985). "A test of Roll's hubris hypothesis of corporate takeovers." Working paper, Southern Methodist University, School of Business; Ruback, R. S., and W. H. Mikkelson. (1984). "Corporate investments in common stock." Working paper, Massachusetts Institute of Technology, Sloan School of Business; and Ruback, R. S. (1982). "The Conoco takeover and stockholder returns." *Sloan Management Review*, 14, pp. 13–33.

16 This section of the chapter draws on Barney, J. B. (1988). "Returns to bidding firms in mergers and acquisitions: Reconsidering the relatedness hypothesis." *Strategic Management Journal*, 9, pp. 71–78.

17 See Turk, T. A. (1987). "The determinants of management responses to interfirm tender offers and their effect on shareholder wealth." Unpublished doctoral disserta tion, Graduate School of Management, University of California at Irvine. In fact, this is an example of an anti-takeover action that can increase the value of a target firm. These anti-takeover actions are discussed later in this chapter.

18 See Bower, J. (1996). "WPP-integrating icons." Harvard Business School Case No. 9-396-249.

19 See Jemison, D. B., and S. B. Sitkin. (1986). "Corporate acquisitions: A process perspective." *Academy of Management Review*, 11, pp. 145–163.

20 Blackwell, R. D. (1998). "Service Corporation International." Presented to The Cullman Symposium, October, Columbus, OH.

21 R. Walkling and M. Long (1984). "Agency theory, managerial welfare, and takeover bid resistance." *Rand Journal of Economics*, 15(1), pp. 54–68; R. D. Kosnik (1987). "Greenmail: A study of board performance in corporate governance." *Administrative Science Quarterly*, 32, pp. 163–185; J. Walsh (1989). "Doing a deal: Merger and acquisition negotiations and their impact upon target company top management turnover." *Strategic Management Journal*, 10, pp. 307–322; L. Y. Dann and H. DeAngelo (1983). "Standstill agreements, privately negotiated stock repurchases, and the market for corporate control." *Journal of Financial Economics*, 11, pp. 275–300; M. Bradey and L. Wakeman (1983). "The wealth effects of targeted share repurchases." *Journal of Financial Economics*, 11, pp. 301–328; H. Singh and F. Haricento (1989). "Top management tenure, corporate ownership and the magnitude of golden parachutes." *Strategic Management Journal*, 10, pp. 143–156; T. A. Turk (1987). "The determinants of management responses to interfirm tender offers and their effect on shareholder wealth." Unpublished doctoral dissertation, Graduate School of Management, University of California at Irvine.

22 Cartwright, S., and C. Cooper. (1993). "The role of culture compatibility in successful organizational marriage." *The Academy of Management Executive*, 7(2), pp. 57–70; Chatterjee, S., M. Lubatkin, D. Schweiger, and Y. Weber. (1992). "Cultural differences and shareholder value in related mergers: Linking equity and human capital." *Strategic Management Journal*, 13, pp. 319–334.

23 Jacobsen, D. (2012). "Six big mergers killed by culture." *Globoforce*, September 22.

24 See Walsh, J., and J. Ellwood. (1991). "Mergers, acquisitions, and the pruning of managerial deadwood." *Strategic Management Journal*, 12, pp. 201–217; and Walsh, J. (1988). "Top management turnover following mergers and acquisitions." *Strategic Management Journal*, 9, pp. 173–183.

25 See Haspeslagh, P., and D. Jemison. (1991). *Managing acquisitions: Creating value through corporate renewal*. New York: Free Press.

Case 3–1: National Hockey League Enterprises Canada: A Retail Proposal

IVEY | Ivey Publishing

Richard Ivey School of Business
The University of Western Ontario

Elizabeth Gray prepared this case under the supervision of Elizabeth M.A. Grasby solely to provide material for class discussion. The authors do not intend to illustrate either effective or ineffective handling of a managerial situation. The authors may have disguised certain names and other identifying information to protect confidentiality.

In July 1998, Glenn Wakefield, vice-president of National Hockey League Enterprises Canada (NHLEC), was faced with an opportunity to pursue the development of a retail outlet solely dedicated to Brand NHL merchandise. If pursued, Wakefield had to select one of three implementation options: NHLEC could retain managerial and financial control of the facility, control could be relinquished to a management firm, or floor space could be rented in a department store where NHLEC would maintain partial control over operations. Opening a flagship store would be a shift in the organization's strategy and Wakefield wondered if it was the right thing to do.

The National Hockey League

The National Hockey League (NHL), a professional hockey organization then housing 27 teams in total, was divided into two conferences, each consisting of three divisions (see Exhibit 1). Each team received representation from the NHL division responsible for officiating, scouting, and public relations as well as the marketing division, National Hockey League Enterprises. Additionally, each NHL team employed its own marketers who were responsible for promoting the team and selling tickets to the team's games.

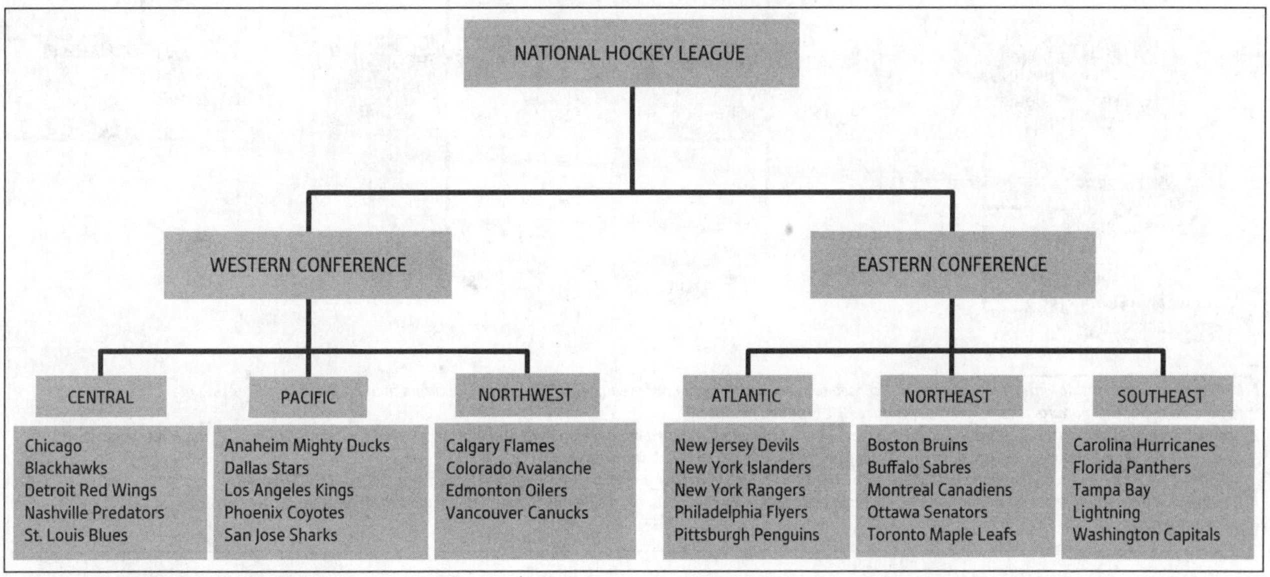

Exhibit 1 National Hockey League

National Hockey League Enterprises

National Hockey League Enterprises (NHLE) managed the promotion of the game, the licensing of NHL merchandise, and the exploitation of corporate marketing partnerships. NHLE was a large enterprise with job descriptions ranging from "Asia/Pacific Promotions" to "Grassroots Development". NHLE was housed in downtown New York, New York, U.S.A.

National Hockey League Enterprises Canada

NHLE's Canadian counterpart, the National Hockey League Enterprises Canada (NHLEC), was located in Toronto, Ontario, Canada. NHLEC was a relatively small operation under the managerial control of the New York office (an organizational chart is given in Exhibit 2).

One of NHLEC's primary strategic goals was to develop a distinct brand image. The ever-increasing number of licensees and retailers for NHL-branded merchandise was becoming too fragmented. Wakefield wanted the brand's image to be presented consistently to consumers at the retail level. He believed this approach would, in turn, translate into increased sales of NHL-brand merchandise and also increased recognition of the NHL. The greatest obstacle in achieving this goal lay not with the independent retailer, but with the larger department store chains such as Wal-Mart. NHLEC relied on these large retailers to push crucial sales volume but the end result was scattered NHL merchandise and an inconsistent brand image presented to the consumer. Frequent buyer turnover, power struggles and turf wars among the buyers, and the sheer size of these retailers had all contributed to NHLEC's difficulties in developing brand equity at a mass-market consumer level.

A New Approach

Wakefield had to find a way to convince large retailers that there was a better way to display and promote

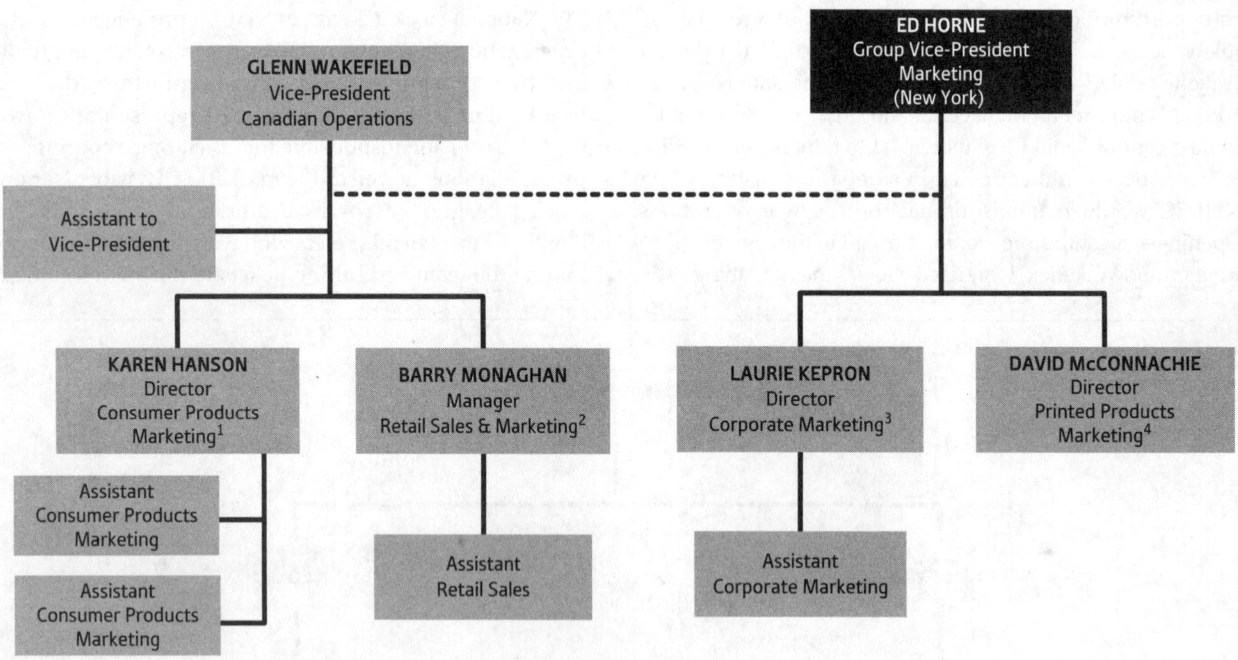

1. Managed the relationship with all manufacturers licensed to print an NHL or member team logo. These manufacturers then paid NHLEC a licensing fee (a percentage of the manufacturers' sales) to produce NHL branded products.

2. Coordination of all retail stores carrying NHL brand merchandise. Activities included the development and maintenance of the relationships with these retailers. These activities included promotional incentives for retailers to boost sales of NHL brand merchandise.

3. Responsible for governing partnerships with large corporations; currently managing relationships with Air Canada and McDonald's Corporation.

4. Governed all printed products related to the NHL, including PowerPlay Magazine™, season schedule pamphlets, trading cards, and corporate sponsor print material.

Exhibit 2 National Hockey League Enterprises Canada Organizational Chart

NHL products. One potential solution would be to focus NHLEC's selling efforts toward the general merchandise manager, rather than (and one step above) the individual buyer, encouraging a more coordinated purchase and display effort. Another option would be the introduction of the NHL's own store. This flagship store would sell merchandise purchased from NHL licensees. This store would be used to illustrate to these large retailers the positive effects that a consistent NHL brand image could have on sales.

The Industry

While the apparel industry experienced rapid growth throughout the 1980s, the recession in the early 1990s had hurt apparel sales (see Exhibits 3 and 4). Recovery from the recession had been gradual and it was a well-known fact that apparel sales were tied tightly to the overall level of economic activity (see Exhibit 5 for Gross Domestic Product data and Exhibit 6 for Canadian disposable income and expenditure on clothing).

With the introduction of both the Canada-U.S. Free Trade Agreement (FTA) and the North American Free Trade Agreement (NAFTA) in the late 1980s, Canadians had witnessed a multitude of lower priced imports entering the market. Within the last decade, there had been a restructuring of the retail apparel industry. Consolidation and the emergence of U.S.-based retail giants such as Wal-Mart had resulted in a highly concentrated retail industry. These large Canadian retailers had sought to narrow their supplier base and increase their margins. In addition, the Canadian dollar was trading at a record low (around U.S. $0.66).

Although Wakefield wondered what impact all of this would have on small NHL licensees and what the NHL store might do for these retailers, his review of the retail industry convinced him that the timing was right for such a venture. GDP for both Canada and Ontario was expected to grow steadily at a rate of three per cent into the next century. Additionally, lower unemployment, reduced housing costs, and general consumer confidence were predicted to characterize the years to come.

Demographics

Consumer demand was also driven by demographic factors, the first of which was population. Refer to Exhibit 7 for selected population growth statistics. The "baby boom" and "baby boom echo[1]" population accounted for 56 per cent of the total population, with this group driving growth

Exhibit 3 Retail Sales in 1996–1997 ($Billions) and Growth Rate for Canada and Ontario

	1996	1997	Growth Rate
Canada	217.0	232.7	+7.2
Ontario	78.6	84.4	+7.4

Exhibit 4 Canadian Apparel Retail Sales ($Billions) and Growth Rate (%) 1988–1997

	1988	1989	1990	1991	1992	1993	1994	1995	1996	1997
Retail Sales	14.3	15.5	16.3	14.9	15.5	14.0	14.6	15.2	15.8	16.4
Growth Rate		+8.4	+5.2	-8.6	+4.0	-9.7	+4.3	+4.1	+3.9	+3.8

Exhibit 5 GDP ($Billions) and Growth Rates (%) for Canada and Ontario 1987–1996

	1987	1988	1989	1990	1991	1992	1993	1994	1995	1996
Canada										
GDP	551.5	606.9	650.7	669.5	676.5	690.1	712.9	747.3	776.3	797.8
Growth Rate		+10.0	+7.2	+2.9	+1.0	+2.0	+3.3	+4.8	+3.9	+2.8
Ontario										
GDP	226.8	253.1	276.1	277.6	278.5	282.8	288.6	300.8	314.1	323.0
Growth Rate		+11.6	+9.1	+0.5	+0.3	+1.5	+2.1	+4.2	+4.4	+2.8

Exhibit 6 Canadian Disposable Income ($Billions), Growth Rates (%), and Clothing Expenditure (%) 1994–1997

	1994	1995	1996	1997
Disposable Income	493.6	510.8	518.2	523.7
		+3.5	+1.4	+1.1
Expenditure on Clothing	23.0	23.9	23.9	24.7
		3.9	0.0	+3.3
Expenditure on clothing as a percentage of disposable income	4.7	4.7	4.6	4.7

Exhibit 7 Populations and Growth Rates (%) for Canada, Ontario and Toronto

	1981	1991	1996	Growth Rate (Arithmetic)
Canada	24,343,181	27,296,859	28,846,761	9.2%
Ontario	8,625,107	10,084,885	10,753,573	24.6%
Toronto		3,893,046	4,263,757	10.0%

in consumer demand. As baby boomers aged, their needs in terms of apparel were likely to include a greater emphasis on quality, comfort, functionality, value, and service; whereas, by 1996, those in the "baby boom echo" phase had entered their teenage years, a time when people were typically more fashion-conscious.

Other Trends

Canadians were spending a greater portion of their disposable income on consumer goods such as computers, electronics, and leisure products—leaving less for apparel. Also, as consumers became more knowledgeable about products, they placed increased importance on the price-value relationship. Today's consumers demanded "value"—high quality merchandise at reasonable prices and had begun to shop at more inexpensive retail stores. Furthermore, today's consumers spent less time shopping for apparel. Since less time was spent shopping, consumers looked for reliable indicators of product quality and service prior to the purchase. In addition to these changes in consumer behavior, there was a trend towards relaxation of the dress code in the work place.

As consumers became more knowledgeable about products and demanded more from retailers, quick response (QR) technologies—such as electronic data interchange (EDI)—were being utilized to provide top-notch service to customers. These technologies allowed retailers to immediately process, store, and forward point-of-sale statistics to the manufacturer who, in turn, could replenish inventory levels.

Alternatives

Wakefield identified three models for establishing a NHLEC retail presence. In the first model, NHLEC would have complete managerial control over the location and operation of the retail store. There were three viable locations to choose from: Vancouver, Toronto, and Montreal. Investment funds of $2,200,000 for start-up and approximately $800,000 in working capital would be required. He wondered how NHLEC could raise those kinds of funds. He also knew that if the venture was not profitable, NHLEC would have to absorb the loss and NHLEC's budget was simply not large enough to sustain significant losses. If he decided to pursue this option, Wakefield would have to convince New York to give the go-ahead.

The location would need to be 15,000 square feet in total, with 10,000 of that being retail space. The average lease range for a downtown Toronto location was $50 to $60 per square foot. Wakefield estimated the store could generate $750 revenue per retail square foot per year. Cost of goods sold was estimated to be 50 percent of sales. Salaries and wages were estimated at 10 percent and other miscellaneous costs at 15 percent. Net income would be taxed at 45 percent and the prime lending rate was currently at 6.5 percent (borrowers would typically pay an interest rate of prime plus one and a half percent).

In the second model, NHLEC would hire and relinquish all control to a management firm that would handle all the operational and administrative functions. In turn, NHLEC would collect a licensing fee—15 percent of gross revenue—from the management firm. Typically, a management firm would rent a much smaller space, likely around 4,000 square feet, and might require NHLEC to invest as much as $500,000 for furnishings and fixtures. While he knew that several of these firms existed, he also knew that it was often a challenge to persuade them to adopt a project. How could he pitch the idea to such a firm?

In the third model, NHLEC could rent floor space in a major department store (i.e., The Bay, Sears, etc.). Wakefield estimated the location would be 200 square feet in size and would generate $200 revenue per square foot per year. The department store usually charged an operating fee of 10 percent of sales to manage the area and a lease rate equal to 50 percent of revenues. An initial investment in inventory of $6,000 and another $6,000 would be needed to equip the space with fixtures and signage.

With these three options before him, Wakefield sat down to write out his proposal. He knew each proposal would have to be evaluated based on the following criteria:

- Maintaining sufficient control to present the proper "Brand NHL" image.
- Limiting NHLEC's investments—both financial and human resources.
- Establishing a profitable retail outlet.

Glenn was unsure how important this last criterion was in the face of the project's true objective to increase the exposure of "Brand NHL".

End Note

1. Children of the "baby boom."

Case 3-2: Rayovac Corporation: International Growth and Diversification Through Acquisitions[1]

School of Business
D'Amore-McKim
Northeastern University

Ivey | Publishing

David T.A. Wesley prepared this case under the supervision of Professor Ravi Sarathy solely to provide material for class discussion. The authors do not intend to illustrate either effective or ineffective handling of a managerial situation. The authors may have disguised certain names and other identifying information to protect confidentiality.

In 2005, Rayovac announced acquisitions totalling $1.5 billion, which encompassed the purchases of United Industries and of Tetra Holdings and aimed at making Rayovac the most, "significant global player in the pet supplies industry."[2] These acquisitions were the latest in a series, going back to 1999, that gave Rayovac significant market presence in new product categories, including lawn and garden care, household insecticides and pet foods (see Exhibit 1). Through such acquisitions, Rayovac grew from $400 million in sales in 1996 to approximately $2.8 billion in 2005. In recognition of this major shift in both composition and direction, the company changed its name from Rayovac to Spectrum Brands.

Company Background[3]

Rayovac was established in Madison, Wisconsin, in 1906 as the French Dry Battery Company. After changing its name to Rayovac in 1921, the company became one of the best known battery brands in the United States and quickly established itself as the leading marketer of value-brand batteries in North America.

In 1996, after seeing its market share steadily eroded by Duracell, Energizer, and Panasonic (owned by Matsushita), the company was purchased by private equity firm Thomas H. Lee Partners (THL). At the time, revenues were approximately $400 million. THL sought to revive the Rayovac brand name by growing the company through acquisitions. Initially, acquisitions focused on the battery business, but later included businesses focused on shaving products and personal care. This strategy met with some success as Rayovac increased its U.S. market share from 27 percent to 34 percent between 1996 and 2001.

Historically, most of the company's growth had been in North America. However, beginning in 2002, the company began to selectively acquire battery manufacturers and distributors in key foreign markets in an effort to establish a strong global presence. Then in 2003, the company acquired Remington Products in its first move to diversify away from consumer batteries.

According to David A. Jones, chief executive officer (CEO) of Rayovac Corporation, the company's diversification efforts had only begun. He explained:

> *We set out consciously for the first five or six years to globalize the battery and lighting business, which we've done, and we have consciously now, for some period of time, been looking for the right diversification moves . . . . There are other things that, over time, we'll become interested in and you'll probably see us move towards.*[4]

The Global Battery Business

In 2003, the global battery market was worth approximately $24 billion, with the United States accounting for about one-third of total consumption. Between 1990 and 2000, the

Exhibit 1 Rayovac Acquisitions (1999 to 2005) (in $ millions)

Year	Company Acquired	Price Paid	EBITDA	Key characteristics of acquired company
1999	ROV Ltd.	155	41.0	Leading Latin-American battery manufacturer (except Brazil)
Oct. 2002	Varta	258	41.2	Leading Europe-based battery manufacturer of general batteries and the market leader in Germany and Latin America
Sept. 2003	Remington Products	322	48.8	Largest selling brand in the United States in the combined dry shaving and personal-grooming products categories, on the basis of units sold; share similar distribution channels, sales outlets. Mid-tier brand competes with Braun, not wet shavers.
Jan. 2004	Ningbo Baowang Battery Co., China	31 (for 85% stake)	3.4	Manufactures alkaline and heavy-duty batteries in China
June 2004	Microlite Brazil	38	(6.4)	Owned Rayovac brand name in Brazil; leading Brazilian brand with 49% market share in alkaline and zinc carbon segments
Jan. 2005	United Industries	1,504	150.0	Significant presence in lawn and garden care products, and pet supplies
April 2005	Tetra Holding	555	52.9	Pet food for fish and reptiles, aquarium accessories; No. 1 or No. 2 in market share in every major segment and market—United States, Japan, Germany, United Kingdom and France

Source: Company files.

United States achieved an annual growth rate of 7.4 percent in alkaline battery products. Rayovac Corporation accompanied this trend but lagged behind Duracell and Energizer in the United States. The intensely competitive U.S. battery market led to considerable price discounting and required significant advertising and promotion expenditures. Rayovac, as the No. 3 player, had to carefully choose its competitive strategy, its product line composition and features, its price points, its cost position, its distribution channels and its advertising strategy in order to be able to close the competitive gap.

Gillette, owner of the Duracell brand, had annual revenues of $9 billion, followed by Energizer Holdings, with revenues of $1.7 billion. Although Rayovac was in third place in the United States, globally, it was the worldwide leader in hearing aid batteries, the leading manufacturer of zinc carbon household batteries in North America and Latin America, and the leading marketer of rechargeable batteries and batterypowered lights in the United States.

Both Energizer and Duracell produced premium brands that sold for approximately 15 percent above comparable Rayovac products. Jones believed that Rayovac's value position distinguished it from its premium brand competitors. He explained:

For any brand, whether it's a value brand or premium brand, you have to have high quality products. And the facts are on our side. Our products are very good, high quality products. But once you have that, certainly our point of differentiation is value. You can buy our products for 10 percent to 15 percent lower than our competitors . . . . We're actively outselling our value proposition, because we've tried to create a business model and a business plan different from Duracell and Energizer. Our products are as good as those two fine companies but sell at value price.[5]

For several years, battery manufacturers experienced strong growth worldwide due to the increased use of personal electronic devices, such as portable music players, fitness monitors, handheld computers (PDAs) and gaming devices. Portable lighting was another significant Rayovac product category, with 2003 global sales approaching $3 billion, of which flashlights represented about half of the market.

With the proliferation of personal electronic devices, average household battery consumption increased from approximately 23 batteries per year in 1986 to 44 batteries per year in 2000. As incomes grew, consumption in developed countries switched from zinc carbon to the better performing and higher-priced alkaline batteries, a trend that Rayovac expected to be duplicated in emerging markets. According to Rayovac, the company's strategy of raising brand awareness and increasing the number of distribution channels allowed it to take better advantage of market growth than its competitors. Kent Hussey, Rayovac chief operating officer (COO), underlined the central role of brands, noting:

> *We believe that brands are very important. Being able to easily identify high-quality products that deliver on the value proposition and have recognizable brand names is very important in terms of marketing to consumers. Having that brand name that the consumer can identify and find on the shelf is key. We think that one of Rayovac's core competencies is our expertise in marketing branded consumer products, and it's really the focus of our entire business.*[6]

From the 12 months ended September 30, 1996, through the 12 months ended April 1, 2001, Rayovac grew net sales and adjusted income from operations from $417.9 million to $675.3 million and from $27 million to $83.3 million, respectively. This represented an 11.3 percent and 28.4 percent compound annual growth rate in net sales and adjusted income from operations, respectively. In addition, adjusted income from operations margins improved from 6.5 percent for the 12 months ended September 30, 1996, to 12.3 percent for the 12 months ended April 1, 2001 (see Exhibits 2 to 5).

Rayovac's ability to distribute its products to customers was constrained to some extent by the emergence of large retailers that controlled access to large numbers of consumers. Wal-Mart Stores, Inc., alone accounted for 21 percent of Rayovac's annual sales. Other significant outlets were Home Depot, Lowe's, and Target. Rayovac also sold through discount channels such as "dollar stores."

Acquisitions

Varta AG (Germany)

In 2002, Rayovac acquired the consumer battery business of Varta AG of Germany for $258 million.[7] Varta was the leading European-based manufacturer of general batteries with 2001 revenues of $390 million. Prior to the acquisition, 73 percent of Rayovac's revenues came from North America while 86 percent of Varta's revenues came from Europe. The largest overlap was in Latin America where combined operations solidified Rayovac's market lead, excluding Brazil. The acquisition allowed the two companies to consolidate production and distribution in Latin America and to close redundant manufacturing plants.

The complementary geographic distribution of the two companies' production facilities and distribution channels was expected to give greater access to global sourcing

Exhibit 2 Rayovac Financial Summary (for years ending September 30) (in $ millions)

	2004	2003	2002	2001	2000
Income Statement					
Net Sales	1,417.19	922.12	572.74	616.17	630.91
Cost of Goods Sold	811.89	549.51	334.15	361.17	371.47
Pretax Income	90.53	23.04	45.68	17.50	57.95
Net Income	55.78	15.48	29.24	11.53	38.35
Balance Sheet					
Assets					
Total Current Assets	650.51	666.82	259.32	303.09	291.17
Net PP&E	182.40	150.61	102.59	107.26	111.90
Total Assets	1,635.97	1,545.29	533.23	566.50	569.02
Liabilities and Shareholders' Equity					
Total Current Liabilities	398.66	397.01	118.78	144.54	186.48
Long-Term Debt	806.00	870.54	188.47	233.54	272.82
Total Liabilities	1,318.55	1,343.29	358.44	408.91	488.32
Total Shareholders' Equity	316.04	202.00	174.79	157.59	80.70
Total Liabilities and Shareholders' Equity	1,635.97	1,545.29	533.23	566.50	569.02
Cash Flow Statement					
Net Cash Flows from Operations	104.86	76.21	66.83	18.05	32.84
Net Cash Flows from Investing	(68.58)	(446.40)	(15.47)	(18.27)	(17.95)
Net Cash Flows from Financing	(131.02)	471.85	(56.71)	1.67	(16.00)

Source: Company 2004 Annual Report.

Exhibit 3 Rayovac Corporation and Subsidiaries Consolidated Balance Sheets (for years ending September 30) (in $ millions)

	2004	2003	2002	2001	2000
Assets					
Cash	15.79	107.77	9.88	11.36	9.76
Receivables	269.98	255.21	128.93	160.94	147.77
Total Inventories	264.73	219.25	84.28	91.31	100.68
Other Current Assets	100.02	84.58	36.24	39.48	32.97
Total Current Assets	650.51	666.82	259.32	303.09	291.17
Property, Plant and Equipment	182.40	150.61	102.59	107.26	111.90
Deferred Charges	60.38	76.61	51.90	37.08	43.84
Intangibles	742.68	651.25	119.43	119.07	122.11
Total Assets	1,635.97	1,545.29	533.23	566.50	569.02
Liabilities					
Accounts Payable	228.05	172.63	76.16	81.99	97.86
Current Long-Term Debt	23.90	72.85	13.40	24.44	44.82
Accrued Expense	56.44	41.47	22.09	38.12	43.81
Income Taxes	21.67	20.57	7.14	n/a	n/a
Other Current Liabilities	68.60	89.49	n/a	n/a	n/a
Total Current Liabilities	398.66	397.01	118.78	144.54	186.48
Deferred Charges/Inc.	7.27	n/a	20.96	7.43	8.24
Long-Term Debt	806.00	870.54	188.47	233.54	272.82
Other Long-Term Liabilities	106.61	75.73	30.23	23.40	20.78
Total Liabilities	1,318.55	1,343.29	358.44	408.91	488.32
Shareholders' Equity					
Minority Interest	1.38	n/a	n/a	n/a	n/a
Common Stock	0.64	0.62	0.62	0.62	0.57
Capital Surplus	224.96	185.56	180.82	180.75	104.20
Retained Earnings	220.48	164.70	149.22	119.98	108.45
Treasury Stock	130.07	130.07	130.07	130.07	129.98
Total Shareholders' Equity	316.04	202.00	174.79	157.59	80.70
Total Liabilities and Shareholders' Equity	1,635.97	1,545.29	533.23	566.50	569.02

Source: Company 2004 Annual Report.

and distribution opportunities and generate cost savings of between $30 million and $40 million through the consolidation of production plants and administration. As a direct result of the Varta acquisition, Rayovac became the market leader in consumer batteries in Germany and Austria and the second leading producer in Europe.

ROV Ltd. and Microlite (Latin America)

Rayovac was the leading producer of zinc carbon batteries in Latin America, a region where the company enjoyed strong brand recognition. However, Latin America was plagued by frequent economic downturns, and consumers had relatively low purchasing power. Despite the region's volatility, Latin America played an important role in the company's geographic diversification strategy.

In the late 1990s, Latin America was one of Rayovac's fastest growing markets, where it had distribution agreements with Ahold, Woolworths, Makro, and several other large supermarket and box-store chains. A large part of the company's growth came from its 1999 acquisition of Miami-based ROV Limited for $155 million. ROV, which was spun off from Rayovac in 1982, was Rayovac's largest distributor of batteries in Latin America, with approximately $100 million in revenues, compared to Rayovac's regional preacquisition revenues of less than $20 million.

However, shortly after the ROV Limited acquisition, Latin America sales took a turn for the worse. All three major manufacturers saw declines of approximately 30 percent. Rayovac also saw delinquent accounts increase to nearly $5 million, which Rayovac attempted to mitigate by withholding future product shipments. As a result, Rayovac decreased receivables for Latin America from $50 million to $41 million. Fixed costs were also reduced by $12 million, including process rationalization and a reduction in staff by 120 people.

Exhibit 4 Rayovac Corporation and Subsidiaries Statement of Operations Data (for years ending September 30) (in $ millions)

	2004	2003	2002	2001	2000	1999	1998
Net sales	1,417.2	922.1	572.7	616.2	703.9	564.3	495.7
Cost of goods sold	811.9	549.5	334.1	361.2	358.2	293.9	258.3
Other special charges[1]	(0.8)	21.1	1.2	22.1	-	1.3	-
Gross profit	606.1	351.5	237.4	232.9	345.7	269.1	237.4
Operating expenses:							
Selling expense	293.1	185.2	104.4	119.6	195.1	160.2	148.9
General and administrative expense	121.3	80.9	56.9	46.6	50.5	37.4	32.4
Research and development expense	23.2	14.4	13.1	12.2	10.8	9.8	9.4
Other special charges[2]	12.2	11.5	-	0.2	-	8.1	6.2
	449.9	291.9	174.4	178.6	256.4	215.5	196.9
Income from operations	156.2	59.6	63.0	54.4	89.3	53.6	40.5
Interest expense	65.7	37.2	16.0	27.2	30.6	16.3	15.7
Non-operating expense	-	3.1	-	8.6	-	-	-
Other (income) expense, net	0.1	(3.6)	1.3	1.1	0.7	(0.3)	(0.2)
Income before income taxes and extraordinary item	90.5	23.0	45.7	17.5	58.0	37.6	25.0
Income tax expense	34.3	7.6	16.4	6.0	19.6	13.5	8.6
Income before extraordinary item	56.2	15.5	29.2	11.5	38.4	24.1	16.4
Extraordinary item[3]	(0.4)	-	-	-	-	-	(2.0)
Net income	55.8	15.5	29.2	11.5	38.4	24.1	14.4

Notes:

[1]Related to plant closings, restructuring, process rationalization and severance pay.

[2]Ibid.

[3]Loss from discontinued operations (2004) and expense associated with the repurchase of shares (1998).

Source: Company 2004 Annual Report

Exhibit 5 Rayovac Corporation and Subsidiaries Consolidated Statements of Cash Flows (for years ending September 30) (in $ millions)

	2004	2003	2002	2001	2000
Net Income (Loss)	55.78	15.48	29.24	11.53	38.35
Depreciation/Amortization	44.75	36.95	22.05	24.86	22.33
Net Increase (Decrease) in Assets/Liabilities	(13.12)	14.38	10.48	(37.67)	(30.07)
Cash Flow from Discontinued Operations	0.38	n/a	n/a	8.59	n/a
Other Adjustments-Net	17.08	9.39	5.06	10.74	2.23
Net Cash Flow from Operations	104.86	76.21	66.83	18.05	32.84
Increase (Decrease) in Prop. Plant and Equip	(26.86)	(25.99)	(15.47)	(18.83)	(17.95)
(Acquisition) Disposal of Subsidiary. Business	(41.71)	(420.40)	n/a	n/a	n/a
Increase (Decrease) in Securities Investments	n/a	n/a	n/a	0.56	n/a
Other Cash Flow from Investing	(0.34)	n/a	(0.24)	(69.65	n/a
Net Cash Flow from Investing	(68.58)	(446.40)	(15.47)	(18.27)	(17.95)
Issue (Repayment) of Debt	(1.35)	(29.93)	n/a	n/a	n/a
Increase (Decrease) in Borrowing	(150.46)	501.61	(56.22)	3.90	(15.74)
Net Cash Flow from Financing	(131.02)	471.85	(56.71)	1.67	(16.00)
Effect of Exchange Rate on Cash	2.75	(3.77)	3.88	0.16	(0.20)
Cash or Equivalents at Year Start	107.77	9.88	11.36	9.76	11.07
Cash or Equivalents at Year End	15.79	107.77	9.88	11.36	9.76
Net Change in Cash or Equivalent	(91.99)	97.89	(1.48)	1.60	(1.31)

In 2004, the company was able to offset this decline through its acquisition of Microlite S.A., the largest producer of consumer batteries in Brazil and owner of the Rayovac brand name in Brazil, for $38 million.[8] The Microlite acquisition allowed Rayovac to immediately realize a 50 percent market share in Latin America's largest consumer market.[9] Rayovac replaced Microlite's management team with Rayovac veterans who proceeded to reduce costs, increase efficiency, and improve product packaging. The latter allowed Rayovac to increase prices by 16 percent. Regional competitors, following Rayovac's lead, also raised prices.

When Rayovac acquired Microlite, the business was undercapitalized and losing money. Its precarious situation made it a high risk for lenders who, in turn, charged very high interest rates. Rayovac immediately proceeded to recapitalize the business and to replace high-rate debt with Rayovac-backed debentures. The reduction in interest payments immediately improved the acquired company's financial results. According to Chief Executive Officer David A. Jones, the results exceeded company expectations.

> *We were frankly surprised by how fast the actions took hold. It didn't surprise us that we were going to make it profitable. I think in the future it's going to be a star performer. Our numerical distribution is high because of the dominance of the brand in the marketplace.*[10]

As a result of the Microlite acquisition, Rayovac expected to increase total Latin American revenues by approximately 50 percent in 2005.

China

In the same year that Rayovac acquired Microlite, the company acquired 85 percent of Ningbo Baowang for $24 million. Located in Ninghai, China, Ningbo Baowang was a major exporter of private label branded batteries with annual revenues of $6.4 million. The company also sold its own Baowang brand throughout China.

By acquiring a Chinese manufacturer, Rayovac hoped to both increase its presence in the rapidly growing Asia market and to add a low-cost manufacturing subsidiary from which to export Rayovac and Varta branded batteries to its global markets. Rayovac replaced Ningbo Baowang's existing management with its own company managers in order to implement Rayovac process controls and management policies more efficiently. It also installed new manufacturing equipment that would allow it to produce one billion Rayovac branded batteries a year beginning in 2005.[11] Explained Jones:

> *China is going to be the growth vehicle for all the alkaline capacity needs in the future. We have a very large plant in Fennimore; we have a very large plant in Dischingen in Germany (see* Exhibit 6*). Those plants are running near capacity and so, as alkaline grows around the world, all the future capacity needs are going to come out of that China plant.*[12]

Remington Products Company

In 2003, Rayovac diversified its product offering by acquiring Remington Products for $322 million.[13] Remington was established in 1816 and was recognized as one of America's oldest consumer brands. The company focused on personal care products but was best known for its electric shavers. In this category, Remington was the No. 2 brand in North America with 35 percent market share, compared with 40 percent for Norelco and less than 20 percent for Braun. Other "personal grooming" products included hair dryers, curling irons and hot air brushes. In the four years leading up to its acquisition, Remington experienced a compound annual growth rate in excess of 10 percent.

In 2003, global sales of electric shaving and grooming products were around $3 billion, growing at about three percent annually. The global market for other electric personal case products, such as hair dryers, curling irons, hot air brushes and lighted mirrors, was estimated at $2 billion, with annual unit sales growth also at three percent.

Remington was considered a low-cost producer with capital expenditures of approximately one percent of revenues. Production was mainly outsourced to low-cost Far East suppliers, particularly in mainland China. Therefore, any synergies between the two companies would be limited to administration, purchasing, and distribution, with estimated annual savings of approximately $23 million. Rayovac also planned to use its established international distribution network to expand the presence of Remington products outside North America, which accounted for 64 percent of that company's sales in 2002. The Varta distribution network in particular would be used to increase the presence of Remington products in Europe. According to Jones:

> *In 1996, we were selling our products in 36,000 stores principally the United States. We are now selling in over a million stores. Remington is selling in 20,000 stores in the Unieted States. There are a lot more in the United States. and a lot of retailers around the world that we currently do business with. We think some of the Remington product line is applicable, and we think because our sales organizations are on the ground and have strong relationships with retailers, we could build the Remington brand name globally.*
>
> *Remington represents a very logical diversification for Rayovac due to its product offerings, brand positioning and customer similarities, and represents the first*

Exhibit 6 Rayovac Corporation and Subsidiaries Manufacturing and Distribution Centers 2004

Facility	Function	Ft^2
North America		
Fennimore, Wisconsin[1]	Alkaline Battery Manufacturing	176,000
Portage, Wisconsin[1]	Zinc Air Button Cell and Lithium Coin Cell Battery Manufacturing and Foil Shaver Component Manufacturing	101,000
Dixon, Illinois[2]	Packaging and Distribution of Batteries and Lighting Devices and Distribution of Electric Shaver and Personal Care Devices	576,000
Nashville, Tennessee[2]	Distribution of Batteries, Lighting Devices, Electric Shaver. and Personal Care Devices	266,700
Bridgeport, Connecticut[1,3]	Foil Cutting Systems and Accessories Manufacturing	167,000
Asia		
Ninghai, China[1]	Zinc Carbon and Alkaline Battery Manufacturing & Distribution	274,000
Europe		
Dischingen, Germany[2]	Alkaline Battery Manufacturing	186,000
Breitenbach, France[1]	Zinc Carbon Battery Manufacturing	165,000
Washington, UK[2]	Zinc Air Button Cell Battery Manufacturing & Distribution	63,000
Ellwangen, Germany[2]	Battery Packaging and Distribution	312,000
Latin America		
Guatemala City, Guatemala[1]	Zinc Carbon Battery Manufacturing	105,000
Ipojuca, Brazil[1]	Zinc Carbon Battery Component Manufacturing	100,000
Jaboatoa, Brazil[1]	Zinc Carbon and Alkaline Battery Manufacturing	516,000
Manizales, Colombia[1]	Zinc Carbon Battery Manufacturing	91,000

[1]Facility is owned.
[2]Facility is leased.
[3]Facility closed September 30, 2004.

step of hopefully several other diversification moves over the next few years as we build Rayovac into a much larger, more diversified consumer products company.[14]

Integrating Remington into Rayovac involved closing several Remington manufacturing and distribution facilities, integrating all functional departments of the two companies and absorbing Remington's worldwide operations into Rayovac's existing North American and European operations, thereby creating a global organization and infrastructure. This included merging sales management, marketing, and field sales of the two companies into a single North American sales and marketing organization. Similarly, research and development (R&A) would be merged into Rayovac's research facility at the company's headquarters in Wisconsin. From a total of 20 plants in 1996, Rayovac reduced its plants to nine by the end of 2004 while still quadrupling sales and unit volume. The number of suppliers was reduced to 40 percent of 1996 levels, while average procurement per supplier rose tenfold. Remington also focused on matching the product performance of its two major rivals, Braun and Norelco, in terms of consumer attributes, features, functionality, and overall quality.

Following these acquisitions, Rayovac products were sold by 19 of the world's top 20 retailers and were available in over one million stores in 120 countries. Company revenues increased to approximately $1.5 billion, and employees numbered more than 6,500 worldwide. The company also realized annual cost savings of more than three percent of cost of goods sold.

Lawn and Garden Care, Insecticides and Pet Supplies

In 2005, Rayovac announced its intention to acquire two pet supply companies for more than $2 billion and to change its name to Spectrum Brands. The first of these acquisitions was United Industries Corporation, which Rayovac acquired for $1.5 billion, funded with cash payments of $1 billion, stock

issued from Treasury totalling $439 million with acquisition related expenses, and assumed debt totalling $36 million. To fund the acquisition, Rayovac issued $1.03 billion in new long-term debt.[15]

United Industries

United Industries was the leading North American producer of consumer lawn and garden care products, household insect control products and specialty pet supplies. The company had about 24 percent market share in lawn products, such as fertilizers and pesticides, which it sold under the brand name Spectrum. In insect control (mosquito repellents), it had an 18 percent market share. Retails sales of household insect control products in the United States was approximately $1 billion in 2003, growing at four percent a year, with sales likely to increase as public awareness increased of insect-borne diseases such as the West Nile virus.

The U.S. pet supplies market was estimated at $8 billion in 2004, while the European market was about $4 billion. Annual growth in the pet supplies category was between six percent and eight percent. With increased incomes, more households were likely to have pets and to treat them as household members, spending increasing amounts on feeding and care. The U.S. pet supplies industry was highly fragmented, with over 500 manufacturers, primarily small firms. The industry was not significantly affected by business cycles. The rise of pet superstores, such as Petco and Pet Smart, provided a competitive opportunity for larger companies, such as Rayovac, with strong distribution channels.

The lawn and garden segment also enjoyed favorable demographic trends. People over age 45 were more likely to pursue gardening compared to the general population, a group whose cohort was increasing as the North American, European, and Japanese populations increased in average age. About 80 percent of U.S. households participated in some form of lawn and garden activity. In 2003, North American industry revenues were approximately $3.2 billion, growing at approximately four percent annually. Lawn and garden care product sales, as well as insecticide sales, were seasonal. Garden product sales typically fell off when the weather was wet and cold.[16]

The Scotts Miracle-Gro Company was the largest producer of home gardening supplies, with annual net sales of $2 billion. Scotts led the market in almost every product category and every region in which it conducted business. Its major brands included Scotts, Miracle-Gro, and Ortho fertilizers and herbicides. It was also the sole distributor in the home gardening segment for Monsanto's Roundup brand herbicides.[17]

Central Garden and Pet Company was a distant third, with $1.2 billion in annual revenues. Central Garden's pet products included pet food, aquarium products, pest control products, cages, pet books, and other small animal products. Lawn and garden products included grass seed, wild bird food, herbicides, insecticides, and outdoor patio furniture. The company's products were sold under more than 16 different brand names.[18]

United itself had just completed two significant acquisitions in 2004 as it expanded geographically and diversified away from its roots in pesticides. In 2004, it entered the pet supply business with its acquisition of United Pet Group, Inc. (UPG) for $360 million. UPG derived approximately half its sales from aquarium supplies, while the remainder consisted of a variety of supplies for small household pets, excluding pet food. As United was still in the process of integrating UPG when it was acquired by Rayovac, Jones expected its integration to be considerably more complicated than previous acquisitions, taking up to three years to complete (compared to less than one year for Remington and Varta). Nevertheless, Jones reasoned that any company that sold its products through major retail chains, such as Wal-Mart, was a fair acquisition target. He explained:

> *As a larger and more significant supplier of consumer products, we believe the postacquisition Rayovac will enjoy stronger relationships with our most important global retailer customers. For instance, United does a substantial business with Wal-Mart, Home Depot, and Lowe's, all of whom are important relationships for Rayovac today and all of whom will become even more significant.*[19]

Many of the cost savings associated with the integration of United Industries were expected in marketing and distribution, as existing networks increased cross-selling to department store customers. Other savings were expected in administration and purchasing.[20] According to Rayovac Chief Operating Officer Kent Hussey, his company's strong presence in Asia and Europe provided it with more sophisticated sourcing and distribution opportunities than those available to United, which had a limited presence outside of North America. Hussey explained:

> *Rayovac operates on a global scale. From a purchasing perspective, significant sourcing capabilities exist in the Far East. I think, with our experience and our infrastructure, we can accelerate dramatically, purchasing leverage and sourcing in the Far East. And then finally, in manufacturing in distribution, we can use our expertise very quickly to help rationalize, eliminate redundancies and improve the efficiency of the overall supply chain. It really is very much operationally driven. There*

are clearly some administrative synergies here in IT and finance and administration, but the bulk of this is really operationally focused.[21]

Jones added that Rayovac also planned to use its global network to expand United Industries' distribution beyond North America.

> *While United is a North American business now, that is not to say it will be only a North American business in the future. Our European teams are actively looking at the categories that United participates in and looking at where we can potentially expand there or in Latin America by taking advantage of obvious distribution opportunities and customer relationships that we have in regions other than North America.*[22]

Rayovac further argued that industry consolidation in pet supplies was needed, "in order to meet the requirements of global retailers." According to Jones, pet supplies was the fastest growing retail category but one that was highly fragmented. Rayovac intended to increase its participation by further acquiring and consolidating pet supply companies. "We think we can actually accelerate consolidation," he noted. "Pet is going to be a major growth platform and opportunity for further acquisitions." [23]

United's 2004 revenues of around $950 million came mainly from major chains, such as Home Depot, Lowe's, Wal-Mart, Petco, and PetSmart. Through increased sales and cost savings, Rayovac anticipated "gross synergies" of between $70 million and $75 million over the first three years. Boston-based private equity firm Thomas Lee Partners, which had acquired United in 1999, would end up with nearly 25 percent ownership in Rayovac, as well as two seats on Rayovac's 10-member board of directors. Thomas H. Lee Partners had previously invested in Rayovac in 1995, and helped take it public in 1997. In addition, David Jones, Rayovac chairman and CEO, had served on United's board between 1999 and 2003. THL acquired significant stakes in growth companies, and at the time of the United acquisition, managed over $12 billion of committed capital. Some of its major deals include Warner Music, Houghton Mifflin Co., Snapple Beverage, and Fisher Scientific.

Tetra Holdings

Rayovac's interest in pet supplies was further realized with the acquisition of Tetra Holdings of Germany less than two months after the United deal for $555 million (see Exhibit 7), of which $500 million was financed with long-term debt (Table 1 summarizes Rayovac debt as of July 2005, following the United and Tetra acquisitions).[24] Tetra was founded in 1955 by Dr. Ulrich Baensch, the inventor of flaked fish food. The company supplied pet fish and reptile products in 90 countries and had annual

Exhibit 7 Pre and Post 2005 Acquisitions Consolidated Balance Sheets (in $ millions)

	Period ending Jul 3, 2005	Period ending Sep 30, 2004
Cash	27.0	15.8
Receivables	462.6	289.6
Inventories	470.3	264.7
Prepaid Expenses	99.6	80.4
Total Current Assets	1,059.4	650.5
Net Plant and Equipment	310.7	182.4
Goodwill	1,432.6	320.6
Net intangible Assets	1,169.7	422.1
Other assets	83.7	60.4
Total assets	4,056.1	1,636.0
Accounts Payable	280.2	228.1
Accrued Liabilities	261.2	146.7
Current L-T debt	38.8	23.9
Total Current Liabilities	580.2	398.7
Long-term Debt	2,298.0	806.0
Employee benefits	73.8	69.2
Other Liabilities	259.2	44.6
Shareholders' Equity	845.0	316.0
Total Liabilities and Equity	4,056.1	1,636.0

Table 1 Rayovac Debt (as of July 2005)

Debt	Amount $ Millions	Interest Rate %
Senior Subordinated Notes, due February 1, 2015	700.0	7.4
Senior Subordinated Notes, due October 1, 2013 (*pre-existing*)	350.0	8.5
Term Loan, U.S. dollar, expiring February 6, 2012	653.7	5.3
Term Loan, Canadian dollar, expiring February 6, 2012	71.0	4.7
Term Loan, Euro expiring February 6, 2012	138.0	4.7
Term Loan, Euro Tranche B, expiring February 6, 2012	340.4	4.4
Revolving Credit Facility, expiring February 6, 2011	28.3	7.3
Euro Revolving Credit Facility, expiring February 6, 2011	3.6	4.4

sales of $233 million in 2004 (compared to $179 million in 2001). Tetra was purchased by Warner-Lambert in 1974 and was later spun off when Warner Lambert was acquired by Pfizer in 2000, and Pfizer decided to shed, "poorer performing consumer brands."[25] Jones justified his company's latest acquisition by noting:

> *The combination of Tetra with United Pet Group means Rayovac will become the world's largest manufacturer of pet supplies, a position with which we can leverage our company's worldwide operations.*

Commenting on the Tetra acquisition, Kent Hussey remarked:

> *Tetra is a globally recognized brand name in the pet supplies category, one that consumers know and trust. It gives us entry into the pet supplies category literally around the world, and it's a brand that virtually every pet supply retailer considers a must-have brand in terms of consumer loyalty. If the retailer doesn't have that product on the shelf, he is missing significant sales opportunities. That makes Tetra a very attractive asset for us."*[26]

Throughout its history, Rayovac had been primarily a battery company. After the Tetra and United acquisitions, for the first time in its history, Rayovac's battery division accounted for only slightly more than a third of total sales, significantly less than the combined sales for lawn, garden and pet care products (see Table 2 and Exhibit 8). Furthermore, with the United and Tetra acquisitions, more than a third of total sales came from international sources. Tetra, for example, obtained 40 percent of its sales from Europe, 40 percent from the United States, and 20 percent from Japan. Correspondingly, the company incurred a third of its total operating expenses in foreign currencies.

Investment analyst Alyce Lomax described Rayovac's move into pet supplies as "diworseification,"[27] a term that described, "companies that lose their primary focus in their quest to jumpstart growth through diversification."[28] Even so, most analysts hailed the deal, while investors sent the company's stock up nearly 10 percent immediately following the announcement. Overall, the company's stock had risen from about $15 to around $45 in the two years since its acquisition of Remington (see Exhibit 9).

Table 2 Rayovac: Percentage of Sales from Major Product Lines

% of Sales	October 2004	June 2005
Batteries	65	35
Shaving	21	11
Personal care	8	5
Lighting	6	3
Pet Supplies		20
Lawn & Garden		20
Household Insecticides		6

Exhibit 8 Rayovac And Its Competitors, Percentage of Market Share by Major Product Line (as of 2005)

Brand	Batteries			U.S. Shaving and Grooming	U.S. Lawn and Garden	U.S. Household Insecticide	U.S. Pet Supplies
	U.S.	*L.A*	*Europe*				
Duracell	37	9	28	24 *(Braun)*			
Energizer	26	19	22				
Rayovac/ Spectrum Brands	21	41	26 *(Varta)*	29 *(Remington)*	24	18	7
Panasonic		20					
Norelco				43			
Scotts					49		
Central Garden					8		8
S C Johnson						42	

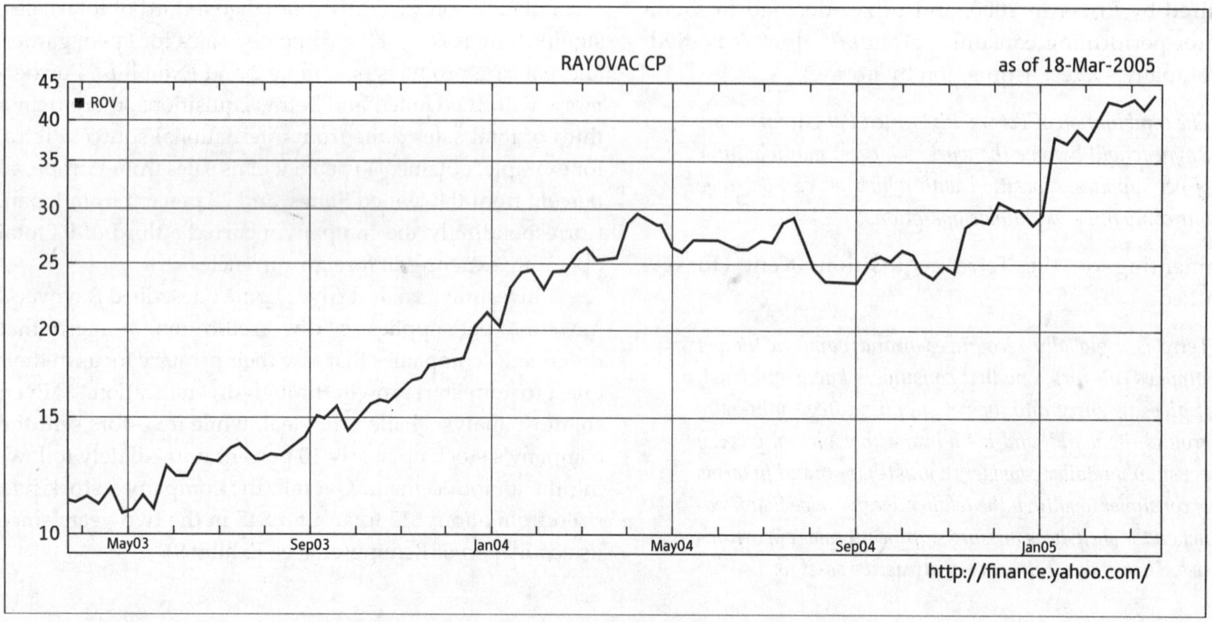

Exhibit 9 Rayovac Corporation Stock Chart

Note: The chart includes data up to and including the announced acquisition of Tetra Holdings on March 15, 2005.

End Notes

1 This case has been written on the basis of published sources only. Consequently, the interpretation and perspectives presented in this case are not necessarily those of Rayovac Corporation or any of its employees.

2 Rayovac Buys Pet Supplies Company, *Reuters*, March 15, 2005.

3 Portions adapted from Rayovac Corporation, Prospectus Supplement, June 20, 2001.

4 "Rayovac to Acquire Remington Products," Company Conference Call, *Fair Disclosure Wire*, August 22, 2003.

5 Transcript "In The Game," *CNNfn*, March 9, 1999.
6 SunTrust Robinson Humphrey Conference, Interview with Kent Hussey, Rayovac Corporation, *Wall Street Transcript*, April 2005.
7 The acquisition did not include Microlite, SA, a Brazilian joint venture that Rayovac acquired separately in 2004. It also excluded Varta's automotive and micro-power divisions.
8 "Rayovac Gains Worldwide Rights to Brand Name, " *Atlanta Business Chronicle*, June 1, 2004.
9 Brazil represented 30 percent of total Latin American market for consumer goods.
10 "Event Brief of Q1 2005 Rayovac Earnings, " Conference Call, *Fair Disclosure Wire*, January 25, 2005.
11 "Rayovac to Acquire 85% of Ningbo Baowang China Battery Company, " *PR Newswire*, January 19, 2004.
12 Ibid.
13 The purchase price represented 6.9 times Remington's 2002 EBITDA of $47 million.
14 "Rayovac to Acquire Remington Products, " Company Conference Call, *Fair Disclosure Wire*, August 22, 2003.
15 "Rayovac Taps BofA, Citigroup For Add-On To Back Tetra Buy, " *Bank Loan Report*, April 4, 2005.
16 Seasonality also affected Rayovac's other products, such as batteries and electric shavers, sales of which surged during the holiday season (quarter ending December 31).
17 Background information on Scotts Miracle-Gro Company was adapted from the company's investor relations website, *investor.scotts.com*, August 30, 2005.
18 Background information on Central Garden and Pet Company was adapted from the company's investor relations website, *www.centralgardenandpet.com*, August 30, 2005.
19 "Rayovac Acquisition Update," *Fair Disclosure Wire*, January 4, 2005.
20 Rayovac anticipated $75 million in cost savings during the first three years.
21 "Rayovac Acquisition Update," *Fair Disclosure Wire*, January 4, 2005.
22 Ibid.
23 Ibid.
24 "Rayovac Taps BofA, Citigroup For Add-On To Back Tetra Buy," *Bank Loan Report*, April 4, 2005.
25 "Tetra Under The Hammer?" *UK Pets*, December 17, 2001.
26 Rayovac Corporation, *The Wall Street Transcript*, April 2005.
27 "Will Pets Juice Rayovac?" *Motley Fool*, March 16, 2005.
28 "Diworseification" was first coined by mutual fund manager Peter Lynch in his book "One Up On Wall Street : How To Use What You Already Know To Make Money In The Market" (Simon & Schuster; 2000).

Case 3-3: Activision's Crush on Mobile Gaming

Introduction

On November 2, 2015, Activision-Blizzard announced it would purchase mobile gaming giant, King Entertainment for $5.9 billion. The all cash deal was expected to close in March 2016. Activision-Blizzard was formed in 2008 as a merger of Activision and the interactive entertainment division of Vivendi (Blizzard). Activision-Blizzard was best known for its Call of Duty, World of Warcraft, Skylanders, Starcraft, and Destiny game franchises. In 2014, the company reported revenues of about $4.4 billion and was the number 3 video game (software) company in the world behind Tencent, and Microsoft.

King Entertainment PLC was founded in 2003 as a social games company. The company, headquartered in Ireland, was primarily known for its best-selling mobile game, Candy Crush Saga. The company's revenues came in at about $2.6B in 2014, with Candy Crush Saga generating nearly 50% of revenues despite about 98% of Candy Crush players being non-payers on the "free to play" service. King was the largest mobile gaming company in 2014 with an estimated 10% global market share.

At the time of the acquisition announcement, mobile gaming companies largely had been unable to repeat their successes as a "formula" for developing a popular mobile game had proven to be elusive. Meaning, most mobile games were "one hit wonders." Wacky games like Flappy-Bird and Plants vs. Zombies appeared to have chances to succeed as good as apps associated with established game franchises. Despite its success in PC and online gaming, Activision-Blizzard had had little success in cracking the mobile gaming market. Activision's revenues from mobile games and accessories had fallen from $629 million in 2012 to $418 million in 2015. Given the large number of failures and crowded mobile marketplace, investors worried that Activision-Blizzard would be making a nearly $6 billion mistake in purchasing King Entertainment. Moreover, the business models of Activision-Blizzard and King Entertainment were fundamentally different—and some observers noted, perhaps fundamentally incompatible.

Global Video Industry

As Table 1 shows, the global video game industry generated revenues of an estimated $81.5 billion in 2014 up about 16% compared to 2013 – excluding global game hardware sales of roughly $20 billion. Troublingly, the video game market rose about 9% in 2015, but all of the growth occurred in the mobile segment. Mobile revenues jumped 37% compared to 2014, but PC games and online game revenues declined about (−2%). Video games were broken into three large categories by technology platform. Console games accounted for about 45% of global revenues followed by PC games with an estimated 35% share of the market in 2014. Mobile games brought in about 27% of industry revenues in 2014 and 33% in 2015.[1]

Physical distribution of consoles and games was concentrated in electronics stores, big box retailers, and on e-commerce sites. For example, Best Buy sold an estimated 17% of video games in the U.S. market. Walmart accounted for 11% of Activision's global revenues in 2015. However, digital downloads were rapidly replacing physical copies of games. Consumers purchased digital downloads (DLC) games on each console's websites, mobile application stores, and on the Steam digital gaming platform. Steam, a division of Valve, accounted for about 75% of the $10 billion global market of digital PC game content transactions in 2013.[2] Note that the console game hardware manufacturers also accounted for a substantial portion of game revenues worldwide. To illustrate, Sony and Microsoft accounted for 18% and 13% of Activision's revenues in 2015.

The top 4 video game markets—China, the United States, Japan, and South Korea—generated about two-thirds of global video game sales despite making up just 40% of the world's 3.1 billion internet users. Germany, the UK, France and Canada made up an additional 12% of global video game sales in 2014.[3]

Mobile Gaming Segment

Table 2 shows revenues of the mobile gaming segment of the global video game industry by company in 2014 and 2015. In contrast to the overall video game market, the U.S. market dominated the mobile gaming segment. The United States made up 32% of the worldwide mobile game market followed by Japan with 26% of the market. South Korea followed with about a 10% market share and the UK held an estimated 7% of the mobile game market. Although China was the largest video game market in the world with about a 24% market share, it only accounted for about 5% of the

Table 1 Global Video Game Market 2014-2015
Top 25 Companies in Game Software Development, Publishing, & Distribution ($ in millions)

	2014 Growth		2015 Growth			2014 Growth		2015 Growth	
Company	**Revenues**	**vs. 2013**	**Revenues**	**vs. 2014**		**Revenues**	**vs. 2013**	**Revenues**	**vs. 2014**
Tencent	$7,211	37%	$8,725	21%	Nexon	$1,446	−2%	$1,581	9%
Sony	6,040	40%	$5,892	−2%	Disney	1,280	9%	1,180	−8%
Microsoft	5,023	7%	$6,409	28%	DeNa	998	−38%	938	−6%
EA	4,453	22%	$4,273	−4%	Take Two	978	−60%	1,337	37%
Activision-Blizzard	4,409	−4%	$4,665	6%	Facebook	974	10%	847	−13%
Apple	3,199	59%	$4,432	39%	Square Enix	949	12%	1,218	28%
Google	2,623	118%	$2,961	13%	GREE	883	34%	Not in top 25	NA
King.com	2,260	20%	$2,000	−12%	Konami	841	−18%	1,017	21%
Nintendo	2,092	−13%	$1,941	−7%	NCSoft	769	7%	Not in top 25	NA
Ubisoft	1,806	33%	$1,022	−43%	Changyou	755	2%	Not in top 25	NA
Warner	1593	NA	$2,214	39%	Sega	735	0%	785	7%
NetEase	1,586	11%	$2,792	76%	Zynga	692	−21%	764	10%
GungHo	1,447	−7%	$1,282	−11%	Bandai Namco	681	−16%	1,668	145%
Total Market	$81,500	16%	$91,800	13%	Mobile Gaming	$21,700	27%	$30,400	40%

Source: NewZoo.Com Accessed 2\7\17.

world's mobile game sales due to relatively low penetration of smartphones.

In the US market, Apple's app store beat Google's Play store by 3:1 in mobile game sales in 2014. The two stores combined accounted for nearly 100% of the U.S. mobile game market. Industry observers attributed Apple's dominance to two factors. First, Apple iPhone and tablet users tended to be more affluent than Android consumers. Second, Apple reportedly had 800 million iTunes accounts and 400 million credit card numbers on file—making mobile game purchases quick and easy for Apple users. Outside the United States, Google's Android system was more popular. The Google Play store generated more than 50% of mobile game purchases in Japan and 80% of them in South Korea.[3]

Reportedly, the median lifetime revenue for mobile games sold through Apple's app store was a mere $3,000. While it only cost about $130,000 to fully develop a mobile game, most games lost money for the developer. Overall, there were about 19 million software developers and 8.7 million mobile apps developers in the world in 2014. An estimated 60% of mobile app developers lived, "below the app poverty line" i.e., made less than $500 per app per month.[4] Only about 4% of all mobile games had lifetime revenues of over $1 million. Less than 2% of all mobile gamers purchased anything at all, as nearly all mobile gamers played for free. A tiny fraction of mobile gamers (0.15%), so-called "whales" accounted for over 50% of all mobile gaming revenues. One Japanese company supposedly had a "whale" that spent over $10,000 per month on app purchases. In response, the company dedicated one employee to that customer to ensure that she was satisfied with the game so as to earn her repeat business. On average, mobile games retained only 15% of players 30 days after installation and a paltry 4% of players after three months, which made attentiveness to a game's "whales" critical to success. Moreover, the life cycle of mobile games had compressed significantly. According to App Annie, mobile game maturity plunged from 50 weeks in 2014 to 17 weeks in 2015—meaning that

Table 2 Global Mobile Game Industry Revenues by Company 2014

	2014	
Colopl	$598	
EA Mobile	524	
Gamevil	131	
Gungho	1,447	
Kabam	400	
King	2,260	
Machine Zone	600	
Netmarble	580	
Rovio	171	
SGN	280	
Supercell	1,700	
Zynga (Mobile Only)	416	
All Others	12,593	
Total Global Mobile Gaming	$21,700	
Apple App Store	1,500,000	Game Titles Available
Google Play Store	1,600,000	Game Titles Available

Source: NewZoo.com estimates.

the average mobile game launched in 2015 received nearly all of its potential downloads in 4 months. In 2012, it took mobile games over 10x longer to reach maturity.

Note that PC game developers were not much better off. The average game on Steam sold only 32,000 copies—better than mobile apps, but development costs were considerably higher for PC games. (To illustrate, Activision-Blizzard invested nearly $1.8 billion in product development from 2012-2014.) While Activision had 19% net margin in 2015, the majority of both mobile and PC game developers were unprofitable.

Activision-Blizzard

Activision-Blizzard (ACTV) was a game developer and publisher. The U.S. based company had one of the largest and most popular game franchises in the world, Call of Duty. Call of Duty was a first person shooter game played primarily on game consoles like X Box, and Playstation. According to Activision management, Call of Duty was so popular that 125 million people played the game from 2010-2014. As of June 2014, players had logged in a cumulative total of 25 billion hours. Players paid between $60 and $75 for a copy of Call of Duty, depending upon their gaming platform.

The company also owned the world's most popular MMORPG (massively multi-player on line role playing game) World of Warcraft. Unlike console games that garnered revenues mainly from the one-time sale of games and follow up "expansion packs," World of Warcraft's 5.6 million players paid monthly subscription fees ranging from $13 to $15 per month in addition to an upfront cost of roughly $50 to begin playing the game.

Activision-Blizzard also had been successful in establishing newer game franchises that were extremely popular with gamers. The company's Skylanders franchise was launched in 2007 and Destiny was introduced in 2013. The three franchises and World of Warcraft together accounted for 71% of Activision's sales in 2015.

Activision-Blizzard's Strategy

Although the Activision-Blizzard merger had occurred several years earlier, the two companies still operated somewhat separately in 2015. Activision primarily was a game publisher that saw itself as a "franchise creator." The division's management team planned to use a 4-pronged approach to creating shareholder value. Namely, it intended to 1. broaden the company's reach; 2. deepen player engagement with its games; 3. earn player investment; and 4. use its scale to create more value.[5] Broadening reach was management's way of saying that the company intended to geographically diversify, expand its game capabilities to different technology platforms, and to target new demographic segments of the gaming market. Deepening engagement meant creating game communities and social networks as well as personalizing games. Part of this effort had led management to announce in 2015 that it would expand the Call of Duty franchise to include TV and movies. Earning player investment would be accomplished through add-on content sales, season passes, and character/world investments through in game purchases. Similarly, the Blizzard division intended to: 1) provide epic entertainment through superior content and gaming experiences; 2) deepen player engagement; and 3) aggressively expand its community to include e-sports.[6] In 2014, over 100 million people worldwide watched e-sports—more than viewed NHL and nearly as many viewers as MLB. Blizzard management felt the division had a strong competitive advantage stemming from its ownership of "the most iconic franchises in the world" along with a proven track record in innovation and proprietary analytics. In addition, the division had 70 million direct connections with consumers. Table 3 shows the company's breakdown of results by operating segment for 2012-2015.

Table 3 Activision-Blizzard Results by Segment

Revenues from Operating Segments	2012	2013	2014	2015
Activision	$3,072	$2,895	$2,686	$2,700
Blizzard	1,609	1,124	1,720	1,565
Distribution	306	323	407	356
Net Effect from Deferral of Net Revenues	−131	241	−405	43
Consolidated Net Revenues	$4,856	$4,583	$4,408	$4,664
Segment Income From Operations	**2012**	**2013**	**2014**	**2015**
Activision	$970	$971	$763	$868
Blizzard	717	376	756	561
Distribution	11	8	9	37
Net Effect from Deferral of Net Revenues and Related COGS, Amt. of Intangibles, Stock-based Compensation & Banking Fees	−247	17	−345	−147
Consolidated Operating Income	$1,451	$1,372	$1,183	$1,319

Source: Activision-Blizzard 2015 10K Annual Report.

Overall Results

Given the company's strong gaming line up and scale, it was not surprising that Activision-Blizzard was a profitable company. As Table 4 shows, Activision-Blizzard had a net margin of about 19% in 2014. However, its return on assets was an uninspiring 5%. Moreover, the company had experienced revenue declines and some margin compression over the previous three years. While some of the company's game franchises were growing, World of Warcraft's popularity had declined in recent years. In addition, the console game manufacturers had recently released new hardware versions. Although demand for the new consoles was growing rapidly, the transition from old hardware to new hardware had negatively impacted sales of console games, which accounted for well over half of Activision-Blizzard's revenues. Management expected console game sales to catch up and surpass their previous levels, but the transition to new hardware was expected to take several years.

Also, game development costs had increased substantially. While the first Call of Duty game cost an estimated $8.5 million to develop in 2004, development costs skyrocketed over the next decade. While Activision-Blizzard's once extremely popular Guitar Hero game cost only $1.7 million to develop in 2005, development costs for a similar, competing title (Rock Band) had jumped to $20 million by 2007. Indeed, Call of Duty 2: Advanced Warfare launched in 2009 had a production budget of $40-$50 million with total costs including marketing and distribution coming in at $200 million. In 2008, Blizzard management disclosed that the company had spent over $200 million to maintain World of Warcraft from 2004-2008. ACTV reportedly paid game-developer, Bungie, $140 million to develop Destiny. The game, launched in September 2014, had captured 25 million registered players by September 2015.

By the end of 2015, revenues had rebounded modestly —up 5.8%—and net profits had risen 6.8%. Nevertheless, investors were uneasy about Activision-Blizzard's longer term prospects due to the highly competitive nature of the market and frequent technology changes. Still, all of the console games in the top ten in 2015 were established franchises with an average age of 15 years. Moreover, Activision-Blizzard owned three of the top ten best-selling console games —Call of Duty, Skylanders, and Destiny.[7]

King Entertainment Acquisition: Searching for New Growth Vehicles

In addition to the announced move into TV and movie content with the Call of Duty franchise, ACTV management wanted to move into the mobile gaming market to cover

Table 4 Activision-Blizzard Selected Financials ($ in millions)

	2012	2013	2014	2015
Product Sales	$3,620	$3,201	$2,786	$2,447
Subscription, licensing and other	1,236	1,382	1,622	2,217
Total Net Revenues	$4,856	$4,583	$4,408	$4,664
Cost of Sales - Product Costs	1,116	1,053	999	921
Cost of Sales - On Line	263	204	232	224
Cost of Sales - Software royalties and amortization	194	187	260	412
Cost of Sales - Intellectual property licenses	89	87	34	28
Gross Profit	$3,194	$3,052	$2,883	$3,079
Gross Margin	65.8%	66.6%	65.4%	66.0%
Product Development	604	584	571	646
Sales and Marketing Expenses	578	606	712	734
General and Administrative Expenses	561	490	417	380
Total SG&A	$1,743	$1,680	$1,700	$1,760
Operating Profit	1,451	1,372	1,183	1,319
Operating Margin	29.9%	29.9%	26.8%	28.3%
Interest & Other Income (Expense)	7	−53	−202	−198
Pretax Income	1,458	1,319	981	1,121
Taxes	309	309	146	229
Tax Rate	21.2%	23.4%	14.9%	20.4%
Net Income	1,149	1,010	835	892
Net Margin	23.7%	22.0%	18.9%	19.1%
E.P.S. Fully Diluted	$1.01	$0.95	$1.13	$1.19
Selected Balance Sheet Figures	**2012**	**2013**	**2014**	**2015**
Total Assets	$14,200	$14,012	$14,746	$15,251
Total Debt	0	4,693	4,324	4,079
Total Liabilities	2,883	7,390	7,409	7,183
Shareholders' Equity	11,317	6,622	7,233	8,068
Total Liabilities & Equity	$14,200	$14,012	$14,642	$15,251

all technology platforms and to appeal to new customers. As a result, the company agreed to purchase King Entertainment for $5.9 billion. Headquartered in Ireland, King's business was very different from ACTV's gaming business. While 100% of ACTV's customers always paid for a game, often paid for a subscription, and sometimes made in game purchases, nearly 100% of King's customers played the company's games for free. In fact, less than 2% of King's "customers" spent any money at all on its games or in game virtual game accessories. The company summed up its approach to gaming in its 2014 annual report (20-F) by saying, "we have designed our mobile and social games with the following characteristics . . . anytime, anywhere, seamlessly synchronized across platforms and devices, highly engaging (easy to learn, but hard to master), inherently social, and free-to-play. Most players can reach the highest

In 2004, the company was able to offset this decline through its acquisition of Microlite S.A., the largest producer of consumer batteries in Brazil and owner of the Rayovac brand name in Brazil, for $38 million.[8] The Microlite acquisition allowed Rayovac to immediately realize a 50 percent market share in Latin America's largest consumer market.[9] Rayovac replaced Microlite's management team with Rayovac veterans who proceeded to reduce costs, increase efficiency, and improve product packaging. The latter allowed Rayovac to increase prices by 16 percent. Regional competitors, following Rayovac's lead, also raised prices.

When Rayovac acquired Microlite, the business was undercapitalized and losing money. Its precarious situation made it a high risk for lenders who, in turn, charged very high interest rates. Rayovac immediately proceeded to recapitalize the business and to replace high-rate debt with Rayovac-backed debentures. The reduction in interest payments immediately improved the acquired company's financial results. According to Chief Executive Officer David A. Jones, the results exceeded company expectations.

> *We were frankly surprised by how fast the actions took hold. It didn't surprise us that we were going to make it profitable. I think in the future it's going to be a star performer. Our numerical distribution is high because of the dominance of the brand in the marketplace.*[10]

As a result of the Microlite acquisition, Rayovac expected to increase total Latin American revenues by approximately 50 percent in 2005.

China

In the same year that Rayovac acquired Microlite, the company acquired 85 percent of Ningbo Baowang for $24 million. Located in Ninghai, China, Ningbo Baowang was a major exporter of private label branded batteries with annual revenues of $6.4 million. The company also sold its own Baowang brand throughout China.

By acquiring a Chinese manufacturer, Rayovac hoped to both increase its presence in the rapidly growing Asia market and to add a low-cost manufacturing subsidiary from which to export Rayovac and Varta branded batteries to its global markets. Rayovac replaced Ningbo Baowang's existing management with its own company managers in order to implement Rayovac process controls and management policies more efficiently. It also installed new manufacturing equipment that would allow it to produce one billion Rayovac branded batteries a year beginning in 2005.[11] Explained Jones:

> *China is going to be the growth vehicle for all the alkaline capacity needs in the future. We have a very large plant in Fennimore; we have a very large plant in Dischingen in Germany (see* Exhibit 6*). Those plants are running near capacity and so, as alkaline grows around the world, all the future capacity needs are going to come out of that China plant.*[12]

Remington Products Company

In 2003, Rayovac diversified its product offering by acquiring Remington Products for $322 million.[13] Remington was established in 1816 and was recognized as one of America's oldest consumer brands. The company focused on personal care products but was best known for its electric shavers. In this category, Remington was the No. 2 brand in North America with 35 percent market share, compared with 40 percent for Norelco and less than 20 percent for Braun. Other "personal grooming" products included hair dryers, curling irons and hot air brushes. In the four years leading up to its acquisition, Remington experienced a compound annual growth rate in excess of 10 percent.

In 2003, global sales of electric shaving and grooming products were around $3 billion, growing at about three percent annually. The global market for other electric personal case products, such as hair dryers, curling irons, hot air brushes and lighted mirrors, was estimated at $2 billion, with annual unit sales growth also at three percent.

Remington was considered a low-cost producer with capital expenditures of approximately one percent of revenues. Production was mainly outsourced to low-cost Far East suppliers, particularly in mainland China. Therefore, any synergies between the two companies would be limited to administration, purchasing, and distribution, with estimated annual savings of approximately $23 million. Rayovac also planned to use its established international distribution network to expand the presence of Remington products outside North America, which accounted for 64 percent of that company's sales in 2002. The Varta distribution network in particular would be used to increase the presence of Remington products in Europe. According to Jones:

> *In 1996, we were selling our products in 36,000 stores principally the United States. We are now selling in over a million stores. Remington is selling in 20,000 stores in the Unieted States. There are a lot more in the United States. and a lot of retailers around the world that we currently do business with. We think some of the Remington product line is applicable, and we think because our sales organizations are on the ground and have strong relationships with retailers, we could build the Remington brand name globally.*
>
> *Remington represents a very logical diversification for Rayovac due to its product offerings, brand positioning and customer similarities, and represents the first*

Exhibit 6 Rayovac Corporation and Subsidiaries Manufacturing and Distribution Centers 2004

Facility	Function	Ft²
North America		
Fennimore, Wisconsin[1]	Alkaline Battery Manufacturing	176,000
Portage, Wisconsin[1]	Zinc Air Button Cell and Lithium Coin Cell Battery Manufacturing and Foil Shaver Component Manufacturing	101,000
Dixon, Illinois[2]	Packaging and Distribution of Batteries and Lighting Devices and Distribution of Electric Shaver and Personal Care Devices	576,000
Nashville, Tennessee[2]	Distribution of Batteries, Lighting Devices, Electric Shaver. and Personal Care Devices	266,700
Bridgeport, Connecticut[1,3]	Foil Cutting Systems and Accessories Manufacturing	167,000
Asia		
Ninghai, China[1]	Zinc Carbon and Alkaline Battery Manufacturing & Distribution	274,000
Europe		
Dischingen, Germany[2]	Alkaline Battery Manufacturing	186,000
Breitenbach, France[1]	Zinc Carbon Battery Manufacturing	165,000
Washington, UK[2]	Zinc Air Button Cell Battery Manufacturing & Distribution	63,000
Ellwangen, Germany[2]	Battery Packaging and Distribution	312,000
Latin America		
Guatemala City, Guatemala[1]	Zinc Carbon Battery Manufacturing	105,000
Ipojuca, Brazil[1]	Zinc Carbon Battery Component Manufacturing	100,000
Jaboatoa, Brazil[1]	Zinc Carbon and Alkaline Battery Manufacturing	516,000
Manizales, Colombia[1]	Zinc Carbon Battery Manufacturing	91,000

[1]Facility is owned.
[2]Facility is leased.
[3]Facility closed September 30, 2004.

step of hopefully several other diversification moves over the next few years as we build Rayovac into a much larger, more diversified consumer products company.[14]

Integrating Remington into Rayovac involved closing several Remington manufacturing and distribution facilities, integrating all functional departments of the two companies and absorbing Remington's worldwide operations into Rayovac's existing North American and European operations, thereby creating a global organization and infrastructure. This included merging sales management, marketing, and field sales of the two companies into a single North American sales and marketing organization. Similarly, research and development (R&A) would be merged into Rayovac's research facility at the company's headquarters in Wisconsin. From a total of 20 plants in 1996, Rayovac reduced its plants to nine by the end of 2004 while still quadrupling sales and unit volume. The number of suppliers was reduced to 40 percent of 1996 levels, while average procurement per supplier rose tenfold. Remington also focused on matching the product performance of its two major rivals, Braun and Norelco, in terms of consumer attributes, features, functionality, and overall quality.

Following these acquisitions, Rayovac products were sold by 19 of the world's top 20 retailers and were available in over one million stores in 120 countries. Company revenues increased to approximately $1.5 billion, and employees numbered more than 6,500 worldwide. The company also realized annual cost savings of more than three percent of cost of goods sold.

Lawn and Garden Care, Insecticides and Pet Supplies

In 2005, Rayovac announced its intention to acquire two pet supply companies for more than $2 billion and to change its name to Spectrum Brands. The first of these acquisitions was United Industries Corporation, which Rayovac acquired for $1.5 billion, funded with cash payments of $1 billion, stock

In 2004, the company was able to offset this decline through its acquisition of Microlite S.A., the largest producer of consumer batteries in Brazil and owner of the Rayovac brand name in Brazil, for $38 million.[8] The Microlite acquisition allowed Rayovac to immediately realize a 50 percent market share in Latin America's largest consumer market.[9] Rayovac replaced Microlite's management team with Rayovac veterans who proceeded to reduce costs, increase efficiency, and improve product packaging. The latter allowed Rayovac to increase prices by 16 percent. Regional competitors, following Rayovac's lead, also raised prices.

When Rayovac acquired Microlite, the business was undercapitalized and losing money. Its precarious situation made it a high risk for lenders who, in turn, charged very high interest rates. Rayovac immediately proceeded to recapitalize the business and to replace high-rate debt with Rayovac-backed debentures. The reduction in interest payments immediately improved the acquired company's financial results. According to Chief Executive Officer David A. Jones, the results exceeded company expectations.

> *We were frankly surprised by how fast the actions took hold. It didn't surprise us that we were going to make it profitable. I think in the future it's going to be a star performer. Our numerical distribution is high because of the dominance of the brand in the marketplace.*[10]

As a result of the Microlite acquisition, Rayovac expected to increase total Latin American revenues by approximately 50 percent in 2005.

China

In the same year that Rayovac acquired Microlite, the company acquired 85 percent of Ningbo Baowang for $24 million. Located in Ninghai, China, Ningbo Baowang was a major exporter of private label branded batteries with annual revenues of $6.4 million. The company also sold its own Baowang brand throughout China.

By acquiring a Chinese manufacturer, Rayovac hoped to both increase its presence in the rapidly growing Asia market and to add a low-cost manufacturing subsidiary from which to export Rayovac and Varta branded batteries to its global markets. Rayovac replaced Ningbo Baowang's existing management with its own company managers in order to implement Rayovac process controls and management policies more efficiently. It also installed new manufacturing equipment that would allow it to produce one billion Rayovac branded batteries a year beginning in 2005.[11] Explained Jones:

> *China is going to be the growth vehicle for all the alkaline capacity needs in the future. We have a very large plant in Fennimore; we have a very large plant in Dischingen in Germany (see* Exhibit 6*). Those plants are running near capacity and so, as alkaline grows around the world, all the future capacity needs are going to come out of that China plant.*[12]

Remington Products Company

In 2003, Rayovac diversified its product offering by acquiring Remington Products for $322 million.[13] Remington was established in 1816 and was recognized as one of America's oldest consumer brands. The company focused on personal care products but was best known for its electric shavers. In this category, Remington was the No. 2 brand in North America with 35 percent market share, compared with 40 percent for Norelco and less than 20 percent for Braun. Other "personal grooming" products included hair dryers, curling irons and hot air brushes. In the four years leading up to its acquisition, Remington experienced a compound annual growth rate in excess of 10 percent.

In 2003, global sales of electric shaving and grooming products were around $3 billion, growing at about three percent annually. The global market for other electric personal case products, such as hair dryers, curling irons, hot air brushes and lighted mirrors, was estimated at $2 billion, with annual unit sales growth also at three percent.

Remington was considered a low-cost producer with capital expenditures of approximately one percent of revenues. Production was mainly outsourced to low-cost Far East suppliers, particularly in mainland China. Therefore, any synergies between the two companies would be limited to administration, purchasing, and distribution, with estimated annual savings of approximately $23 million. Rayovac also planned to use its established international distribution network to expand the presence of Remington products outside North America, which accounted for 64 percent of that company's sales in 2002. The Varta distribution network in particular would be used to increase the presence of Remington products in Europe. According to Jones:

> *In 1996, we were selling our products in 36,000 stores principally the United States. We are now selling in over a million stores. Remington is selling in 20,000 stores in the Unieted States. There are a lot more in the United States. and a lot of retailers around the world that we currently do business with. We think some of the Remington product line is applicable, and we think because our sales organizations are on the ground and have strong relationships with retailers, we could build the Remington brand name globally.*
>
> *Remington represents a very logical diversification for Rayovac due to its product offerings, brand positioning and customer similarities, and represents the first*

Exhibit 6 Rayovac Corporation and Subsidiaries Manufacturing and Distribution Centers 2004

Facility	Function	Ft²
North America		
Fennimore, Wisconsin[1]	Alkaline Battery Manufacturing	176,000
Portage, Wisconsin[1]	Zinc Air Button Cell and Lithium Coin Cell Battery Manufacturing and Foil Shaver Component Manufacturing	101,000
Dixon, Illinois[2]	Packaging and Distribution of Batteries and Lighting Devices and Distribution of Electric Shaver and Personal Care Devices	576,000
Nashville, Tennessee[2]	Distribution of Batteries, Lighting Devices, Electric Shaver. and Personal Care Devices	266,700
Bridgeport, Connecticut[1,3]	Foil Cutting Systems and Accessories Manufacturing	167,000
Asia		
Ninghai, China[1]	Zinc Carbon and Alkaline Battery Manufacturing & Distribution	274,000
Europe		
Dischingen, Germany[2]	Alkaline Battery Manufacturing	186,000
Breitenbach, France[1]	Zinc Carbon Battery Manufacturing	165,000
Washington, UK[2]	Zinc Air Button Cell Battery Manufacturing & Distribution	63,000
Ellwangen, Germany[2]	Battery Packaging and Distribution	312,000
Latin America		
Guatemala City, Guatemala[1]	Zinc Carbon Battery Manufacturing	105,000
Ipojuca, Brazil[1]	Zinc Carbon Battery Component Manufacturing	100,000
Jaboatoa, Brazil[1]	Zinc Carbon and Alkaline Battery Manufacturing	516,000
Manizales, Colombia[1]	Zinc Carbon Battery Manufacturing	91,000

[1]Facility is owned.
[2]Facility is leased.
[3]Facility closed September 30, 2004.

step of hopefully several other diversification moves over the next few years as we build Rayovac into a much larger, more diversified consumer products company.[14]

Integrating Remington into Rayovac involved closing several Remington manufacturing and distribution facilities, integrating all functional departments of the two companies and absorbing Remington's worldwide operations into Rayovac's existing North American and European operations, thereby creating a global organization and infrastructure. This included merging sales management, marketing, and field sales of the two companies into a single North American sales and marketing organization. Similarly, research and development (R&A) would be merged into Rayovac's research facility at the company's headquarters in Wisconsin. From a total of 20 plants in 1996, Rayovac reduced its plants to nine by the end of 2004 while still quadrupling sales and unit volume. The number of suppliers was reduced to 40 percent of 1996 levels, while average procurement per supplier rose tenfold. Remington also focused on matching the product performance of its two major rivals, Braun and Norelco, in terms of consumer attributes, features, functionality, and overall quality.

Following these acquisitions, Rayovac products were sold by 19 of the world's top 20 retailers and were available in over one million stores in 120 countries. Company revenues increased to approximately $1.5 billion, and employees numbered more than 6,500 worldwide. The company also realized annual cost savings of more than three percent of cost of goods sold.

Lawn and Garden Care, Insecticides and Pet Supplies

In 2005, Rayovac announced its intention to acquire two pet supply companies for more than $2 billion and to change its name to Spectrum Brands. The first of these acquisitions was United Industries Corporation, which Rayovac acquired for $1.5 billion, funded with cash payments of $1 billion, stock

Table 3 Activision-Blizzard Results by Segment

Revenues from Operating Segments	2012	2013	2014	2015
Activision	$3,072	$2,895	$2,686	$2,700
Blizzard	1,609	1,124	1,720	1,565
Distribution	306	323	407	356
Net Effect from Deferral of Net Revenues	−131	241	−405	43
Consolidated Net Revenues	$4,856	$4,583	$4,408	$4,664
Segment Income From Operations	**2012**	**2013**	**2014**	**2015**
Activision	$970	$971	$763	$868
Blizzard	717	376	756	561
Distribution	11	8	9	37
Net Effect from Deferral of Net Revenues and Related COGS, Amt. of Intangibles, Stock-based Compensation & Banking Fees	−247	17	−345	−147
Consolidated Operating Income	$1,451	$1,372	$1,183	$1,319

Source: Activision-Blizzard 2015 10K Annual Report.

Overall Results

Given the company's strong gaming line up and scale, it was not surprising that Activision-Blizzard was a profitable company. As Table 4 shows, Activision-Blizzard had a net margin of about 19% in 2014. However, its return on assets was an uninspiring 5%. Moreover, the company had experienced revenue declines and some margin compression over the previous three years. While some of the company's game franchises were growing, World of Warcraft's popularity had declined in recent years. In addition, the console game manufacturers had recently released new hardware versions. Although demand for the new consoles was growing rapidly, the transition from old hardware to new hardware had negatively impacted sales of console games, which accounted for well over half of Activision-Blizzard's revenues. Management expected console game sales to catch up and surpass their previous levels, but the transition to new hardware was expected to take several years.

Also, game development costs had increased substantially. While the first Call of Duty game cost an estimated $8.5 million to develop in 2004, development costs skyrocketed over the next decade. While Activision-Blizzard's once extremely popular Guitar Hero game cost only $1.7 million to develop in 2005, development costs for a similar, competing title (Rock Band) had jumped to $20 million by 2007. Indeed, Call of Duty 2: Advanced Warfare launched in 2009 had a production budget of $40-$50 million with total costs including marketing and distribution coming in at $200 million. In 2008, Blizzard management disclosed that the company had spent over $200 million to maintain World of Warcraft from 2004-2008. ACTV reportedly paid game-developer, Bungie, $140 million to develop Destiny. The game, launched in September 2014, had captured 25 million registered players by September 2015.

By the end of 2015, revenues had rebounded modestly —up 5.8%—and net profits had risen 6.8%. Nevertheless, investors were uneasy about Activision-Blizzard's longer term prospects due to the highly competitive nature of the market and frequent technology changes. Still, all of the console games in the top ten in 2015 were established franchises with an average age of 15 years. Moreover, Activision-Blizzard owned three of the top ten best-selling console games —Call of Duty, Skylanders, and Destiny.[7]

King Entertainment Acquisition: Searching for New Growth Vehicles

In addition to the announced move into TV and movie content with the Call of Duty franchise, ACTV management wanted to move into the mobile gaming market to cover

Table 4 Activision-Blizzard Selected Financials ($ in millions)

	2012	2013	2014	2015
Product Sales	$3,620	$3,201	$2,786	$2,447
Subscription, licensing and other	1,236	1,382	1,622	2,217
Total Net Revenues	$4,856	$4,583	$4,408	$4,664
Cost of Sales - Product Costs	1,116	1,053	999	921
Cost of Sales - On Line	263	204	232	224
Cost of Sales - Software royalties and amortization	194	187	260	412
Cost of Sales - Intellectual property licenses	89	87	34	28
Gross Profit	$3,194	$3,052	$2,883	$3,079
Gross Margin	65.8%	66.6%	65.4%	66.0%
Product Development	604	584	571	646
Sales and Marketing Expenses	578	606	712	734
General and Administrative Expenses	561	490	417	380
Total SG&A	$1,743	$1,680	$1,700	$1,760
Operating Profit	1,451	1,372	1,183	1,319
Operating Margin	29.9%	29.9%	26.8%	28.3%
Interest & Other Income (Expense)	7	−53	−202	−198
Pretax Income	1,458	1,319	981	1,121
Taxes	309	309	146	229
Tax Rate	21.2%	23.4%	14.9%	20.4%
Net Income	1,149	1,010	835	892
Net Margin	23.7%	22.0%	18.9%	19.1%
E.P.S. Fully Diluted	$1.01	$0.95	$1.13	$1.19
Selected Balance Sheet Figures	**2012**	**2013**	**2014**	**2015**
Total Assets	$14,200	$14,012	$14,746	$15,251
Total Debt	0	4,693	4,324	4,079
Total Liabilities	2,883	7,390	7,409	7,183
Shareholders' Equity	11,317	6,622	7,233	8,068
Total Liabilities & Equity	$14,200	$14,012	$14,642	$15,251

all technology platforms and to appeal to new customers. As a result, the company agreed to purchase King Entertainment for $5.9 billion. Headquartered in Ireland, King's business was very different from ACTV's gaming business. While 100% of ACTV's customers always paid for a game, often paid for a subscription, and sometimes made in game purchases, nearly 100% of King's customers played the company's games for free. In fact, less than 2% of King's "customers" spent any money at all on its games or in game virtual game accessories. The company summed up its approach to gaming in its 2014 annual report (20-F) by saying, "we have designed our mobile and social games with the following characteristics . . . anytime, anywhere, seamlessly synchronized across platforms and devices, highly engaging (easy to learn, but hard to master), inherently social, and free-to-play. Most players can reach the highest

Table 3 Activision-Blizzard Results by Segment

Revenues from Operating Segments	2012	2013	2014	2015
Activision	$3,072	$2,895	$2,686	$2,700
Blizzard	1,609	1,124	1,720	1,565
Distribution	306	323	407	356
Net Effect from Deferral of Net Revenues	−131	241	−405	43
Consolidated Net Revenues	$4,856	$4,583	$4,408	$4,664
Segment Income From Operations	**2012**	**2013**	**2014**	**2015**
Activision	$970	$971	$763	$868
Blizzard	717	376	756	561
Distribution	11	8	9	37
Net Effect from Deferral of Net Revenues and Related COGS, Amt. of Intangibles, Stock-based Compensation & Banking Fees	−247	17	−345	−147
Consolidated Operating Income	$1,451	$1,372	$1,183	$1,319

Source: Activision-Blizzard 2015 10K Annual Report.

Overall Results

Given the company's strong gaming line up and scale, it was not surprising that Activision-Blizzard was a profitable company. As Table 4 shows, Activision-Blizzard had a net margin of about 19% in 2014. However, its return on assets was an uninspiring 5%. Moreover, the company had experienced revenue declines and some margin compression over the previous three years. While some of the company's game franchises were growing, World of Warcraft's popularity had declined in recent years. In addition, the console game manufacturers had recently released new hardware versions. Although demand for the new consoles was growing rapidly, the transition from old hardware to new hardware had negatively impacted sales of console games, which accounted for well over half of Activision-Blizzard's revenues. Management expected console game sales to catch up and surpass their previous levels, but the transition to new hardware was expected to take several years.

Also, game development costs had increased substantially. While the first Call of Duty game cost an estimated $8.5 million to develop in 2004, development costs skyrocketed over the next decade. While Activision-Blizzard's once extremely popular Guitar Hero game cost only $1.7 million to develop in 2005, development costs for a similar, competing title (Rock Band) had jumped to $20 million by 2007. Indeed, Call of Duty 2: Advanced Warfare launched in 2009 had a production budget of $40-$50 million with total costs including marketing and distribution coming in at $200 million. In 2008, Blizzard management disclosed that the company had spent over $200 million to maintain World of Warcraft from 2004-2008. ACTV reportedly paid game-developer, Bungie, $140 million to develop Destiny. The game, launched in September 2014, had captured 25 million registered players by September 2015.

By the end of 2015, revenues had rebounded modestly —up 5.8%—and net profits had risen 6.8%. Nevertheless, investors were uneasy about Activision-Blizzard's longer term prospects due to the highly competitive nature of the market and frequent technology changes. Still, all of the console games in the top ten in 2015 were established franchises with an average age of 15 years. Moreover, Activision-Blizzard owned three of the top ten best-selling console games —Call of Duty, Skylanders, and Destiny.[7]

King Entertainment Acquisition: Searching for New Growth Vehicles

In addition to the announced move into TV and movie content with the Call of Duty franchise, ACTV management wanted to move into the mobile gaming market to cover

Table 4 Activision-Blizzard Selected Financials ($ in millions)

	2012	2013	2014	2015
Product Sales	$3,620	$3,201	$2,786	$2,447
Subscription, licensing and other	1,236	1,382	1,622	2,217
Total Net Revenues	$4,856	$4,583	$4,408	$4,664
Cost of Sales - Product Costs	1,116	1,053	999	921
Cost of Sales - On Line	263	204	232	224
Cost of Sales - Software royalties and amortization	194	187	260	412
Cost of Sales - Intellectual property licenses	89	87	34	28
Gross Profit	$3,194	$3,052	$2,883	$3,079
Gross Margin	65.8%	66.6%	65.4%	66.0%
Product Development	604	584	571	646
Sales and Marketing Expenses	578	606	712	734
General and Administrative Expenses	561	490	417	380
Total SG&A	$1,743	$1,680	$1,700	$1,760
Operating Profit	1,451	1,372	1,183	1,319
Operating Margin	29.9%	29.9%	26.8%	28.3%
Interest & Other Income (Expense)	7	−53	−202	−198
Pretax Income	1,458	1,319	981	1,121
Taxes	309	309	146	229
Tax Rate	21.2%	23.4%	14.9%	20.4%
Net Income	1,149	1,010	835	892
Net Margin	23.7%	22.0%	18.9%	19.1%
E.P.S. Fully Diluted	$1.01	$0.95	$1.13	$1.19
Selected Balance Sheet Figures	**2012**	**2013**	**2014**	**2015**
Total Assets	$14,200	$14,012	$14,746	$15,251
Total Debt	0	4,693	4,324	4,079
Total Liabilities	2,883	7,390	7,409	7,183
Shareholders' Equity	11,317	6,622	7,233	8,068
Total Liabilities & Equity	$14,200	$14,012	$14,642	$15,251

all technology platforms and to appeal to new customers. As a result, the company agreed to purchase King Entertainment for $5.9 billion. Headquartered in Ireland, King's business was very different from ACTV's gaming business. While 100% of ACTV's customers always paid for a game, often paid for a subscription, and sometimes made in game purchases, nearly 100% of King's customers played the company's games for free. In fact, less than 2% of King's "customers" spent any money at all on its games or in game virtual game accessories. The company summed up its approach to gaming in its 2014 annual report (20-F) by saying, "we have designed our mobile and social games with the following characteristics . . . anytime, anywhere, seamlessly synchronized across platforms and devices, highly engaging (easy to learn, but hard to master), inherently social, and free-to-play. Most players can reach the highest

level of a game without making a purchase. For those who do, we price our virtual items relative to the entertainment value they deliver." "Our mission is to delight the world with brilliant games that create moments of magic."[8] The company's four category-leading franchises were Candy Crush, Farm Heros, Bubble Witch, and Pet Rescue. Candy Crush Soda Saga became the number 6 mobile game after its launch in 2014. At the end of 2014, King owned three of the top ten games offered in the Apple App store and four of the top ten games offered in the Google Play store in the US market.

In contrast to most mobile game companies, King Entertainment management felt that developing long-term relationships with an extensive user network was the single most important contributor to long-term success. As a result, the company offered all of its mobile games "advertisement free." Historically, King collected a small amount of advertising revenue from its tournament side, but had completely discontinued the practice by the end of 2Q, 2013. King generated revenues primarily through the sale of virtual items within its games. According to the 10K, "Virtual items available for purchase include extra lives, allowing players to extend the duration of their game session, skill-enhancing boosters, helping our players progress through games more quickly and access to content, hastening players' access to new episodes." A typical in-app purchase for an "extra life" on Candy Crush cost players $0.99. The most expensive item, a virtual bomb cooler, cost $1.99. However, other games charged as much as $99 for their most expensive virtual items. During 2014, King switched from in-game purchases of discrete items to in-game purchases of so-called "virtual currency." Management felt the transition to virtual currency had a positive impact on the monetization of players over time.

The company's strategy was to: 1) maintain and grow its casual [game] leadership; 2) prioritize engagement and monetization across its portfolio of casual games by introducing new titles, content and features, launching franchise extensions and titles and concentrating on social engagement as a core game-driver; 3) focus on product innovation by launching innovative products within its classic casual genre and adjacent game genres of broad appeal, and by introducing new monetization features that appeal to its players; and 4) reinforce its player network by strengthening its network through investing in the reactivation of historical players, monetizing the hundreds of millions of players in its network, continuing to promote player adoption of additional games across its portfolio, and acquiring new-to-network players. Nevertheless, King had only been successful in monetizing 8,344,000 of its 533,000,000 monthly active users or about 1.6% of the total as of the end of 2014. This figure was made up of 356 million monthly unique users and about 177 million repeat players per month.

King Entertainment management believed that game development was a core strength of the company. According to King's 2014 annual report, the company had developed 195 game IPs (intellectual properties) between 2003-2013. King typically introduced new casual game IPs in a tournament format on its royalgames.com website, allowing it to gather feedback on the games quickly. The company then modified its new games for launch on mobile devices and on Facebook. Management felt that this approach had allowed King to establish its category-leading franchises. The company also had adopted some principles of entrepreneurship—namely, rapid prototyping in adjacent game categories by small development teams. In management's view, this approach reduced the risk associated with new game launches as well as the costs. In fact, the company claimed that it was able to, "deliver performance, resilience, and high scalability at a fraction of comparable industry costs." King's annual report noted that its scalable proprietary server infrastructure built on commodity hardware accommodated an average of 149 million daily active users playing its games 1.5 billion times per day.

While King Entertainment's growth had been nothing short of spectacular since its founding, investors had become concerned about the company's ability to maintain its results. Some of the factors that had impacted Activision-Blizzard's margins also came into play for King. Namely, product development costs had increased significantly for the company over the past two years. While the company's original games were inexpensive to develop, the process of searching for new game concepts to develop and market that would be large enough to maintain the company's size was quite expensive. Unfortunately for King, the costs to develop a "one off" mobile game for its indie competitors remained inexpensive at approximately $130,000 per app. Moreover, marketing costs had skyrocketed from $55 million in 2012 to $455 million in 2014. In 2015, revenues began to decline as Candy Crush lost some of its popularity and the company was unable to compensate for lost revenues with its new product introduction. King's revenues and operating profits fell (−11%), while return on assets dropped from about 40% in 2014 to less than 34% in 2015. King's results left Activision investors wondering whether the acquisition would pay off or lead to protracted revenue declines and margin compression in the future.

Table 5 King Entertainment Results ($ in millions)

	2012	2013	2014	2015
Revenues	$164.4	$1,884.3	$2,269.4	$2,012.6
Cost of Sales	54.7	584.4	716.7	636.3
Gross Profit	$109.7	$1,299.9	$1,552.7	$1,376.3
Gross Margin	66.7%	69.0%	68.4%	68.4%
Research & Development	28.6	110.5	177.9	198.4
Sales and Marketing	55.2	376.9	455.4	344.8
General and Administrative Expenses	14.9	96.5	184.2	178.4
Total SG&A	$98.7	$583.9	$817.6	$721.7
Operating Profit	$11.1	$716.0	$735.1	$654.6
Operating Margin	6.8%	38.0%	32.4%	32.5%
Other Income (Expense)	0.1	−1.7	33.2	21.2
Pretax Income	11.1	714.2	768.3	675.8
Taxes	3.3	146.7	193.4	159.0
Tax Rate	29.5%	20.5%	25.2%	23.5%
Net Income	$7.8	$567.6	$574.9	$516.8
E.P.S. - Fully Diluted	$0.02	$1.75	$1.79	$1.62
Total Current Assets	$61.3	$631.6	$1,296.1	$1,304.9
Intangible Assets	3.8	9.2	48.6	104.7
Property, Plant & Equipment (Net)	3.0	14.3	34.3	56.5
Total Assets	$75.2	$811.5	$1,441.8	$1,534.1

Sources: King Entertainment 20-F filings, King Entertainment 4Q:15 Results Press Release.

References

1. NewZoo.com estimates. www.newzoo.com Accessed 10/2015.
2. Wikipedia- Steam (Software) https://en.wikipedia.org/wiki/Steam_%28software%29 Accessed 10/2015.
3. NewZoo.com estimates. www.newzoo.com Accessed 10/2015.
4. Vision Mobile: 'App poverty line' represents 60% of all developers. By Shane Schick July 10, 2015. FierceWireless.com http://www.fiercewireless.com/developer/vision-mobile-app-poverty-line-represents-60-all-developers Accessed 10/2015.
5. Activision-Blizzard Investor Day 2015 Presentation. http://investor.activision.com/events.cfm
6. Ibid.
7. Ibid.
8. King Entertainment 2015 20-F Annual Report.

Appendix

Analyzing Cases and Preparing for Class Discussions

This book, properly understood, is really about how to analyze cases. Just reading the book, however, is no more likely to fully develop one's skills as a strategist than reading a book about golf will make one a golfer. Practice in applying the concepts and tools is essential. Cases provide the opportunity for this necessary practice.

Why the Case Method?

The core of many strategic management courses is the case method of instruction. Under the case method, you will study and discuss the real-world challenges and dilemmas that face managers in firms. Cases are typically accounts of situations that a firm or manager has faced at a given point in time. By necessity, cases do not possess the same degree of complexity that a manager faces in the real world, but they do provide a concrete set of facts that suggest challenges and opportunities that real managers have faced. Very few cases have clear answers. The case method encourages you to engage problems directly and propose solutions or strategies in the face of incomplete information. To succeed at the case method, you must develop the capability to analyze and synthesize data that are sometimes ambiguous and conflicting. You must be able to prioritize issues and opportunities and make decisions in the face of ambiguous and incomplete information. Finally, you must be able to persuade others to adopt your point of view.

In an applied field like strategic management, the real test of learning is how well you can apply knowledge to real-world situations. Strategic management cases offer you the opportunity to develop judgment and wisdom in applying your conceptual knowledge. By applying the concepts you have learned to the relatively unstructured information in a case, you develop judgment in applying concepts. Alfred North Whitehead discussed the importance of application to knowledge:

> *This discussion rejects the doctrine that students should first learn passively, and then, having learned, should apply knowledge. . . . For the very meaning of the things known is wrapped up in their relationship beyond themselves. This unapplied knowledge is knowledge shorn of its meaning.*
>
> Alfred North Whitehead (1947). *Essays in Science and Philosophy*. New York: Philosophical Library, Inc. pp. 218–219.

Thus, you gain knowledge as you apply concepts. With the case method, you do not passively absorb wisdom imparted from your instructor, but actively develop it as you wrestle with the real-world situations described in the cases.

How to Analyze Cases

Before discussing how to analyze a case, it may be useful to comment on how *not* to prepare a case. We see two common failings in case preparation that often go hand-in-hand. First, students often do not apply conceptual frameworks in a rigorous and systematic manner. Second, many students do not devote sufficient time to reading, analyzing, and discussing a case before class. Many students succumb to the temptation to quickly read a case and latch on to the most visible issues that present themselves. Thus, they come to class prepared to make only a few superficial observations about a case. Often, they entirely miss the deeper issues around why a firm is in the situation that it is in and how it can better its performance. Applying the frameworks systematically may take more time and effort in the beginning, but it will generally lead to deeper insights about the cases and a more profound understanding of the concepts in the chapters. As you gain experience in this systematic approach to analyzing cases, many of you will find that your preparation time will decrease. This appendix offers a framework that will assist you as you analyze cases. The framework is important, but no framework can substitute for hard work. There are no great shortcuts to analyzing cases, and there is no single right method for preparing a case. The following approach, however, may help you develop your ability to analyze cases.

1. **Skim through the case very quickly.** Pay particular attention to the exhibits. The objective in this step is to gain familiarity with the broad facts of the case. What apparent challenges or opportunities does the company face? What information is provided? You may find it especially useful to focus on the first and last few paragraphs of the case in this step.
2. **Read the case more carefully and make notes, underline, etc.** What appear to be important facts? The conceptual frameworks in the chapters will be essential in helping you identify the key facts. Throughout the course, you will want to address central questions such as the following:

    - What is the firm's performance?
    - What is the firm's mission? strategy? goals?
    - What are the resources involved in the firm's value chain? How do they compare to competitors on cost and differentiation?
    - Does the firm have a competitive advantage?
    - Are the firm's advantages and disadvantages temporary or sustainable?
    - What is the value of the firm's resources?
    - Are the firm's resources rare?
    - Are the firm's resources costly to imitate?
    - Is the firm organized sufficiently to exploit its resources?

    Depending on the case, you may also want to consider other frameworks and questions, where appropriate. Each chapter provides concepts and frameworks that you may want to consider. For example:

    - What are the five forces? How do they influence industry opportunities and threats? (Chapter 2)

- What are the sources of cost differences in an industry? (Chapter 4)
- What are the bases and potential bases for product differentiation in an industry? (Chapter 5)

Each chapter suggests more specific questions and concepts than those above. You will want to consider these concepts in detail. In some cases, the instructor may offer direction about which concepts to apply to a given case. In other instances, you may be left to use your judgment in choosing which concepts to focus on in analyzing a case.

3. **Define the basic issues.** This is perhaps the most important step and also the stage of analysis that requires the most wisdom and judgment. Cases are rarely like tidy problem sets where the issues or problems are explicitly stated and the tools needed to address those issues are prescribed. Generally, you need to determine what the key issues are. In doing this, it may help for you to begin by asking: What are the fundamental issues in the case? Which concepts matter most in providing insight into those issues? One trap to avoid in defining basic issues is doing what some decision-making scholars label "plunging-in," which is drawing conclusions without first thinking about the crux of the issues involved in a decision.[1] Many students have a tendency to seize the first issues that are prominently mentioned in a case. As an antidote to this trap, you may want to consider a case from the perspective of different conceptual frames.
4. **Develop and elaborate your analysis of the key issues.** As with all of the steps, there is no substitute for painstaking work in this stage. You need to take the key issues you have defined in Step 3, examine the facts that you have noted in Step 2, and assess what are the key facts. What does quantitative analysis reveal? Here it is not just ratio analysis that we are concerned with. Just as body temperature, blood pressure, and pulse rate may reveal something about a person's health but little about the causes of a sickness, ratio analysis typically tells us more about the health of a company than the causes of its performance. You should assemble facts and analysis to support your point of view. Opinions unsupported by factual evidence and analysis are generally not persuasive. This stage of the analysis involves organizing the facts in the case. You will want to develop specific hypotheses about what factors relate to success in a particular setting. Often, you will find it helpful to draw diagrams to clarify your thinking.
5. **Draw conclusions and formulate a set of recommendations.** You may be uncomfortable drawing conclusions and making recommendations because you do not have complete information. This is an eternal dilemma for managers. Managers who wait for complete information to do something, however, usually act too late. Nevertheless, you should strive to do the most complete analysis that you can under reasonable time constraints. Recommendations should also flow naturally from your analysis. Too often, students formulate their recommendations in an ad hoc way. In formulating recommendations, you should be clear about priorities and the sequence of actions that you recommend.
6. **Prepare for class discussion.** Students who diligently work through the first five steps and rigorously examine a case should be well prepared for class discussion. You may find it helpful to make some notes and bring them to

[1] J. E. Russo and P. J. H. Schoemaker (1989). *Decision Traps: The Ten Barriers to Brilliant Decision-Making and How to Overcome Them*. New York: Fireside.

class. Over the years, we have observed that many of the students who are low contributors to class discussions bring few or no notes to class. Once in class, a case discussion usually begins with a provocative question from the instructor. Many instructors will "cold call"—direct a question to a specific student who has not been forewarned. Students who have thoroughly analyzed and discussed the case before coming to class will be much better prepared for these surprise calls. They will also be better prepared to contribute to the analysis, argument, and persuasion that will take place in the class discussion. Discussions can move rapidly. You will hear new insights from fellow students. Preparation helps you to absorb, learn, and contribute to the insights that emerge from class discussion.

Summary

Students who embark in the case method soon learn that analyzing cases is a complex process. Having a clear conceptual approach such as the VRIO framework does not eliminate the complexity. This systematic approach, however, does allow the analyst to manage the complexity of real-world business situations. In the end, though, neither cases nor real-world businesses conclude their analyses with tidy solutions that resolve all the uncertainties and ambiguities a business faces. However, the case method coupled with a good theory such as the VRIO approach and hard work do make it more likely that you will generate valuable insights into the strategic challenges of firms and develop the strategic skills needed to lead a firm.

TABLE A.1 Black-Scholes Option Pricing Table

	0.05	0.10	0.15	0.20	0.25	0.30	0.35	0.40	0.45	0.50
0.50	*	*	*	*	0.0003	0.0015	0.0044	0.0094	0.0167	0.0261
0.60	*	*	*	0.004	0.0024	0.0070	0.0144	0.0243	0.0366	0.0506
0.70	*	*	0.0005	0.0035	0.0103	0.0204	0.0333	0.0482	0.0645	0.0820
0.75	*	0.0001	0.0018	0.0077	0.0178	0.0310	0.0463	0.0632	0.0810	0.0997
0.80	*	0.0005	0.0050	0.0148	0.0283	0.0442	0.0615	0.0799	0.0989	0.1183
0.82	*	0.0010	0.0072	0.0186	0.0334	0.0502	0.0682	0.0870	0.1063	0.1259
0.84	*	0.0018	0.0099	0.0230	0.0390	0.0566	0.0752	0.0943	0.1139	0.1337
0.86	*	0.0031	0.0133	0.0280	0.0450	0.0633	0.0824	0.1019	0.1216	0.1415
0.88	0.0001	0.0051	0.0175	0.0336	0.0516	0.0705	0.0899	0.1096	0.1295	0.1494
0.90	0.0003	0.0079	0.0225	0.0399	0.0586	0.0779	0.0976	0. 1175	0.1374	0.1573
0.92	0.0010	0.0118	0.0283	0.0467	0.0660	0.0857	0.1055	0.1255	0.1454	0.1653
0.94	0.0027	0.0169	0.0349	0.0542	0.0738	0.0937	0.1136	0. 1336	0.1535	0.1733
0.96	0.0060	0.0232	0.0424	0.0622	0.0821	0.1020	0.1219	0.1418	0.1616	0.1813
0.98	0.0116	0.0309	0.0507	0.0707	0.0906	0. 1105	0.1304	0.1501	0.1698	0.1894
1.00	0.0199	0.0399	0.0598	0.0797	0.0995	0.1192	0.1389	0.1585	0.1780	0.1974
1.02	0.0311	0.0501	0.0695	0.0891	0.1086	0.1281	0.1476	0.1670	0.1862	0.2054
1.04	0.0445	0.0613	0.0799	0.0988	0.1180	0.1372	0.1563	0.1754	0.1945	0.2134
1.06	0.0595	0.0734	0.0907	0.1090	0.1276	0. 1463	0.1651	0.1839	0.2027	0.2214
1.08	0.0754	0.0863	0.1020	0.1193	0.1373	0. 1556	0.1740	0.1925	0.2109	0.2293
1.10	0.0914	0.0996	0. 1136	0.1299	0.1472	0.1649	0.1829	0.2010	0.2191	0.2372
1.12	0.1073	0.1132	0.1255	0.1407	0.1572	0. 1743	0.1918	0.2095	0.2273	0.2451
1.14	0.1229	0.1270	0.1376	0.1516	0. 1672	0.1837	0.2007	0.2018	0.2354	0.2529

1.16	0.1380	0. 1407	0.1497	0.1626	0. 1773	0. 1932	0.2096	0.2264	0.2435	0.2606
1.18	0.1525	0.1544	0.1619	0.1736	0.1874	0.2026	0.2185	0.2349	0.2515	0.2683
1.20	0.1667	0.1679	0.1741	0.1846	0. 1975	0.2120	0.2273	0.2432	0.2595	0.2759
1.25	0.2000	0.2004	0.2040	0.2119	0.2227	0.2353	0.2492	0.26398	0.2791	0.2946
1.30	0.2308	0.2309	0.2329	0.2385	0.2473	0.2583	0.2707	0.2841	0.2983	0.3129
1.35	0.2593	0.2593	0.2604	0.2643	0.2713	0.2806	0.2916	0.3039	0.3169	0.3306
1.40	0.2857	0.2857	0.2863	0.2889	0.2994	0.3023	0.3120	0.3230	0.3351	0.3478
1.45	0.3103	0.3103	0.3106	0.3124	0.3166	0.3232	0.3316	0.3416	0.3526	0.3645
1.50	0.3333	0.3333	0.3335	0.3346	0.3378	0.3432	0.3506	0.3595	0.3696	0.3806
1.75	0.4286	0.4286	0.4286	0.4287	0.4294	0.4313	0.4347	0.4395	0.4457	0.4530
2.00	0.5000	0.5000	0.5000	0.5000	0.5001	0.5007	0.5022	0.5047	0.5083	0.5131
2.50	0.6000	0.6000	0.6000	0.6000	0.6000	0.6001	0.6003	0.6009	0.6021	0.6041

	0.55	**0.60**	**0.65**	**0.70**	**0.75**	**0.80**	**0.85**	**0.90**	**0.95**	**1.00**
0.50	0.0375	0.0506	0.0651	0.0808	0.0976	0.1151	0.1333	0.1520	0.1712	0.1906
0.60	0.0661	0.0827	0.1003	0.1185	0.1373	0.1565	0.1761	0.1958	0.2157	0.2356
0.70	0.1003	0.1191	0.1384	0.1580	0.1778	0.1977	0.2176	0.2376	0.2575	0.2773
0.75	0.1188	0.1383	0.1580	0.1779	0.1978	0.2178	0.2377	0.2575	0.2772	0.2968
0.80	0.1380	0.1578	0.1777	0. 1977	0.2176	0.2374	0.2572	0.2768	0.2963	0.3156
0.82	0.1457	0.1657	0.1856	0.2055	0.2254	0.2452	0.2648	0.2843	0.3037	0.3228
0.84	0.1536	0.1735	0.1935	0.2133	0.2331	0.2528	0.2724	0.2918	0.3110	0.3300
0.86	0.1614	0.1814	0.2013	0.2211	0.2408	0.2604	0.2798	0.2991	0.3181	0.3370
0.88	0.1693	0.1892	0.2091	0.2288	0.2484	0.2679	0.2872	0.3063	0.3252	0.3439
0.90	0.1772	0.1971	0.2168	0.2364	0.2559	0.2752	0.2944	0.3134	0.3321	0.3507
0.92	0.1852	0.2049	0.2245	0.2440	0.2634	0.2825	0.3016	0.3204	0.3390	0.3507
0.94	0.1931	0.2127	0.2322	0.2515	0.2707	0.2898	0.086	0.3272	0.3457	0.3639
0.96	0.2010	0.2204	0.2398	0.2590	0.2780	0.2969	0.3156	0.3340	0.3523	0.3704
0.98	0.2088	0.2282	0.2473	0.2664	0.2852	0.3039	0.3224	0.3407	0.3588	0.3767
1.00	0.2167	0.2358	0.2548	0.2737	0.2923	0.3108	0.3292	0.3473	0.3652	0.3829
1.02	0.2245	0.2434	0.2622	0.2809	0.2994	0.3177	0.3358	0.3538	0.3715	0.3890
1.04	0.2323	0.2510	0.2696	0.2880	0.3063	0.3244	0.3424	0.3601	0.3777	0.3890
1.06	0.2400	0.2585	0.2769	0.2951	0.3132	0.3311	0.3489	0.3664	0.3838	0.4010
1.08	0.2477	0.2659	0.2841	0.3021	0.3200	0.3377	0.3552	0.3726	0.3898	0.4068
1.10	0.2553	0.2733	0.2912	0.3091	0.3267	0.3442	0.3615	0.3787	0.3957	0.4125
1.12	0.2629	0.2806	0.2983	0.3158	0.3333	0.3506	0.3677	0.3747	0.4015	0.4181
1.14	0.2704	0.2878	0.3052	0.3226	0.3398	0.3569	0.3738	0.3906	0.4072	0.4236
1.16	0.2778	0.2950	0.3121	0.3292	0.3462	0.3631	0.3798	0.3964	0.4128	0.4291
1.18	0.2852	0.3021	0.3190	0.3358	0.3525	0.3692	0.3857	0.4021	0.4184	0.4344
1.20	0.2925	0.3091	0.3257	0.3423	0.3588	0.3722	0.3916	0.4077	0.4238	0.4397
1.25	0.3104	0.3262	0.3422	0.3581	0.3741	0.3900	0.4058	0.4214	0.4370	0.4524
1.30	0.3278	0.3429	0.3582	0.3735	0.3888	0.4042	0.4194	0.4346	0.4497	0.4647
1.35	0.3447	0.3591	0.3736	0.3883	0.4031	0.4178	0.4326	0.4473	0.4619	0.4765
1.40	0.3611	0.3747	0.3886	0.4026	0.4168	0.4310	0.4453	0.4595	0.4737	0.4878
1.45	0.3769	0.3898	0.4030	0.4165	0.4301	0.4438	0.4575	0.4713	0.4851	0.4987
1.50	0.3923	0.4044	0.4170	0.4298	0.4429	0.4561	0.1693	0.4826	0.4959	0.5092
1.75	0.4613	0.4703	0.4799	0.4900	0.5005	0.5112	0.5222	0.5334	0.5447	0.5560
2.00	0.5188	0.5553	0.5326	0.5404	0.5488	0.5575	0.5666	0.5760	0.5856	0.5953
2.50	0.6067	0.6101	0.6142	0.6190	0.6243	0.6301	0.6363	0.6430	0.6499	0.6571

Glossary

above-average accounting performance: when a firm's accounting performance is greater than the industry average

above-normal economic performance: when a firm earns above its cost of capital

absorptive capacity: the ability of firms to learn

accounting performance: a measure of a firm's competitive advantage; calculated from information in the firm's published profit and loss and balance sheet statements

accounting ratios: numbers taken from a firm's financial statements that are manipulated in ways that describe various aspects of the firm's performance

acquisition: a firm purchases another firm

acquisition premium: the difference between the current market price of a target firm's shares and the price a potential acquirer offers to pay for those shares

activity ratios: accounting ratios that focus on the level of activity in a firm's business

adverse selection: an alliance partner promises to bring to an alliance certain resources that it either does not control or cannot acquire

after-tax cost of debt: the cost of debt multiplied times one minus a firm's marginal tax rate (assuming that the interest on debt is tax deductible)

agency problems: parties in an agency relationship differ in their decision-making objectives

agency relationship: one party in an exchange delegates decision-making authority to a second party

agent: a party to whom decision-making authority is delegated

architectural competence: the ability of a firm to use organizational structure and other organizing mechanisms to facilitate coordination among scientific disciplines to conduct research

auction: in mergers and acquisitions, a mechanism for establishing the price of an asset when multiple firms bid for a single target firm

audit committee: subgroup of the board of directors responsible for ensuring the accuracy of accounting and financial statements

average accounting performance: when a firm's accounting performance is equal to the industry average

backward vertical integration: a firm incorporates more stages of the value chain within its boundaries and those stages bring it closer to gaining access to raw materials

barriers to entry: attributes of an industry's structure that increase the cost of entry

below-average accounting performance: when a firm's accounting performance is less than the industry average

below-normal economic performance: when a firm earns less than its cost of capital

Black-Scholes formula: used to determine an option's value depending on five variables: (1) the value of the underlying financial asset, (2) the option's exercise price, (3) the time to an option's maturity, (4) the variance in the price of the asset on which an option is written, and (5) the risk-free rate of interest

board chair: the person who presides over the board of directors; may or may not be the same person as a firm's senior executive; also known as Chairman of the Board

board of directors: a group of 10 to 15 individuals drawn from a firm's top management and from people outside the firm whose primary responsibilities are to monitor decisions made in the firm and to ensure that they are consistent with the interests of outside equity holders

business cycle: the alternating pattern of prosperity followed by recession followed by prosperity

business model: the set of activities that a firm engages in to create and appropriate economic value

business strategy: a firm's theory of how to gain competitive advantage in a single business or industry

business-level strategies: actions firms take to gain competitive advantages in a single market or industry

buyers: those who purchase a firm's products or services

capabilities: a subset of a firm's resources, defined as tangible and intangible assets, that enable a firm to take full advantage of other resources it controls

Capital Asset Pricing Model (CAPM): a model used to estimate the cost of equity

causally ambiguous: imitating firms do not understand the relationship between the resources and capabilities controlled by a firm and that firm's competitive advantage

chairman of the board: the person who presides over the board of directors; may or may not be the same person as a firm's senior executive

chief executive officer (CEO): person to whom all functional managers report in a U-form organization; the person to whom all divisional personal and corporate staff report to in an M-form organization: responsible for strategy formulation and implementation

chief operating officer (COO): reports to CEO; primary responsibility is strategy implementation

closely held: a firm that has not sold many of its shares on the public stock market

collusion: two or more firms in an industry coordinate their strategic choices to reduce competition in that industry

compensation policies: the ways that firms pay employees

competitive advantage: a firm creates more economic value than rival firms

competitive disadvantage: a firm generates less economic value than rival firms

competitive dynamics: how one firm responds to the strategic actions of competing firms
competitive parity: a firm creates the same economic value as rival firms
competitor: any firm, group, or individual trying to reduce a firm's competitive advantage
complementary resources and capabilities: resources and capabilities that have limited ability to generate competitive advantage in isolation but in combination with other resources can enable a firm to realize its full potential for competitive advantage
complementor: when the value of a firm's products increases in the presence of another firm's products
conduct: (as in structured conduct performance model) the strategies that firms in an industry implement
conglomerate merger: a merger or acquisition where there are no vertical, horizontal, product extension, or market extension links between the firms
conscious parallelism: when a firm consciously makes price and output decisions in order to reduce competition, but does not directly communicate with its competition
consolidation strategy: strategy that reduces the number of firms in an industry by exploiting economies of scale
controlling share: when an acquiring firm purchases enough of a target firm's assets to be able to make all the management and strategic decisions in the target firm
core competence: the collective learning in an organization, especially how to coordinate diverse production skills and integrate multiple streams of technologies
corporate competence: exists when a firm develops managerial skills, technical knowhow, experience, and wisdom in managing a diversified corporation
corporate diversification strategy: when a firm operates in multiple industries or markets simultaneously
corporate staff: upper-level managers who provide information about a firm's external and internal environments to the firm's senior executive
corporate strategy: a firm's theory of how to gain competitive advantage by operating in several businesses simultaneously
corporate-level strategies: actions firms take to gain competitive advantages by operating in multiple markets or industries simultaneously
cost centers: divisions are assigned a budget and manage their operations to that budget
cost leadership business strategy: focuses on gaining advantages by reducing costs below those of competitors
cost of capital: the rate of return that a firm promises to pay its suppliers of capital to induce them to invest in a firm
cost of debt: the interest that a firm must pay its debt holders to induce them to lend money to the firm
cost of equity: the rate of return a firm must promise its equity holders to induce them to invest in the firm
crown jewel sale: a bidding firm is interested in just a few of the most highly regarded businesses being operated by the target firm, known as its *crown jewels*, and the target firm sells these businesses
culture: the values, beliefs, and norms that guide behavior in a society and in a firm
cumulative abnormal return (CAR): performance that is greater (or less) than what was expected in a short period of time around when an acquisition is announced
current market value: the price of each of a firm's shares multiplied by the number of shares outstanding
customer-switching costs: customers make investments in order to use a firm's particular products or services that are not useful in using other firms' products
cut throat competition: when a firm's profit maximizing decision sets its price below its marginal costs
dead weight loss: a reduction in social welfare due to the actions of a monopolist
debt: capital from banks and bondholders
declining industry: an industry that has experienced an absolute decline in unit sales over a sustained period of time
deep-pockets model: a firm that takes advantage of its monopoly power in one business to subsidize several different businesses
demand management: when a firm increases or decreases prices depending on historical patterns to try to make sure that supply and demand balance
demographics: the distribution of individuals in a society in terms of age, sex, marital status, income, ethnicity, and other personal attributes that may determine their buying patterns
depression: a severe recession that lasts for several years
direct duplication: the attempt to imitate other firms by developing resources that have the same strategic effects as the resources controlled by those other firms
diseconomies of scale: a firm's costs begin to rise as a function of the volume of production
distinctive competence: a valuable and rare resource or capability
distribution agreements: one firm agrees to distribute the products of others
diversification economies: sources of relatedness in a diversified firm
divestment: a firm sells a business in which it had been operating
division: each business that a firm engages in, also called a strategic business unit (SBU)
dominant logic: common theory of how to gain competitive advantages shared by each business in a diversified firm
dominant-business firms: firms with between 70 percent and 95 percent of their total sales in a single product market
economic climate: the overall health of the economic systems within which a firm operates

economic measures of competitive advantage: measures that compare a firm's level of return to its cost of capital instead of to the average level of return in the industry
economic value: the difference between the perceived benefits gained by a customer who purchases a firm's products or services and the full economic cost of these products or services
economic value added (EVA): calculated by subtracting the cost of the capital employed in a division from that division's earnings
economies of scale: the per-unit cost of production falls as the volume of production increases
economies of scope: exists when the value created by several businesses operated together is greater than the value of these businesses operated separately
emergent strategies: theories of how to gain competitive advantage in an industry that emerge over time or have been radically reshaped once they are initially implemented
emerging industries: newly created or newly re-created industries formed by technological innovations, change in demand, or the emergence of new customer needs
empty core Industries: exist when four industry conditions are present: (1) capacity in this industry is added in large increments, relative to demand, (2) there are large unavoidable sunk costs associated with adding this extra capacity, (3) demand fluctuates in difficult to predict ways, and (4) there is limited product differentiation
environmental threat: any individual, group, or organization outside a firm that seeks to reduce the level of that firm's performance
equity: capital from individuals and institutions that purchase a firm's stocks
equity alliance: cooperating firms supplement contracts with equity holdings in alliance partners
escalation of commitment: an increased commitment by managers to an incorrect course of action, even as its limitations become manifest
event study analysis: evaluates the performance effects of acquisitions for bidding firms
executive committee: typically consists of the CEO and two or three functional senior managers
expected market return: the return an investor expects to receive from investing in a fully diversified portfolio of stocks
explicit collusion: firms directly communicate with each other to coordinate levels of production, prices, and so forth (illegal in most countries)
external analysis: identification and examination of the critical threats and opportunities in a firm's competitive environment
finance committee: subgroup of the board of directors that maintains the relationship between the firm and external capital markets
financial resources: all the money, from whatever source, that firms use to conceive and implement strategies
firm-specific human capital investments: investments made by employees in a particular firm over time, including understanding the culture, policies, and procedures and knowing the people to contact to complete a task, that have limited value in other firms
firm-specific investments: the value of stakeholders' investments in a particular firm is much greater than the value those same investments would be in other firms
first-mover advantages: advantages that come to firms that make important strategic and technological decisions early in the development of an industry
flexibility: how costly it is for a firm to alter its strategic and organizational decisions
formal management controls: a firm's budgeting and reporting activities that keep people higher up in a firm's organizational chart informed about the actions taken by people lower down in the organizational chart
formal reporting structure: a description of who in the organization reports to whom
forward vertical integration: a firm incorporates more stages of the value chain within its boundaries and those stages bring it closer to interacting directly with final customers
fragmented industries: industries in which a large number of small- or medium-sized firms operate and no small set of firms has dominant market share or creates dominant technologies
free cash flow: the amount of cash a firm has to invest after all positive net present-value investments in its ongoing businesses have been funded
friendly acquisitions: the management of a target firm wants the firm to be acquired
functional manager: a manager who leads a particular function within a firm, such as manufacturing, marketing, finance, accounting, or sales
functional organizational structure: the structure a firm uses to implement business-level strategies it might pursue where each function in the firm reports to the CEO
general environment: broad trends in the context within which a firm operates that can have an impact on a firm's strategic choices
generic business strategies: another name for business-level strategies, which are cost leadership and product differentiation
geographic market diversification strategy: when a firm operates in multiple geographic markets simultaneously
golden parachutes: incentive compensation paid to senior managers if the firm they manage is acquired
greenmail: a target firm's management purchases any of the target firm's stock owned by a bidder for a price that is greater than its current market value
harvest strategy: a firm engages in a long, systematic, phased withdrawal from a declining industry, extracting as much value as possible

hedonic prices: that part of the price of a product or service that is attributable to a particular characteristic of that product or service
holdup: one firm makes more transaction-specific investments in an exchange than partner firms make and the firm that has not made these investments tries to exploit the firm that has made the investments
horizontal merger: a firm acquires a former competitor
hostile takeovers: the management of a target firm does not want the firm to be acquired
human resources: include the training, experience, judgment, intelligence, relationships, and insight of individual managers and workers in a firm
imperfectly imitable: resources and capabilities that are more costly for other firms to imitate, compared to firms that already possess them
increasing returns industries: another name for network industries
increasing returns to scale: in network industries, the value of a product or service increases as the number of people using those products or services increases
industry culture: norms of acceptable behaviors that exist among firms in an industry
industry recipe: the standard operating procedures, acceptable forms of competition, and norms of behavior for firms in an industry
industry social structure: accepted norms of behavior and competition that often evolve in industries
inelastic in supply: the quantity of supply is fixed and does not respond to price increases, such as the total supply of land, which is relatively fixed and cannot be significantly increased in response to higher demand and prices
Informal management controls: include a firm's culture and the willingness of employees to monitor each other's behavior
Institutional owners: pension funds, corporations, and others that invest other peoples' money in firm equities
intermediate products or services: products or services produced in one division that are used as inputs for products or services produced by a second division
internal analysis: identification of a firm's organizational strengths and weaknesses and of the resources and capabilities that are likely to be sources of competitive advantage
internal capital market: when businesses in a diversified firm compete for corporate capital
invented competencies: illusory inventions by creative managers to justify poor diversification moves by linking intangible core competencies to completely unrelated businesses
joint venture: cooperating firms create a legally independent firm in which they invest and from which they share any profits that are created
learning curve: a concept that formalizes the relationship between cumulative volumes of production and falling per-unit costs
learning race: both parties to an alliance seek to learn from each other, but the rate at which these two firms learn varies; the first party to learn "wins" the race and may withdraw from the alliance
legal and political conditions: the laws and the legal system's impact on business, together with the general nature of the relationship between government and business
leverage ratios: accounting ratios that focus on the level of a firm's financial flexibility
licensing agreements: one firm allows others to use its brand name to sell products in return for some fee or percentage of profits
limited corporate diversification: all or most of a firm's business activities fall within a single industry and geographic market
liquidity ratios: accounting ratios that focus on the ability of a firm to meet its short-term financial obligations
management control systems: a range of formal and informal mechanisms to ensure that managers are behaving in ways consistent with a firm's strategies
managerial hubris: the unrealistic belief held by managers in bidding firms that they can manage the assets of a target firm more efficiently than the target firm's current management
managerial know-how: the oft-taken for granted knowledge and information that are needed to compete in an industry on a day-to-day basis
managerial perquisites: activities that do not add economic value to the firm but directly benefit the managers who make them
managerial risk aversion: managers unable to diversify their firm-specific human capital investments may engage in less risky business decisions than what would be preferred by equity holders
market extension merger: firms make acquisitions in new geographical markets
market for corporate control: the market that is created when multiple firms actively seek to acquire one or several firms
market leader: the firm with the largest market share in an industry
market uncertainty: the extent to which managers do not understand how a new product or service will be received in the market
matrix structures: one employee reports to two or more people
mature industries: an industry in which, over time, ways of doing business have become widely understood, technologies have diffused through competitors, and the rate of innovation in new products and technologies drops
merger: the assets of two similar-sized firms are combined
M-form (multidivisional): an organizational structure for implementing a corporate diversification strategy whereby each business a firm engages in is managed through a separate profit-and-loss division

mission: a firm's long-term purpose
mission statement: written statement defining both what a firm aspires to be in the long run and what it wants to avoid in the meantime
monopolistic competition: a market structure where within the market niche defined by a firm's differentiated product, a firm possesses a monopoly
monopolistic industries: industries that consist of only a single firm
monopolistically competitive industries: industries in which there are large numbers of competing firms and low-cost entry and exit, but products are not homogeneous with respect to cost or product attributes; firms are said to enjoy a "monopoly" in that part of the market they dominate
monopoly: when a single firm is operating in an industry
moral hazard: partners in an exchange possess high-quality resources and capabilities of significant value to the exchange but fail to make them available to the other partners
mutual forbearance: a form of tacit collusion whereby firms tacitly agree to not compete in one industry in order to avoid competition in a second industry
network industries: industries in which a single technical standard and increasing returns to scale tend to dominate; competition in these industries tends to focus on which of several competing standards will be chosen
new competitors: firms that have either recently started operating in an industry or that threaten to begin operations in an industry soon
niche strategy: a firm reduces its scope of operations and focuses on narrow segments of a declining industry
nominating committee: subgroup of the board of directors that nominates new board members
nonequity alliance: cooperating firms agree to work together to develop, manufacture, or sell products or services, but they do not take equity positions in each other or form an independent organizational unit to manage the cooperative efforts
normal economic performance: a firm that earns its cost of capital
objectives: specific, measurable targets a firm can use to evaluate the extent to which it is realizing its mission
office of the president: together, the roles of chairman of the board, CEO, and COO
oligopolies: industries characterized by a small number of competing firms, by homogeneous products, and by costly entry and exit costs
oligopoly: when a few firms are operating in an industry
operations committee: typically meets monthly and usually consists of the CEO and each of the heads of the functional areas included in the firm
opportunism: a firm is unfairly exploited in an exchange
option to abandon: a firm's ability to make choices that enhance their ability to abandon a particular strategy
option to contract: a firm's ability to make choices that enhance their ability to get smaller and reduce investment in a strategy, should that option turn out to be valuable in the future
option to defer: a firm's ability to make strategic choices that enhance its ability to defer additional investment in a strategy until some later period
option to expand: a firm's ability to make choices that enhance its ability to expand its strategy beyond its current boundaries
option to grow: a firm's ability to make choices that enhance their ability to "grow" an investment in the future, should that option turn out to be valuable
option to shut down and restart: a firm's ability to make choices that enhance its ability to shut down and restart a business should this option be valuable in the future
organizational chart: a depiction of the formal reporting structure within a firm
organizational resources: a firm's formal reporting structure; its formal and informal planning, controlling, and coordinating systems; its culture and reputation; and informal relations among groups within a firm and between a firm and those in its environment
Pac Man defense: fending off an acquisition by a firm acquiring the firm or firms bidding for it
path dependence: events early in the evolution of a process have significant effects on subsequent events
pecuniary economies: sources of relatedness in market power between bidding and target firms
perfect competition: when there are numerous competing firms in an industry, when these firms are of similar size, when there is little product differentiation among them, and when there is free entry and exit in an industry
perfectly competitive: when there are large numbers of competing firms, the products being sold are homogeneous with respect to cost and product attributes, and entry and exit costs are very low
performance: (in the structure-conduct-performance model) performance of individual firms and performance of the industry
personnel and compensation committee: subgroup of the board of directors that evaluates and compensates the performance of a firm's senior executive and other senior managers
physical resources: all the physical technology used in a firm
poison pills: a variety of actions that target firm managers can take to make the acquisition of the target prohibitively expensive
policy choices: choices firms make about the kinds of products or services they will sell—choices that have an impact on relative cost and product differentiation position
policy of experimentation: exists when firms are committed to engage in several related product differentiation efforts simultaneously

positioning options: when a firm makes multiple small investments in an uncertain technology and waits to increase its investments until technological uncertainty is resolved
predatory pricing: setting prices so that they are less than a business's costs
present value: equal to the sum of cash flows generated by choosing and implementing a particular strategy, discounted by how risky they are
price leader: a firm that sets "acceptable" industry prices or "acceptable" profit margins in an industry
price takers: where the price of the products or services a firm sells is determined by market conditions and not by the decisions of firms
principal: the party who delegates the decision-making authority
privately held: a firm that has stock that is not traded on public stock markets and that is not a division of a larger company
processes: the activities a firm engages in to design, produce, and sell its products or services
process innovation: a firm's effort to refine and improve its current processes
process manufacturing: when manufacturing is accomplished in a continuous system; examples include manufacturing in chemical, oil refining, and paper and pulp industries
product differentiation: a business strategy whereby firms attempt to gain a competitive advantage by increasing the perceived value of their products or services relative to the perceived value of other firms' products or services
product diversification strategy: a firm operates in multiple industries simultaneously
product extension merger: firms acquire complementary products through merger and acquisition activities
productive inputs: any supplies used by a firm in conducting its business activities, such as labor, capital, land, and raw materials, among others
product-market diversification strategy: a firm implements both product and geographic market diversification simultaneously
profitability ratios: accounting ratios with some measure of profit in the numerator and some measure of firm size or assets in the denominator
profit-and-loss centers: profits and losses are calculated at the level of the division in a firm
proprietary (secret or patented) technology: secret or patented technology that gives incumbent firms important advantages over potential entrants
question of imitability: "Do firms without a resource or capability face a cost disadvantage in obtaining or developing it compared to firms that already possess it?"
question of organization: "Is a firm organized to exploit the full competitive potential of its resources and capabilities?"
question of rarity: "How many competing firms already possess particular valuable resources and capabilities?"
question of value: "Does a resource enable a firm to exploit an external opportunity or neutralize an external threat?"
real assets: tangible resources that can have an impact on a firm's production, including land, buildings, raw materials, finished goods inventories, distribution systems, information technology, and so forth
real options: investments in real assets that create the opportunity for additional investments in the future
recession: a period of relatively low prosperity; demand for goods and services is low and unemployment is high
related corporate diversification: less than 70 percent of a firm's revenue comes from a single product market and its multiple lines of business are linked
related-constrained: the businesses in which a firm operates share the same economies of scope
related-linked: the different businesses that a single firm pursues realize different types of economies of scope
reputation: beliefs customers hold about a firm
residual claimants view: equity holders receive payment on their investment in a firm after all legitimate claims by a firm's other stakeholders are satisfied
resource heterogeneity: for a given business activity, some firms may be more skilled in accomplishing the activity than other firms
resource immobility: resources controlled by some firms may not diffuse to other firms
resources: the tangible and intangible assets that a firm controls, which it can use to conceive and implement its strategies
retained earnings: capital generated from a firm's ongoing operations that is retained by a firm
risk-free rate of return: the interest earned on a risk-free asset (typically an investment in a government bond)
risky: when the outcome of a decision is not known with certainty, but the possible outcomes associated with that decision, and their probability, are known before a decision is made
scouting options: when firms make several new offerings available to consumers, and invest once consumer preferences become clear
senior executive: the president or CEO of a firm
shakeout period: period during which the total supply in an industry is reduced by bankruptcies, acquisitions, and business closings
shared activities: potential sources of operational economies of scope for diversified firms
shared business-level competence: focuses on learning, know-how, and experience that develops in a business within a diversified firm that can then be leveraged in other businesses within that firm

shark repellents: a variety of relatively minor corporate governance changes that, in principle, are supposed to make it somewhat more difficult to acquire a target firm
single-business firms: firms with greater than 95 percent of their total sales in a single product market
skunk works: temporary teams whose creative efforts are intensive and focused
social welfare: the overall good of society
socially complex: resources and capabilities that involve interpersonal, social, or cultural links among individuals
soft signal: suggests that a firm will not aggressively respond to cheating on collusive agreements
specific international events: events such as civil wars, political coups, terrorism, wars between countries, famines, and country or regional economic recessions, all of which can have an enormous impact on the ability of a firm's strategies to generate competitive advantage
stakeholders: all groups and individuals who have an interest in how a firm performs
standstill agreements: contract between a target and a bidding firm wherein the bidding firm agrees not to attempt to take over the target for some period of time
stepping-stone options: when firms avoid making large technology or product investments and instead make numerous small investments, and adjust quickly
stock grants: payments to employees in a firm's stock
stock options: employees are given the right, but not the obligation, to purchase a firm's stock at predetermined prices
strategic alliance: whenever two or more independent organizations cooperate in the development, manufacture, or sale of products or services; a form of exchange governance between market exchanges and hierarchical exchanges; examples include licensing arrangements, manufacturing agreements, and joint ventures
strategic flexibility: firm's ability to choose among several different strategic options
strategic management process: a sequential set of analyses that can increase the likelihood of a firm's choosing a strategy that generates competitive advantages
strategic options: when firms have the ability, but not the obligation, to invest in a particular strategy
strategically valuable assets: resources required to successfully compete in an industry, including access to raw materials, particularly favorable geographic locations, and particularly valuable product market positions
strategy: a firm's theory about how to gain competitive advantage
strategy implementation: a firm adopting organizational policies and practices that are consistent with its strategy
structure: (in the structure-conduct-performance model) industry structure measured by such factors as the number of competitors in an industry, the heterogeneity of products in an industry, the cost of entry and exit in an industry, and so forth
structure-conduct-performance (S-C-P) model: theory suggesting that industry structure determines a firm's conduct, which in turn determines its performance
substitutes: products or services that meet approximately the same customer needs but do so in different ways
substitution: developing or acquiring strategically equivalent, but different, resources as a competing firm
supermajority voting rules: an example of a shark repellent that specifies that more than 50 percent of the target firm's board of directors must approve a takeover
suppliers: firms that make a wide variety of raw materials, labor, and other critical assets available to firms
supply agreements: one firm agrees to supply others
sustainable distinctive competencies: valuable, rare, and costly-to-imitate resources or capabilities
sustained competitive advantage: a competitive advantage that lasts for a long period of time; an advantage that is not competed away through strategic imitation
tacit collusion: firms coordinate their production and pricing decisions not by directly communicating with each other, but by exchanging signals with other firms about their intent to cooperate; special case of tacit cooperation
tactics: the specific actions a firm takes to implement its strategies
technical economies: sources of relatedness in marketing, production, and similar activities between bidding and target firms
technical uncertainty: the extent to which managers understand the process by which a new product or service will be developed before that process is undertaken
technological hardware: the machines and other hardware used by firms
technological leadership strategy: firms make early investments in particular technologies in an industry
technological software: the quality of labor–management relations, an organization's culture, and the quality of managerial controls in a firm
temporary competitive advantage: a competitive advantage that lasts for a short period of time
tender offers: a bidding firm offers to purchase the shares of a target firm directly by offering a higher-than-market price for those shares to current shareholders
thinly traded market: a market where there are only a small number of buyers and sellers, where information about opportunities in this market is not widely known, and where interests besides purely maximizing the value of a firm can be important
tough signal: suggests that a firm will aggressively respond to cheating on collusive agreements
transaction specific: whenever an investment's value in its first-best use (in this case, within the alliance) is much greater than its value in its second-best use (in this case, outside the alliance)

transaction-specific investment: whenever an investment's value in its first-best use is much greater than its value in its second-best use

transfer-pricing system: using internally administered "prices" to manage the movement of intermediate products or services among divisions within a firm

transnational strategy: actions in which a firm engages to gain competitive advantages by investing in technology across borders

U-form structure: organization where different functional heads report directly to CEO; used to implement business level strategies

uncertain: when the outcome of a decision is not known with certainty, and the possible outcomes associated with that decision, and their probability, are also not known before a decision is made

uncertainty: when the outcome of a decision is not known with certainty, and the possible outcomes associated with that decision, and their probability, are also not known before a decision is made

unfriendly acquisitions: the management of the target firm does not want the firm to be acquired

unrelated corporate diversification: less than 70 percent of a firm's revenues is generated in a single product market and a firm's businesses share few, if any, common attributes

value added as a percentage of sales: measures the percentage of a firm's sales that are generated by activities done within the boundaries of a firm; a measure of vertical integration

value chain: that set of activities that must be accomplished to bring a product or service from raw materials to the point that it can be sold to a final customer

vertical integration: the number of steps in the value chain that a firm accomplishes within its boundaries

vertical merger: when a firm vertically integrates, either forward or backward, through its acquisition efforts

visionary firms: firms whose mission is central to all they do

VRIO framework: four questions that must be asked about a resource or capability to determine its competitive potential: the questions of value, rarity, imitability, and organization

weighted average cost of capital (WACC): the percentage of a firm's total capital that is debt multiplied by the cost of debt plus the percentage of a firm's total capital that is equity times the cost of equity

white knight: another bidding firm that agrees to acquire a particular target in place of the original bidding firm

winner take all strategy: when a firm is an early mover in a network industry and builds a large market share quickly, it may obtain an almost unassailable advantage

zero-based budgeting: corporate executives create a list of all capital allocation requests from divisions in a firm, rank them from most important to least important, and then fund all the projects the firm can afford, given the amount of capital it has available

Company Index

NOTES: In the page references, the number after "*n*" refers to the number of the end note in which the name is cited.

Name Index

Notes: In the page references, the number after "n" refers to the number of the end note in which the name is cited

Subject Index